PROFESSIONAL SALES————— MANAGEMENT

McGraw-Hill Series in Marketing

PROFESSIONAL SALES MANAGEMENT

Second Edition

Rolph E. Anderson
Drexel University

Joseph F. Hair, Jr.
Louisiana State University

Alan J. Bush
Memphis State University

McGraw-Hill, Inc.

New York   St. Louis   San Francisco   Auckland   Bogotá   Caracas
Lisbon   London   Madrid   Mexico   Milan   Montreal   New Delhi   Paris
San Juan   Singapore   Sydney   Tokyo   Toronto

For their steadfast love and understanding,
this book is dedicated:
to Sallie, Rachel, Stuart, and Susannah,
to Dale and Joey,
and to Victoria.

PROFESSIONAL SALES MANAGEMENT

Copyright © 1992, 1988 by McGraw-Hill, Inc. All rights reserved. Printed in the United States of America. Except as permitted under the United States Copyright Act of 1976, no part of this publication may be reproduced or distributed in any form or by any means, or stored in a data base or retrieval system, without the prior written permission of the publisher.

2 3 4 5 6 7 8 9 0 HAL HAL 9 0 9 8 7 6 5 4 3 2

ISBN 0-07-001686-0

This book was set in Meridien by General Graphic Services, Inc.
The editors were Bonnie K. Binkert, Mimi Melek, and Laura D. Warner; the production supervisor was Leroy A. Young.
Cover photograph by R. Wickham.
Arcata Graphics/Halliday was printer and binder.

Library of Congress Cataloging-in-Publication Data

Anderson, Rolph E.
    Professional sales management / Rolph E. Anderson, Joseph F. Hair, Jr., Alan J. Bush. — 2nd ed.
        p.   cm. — (McGraw-Hill series in marketing)
    Includes bibliographical references and index.
    ISBN 0-07-001686-0
    1. Sales management.   2. Marketing—Management.   I. Hair, Joseph F.   II. Bush, Alan J.   III. Title.   IV. Series.
HF5438.4.A527   1992
    658.8′1—dc20   91-43810

ABOUT THE AUTHORS

Rolph E. Anderson is the Royal H. Gibson, Sr., Professor of Business Administration and head of the Department of Marketing at Drexel University. He earned his Ph.D. from the University of Florida and his M.B.A. and B.A. degrees from Michigan State University. He is the author or coauthor of several current leading textbooks: *Multivariate Data Analysis,* 3d ed. (Macmillan, 1992), *Professional Sales Management* (McGraw-Hill, 1988), and *Professional Personal Selling* (Prentice-Hall, 1991). His research has been widely published in the major professional journals in his field, and he is a recipient of the Mu Kappa Tau award for the best article published in the *Journal of Personal Selling and Sales Management.* A dedicated teacher, he has won awards for excellence in the classroom. Among various professional organizations he has served are the following: president, Southeast Institute for Decision Sciences; secretary, Academy of Marketing Science; vice president for programming and member of the Board of Directors, American Marketing Association (Philadelphia chapter); National Council member, Institute for Decision Sciences; and co-chairperson, 61st International American Marketing Association Conference. He is a member of the editorial boards of several journals, including the *Journal of Personal Selling and Sales Management, Review of Business and Economics, Review of Business,* the *Journal of Managerial Issues,* and the *Journal of Marketing Channels.* Prior to entering academia, Dr. Anderson worked for three Fortune 500 companies, and in his last position was new-product development manager for the Quaker Oats Company. Active as a business and government consultant, he is also a retired Naval Reserve captain. Married and the father of two children, he is listed in *Who's Who in American Education,* and *Who's Who in America.*

Joseph F. Hair, Jr., is professor and chairman of the Department of Marketing, College of Business Administration, at Louisiana State University. He was a United States Steel Foundation Fellow at the University of Florida, Gainesville, where he earned his Ph.D. in marketing in 1971. He is the author or coauthor of four books, including *Multivariate Data Analysis,* 3d ed. (Macmillan, 1992), *Professional Sales Management* (McGraw-Hill, 1988), *Sales Management* (Random House, 1983), and *Effective Selling,* 8th ed. (South-Western, 1989). He has written numerous articles for professional journals such as the *Journal of Marketing Research,* the *Journal of Experimental Education, Business Horizons,* the *Journal of Retailing, Managerial Planning,* the *Journal of Business/Chicago,* the *Journal of Ad-*

vertising Research, Medical and Marketing Media, Drugs in Health Care, Multivariate Behavioral Research, and the *Journal of Medical and Pharmaceutical Marketing.* Currently secretary-treasurer of the Southwestern Marketing Association and secretary of the Academy of Marketing Science, he has also served as president of the Southern Marketing Association; president and vice president for academic affairs of the American Institute for Decision Sciences, Southeast Section; program chairperson, proceedings editor, vice president, and council member of the Decision Sciences Institute; and treasurer and program chairperson of the Southern Marketing Association. He has been retained as a marketing consultant by firms in the food, lodging, transportation, banking, utilities, and electronics industries, as well as by the U.S. Department of Agriculture and the U.S. Department of the Interior. He has also provided expert testimony in a wide variety of cases, most often in the areas of marketing and marketing research. He has planned and presented executive development and management training programs for numerous companies in a wide variety of industries.

Alan J. Bush is associate professor of marketing at Memphis State University. He earned his Ph.D. and M.B.A. degrees from Louisiana State University. His research has been published in numerous marketing journals, including the *Journal of Marketing Research,* the *Journal of Business Research,* the *Journal of Advertising Research,* the *Journal of Retailing,* the *Journal of Advertising,* the *Journal of Public Policy and Marketing, Psychology and Marketing,* and *Industrial Marketing Management.* He is very active in both national and regional professional associations, currently serving as vice president of research and publications for the Southern Marketing Association and faculty adviser for the kappa chapter of Pi Sigma Epsilon.

CONTENTS

PREFACE

In the decade ahead, sales managers and salespeople will be facing more challenges and opportunities than at any time in the history of this country. No job will be more important than sales in the effort to increase our worldwide competitiveness. With intensifying competition from foreign products and services, the performance levels of sales managers and salespeople will affect not just their own careers but the economic health of the nation as a whole.

Successful sales professionals will have to adapt to several dramatic trends, including (1) growing consumer and buyer expertise, (2) rising customer standards and expectations, (3) intense domestic and foreign competition, (4) revolutionary developments in communications and computer technology, and (5) the influx of women and minorities into sales careers. Successful adaptation to these trends will have to be based on a significant broadening of the concept of sales management. There will need to be an increased meshing of marketing and sales activities. Field sales managers will require a greater knowledge of headquarters marketing functions, and the headquarters marketing team will need a better understanding of selling and sales management. The most successful sales managers will develop and apply marketing concepts, strategic planning processes, financial analysis techniques, motivation and leadership skills, effective communication methods, managerial and interpersonal abilities, the latest communication and computer technologies, and an eclectic comprehension of the behavioral and decision sciences.

Professional Sales Management integrates sales and marketing management while illustrating how the entire marketing organization (both field and headquarters) must function as a team, working with customers (organizations or consumers) to solve problems of mutual interest. Emphasis is on relationship selling, which seeks to establish long-run partnerships with customers based on trust, quality, service, and mutual respect. More attention is given to industrial sales than to consumers sales because most graduating students will be selling products and services to businesses. Discussions and examples of the diverse sales concepts, issues, and activities strive to provide an appropriate balance among the theoretical, analytical, and pragmatic approaches by blending the most progressive applications from the sales practitioner's world with the latest research findings from academia.

Though *Professional Sales Management* is designed primarily for use at the upper level in colleges and universities, some progressive junior colleges may wish to adopt it for students planning to enter sales careers after earning their associate's degree. All chapters of the text have been successfully pretested by undergraduate students at Louisiana State University and Memphis State University and with undergraduate and M.B.A. students at Drexel University. Individual chapters have been pretested at several other universities around the country.

Organization of the Book

The overall objective of this book is to help the sales managers and salespeople of today and tomorrow prepare for the challenging and exciting years ahead, so that the transition from sales to sales management to marketing is a natural progression, not a traumatic step, for the young manager. To this end, *Professional Sales Management* is divided into six major parts, with a total of seventeen chapters, plus two appendixes.

Part One provides an overview and integration of personal selling and sales management with headquarters marketing management. Chapter 1 covers the eclectic, expanding role of the professional sales manager, who is fast becoming a respected member of marketing management and is concerned with long-run strategic planning and profitability. The contemporary performance of sales managers is analyzed, and methods are recommended to improve the selection, training, and evaluation of sales managers for improved sales force performance. Finally, the chapter describes several megatrends that will significantly impact on the performance of sales managers in the decade ahead. Chapter 2 explains how the growing responsibilities of contemporary sales representatives require them to operate more like marketing managers than sellers of products or services. Sales careers are viewed from the standpoints of income, perquisites, lifestyle, and advancement opportunities. The variety of sales positions from responsive selling to creative selling is examined. The chapter stresses how the professional salesperson works with a team of backup specialists to help solve customer problems.

Part Two covers planning and organizing the sales force. Chapter 3 focuses on strategic sales planning and budgeting. Planning is shown to be the most basic function of the sales manager because it creates the essential framework for all other sales decision making. The value of a sales management information system to strategic and tactical planning is illustrated, and the proactive planning process is explained step by step. Periodic sales audits are depicted as critical to the success of the entire sales function, not only to evaluate the results of an implemented plan but to provide a complete "health examination" on which to construct more realistic future plans. Finally, the purposes, benefits, and preparation of an annual sales budget are discussed. Chapter 4 addresses the sales management task of estimating market potentials and forecasting sales. Sales forecasting is viewed as the starting point for all sales and marketing planning, production scheduling, cash-flow projections, financial planning, capital investment, procurement, inventory management, human resource planning, and budgeting. After analyzing the various concepts and methods of estimating demand, the chapter illustrates the application of the most widely used forecasting techniques, including judgment, counting, time series, and causal methods. A comparative analysis of forecasting methods closes the chapter.

Chapter 5 deals with organizing the sales force. Structural designs for sales organizations, ranging from extremely mechanistic to extremely organic, are analyzed. Evolution of the sales department within the marketing organization is reviewed. Techniques for determining the optimal sales force size are illustrated, and the advantages and disadvantages of employing a direct sales force rather than independent sales agents are presented.

Part Three concentrates on the development of the sales force. Chapter 6 explains the sales force recruiting process, the sources of good candidates, the legal rights of sales applicants, the critical distinction between a job analysis and a job description, the basic qualifications needed for sales positions, and the key attributes of "supersalespeople." Chapter 7 describes the procedures and tools used to select the best applicants and explains what sales managers look for in application forms and interviews. Legal considerations in interviewing and testing are studied. The important step of socialization, or helping the individual integrate into the sales organization, is also considered. Chapter 8 presents the many aspects of training and retraining sales representatives. After analysis of why salespeople fail, the topics investigated are the assignment of responsibility for sales training; training program content; the latest methods and technologies for training; evaluation of training; and the benefits of continual training, retraining, and executive training.

Part Four focuses on directing the sales force and includes five chapters. Chapter 9 sets up an overall conceptual framework for understanding the major determinants of salesperson and sales force performance. Chapter 10 presents alternative approaches for assigning and managing sales territories to achieve sales objectives effectively and efficiently. It outlines the procedures for setting up and revising sales territories, and for routing and maximizing productive selling time, and it shows applications of the newest technologies in time and territory management. Chapter 11 deals with the different types of sales quotas; their purposes; and how they are developed, measured, and administered. Chapter 12 examines various compensation plans and how they need to be modified with changing market conditions. The chapter also considers what can be done about rapidly rising selling costs and analyzes some alternatives to making personal sales calls. Different plans for reimbursement of sales expenses incurred by sales reps are also presented. Chapter 13 focuses on motivating the sales force. It describes the various theories of motivation and considers nonfinancial as well as financial rewards. Most important, it refutes blanket approaches to motivation and recommends a hierarchical segmentation strategy to motivate the sales force. Sales contests, sales meetings, and various other motivational tools are discussed. Chapter 14 is concerned with the important topic of leading the sales force. After leadership is defined, interrelationships among communication, motivation, and leadership are explained. Verbal as well as nonverbal forms of communication are evaluated, and transactional analysis is presented as an effective approach to communicating with salespeople. Major leadership theories are described and evaluated, and then the sources of leader power are identified. The chapter concludes with analysis of the appropriate style of sales management leadership for different stages of sales force maturity.

Part Five discusses controlling and evaluating sales force performance. Chapter 15 relates sales volume, costs, and profit analyses to various market segments, including products, customers, salespeople, territories, and marketing activities. Some sources of sales information are described, and the concept of input-output efficiency is explained. The value of cooperation between marketing and accounting departments is shown, and then procedures for conducting sales, cost, and profitability analyses are explained step by step. There is an analysis of arguments for using contribution costs rather than full costs in allocating costs to market segments, and specific examples show the impact of each approach on overall organization profitability. Return on assets measured, a useful criterion for measuring sales manager performance, is presented and illustrated by easy-to-follow examples. Chapter 16 investigates state-of-the-art techniques for setting performance standards for sales representatives and objectively measuring actual performance. The use of sales audits to evaluate the entire sales force is also examined.

Part Six considers the environment for personal selling and sales management. Chapter 17 focuses on ethics, social responsibility, and the legal environment for selling and sales management. It presents the different concepts of business ethics and the conflicts among them. Then it analyzes the ethical concerns of salespeople in dealing with the company, coworkers, customers, and other salespeople. Major ethical concerns of sales managers are discussed, along with a pragmatic approach to making ethical decisions. The evolution of corporate social responsibility is traced, and the different levels of social responsibility at which a company can operate are depicted. A process for making socially responsible decisions is presented, and the use of social audits is explained and illustrated. Finally, the legislation affecting selling and sales management in local, state, federal, and international sales situations is analyzed.

Appendix A provides a comprehensive, in-depth analysis of the personal selling process and presents a host of techniques and real-world examples for improving selling performance. (Many instructors will want to assign Appendix A as the first chapter for students to read in order to prepare them for the study of sales management.) Appendix B is designed to help students who are considering a career in sales. It explains how to conduct a self-analysis prior to choosing a career, and then uses the personal selling process to show students how to sell their services effectively to prospective employers.

Changes in the Second Edition

The second edition had the following objectives:

- *To update the statistics and trends in sales force management.* Many developments (war in the Middle East, increasing gas prices, recession, etc.) in the late 1980s and early 1990s have had an impact on sales management.

- *To analyze new forces in the selling environment.* The environmental trends of the late 1980s and early 1990s led to changes in the selling environment such as greater emphasis on controlling costs, more competitive markets, more women and minorities in sales.

- *To emphasize the global market facing sales managers today.* Sales managers of the 1990s must be prepared to deal with the challenge of foreign competitors in the United States as well as the potential opportunities existing in foreign markets.

- *To stress the role of ethics in sales management decision making.* Business ethics is one of the most important, yet perhaps most misunderstood, concerns in the world of business today. Sales managers of the 1990s must be able to recognize the role of ethics in sales management decision making.

- *To emphasize the importance of analytical skills for today's sales managers.* Sales managers of the 1990s will need to sharpen their analytical skills if they are to function in the very competitive selling environment of the 1990s. More competition, advancing technologies, new products, and changing markets are just a few characteristics of today's selling environment that make analytical skills so important for sales managers.

- *To describe the increasing importance of computers, telecommunications, and other new technologies in improving sales management planning and sales force performance.* The sales manager's job has changed dramatically in the last decade due to changes in technology. The successful sales manager of the 1990s will be one who can blend the latest in computer technologies with analytical and interpersonal skills.

These objectives are reflected in some distinctive features and substantial revisions in the second edition:

- *Chapter 1: Professional Sales Management.* Emphasizes the role of the sales manager in the tough, competitive selling environment of the 1990s. The megatrends affecting sales managers in the 1990s have been updated.

- *Chapter 2: Personal Selling.* Updates the trends in the personal selling environment. Sections on women in sales, minorities in sales, and relationship selling have been expanded.

- *Chapter 6: Recruiting the Sales Force.* Thoroughly discusses the importance of recruiting in the 1990s, a decade when recruiters will see the pool of qualified candidates shrink because of changing demographics.

- *Chapter 7: Selecting the Sales Force.* Expands the discussion of sales force socialization and adds a section on sales force selection in multinational companies.

- *Chapter 8: Training the Sales Force.* Now emphasizes sales training to build partnerships and long-term relationships. Additions include a discussion of storytelling and sales training, as well as an academic discussion on evaluating sales training programs.

- *Chapter 13: Motivating the Sales Force.* Adds a section on emerging perspectives on motivation which includes goal-setting theory and the Japanese style of motivation. Also includes a section on motivating salespeople over time.

- *Chapter 14: Leading the Sales Force.* Integrates a more detailed discussion of how leadership is critical for successful managers. Additions include a discussion on the concept of substitutes for leadership and a new section on listening skills.

- *Chapter 17: Ethics, Social Responsibility, and the Legal Environment.* Amplifies the discussion of ethics in sales management by incorporating a contingency framework for ethical decision making for the selling environment. Also adds a section on managing unethical sales force behavior.

Two more distinctive features of the second edition are the Ethics Scenarios and the In-Basket Exercises added to each chapter.

- *Ethics Scenarios.* Each chapter incorporates an ethics situation dealing with a topic in that chapter. These scenarios have been developed with no right or wrong answers. The goal is to place a student in a sales manager's role when facing ethical dilemmas. The exercises are excellent in generating class discussion since students' ethical standards vary considerably. Additionally, the scenarios place students in real-world situations where their own ethical decision-making abilities are challenged.

- *In-Basket Exercises.* A real-world In-Basket Exercise has been added to each chapter to place students in a sales manager's role in order to work on decision-making skills. Having several alternative solutions, these exercises are also excellent at generating class discussion.

The cases have also been changed for the second edition. The instructor has two options in case assignments:

- There are two cases at the end of each chapter which focus on the chapter material. Many completely new cases have been added to the second edition. All others have been revised.

- A completely new set of integrated cases has been added at the end of Parts One through Five of the text. These CHEMCO cases are more comprehensive as they integrate subjects from each chapter within that part of the text. All five integrated cases are from a real-world company database. A diskette providing the company data is also available for students. The goal of the integrated cases is to sharpen students' analytical skills with real-world sales management decision-making experience.

Improved Pedagogical Aids

The second edition is accompanied by extensive supplementary materials:

- A comprehensive, extensively revised Instructor's Manual containing chapter outlines, teaching aids, alternative course organizations, learning objectives, classroom discussion questions, solutions to text problems and questions, discussions and solutions relating to Ethics Scenarios and In-Basket Exercises, a film and videotape bibliography, and transparency masters.

- A completely revised test bank of analytical multiple-choice questions. Correct answers and text page references are provided for ease of use. The test bank is also available in computerized form.

- Numerous IBM PC-based computer exercises emphasizing sales management applications and designed to amplify the textbook, available in a separate book of Lotus-based exercises.

Acknowledgments

Long-term efforts, both large and small, are needed from many talented people to give life to a college textbook, and the authors gratefully acknowledge their debt to those who contributed to *Professional Sales Management*.

First, we recognize the enormous, unpayable debt we owe to all those scholars and practitioners who have advanced the study and practice of selling and sales management over the years and thereby enabled us to make our own contribution. Second, we are especially appreciative to our marketing colleagues (professors, business executives, and students) who contributed case material or read the manuscript as it developed and offered their candid suggestions about how to improve the presentation of material. Among these people, our special thanks go to Sandra Hart and Jack Degan, of Texas Wesleyan University; Ronald F. Bush and Richard Sjolander, of the University of West Florida; Joyce L. Grahn, of the University of Wisconsin—Eau Claire; William Moncrief, of Texas Christian University; Bob Powell, of Piccadilly Cafeterias, in Baton Rouge, Louisiana; Debbie Boswell, Colleen Terro, S. Michael Carlson, William Simmons, Suzanne Desonier, Randy Russ, Jill A. Cavell, Frank Notturno, B. Mitchell Griffin, Dan L. Sherrell, and Paul W. Johnston, of Louisiana State University; E. Stephen Grant, Molly Inhofe, Philip Nitse, and Steve Remington, of Memphis State University.

McGraw-Hill and the authors would like to express their thanks for the many useful comments and suggestions provided by colleagues who reviewed this text during the course of its development, especially to Daniel Bosse, Southern Illinois University at Edwardsville; Burton J. Brodo, Wharton School of Business; Andrew A. Brogowicz, Western Michigan University; Kenneth Evans, Arizona State University; Noel Mark Lavenka, Loyola University of Chicago; Peggy Liebman, Trenton State University; Lynn Metcalf, California State Polytechnic University; and David Szymanski, Texas A&M University. We were also fortunate to have the talented help of Molly Inhofe in revising the supplements for the text.

Next, we want to thank Dean James Henry, at Louisiana State University, and Dean Paul Dascher, at Drexel University, for their continuing support of our writing efforts. We also gratefully acknowledge the valuable assistance of our secretarial staffs, Nora Fierro, Frances Hughes, Berrenice Strickland, and Mary Rhein.

Most important to the initiation and completion of *Professional Sales Management* was the professional McGraw-Hill team who diligently and creatively guided it throughout the various stages of development. Bonnie Binkert, Mimi Melek, and Laura Warner served as editors; Charles Carson was the text designer; and Leroy Young supervised production. Their dedicated work on this book was first-rate in every way, and we believe the finished product reflects well on them.

Finally, we want to acknowledge all our students—past, present, and future—who make our teaching and writing enjoyable and meaningful.

Rolph E. Anderson
Joseph F. Hair, Jr.
Alan J. Bush

PART ONE

OVERVIEW OF PERSONAL OF PERSONAL SELLING AND SALES MANAGEMENT

1

PROFESSIONAL
SALES
MANAGEMENT

LEARNING OBJECTIVES

When you finish this chapter, you should understand:

▲ The role, responsibilities, and duties of the sales manager
▲ Position titles and responsibilities of sales managers at different hierarchical levels
▲ Why and how to integrate sales and marketing management
▲ How well sales managers are performing in their jobs
▲ Why sales managers are not doing a better job
▲ Why the concept of the sales manager's job is expanding
▲ Why sales managers need top-management support
▲ What megatrends are impacting on sales management
▲ How to develop people to handle the increasingly eclectic job of sales manager

---

A DAY ON THE JOB

Ken McWain is a sales manager for the Paper Packaging Ink Group of BASF Corporation, where his group is responsible for approximately $35 million in sales each year. Ken manages seventeen salespeople who market ink for corrugated boxes and single-wall and multiwall bags. He finds sales management extremely exciting and challenging as he markets ink to industrial users. "When you're selling a commodity-type product like ink, products, prices, and even services are very similar. In a competitive situation like this, the salespeople become the key differentiator. One of the most challenging aspects of sales management is that you cannot manage all salespeople alike. Salespeople can be very different from each other, and this makes it extremely important for sales managers to know their salespeople very well. You've got to know what makes each of them tick so that you can direct and motivate them to their optimal level." Among his sales force, Ken is perhaps best known for his strong support of customer involvement. "I believe sales managers should get out and ride with their salespeople, go to lunch with them and their clients, and advise salespeople to interact with their customers as often as possible." There are two aspects of sales management that Ken especially enjoys: "I believe good sales managers should also be teachers and cheerleaders. I personally believe in teaching by example." Regarding being a cheerleader, he says: "Everyone needs recognition and praise. You can never give your salespeople enough praise!" This kind of sales management philosophy enabled Ken to move BASF's Paper Packaging Ink Group from being a follower in the industry to being one of its market leaders.[1]

WHAT IS A SALES MANAGER?

A sales vice president from Mead Johnson & Company describes the sales manager in the following way:

A [sales] manager is many things to many people! He is a teacher, a trainer, and a coach. He is a recruiter, an employer, and a counselor. He is a leader of his group, and a follower and implementor of company policies, plans, and programs. He is a decision-maker who accepts responsibility for his decisions and teaches others the fine art of decisiveness.

Yes, a [sales] manager is many things to many people. He is a communicator and a catalyst. He is a planner, an organizer, and a prognosticator. He is a conductor, an orchestrator, and a skillful manipulator. He is an amalgamator, a consolidator, directing and uniting the efforts of many toward the achievement of common goals.

Yes, a [sales] manager is many things to many people. He is a teammate, a referee, and an umpire. He is an advisor, a supervisor, and a friend. He is a developer and supporter of his people but at times he must also be an executioner. He must handle the broken dreams of some and the good fortune of others, sharing in their disappointment just as he shares in their happiness.

Yes, a [sales] manager is many things to many people. He is a psychologist, an analyst, and strategist. He is a delegator, a motivator, and an evaluator. He is a successful mentor who understands each individual's need for self-fulfillment, economic growth, and personal prestige. He is an artist, slowly and carefully helping others to carve and mold their futures.

Yes, a [sales] manager is many things to many people. He is an instigator, an innovator, and a creator of new ideas and promotions. He is an over-achiever rising to the challenge of a new forecast each year. He has the strength and courage to handle unanticipated difficulties and events. He is an opportunist and a worthy adversary.

Yes, a [sales] manager is many things to many people.[2]

Sales managers are paid to plan, lead, and control the personal selling activities of an organization. In carrying out these responsibilities, sales managers (1) prepare sales plans and budgets; (2) set sales force goals and objectives; (3) estimate demand and forecast sales; (4) determine the size and structure of the sales force organization; (5) recruit, select, and train salespeople; (6) design sales territories, set sales quotas, and define performance standards; (7) compensate, motivate, and lead the sales force; (8) conduct sales volume, cost, and profit analyses; (9) evaluate sales force performance; and (10) monitor the ethical and social conduct of the sales force. Few, if any, jobs in an organization are more important, because sales is the only activity that directly generates income: all other activities support this revenue-producing function. Unless products and services can be profitably sold, the organization will not survive. In short, the ultimate success or failure of any business depends on how well it can sell products. The next example shows what it takes to be a sales manager at Procter & Gamble.

WHAT IT TAKES TO BE A SALES MANAGER AT PROCTER & GAMBLE

Sales managers have to be effective managers of people, good decision makers, creative problem solvers, and outstanding communicators. They also must work closely with other disciplines as part of the overall marketing team, helping to coordinate and focus the efforts of Product Development, Manufacturing, Market Research, and Advertising. For example, sales managers must jointly develop national marketing objectives and strategy with Advertising, and then tailor these plans to suit regional differences, the competitive environment, consumer preferences, and so on. The sales manager is also responsible for "making it happen" in the marketplace. In addition, sales managers use consumer data from Market Research to demonstrate the benefits of P&G products to their accounts, helping create strong brand support. And, they make recommendations to Product Development, based on responses from accounts, which may result in an improved product or better packaging.

To be happy in Sales Management, you have to love challenges because you'll be getting them every day. You have to be tough enough to cope when a customer turns you down, creative enough to solve problems for your accounts, motivated enough to set lofty goals for yourself and then strive to exceed them. And you have to love working with people, because that's the essence of the job.

Because P&G sales managers' responsibilities require working with all disciplines in the Company, a career in Sales Management provides the kind of broad experience important to assuming general management responsibility.[3]

Not-for-profit organizations as well as businesses employ sales representatives—no matter what their euphemistic title may be—and so they also need sales managers. For example, recruiters for all-voluntary military services, fundraisers for political parties, and admissions people for universities are all engaged in selling. As proven every day, selling and sales management concepts and techniques are as applicable to noncommercial as to commercial organizations.

EXHIBIT 1-1

Sales Management Hierarchy with Corresponding Responsibilities

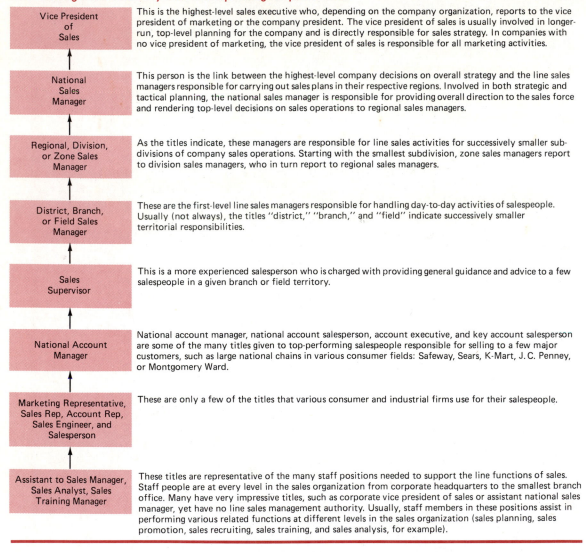

Vice President of Sales
This is the highest-level sales executive who, depending on the company organization, reports to the vice president of marketing or the company president. The vice president of sales is usually involved in longer-run, top-level planning for the company and is directly responsible for sales strategy. In companies with no vice president of marketing, the vice president of sales is responsible for all marketing activities.

National Sales Manager
This person is the link between the highest-level company decisions on overall strategy and the line sales managers responsible for carrying out sales plans in their respective regions. Involved in both strategic and tactical planning, the national sales manager is responsible for providing overall direction to the sales force and rendering top-level decisions on sales operations to regional sales managers.

Regional, Division, or Zone Sales Manager
As the titles indicate, these managers are responsible for line sales activities for successively smaller subdivisions of company sales operations. Starting with the smallest subdivision, zone sales managers report to division sales managers, who in turn report to regional sales managers.

District, Branch, or Field Sales Manager
These are the first-level line sales managers responsible for handling day-to-day activities of salespeople. Usually (not always), the titles "district," "branch," and "field" indicate successively smaller territorial responsibilities.

Sales Supervisor
This is a more experienced salesperson who is charged with providing general guidance and advice to a few salespeople in a given branch or field territory.

National Account Manager
National account manager, national account salesperson, account executive, and key account salesperson are some of the many titles given to top-performing salespeople responsible for selling to a few major customers, such as large national chains in various consumer fields: Safeway, Sears, K-Mart, J.C. Penney, or Montgomery Ward.

Marketing Representative, Sales Rep, Account Rep, Sales Engineer, and Salesperson
These are only a few of the titles that various consumer and industrial firms use for their salespeople.

Assistant to Sales Manager, Sales Analyst, Sales Training Manager
These titles are representative of the many staff positions needed to support the line functions of sales. Staff people are at every level in the sales organization from corporate headquarters to the smallest branch office. Many have very impressive titles, such as corporate vice president of sales or assistant national sales manager, yet have no line sales management authority. Usually, staff members in these positions assist in performing various related functions at different levels in the sales organization (sales planning, sales promotion, sales recruiting, sales training, and sales analysis, for example).

Sales managers' responsibilities vary widely. Depending on the nature of the organization and the attitude of top management toward the sales function, the sales manager's responsibilities and duties vary on a long continuum. In some companies, the sales manager may be little more than a supervisor of the sales force, a kind of "supersalesperson" who shows the others how to do it. Some organizations assign forecasting, planning, budgeting, and profit responsibilities to the sales manager, while in others the sales manager is the marketing manager in every way but position title. Depending on their hierarchical level, sales managers may have several different position titles and responsibilities, as Exhibit 1-1 reveals.

BASIC RESPONSIBILITIES OF A SALES MANAGER

Exhibit 1-2 presents a framework for sales management decision making and indicates chapters where each component is discussed. The sales manager must accomplish his or her duties within the larger framework of organizational objectives, marketing strategies, and target markets while continuously monitoring the *macroenvironment* (technological, competitive, economic, legal, cultural, and ethical factors) and the company's *stakeholders* (employees, suppliers, the financial community, the media, stockholders, special interest groups, the government, and the general public).

Chapters 1 and 2 and Appendixes A and B will help you understand the overall roles of sales manager and salesperson. Specific sales management functions will be discussed in subsequent chapters, but it is important that a short, general description of each is offered at this point to provide a conceptual framework for understanding the chapters to follow.

EXHIBIT 1-2

A Framework for Sales Management Decision Making

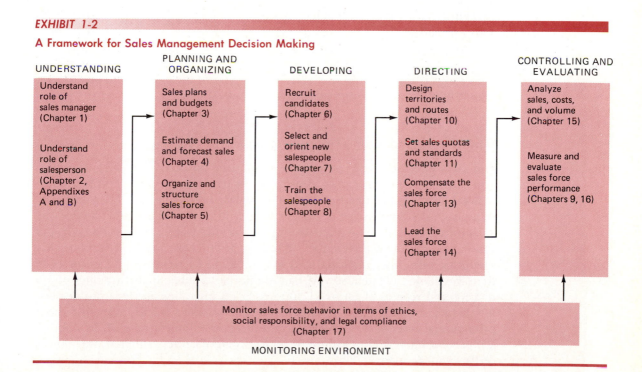

UNDERSTANDING	PLANNING AND ORGANIZING	DEVELOPING	DIRECTING	CONTROLLING AND EVALUATING
Understand role of sales manager (Chapter 1)	Sales plans and budgets (Chapter 3)	Recruit candidates (Chapter 6)	Design territories and routes (Chapter 10)	Analyze sales, costs, and volume (Chapter 15)
Understand role of salesperson (Chapter 2, Appendixes A and B)	Estimate demand and forecast sales (Chapter 4)	Select and orient new salespeople (Chapter 7)	Set sales quotas and standards (Chapter 11)	Measure and evaluate sales force performance (Chapters 9, 16)
	Organize and structure sales force (Chapter 5)	Train the salespeople (Chapter 8)	Compensate the sales force (Chapter 13)	
			Lead the sales force (Chapter 14)	

Monitor sales force behavior in terms of ethics, social responsibility, and legal compliance (Chapter 17)

MONITORING ENVIRONMENT

Sales Planning and Budgeting

Planning is the first job of all sales managers because the plan provides the direction and strategy for all other sales management decisions and activities. Plans are made at each hierarchical level in the company. At the level of the chief executive officer (CEO), planning is largely oriented toward refining the company's mission, setting corporate goals and objectives, devising overall strategies, and developing total budgets. In contrast, even at the highest sales management levels, planning tends to be tactical; sales planners are concerned with yearly or quarterly goals and objectives, departmental policies, and budgets. Planning by first-level sales managers is usually focused on monthly, weekly, or even daily activities. No matter the hierarchical level where planning is being done, however, the critical part of the process is determining organizational goals and objectives.

Sales goals give the sales force broad, long-run direction and general purpose, while *sales objectives* make explicit what results are to be achieved within a specified time period. For example, one goal of the sales force may be to become recognized as the most service-oriented in the industry, whereas a sales objective may be to achieve sales of $35 million by the end of the year. For an individual salesperson, a major goal could be improved travel scheduling and routing to increase time spent with customers, while the salesperson's objectives may be to achieve a certain level of dollar sales, profit, or new accounts in a set time period.

Funding is needed to implement any plan, so preparation of the budget is a critical part of the planning process. A *sales budget* is simply a financial plan of expenditures needed to accomplish the projected goals and objectives. In other words, preparing a sales budget is the process of assigning dollar costs to the various components of the plan. The purpose of the budget is to ensure that organizational resources are allocated in the most efficient way over the period of the plan.

Estimating Demand and Forecasting Sales

The sales forecast is the cornerstone supporting all other company decisions. Thus, forecasting errors can be disastrous. For example, General Motors forecast that gasoline would cost $3.60 per gallon by late 1986 or early 1987. As a result, its product mix emphasized compact and subcompact cars instead of larger ones. As it turned out, gasoline prices during that period were as low as 65 cents per gallon, and customer preferences shifted toward midsize and larger cars. Highly optimistic sales forecasts lured GM into building far more small cars in 1986 than the market wanted, so GM had to offer automobile financing rates of 2.9 percent and rebates of up to $1,500 to sell off huge inventories from dealers' lots before shipping 1987 models. Ford and Chrysler quickly matched those promotional incentives, and American Motors one-upped them all by offering a 0 percent interest rate. Naturally, all four manufacturers suffered huge losses on automobile loans to customers.

Sales managers should estimate *market potential* for the industry and *sales potential* for the company before developing a final *sales forecast* on which to base all operational planning and budgeting for their sales force. Shrewd sales managers employ both quantitative and qualitative approaches and study the similarities and differences between the two sets of results before deciding on the final sales forecast. After all, the final sales forecast can determine the success or failure of the company.

Determining the Size and Structure of the Sales Organization

The number of salespeople and the way they are organized affect several sales management decisions, including job descriptions, compensation methods, sales forecasts, budgets, territory assignments, supervision, motivation, and evaluation of sales force performance. Considerable experience and various guidelines are available to help sales managers determine the optimal number of salespeople to hire and the best way to structure the sales force (geographically, by product, by customer type, or by some combination of these factors). In some companies, the sales manager must also decide whether to substitute independent *manufacturing representatives* for some or even all members of the direct sales force. Adjustments may be needed in both sales force size and structure in response to changes in marketing strategy or fluctuations of the uncontrollable variables in the marketing environment. In all cases, the overriding purpose in selecting a particular organizational structure and size should be to optimize the attainment of sales objectives and goals.

Recruiting, Selecting, and Training Salespeople

Recruiting is the task of attracting qualified applicants for employment. It includes identifying sources of potential sales recruits, methods of reaching them, and strategies for attracting them to apply for a sales job. Once applicants have been recruited, the sales manager must devise a system for measuring applicants against predetermined job requirements. This involves analysis of the numerous tools and techniques available for processing applicants. Finally, the decision to select or reject each applicant must be made.

New salespeople need to be assimilated, or blended smoothly, into the sales organization. Included in the assimilation process are an explanation of job responsibilities and managerial expectations, introduction to coworkers, and help for the new salesperson as he or she adjusts socially and psychologically to the organization—and sometimes to the community, as well.

Traditionally, training and retraining of salespeople have focused mainly on sales techniques, but more progressive firms are trying to expand the perspectives of their salespeople by blending sales and marketing concepts with sales training. This broader-based training not only helps salespeople to see how their jobs fit into the overall organization but also prepares them for future responsibilities as sales and marketing managers. Any time a salesperson is promoted to sales management or receives significantly broader or different responsibilities, it is a good idea to consider additional training. In designing a training program, the sales manager must answer several questions: Who should receive the training? Who should do the training? Where, when, and how should the training be accomplished? What should be taught?

Allocating Sales Force Efforts and Setting Sales Quotas

To effectively allocate sales force efforts, the sales manager must first design sales territories. A *sales territory* is a market segment or group of present and potential customers who share some common characteristics relevant to purchasing behavior. Territories should be compared on the basis of sales potential, which in turn decides individual *sales quotas* (the motivational targets assigned to the sales force as a whole and to salespeople individually). After sales territories have been determined, management may design a formal pattern, or *routing,* for sales representatives to follow in calling on customers. Some sales managers prefer to have the salespeople assume responsibility for scheduling and routing themselves, but in either case a predetermined plan should be carried out.

Few salespeople make optimal use of their most precious resource: time. Thus, one of the most important jobs of sales managers is to train and retrain their salespeople in techniques for improving the management of time and territory.

Compensating, Motivating, and Leading the Sales Force

Decisions about sales force compensation ought to include both financial and nonfinancial incentives. Besides basic salary and commissions, *financial compensation* should include reimbursement of sales expenses and transportation. *Nonfinancial incentives* may include use of a company car, office space, secretarial help, and special company benefits such as life insurance, a retirement plan, and health care.

The level, components, and structure of compensation should be carefully considered by the sales manager. A fair and rational pay structure for different positions in the sales organization—sales trainees, junior salespeople, senior salespeople, and sales managers—plays a major role in the retention of superior performers.

Sales managers must continuously strive to keep the sales force highly motivated. *Motivation* is personal and must arise first within the individual salesperson, but sales managers can help create the type of working environment and incentives that boost the morale and enthusiasm of the salespeople. In addition to understanding how organizational culture, sales quotas, compensation methods, and sales management style can affect sales force motivation, it is important for sales managers to understand the personal needs and aspirations of each salesperson. A sales manager must realize that most employees seek fulfillment beyond working conditions and financial rewards.

Closely linked to sales force motivation is *leadership.* Leadership goes far beyond administrative and supervisory functions. *Administration* tends to be identified with the largely ''nonpeople,'' policy-making activities of management, and *supervision* is concerned with monitoring the daily work of a group of people. But sales managers with leadership ability can inspire salespeople to extraordinary accomplishments, making their work personally meaningful and helping them to achieve more than they ever thought they could.

Sales force leadership ought to be proactive and flexible. With even subtle changes in market conditions or the maturity of the sales force, sales managers may need to adjust their leadership style, ranging from autocratic control to free reign.

Analyzing Sales Volume, Cost, and Profit

To accomplish the bottom-line goal of improved profitability, sales managers must analyze volume, cost, and profit relationships across product lines, territories, customers, salespersons, and sales and marketing functions. These analyses seek to identify unprofitable sales units so that sales managers can take timely corrective action to allocate sales force efforts better and improve profitability.

Measuring and Evaluating Sales Force Performance

Sales force performance must be measured and evaluated to determine commissions and bonuses for salespeople and sales managers and to make promotion decisions. The overall purpose of performance evaluation, however, is to improve organizational profitability by improving sales force efforts.

Any meaningful system for evaluating salespeople requires job descriptions and mutual agreement regarding performance standards. Standards for the measurement of performance may include (1) salesperson-to-salesperson comparisons, (2) current-to-past performance comparisons, and (3) actual-to-expected performance comparisons. For effective managerial control and evaluation, standards of performance must be established, actual performance compared to the predetermined standards, and appropriate corrective action taken to improve performance.

Not to be overlooked in evaluating sales force performance is how well ethical guidelines and standards of social responsibility are being met. Nothing will destroy the credibility and performance of salespeople faster than the per-

---

ETHICS IN SALES MANAGEMENT: PLAYING BY THE RULES

You are a sales manager for a large chemical company, and you have reason to suspect that one of your *top* salespeople isn't always playing by the rules. You know that on occasion he has taken friends out to lunch and charged it to the company. At other times, you have caught him conducting personal business (long-distance telephone calls, for instance) on company time. You have overlooked these things in the past because of the large sales volume he brings into the company. One evening, though, on your way out of the office, you overhear a conversation between this top sales performer and another one of your salespeople. Your top salesperson comments: ''I personally think it's okay to withhold certain information about a product in order to make a big sale as long as no one can get injured by the product. Things are getting real tough in our industry, and sometimes you've got to do whatever it takes to get a sale!''

What do you do?

ception by potential customers that they do not operate in an ethical or socially responsible manner. A sales manager's job today is becoming more challenging due to the increasing number of ethical considerations that occur in selling situations on a day-to-day basis. The *Ethics* scenario on page 11 exemplifies this challenge.

Monitoring the Marketing Environment

While carrying out all their basic responsibilities, sales managers must also satisfy target customers within the constraints of a continuously changing marketing environment. Every corporation has many stakeholders who share a vested interest in corporate activities, and an increasing number of companies are becoming *proactive* as well as *reactive* in dealing with these indirect partners in the business. For example, large companies usually have political action committees (PACs) that try to influence legislation and public affairs departments to promote the company to stockholders, the financial community, and the media. Beyond these influencing publics, or stakeholders, is the larger macroenvironment, which often brings dramatic, unexpected changes in technology, economic conditions, competitors, laws, culture, and ethical standards. Avon Products, the well-known, door-to-door cosmetics company, found it necessary to adjust to major shifts in its marketing environment, as the next example describes.

AVON CALLING . . . OR MAILING OR TELEPHONING

With 52 percent of American women working outside the home, Avon Products is finding fewer potential customers at home and is encountering increasing difficulty in recruiting sales representatives. Traditionally, "Avon ladies" have worked only part-time for relatively low pay and without such basic benefits as medical insurance or paid vacations. Thus, of 600,000 recruits only about 180,000 continue with the company for more than a year. In recent years, Avon's profit margins and stock price have dropped dramatically. In addition, attempts to diversify through acquisitions have seen long-term debt soar. In an effort to increase the number of sales representatives, Avon is offering higher commissions and improved training programs. Beyond these measures, Avon is exploring direct-mail and telephone sales. But the real question for Avon may be whether or not direct selling can continue to be a viable way to sell cosmetics in the new marketing environment.

Sloppy monitoring of the organization's marketing environment can result in severe setbacks or even threaten survival. But it is not sufficient merely to take a defensive posture with respect to the uncontrollable environment. Successful sales managers must be alert for new market opportunities as well as threats to existing markets. For example, there are ninety-two producers of bottled water in the United States, and any one of them might have captured the market that Perrier now dominates by observing such factors as aging population, weight concerns, and status consciousness. But the "attennae" of the other bottlers were not sufficiently sensitive and alert to the changing tastes and preferences of consumers to see this emerging opportunity. Similarly, several

EXHIBIT 1-3

Unrecognized Opportunities in Their Own Markets

Company or Industry	Product
Levi	Designer jeans
Converse, Keds	Running shoes
IBM	Microcomputers
Anheuser-Busch	Light beers
Coca-Cola, Pepsi-Cola	Diet soft drinks
Swiss watchmakers	Digital watches

well-known companies and even whole industries have failed to recognize emerging opportunities in their own markets, as Exhibit 1-3 illustrates.

As the organization's "eyes and ears" in the marketplace, the sales force has a special responsibility to identify opportunities and threats and report back to headquarters. A successful early-warning system operating from the field can be invaluable to short-run tactics and long-run achievement of organization objectives. Both marketing and sales executives should keep in mind that the highest profits are usually obtained by exploiting opportunities, not by solving problems. To the sensitive observer, however, there is an opportunity in almost every problem. Recently, even giant IBM has moved beyond traditional products and services to turn a growing customer problem into a market opportunity (see the example that follows).

IBM: A SERVICE-ORIENTED SELLER OF PROFESSIONAL SERVICES

Sometimes, a change in the marketing environment creates an opportunity for alert management. IBM built its reputation by providing excellent service on its computers and office products. Beyond providing repair service on the products it has sold, IBM is now becoming a major seller of professional services, especially the planning, design, and management of complex computer systems. To develop its professional services, IBM has created a customer sector organization, which consists of several hundred employees who are experts on various industries. These experts help IBM's thousands of salespeople obtain work for the company's technical consultants and designers.

As companies attempt to build companywide networks of increasingly complex computer hardware and software, many are becoming so frustrated that they are turning to outside experts for help. General Motors Corporation spent over $2.5 billion to buy Electronic Data Systems Corporation in order to have an in-house provider of professional services to solve its computer networking problems.

United Airlines has chosen IBM to develop a new computer system to link travel agents with United's reservations network. IBM also recently announced a $25 million contract to develop software and a network to automate administrative tasks for Hospital Corporation of America, a large corporation that operates private hospitals. Finally, IBM is building a new computer system to manage the huge inventories of small items stocked by 8,000 Tru-Value and V&S Variety Stores. With increasing income from its professional services organization, IBM hopes to smooth out the ups and downs of its hardware sales.[4]

INTEGRATING SALES AND MARKETING MANAGEMENT

Without thoroughly understanding the larger marketing framework within which the sales manager operates, few sales managers can appreciate the importance of integrating sales force planning efforts with overall marketing planning and strategies. Sales management involves a specialized set of responsibilities and activities within the larger field of marketing management. In a broad sense, sales managers are really marketing managers with the specific task of managing the sales force. Many knowledgeable people believe that the sales manager heads the most important of all marketing activities—the critical revenue-generating function, which determines the success or failure of the overall marketing plan.

The Field Sales Force and Headquarters Marketing

An organization's marketing team usually consists of two basic groups: the *field sales force* and the *headquarters marketing team*. In contrast to the sales force personnel who are out in their territories with customers, the headquarters marketing people provide support and service functions that can significantly help the sales manager in performing his or her job. This support includes:

- *Advertising.* Coordination of product or service advertising, usually through an outside agency
- *Sales promotion.* Development of brochures, catalogs, direct-mail pieces, and the like
- *Sales aids.* Preparation of audiovisuals, flip charts, and other materials for sales presentations
- *Trade shows.* Coordination of arrangements for participation in trade shows
- *Product publicity.* Preparation and distribution of news releases to various media about products and services
- *Marketing research.* Collection and interpretation of data concerning markets, products, customers, sales, and other factors
- *Marketing and sales planning.* Assistance in the preparation of marketing and sales plans
- *Forecasting.* Preparation of sales forecasts and prediction of market trends
- *Product planning and development.* Help in planning and developing new or improved products
- *Market development.* Support for entering new markets
- *Public relations.* Help in explaining the actions of the sales force to the company's various stakeholders, including employees, the media, special interest groups, suppliers, government agencies, legislators, the financial community, company stockholders, and the general public

Though precise responsibilities vary among organizations and industries, these support activities are either handled by in-house marketing personnel or subcontracted to outside specialists such as advertising agencies, marketing-research houses, consulting organizations, and public relations firms. Sales managers need to interact frequently with many of these headquarters marketing managers or outside specialists.

Most sales managers and headquarters marketing services staffs could do a much better job of working together to their mutual benefit. By establishing friendly, cooperative relationships with the headquarters marketing managers, sales managers may obtain extra support and services to measurably improve sales force performance. Sales managers who create or allow continuation of a relationship of animosity, rivalry, or indifference toward headquarters marketing people do their salespeople, their customers, and themselves a disservice.

Many of the people who provide critical marketing services for the sales force may not have much understanding of the sales job. When asked "How well do the people providing this service understand your business?" line sales and marketing managers responded as follows:

Services	Little or No Understanding	Moderate Understanding	Great Understanding
Advertising	19%	50%	31%
Sales promotion	6	50	44
Sales aids	13	67	20
Trade shows	21	50	29
Product publicity	36	28	36
Marketing research	10	50	40
Marketing/sales planning	11	67	22
Forecasting	10	70	20
Product development	12	38	50
Market development	12	44	44

Source: Vaughan C. Judd, "Help Marketing Services Get with It," *Sales & Marketing Management*, Oct. 6, 1980, p. 46.

If sales managers would take time to explain how each requested service is to be used, the quality of the marketing services could improve significantly.

Team Selling

When complex product systems such as business services or computer installations are being sold, team selling is frequently employed and the sales representative acts as the team coordinator in contacts with the buyer organization. Instead of having a lone salesperson contacting a single corporate purchasing agent, more and more companies are selling on many different levels by interlocking their research, engineering, production, marketing, and upper-management people with their customers. With this approach, the salesperson operates as an account coordinator or manager. Once established, relationships between buyer and seller teams tend to be continuous and based on respect, performance, trust, and understanding. Key members of the sales team usually include:

- *Top management.* Increasingly, top management is becoming a central part of the selling team, especially in the initial stages of contact with national accounts or during negotiations of major contracts. For example, in Singer Business Machines' opening sales strategy, a top manager writes a letter that requests a meeting with the prospective customer's top operating officer. Seldom is Singer turned down at this level. At this first meeting, the regional sales manager, the local salesperson, and a systems engineer attend along with the key manager to discuss how the system can benefit the client. If promising, this meeting is followed by a series of conferences and demonstrations that involve people throughout the prospect's organization.

- *Technical specialists.* These specialists work with sales representatives to provide technical advice and information sought by the customer before, during, and after the purchase. IBM assigns a technical specialist to work with each of its marketing representatives as part of a consultative team to anticipate and solve customer problems.

- *Customer service representatives.* These representatives assist in the installation, maintenance, and regular servicing of the products and systems that customers purchase.

Besides forming sales teams, many organizations utilize two specialized categories of salespeople to round out their selling efforts or sometimes to substitute entirely for a direct sales force:

- *Inside salespeople,* who sell from the office via telephone. They frequently respond to unsolicited inquiries from prospective customers, and they also generate leads for the direct sales force to follow up. *Telemarketing* has become so popular that some companies are bringing all their salespeople back to headquarters. Louisiana Oil & Tire Company brought all ten of its traveling salespeople inside for telemarketing training. Since then, the company's phone bill has increased by $6,000 a month, but other sales expenses have declined by $15,000 a month and sales volume has doubled.[5]

- *Manufacturers' representatives,* independent manufacturers' agents (usually called manufacturers' "reps") who are paid a commission on the sales they generate. Employing reps is a relatively low-risk way to expand the sales force because the cost-to-sales ratio is fixed. Manufacturers' reps are entrepreneurial, independent salespeople who specialize in certain markets and usually sell the products of several noncompeting companies. Many companies use manufacturers' reps to do specialized selling or to increase call frequencies on certain customers. Quaker Oats Company finds that manufacturers' reps enable it to increase call frequencies on supermarkets so that in-store stocks are replenished at least weekly. Working closely together, the direct sales force, inside salespeople, and manufacturers' representatives can make up a well-rounded, synergistic sales force.

Substitutability of Promotion Elements

Another compelling reason for cooperation between the field sales force and headquarters marketing is the partial substitutability of the four promotional tools (advertising, personal selling, publicity, and sales promotion). Advertising is the most efficient tool in obtaining customer *awareness* of new products and services, whereas customer *comprehension* is influenced about equally by advertising and personal selling. *Closing the sale,* however, can best be done by the salesperson. All types of promotion, especially advertising and follow-ups by the salespeople, can favorably enhance customer evaluation and satisfaction with products and services after purchase.

In many organizations, personal selling is the largest single operating expense—often as much as 15 percent of sales. Selling expenses cover salaries, commissions, travel, and the cost of operating sales branches. Collectively, American firms annually spend more than twice as much on personal selling as on advertising. The decision to use a sales force often boils down to the relative costs and benefits of personal selling and advertising. As Exhibit 1-4 shows, personal selling is considered the most important of the promotion tools in the marketing of industrial goods, but advertising is most important in the marketing of consumer goods. In most cases, the time, money, and effort put into other elements of promotional strategy would be unprofitable without successful sales management and personal selling—and profit is truly the bottom line.

EXHIBIT 1-4

Characteristics and Relative Importance of the Four Elements of Promotion

	Personal Selling	Advertising	Sales Promotion	Publicity
Form of communication	Personal	Nonpersonal	Nonpersonal	Nonpersonal
Contact with prospect	Direct	Indirect	Indirect	Indirect
Message flexibility	Flexible	Inflexible	Inflexible	Inflexible
Prospect feedback	Direct	Indirect	Indirect	Indirect
Cost per contact	High	Low	Moderate to high	None
Relative importance for consumer marketing	3	1	2	4
Relative importance for industrial marketing	1	3	2	4

Top-Management Support for Sales Managers

Any sales manager knows that the attitudes of top management are a powerful influence on how the sales organization functions. Thus, it is in the best interest of sales managers to encourage top management to create the climate and profit orientation that will enable the sales organization to function most effectively and efficiently. Top management can achieve this by:

- Developing and fostering a companywide managerial orientation through up-to-date and *meaningful job descriptions for all managers* as well as their subordinates

- Establishing and maintaining *open channels of communication* with managers throughout the organization, with special care taken to include the field sales force managers in headquarters communications

- Including sales managers in *training programs with other functional managers in the organization* and encouraging special training seminars for sales managers at which they can discuss, with the guidance of a skilled moderator, their common problems

- Providing sales managers with necessary *tools and incentives for managing*, including:

  1. *Managerial performance criteria,* such as profit contribution, return on assets managed, development and maintenance of customers, sales force retention and development goals, sales-to-costs ratios, and market-share changes

  2. *Decision-oriented reports from headquarters,* which allow analyses of customers, products, territories, salespeople, and functions in terms of cost and profit, instead of the traditional accounting-oriented reports that summarize total organization expenses

HOW ARE SALES MANAGERS PERFORMING?

Sales managers have a difficult job, and they are bound to be criticized by some organization members no matter how well they handle their duties. A study in *Sales & Marketing Management* identified a number of complaints that salespeople have about their own sales managers; Exhibit 1-5 summarizes the results. Some of the common complaints are that sales managers don't spend enough time with their salespeople; they don't listen to their salespeople's concerns; they don't take their salespeople's concerns seriously; and they don't follow up. Although some of the criticism may be unfair, there is considerable evidence that sales activities in the United States are not being performed as effectively as they could be. The responsibility for this must lie with sales managers. A survey of over 10,000 industrial buyers revealed these serious deficiencies:

- 96 percent said the salespeople did not ask for a commitment on an order form, apparently because they had "lost control" of the selling situation.

EXHIBIT 1-5

Complaints of Salespeople about Their Sales Managers

- They believe that they have to solve problems personally if those problems are going to be solved.
- They don't teach us problem-solving skills.
- They have too many salespeople to manage.
- The paperwork is killing me!
- Their territories are too large to administer.
- They never discuss long-term goals.
- When we're doing well, please communicate with us! Don't wait until performance slips.
- It's up to them to initiate and sustain direct communication.
- Please ask us, once in a while, how *you* are performing!
- Their management style often becomes a hodgepodge of directives mixed with intimidation and persuasion.

Source: Adapted from Jack Carew, "When Salespeople Evaluate Their Managers . . . ," *Sales & Marketing Management,* March 1989, pp. 24–27.

- 89 percent said the salespeople did not know their products.
- 88 percent said the salespeople did not present or demonstrate the products they were selling; what they appeared to be selling was price.
- 85 percent said the salespeople lacked empathy.
- 82 percent said they would not buy from the same salespeople or companies again and cited "neglect" and "indifference" as the major reasons.[6]

Another study examined 257 *Fortune* 500 companies and found that:

- 83 percent do not determine an approximate duration for each sales call.
- 77 percent do not use the computer in time and territory management.
- 72 percent do not set profit objectives for accounts.
- 63 percent do not use prescribed routing patterns in covering territories.
- 54 percent do not conduct organized studies of their sales representatives' use of time.
- 51 percent do not determine the number of calls it is economical to make on an account.
- 51 percent do not use a planned sales presentation.
- 30 percent do not use call schedules for their sales forces.
- 25 percent do not have a system for classifying customers according to potential.
- 24 percent do not set sales objectives for customer accounts.
- 19 percent do not use a call-report system.[7]

EXHIBIT 1-6

Comparative Analysis of Top Problems in Sales Force Management

Sales Force Management Problems	Ranked per Frequency	
	1979	1959
Poor utilization of time and planned sales effort	1	1
Inadequacy in sales training	2	21
Wasted time in office by salespersons	3	6
Too few sales calls during working hours	4	3
Inability of salespersons to overcome objections	5	5
Indifferent follow-up of prospects by salespersons	6	7
Lack of creative, resourceful sales techniques	7	2
Inability to meet competitive pricing	8	15
Lack of sales drive and motivation	9	8
Recruitment and selection of sales personnel	10	11

Source: Adapted from Jack Dauner and Eugene M. Johnson, "Poor Utilization of Time and Planned Sales Efforts," *Training and Development Journal,* January 1980, p. 9.

Longitudinal as well as cross-sectional studies are available to help consider the problems of sales management. A 1979 survey of several hundred sales executives revealed that "inadequacy in sales training" was the second most important problem plaguing sales managers. Surprisingly, this problem ranked twenty-first in a similar survey done twenty years earlier, but the top problem in both surveys was "poor utilization of time and the planned sales effort," as Exhibit 1-6 shows. One might argue that almost all the problems in the two surveys might be overcome by a good training program and that the sales manager must take ultimate responsibility for these problems.

There is some indication that sales managers are progressively improving in regard to these problems. A 1990 study of 1,000 buyers who deal directly with salespeople in the food industry revealed some interesting findings on how today's salespeople are doing. Overall, the salespeople were evaluated rather favorably for their punctuality, courtesy, honesty, positive attitude, and appearance. The buyers gave the salespeople low marks for knowing about promotional techniques, providing buyers with assistance, keeping them informed, following up on orders, and motivating store personnel.[8] While sales managers appear to be improving in many areas, there is still a lot of work to be done. The next example illustrates an innovative approach recently undertaken by General Electric to improve its sales managers.

IMPROVING SALES MANAGERS AT GENERAL ELECTRIC

As part of General Electric Corporation's management development program, sales managers are evaluated not only by their managers and peers but also by their salespeople. According to James P. Baughman, manager of corporate development at GE, a manager's peers and *subordinates* are asked to fill out an evaluation questionnaire whenever the manager is scheduled for a corporate training session. The results from these questionnaires become a part of the sales manager's overall training program. For example, when the day sales managers receive training on motivation, the individual feedback on motivation provided by their salespeople is incorporated into the training session. The important thing to note about GE's evaluation process is that it is *not* part of the company's formal performance evaluation program. The feedback from the salespeople is used for developmental reasons and does not affect the sales manager's performance appraisal or compensation. And how do sales managers like the idea of being evaluated by their salespeople? "They love it," Baughman says, "as long as the results stay outside the chain of command."[9]

WHY AREN'T SALES MANAGERS DOING A BETTER JOB?

The major reasons for the failure of sales managers to perform at higher levels are (1) poor selection criteria for promotion to sales management, (2) inadequate sales management training programs, (3) lack of a marketing orientation in handling sales operations, and (4) insufficient blending of sales and marketing activities.[10]

Illogical Selection of Sales Managers

Through no fault of their own, newly selected sales managers are probably marketing's best example of the Peter Principle: "In a hierarchy, every employee tends to rise to his level of incompetence." Despite many articles by marketing scholars and practitioners who stress that a supersalesperson does not necessarily make a good sales manager, the reward for a sales rep who does an outstanding selling job for a couple of years is still usually promotion to sales management—a position for which he or she may be ill-prepared.

Ironically, the very skills that enable a person to be an excellent salesperson may prevent him or her from being a good sales administrator. As Exhibit 1-7 indicates, as individuals climb up the managerial staircase, the skills needed change from selling to supervisory, to managerial, to administrative and leadership. But at all levels, interpersonal skills are needed to serve effectively as the vital link between the sales force and higher management. Although most new sales managers readily learn to use the language of management to talk about such functions as planning, directing, and motivating, few seem to really understand and practice good management.

Some sales organizations suffer because the sales manager remains too involved in "doing" instead of managing. Time devoted to determining how to accomplish work through other people is managing. Time spent on performing activities that subordinates could do is doing. New sales managers often unconsciously become involved in doing because they feel comfortable in continuing to apply the same skills that earned them promotion to sales management. The difference between a skillful sales manager and a mere "doer" can make a significant impact on the success of the sales force efforts.

EXHIBIT 1-7

Changes in Ability Requirements as Position Changes

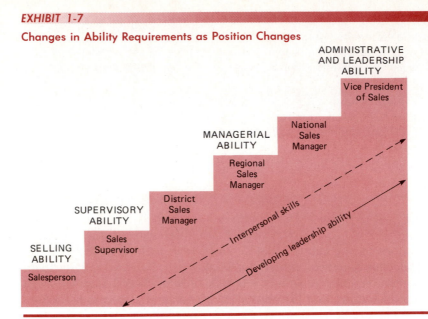

Even in small businesses where the size of the sales force restricts the amount of time that can be devoted to managing, the sales manager still should recognize that management tasks come first. For example, when sales managers make sales calls on their own, they are not managing. But when they make calls with the salespeople to analyze the latter's presentations, they are performing management duties. Subordinates usually recognize when a manager is doing rather than managing, and few sales managers enhance their own stature with the sales force by preempting salespeople's jobs.

Inadequate Training

Compounding the problem of poor selection criteria for promotion to sales management is the inadequacy of sales management training programs. While many companies spend $10,000 to $30,000 to train each new salesperson, most of these same companies fail to train sales managers adequately. One early study by the American Management Association found that 78 percent of sales managers had never received any specific training for their roles or were dissatisfied with their limited training.[11] In a more recent study of sales managers from a cross section of sixteen industries, less than half indicated that their companies provided any sales management training at all.[12] Even when sales management training is provided, it usually emphasizes company policies and procedures. Seldom is adequate and sound training provided in what constitutes effective management practice or what the holistic role of the successful sales manager should be.

Often, top management takes the shortsighted view that the activities of sales managers are too critical to company success to take these people away from their daily work for managerial training. If such an attitude permeates an organization, it can cause sales managers to perpetuate poorly planned field selling, whereas improved managerial skills might result in more effective strategies and tactics for producing profitable sales. As the linchpin between the selling and buying organizations, sales managers are too essential to organizational success to be excluded from managerial training. Furthermore, over the long run, managerial training for sales managers is even more critical to the organization because such a high percentage of company presidents come from sales backgrounds. A recent study of 1,000 companies by the executive search firm Heidrick and Struggles found that 31 percent of CEOs came from selling and marketing backgrounds.[13]

Orientation toward Sales, not Marketing

Despite the critical necessity for sales managers to understand and practice sound marketing, many sales managers still give little more than lip service to application of the marketing concept. Sales managers and salespeople who employ a narrow selling orientation focus on products and the "sell"—that is, they emphasize their own needs. In contrast, a marketing orientation focuses on serving by emphasizing the customer's needs. For example, Hewlett-Packard Company, manufacturer of precision electronic devices, puts the customer orientation into practice: its salespeople, called "field engineers," are instructed to take the customer's side in any dispute with HP.

Selling-oriented sales managers too often tend to think in terms of sales volume, short-run tactics in response to competitive actions, individual accounts, and fieldwork instead of market analysis. In contrast, marketing-oriented sales managers think in terms of profit planning; long-run trends, threats, and opportunities; market segments or customer types; and information systems. Exhibit 1-8 contrasts basic differences in the orientation of progressive and traditional sales managers.

Insufficient Blending of Sales and Marketing Functions

Marketing experience is fast becoming a requirement for sales management positions in excellent companies. Companies are looking for more versatile, well-rounded sales managers these days. Strong financial capability, as well as solid marketing experience, is being sought.[14] For better sales and marketing coordination, General Foods has division sales managers with dual reporting responsibilities. Not only do they report directly to a national sales manager, but they also have a direct relationship with the head of the marketing division. The idea is to keep division managers more closely informed about how their particular product lines are being marketed and sold. Yet, in many companies today, sales managers are still kept in the dark when it comes to sharing marketing information. For example, control reports sent to sales managers often contain only overall sales performance, sales expense, and budget data—not profit figures, which are solely for the eyes of top management. To do their jobs well, sales managers need profit information and accountability. Otherwise, they will

---

EXHIBIT 1-8

Marketing-Oriented versus Selling-Oriented Sales Managers

Marketing-Oriented Sales Managers Think in Terms of:	Selling-Oriented Sales Managers Think in Terms of:
Profit planning. Planning marketing mixes, product mixes, and customer segments to achieve profits and market-share targets	*Sales volume.* Increasing current sales to meet quotas and earn commissions or bonuses. Usually not sensitive to profit differences among customer or product categories
Long-run outlook. Continuously analyzing opportunities for profitable new products, markets, and strategies to assure long-run growth	*Short-run outlook.* Committing to today's products, markets, customers, and strategies
Market segments. Developing strategies to deal effectively and efficiently with customer groupings and types	*Individual customers.* Focusing on specific account satisfaction
Information systems. Continuously analyzing markets, plans, and controls to improve efforts toward organizational goals	*Field work instead of desk work.* Preferring to sell to customers instead of devising plans and and strategies for implementation

Source: Adapted from Philip Kotler, "From Sales Obsession to Marketing Effectiveness," *Harvard Business Review,* November–December 1977, pp. 67–75.

---

tend to focus on large sales volume, which may be more unprofitable for the company than smaller, more specialized sales.

A sales volume orientation is often evidenced by companies that require the sales manager to handle several large accounts in person. Although this may be necessary in a small company, sales managers in large companies should seldom make personal sales calls except in support of the sales representatives handling the account. Sales managers generally have little enough time for their critical managerial planning and profitability analysis functions without the added burden of making sales calls and servicing accounts.

Both the field sales and headquarters marketing groups need to appreciate that they are key players on the same team. They must cooperate to achieve organization objectives. If either is viewed as an activity isolated and remote from the other, poor communication and even rivalry can separate the marketing staff and sales force to the detriment of overall company performance.

Cross-disciplinary training is another approach to achieving organizational synergism. Some companies periodically bring sales managers into headquarters for training in finance and operations as well as marketing. Broad managerial training in several functional areas can greatly enhance the value of sales managers to their companies and help prepare them for promotion to higher management levels. Too many managers who make it to the penultimate levels have never had functional managerial experience outside their area of specialization and often have had only limited contact with customers, who are the raison d'être of any organization. Such specialized backgrounds can nurture very narrow perspectives on the company's challenges and opportunities. They also leave the company vulnerable to being blindsided by an unexpected source of competition or development in the macromarketing environment.

MEGATRENDS AFFECTING SALES MANAGEMENT

Several dramatically accelerating trends make the sales manager's job complex:[15]

- Intense foreign competition
- Rising customer expectations
- Increasing buyer expertise
- Revolutionary developments in computer technology and communications
- Influx of women and minorities into sales careers
- Growing emphasis on controlling costs[16]

To adapt successfully to these "megatrends," progressive companies are significantly broadening the concept of sales management. There is an increased integration of marketing and sales functions. Field sales managers are gaining a better knowledge of headquarters marketing activities, and the headquarters marketing team is obtaining a better understanding of selling and sales management. The best sales managers are developing and applying concepts and techniques from the behavioral sciences, marketing management, strategic planning, financial analysis, communication theory, general management, and the decision sciences.

The sections that follow examine each megatrend.

Intense Foreign Competition

Businesses based in Asia—notably, in Japan, South Korea, Hong Kong, and Taiwan—have captured huge market shares of the most basic U.S. industries: automobiles, steel, electronic components, home appliances, industrial chemicals, textiles, and machine tools. The U.S. home market has become the world's most attractive market for foreign sellers, and the battle for domestic and world markets is expected to continue. Unless the United States can develop and market innovative, top-quality, cost-competitive products that match or exceed those of any competitor, its domestic market shares will be lost to foreign imports. The economic health of the United States will depend partially on how well salespeople and sales managers do their jobs as industry faces intensifying competition from foreign products and services.

Rising Customer Expectations

Consumers are becoming less and less tolerant of product and service limitations. Even though today's customers may accept some shortcomings, they will quickly switch to better products and services when they appear, as the success of foreign products in the United States has demonstrated. Instead of putting so much sales and marketing effort into persuading prospects that superficially altered products are "new and improved," businesses must focus more attention on developing significant innovations in products and services and ensuring in-depth customer satisfaction. Successful sales and marketing managers are becoming less defensive about their own company's offerings and trying to look at products and services from the perspective of their most critical customers.

As the eyes and ears of the company in the market, the sales organization will play a larger role in monitoring customer satisfaction and complaint resolution. Companies such as Johnson & Johnson and Worthington Industries are already showing the way by requiring their senior executives to make monthly sales calls to stay in direct touch with customers and learn about their problems and satisfactions.

Increasing Buyer Expertise

With budget and profit squeezes, buyers of all kinds (consumers, producers, resellers, and governments) are becoming increasingly skillful at obtaining value for their dollars. Many consumers are beginning to treat more purchases (even of clothing) like long-term investments—an attitude that has long prevailed in many European countries. At the same time, organizations are developing more efficient purchasing processes and using buying committees consisting of purchasing, engineering, and operations managers. The new purchasing processes require a new attitude on the seller's part. The seller must place less emphasis on persuasive selling techniques and more on fostering long-term relationships of trust, respect, and understanding with buying organizations. A talented new type of professional salesperson is needed to convey the new attitude in sales presentations to buying committees and to function as a consultative account coordinator.

Revolution in Computer Technology and in Communications

An electronic revolution is well under way in communications and computer technology. Sales managers cannot afford to miss out on this revolution because it offers great opportunities to win competitive advantages with customers. Among the important technological innovations for sales management are (1) portable and desktop computers, (2) videotape presentations, (3) videoconferencing, (4) mobile communications equipment, and (5) electronic sales offices.

Computers. Instead of working with pages of numbers and computer printouts, today's sales manager can use a personal computer (PC) to call up charts, tables, and figures of various kinds to obtain an instant reading on the marketplace and sales force performance. About 80 percent of all information processed by the human brain originates as visual images, so computer graphics are significantly enhancing the ability of sales managers to quickly grasp the "big picture" and to obtain early warning of discrepancies from planned performance. At American Hoechst, sales managers utilize a computer mapping system to project the revenue change that would result from different realignments of salespeople. General Mills has installed a software package that allows managers to use the company's graphics system from any remote terminal in the United States. This enables sales managers to simulate various scenarios and to ask "what if" questions about different strategies and tactics before committing actual resources. General Electric sales managers use an online sales control system to cut the time between salesperson observation and sales manager awareness to only minutes. Regional sales managers use their computers to call up data banks, specify any status reports they desire, and receive summaries that reflect all sales activities up to the time they keyed in their requests. According to one GE sales manager, it is the "most tremendous advance we've had in sales management in my thirty years in the business."

To provide field insurance agents with instant access to competitive insurance products and prices, IBM developed its Insurance Value-Added Network Service (IVANS). This computer-based system allows agents to compare insurance coverage and prices among twenty-seven competitive companies before preparing proposals for their clients. In 1985, over half of all insurance agents were using computer-assisted selling.[17]

In a recent national survey, sales managers listed the use of information and computer technology as one of the most important resources for their profession in the 1990s.[18] Exhibit 1-9 shows that computers are already a major part of most sales managers' activities at both the headquarters and the regional office levels. Some experts are predicting an even greater emphasis on laptop personal computers for the sales force during the 1990s. One estimate predicts that while shipments of business PCs will rise 120 percent during the early 1990s, shipments of laptops will soar 174 percent during that same time period.[19]

EXHIBIT 1-9

How Computers Are Being Used in Sales Management

Sales Management Activity	At Company Headquarters, %	At Company's Regional Office, %
Monitor sales data for analysis	94	65
Track sales	88	71
Track competitive activity	47	47
Prepare sales budgets	81	44
Align sales territories	50	17
Order inquiries	67	57
Enter orders	67	33
Develop sales presentations	67	64
Plan promotions	67	47

Source: Thayer C. Taylor, "How the Game Will Change in the 1990s," *Sales & Marketing Management*, June 1989, pp. 52–61.

Videotape presentations.   Sales presentations are being brought dramatically to life through the use of videotapes. Over 480 salespeople at twenty-seven branch offices of Fisher Scientific Company use videotapes to demonstrate the company's products, equipment, and furniture for educational, medical, and industrial laboratories. It was not possible to show the diverse quality and features of the equipment on static catalog pages.

Fifty salespeople in American Saw & Manufacturing's Industrial Division share twenty portable video tape recorders. One unique use of the equipment was the preparation of instructional tapes in Spanish to win the account of a Chicago manufacturer whose employees did not understand English very well.

Videotapes are especially valuable when the sales manager wants to communicate an identical message to all salespeople. American Saw also uses monthly tapes as a company newsletter and morale booster for employees in the home office and field sales offices.

Videoconferencing.   Finding that the cost of travel and employee "downtime" are escalating yearly because of conferences, many companies are turning to videoconferencing. For example, Hewlett-Packard Company introduced a new business minicomputer to its 84,000 employees all at once via a videoconference that linked eighty-six offices in the United States and Canada and eighteen offices in Europe.

When Merrill Lynch broadcast an hour-long presentation called "Strategies for High-Yield Investments" to 30,000 customers assembled in thirty hotels around the country, a stunning 35 percent of the viewers bought one of the products suggested. Merrill Lynch was so delighted by these results that it installed a permanent video network connecting all 500 sales offices. A. L. Williams Corporation, the largest life insurance marketing agency in the United States, has installed videoconferencing equipment in 1,000 of its 5,600 sales offices to provide training and information to its 100,000-member field sales force. J. C. Penney, Sears, Exxon, Xerox, 3M, and IBM are rapidly expanding their videoconferencing networks, and many smaller companies are following suit as transmission costs decline and travel savings increase.

J. C. Penney is not only a dedicated user of videoconferences in sites at 110 stores and 50 regional offices but a profitable provider of videoconferencing services for *Fortune* 500 companies like NBC, ABC, Procter & Gamble, Pizza Hut, and Nippon Electronic Company. The American Management Association uses the U.S. Chamber of Commerce's American Business Network to produce "Seminars by Satellite," which teaches field and telephone selling techniques. The program has proved to be the most cost-effective way for the AMA to train large numbers of people.[20]

Mobile communications equipment.   Sales managers no longer have to wait anxiously for traveling salespeople to call in before being able to convey essential instructions or information to them. Automobile telephones and electronic pagers (beepers) are making it possible to contact salespeople wherever they are, whether it be in a traffic jam or walking across a parking lot in a distant city. Mobile communications devices also enable the salesperson to call ahead to customers to warn about an unavoidable delay, such as being stuck in traffic. The salesperson can also call the home office to obtain up-to-the-minute information while heading for a sales call. Kent H. Landsberg Company, a distributor of corrugated paper products in Montebello, California, has equipped its entire 100-person sales force with mobile telephones, pagers, and two-way radios. Landsberg's sales managers and sales reps consider the equipment vital in maintaining instant contact with each other, key support people in the main office, and drivers in company delivery vehicles who can check on customer orders. Since they have instant access to each other, the members of the sales force meet only every two weeks or so for general sales meetings.

High-tech sales offices.   With the development of integrated circuits and miniature microprocessors, large and medium-sized sales offices may soon be functioning efficiently in a "paperless" environment. Word processors have already replaced electronic and magcard typewriters in many offices, and instead of keeping bulky files, some companies are using high-speed laser copiers to convert incoming paper into retrievable electronic files. Badische Corporation (a chemical producer based in Williamsburg, Virginia) utilizes a microprocessor-controlled remote dictation system that permits salespeople to phone in up to eighteen hours of dictation, thereby drastically reducing the paperwork burden on salespeople. In modern electronic sales offices, sales managers can use their own desktop PCs to call up a customer record for review, to edit the draft of a report, or to deliver a memorandum simultaneously to salespeople scattered nationwide. Sales offices of the future will combine several functions and technologies into single, portable desktop units and use diverse electronic equipment connected through local and long-distance networks. Multifunctional terminals will include software (computer programs) for special applications and will use English as an operating language. Terminals will be tailored to suit the needs of individual sales managers and will be capable of data manipulation and analysis; intelligent copying, printing, and transmission; automatic scheduling; computer graphics; electronic files storage; and manipulation of electronic mail, voice mail, and the like. Networks will allow microimages to be sent directly to terminals or computers; data from computers will go directly to laser printers for high-quality printout; and data or graphics will be relayed through a teleconferencing network. All these technological changes are definitely helping sales managers cope with the complex environmental and competitive challenges of the 1990s.

Influx of Women and Minorities into Sales Careers

The composition of America's sales force is changing rapidly as women and minorities are increasingly recognizing the excellent career opportunities in sales. In the mid-1980s, about 30 percent of the nearly 3 million sales reps in the United States were women. (Interestingly, they were concentrated largely in real estate.) By the end of 1990, the number of female sales reps had soared to 50 percent in some industries. According to U.S. Labor Department statistics, manufacturing firms employ over 4,000 female sales managers, and the experiences of such diverse companies as General Tire & Rubber, Philip Morris, RCA, R. J. Reynolds Tobacco, Del Monte, IBM, Wang Laboratories, Viking Press, Continental Air Transport, Hoffmann-La Roche, Jewel Companies, and Xerox prove that women are performing successfully in the role. Not only is the number of women in selling climbing rapidly, but the Research Institute of America reports that roughly 25 percent of companies now employ blacks in the sales force. The 1964 Civil Rights Act has stimulated the hiring of women and minorities, but many companies claim that they still have limited success in attracting minorities to industrial sales jobs.

Emphasis on Controlling Costs

Sales managers are emphasizing cost control as an important means of adapting to the new selling environment of the 1990s. With retail consolidation and foreign ownership of major chains, there is more buying power in fewer hands today. Retailers can use this power to cut their own costs by shifting more of their in-store labor burden to manufacturers. Thus, the relationship between the manufacturer's sales force and the large retailers is very different from what it was a few years ago. The sales rep of the 1990s will deal with a well-informed, powerful buyer. The key for sales managers is to provide the sales force with better training in controlling costs and improving effectiveness in this new selling environment.

DEVELOPING SALES MANAGERS FOR TOMORROW

To successfully adapt to the megatrends that are affecting business today and to enable sales managers to help move their companies toward competitive excellence in the fiercely competitive markets of tomorrow, companies must significantly broaden the concept of the sales manager's job. Companies must emphasize the selection and training of sales managers. Specifically, top management must ensure that (1) sales managers are selected on the basis of appropriate managerial criteria, (2) newly promoted sales managers are taught basic marketing concepts and strategies, (3) sales activities are fully integrated with overall marketing programs, and (4) broad training is provided to develop talented salespeople into men and women who are capable of handling the most eclectic job in marketing—sales management.

In the words of one sales manager: "Unless tomorrow's sales managers can innovate and automate, they'll evaporate."

SUMMARY

Sales managers plan, lead, and control the personal selling activities of an organization. Although sales managers' responsibilities vary widely across companies, their basic duties are to (1) prepare sales plans and budgets; (2) set sales force goals and objectives; (3) estimate demand and forecast sales; (4) determine the size and structure of the sales force; (5) recruit, select, and train the salespeople; (6) determine sales territories, sales quotas, and performance standards; (7) compensate, motivate, and lead the sales force; (8) conduct sales volume, cost, and profit analyses; and (9) evaluate sales force performance, including ethical and social conduct. While carrying out their responsibilities, sales managers must be proactive leaders rather than mere reactive monitors of the sales environment.

Field sales activities and headquarters marketing functions must be blended if the overall company marketing efforts are to be effective and efficient. Headquarters marketing support for sales may include any or all of the following: advertising, sales promotion, sales aids, trade shows, product publicity, marketing research, marketing and sales planning, forecasting, product planning and development, market development, and public relations. A compelling reason for cooperation between the field sales force and headquarters marketing is the partial substitutability of the four promotional tools.

Sales managers are not generally perceived as performing as well as they should for these reasons: (1) poor selection criteria for promotion to sales management, (2) inadequate sales management training programs, (3) lack of a marketing orientation in handling sales operations, and (4) insufficient blending of sales and marketing activities.

For sales managers to do an optimal job, top-management support for sales managers is important. Managerial performance criteria such as profit accountability and decision-oriented reports from headquarters can help significantly in enabling sales managers to increase the productivity and profitability of the sales force.

Several megatrends are making the sales manager's job increasingly complex. Companies will need to significantly broaden the concept of a sales manager's job and emphasize the selection and training of top-notch men and women to handle what has become marketing's most eclectic job.

STUDY QUESTIONS

1. Project yourself to the year 2001 and describe what the sales manager's job will be like then. Explain.

2. Why do you think many companies are unable to recognize emerging opportunities in their own markets until long after competitors have captured major shares? As a top sales manager, what would you propose to avoid such myopia in the future?

3. You work for a large machine tool manufacturer and have been recently promoted from the sales force in another region to the position of sales manager. How would you go about ensuring a good working relationship with the headquarters marketing staff?

4. What kind of criteria would you propose to use in selecting salespeople for promotion to sales manager?

5. What kind of training would you provide to new sales managers? What about training for more experienced sales managers?

6. What criteria would you use to evaluate the performance of a sales manager?

7. Write a job description for the position of sales manager. Which responsibilities would you consider most important? Why?

8. Develop a scenario in which the technological innovations for sales management would prove beneficial in a work environment.

IN-BASKET EXERCISE

You are a sales manager for a small midwestern company, and you just received a memo from your company president indicating that your firm will soon be switching all sales and marketing activities to personal computers. Although your salespeople have been doing everything manually for years—and have been successful in the market—you feel that the majority will welcome the new technology. However, you do have a few older, very successful salespeople who may resist changing over to the computer-based system. You don't want to upset or alienate these individuals, as they are extremely important to your sales force and often act as "coaches" or "big brothers" to your newer salespeople.

How will you handle this situation while keeping sales force morale high?

CASE 1-1

THE COMPLEXITY OF THE SALES MANAGER'S JOB AT BASLER, INC.

Basler, Inc., is a well-established medical firm. While Basler is much smaller than most of its competitors, its credentials in the medical profession have always been impeccable. It is regarded as a stable, conservative organization that has consistently provided the medical profession with reliable and safe drugs.

Basler, Inc., was formed in 1908 by two medical professionals, Jim Bastrop and Ken Draeler. Jim Bastrop was a respected professor of medicine at the Harvard Medical School, and Ken Draeler was the administrator of Boston General Hospital. The idea of Basler, Inc., was conceived by Draeler to market his best friend Bastrop's brilliant medical discoveries. Even after Bastrop's initial and unexpected success, the two partners never strayed from their original philosophy: "We are a small company producing big-value drugs." Both Bastrop and Draeler vehemently opposed any commercial ventures and rejected many offers by private sources to expand Basler's operations. This philosophy was endorsed by the next generation of Basler's management. Draeler's son Gareth, a brilliant

scientist, helped build Basler's reputation through the invention of several "miracle drugs." His team of scientists was responsible for the development of Flumen and Gradior. Flumen is the mainstay of Basler's product offerings. It is considered to be the best drug in the treatment of Parkinson's disease; Gradior is regarded as one of the leading retardants of progressive Alzheimer's disease.

Gareth was opposed to the idea of Basler's becoming a huge medical firm offering its stock to the public. In 1987, the reins of Basler's management were passed on to Robert Bastrop, Jim Bastrop's grandson. Robert Bastrop was the first nonscientist to head Basler. He was also the first professional manager to become Basler's president.

The Robert Bastrop Era

Robert Bastrop, a Harvard M.B.A., made it very clear when he took over as president and CEO that Basler was going to see drastic changes in style and philos-

Case prepared by Anil Menon, Texas Tech University. Used with permission.

ophy. He actively pursued and encouraged proposals for rapid-growth strategies. Most of the employees supported the expansion moves but did not want to see such rapid change.

In 1989, Basler acquired Gyro Labs, a small, technologically oriented medical research firm. The scientists at Gyro were considered brilliant and highly aggressive. Gyro's creative genius was in the use of high-tech ideas such as gene splicing to develop retardants for cancerous growths. In the merger of Basler and Gyro, Basler could provide Gyro Labs with the financial resources needed to support its research efforts, and Gyro was expected to help Basler achieve its objective of fast growth and a reputation for progressive research. But analysts expressed concerns over the stylistic chasm between these two firms. Robert Bastrop did not share these concerns and expressed great optimism about Basler's future. There was a lot of excitement at Basler and Gyro over the merger.

The New Sales Organization

To maintain closer control on the initial operations of the merged Basler/Gyro Labs, Bastrop decided to reorganize the New England region's sales force. The New England region was Basler's strongest region and the location of Basler's headquarters. As before the merger, Gyro Labs marketed only in New England.

The new sales force was composed of the ten Basler veteran salespeople and the eight salespeople that Gyro had employed before the merger. (All but one Gyro salesperson remained with the newly merged firm.) Bastrop decided to use a team selling approach. He created teams of two sales representatives, one from each of the two firms. The logic for this structure was simple: The combined product lines of Basler and Gyro Labs would be distributed through the existing Basler network of doctors, hospitals, and pharmacies. The senior Basler sales representative was to help the younger Gyro sales rep fit into the Basler network.

The Problem Begins

On July 21, 1991 (one year after the reorganization), Robert Bastrop called in Jack Hanna, the district manager for the New England region, to discuss the sales force performance. A frustrated and angry Jack Hanna bluntly said, "Robert, I have told you this a dozen times already. It is not working out. My people are angry and can't work with those young wheeler-dealers from Gyro." Bastrop replied, "Jack, I have told you a dozen times: Those people from Gyro are now our people." "I don't care," Hanna responded. "They all want to do their own thing. They show no respect and are pushy." Hanna also charged that the young Gyro sales force was not loyal to Basler and used highly questionable tactics to make a sale.

Robert Bastrop calmed Hanna down and suggested that they go over the sales force performance on an individual basis.

In the discussion, Hanna summarized the characteristics of the seven selling teams.

Green and Ford. Arthur Green is a Basler veteran. He has been with Basler for over eighteen years. He is considered a very steady worker. However, in recent years he has been making fewer calls on potential new accounts. Thirty-year-old James Ford was Gyro's top salesperson. He is a very aggressive salesperson even by Gyro's standards and the unofficial leader of the Gyro sales force. He considers himself a professional. He is known to have ridiculed Green's "detail-work mentality." Ford works an average of seventy hours a week. He is reported to miss weekly sales meetings because "they are boring and useless."

Green is angry with Ford because Ford refuses to go along on many of his calls on long-time customers. Ford does not consider those calls potentially useful; Ford has already complained to Hanna that Green makes calls on the basis of friendship and not on sales potential. Ford refuses to "waste his time."

Hayes and Fields. Edward Hayes has worked with Basler for about twelve years. He is considered a hard-working but very slow worker. He has been quite content working with Fields, but he still does not approve of the merger. He calls it "more stupid than trying to mix oil and water."

Kevin Fields is 28 years old and is a frustrated scientist who could not make it through graduate school. He likes to read scientific journals and attends scientific meetings regularly. He is not very ambitious and is satisfied with the close contact he has with the medical profession.

Hale and Hargrove. Tom Hale is the youngest of the Basler salespeople. He is 43 years old and is considered one of the steadier salespeople. He is, however, very dissatisfied because his new partner is an aggressive woman, Lisa Hargrove. He considers Hargrove to be a shrewd and highly motivated woman. Hale claims that Hargrove is always on the lookout for ideas for new drugs. He voiced the complaint of many of the Basler salespeople: "These young Gyro salespeople should realize that we are in detail work, not prospecting for new products. Let's leave that to the R&D department." Hale claims that Hargrove's obsession for prospecting has led her to date a competitor's lab assistant. He says she hopes to get secrets out of him. Hargrove has denied this association and refuses to say anything more since "it is none of Basler's damn business."

Lisa Hargrove is a pretty and energetic woman in her early thirties. She shocks most of the older Basler salespeople with her explicit vocabulary. She is considered to be a vocal feminist and has consistently complained that Hale does not introduce her to many of the doctors and scientists. She alleges that Hale does not like women in business and is condescending toward her.

Grace and Gonzales.   Richard Grace has been with Basler for eight years. He has always been one of the top salespeople at Basler. However, he recently separated from his wife, is depressed, and seems to be drinking heavily. Grace and Gonzales's quota has been achieved for the year, but Gonzales did all the work and Hanna knows it. Gonzales does not want to get Grace into trouble, but he feels that Grace's problems are his own and that he has no time to "baby-sit" a grown man. Gonzales has given Hanna an ultimatum: "Tell Grace to shape up or team me up with someone else. I don't care about his problems, and I don't want to work with him forever."

Hamm and Kemp.   Todd Hamm has been with Basler for twenty-two years. He is a steady worker. He is completely satisfied with his partner, Kemp. In fact, Todd Hamm and Greg Kemp are known to socialize. Kemp is now dating Hamm's daughter. Greg Kemp is also satisfied with the team. He feels that his skills have been sharpened because of Hamm's criticisms. He does not understand why the others cannot get along. He enjoys Hamm's company and thinks they can work together even if he breaks up with Hamm's daughter.

Jones and Hinkle.   Gary Jones is the oldest salesperson in the sales force. He is 60 years old. He is slowing down and thinking of retiring. He is opposed to the merger and is very distrustful of the new salespeople. Jones is known for his contempt of the new "yuppie" groups. He considers the younger generation to be devoid of any redeeming qualities.

Mark Hinkle is the only married salesperson from Gyro. He is 33 years old, and his wife was the runner-up in the 1980 Miss Tennessee beauty pageant. The couple is known to have very expensive tastes. Hinkle drives a Porsche 911 Turbo and lives in the exclusive section of Cambridge, Massachusetts. He is constantly on the lookout for opportunities to make more money. His loyalty to Basler or Gyro can be considered suspect at best. He is dissatisfied with the merger because he has to mix with "boring straitlaced old people." However, he loves Robert Bastrop's leadership and considers his future at Basler very bright. He traveled 600 miles at his own expense to help a client with a problem.

Wells and Thompson.   Bill Wells and Hank Thompson make a reasonably steady team. Wells is receptive to younger salespersons and their methods of operation, but he is frustrated with Thompson's frequent visits to universities to "chat" with the professors. He finds Thompson's reason ("You never know when you can hit pay dirt.") rather weak. In fact, Wells suspects that some of those visits may be for personal medical information. Wells had overheard a member of the clerical staff comment that Thompson reportedly tested positive for the HIV virus. These suspicions were reinforced by Thompson's visits with young interns at the different medical schools. What really makes Wells suspect that some of these visits are personal in nature is that Thompson often tactfully gains private access to the people he visits, thus leaving Wells waiting in a reception area. Wells believes that too many of these visits have been a waste of company time and money. Thompson argues that he is developing future prospects.

After hearing Hanna out, Bastrop stated, "I agree that we have a communication problem, but I am not ready to throw in the towel. I still feel it is a good idea to team sell. Jack, you have to do a good job of selling this concept to the salespeople." Hanna left with the feeling that he was not going to get any sympathy from Bastrop. He reflected that if he were to attack the situation before it got completely out of hand, he would have to do something dramatic. Unsure what he could do, given Bastrop's comments, it crossed Hanna's mind that perhaps his best option would be to seek a sales management position elsewhere.

Questions

1. What are the major problems in this case?

2. Does Jack Hanna or Robert Bastrop really understand the situation? Are they serious about solving the problems, or are they on an ego trip?

3. Would you suggest that the new sales organization be reorganized? Would you fire anyone?

4. How would you handle the two groups of salespeople? Which group do you identify with?

5. Is Jack Hanna's consideration to leave Basler, Inc., an appropriate solution to his and the organization's problems?

CASE 1-2

CENTROID COMPUTER CORPORATION: THE NEW SALES MANAGER

Centroid Computer Corporation is a Dallas-based manufacturer of personal computers, monitors, interactive terminals, disk drives, and printers. In the last five years Centroid expanded into the development of a variety of software packages for its computers. The firm's growth in the past three years can only be described as explosive. Centroid grew from less than $2 million in annual sales to almost $5 million.

Centroid distributes its products through company-owned retailers as well as franchises. It also has a sales force of eighty-seven salespeople who call directly on small businesses. Most major metropolitan cities have at least one salesperson, and several have two. There are eight regional sales managers and one national sales manager.

Six months ago Alan Black was promoted to regional sales manager for the southeastern region. Alan grew up in Atlanta, Georgia, and graduated from the University of Georgia. He spent two years with IBM as a salesperson and then joined Centroid three years ago. He was based in Atlanta and has consistently been among the top five salespersons in the company, winning sales awards every year.

Alan's region includes Georgia, Florida, Alabama, Mississippi, Tennessee, North Carolina, and South Carolina. As regional sales manager, Alan must supervise nine salespeople in the seven states. He is also permitted to do some selling, but his primary responsibility is managing the sales force.

Since being promoted to sales manager, Alan has spent a great deal of time in the field working with his salespeople. His years of selling computers gave him many innovative ideas, and he wanted to pass them along so all his salespeople would be "super-salespeople" as he had been. It has not been uncommon for Alan to spend two or three days per month with each salesperson, telling about his ways to contact customers and make a sale.

Since Alan was such a supersalesperson, his bosses saw little need to train him when he was promoted to sales manager. Besides, the top managers were so busy handling the growth that they had little time to think about the field. That is one of the reasons they promoted outstanding salespeople like Alan to sales manager.

In the last couple of months, the national sales manager has received a couple of complaints from salespeople in the southeastern region about Alan's spending so much time with them. In fact, they say that on a number of occasions Alan actually made the sales presentations. The salespeople say he is confusing their customers and belittling their efforts. One of the complainants reported that she now had a credibility problem with several clients. She stated, "When we made sales calls together, he would allow me to take the lead and handle the call as I normally would. That was fine, but the clients' perception was that Alan was there to evaluate me. Three of my most promising clients asked why Alan was not satisfied with my performance." The other complainant offered similar comments but reported that if Alan disapproved of the presentation, he would take over in such a manner that "it was clear he was there to teach me a lesson." He stated, "One of my clients asked: 'Was he here to sell us equipment or to put you in your place?' "

Questions

1. Do you believe Alan is doing a good job in his new sales management position? Why or why not?

2. As national sales manager, how would you handle this problem with Alan?

3. Describe the functions Alan should be performing. What should the approximate allocation of his time be in performing these functions?

4. Do you believe that Alan's behavior will have a long-term negative effect on those salespeople who have had a problem with his means of training? If so, what could Alan do to moderate the situation?

REFERENCES

1. Based on personal interview with Ken McWain, June 1990.
2. Don Powell, *Sales & Marketing Management*, Apr. 6, 1981, p. 28.
3. Procter & Gamble, Recruiting Brochure, 1986–1987.

4. John Marcom, Jr., "IBM Service Strategy Changes with the Times," *Wall Street Journal,* Aug. 25, 1986, p. 6.
5. "Rebirth of a Salesman: Willy Loman Goes Electronic," *Business Week,* Feb. 27, 1984, pp. 103–104.
6. Robert Evans, "Training, Employee Orientation Hike Sales Rep Performance," *Marketing News,* Nov. 13, 1981, pp. 1, 16.
7. Robert Vizza, "Managing Time and Territories for Maximum Sales Success," *Sales Management,* July 15, 1971, pp. 31–36.
8. Hugh Lendrum, "What's Wrong with These Sales Forces?" *Sales & Marketing Management,* March 1990, pp. 54–56.
9. Jack Carew, "When Salespeople Evaluate Their Managers . . . ," *Sales & Marketing Management,* March 1989, pp. 24–27.
10. Rolph E. Anderson and Bert Rosenbloom, "Electric Sales Management: Strategic Response to Trends in the Eighties," *Journal of Personal Selling and Sales Management,* November 1982, pp. 41–46.
11. Velma A. Adams, "Field Sales Managers Cry: 'Give Us More Training,' " *Sales Management,* Apr. 16, 1965, pp. 25–27.
12. John I. Coppett and William A. Staples, "An Exploratory Study of Training Programs for New First Level Sales Managers," *Akron Business & Economic Review,* Fall 1980, pp. 36–41.
13. "Industrial Newsletter," *Sales & Marketing Management,* June 4, 1984, p. 29.
14. Bert Rosenbloom and Rolph E. Anderson, "The Sales Manager: Tomorrow's Super Marketer," *Business Horizons,* March–April 1984, pp. 50–56.
15. Ibid.
16. Thayer C. Taylor, "How the Game Will Change in the 1990s," *Sales & Marketing Management,* June 1989, pp. 52–61.
17. Marcom, op. cit.
18. Taylor, op. cit.
19. Thayer C. Taylor, "For Reps, the Future Is in Their Laps," *Sales & Marketing Management,* April 1989, p. 89.
20. "The Rediscovery of Video Teleconferencing," *Training,* September 1986, pp. 28–43; "New Ways to Keep in Touch," *U.S. News & World Report,* Apr. 28, 1986, pp. 54–55.

2

PERSONAL SELLING

LEARNING OBJECTIVES

When you finish this chapter, you should understand:

- ▲ The increasing professionalism demanded in today's sales positions
- ▲ The career alternatives available in personal selling
- ▲ The variety of sales jobs, from responsive selling to creative selling of intangible products
- ▲ How selling has evolved and developed in the United States
- ▲ How the salesperson is increasingly becoming a micromarketing manager

A DAY ON THE JOB

It has been only a year since Tiffany Morrison graduated from Syracuse University and entered the personal selling field with the Eastman Kodak Company. Already, as a copy-products sales representative for Kodak, Tiffany finds the field of personal selling challenging, competitive, and rewarding. "My typical day consists of calling on current customers to maintain their level of satisfaction with our products, while also attempting to get new business by replacing competitors' equipment with our products. Also, my day consists of writing proposals and making lots of phone calls!"

While Tiffany believes a sales job can sometimes be extremely competitive and stressful, she also feels that the rewards outweigh the drawbacks. She has a company car, an expense account, and a corporate American Express card, and she recently received a cash bonus for being named the "district sales representative of the month." Tiffany believes that being a woman or being young can sometimes work against a sales rep: "Most decision makers and purchasing agents tend to be older and may be hesitant to make a major financial commitment based on the advice of someone in their midtwenties. There are no absolutes in selling. The bottom line is that if you know your product and are credible, your sex, race, or age won't come into play when someone is making an objective buying decision for a company."[1]

SLICES OF THE SELLING LIFE

Creativity in Sales
Carlos Barba: Media Sales

Carlos Barba promotes a television network to viewers and sells its advertising time to sponsors. One of Barba's creative selling ideas focused on increasing the station's prime-time ratings while simultaneously promoting the customer's product. It all revolved around a soap opera which the station showed every weeknight. Barba knew that a lot of the viewers were housewives, and he offered them a chance to win a pair of emerald earrings, which would be delivered by the handsome male star of the show. All the viewers had to do was mail in the box top from a package of Bufferin, and the winner's name would be drawn out of a hat. Barba sold Bristol-Myers, which makes Bufferin, on cosponsoring the contest.

Shortly into the contest, Barba got a frantic call from his ad agency demanding that he "stop the contest." The people at Bristol-Myers were receiving hundreds of phone calls from drugstore managers who were complaining about a "run on Bufferin!" It appears that consumers were picking up ten to fifteen packages of Bufferin apiece. The problem, however, was that people were coming in and taking the packages from the shelves and leaving the bottles behind!

Barba immediately called his lawyer, who informed him that the contest had to continue in accordance with FTC regulations. At the same time, Barba received a call from the post office telling him that the station's mail delivery had been suspended because of the enormous number of letters from entrants of this contest. Barba's unique idea was turning into a nightmare. He quickly decided to run a bulletin during the show saying that it was no longer necessary to send in the box top from the Bufferin package. Instead, a 3 by 5 index card could be used to enter the contest.

The impact from this creative idea was astonishing. Approximately 789,000 letters were mailed to the station during the contest's ten-week run. The bulk of mail was so large that the letters were kept in an empty swimming pool, and the contest created such a stir that *The New York Times* picked up the story. Response to the contest was called one of the biggest ever received by a television station. This is just one example of how creativity is a big part of a sales career. It also shows how sales can be a challenging and rewarding career.[2]

Selling a Technical Product
Gerry Dalhouse: Manufacturer's Sales Representative

Fifteen years ago, Gerry Dalhouse considered "jumping off a roof" because he believed his career was going nowhere. Now, he enjoys his work so much that he won't even take a vacation. Dalhouse became one of the country's 360,000 manufacturers' sales representatives. Paid strictly on commission, the hardworking salesman for a Chicago machine tool company expects to earn $80,000 this year. The money doesn't come easy. He starts work at 7:30 A.M. and seldom gets back to his suburban home until 8:30 P.M. or later.

A typical day consists of missed connections, long waits in reception rooms, loss of sales to the competition, and hours spent helping customers get an expensive piece of equipment in operation. At one stop, he may be received with open arms; at another, he may be cursed—literally. These frustrations would be the despair of a less energetic man. But the good-natured Dalhouse thrives on the challenge, trading jokes with customers to ease the tensions. Much of Dalhouse's time is spent walking around the noisy back shops of the small manufacturers and machine shops he calls on in the Chicago suburbs. Sometimes he will sell a machine worth more than $100,000 to a plant executive while shouting over the racket of a busy factory.

Most manufacturers pay their representatives a base salary plus commission, and the biggest opportunities are in fields that demand technical expertise: drugs, chemicals, electrical equipment, and machinery. Although a college degree is increasingly desirable, the type and level of education needed depend largely on the product being sold. In drug sales, for example, training at a pharmacy college is often needed. In other areas, it's mostly a matter of having a pleasant personality and a thorough knowledge of product line and customer needs. Dalhouse, for one, has a liberal arts degree from Northwestern University and seventeen years of experience in machine tool selling. It's that kind of expertise that is the key to success in the job, not glad-handing, which is why Dalhouse is scornful of all the talk about "three-martini lunches."

"Most of my clients are too busy for that kind of thing and so am I," he says. Lunch for him is usually an apple or a sandwich eaten while driving to a client who is having machine problems. He says that his best customers—some buy $500,000 worth of machines each year—don't want to bother having lunch with him. "They want someone who can service them after they buy and who knows something about the machine tool business."

Early in his career, Dalhouse worried about the image of his freewheeling profession, but he wouldn't trade the job now, even for one that offered more security. "A lot of people think my job is ridiculously simple," he observes. "They say I make big money peddling a bunch of machines with little wheels that go around. Well, I happen to think it is much more than that."[3]

Selling an Intangible Product
Lynn Hutchings: Insurance Agent

At whatever he does, Wyoming life insurance agent Lynn Hutchings is driven to succeed.

A couple of years ago Hutchings took up jogging for a "little exercise." Recently, he finished the 26.2-mile Las Vegas marathon in three hours, forty-three minutes—an excellent time for a beginner. He still runs about 70 miles a week and hopes to improve his Las Vegas time in the upcoming St. George marathon in Utah.

When he's not running, Lynn Hutchings at age 32 is one of the nation's most successful insurance salesmen. For nine straight years, he has been his company's best agent. He sold over $35 million worth of life insurance in one year while earning an income of over $250,000 for himself. Most remarkably, Hutchings has done all this from a one-man office in Rock Springs, a dusty Wyoming town of 25,000 people. His father was a cook and his mother was a waitress, and there was little income as he grew up in Evanston, Wyoming. After high school, he sold auto parts for several years. When he was 22, Farm Bureau Company hired him and assigned him to Rock Springs. "At the time," he recalls, "we had no business there at all, so maybe they sent me in because there was nothing I could screw up." Hutchings maintains: "I'm not really any different than anyone else—I just work harder." His week begins at 5:30 Sunday afternoon with four to five hours of phone calls to line up appointments. In the following five days, he works sixty or more hours, visiting as many as six prospective customers per day. He doesn't stop to eat, nor does he take clients out for a drink or a meal.

His tangible rewards are many: a ten-room house in Rock Springs, a $200,000 second home in the Teton Mountains of northwestern Wyoming, four automobiles, and a $75,000 Bellaneo Turbo Viking airplane.

His intense drive and self-confidence are important assets. As his boss says of Hutchings: "when Lynn gets his nose bloodied, he isn't discouraged. He just keeps on charging."[4]

THE SALES PROFESSIONAL

Tiffany Morrison, Carlos Barba, Gerry Dalhouse, and Lynn Hutchings are involved in different types of sales activity, but their stories illustrate more accurately the diverse opportunities, challenges, and responsibilities faced by today's professional salespeople than do the old stereotypes of the legendary "traveling salesman." Yesterday's salesmen (yes, they were mostly male) would barely recognize the modern sales representative. So changed is selling today from only a few decades ago that it is almost a different profession, as Exhibit 2-1 suggests.

"Gone forever is the typical, slap-on-the-back, 'Did ja hear the one about . . .' salesperson. Brashness and puffery have been largely replaced by a polished professionalism that reflects the ever-increasing demands by customers on the sales reps' time, know-how, and ability to serve."[5] Personality, of course, will always be a factor in successful selling, but you cannot get by on personality alone. Seat-of-the-pants selling will not get the job done anymore. No longer can the enthusiastic "personality boy" learn a few sales tricks and then go on to sell successfully over the long run. Selling has increased in complexity as products and services have become more technical, competition more intense, and buyers more sophisticated. In addition, purchase decisions are now shared by several layers of management and technical experts, a process that necessitates interaction among counterparts in the buyer and seller organizations. Today's top salespeople are largely made, not merely born. Success usually comes from a combination of innate ability and acquired skills. A recent study of purchasing agents indicated that of fifteen personal qualities, "reliability, credibility" was considered extremely or very important by 98 percent of the agents. Exhibit 2-2 summarizes the study, and Exhibit 2-3 gives an idea of what qualities buyers like and do not like in salespeople.

EXHIBIT 2-1

What's New about Professional Selling

- Greater knowledge of product and product systems required
- Increased understanding of customers' problems necessary
- More knowledgeable plant and purchasing people in the buyer's organization
- Higher expectations by customers that sellers will solve their problems
- More technical products and processes being sold
- Increased emphasis on "systems selling"
- More pressure on buyers to make the right purchases
- Need for salespeople to understand the use of computer analysis in comparing alternative product or system benefits for customers
- More professional reading and studying required by salespeople
- Less small talk between buyers and sellers
- Contact with a wider variety of people in the customer's organization as several layers of management and staff specialists become involved in purchasing decisions
- More time spent in the customer's working environment to enable the salesperson to fully understand customer problems
- Increasingly specialized professional buyers
- More team selling required for product systems
- Emphasis on establishment of long-term relationships between sellers and buyers
- Increased use of sophisticated technical aids such as computers, videocassettes, and videoconferences
- More effective use of the selling organization's backup team of marketing specialists

EXHIBIT 2-2

What Do Buyers Like Most in a Salesperson?

	Percentage of Buyers
Most valued:	
Reliability, credibility	98.6
Professionalism, integrity	93.7
Product knowledge	90.7
Innovativeness in problem solving	80.5
Presentation, preparation	69.7
Least valued:	
Supplies market data	25.8
Appropriate frequency of calls	27.3
Knowledge of competitor's products	31.2
Knowledge of buyer's business and negotiation skills	45.8

Source: "PAs Examine the People Who Sell to Them," *Sales & Marketing Management*, Nov. 11, 1985, p. 39.

EXHIBIT 2-3

The Good, the Bad, and the Ugly

Here, in their own words, are some qualities that buyers say they like, don't like, and just plain hate in salespeople.

The Good	The Bad	The Ugly
Honest	No follow-up	Wise attitude
Loses a sale graciously	Walks in without an appointment	Calls me dear or sweetheart (I am a female)
Admits mistakes	Begins by talking sports	Gets personal
Has problem-solving capabilities	Puts down competitors' products	Doesn't give purchasing people credit for any brains
Friendly but professional	Poor listening skills	A whiner
Dependable	Too many phone calls	A bull-shooter
Adaptable	Lousy presentation	Wines and dines me
Knows my business	Fails to ask about needs	Plays one company against another
Well prepared	Lacks product knowledge	Pushy
Patient	Wastes my time	Smokes in my office

Source: "PAs Examine the People Who Sell to Them," Sales & Marketing Management, Nov. 11, 1985, p. 39.

The knowledge and skills needed to meet the complex and competitive market conditions of today are acquired through intensive training and practice, often in corporate schools. Xerox, for example, has its own International Center for Training and Management Development in Leesburg, Virginia, where a thousand students at a time are trained, housed, and fed. AT&T has a similar training facility in Denver, Colorado.

The Importance of Personal Selling

It is estimated that about 55 percent of total sales expenses in U.S. industry pertain to personal selling, 36 percent to advertising, and 9 percent to sales promotion. Seven million people, or 10 percent of the total labor force, are in personal selling jobs. It can be said that sales personnel are "the movers and shakers behind America's free-enterprise economy."[6] The great entrepreneur Marshall Field once described the distance between the salesperson and the prospect as "the most important three feet in business."[7] All the other marketing activities—market research, product development, pricing, sales promotion, and advertising—can bring the football 99 yards up the field, but the last yard must almost always be covered by the salesperson.

In celebrating National Salesperson's Month, then President Carter described salespeople as "intelligent, aggressive, well informed," and necessary to our consumer-oriented economy. Further, he said:

Salespeople stimulate the competitive forces that make our economy one of the most productive in the world, as well as the most responsive to consumer wants and needs. Salespeople stimulate industrial innovation and speed the distribution process, enabling producers to maximize output and improve efficiency. A professional and responsive salesforce helps buyers spend their money wisely and effectively. On behalf of a grateful nation, I welcome this opportunity to commend the sales profession.[8]

The Seller's Personal Representative

In contrast to the impersonal mass communication of advertising, *personal selling* is face-to-face interaction with potential buyers. Thus, it is the most flexible means of promotion as well as the most expensive. Personal selling's distinguishing feature is two-way seller-buyer communication with immediate feedback in the form of verbal exchanges, expressions, gestures, and the like. Personal selling is the best means of tailoring the firm's offering to the unique needs of each market segment.

From the customer's perspective, the salesperson is the personification of the seller's organization. The salesperson is likely to be blamed for late delivery, billing errors, faulty product quality, or anything else that may go wrong. Conversely, the customer may credit the salesperson for all services provided by the seller's organization. Sales representatives can significantly enhance or detract from the seller's image in the market, for they are the critical contact with the customers. When organizational activities are truly integrated and oriented toward customer satisfaction, there is an attitude of teamwork among departments that yields synergistic company efforts and results. As the seller's personal representative, a salesperson might encounter circumstances that test his or her own ethics. The accompanying *Ethics* scenario describes such a situation.

ETHICS IN SALES MANAGEMENT:
A DISAGREEMENT WITH YOUR SUPERVISOR

You have just been hired as a sales management trainee for a large consumer goods company. All your hard work in college has paid off, as you feel you have landed your "dream job." You are getting along with all your coworkers, and one of the highest-performing sales managers in the company is training you. Things couldn't be better. After a month on the job, however, you begin to have second thoughts about some of your sales manager's instructions. He doesn't think twice about telling you to promise unrealistic delivery dates to top customers or to "guesstimate" certain cost figures when your customers are in a hurry. This highly respected sales manager appears to be operating under the premise that "exceptions to company policy and procedures are a way of life!"

You're not sure how to handle this issue. You certainly don't want to "ruffle anyone's feathers," yet you also don't want to jeopardize a promotion by doing anything questionable.

What do you do?

Increasing Professionalism in Selling

Indications are that the importance of sales representatives in overall marketing strategy will continue to increase. Some authorities have gone so far as to predict that sales representatives will eventually become the most critical members of the marketing team and that they will be backed up by the rest of the marketing organization. Many would argue that this is already true but that marketing executives have yet to fully understand the salesperson's role. Along with their expanded responsibilities, sales reps will need more education and training, but they will simultaneously benefit from higher compensation, more prestige, and greater opportunities for promotion.

At one time it was thought that a college degree was unnecessary for a salesperson. But today most sophisticated managements recognize that a college education substantially enhances the value of a salesperson to the organization. Not only does a college education broaden a person, promote self-confidence, and improve analytical abilities; it also increases the personal interaction skills so essential to selling. Many prospective buyers and managers who influence the purchase decisions of organizations have college educations and often even graduate degrees. It is important for sales reps to be able to gain their respect by talking on their level. A high school graduate may have a difficult time interacting with a buyer who holds a college degree.

Individuals with college degrees entering sales positions are highly compensated. For example, starting salaries in 1990 ranged from $27,828 to $48,000 a year. Morever, the average salary for a salesperson with an M.B.A. in 1990 was $40,008, much higher than the salary for someone in market research.[9] One well-known company studied the academic backgrounds of salespeople and sales management candidates who had been with the firm for three years. Results revealed that 84 percent of all promotions in the sales force had gone to people with college degrees, even though nearly 40 percent of those in the study did not finish college. As a consequence, the company reevaluated its recruiting sources to reduce the costly turnover of salespeople.[10]

Although sales careers are often viewed with mixed feelings by college students (largely owing to erroneous stereotyping based on contact with door-to-door salespeople), sales is rapidly being recognized as the preferred entry-level position in a successful marketing career. Sales positions are swiftly expanding in responsibilities and required professionalism, and their titles are being changed to reflect this. Many top corporations call their salespeople "marketing representatives" and train them intensively to ensure that they retain a marketing perspective even while engaged in personal selling. General Foods prefers the title "account executive," and more technically oriented firms frequently use the term "sales engineer." Whatever the title, the more progressive organizations are keenly aware of the importance of being represented by talented professionals in dealing with customers who determine the success or failure of the enterprise. The example that follows describes IBM's approach to ensuring that its marketing representatives are truly professional.

THE PROFESSIONAL SALESPERSON AT IBM

IBM marketing representatives [who sell office products] generally deal with customers at all levels of management due to the importance of IBM products and systems to their [customers'] business. New marketing representatives undertake an extensive and thorough education program. It includes on-the-job instruction and specialized training at Marketing's education center in Dallas. There, marketing representatives learn the product line and receive individual guidance in marketing word processing products and systems. The learning process never stops. Continual education in new products and marketing techniques is essential in a marketing representative's career. Office Products Division (OPD) marketing representatives begin their careers in either office product sales, office systems sales, or a combination of both. As OPD marketing reps complete their training, they are assigned to branch offices and given individual territories. That territory and the customers within it are theirs, and theirs alone, to manage—much like an independent business. Calling on customers, they have IBM's image, product quality, service organization, and resources behind them. But their basic work environment is the branch office and their own marketing territories. Marketing representatives sell solutions to problems by selling IBM products such as computers and typewriters to customers. These products are often in the form of complex electronic systems that process information. Working closely with marketing representatives, systems engineers plan the systems, oversee their installation, and train the customer on their use. Marketing reps and systems engineers are key positions because they are the first line of contact with customers. One of IBM's basic objectives is to strive to provide the best customer service of any company in the world. Marketing reps must appreciate problems customers face, for they often serve in a consulting role to executives in large and small companies. They must like to analyze problems and communicate solutions, for the role of IBM's products is to help customers perform tasks in more productive ways. Marketing representatives and systems engineers occupy positions that complement each other. Marketing reps and systems engineers may begin as junior members of an account team or be assigned territorial responsibility for small systems or office products equipment. In time, they may be assigned responsibility for one or more accounts. Eventually, they may become account executives serving a large national account.

To sell these types of systems, which often represent substantial capital investment, IBM marketing reps must know two things. They must know IBM's business—that is, they must know in depth the capabilities of the products and systems they recommend. Second, they must know their customer's business if their recommendations are to carry any weight. They must know the kinds of problems their customers face in their daily operations. In short, they must be specialists who can bridge both worlds.[11]

SALES AS A CAREER

Sales is one of the most exciting, financially rewarding, and challenging of careers. Unlike many jobs, few people ever complain about a sales career being boring. It can hardly be boring, for it deals with human beings and their wants, which are always changing. Many sales representatives have work freedom much like an entrepreneur or independent business owner yet enjoy the security and benefits of employment with a company. The example that follows describes sales careers at Procter & Gamble. This description is similar to that of other large marketing-oriented firms.

SALES CAREERS AT P&G

Lou Pritchett, Procter & Gamble's Vice President of Sales, says, "Sales is where the action is. It's the salesperson who must present a brand to our customers, in opposition to our competitors' salespeople, and make things happen."

The challenge you face in sales is to become the acknowledged expert on your brands, categories, customers, and the marketplace. Your responsibility is to develop and execute selling strategies needed to drive the business ahead. You must analyze the business, identify opportunities, and then develop specific plans to capitalize on them. Sometimes you work alone, but more often you must skillfully manage others to achieve your goals. As a member of P&G Sales, you also must be an "entrepreneur," and your own boss.

Obviously, as a member of P&G's Sales Team, you're no mere order-taker. You must be a creative merchandiser with business-building ideas. As your knowledge increases, you'll develop creative solutions for the day-to-day problems and challenges that are an inevitable part of the business: a newspaper advertising theme tieing in your brands; a unique promotion relating your brands with a topic in the national or local spotlight; an innovative selling idea specifically aimed at the demographics of your area; or a tailored solution to a warehouse-to-store distribution problem. This kind of creativity and results-oriented thinking are the hallmark of the P&G salesperson.

You'll manage your own business with the support of other experts from Product Development, Manufacturing, Advertising, Management Systems, and Finance. But the decisions are yours to make: how to organize your sales territory; the order, frequency, and timing of your visits to accounts; the merchandising strategies you develop to build their business. You'll have advertising and display funds to use as merchandising incentives, and the responsibility for executing various types of merchandising contracts.[12]

Income

Sales representatives are among the best paid people in business. In 1989, as shown in Exhibit 2-4, sales trainees earned an average of $25,079, senior salespeople earned $58,981, and sales supervisors (who direct other salespeople and may call on key accounts) earned nearly $62,282 annually. Sources show that salespeople who worked for industrial products companies or were paid salary plus commissions earned significantly more than salespeople working for service or consumer products companies or those paid straight salary. Some top salespeople earn $100,000 or more in salary and commissions, and a rare few in some select fields make over $1 million annually.

Sales and marketing executives who earn the highest base salaries are employed by food and beverage manufacturers; or by the manufacturers of chemicals, pharmaceuticals, or rubber or plastic products; or by insurance companies with annual sales of $100 million or more. These highly paid executives supervise sales forces of fifty or more people, are usually in the northeastern or Pacific Coast states, and hold graduate degrees. Sales and marketing executives with the highest total compensation, however, work for electrical equipment distributors with annual sales of less than $100 million. These executives oversee fifty or more salespeople, reside in the midwest, and hold graduate degrees. Students and others who are laboring under the misconception that a college degree is not important for sales should take note that the top executives not only have college degrees but graduate degrees as well.

Sales executives are probably more objectively evaluated than most employees, since their sales contributions are more subject to direct measurement

EXHIBIT 2-4

How Salespeople's Total Compensation Is Growing

Sales trainee: Anyone who is learning about the company's products, services, and policies, as well as proven sales techniques, in preparation for sales assignments.

Senior salesperson: A salesperson at the highest level of selling responsibility, and completely familiar with the company's products, services, and policies. He or she usually has years of experience and is assigned to major accounts and territories.

Sales supervisor: A veteran salesperson, with the primary function of directing activities of other salespeople and trainees. He or she may also sell to selected key accounts.

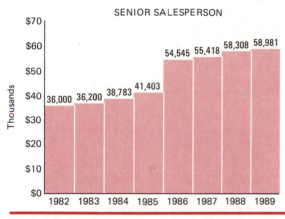

Source: Sales & Marketing Management, Feb. 26, 1990, p. 75.

and rewards tend to be commensurate with accomplishments. In other words, a talented sales representative will not be overlooked in the evaluation process, as company employees in less "measurable" jobs may be.

Perquisites

Not only does a sales position offer the potential of high earnings, but there are frequently expense-account benefits (which permit enjoyment of the good life while wooing customers) and tax write-offs for home office expenses (which allow salespeople to live better than their basic incomes suggest).

Route to the Top

A sales career is undoubtedly one of the surest and fastest routes to the top of an organization. One survey of 1,708 top-level managers in *Fortune* 500 companies showed that many of these executives began their business careers in either sales or marketing positions.[13]

One of the major reasons for corporate success via the sales route is that, of all employees, salespeople have the closest relationships with customers, and thus they learn the business from the perspective of those who determine its ultimate success or failure. Also, sales reps are usually the last to be fired in any cutback of company personnel because reducing the sales force normally results in a reduction of sales revenue.

Shortage of Qualified Salespeople

Despite the many opportunities and high compensation in selling, there always seems to be a shortage of qualified salespeople. Over 300,000 new salespeople, not counting replacements, are needed each year. Annual openings for manufacturers' sales forces alone will average about 26,000 in the 1990s. By 2000 there will be about 720,000 industrial sales reps in the United States.

Owing in part to the shortage of qualified salespeople, selling is inefficient compared with what it could be. Many salespeople are poor planners and organizers, so they waste time waiting to see customers, call on the wrong accounts, spend too much time with people who do not have the power to make a purchase decision, and fail to design sales presentations which focus on the prospect's needs.

Research has shown that the majority of sales are made by a minority of the salespeople and that annual turnover is 60 percent or higher in many industries.[14] Sales managers often must accept marginal people because of misconceptions about sales careers: (1) all sales jobs require extensive overnight traveling, (2) sales jobs are all like telephone sales, door-to-door selling, or retail clerking, (3) salespersons are usually in a less powerful position than customers. In addition, many people lack awareness of the numerous excellent industrial sales positions available in manufacturing, wholesaling, and retailing. Sales managers must develop programs to overcome these misconceptions so that they can recruit a large pool of qualified applicants.

WOMEN IN SALES

Nearly half of all women in the United States—more than 50 million—are working today outside the home. Yet these working women still earn less than 60 percent of men's pay for essentially equal work, a gap that is wider today than it was over twenty years ago. Despite equal employment opportunity legislation, over half of U.S. businesses employed no women as industrial sales representatives as recently as 1984, although many women worked in retail (in-store) sales jobs. Companies are increasingly hiring female sales reps, but women still account for a relatively small percentage of the sales force. For example, as recently as 1987, women made up only about 16 percent of the national sales force. These are some of the reasons often given for not employing female sales reps:

1. Sales jobs are too tough for women.
2. Customers prefer to deal with men.

3. Women are unreliable because of marriage, pregnancy, and other "women's problems."

4. Women take advantage of their sex in selling situations or might cause sex-related problems within the sales force.

5. Women cannot sell as well as men.

New Opportunities for Women

Rather than be discouraged by such myths as those cited above, women should be assured that times have changed dramatically and that career opportunities for them in sales have expanded tremendously. The proportion of women in U.S. field sales forces skyrocketed between 1981 and 1987, more than doubling from 7.3 to 17.6 percent.[15] Dow Chemical Company's industrial sales staff is now 15 percent female, up from 10 percent five years ago. American National Insurance Company doubled the number of women in its sales force during the same period. At McCormick & Company of Hunt Valley, Maryland, women make up 29 percent of the sales force, compared with 15 percent in 1985.[16] The proportion of women in today's sales forces varies depending on the type of industry. As Exhibit 2-5 indicates, women have made great strides in sales in such industries as textiles and apparel, utilities, and financial services, where the percentage of females ranges from 40 to 61 percent. The downside, however, is that in certain industries, such as general machinery, aerospace, and transportation equipment, women represent only a very small percentage of the sales force. Many experts are predicting, however, that since college-educated women

---

EXHIBIT 2-5

Women in Sales

	Percentage of Sales Force	
	1981	1987
The top industries:		
Textile and apparel	21	61
Utilities	48	59
Banks and financial services	24	58
Housewares	37	50
Publishing	31	49
Food products	10	40
The bottom industries:		
General machinery	1	0
Aerospace	1	0
Transportation equipment	2	1
Tools and hardware	4	2
Automotive parts	4	2
Fabricated metal products	4	3

Source: "'Pink Ghetto' in Sales for Women," Sales & Marketing Management, July 1988, p. 80.

are entering sales at a faster pace than college-educated males, especially in engineering, the potential for women in male-dominated sales positions should be extremely good.

Many women are also advancing into sales management positions. According to U.S. Labor Department statistics, manufacturing firms now employ almost 5,000 female sales managers. The experiences of such companies as Del Monte, General Tire & Rubber, Philip Morris, RCA, R. J. Reynolds Tobacco, Wang Laboratories, Viking Press, Continental Air Transport, Hoffmann–La Roche, Jewel Companies, and Xerox prove that women are performing successfully as sales managers. Philip Morris has over 150 female sales representatives—18 percent of its sales force—and many have already been promoted to sales management with strong prospects for making it to the top-management rungs.[17]

Affirmative action.   Of course, government affirmative action pressures have helped women enter industrial sales. But once hired, the "token" saleswoman has proved that she is equal to or better than the typical salesman. In the words of a sales rep for NCR: "It doesn't matter whether I was hired as a token female or not, I can do the job. All I needed was the chance to prove it."[18]

Objective evaluation.   Sales jobs give women and minorities a chance to provide objective proof of their performance capabilities. While women and minorities in other careers often complain that they are judged subjectively by a possibly biased superior, performance is easily measurable in a sales job, so individuals are generally rewarded in direct proportion to their sales productivity. According to the College Placement Council, salary offers made to women graduates trying for industrial sales or marketing jobs are nearly identical to those made to men.

Advantages and Disadvantages for Women in Sales

Rosemarie Sena, a senior vice president with Wall Street's Shearson, Hayden Stone, Inc., earns over $300,000 yearly by selling stock research to institutions and managing individual stock portfolios. She claims: "If a woman is good at sales at all, she's apt to be better than a man," for women have two advantages: novelty and better-developed social skills. The first wins them five minutes of the prospective customer's time, and the second enables them to make the most of it.[19]

Progressive organizations actively seek female sales reps for very profit-oriented reasons. First, the buyer will nearly always agree to see saleswomen, even after refusing to see salesmen from the same company. Second, women are more easily remembered, and this recall is transferred to the product lines and companies the women represent. Third, women tend to be better listeners than men, and listening is an essential for successful selling.[20]

Beyond facing the difficulties common to all salespeople, such as long and irregular working hours, extensive travel and entertaining, occasionally difficult customers, and blunt rejections, women may also confront special problems. They may encounter unwelcome sexual overtures or customers who refuse to talk to a saleswoman. But if the saleswoman is persistent and straightforward, she can almost always overcome initial problems. For example, when a customer comments, "I want to do business with a man," a saleswoman for Alcoa simply says: "Fine, I'm your man," and that usually gains acceptance for her. Some of these unique problems were uncovered in a recent study on women in sales; the results of this study are summarized in Exhibit 2-6.

A number of support systems exist specifically for women in selling. New saleswomen or sales managers can receive advice from professional organizations designed to help women get ahead in their specialized fields. Two such groups are the National Association for Professional Saleswomen and the National Association of Business & Industrial Saleswomen. Several women have found the confidence to leave dead-end jobs for better-paying careers in sales after interacting with successful saleswomen at meetings of these organizations.

Today, there are no objective reasons why women cannot be as successful as men in sales careers. Almost all the women who have entered sales careers with reservations are now happy that they did so, and most of the companies that employed them with equal reservations report that the women are "eager, talented, and right at home" in sales.

EXHIBIT 2-6

Job-Related Concerns of Saleswomen

Professional Concerns

- Sustaining interest and maintaining credibility throughout the sales call
- Handling heavy luggage and sample cases
- Car breaking down or getting lost at night in an unfamiliar territory
- Taking married male clients to dinner
- How clients and peers perceive them on the job (e.g., too feminine, too aggressive)
- Dealing with sales managers who really believe "a woman's place is in the home."
- Reaction of sales manager and/or client if meeting, trip, or appointment is cancelled because of a sick child

Personal Concerns

- Planning trips to work out with family plans
- Dealing with friends and clients concerning why they travel, how their husbands feel, who takes care of the children, etc.
- Unwelcome advances from men (e.g., prospects, clients, colleagues)
- Growing dependent on male sales managers
- Clients' perceptions of their relationships with sales managers and male colleagues when they travel together
- A single woman's difficulty in establishing and maintaining a social life
- Dealing with husbands when they have a more successful or more "glamorous" job than he does

Source: Bobbi Linkemer, "Women in Sales: What Do They Really Want?" *Sales & Marketing Management,* January 1989, pp. 61–65.

MINORITIES IN SALES

Not only is the number of women in selling climbing sharply, but the number of blacks, Hispanics, Orientals, native Americans, handicapped, and older workers is increasing in U.S. sales forces, too. Beyond the strong legal and moral pressure to hire more people from these "protected groups" under civil rights law, an overriding practical reason is that the number of white males from 16 to 24 (who make up the majority of today's sales trainees) is declining while the number of minorities in this age group is growing rapidly.

Many sales organizations that have hired older people and minorities as sales representatives have been delighted with the results. One-fifth of the people in Texas Refinery Corporation's sales force of 3,000 are over 65, and one salesperson is 84. A few years ago, the company's "rookie of the year" was a 74-year-old man who earned $45,000 in commissions.[21] On the basis of studies of thousands of salespeople, Greenberg and Bern concluded: "Our experience shows that a man of 50 may have more open-mindedness and youthful vigor than a man half his age; . . . and that race has nothing to do with the ability to sell."[22] Another recent study found that successful salespeople do not fit any stereotype and that a large pool of sales talent among older people and minorities is waiting to be tapped.[23]

The 1964 Civil Rights Act was a legal stimulus to encourage the hiring of minority sales reps, but for years many companies had little success in attracting them to industrial sales jobs. This began changing in the early 1980s as the number of minorities interested in business increased substantially and sales managers became more creative in developing recruiting sources, messages, and media to attract minorities. Minority employees with sales potential now serving in secretarial, clerical, or factory positions are increasingly being considered for sales force openings. Local chapters of the National Association for the Advancement of Colored People (NAACP), the Urban League, and similar groups usually have employment referral services with whom many employers work closely. Colleges with large minority enrollments have become attractive recruiting grounds for companies seeking sales candidates, and college instructors of sales and marketing courses are often consulted about talented minority students who may be interested in sales careers. Advertisements for sales recruits are being placed in newspapers, radio and television programs, and magazines that appeal to minority audiences. Finally, many employers are striving to establish closer personal contacts with prominent minority business executives and community leaders in order to find help in attracting candidates for sales.

All major companies doing business in the United States have policy statements that reflect legal requirements with regard to equal employment opportunity. Nearly all the policies specify that the company does not discriminate against any employee or applicant for employment because of race, color, religion, sex, age, or national origin. In cases of noncompliance, the Equal Employment Opportunity Commission (EEOC) and state agencies may take legal action against employers and levy heavy financial penalties. A few years ago,

AT&T agreed to make back payments of almost $15 million to 15,000 employees. Beyond a policy statement, any company (with fifty or more employees) seeking federal government contracts must submit a written affirmative action program to the Office of Federal Contract Compliance (OFCC) of the Department of Labor. Without doubt, there will be expanding job opportunities in sales careers for minorities and older people who have a strong interest in sales and are willing to work hard.

VARIETY OF SALES JOBS

Sales positions differ greatly. No two seem exactly alike. Even in trying to classify sales positions, one finds a wide range of requirements and some overlap. The tasks and responsibilities of an IBM marketing representative who calls on large companies to demonstrate the features, functions, and benefits of a sophisticated computer are quite different from those of a real estate salesperson who attempts to sell homes to families. Nevertheless, there are many similarities, and the processes and techniques applied in each of these creative selling situations are closely related. Most firms require many different types of salespeople to perform different selling tasks. Size and characteristics of potential accounts, product complexity and price range, types of distribution channels, and intensity of advertising all influence the type of salespeople hired for sales assignments.

The basic sales categories are (1) order processing, (2) creative selling, and (3) missionary sales. Selling situations can be classified in several ways, and most sales jobs do not fall neatly into one category or another. In fact, some salespeople do all three basic tasks to some degree. The annual survey conducted by *Sales & Marketing Management* uses the categories shown in Exhibit 2-7 to classify salespeople. However, a more general taxonomy is (1) response selling, which includes both inside order taker and outside order taker; (2) trade selling; (3) missionary selling; (4) technical selling; and (5) creative selling.

Response selling implies that the salesperson merely reacts or responds to the customer's demands. Salespersons in response selling are either ''inside'' order takers (such as retail clerks who stand behind counters or wait to serve customers) or ''outside'' order takers (such as route drivers whose primary job is to deliver products, e.g., soft drinks, milk, bread, or fuel oil, and replenish inventories). Salespeople in such situations may generate some sales by having a pleasant personality and suggesting complementary products, but generally they create few sales. Usually, the main selling tasks are left to higher-level sales personnel in the organization.

Trade selling is similar to response selling in that the salesperson is primarily an order taker. But field service is more important in trade selling than in response selling. Most sales representatives of wholesalers are concerned with repeat sales to regular trade customers of such items as food, textiles, clothing, and household products. Trade selling consists largely of taking orders, expediting orders, restocking shelves, obtaining more shelf space, setting up displays, rotating stock, providing in-store demonstrations, and distributing samples to

---

EXHIBIT 2-7

The Five Types of Salespeople

Account representative. A salesperson who calls on a large number of already established customers in, for example, the food, textile, apparel, and wholesaling industries. Much of this selling is low-key, and there is minimal pressure to develop new business.

Detail salesperson. A salesperson who, instead of directly soliciting an order, concentrates on performing promotional activities and introducing products. The medical detail salesperson, for example, seeks to persuade doctors, the indirect customers, to specify the pharmaceutical company's trade name product for prescriptions. The firm's actual sale is ultimately made through a wholesaler or direct to pharmacists who fill prescriptions.

Sales engineer. A salesperson who sells products for which technical know-how and the ability to discuss technical aspects of the product are extremely important. The salesperson's expertise in identifying, analyzing, and solving customer problems is another critical factor. This type of selling is common in the chemical, machinery, and heavy equipment industries.

Industrial products salesperson, nontechnical. This salesperson sells a tangible product to industrial or commercial purchasers. A high degree of technical knowledge is not required. Organizations that sell packaging materials or standard office equipment use this type of sales rep.

Service salesperson. A salesperson who sells intangibles such as insurance and advertising. Unlike the four preceding types, those who sell services must be able to sell the benefits of intangibles.

Source: Adapted from *Sales & Marketing Management*, Feb. 25, 1986, p. 24.

---

store customers. More often than not, trade sellers are discouraged from using a hard sell with prospective buyers.

Missionary selling tries to influence the "decider" instead of the purchaser or user of the product. Missionary salespersons assist customers in selling to their own customers. The "detail person" in the pharmaceutical business introduces and explains the products of drug manufacturers to medical doctors. Although doctors seldom buy or use the drugs themselves, they become the missionary salespersons' target market. Missionary salespeople try to build goodwill, educate the deciders, and provide various services. Distilleries, brewers, pharmaceutical houses, food manufacturers, transportation firms, and public utilities commonly use missionary salespeople to help customers improve their bottom line.

Technical selling attempts to solve the customer's problems through the advice of technically trained salespeople. Technical selling resembles professional consulting and is common in such industries as steel, chemicals, heavy machinery, and computers. The technical help typically concerns use of complex products, system design, product characteristics, and installation procedures. Often, this type of salesperson is called a "sales engineer" to stress the technical nature of the job.

Creative selling calls for the salesperson to create demand among present and potential customers for two types of products and services: *tangibles* (such as automobiles, office supplies, real estate, typewriters, or college textbooks) and *intangibles* (such as insurance policies, educational courses, stocks and bonds, consulting services, and advertising services). Creative selling involves two distinct jobs: sales maintenance and sales development. The objective of sales maintenance is the creation of sales from present customers by maintaining and building on the good relationships already established. Sales development, however, concerns the creation of new customers, not just additional sales. When salespeople are expected to do both tasks, sales maintenance work usually drives out the more difficult sales development activities. Instead of calling on new prospects, where the expenditure of time may be unprofitable, most salespeople prefer to return to a known, friendly customer, where a profitable payoff is more likely.

This five-category taxonomy was recently updated and expanded to six categories on the basis of a study involving 1,393 salespeople in fifty-one industrial selling organizations. The new taxonomy includes (1) missionary selling, (2) trade services, (3) trade seller, (4) order taker, (5) institutional seller, and (6) residual seller.[24] The major differences between this taxonomy and the ones previously discussed center on the trade services (groups that emphasize service to retail and wholesale buyers), trade sellers (those who rely on bids, financing, and credit to make an initial sale), and institutional sellers (those who sell to an ultimate user that is either a manufacturer or institution).

CONTINUUM OF SALES TASKS

A continuum that represents the difficulty or complexity of sales tasks ranges from responsive selling (order taking) to the highly creative selling necessary in obtaining new business (order getting). Exhibit 2-8 provides examples of the types of activities involved in each major stage of the sales continuum, from sales support to sales maintenance to missionary work to sales development. Note that selling intangibles to new customers requires the highest level of creativity. Exhibit 2-9 presents another view of the varying intricacy of sales tasks. It shows how the specific characteristics of a given selling assignment determine its complexity and the level of preparation needed by the salesperson. With increasing complexity of the sales tasks, the salesperson needs more training, higher compensation, greater independence, and fewer customers.

SELLING ERAS

Selling approaches are continually evolving. An early era focused on *social selling* by extroverted salesmen who "knew the territory." Professor Harold Hill of *The Music Man* typifies such salesmen, who sold by dint of their flamboyant personalities and personal contacts in the territory. Similarly, Willy Loman of *Death of a Salesman* was convinced that you had to be well liked to be successful; he

EXHIBIT 2-8

The Sales Continuum

SERVICE
SELLING

CREATIVE
SELLING

Arousing demand and
influencing demand

Assistance in bringing
the sale to completion

Support	Maintenance	Missionary	Development

Service
representative

Technical
specialist

Order
taker

Detail
salesperson

Technical-use
salesperson

New–business
intangibles

Inside
salesperson

Driver
salesperson

Trade
salesperson

Factory
salesperson

New–business
tangibles

began to worry that people did not like him as he grew older, and his sales fell off.

Between the world wars salespeople began differentiating themselves by thoroughly learning their product lines and communicating product features and benefits to potential customers. Customers, however, were largely left with the responsibility of relating these product benefits to their particular set of needs. The prevailing view was that the products sold themselves if their features were accurately communicated. This was an updated version of the old production-oriented belief that the world would beat a path to your door if you built a better mousetrap.

Another sales era stressed programmed (canned) sales messages and sales formulas. These formulas might consist of ten easy steps to successful selling or the use of such acronyms as AIDA (attention, interest, desire, action) to help salespeople become more systematic and effective in dealing with potential buyers. Almost everyone has been approached and trapped into listening to one of these canned sales talks at one time or another. Canned sales presentations—or, more euphemistically, "structured, company-prepared, and planned presentations"—can be very effective when used as a guide but not when followed by rote.

The emphasis in today's changing selling environment is on identifying and solving customer problems via *consultative selling*. The consultative selling era is an outgrowth of the marketing concept, as it positions salespeople as extensions of their clients' buying center. Salespeople act as consultants who help customers achieve personal objectives and improve profits. They do this by recommending the best solutions to customers' problems—even if the solution sometimes fails

EXHIBIT 2-9

Complexity of the Sales Task

NATURE OF SELLING EFFORT:	Simple	Moderately simple	Moderately complex	Complex
CHARACTERISTICS OF THE TASK:				
Sales activity	Delivery			Problem solving
Degree of information communicated	Low			High
Needs served	Personal; physical			Intellectual; psychological
Customer type	Consumer; retailer			Industrial; commercial
PROFIT IMPACT:	Low			High
SALES FORCE NEEDS:				
Training	Less			More
Compensation	Low			High
Independence	Low			High
Number of customers	High			Low
EXAMPLES:				
Consumer selling	Milk	Clothing	Real estate; insurance	Stock; bonds
Industrial or commercial selling	Simple industrial supplies		Industrial equipment	High-volume OEM components
			Fashion at wholesale	Large private-label sales

Source: Modified from Benson P. Shapiro, "Manage the Customer, Not Just the Sales Force," Harvard Business Review, September-October 1974, pp. 236–237.

to include the purchase of the sales rep's products. Sales managers engaged in consultative selling recognize the importance of developing positive long-term relationships with clients.

Salespeople in a variety of industries are increasingly using the consultative sales approach. For example, AMP of Canada Ltd., the world's leading producer of electrical and electronic interconnection systems and devices, recently moved to a consultative selling approach. Free trade and globalization have placed many of AMP's customers in fiercely competitive markets, where factors such as world-class quality, flexible manufacturing, and shortened product life cycles are all prerequisites for survival. By moving to a consultative selling approach,

AMP was better able to understand its customers' needs and requirements, and this contributed to an increase in its market share.[25] The next example illustrates how Quaker Chemical views consultative selling.

CONSULTATIVE SELLING AT QUAKER CHEMICAL

Every year, as many as a dozen sales engineers may earn more than Peter Benoliel, president of Quaker Chemical Corporation in Conshohocken, Pennsylvania. The company produces a line of industrial cleaners, lubricants, additives, and other chemical products designed to solve problems for customers in a host of manufacturing industries.

Benoliel candidly admits that the success of his organization depends heavily on the marketing team, with its blend of technical expertise and sales know-how. "Quaker," he says, "is willing to pay well to get results. We have a very aggressive sales program. We present ourselves and try to achieve a position as consulting engineers. Our approach is to go in and address ourselves to the total process, and we usually have a pretty good knowledge of the process." One Quaker salesman, Benoliel notes, succeeded so well that the manager of the steel plant he served frankly acknowledged him as the person who knew the most about the plant's operation.

"We present ourselves as problem solvers," says Benoliel, "but the customer seldom comes to Quaker to seek help. Usually, it's the Quaker salesman who finds the problem, tries to convince the customer that he has a problem, and sells him on the idea that Quaker has the means to solve the problem. Often this requires the salesman to suggest development of an entirely new product or system of products."

Quaker Chemical's sales engineers are paid relatively modest base salaries, supplemented by a commission based on the price of the materials sold. "There's no limit to what they can earn," states Benoliel, who is himself a veteran of the sales and engineering sector.[26]

A recent study summarized the requirements for successful consultative selling in today's competitive selling environment.[27] The requirements were:

1. Clients must view sales reps as "purchasing experts." It is very important for salespeople to create an impression that they possess superior skills and/or knowledge related to the client's purchasing decision.

2. Salespeople must identify key members of the client's buying center as well as the input each member has in the decision-making process.

3. Salespeople must become thoroughly familiar with their clients' decision-making processes. The consultative sales rep should be able to identify alternative products and vendors the client has under consideration, key choice criteria of the client, beliefs about product and vendor performance held by the client, and procedures employed in the client's alternative evaluation process.

4. Salespeople should encourage their clients to make decisions that maximize the clients' benefits, but at the same time they should ensure a fair evaluation of their own product.

Adherence to these requirements can hopefully strengthen the bond between buyer and seller and ultimately lead to a long-term relationship.

In a recent interview, Howard Anderson, founder and managing director of the Yankee Group of Boston, introduced yet another era of personal selling. He dubbed this the "era of powerful tools," in which everything from software applications to voice mail and artificial intelligence will be used to help make the salesperson more productive in the future. Furthermore, many companies today are spending an extraordinary 25 percent of their management information system (MIS) budget to support sales and marketing functions. Mr. Anderson also stated that one of the changes during this power tools era will be the elimination of the traditional sales branch office. Companies are already moving in the direction of the "integrated customers" mode, in which customers and suppliers will be linked via a common data base, thus making the sales branch office unnecessary.[28] As selling changes in the 1990s, so does the emphasis on marketing in the sales force.

EXPANDING MARKETING RESPONSIBILITIES IN SELLING

As customers become more sophisticated and as their expectations for product and service performances rise, sales representatives must continuously raise their own standards of performance and strive for increasing professionalism. Enlightened managements are steadily enlarging the marketing-oriented role for their professional sales forces.

Instead of merely selling products, today's sales representatives are expected to understand the customers' spectrum of existing and potential problems while achieving both buyer and seller objectives. Beyond skillful application of the personal selling process (which is discussed in depth in Appendix A), these new consultative sales reps are accepting responsibility as *field marketing managers* with profit objectives for a designated territory or market. These expanding responsibilities require performance of a diversity of interactive roles, including the following:

1. *Market analysts and planners* monitor competitors' actions and changes in the uncontrollable marketing environment and devise strategies to adjust to these changes by successfully satisfying customers.

2. *Sales forecasters* help sales management in estimating future sales and setting sales quotas in the sales reps' assigned market.

3. *Opportunity managers* are sensitive to unsatisfied or even unrecognized customer needs and potential problems calling for new products, new markets, or innovative marketing mixes.

4. *Students of buyer behavior* are aware of customer decision processes and the motivations that influence the buyer to buy.

5. *Intelligence gatherers* are alert and conscientious about providing feedback from the field to headquarters marketing for strategic planning purposes.

6. *Team coordinators* effectively utilize their backup specialists in marketing research, traffic management, engineering, finance, operations, and customer services to solve customer problems.

7. *Allocators of scarce products* are perceived by customers as efficient and fair in allocating scarce products and services.

8. *Marketing cost analysts* are aware of the differential costs associated with selling separate products to different customers and territories so that they can concentrate on profitable sales—not merely on sales volume or sales quotas.

Performing Nonselling Tasks

In their range of activities, contemporary sales reps are required to do several "nonselling" jobs beyond the traditional servicing of customer accounts. For example, sales representatives are called on to counsel and regain the goodwill of unhappy customers; to gather and analyze marketing information about competition; to anticipate changing customer needs and problem areas for new-product development opportunities; and to accurately communicate to headquarters the nuances of customer concerns about financing, product quality, delivery, services, promotional support, and the like. With this increased emphasis on nonselling tasks, new forms of compensation are necessary (see Chapter 12).

Establishing Long-Run Partnerships

In the modern era of consultative selling, companies do not make purchases; they establish relationships. Salespeople provide an irreplaceable market element, for they serve as the personal link between the selling and buying systems. They are responsible for establishing and maintaining buyer-seller interfaces that are mutually beneficial. A top marketing executive at IBM claims that today's salesperson must establish a "long-range partnership" with the customers. "The installation of a data processing system," he declares, "is only the beginning, not the end, of IBM's marketing effort. Buyers want to know if they can expect the salesperson's help on a regular basis. There are few quick sales today." As customer problems have increased in complexity, salespeople have had to interrelate sophisticated product systems to provide comprehensive solutions. Coordinating the sale of complex product systems has expanded the time necessary to complete sales transactions. It may take a year to get to know a potential customer and his or her range of problems. "You have to gear yourself psychologically for a long haul," says a regional sales manager for Singer's Business Machines Group who almost quit the company after going a year without making a sale. Illustrative of the long-run commitment often necessary to make complex sales today is the next story, of a Honeywell computer sales representative.

A BIG SALE IS WORTH THE WAIT

At the age of 29, Kim Kelley is already something of a legend around Honeywell, Inc. "He's the one who cried when he made his sale, isn't he?" a fellow Honeywell salesperson asks with a chuckle.

Indeed he is. Kim stood there in his customer's office last June and bawled like a baby. And for good reason. Kim had just shaken hands on an $8.1 million computer sale to the state of Illinois. He had spent three years laying the groundwork for it, and for three solid months, he had been working six days a week, often 14 hours a day, competing against salespeople from four other computer companies—Burroughs, Univac Division of Sperry Rand, Control Data, and IBM.

It was a make-or-break situation for Kim Kelley, and standing there with tears of joy and relief streaming down his cheeks, he knew that he had it made. A bright future with Honeywell was assured, and he had just made an $80,000 commission.

Now Kim is stalking other big game. He put the finishing touches on a campaign with A. E. Staley Manufacturing Co. in December and expects to close the $1.8 million deal in February. It was a relatively easy sale to a long-time Honeywell customer that Kim had worked diligently with to provide special service. Next, the Illinois Department of Revenue is "going on the front burner," Kim says. His goal: an $8 to $10 million sale of dual computers sometime this year.

When Honeywell recently rewarded Kim by promoting him to Sales Manager, he requested "demotion" in order to avoid going on straight salary. Honeywell refused but did allow Kim a special status whereby he runs an 18-person sales office but stays on commission plus salary. Kim says he expects to move high in management eventually, but right now, "I can't afford the pay cut."[29]

Coordinating Buyer-Seller Teams

When selling complex product systems such as computer installations, the seller frequently employs team selling, and the sales representative acts as the team coordinator in contacts with the buyer organization. In the words of a marketing vice president for Transamerica Corporation:

> A few years back . . . it was usually the salesman out there alone, pitting his wits against the resistance of a single corporate purchasing agent. Now, more and more companies are selling on many different levels, interlocking their research, engineering, marketing, and upper management with those of their customers. This way, today's salesperson becomes a kind of committee chairman within his company. Some manufacturers call them account managers. Either way, their job is to exploit the resources of his company in serving the customer.[30]

To make a major sale, it is essential for the buyer to feel that the seller is on his or her team. An example of this buyer-seller teamwork is evidenced by the comments of an Armco Steel Corporation salesperson.

> I try to find out as much as I can about a prospect's company, the products he makes, what problems he has in selling them. Suppose he makes oil pipes. I bring in our market-development people to help him find new markets for them. Or maybe, he has a manufacturing problem requiring technical help. I bring in our welding engineer. If a customer says Company A shipped him plates below a quality standard, I suggest he contact someone in our metallurgy department who can tell him what grade steel will solve his problem. Even when I learn that one of my competitors has stock that my customer needs, I pass the news along to the customer. I try to be as honest with a customer as I can.[31]

Salespeople in all industries need headquarters marketing support to coordinate buyer-seller teams and satisfy customers, but they do not always get it. For instance, the insurance industry spends thirty times as much for advertising as it does for marketing research.[32] Such statistics suggest that the insurance industry encourages its salespeople to operate more under the selling concept than the marketing concept; that is, a salesperson is oriented more toward selling policies than toward understanding potential customers' needs and problems. It is difficult for the salesperson to establish long-run relationships of respect and trust with customers unless the seller's top management is clearly committed to the marketing concept. Failure to make this commitment forces the sales force to spend more time in the costly process of seeking new customers (sales development) than in the more efficient process of sales maintenance, which provides repeat and expanding sales plus customer referrals.

Increasing Sales Productivity and Profits

"A sales order is no longer the measure of [sales representative] success," declares a regional sales manager for Borg-Warner Chemicals, a subsidiary of Chicago-based Borg-Warner Corporation. "We now require him to manage a segment of our business."[33]

Volume versus profit orientations.   Not only industrial firms but even consumer-oriented firms have been operating under the selling concept until recently. According to a vice president of marketing for Del Monte Corporation: "Historically, most food companies have been case-volume oriented. As long as we could push out a lot of volume, we let the profits take care of themselves. That's no longer true. As products multiply and the competition for shelf space increases, salespeople have to be far more sophisticated in their approach to product management, and the company has to learn to identify those with the most profit potential." To develop that potential, Del Monte restructured its entire field sales force by expanding from nine regional divisions to twenty-one. With this new system Del Monte's actual selling is handled by an account representative, who makes the calls on retailers and writes the orders. One level below the account representative is the sales rep, who works with store managers on shelf management, restocking, display, and other merchandising chores. Sales representatives are also information gatherers. Using a computerized system called Key Facts, Del Monte's salespeople fill out a form on each store visit. The form lists shelf position, pricing, advertising support, and other basic marketing data. These data are fed into the computer for later comparison against actual product performance to determine maximum profitability.

Reassignment of routine duties.   Hunt-Wesson Foods, Gillette, Allied Chemical, and several other firms are trying new ways to free salespeople from routine duties. Gillette, for instance, employs an auxiliary force of 150 middle-aged homemakers who operate one level below the individual store salespeople. The women work twenty-four hours a week and handle retail displays, distribution, and stock replenishment. Twenty years ago, Gillette salespeople spent 30 percent of their time calling on customers and 70 percent working on store displays, distribution, and order taking. Today, the salespeople spend 85 percent of their time with customers and only 15 percent on routine requirements.

Advanced sales aids.   Modern salespeople have an array of advanced sales aids: cellular mobile telephones, audiovisual cassettes, special slide projectors, videodisc players, pocket pagers (beepers), and remote portable computers that connect with headquarters marketing information. Goya Foods, Inc., is a Hispanic-owned company that sells rice, beans, and other staples to supermarkets and *bodegas* (general stores) across the nation. Goya equips its salespeople (who sell direct to retail outlets, not through wholesalers or brokers) with pocket computer terminals that can store orders from up to twenty stores. When they use up the portable electronic memory, the Goya salespeople simply telephone their orders from their pocket computers to a central computer at the main office, where orders are promptly prepared for next-day delivery.[34]

With the soaring costs of cold calls (industrial sales calls cost $64 in 1973, nearly $100 in 1979, and over $250 in 1990), many companies are selecting high-potential prospects by computer. Modern computer technology and multivariate data analysis techniques have provided salespeople and sales managers with methods for developing precise sales forecasts. They facilitate equitable assignment of sales territories, efficient routing and scheduling of salespeople, marketing cost analysis, effective time management, account tracking, and performance evaluation.

General Electric's Lamp Division uses computers to produce the Personalized Lighting Cost Analysis for customers. It provides a potential client with detailed comparative data on initial installation costs, annual operating costs, and total owning and operating costs for various types of lighting systems. Warn-Belleview, Inc., a manufacturer of locking hubs and power winches, took advantage of General Electric's computer analysis when highway rerouting forced the company to build a new plant. The computer determined that putting in a Lucalox lighting system would have the highest initial installation cost but the lowest total operating costs. Warn-Belleview selected this lighting system from among several alternatives with different costs and benefits.

In the same way, computers are aiding selling and sales management in consumer sales. In real estate sales, computers are matching prospects' housing needs with features of available homes, thereby making more efficient use of the time buyer and seller spend together. Use of computers in selling and sales management is only in its infancy, but its application is growing rapidly.

Transportation and communication.   Improved transportation and communication methods have permitted today's salespeople to remain in touch with customers over a larger territory. The president of a Houston industrial goods firm describes a top salesperson's day: "He starts his day flying out nonstop from North Carolina to Chicago, then gets a midafternoon plane to Los Angeles to make two or three calls, and catches a night plane to Dallas. It's a fast-moving situation today. A few years ago, because of aircraft and flight scheduling, we couldn't do this."

Nationwide advertising and videoconferencing and worldwide communication via orbiting satellites help introduce salespeople, their companies, and products to perspective customers, thereby saving valuable time in the selling process. Another recent innovation, *facsimile transmission*—instant transmission of written words, drawings, graphs, and the like, over ordinary telephone lines—is already one of the leading forms of communication in the 1990s.

One controversial device that life insurance companies, cosmetic firms, churches, and political candidates have used effectively is the automatic telephone dialer. The equipment presents prerecorded sales messages, often from celebrity callers, such as Zsa Zsa Gabor or the Reverend Jesse Jackson. Government restraints have restricted such uninvited calls to people's homes since many complaints have been voiced. Nevertheless, these automatic sales messages have proved very successful, and their use will probably continue in the foreseeable future. As technology advances on all fronts, professional consultative salespeople will continue to apply appropriate innovations to more effectively and efficiently communicate with customers.

Avoiding Job Myopia

Do not assume that all contemporary salespeople are sophisticated professionals. Recognize that too many salespeople today are still not truly integrated into the total marketing team. As a result, they are ill-informed and ill-prepared to fully serve their customers or their companies. They suffer from personal "marketing myopia" in that their jobs have been defined too narrowly in terms of selling rather than in terms of marketing. The effective salesperson needs to be a marketing problem solver who can grasp the full range of customer problems and match current and future customer needs with his or her company's current and future offerings. Through this marketing management orientation, an entry-level sales position can be one of the most accessible ways to begin a marketing management career, and the transition from sales representative to sales manager to vice president of marketing is not a series of traumatic steps, but a natural career progression.

SUMMARY

The top salespeople of today are professionals who combine innate ability and acquired skills. The knowledge and skills needed to meet current complex and competitive market conditions are acquired through intensive training and practice. The distinguishing feature of personal selling is two-way seller-buyer communication with immediate feedback in the form of verbal exchanges, expressions, and gestures. Sales representatives can significantly enhance or detract from the seller's image in the market, for they are the critical contact with the customers.

Many sales representatives have the freedom of entrepreneurs or independent business owners in structuring their work, yet they enjoy the security and benefits of employment with a company. Despite the many opportunities and high compensation in selling, there are shortages of qualified salespeople. Although the number of women in sales is still relatively small, many companies are finding that women are as good as, and often better than, their male counterparts. Today, there are no objective reasons why women cannot be as successful as men in sales careers. There are also increasing numbers of minorities entering sales, and the need for minority group sales reps is growing rapidly.

There are three basic sales categories: order processing, creative selling, and missionary sales. Within these categories five types of salespeople have been identified: account representative, detail salesperson, sales engineer, industrial products salesperson (nontechnical), and service salesperson.

A continuum of sales-task difficulty and complexity ranges from responsive selling (order taking) to the highly creative selling necessary in obtaining new business (order getting). With the increasing complexity of sales tasks, the salesperson needs more training, higher compensation, greater independence, and fewer customers.

Selling approaches are continuously evolving to meet the demands of the market. An early era focused on social selling by extroverted salesmen. In the time between the world wars, salespeople began to communicate product features and benefits to potential customers, but customers were left to relate these benefits to their needs. Another era stressed programmed (canned) sales messages and sales formulas to help salespeople become more systematic and effective in dealing with potential buyers. Recently, the emphasis has shifted to identifying and solving customer problems. This approach often involves teams of sales representatives with complementary skills who sell product systems of complex design to multiple levels in a customer's organization.

As customers become more sophisticated and as their expectations for product and service performance rise, sales representatives must continue to raise their own standards of performance and strive for increasing professionalism. Instead of merely selling products, today's sales representatives are expected to understand the customer's spectrum of existing and potential problems while achieving both buyer and seller objectives. In their range of activities, contemporary sales reps are required to do nonselling jobs beyond traditional servicing of customer accounts. Also, sales representatives must focus not only on selling the product but on establishing a long-term relationship and coordinating buyerseller interfaces and on increasing sales productivity.

Computers have become an increasingly important tool to the sales representative. They can be used to cut down on the time needed to perform market analysis and to identify potential customers. Sales managers are also using computers for assigning territories and for scheduling, routing, and budgeting. The effective salesperson needs to be a marketing problem solver who can grasp the full range of customer problems and match current and future customer needs with his or her company's current and future offerings.

STUDY QUESTIONS

1. Explain why there is a continuing shortage of qualified salespeople.

2. Compare the responsibilities of different sales positions from responsive selling to creative selling. Be sure to give examples.

3. Describe a hypothetical complex selling situation in which a system of products (say, an information processing system) is being sold by a team of seller experts to a team of buyer experts.

4. In what ways should a sales rep function as a marketing manager?

5. Why do you think women and minorities have been underrepresented in company sales forces? Do you feel that there are increasing opportunities for them now? How do sales jobs compare with other options for women and minorities?

6. What should be the responsibilities of the professional sales rep to the customer?

7. Why are many companies seeking people with marketing experience for sales positions? Do you agree or disagree with this approach?

8. Why is personal selling an effective means of sales promotion? Is it always most important? Why or why not?

9. In the words of one well-seasoned sales representative, "Selling means getting out there and finding some sucker. All that's necessary is to have the gift of gab and a little larceny in your heart." Comment.

10. Why do you think the emphasis has shifted in recent years from the structured sales presentation to the consultative sales approach?

IN-BASKET EXERCISE

You are the southwestern regional sales manager for a construction tools company. Your salespeople drive vans or pickup trucks to construction sites to demonstrate tools and take orders from construction site foremen. Today, you received a memo from the vice president of human resources stating that the number of women on your sales force is far below the EEOC standards for the company. Moreover, the memo indicates that a strong possibility exists for fines and/or legal action if more women are *not hired!* The vice president wants you to employ additional women, but this is problematic. Sales have been relatively flat because of a decline in building construction, and currently there are *no* positions open for additional salespeople.

How would you handle this situation?

CASE 2-1

WOMEN IN SALES?

Vivian Long is an undergraduate marketing major in her senior year at Republic State University. She has been interviewing for jobs over the past few months and is confused regarding which type of job she should select. She has been interviewed by retailers, banks, advertising agencies, consumer products companies, industrial products distributors, and manufacturers.

Vivian already has two job offers, and she expects to get a third from an industrial products distributor.

One of her job offers is from a regional retail department store chain. The position is buyer trainee, and the salary is $20,000 for the first year. The company is growing rapidly, and she could probably be promoted to buyer within two years. The people at the department store are pleasant, but Vivian is not sure she wants to pursue a career in retailing. The other job offer is from a local bank. The position consists primarily of work as a research analyst in the marketing department, but Vivian would spend some time doing advertising research with the bank's ad agency. The position is appealing because she would go directly into marketing activities, but the salary is only $15,500.

The position Vivian thinks she is most interested in is the one with the industrial products distributor. The distributor handles drill bits, tools, fasteners, and other equipment used in the construction industry. The company services the construction industry in a five-state area—Louisiana, Mississippi, Alabama, Georgia, and Florida. The sales force consists of thirty-one people who operate from three district offices. There are presently no female salespeople, and although the recruiter for the company was pleasant and somewhat encouraging, Vivian felt that he might be reluctant to hire her because she is a woman.

Vivian has good grades (3.2 average) and has been active in extracurricular activities while in school, including being an officer in the marketing club. Her father worked in the oil fields for years, and she learned a lot from him. One summer she even had a job with a construction company in Houston. She wants the job with the industrial products distributor because the industry has good long-term growth prospects and she believes the opportunity for advancement is better in smaller companies than in large companies. She also likes the flexibility of the sales job. The salary is attractive ($24,000 plus commission and car), but she will have to travel two or three days a week and be away from her boyfriend.

Vivian has the following major concerns: Will people in the industry, including the industrial products distributor, accept and work with a saleswoman in a traditionally male-dominated job? Is there a long-term future for her in industrial sales? Do the other two job offers represent better career opportunities for her?

Questions

1. Discuss the positives and negatives of each of Vivian's job opportunities. Should Vivian accept the industrial sales position? Why or why not?

2. Do you foresee any extra challenges Vivian may experience by being the only woman sales rep on the industrial sales force? Support your answer.

3. Do you foresee any positive inputs to Vivian's career if she chooses the sales job over the other two job opportunities? Why or why not?

4. Is there anything women sales reps can bring into a sales position that might benefit the sales force?

CASE 2-2

PROFESSIONALISM IN SALES?

Kurt Bogner is a senior majoring in marketing at Western State University. He was born in Chicago, but his family moved to California when he was 12 years old. His father is an engineer who originally moved to California to work for an aircraft company but is now with a firm specializing in silicon chip technology for the information processing industry. His father has spent most of his working life in research and has developed several patentable products for his company.

Kurt has been interviewing with a wide variety of firms this semester and already has several offers. While in college he was involved in many outside activities, including playing intramural sports and being an officer in the marketing club. He also held a couple of part-time jobs but still managed to maintain a 2.9 grade-point average. Kurt has put much thought into each of his offers, but the ones he is attracted to most are in sales. Kurt likes to work with people and is drawn to the flexibility and challenge of a sales career.

In addition, the starting salaries for the sales jobs are higher than those for the others, particularly when he considers the commissions, bonuses, expense account, and company car.

While Kurt is convinced that he will enjoy a sales career, he can't forget what some people have said about working in sales. He has discussed job opportunities with his dad several times, and every time he mentions sales positions, his dad says, "Can't you find something better than sales? You don't need a college degree to get a sales job." Additionally, Kurt's roommate, who is an accounting major, can't understand why Kurt wants to go into sales. In one of his typical comments to Kurt, he said, "Sales is a high-pressure, low-status occupation with very little job security. There isn't much professionalism in a field filled with door-to-door salespeople!" Kurt is concerned with these opinions and is starting to have second thoughts about a career in sales.

Questions

1. Do you consider a sales position a prestigious-enough career for a person with a college degree? Why or why not?

2. Why do you think some people have such a low opinion of sales as a career?

3. How might Kurt convince his father and his roommate that sales is a professional career?

REFERENCES

1. Based on personal interview with Tiffany Morrison, June 14, 1990.
2. "Strange Tales of Sales," *Sales & Marketing Management*, June 3, 1985, pp. 42–46.
3. "Big Money in Selling—But 'No Guarantees,'" *U.S. News & World Report*, Nov. 13, 1978, p. 51.
4. *Money*, November 1981, p. 52.
5. "The New Business of Selling," *Industrial Distribution*, June 1975, pp. 37–40.
6. Charles W. Parker, Jr., "200th Year of Selling," *Marketing Times*, January–February 1975, p. A-8.
7. *Marketing News*, May 30, 1980, p. 20.
8. Quoted in *Marketing Times*, January–February 1979, p. 39.
9. "1990 Survey of Selling Costs," *Sales & Marketing Management*, Feb. 26, 1990.
10. Edward C. Bursk and G. Scott Hutchinson (eds.), *Salesmanship and Sales Force Management*, Harvard University Press, Cambridge, Mass., 1971, pp. 109–120.
11. IBM, Office Products Division, Recruiting Brochure, 1986–1987.
12. Procter & Gamble, Recruiting Brochure, 1986–1987.
13. John A. Sussman, "Making It to the Top: A Career Profile of the Senior Executive," *Management Review*, July 1979, p. 16.
14. Jeanne Greenberg and Herbert Greenberg, "Predicting Sales Success—Myths and Reality," *Personnel Journal*, December 1975, pp. 621–627.
15. "'Pink Ghetto' in Sales for Women," *Sales & Marketing Management*, July 1988, p. 80.
16. "A Special News Report on People and Their Jobs in Office, Fields, and Factories," *Wall Street Journal*, Mar. 29, 1988, p. 1.
17. Rayna Skolnik, "A Woman's Place Is on the Sales Force," *Sales & Marketing Management*, Apr. 1, 1985, pp. 34–37.
18. Statement made by one of the author's female students, September 1986.
19. "The Industrial Salesman Becomes a Salesperson," *Business Week*, Feb. 19, 1979, pp. 104–110.
20. Sales Executives Club of New York, *Survey of Women in Sales*, 1976.
21. Maria T. Padillo, "Firm Recruits Older People as Salesmen," *Wall Street Journal*, Apr. 19, 1982, p. 29.
22. Herbert M. Greenberg and Ronald L. Bern, *The Successful Salesman: Man and His Sales Manager*, Auerbach Publishers, Philadelphia, 1972, p. 80.
23. Herbert M. Greenberg and Jeanne Greenberg, "Job Matching for Better Sales Performance," *Harvard Business Review*, September-October 1980, pp. 128–133.
24. William C. Moncrief III, "Selling Activity and Sales Position Taxonomies for Industrial Salesforces," *Journal of Marketing Research*, August 1986, pp. 261–270.
25. Barrie Whittaker, "Increasing Market Share through Marketing Excellence," *Canadian Business Review*, Spring 1990, pp. 35–37.
26. Adapted from *Philadelphia Inquirer*, June 13, 1978, pp. 8C, 13C.
27. Kenneth N. Thompson, "Monte Carlo Simulation Approach to Product Profile Analysis: A Consultative Selling Tool," *Journal of Personal Selling & Sales Management*, Summer 1989, pp. 1–10.

28. Thayer C. Taylor, ''Selling Will Never Be the Same,'' *Sales & Marketing Management*, March 1989, pp. 48–53.
29. Thomas Ehrich, ''To Computer Salesmen, the 'Big-Ticket' Deal Is the One to Look For,'' *Wall Street Journal*, Jan. 22, 1974, pp. 1, 41.
30. ''The New Supersalesman: Wired for Success,'' *Business Week*, Jan. 6, 1973, pp. 45–49.
31. M. B. Rothfeld, ''A New Kind of Challenge for Salesmen,'' *Fortune*, April 1974, pp. 156–166.
32. Consensus estimates obtained from discussions with several insurance industry executives, May 1986 to August 1986.
33. Quoted in *Business Week*, Oct. 26, 1974, p. 54.
34. *Newsweek*, May 17, 1982, p. 84.

OVERVIEW OF PERSONAL SELLING AND SALES MANAGEMENT AT CHEMCO

In an attempt to place the reader in a realistic sales management environment, we have created a series of five integrated cases about a single company. One case appears at the end of each part of the text. The company and its data bank are based on a real company so that the reader can encounter a situation with real-world problems and opportunities.

THE COMPANY

CHEMCO is a medium-sized organization that sells process and formulator chemicals throughout the United States. Its sales force calls on companies that use these chemicals in their operations. The salespeople deal directly with the purchasing agents of those companies. CHEMCO has experienced steady growth in sales over the last three to four years. During this period, its sales force has grown by over 200 percent.

The composition of CHEMCO's sales force is presented in Exhibit 1. The company has a national sales force, divided into Divisions 1 and 2. Division 1 has eight regional managers who supervise twenty-one district sales managers. The district sales managers are responsible for the fifty-five representatives in Division 1. All the division's management personnel (regional managers and

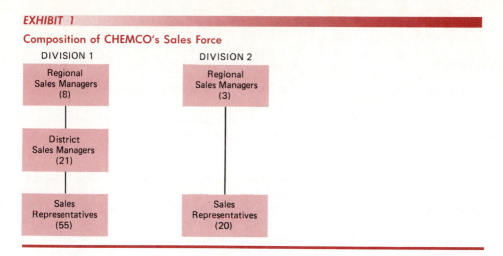

EXHIBIT 1

Composition of CHEMCO's Sales Force

district managers) are male, but eight of its sales reps are female. Division 2 is smaller, with only three regional sales managers directly supervising twenty sales representatives. The regional sales managers and all the sales reps in Division 2 are male. The regional sales managers in both divisions report to the vice president of sales and marketing, and none are involved in any personal selling.

THE DATA BANK

The president of CHEMCO, Al Jorgenson, recently requested a comprehensive study of his company's sales force. Jorgenson believed that his management team had lost touch with the sales force because of the company's recent rapid expansion. A university research team was hired to conduct the study.

A questionnaire was mailed to all the sales personnel, including the regional and district sales managers. Of the recipients, 95 percent responded to the survey; the 5 percent who did not left CHEMCO shortly after the survey was completed. Therefore, the data bank consists of completed questionnaires from eleven regional sales managers, twenty-one district sales managers, and seventy-five salespeople. All the sales managers were briefed about the study and its results. Furthermore, they have been encouraged to use the data bank at any time for solving problems or planning future strategies.

A brief description of the variables in the data base is presented in Exhibit 2. More complete definitions of the variables follow.

- X_1 *job satisfaction.* This variable measures how satisfied a salesperson is with various aspects of his or her job. Salespeople give their opinions on how satisfied they are with such job-related areas as pay, coworkers, promotion opportunities, customers, managers, and the overall company.

EXHIBIT 2

Description of Data-Base Variables

Variable	Description
X_1 Job satisfaction	Individual's overall level of satisfaction with his or her job
X_2 Organizational commitment	Individual's overall level of perceived involvement with and loyalties to the company
X_3 Role perception	Individual's understanding of what is expected of him or her by others
X_4 Job performance	Individual's perception of how he or she is doing on the job
X_5 Propensity to quit	Individual's perception of how likely it is that he or she will quit the job
X_6 Managerial considerations	Individual's perception of his or her managers
X_7 Perceived organizational climate	Individual's perception of the climate of the organization
X_8 Salesperson's self-esteem	Individual's attitude toward himself or herself
X_9 Demographics	Individual's specific characteristics

- X_2 *organizational commitment.* This variable assesses an individual's level of commitment toward the company. Salespeople indicate how loyal they are to the company, how involved they are with their jobs, and what their level of dissatisfaction is with the company.

- X_3 *role perception.* This variable assesses how well a salesperson understands exactly what is expected of him or her by others. Individuals report any level of conflict and uncertainty concerning job expectations.

- X_4 *job performance.* This variable measures how an individual feels about his or her own job performance. Salespeople report their level of performance concerning selling skills, customer relations, fieldwork, technical knowledge, territory management, and the overall job.

- X_5 *propensity to quit.* This variable attempts to assess the likelihood of a salesperson's quitting his or her job. Salespeople answer several questions regarding the possibility of their leaving the company.

- X_6 *managerial considerations.* This variable measures how a salesperson feels about his or her sales managers. Salespeople give their perceptions of their regional and district sales managers.

- X_7 *perceived organizational climate.* This variable assesses how a salesperson views the corporate climate. Salespeople answer questions concerning their feelings about the prestige of the company, the people within the organization, the goal-setting process of the company, and the reward structure of the company.

- X_8 *salesperson's self-esteem*. This variable measures how an individual feels about himself or herself. For example, high self-esteem means the individual has self-respect and feels he or she is doing a good job.

- X_9 *demographics*. This variable measures specific characteristics of a salesperson. Salespeople provide such data as education, income, gender, composition of family, spouse's employment, experience in sales (years), tenure in current job, sales in last two years, and salary earned in last year.

Each of the variables listed above corresponds to several questions on the questionnaire. However, in an attempt to make the data set more manageable, each of the variables X_1 to X_8 has been listed on the diskette as one summary measure, or weighted average, of the responses pertaining to that specific variable. For example, while each salesperson responded to six questions dealing with job satisfaction, only one measure (weighted average) of job satisfaction is given for each salesperson. Thus, each of the seventy-five salespeople has eight data points representing the eight respective variables. All the demographic information (variable X_9) collected in the study is furnished on the diskette. A listing of the complete data bank and all the items is provided in the Instructor's Manual.

QUESTIONS

1. After reading Chapters 1 and 2 of the text, what are your feelings regarding the decision to do a comprehensive survey of CHEMCO's sales personnel? Do you agree or disagree with the president's decision?

2. As one of the regional or district sales managers for CHEMCO, how would you react to this survey? Would you use the data from the survey? Why or why not?

3. Assuming you were to use the data from this survey, how would you do so? What sales management tasks would be easier to accomplish given the results of this study? Be specific.

PART TWO

PLANNING AND ORGANIZING THE SALES FORCE

3

SALES PLANNING AND BUDGETING

LEARNING OBJECTIVES

When you finish this chapter, you should understand:

▲ The overall philosophy and process of sales planning
▲ How strategic sales planning and tactical sales planning differ
▲ The purpose, value, and use of a sales management information system
▲ What is involved in a sales audit
▲ Business portfolio approaches to strategic planning
▲ Some causes of unsuccessful sales planning
▲ The purpose and benefits of a sales budget
▲ How to prepare a sales budget

A DAY ON THE JOB

James Kent began his career in 1960 as a sales trainee with the Forest Products Division of the Owens-Illinois Glass Company. Through the years, James has progressed as a sales rep, national-account sales rep, sales manager, operations manager, and general manager. During this time the Forest Products Division was sold to Great Northern Nekoosa Corporation, which was recently acquired by Georgia-Pacific Corporation. Now, as general manager at Georgia-Pacific, James is actively involved in sales planning for the corrugated box plant. "Typically, the sales territory of a corrugated box plant will be comprised of an area within a 300-mile radius of the plant. Information is then gathered from such sources as chambers of commerce, privately published industrial guides, and state or federal publications on virtually every manufacturing company within a given sales territory. Once the information on the manufacturing companies is accumulated, it is possible to project estimated corrugated box potential by utilizing historical information that tells us typical corrugated usage for various SICs [standard industrial classifications]. Categorizing usage by SICs and using that historical information, we can come up with a relatively accurate forecast of market potential within a city, county, state, or other geographic area." Mr. Kent is aware that totally correct market potentials are difficult to achieve at first: "However, at Georgia-Pacific we know there will be inaccuracies, but follow-up sales calls by local plant sales reps confirm or correct our estimated market potential."[1]

Xerox Corporation, up to the mid-1970s, sold three out of every four copiers bought in the United States, and "xeroxing" became a commonly understood term for photocopying. However, slow response to Japanese competitors such as Canon, Ricoh, and Sharp caused Xerox's market share to fall to only 36 percent by 1984. Shocked into action, Xerox management began intense strategic planning not only to regain dominance of the copier market but also to become a major player in the complex office automation market. Manufacturing costs for copiers were cut in half, and product quality was monitored closely through monthly surveys of 50,000 Xerox customers. Xerox's plans called for a three-tiered training program, costing up to $20 million a year, to convert nearly 4,000 copier salespeople into a general-line sales force knowledgeable in all Xerox products and customer sales strategies. Indicating the company's commitment, Xerox's senior vice president of marketing and planning says: "The program won't be accomplished overnight, which is why we're looking at a three- to five-year time frame."[2]

Without well-thought-out plans, it is difficult to get anything accomplished efficiently and effectively, especially in large companies. Effective sales managers are usually good planners. Planning is the most basic function that sales managers do because it creates the essential framework for all other decision making. Planning requires that sales managers anticipate the possible outcomes and future implications of their current decisions; thus, planning is a method of managing the future. In fact, a succinct definition of "planning" is "making decisions today to create a desired tomorrow."

WHY SHOULD SALES MANAGERS PLAN?

Some sales managers argue that the marketplace changes too fast for any plan to be of much value. These managers are fooling themselves. Without a plan to provide direction—even in dynamic marketing environments—decision making is aimless and disconnected, and it becomes futile to try to achieve objectives effectively and efficiently or to carry out the functions of sales management. For example, sales managers who attempt to recruit and select a sales force without the guidelines of a plan will find themselves continually underhiring, overhiring, and firing employees. Similarly, sales managers who try to organize, train, motivate, or evaluate salespeople without an overall plan will be frequently reorganizing, retraining, and encountering poor morale and high turnover.

Sales managers must make their decisions within an environment where change is continuous—whether in the competitive, technological, political, economic, or social arena. Planning helps minimize environmental shocks, such as the sudden shortage of energy and critical raw materials, or major changes in federal tax laws. If sales managers do not anticipate these changes and make proactive decisions in line with predictions, they will find themselves caught up in a kind of whiplash decision-making process, in which they are battered back and forth by a seemingly capricious marketing environment.

Benefits of Planning

Planning provides several specific benefits. It can *improve morale* when the entire sales organization actively participates in the process. It *provides direction and focus* for organizational efforts, and it can *improve cooperation and coordination* of sales force efforts. Planning also helps *develop individual and collective standards* by which sales force performance can be measured and deviations identified in time to take corrective action. Finally, planning *increases the sales organization's flexibility* in dealing with unexpected developments.

Planning Precision

Accurate and precise planning will improve the quality of decision making in implementing a plan, but planning accuracy depends a great deal on the time period involved. The shorter the time period covered in a particular plan, the more accurate the plan tends to be. Annual sales plans are meaningful only in the context of a longer-range plan. A common practice among larger corporations is "rolling planning," in which a three- or five-year sales plan is prepared or reworked at the beginning of each year and the annual sales plan is revised later in the year.

As a company develops experience in the planning process, more precise financial measurements are included. Objectives are expressed not just in sales volume but in financial terms, such as return on assets managed, cash flow, and contribution margin. Computer simulations of different scenarios are frequently employed to appraise the impact on sales and profits of alternative plans under

EXHIBIT 3-1

Planning at Different Levels of Management

Type	Participants	Focus
Strategic planning	CEO, board of directors, president, top vice presidents	Company mission, goals, and objectives; primary strategies; overall budgeting
Tactical planning	General sales manager, director of marketing research	Departmental, yearly, and quarterly plans; policies, procedures, budgets
Monthly and weekly planning	Regional sales managers	Branch plans and budgets
Daily planning	Sales supervisors and sales representatives	Unit plans and budgets

various assumptions regarding the future marketing environment. Finally, contingency plans are included along with the basic plan to ensure expedient response to specific changes in the marketing environment.

Planning varies greatly from company to company. Large sales organizations often have formal planning divisions or ad hoc committees of sales managers and supervisors from different areas who take part in the planning process. In contrast, smaller firms usually plan in an informal, unwritten way, and the plan may only be found in the minds of a few key managers. Whether formal or informal, written or unwritten, a plan can help an organization to reduce inefficient and wasteful actions and to better coordinate its efforts toward achieving desired goals.

Levels of Organization Planning

Every manager must do some planning, and the more effective planners tend to be the more effective managers. Those at the very top—the CEO, board of directors, president, and vice president—spend greater proportions of their time in planning than do middle-management people. Similarly, middle managers spend more time planning than do supervisory-level people. Top management devotes most of its planning time to long-run strategic planning for the company, while middle managers—such as regional and district sales managers—spend the majority of their planning time on shorter-run tactical plans for their organization. Exhibit 3-1 illustrates the type of planning done at different levels in the organization.

SALES MANAGERS AS PLANNERS AND ADMINISTRATORS

In their roles as planners and administrators, sales managers must (1) define goals and objectives, (2) set policies, (3) establish procedures, (4) devise strategies, (5) direct tactics, and (6) design controls.

Goals and Objectives

Effective sales department planning requires the communication of clear-cut written goals and objectives to all organization members who are expected to participate in their achievement. *Goals* are established as somewhat general, long-range destinations, while *objectives* are specific results desired within a designated time frame, usually that period covered by the annual sales plan. One sales goal for IBM, for example, has always been to be recognized as the most service-oriented sales force in its industry. In fact, sales executives at IBM think the company's best advertisement simply said: "IBM means service." Objectives are usually expressed in terms of annual sales volume targets or quotas, market share, return on assets managed (ROAM), earnings per share of common stock, inventory turnover, back orders, accounts receivable, or employee turnover. Without clearly communicated goals and objectives, sales efforts may not be synergistic and can even be conflicting.

Management by Objectives

A technique used by about 50 percent of *Fortune* 500 companies for improving sales force efficiency, increasing morale, and blending the objectives of the individual salesperson with those of the sales organization is management by objectives (MBO).[3] Under MBO, each salesperson negotiates with the sales supervisor and signs a contract that sets up common objectives and strategies for attaining them. Such planning requires give-and-take between sales managers and salespeople because these MBO contracts become the basis for the organization's operating plans. In many companies, sales representatives must prepare an annual "territorial marketing plan," outlining their strategy for obtaining new customers and increasing sales to current customers. For example, at Brown & Sharpe's Machine Tool Division, each salesperson has a written plan, which is reviewed quarterly with the sales manager.

Sales managers benefit by obtaining the salesperson's intimate knowledge of the marketplace in planning, while the salespeople receive meaningful guidance from the manager in setting personal goals. Progress toward these objectives is regularly reviewed, and any deviations are analyzed for needed corrective action to get back on target. Year-end deviations serve as input for negotiating future MBO contracts and for establishing new objectives, strategies, appraisal methods, and rewards.

Policies and Procedures

Predetermined approaches for handling routine matters or recurring situations efficiently and effectively are called *policies.* For example, there should be a policy regarding product trade-ins or credit terms when customers purchase a new product. Policies enable sales managers to avoid having to answer the same questions over and over and to focus on more crucial decision making, such as strategic sales planning.

Detailed descriptions of specific steps for carrying out an action are called *procedures.* For instance, in providing customers with a refund on a defective product, salespeople should follow a clear-cut series of steps, or procedures, to ensure that the transaction is handled expediently and fairly.

Strategies and Tactics

A *strategy* is an overall program of action, or a plan for using resources to achieve a certain goal or objective, whereas *tactics* are the day-to-day actions comprising the strategic plan. One example of a sales strategy is Honeywell's concentration of its field sales force in small cities as a means of competing against other computer manufacturers, whose resources are concentrated in large cities. Special sales presentation formats for approaching different customer categories are examples of sales tactics.

Controls

For effective control, standards of performance must be established to enable sales managers to compare actual performance to these predetermined standards. If there are unfavorable gaps between actual and planned sales results, the sales manager has two broad possibilities: (1) increase sales efforts to try to get back on course to accomplish the plan, or (2) revise the sales plan, including its objectives, strategies, and tactics, to conform to a new ''reality'' in the marketplace. Which course of action is most appropriate depends on the reasons for the gaps between planned and actual results. In analyzing the situation to determine likely causes for lagging performance, the sales manager will need to consider numerous possibilities: Were the planning assumptions in preparing the sales forecast and performance objectives realistic? Has there been a major strategic or tactical change by competitors? Has there been a significant shift in the tastes or preferences of present customers? Is product quality, price, and service satisfactory? Is advertising and other headquarters marketing support effective? Are the salespeople properly trained and motivated? Only after sorting through the myriad possibilities can the sales manager have confidence in deciding which approach to use to realign planned and actual sales performance.

SALES MANAGEMENT INFORMATION SYSTEMS

For effective sales planning, the sales manager needs information about the market. Sales planning decisions today require highly specialized and quantified information. Companies no longer have small, limited markets where the sales managers know each customer personally. Large, diversified sales organizations increasingly need better market information and more sophisticated technology to handle all the data about their diverse markets and customers.

Increasingly, companies are insisting that their sales forces take on more responsibility for gathering marketing intelligence on a continuous basis for the company management information system (MIS). At American Cyanamid, for example, salespeople are told: ''Don't just sell—get information. What do our customers need? What's the competition doing? What sort of financial package do we need to win the order?" Beyond supplying market information for the MIS, some progressive sales organizations have even set up a specialized sales management information system (SMIS) to collect, process, store, analyze, interpret, and report market and sales information to aid sales management decision making. Salespeople at Andrew Jergens, a company which makes skin care products and toiletries, often wrestle with over 600 products under 19 major brands. Before Jergens computerized its sales force, it was almost impossible to find needed information quickly on so many products. Now, with a sales management information system, sales managers can answer any sales question in ten minutes or less.[4] Frito-Lay revolutionized the food supplier industry while saving more than $20 million a year with a sales information system, as the next example explains.

SALES INFORMATION SYSTEMS AT FRITO-LAY

Several years ago, Frito-Lay, the Snack Foods Division of Pepsico, Inc., envisioned a hand-held computer system that would provide sales distribution information. Although this was long before such technology was perfected, the company soon developed the computer network for its 10,000-plus route salespeople. This market information system revolutionized the way the food-supplier industry operates. Data from the system help the Frito-Lay sales force determine what shelf space needs to be filled, where stale products are gathering dust, how to adjust delivery dates to meet customer requirements, and so on. Frito-Lay officials estimate that the system saves the company more than $20 million a year. The company is now working on a newer and even better information system that will tie PCs to its mainframe decision support system. This new system will extend sales information throughout the company, to its division managers and up to its top decision makers.[5]

At the same time, many customers are converting to centralized computer purchasing, especially for high-volume items. A manager at Magruder Color Company, a New Jersey manufacturer of printing inks and pigments, says: "When our inventories run down to the preprogrammed reorder point, the computer spits out a card and we call up our suppliers and reorder." As customers develop their own management information systems for determining reorder points, size of orders, and suppliers to be considered, it becomes even more important that sales organizations have the required information readily available from the MIS.

What Is an SMIS?

A sales management information system collects information from within the company as well as from customers, suppliers, and other outside sources for the purpose of supporting the decision making of sales managers at both headquarters and field levels. An SMIS will vary from company to company, depending on the structure, culture, and current needs of the sales organization. Specific purposes for which an SMIS can be used include sales planning and analysis by territory, customer, product, or individual salesperson; inventory control; customer service monitoring; accounts receivable review; call-report analysis; time and territory management; and market trend monitoring. An SMIS is not worthy of its name unless it provides sales managers with information that will alert them to emerging market opportunities and enable them to make better decisions. The essential tasks in handling sales data in an SMIS are:

1. *Collection and transmission of the data.* After an alert salesperson hears or observes potentially valuable data, there must be a smoothly functioning communication channel to allow fast and facile relay of the data from the field to sales headquarters.

2. *Accumulation of the data.* All incoming data should be stored in a central place for easy retrieval when needed.

3. *Categorization of the data.* The numerous data inputs must be classified or categorized in some meaningful way.

4. *Analysis of the data.* There must be statistical processing of the data to discover significant relationships.

5. *Circulation of the data analysis.* Various sales and marketing managers should be given the opportunity to study the data and its analysis and to offer their interpretations and insights.

6. *Scenario development.* Emerging patterns and trends in the data must be identified and developed into competitive market scenarios that will help predict the sales and marketing environment.

Several trends have accelerated sales management's need for a planned SMIS:

- *Shift from local to national and international selling.* As sales managers have become increasingly more removed from their markets physically, they have become highly dependent on information flows in reaching decisions.

- *Transition from price to nonprice competition.* As more sales tools are needed to obtain profitable sales, more information is needed on the effectiveness and efficient use of these tools.

- *Growing professionalism of buyers.* With the increasing centralization and growing professionalism of buyers, more detailed and comprehensive information is required to compete for orders successfully.

- *Continuing information explosion.* With the quantity of information doubling about every four or five years, only a computerized SMIS can keep up with managers' needs to gather, process, store, analyze, interpret, and report information to improve productivity and profitability.

In the past, the relationship between people in sales and those in the information systems department was frustrating. However, with the widespread adoption of SMIS in many companies, this relationship is constantly improving. Many marketing-oriented companies such as Borden and General Foods feel that the information systems–sales relationship is critical in today's competitive environment. Borden and General Foods have recently reorganized their information systems departments so that there will be an even closer working relationship between marketing and information systems.[6]

Working with the Market Research Department

For those sales organizations that do not yet have a workable SMIS in place, a valuable source of sales information is the company's market research department. Many firms, large and small, have established formal market research departments to develop information, generally on a project-by-project basis, to assist decision making in various functional areas such as sales, marketing, finance, or operations.

In essence, the market research departments of most companies perform staff functions and often operate independently of the line organizations. This puts the sales department in direct competition with other line departments to obtain market information; therefore, the sales manager needs to develop a close working relationship with the market research personnel in order to influence which areas are investigated.

From the other side, the organization must realize that, regarding the kinds of data that are essential for nearly all decisions on sales activities, the sales manager is perhaps the single most knowledgeable executive in the firm. The sales manager is closest to the customers and knows a great deal about their future buying intentions, so the top sales manager should be a full participant in the highest-level planning process. Thus, as both suppliers and receivers of market information, sales managers need to develop close ties with the market research department. By looking at the top ten areas of market research, one can readily see the importance of the interrelationship between sales and market research departments:

1. Measurement of market potential
2. Determination of market characteristics
3. Market share analysis
4. Sales analysis
5. Competitive product studies
6. New-product acceptance and potential
7. Short-range forecasting
8. Long-range forecasting
9. Study of business trends
10. Establishment of sales quotas and territories

THE PLANNING PROCESS

Planning is one sales management task that is never completed. As Exhibit 3-2 illustrates, it is a continuous process. As soon as the first plan is prepared, something has changed in the marketing environment—perhaps a competitor's actions—which calls for an adjustment in the original plan. Planning allows a

EXHIBIT 3-2

The Sales Management Planning Process

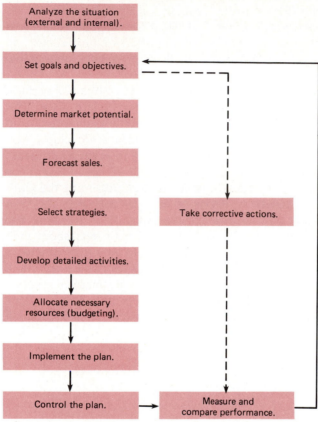

sales manager to be *proactive* rather than merely *reactive* to the future. It allows the sales manager to be instrumental in creating the sales organization's future. Any sales manager involved in the planning process needs to begin by thinking through these questions:

1. *Diagnosis*. Where are we now?
2. *Prognosis*. Where are we headed if no changes are made?
3. *Objectives*. Where should we be headed?
4. *Strategy*. What is the best way to get there?
5. *Tactics*. What specific actions need to be taken, by whom, and when?
6. *Control*. What measures must be monitored if we are to know how we are doing?

Analyzing the Situation

Exhibit 3-2 shows that the planning process begins with an analysis of where the organization is today and where it seems headed if no changes are made. Perspectives can be obtained by reviewing the organization's past performance and by judging its progress against that of the competition and its success in accomplishing objectives and goals. Some key variables to study in the situational analysis include:

- *Market characteristics.* Number and types of potential buyers, their demographic and behavioral profiles, their attitudes and buying patterns, and their servicing needs

- *Competition.* Number and types of competitors; their strengths and weaknesses; their products, prices, brands, market shares, and characteristics; and sales trends for each competitive brand

- *Sales, cost, and profit data for current and recent years.* By product, market, territory, and time period

- *Bundle of benefits offered as perceived by potential customers.* Products, brand names, prices, packages, and service

- *Promotional mix.* Personal selling, advertising, sales promotion, and publicity programs

- *Distribution systems.* Storage and transportation facilities, channels of distribution, and intensity of distribution

Any sales organization ought to utilize the vast amount of both in-house and external information sources available when analyzing its current situation. Usually the best internal sources of information are the product or brand managers and the market research, public affairs, advertising, planning, or marketing services department. The variety and extent of information that can be obtained will vary greatly from company to company, but often it will include some or all of the following: unit and dollar sales, competitive market share analyses, upcoming advertising campaigns and new products, costs for various sales functions, profit margins by product, competitive product studies, customer complaints, proposed federal and state government legislation, and economic forecasts. Most company marketing or commercial research departments have or can obtain current data on customer brand awareness, advertising effectiveness, new-product acceptance, customer satisfaction, and sales organization morale. Additional information on existing and potential competitors, changing elements of the marketing environment, and concerns of stakeholders (anyone with a vested interest in the company) can be acquired through a variety of external sources: trade associations; universities; government, business, and academic publications; and commercial research agencies.

Sales managers and others involved in the planning process at any level need to monitor internal and external events that may make an impact directly or indirectly on their organization. It is particularly important that the organization's major strengths and weaknesses be matched against the opportunities and threats facing it. By building on strengths and shoring up weaknesses, the organization can be in a good position to counter market challenges and exploit opportunities. For a company such as Apple Computer, analysis of the relative strengths and weaknesses of an organization might take the following form:

Strengths

- Our personal computers have the best reputation in the industry for ease of use.
- Our products are among the most innovative in the industry.
- We have strong advertising support for our brands.
- We are particularly strong in the high school and college markets.

Weaknesses

- Our prices are relatively high compared with those of competitive brands.
- Less software is available for our brands than for IBM-compatible machines.
- Our field sales force is small and inexperienced.
- Our products are not widely used in business organizations.

Understanding the relative strengths and weaknesses of an organization is essential for its continued survival and growth, but gaining this understanding requires management that is in close touch with trends in the marketplace. As the next example shows, the once powerful steel companies are in danger of becoming the dinosaurs of this era because their leaders failed to recognize and respond to a changed environment.

U.S. STEEL INDUSTRY: DINOSAUR OF OUR TIMES?

The once powerful steel industry in America seems headed for extinction like the huge dinosaurs of an early era because the leaders of the steel companies failed to recognize their weaknesses in a rapidly changing marketing environment. Steel's limitations, such as its heaviness, have always been known, but when times were good, the major steel companies saw no need to invest in R&D to develop the alloys that would be as strong as steel but much lighter. Unfortunately for the steel industry, the chemical industry created plastics that took huge market shares away from the producers that supplied steel, zinc, aluminum, brass, and copper for automobiles and a great number of other products.

Simultaneously with this threat from the chemical industry, Japanese steel producers were modernizing their plants with the latest technology in preparation for aggressively marketing their products in America. Again, the steel executives were caught flat-footed and unprepared to fight off these foreign invaders even in the domestic market. In stopgap response to their declining sales, the steel companies laid off thousands of employees, closed plants, made acquisitions in unrelated fields, and lobbied for import restrictions on foreign steel.

The steel industry's complacency and disregard of customer needs kept the industry from striving to improve its products. Perhaps sheer size makes some companies feel invincible. Some tough thinking about the strengths and weaknesses of steel from the standpoint of customers might have enabled steel executives to recognize their vulnerability and spurred them to take the actions that their competitors eventually took. Ignominiously, U.S. Steel changed its name to USX as several steel companies struggled to avoid bankruptcy.

Setting Goals and Objectives

Organizations usually have multiple goals and objectives. In many cases, especially in smaller companies, goals are often too vague or inadequately defined, for example: "We want to become one of the best in the industry." Without a clear understanding of what "one of the best" means, the goal is not very meaningful. All units and personnel within an organization should understand overall goals and objectives as well as individual goals and objectives if decision making is to be consistent and complementary in striving for these ends. Goals and objectives must be spelled out explicitly and in order of priority. They also must be consistent and not in conflict with each other, particularly as they pertain to different divisions or departments of a company. Some goals and objectives for a national sales manager employed by a large office-supply manufacturer might include:

Goals

- Implement an SMIS over the next five years.

- Expand our market area over the next ten years to include all the nation's primary metropolitan areas.

- Reduce sales force turnover to below the industry average by the end of the decade.

Objectives

- Increase sales by 15 percent next year.

- Reduce customer complaints by 10 percent next year.

- Reduce sales force turnover by 5 percent next year.

- Increase the number of new-customer accounts by 20 percent next year.

Individual salesperson goals and objectives will be discussed in depth in Chapter 10.

Determining Market Potentials

After overall corporate goals and objectives have been agreed upon, the next step in the planning process is to assess *market potential* (the maximum possible sales for an entire industry) and *sales potential* (the maximum possible sales for a company). Both market and sales potentials are usually estimated for a specified period of time under the most favorable assumptions about the marketing environment and marketing expenditures. Some sales managers, however, prefer to develop three estimates—optimistic, expected, and pessimistic assumptions—to determine market potential and sales potential under different possible scenarios.

Since market potential always assumes a competitive pricing structure, it will always be less than *market capacity*, which is all the units that the market would absorb if the product or service were free. Potentials developed for an organization are generally subcategorized for planning purposes. For example, product potentials are defined in geographic or customer terms such as sales territories. Thus, sales managers who know where sales potential is highest can better allocate the sales force and set sales quotas for individual salespeople. Estimates of customer potentials also help in scheduling sales call frequencies and in carrying out direct-mail promotions in support of the sales force.

Determination of market potential starts with the study of present customers and their buying characteristics (place of purchase, method of payment, product size, and usage rate). Sales managers can then estimate the increased usage rates that might occur if the current product is modified for current customers or repositioned for potential new customers. Finally, sales managers can estimate the market potential for new products being developed by the company's R&D department. Analysis of market potential leads to the development of a more realistic sales forecast for the next quarter or year. Development of market potentials is discussed more fully in Chapter 4.

Forecasting Sales

A *sales forecast* predicts future sales for a prescribed period as an integral part of a marketing plan, which is based on a set of assumptions about the marketing environment. Since an accurate sales forecast is vital to an organization, most firms are constantly striving for more reliable sales forecasts and sales forecasting techniques. Sales forecasting techniques can be quite complex, utilizing mathematical models and high-speed computers. Therefore, some large firms have established separate departments specializing in sales forecasting.

Unfortunately, in most cases, firms devote too little attention to developing an accurate forecasting approach. And when they do, the sales department often plays only a minor role in the forecast, occasionally giving advice about changes in the competitive environment.

Even with the most costly and sophisticated forecasting techniques available, firms still find it difficult to accurately predict the future. The most accurate forecasts for the mid-1980s were altered by the dramatic decline in oil prices and the falling interest rates. Banks and mortgage companies were unprepared for the stampede of home owners trying to refinance their double-digit home mortgages for single-digit mortgages. In the oil states of Texas, Oklahoma, and Louisiana, numerous oil companies and ancillary businesses were forced into chapter eleven bankruptcy proceedings as world surpluses caused oil and natural-gas prices to fall precipitously.

A lesson to learn from these examples is that planning and forecasting must allow for more flexibility in response to abrupt changes in the marketing environment. Firms need to develop alternative sales and budget figures based on different assumptions so that their forecasts and related decisions can be quickly altered if some unexpected event should occur. Finally, a monitoring system should be established that will continually review forecasts to provide early warning when actual sales figures vary from targeted figures.

Selecting Strategies

After organization objectives have been determined and the sales forecasts developed, the next step is to determine the best way to achieve these targets. *Strategic planning* is the process of setting the organization's overall objectives, allocating total resources, and outlining broad courses of action. Strategic decisions give the organization a total plan of action to serve customers better, to take advantage of competitors' weaknesses, and to capitalize on the firm's strengths.[7]

Using military strategy as an analogy (which seems appropriate for today's fierce world competition for markets), strategic planning is the general's art, while tactical planning is the soldier's art. To illustrate: In the movie *Patton,* General Patton is disappointed to learn that General Rommel had been called back to Germany prior to a major battle—Patton feels that he has not been tested against Germany's best general. But Patton's quick-thinking aide points out that generals plan the battle strategies and that Patton's strategy had beaten Rommel's. A reassured Patton smiles, and the aide's promotion chances soar.

Growth strategies.   Exhibit 3-3 depicts four types of growth strategies for sales management. *Market penetration* tries to increase sales of current products in current markets by more intensive market efforts. As an example, Sears is marketing its total "financial network" of services, including insurance from Allstate, investments with Dean Witter, real estate from Coldwell Banker, and banking with Sears Savings Bank. Sears wants to dramatically increase its market penetration by becoming recognized as a full-service center that can handle all its customers' financial transactions.

Market development seeks to open up new markets for current products. To illustrate, the Cross Pen Company continues to enjoy excellent earnings growth because it has concentrated on developing an upscale market beyond the traditional retail consumer market. Cross's market development has focused on

---

EXHIBIT 3-3

Growth Strategies for Sales Management

	Current products	New products
Current markets	Market penetration	Product development
New markets	Market development	Diversification

Source: H. I. Ansoff, *Corporate Strategy,* McGraw-Hill, New York, 1965, p. 109.

corporations, which use high-quality pens as special gifts for customers and as awards for employees.

Product development creates new or improved products for current markets. This can be accomplished in diverse ways by adding new sizes, models with new features, or different-quality versions or by developing creative new alternatives to satisfying the same basic needs. For example, chemicals are gradually being replaced in farming by biogenetics and hydroponics. Biogenetics is breeding strains of plants that are resistant to pests and diseases, thus eliminating the need for pesticides or herbicides. Hydroponics is the science of growing plants indoors in a controlled environment that requires no herbicides, pesticides, or fertilizers.

Above the sales management level, there are other growth strategies: (1) to diversify by purchasing new businesses or product lines and (2) to obtain ownership or control over different levels of the channel of distribution. For example, Firestone Tire & Rubber Company has integrated ''forward'' through ownership of its retail outlets, and Holiday Inn has integrated ''backward'' into manufacturing by acquiring carpet mills and furniture plants.

Smaller or less aggressive large companies sometimes simply follow the leader in their industry, often not knowing where they are going or what dangers await them. They have confidence in the industry leaders and are willing to place their future in the hands of a more powerful, seemingly sophisticated company. Smaller steel companies may have blindly used this approach in following U.S. Steel (now USX). On the other hand, there are companies that are willing to take risks, betting that they can significantly improve their market position. These companies boldly seek out innovative ways of satisfying customers. Chrysler, under Lee Iacocca, is such a company. It has segmented its market and product line, begun a joint venture with Mitsubishi to build Omni and Horizon models, brought back the convertible, and popularized the minivan, and it is producing more cars with half its former plants and one-third fewer people.

Normally, there should be one overriding growth strategy but many tactics to reach sales goals. For example, Apple's primary strategy—especially with its user-friendly Macintosh PC—is to win a major share of the market among relatively unsophisticated computer users. Apple initially focused on winning a major share of the educational market in high schools, colleges, and universities. The reasoning was that students who gain their early experience with the Macintosh personal computer will remain brand-loyal as they move out of school and into the business world. In carrying out this strategy, Apple Computer sold its PCs through authorized Apple dealers and by direct sales to educational institutions. But in mid-1986 President John Sculley decided to change tactics in carrying out the company's long-run strategy. Twenty-three percent of Apple dealers were dropped—over 600 in all (including 103 Sears Business Centers)—leaving Apple with 2,000 remaining dealers nationwide. Apple decided to reduce its dealer base in response to complaints about oversaturation and rampant discounting. Now Apple is substantially increasing its support for its remaining dealers by initiating cooperative advertising plans and a number of dealer development efforts, such as direct mail, telemarketing, and seminars.

Staying with its strategy to sell to the nonexpert computer user, Apple has hired several hundred direct salespeople to sell to middle managers who want uncomplicated ready access to information and the ability to easily generate reports, prepare presentations, manage projects, and send out memos.[8]

The business portfolio approach.   Two major concepts relating to growth are the strategic business unit and the business portfolio matrix. *Strategic business units* (SBUs) are logical divisions of major businesses within multiproduct companies. SBUs are evaluated on the basis of their profit and growth potential just as if they were stand-alone companies. Using the SBU approach, General Electric sold its marginally profitable line of small household appliances to Black & Decker in 1984.

SBUs have several characteristics: (1) distinct mission, (2) separate management, (3) unique customer segments, (4) their own competitors, and (5) planning that is largely independent of other units in the company. Over 20 percent of America's largest manufacturing corporations are using the SBU concept. For example, Campbell Soup Company recently set up eight SBUs: Soups, Beverages, Pet Foods, Frozen Foods, Fresh Produce, Main Meals, Grocery, and Food Service.

In evaluating the strategic business units of a company, the most popular approach is the *business portfolio matrix.* This approach is a simple way to segment the company's activities into groups of well-defined businesses for which distinct strategies should be developed. Three popular business portfolio matrixes are:

- The growth-share matrix developed by the Boston Consulting Group (BCG)
- The industry attractiveness–business strength matrix developed jointly by General Electric and McKinsey and Company
- The life-cycle approach developed by Arthur D. Little, Inc.

Of these three, the most widely used is BCG's growth-share matrix, which plots market share on the horizontal axis and market-growth potential on the vertical axis. It allows all a company's various businesses to be plotted in one of four quadrants labeled "cash cows," "stars," "dogs," or "problem children," as Exhibit 3-4 shows.

Cash cows are high-market-share and low-market-growth products that should be milked for their continuing cash flow. Continuing with the Black & Decker example, tools for professional builders were cash cows throughout most of the company's history, and the large profits they generated allowed Black & Decker to acquire General Electric Corporation's small-appliance business for $300 million. *Stars* are high-market-share and high-market-growth products that are worthy of additional investment. *Dogs* are low-market-share and low-market-growth products that should probably be abandoned as quickly as possible. *Problem children* are low-market-share and high-market-growth products that

EXHIBIT 3-4

The BCG Growth-Share Matrix

Relative market share

	High	Low
High	Stars	Problem children
Low	Cash cows	Dogs

Growth rate

require more cash investment than they are able to generate. Unless problem children can be converted to stars, these products should probably be dropped.

Successful SBUs undergo a number of changes as they go through their life cycles. Successful businesses or products usually begin as problem children and then develop into stars. Eventually, they turn into cash cows, and they become dogs at the end of their life cycle. Sales managers should be cautious about labeling products and businesses too quickly and ignoring the possibility of converting dogs, problem children, or even cash cows into stars. Arm & Hammer baking soda is one example of a cash cow that became a star when its use-versatility potential was recognized and promoted. Arm & Hammer's sales rose dramatically when its baking soda was also promoted as a toothpowder and general deodorizer for the refrigerator, freezer, carpet, and cat-litter box.

Stakeholders.   Marketing planning and strategy must be applied to an organization's relationship with all its stakeholder publics, not just its customers.

Government—whether federal, state, or local—can change its structure, pass laws, issue regulations, and become either a customer or a competitor of the organization. Government actions have ranged from the Product Safety Commission's demanding numerous product recalls to the Food and Drug Administration's banning the sale of products such as cyclamates and saccharin as possible cancer-causing agents to the Department of Agriculture's providing subsidies to tobacco growers at the same time as the Department of Health and Human Services campaigns against cigarette smoking. *Special interest groups* battle either for or against handgun control, nuclear power plants, or tax reform, while the *general public* protests wasteful government spending. *Company employees* demand higher wages and better working conditions. *Stockholders* vote against extravagant executive benefits or commercial dealings with governments that violate human rights. The *financial community* provides either easy or tight credit terms. *Suppliers* make decisions on allocation of scarce commodities. Investigative reporters for the *independent print and broadcast media* expose legal, moral, and ethical violations by business—whether they be misleading advertising claims, faulty product designs, or insider stock trading. Each of these stakeholders influences the sales force operations for better or worse; thus, each must be considered in planning overall marketing strategy and tactics.

Assumptions behind strategies.   When planning strategic decisions, a company must carefully analyze and document any assumptions. Any impulsive or hurried assumptions can cause turmoil for a company's strategic plans. For example, with growing environmental concerns about automobile exhaust, Amoco (Standard Oil of Indiana) assumed that a lead-free gasoline would be a surefire winner, but it was not that easy. The example that follows shows the cost of a faulty assumption.

AMOCO LEAD-FREE GASOLINE

To become a leader in the coming market for a gasoline that would not expel noxious automobile exhaust into the air, Amoco made huge investments to change its refining process and make a lead-free gasoline. Unexpectedly, the largest cost in refining and distributing the new gas turned out to be the thousands of new storage tanks needed at individual gas stations and the fleet of new trucks needed to carry the lead-free gas. In total, Amoco invested over $90 million.

After this costly investment, Amoco naturally thought it could charge a small premium of 2 cents per gallon for the gas. But consumers didn't see the lead-free gasoline as offering any extra value for their money, so sales were poor. Undaunted, Amoco switched its marketing emphasis to a major advertising campaign to educate consumers about this great new product. Market research showed that country-and-western singer Johnny Cash would be the ideal spokesman, so the national advertising campaign was enthusiastically carried out. But still the gas didn't sell. Following more analysis, it was discovered that less than 10 million out of about 100 million cars on the road could use lead-free gas without significantly reducing engine performance.

Fortunately for Amoco, the federal government finally came to the rescue. The Environmental Protection Agency was created to promote mandatory emission-control standards and lead-free gasoline engines for all new automobiles. Gas tanks on the new cars were even made with narrow openings so that only the special nozzles of the lead-free pumps would fit. Thus, as older cars were phased out, lead-free gas soon dominated the market. But if it had not been for government regulations, Amoco might have grievously regretted its assumption that because of environmental concerns, there was a huge consumer market for lead-free gasoline.

Developing Detailed Activities

After the overall strategy has been decided, the planning process must incorporate more detailed activities, or tactics. Tactics focus on the implementation of the strategic plan. Tactical action plans are really the functional subplans that underlie and accomplish the overall strategic plan. Tactical action plans identify what needs to be done, who is responsible, what resources are needed, and what benefits are expected. Exhibit 3-5 shows a sample action plan.

Sales managers must work with the salespeople to ensure that individual tactical plans are compatible with the overall strategy of the sales department and company, but salespeople often need to make on-the-spot tactical decisions in response to unexpected events that occur during the execution of strategy. A salesperson must decide tactics, for example, if a customer is going to place an order with a competitor that has just offered a discount. Can and should the

---

EXHIBIT 3-5

Tactical Action Plan

Velop Manufacturing Company Eastern Region

Goal: To call on 200 new accounts during the first quarter of fiscal year 1992.

Strategy and tactics:

- Develop list of potential new accounts.
- Contract with telemarketing firm to prescreen list to determine likely prospects.
- Assign prescreened prospects to sales force by territory.
- Hold a training workshop to make sure all salespeople know what background material to develop on prospects and where to obtain it.
- Develop timetables and quotas for each salesperson.

Responsibility: Sales manager, Eastern Region

Start date: October 1, 1991

Completion date: December 31, 1991

Resources needed: $18,000 to develop list and contract with telemarketing firm

Benefits:

- Will ensure that new accounts are called on.
- Will facilitate achieving projected 5 percent increase in sales for FY 1992.

---

salesperson match it? Unfortunately, some companies do not allow salespeople any price flexibility, so the battle for that order may be lost.

Special tactics are frequently devised for accomplishing territorial quotas or selling goals. Taking a cue from consumer marketers, for example, Pier-Angeli Company (an industrial distributor of high-quality plumbing and maintenance specialties) prepared an illustrated sales catalog so that customers could see exactly what part they were ordering. Pier-Angeli was the first industrial distributor in its field to offer this catalog service, and customers have responded favorably, giving Pier-Angeli at least a short-run tactical sales advantage over the competition.

Allocating Necessary Resources

Once detailed subplans or tactics are developed, resources (money, people, materials, equipment, time) must be allocated to carry out the plans. The *budget* is the forecast of expenditures required to "buy" the projected revenues. For meaningful sales management, the sales forecast has to be supported by the sales budget. If resources are inadequate, the entire plan—including the sales forecast—must be scaled down. Realistically, budgets are the formal expression of managerial support. Overall, the budget's purpose is to coordinate and control company resources during the period covered by the sales forecast.

Implementing the Plan

Goals, objectives, strategies, and tactics need to be well communicated throughout the organization. Upper-level management wants to know whether department plans tie in smoothly with overall corporate objectives. Sales managers often use management by objectives to involve subordinates in the planning and budgeting process, since subordinates are more apt to accept and carry out plans if they contribute to their preparation. One simple method for ensuring timely implementation of a plan is to show the tasks to be accomplished in a time-sequence format, such as the table in Exhibit 3-6. Columns can represent the time segments (fifty-two weeks or twelve months for the planning period) and rows can list the specific tasks to be done and the responsible person. With more complex projects, a program evaluation and review technique (PERT) network is commonly used for planning and scheduling. PERT diagrams specify the plan's or project's *critical path*, that is, the sequence of tasks that requires the longest time to complete, the time needed to complete each series of activities or events, and the responsible individuals. This scheduling technique is often

EXHIBIT 3-6

Sales Marketing Plan for Fiscal Year 1992

Key Tasks and Responsibility	Sep	Oct	Nov	Dec	Jan	Feb	Mar	Apr	May	Jun	Jul	Aug
Hire three sales reps. (Bill Peters)		[XXXXX]										
Conduct training program. (Melvin Watson)			[XXXXXX]									
Hold national sales meeting. (Greg Roskowski)				[XXXXXXXXXX]								
Evaluate midyear performance. (Julius Smithson)							[XXX]					
Conduct sales contest. (Betty Clark)					[XXXXXXXXXXXXXX]							
Plan telemarketing campaign. (Ralph Compton)								[XXXXX]				
Prepare draft of plans for FY 1993. (Brent Sherman)										[XXXXX]		
Complete sales contest. (Betty Clark)											[XX]	
Plan Hawaii trip for sales contest winners. (Betty Clark)											[XX]	
Submit final FY 1993 plans. (Brent Sherman)												[XX]
Award FY sales bonuses. (Gilbert Waters)												[XX]
Select sales rep of the year. (Carlos Perez)												[XX]
Arrange annual sales banquet. (Elizabeth McGraw)												[X]

implemented by using computers for increased control and dissemination of information.

Regardless of the approach, it is essential that the sales manager ensure that the schedule is closely monitored. Some companies assign full-time project co-ordinators to follow up with those responsible for completion of each task. Since the planning process is based on many assumptions about the external environment, changes or modifications may be necessary in the implementation stage. Sales managers who remain alert to the unexpected will be able to adjust their plans and their implementation in a timely fashion.

Controlling the Plan

A sound planning process demands a built-in monitoring device that will aid management in controlling the plan's operation. This control device should consist of a series of regular measurements that will check progress toward specific objectives and signal deviations in time to take corrective actions and get back on track. Whenever possible, these measurements should be quantitative.

Performance standards and measures.   In Exhibit 3-7, we show three types of performance standards and relate them to seven performance measures. For example, performance can be compared with industry averages. (Of course, when the total industry is performing poorly, it is small consolation to be doing as well as the average company.) Another type of standard is past performance, which can indicate trends, either favorable or adverse. Probably the most meaningful type of standards is managerial expectations because they are based on the organization's objectives, forecasts, and budgetary support. Even if past performance and industry norms are exceeded, failure to meet managerial expectations should be viewed as a disappointing result. All seven of the performance

---

EXHIBIT 3-7

Performance Standards and Performance Measures for Sales Managers

Performance Measures	Industry Averages	Past Performance	Managerial Expectations
Sales volume	Trade publications Annual reports	Sales records	Sales forecast
New accounts	Trade publications	Sales records	MBO contract
Selling costs	Trade publications	Sales records	Budgeted costs
Sales force turnover	Trade publications	Personnel records	MBO contract
Market share	Trade publications	Marketing dept.	Forecast
Profit margins	Trade publications Annual reports	Accounting dept.	Pro forma statement
Customer service	Trade publications Customer surveys	Complaint record Products returned Number of service calls	MBO contract

measures mentioned are not likely to be used in a specific situation. But multiple measures are recommended to adequately monitor and control progress toward achieving goals and objectives.

Each of the three types of standards above reflects the organization's internal measures. However, there are two external measures that may be even more important to the organization's long-run survival: *customer satisfaction* and *societal satisfaction*. Indicators of customer satisfaction or dissatisfaction include repurchase rates, purchase frequencies and quantities, brand and store loyalty, customer perceptions of product quality and organization image, and number of customer complaints. Satisfaction of society is more difficult to measure or even set standards for, since societal expectations for all levels of performance seem to rise continuously. Nevertheless, an organization can track areas that are most likely to affect society, such as product safety and quality standards, equal employment and promotion opportunities for employees, nondiscriminatory treatment of customers and suppliers, promotional truthfulness and disclosure, energy conservation, and protection of the environment. Responsiveness to government initiatives and public interest groups can help organizations in satisfying societal expectations.

Corrective actions.   By establishing clear-cut, meaningful standards, an organization can regularly compare the gap between actual performance and the predetermined standards to ensure timely corrective action. Unless performance is continuously monitored by concerned, decision-oriented management, the entire planning process is a dubious exercise and probably a waste of resources.

CAUSES OF UNSUCCESSFUL PLANNING

Although the planning process inevitably results in creating something called a plan, or a systematic program of action, too many plans are perfunctorily put together, filed away, and not looked at again until next year's plan is due. This does not represent much real planning and is a big waste of time and resources. Merely "going through the planning motions" is probably little better than having no plan at all.

Many organizations, however, do devote much time and effort to their planning process. Moreover, they may use sophisticated computer simulations and quantitative analyses to assist in the process. But despite the serious commitment and technically sophisticated effort put into the planning activity, unsuccessful plans often result. These failures are not restricted to small or novice companies. Large, multinational corporations have had drastic planning failures, too. Consider the failure of technologically innovative Texas Instruments in the personal computer market, for example. TI concentrated on developing the home computer market by offering simple, low-priced computers specifically designed for novices—a market that did not exist in sufficient numbers, so TI dropped out of PC competition after losses of several hundred million dollars.

The most universal cause of unsuccessful planning results from the number of assumptions inherent in each stage of the planning process. Management is constantly making assumptions regarding the future marketing environment. To show the impact of erroneous assumptions, consider the experience of Wilkinson Sword.

THE DULLING AND SHARPENING OF WILKINSON SWORD

Wilkinson Sword's share of the U.S. razor blade market fell to less than 1 percent by early 1985 after having been as high as 8 percent a decade earlier. During its checkered sales history, Wilkinson Sword sold its razors, blades, knives, and scissors through manufacturers' agents or through the sales forces of other companies. Colgate-Palmolive's sales force first carried the line but dropped it in the early 1970s. Then Wilkinson turned to manufacturers' agents for drugstores and brokers for food stores, but its market share kept falling. In 1981, Scripto took on the sales task, but in 1984, Tokai (a Japanese cigarette-lighter manufacturer) acquired Scripto. Assuming that Wilkinson could maintain its unexciting share of the market, Tokai promptly withdrew all advertising and sales support. Without a sales force or promotion of any kind, however, the bottom fell out of Wilkinson sales until survival became the main concern. Finally, Norman Proulx, vice president and general manager at Scripto, was offered the opportunity to take over Wilkinson. He agreed only on the condition that the company have its own direct sales force. With the new sales force, a two-year $23 million advertising campaign, and a strong new product (the Retractor disposable razor), Wilkinson Sword sales rose to $12 million and its market share to 3.5 percent. Wilkinson's new goal is to control 10 percent of the wet-shave market within two years.[9]

APPROACHES TO PLANNING

Dialectic Planning

One approach that parallels the idea of revising assumptions is called *dialectic planning*. Dialectic planning considers the validity or probability of the underlying assumptions in a forecast. This approach calls for a new set of assumptions that sometimes are directly opposite to the first. All previous planning decisions are reevaluated in terms of the new assumptions. Every plan is rigorously challenged at every step and point in time, with consideration given to the second set of assumptions, or counterplan. Forcing management to come up with a totally different second plan enables managers to view the complete planning process from two different and contrasting perspectives and reduces the chance of managerial nearsightedness. However, with two alternatives, management uncertainty may increase, resulting in a delay in decision making or a compromise that can produce undesirable results from either course of action.

Contingency Planning

Another tool used by many organizations to help reduce the risk of a major problem in the future is *contingency planning*. Basically, a contingency plan is a backup to the one adopted and will be executed only if events occur that are beyond the control of the major plan. For example, the electrical systems in many hospitals have redundancy systems, or backup systems, in case the primary system fails. Contingency planning is expensive and time-consuming, but its value has been proved time and again. It should increasingly become a part of an organization's planning process to prepare for an emergency or unlikely turn of events.

Sales Audits

Sales managers can borrow the concepts of the marketing audit and adapt them to their own situations. A *sales audit* might be defined as a systematic and objective evaluation of a sales organization and its selling environment, goals, objectives, policies, strategies, tactics, procedures, and related activities. The purpose of a sales audit is to identify selling opportunities and challenges in order to develop, change, or substantiate a plan to improve overall sales performance. The sales audit goes beyond the normal control system. While the control process seeks to determine whether the organization is doing "things right," an audit also tries to determine whether it is doing the "right things."

A sales audit can be an invaluable tool for the sales manager—not only to evaluate the results of an implemented plan but to provide a complete "health examination" on which to construct more realistic future plans. Exhibit 3-8 shows a listing of the types of questions asked in a sales audit.

SALES BUDGETS

In general, sales managers must decide either what level of sales can be obtained with a given budget or what level of expenditures will be required to reach forecasted sales. A *sales budget* is a financial sales plan outlining how resources and selling efforts should be allocated to achieve the sales forecast. Sales forecasts and sales budgets are interrelated and interdependent planning tools that demand close coordination with other marketing activities. If the sales budget is inadequate, the sales forecast will not be met. Or if the sales forecast is increased, the sales budget must be increased too. As described in Exhibit 3-9, the sales budget is a critical tool for the success of the entire company.

Purposes of the Sales Budget

Sales budgets serve three primary purposes: planning, coordinating, and controlling selling activities.

Planning. To achieve sales department goals and objectives, sales managers must outline essential sales tasks and estimate their costs. Thus, budgeting is a type of *profit planning* in that it is an operational plan expressed in financial terms and designed to provide a guide for action toward achieving the organi-

EXHIBIT 3-8

Sales Environment Audit

Macroenvironment

1. *Demography.* What developments or trends pose opportunities or threats for the sales organization?

2. *Economic.* What developments in income, prices, savings, and interest rates may affect sales activities?

3. *Natural resources.* What is the outlook for the cost and availability of natural resources and energy that may affect sales?

4. *Technology.* What major changes are occurring in production or process technology that may affect sales?

5. *Politics.* What proposed federal, state, and local legislation might affect sales strategy and tactics?

6. *Culture.* What changes in customer and organization lifestyles and values may affect sales operations?

Task Environment

1. *Markets.* What is happening to market segments, size, growth, geographical distribution, and profits?

2. *Customers.* How are different customer segments changing?

3. *Competitors.* Who are the major competitors, their objectives and strategies, their strengths and weaknesses, their sizes, and market shares?

4. *Distribution.* What are the efficiency levels and growth potentials of the different channels for getting products to customers?

5. *Suppliers.* What is the outlook for the availability of vital resources?

6. *Facilitators.* What is the cost and availability outlook for transportation, warehousing, and financial services?

7. *Publics.* What publics pose particular opportunities or problems for the company?

Sales Strategy Audit

1. *Sales mission.* Is the sales mission clearly stated and communicated to the sales force?

2. *Sales goals and objectives.* Are the sales goals and objectives realistic?

3. *Sales strategy.* Is the core sales strategy for achieving the goals and objectives sound?

Sales Organization Audit

1. *Formal structure.* Are the sales activities optimally structured along functional, product, customer, and territorial lines?

2. *Functional efficiency.* Are there good working relationships between sales and marketing?

3. *Interface efficiency.* Are there any problems between sales and manufacturing, R&D, purchasing, or financial management?

Sales Systems Audit

1. *Sales information system.* Is the sales intelligence system producing accurate, timely, and sufficient information?

2. *Sales planning system.* Is sales planning, sales forecasting, and market potential measurement effectively accomplished?

3. *Sales control system.* Does sales management periodically analyze the profitability of products, markets, territories, and salespeople?

4. *New product development system.* Is the sales organization well organized to generate new product ideas?

Sales Productivity Audit

1. *Profitability analysis.* Are there any market segments that the sales force should enter, expand, contract, or withdraw from?

2. *Cost-effectiveness analysis.* Do any marketing activities seem to have excessive costs? Can cost-reducing actions be taken?

Sales Function Audits

1. *Products.* Are product-line objectives reasonable? Are there products that should be phased out, modified, or added?

2. *Price.* Are pricing objectives, policies, strategies, and procedures appropriate for the markets served? Do customers see the company's prices as being in line with the value of its offerings?

3. *Distribution.* Should the mix of distributors, manufacturing agents, and direct selling be changed?

4. *Advertising, sales promotion, and publicity.* Is the promotional mix effectively supporting personal selling?

5. *Sales force.* How is the sales force rated versus competitors' sales forces? Are the procedures adequate for evaluating the performance of salespeople and the overall sales force?

Source: Adapted from Philip Kotler, *Principles of Marketing*, 3d ed., Prentice-Hall, Englewood Cliffs, N.J., 1986, pp. 635–637.

zation's objectives. Though one year is the typical budgeting period, the short-range budget may cover periods of six or even three months. For smooth transition from one period to another, some sales budgets overlap. For example, a twelve-month budget might allow for a three-month overlap period at the beginning and at the end of the year so that the actual budget plan covers eighteen months. Some sales organizations operate on a continuous budget by projecting a month or a quarter ahead as each month or quarter is ended. This procedure forces sales managers to continuously revise and update the budget in response to external and internal opportunities and problems.

EXHIBIT 3-9

The Sales Budget

I am a piece of paper, maybe two or more . . .
I am the promise of the future.

I make people dream dreams and wrestle with ideas . . .
I am the catalyst that converts ideas to decisions.

I am increasing in value every year . . .
I am a gauntlet thrown down at the feet of competition.

I create jobs . . .
I maintain jobs.

I am the difference between hard planning and playing it cozy . . .
I declare the right to be met and, if necessary, exceeded.

I am the means by which to further cooperation . . .
I am one way to earn a promotion.

I am a silent enforcer that demands quality action . . .
I am a benchmark that quantifies performance.

I issue a challenge that professional men acknowledge . . .
I am accused, cursed, agonized over—but also indispensable.

I am often cast in concrete, but I really hate the "clay feet" that come with such rigidity . . .
I am more agreeable to practical flexibility.

I am the basis on which everything in your company depends . . .
I am not the last word in everything—just the first.

I have to be contended with in the end in any case . . .
I am the sales budget.

Source: Robert R. Berg, "The Sales Budget," Sales & Marketing Management, Mar. 14, 1977, p. 49.

Coordinating. To obtain the synergistic results of a coordinated marketing mix, sales budgets need to be closely integrated with the budgets for other marketing functions. Since personal selling is only one element in the promotional mix, the promotional budget must be allocated according to the tasks assigned to each element. The sales budget should reflect a well-thought-out allocation of resources and efforts designed to meet the sales department's goals and objectives. Unless there is a complementary blend of tools in the promotional mix, budgeted funds will not be efficiently employed.

Controlling. Sales budgets also provide financial standards for evaluating actual results versus budgeted figures. Any differences are *budget variances.* Favorable variances indicate areas in which the sales manager might reduce future budgets, while unfavorable variances reveal unanticipated costs requiring analysis and corrective action. A simple illustration of budget variances is provided in Exhibit 3-10. This budget was prepared on a personal computer using a Lotus format,

EXHIBIT 3-10

Budget Variances

| | Budget | Actual | Variances | |
			Favorable	Unfavorable
Sales	$715,000	$733,000	$18,000	
Expenses				
Direct selling	384,000	375,900	8,100	
Sales promotion	107,250	117,328		$10,078
Advertising	87,000	93,281		6,281
Administrative	44,500	43,617	883	
Total expenses	$622,750	$630,126		7,376
Profits (before tax)	$ 92,250	$102,874	10,624	

but many other PC software budgeting packages are available. As the exhibit illustrates, unfavorable variances are easily identified. It is the sales manager's responsibility to determine why sales promotion and advertising expenses exceeded their budget allocations. Keeping expenses below a preset budget may not be the major objective, because expenses may have unfavorable variances when actual sales surpass the sales forecast (as in this case, where sales were $18,000 more than budgeted or forecast). The use of a budget-variances approach enables the sales manager to spot potential problems more quickly or to plan better for unexpected developments such as higher-than-expected sales.

Some sales organizations are turning to a profit-center approach, whereby the sales manager is responsible for both generating sales and controlling costs. But in using the profit-center approach, there is a tendency for sales managers to overstress short-run profits. For example, some sales managers may cut back on customer service or new-account development in the desire for short-run profits, realizing that this neglect may result in lowered profits over the long run but somehow believing that they will find a way to deal with the problem later. By setting goals other than merely financial ends, higher-ranking marketing managers or regional sales managers can guard against the tendency of subordinate sales managers to seek short-run profits at the expense of long-run profits.

Flexible Sales Budgets

To overcome the rigidity of the traditional sales budget, which restricts sales managers to analysis of financial performance after the fact, flexible budgets can be developed. Flexible budgets make use of standard costs (based on past records or managerial judgment) for different revenue forecasts. Flexible budgeting permits the manager to continuously monitor financial performance in terms of standard-cost ratios. For example, the standard cost for promotional materials (brochures, displays, coupons, premiums, and such) might be 15 cents for every dollar of sales, or a ratio of 0.15. After six months $63,000 has been spent on promotional materials while $360,000 worth of revenue has been earned, and the sales manager notes that the ratio has risen to 0.175. Thus, expenditures on promotional materials probably need to be cut back a little. In the past, the use of flexible budgets was limited to larger firms with good computer support. Today, with the widespread availability of low-cost PC hardware and software, even very small businesses can use flexible budgeting.

Top management must make clear that it is wholeheartedly committed to developing realistic budgets and to holding managers responsible for them. If sales managers believe that their reward structure (compensation and promotion) depends to a large extent on achieving budget objectives, they will manage their budgets more carefully. Air Shields, a subsidiary of Naravo Scientific, uses negative budget control. Whenever sales managers go over budget, a calculated amount is deducted from their sales figures, which are one basis for determining their compensation. To earn the maximum compensation at Air Shields, sales managers must stay within budget guidelines, and this same budget pressure is applied throughout the organization, from the top down.

Zero-Base Budgets

In many organizations it is common practice to pad the budget request by following two unwritten rules: request more than you need, and spend all you get. Subordinate sales managers fear that budget surpluses will be taken away in future budgets. So much wasteful spending often takes place near the end of the budget period as managers scramble to spend the rest of the budget allocation. Under such thinking, the budget process becomes somewhat perfunctory, as amounts for inflation are routinely added to last year's fully spent budget prior to any adjustments for changes in overall selling efforts.

One approach to slowing this self-perpetuating budget growth pattern is zero-base budgeting. Zero-base budgeting does not take for granted the continued existence of the sales organization or its separate activities. Each budget must annually stand on its own merits to receive funding. Sales managers using zero-base budgeting start from the ground up by identifying necessary activities, including their associated benefits and costs, in their areas of responsibility. Then each activity is assigned a priority in terms of its contribution to organizational objectives. This process is repeated at each successively higher managerial level until the priorities for all planned activities are clearly identified. Finally, funds are distributed by priority down the array of activities until all available monies are allocated.

Zero-base budgets are most appropriate for activities that are flexible, such as selling and advertising, rather than for mandatory expenditures such as direct labor and material costs for production. Sales managers soon learn that zero-base budgeting can be frustrating because of the increased paperwork involved and the extra time required to prioritize all activities via cost-benefit analysis each year. Yet organizations as diverse as Texas Instruments and Playboy Enterprises have found that it is one way to inhibit the continuing upward spiral of budgets.

Preparation of the Annual Sales Budget

Preparing the annual sales budget is often considered one of the most tedious and unrewarding jobs that the sales manager does. Yet the sales budget should be favorably viewed as an opportunity for profit planning whereby the resources needed to obtain projected sales are ensured or at least requested. Budgeting offers the sales department important advantages by:

- Ensuring a systematic approach to allocating resources (human, material, and financial)
- Developing the sales manager's sensitivity to profitable resource utilization
- Creating awareness of the necessity to coordinate selling efforts with other segments of the organization
- Establishing standards for measuring the performance of the sales organization and its subdivisions
- Involving the entire organization in the profit-planning process, since each subdivision must submit a proposed budget

Most sales organizations have specified procedures, formats, worksheets, and timetables for developing the sales budget. Several steps can be identified in systematic budget preparation.

1. *Review and analyze the situation* beginning with the last budget period's variances. Where, when, and how much were deviations from planned performance, and who was responsible? This review of past budget performance can help the sales manager avoid variances in the coming period. Any changes in the current budget period, such as introduction of new products, changes in the marketing mix, or developments in the uncontrollable marketing environment, must be anticipated and worked into the sales budget. Some common line items in each sales budget include:

- *Salaries.* Salespeople, administrative support, sales supervisors, and managers
- *Direct selling expenses.* Travel, lodging, food, and entertainment
- *Commissions and bonuses*
- *Benefit packages.* Social security, medical insurance, retirement contributions, and stock options
- *Office expenses.* Mailing, telephone, office supplies, and miscellaneous costs
- *Promotional materials.* Selling aids, premiums, contest awards, product samples, catalogs, price lists
- *Advertising*

2. *Communicate sales goals and objectives* and their relative priorities to all management levels to ensure that managers are developing their budgets by using the same assumptions and general guidelines. Encourage the participation of all supervisors and managers in the budget process so that, by contributing to its development, they will accept responsibility for the budget and enthusiastically implement it.

3. *Identify specific market opportunities and problems* so that resources are budgeted in a way that enables sales managers and salespeople to exploit the opportunities and deal with the problems on a timely basis.

4. *Develop a preliminary allocation of resources and selling efforts* to particular activities, customers, products, and territories. Later, revisions can be made in this initial sales budget. But all budgets should be as realistic as possible at each development stage to maximize their favorable impact on the organization. When budget goals are accomplished through a cooperative team effort, a pervasive feeling of organizational confidence is created. Instead of emphasizing punishment for failure to stay within budgets, sales managers ought to stress rewards and public commendations to encourage positive attitudes toward budget goals and pride in their achievement.

5. *Prepare a budget presentation* to ''sell'' the budget proposal to higher management. Each and every component of the organization is usually clamoring for an increased allocation of funds. Unless sales managers can rationally justify each line item in their budgets on the basis of profit contribution, the item will be a candidate for cutting by higher management. Succinct, well-reasoned written and oral budget presentations are worth the effort devoted to them. The presentations are more effective when supported by alternative budget scenarios, which are easy to develop with PC capability.

6. *Implement the budget and provide periodic feedback* to responsible subordinate managers and supervisors so that they have time to take corrective action on budget variances. Although salespeople can be trained to be more budget-conscious, it falls upon the sales manager to ensure that sales revenue and cost ratios are remaining within reasonable budget limits. Exhibit 3-11 shows a quarterly sales budget form, or budget control chart, that sales managers might consider using to monitor budget variances and take timely corrective action. One area in which sales managers will most likely find budget variances is the direct selling expenses of their sales forces. Corrective action may require better time and territory management, which is discussed in Chapter 10.

ETHICS IN SALES FORCE BUDGETING: WINNING THE BUDGET BATTLE

The end of the budget year is rapidly approaching, and it appears that for the second consecutive year, you will be over budget. To make matters even worse, your counterpart in the midwest region is once again on target with his budget. The midwest sales manager has always been somewhat of a rival of yours. Not only is his region the perennial sales leader in the company, but it also ranks near the bottom in selling expenses. One day, at a company sales meeting, you accidentally overhear him talking on the phone with his secretary. From this conversation, it's apparent that one of the reasons the midwest region's budget is met every year is that its sales manager often ''borrows'' other department's time to help with *his* customers. Instead of hiring temporaries, as you often do, he merely gets someone else to help out. By using services his budget is *not* charged for, he's left with that much more in his account. How would you handle this situation?

EXHIBIT 3-11

Quarterly Sales Budget and Budget Control Chart

(*a*) QUARTERLY SALES BUDGET

Line items	January			February			March		
	Budget	Actual	Variance	Budget	Actual	Variance	Budget	Actual	Variance
Sales									
Expenses Salaries Commissions Bonuses Social security Medical insurance Retirement									
Travel Lodging Food Entertainment									
Office expenses Mail Telephone Miscellaneous									
Promotion Samples Catalogs Price lists Selling aids Premiums Awards									
Advertising									

(*b*) BUDGET CONTROL CHART

Sales managers can often be confronted by ethical issues when they are dealing with budget decisions. The *Ethics* scenario on page 108 represents such a situation.

SUMMARY

Sales planning is the primary function of sales managers, since the sales plan provides basic guidelines and direction for all other sales decisions and activities. In their role as planners and administrators, sales managers must set goals and objectives, establish sales policies and procedures, devise strategies and tactics, and implement controls to ensure that goals and objectives are achieved. In order to obtain the information about the market that they need to develop sound sales plans, sales managers should have effective sales management information systems (SMIS).

Prior to beginning the planning process, sales managers should think through the six-stage process of diagnosis, prognosis, objectives, strategy, tactics, and control. The actual steps involved in the sales planning process are (1) analyze the situation, (2) set goals and objectives, (3) determine market potential, (4) forecast sales, (5) select strategies, (6) develop detailed activities, (7) allocate necessary resources (budgeting), (8) implement the plan, and (9) control the plan. One of the most popular approaches to strategic planning is the business portfolio approach, which categorizes strategic business units on the basis of a market-growth–market-share matrix. Before beginning the sales planning process, the manager should undertake a sales environment audit to identify potential opportunities and challenges to the sales organization.

Sales budget planning is a vital part of the sales planning process. Essentially, the sales budget is a financial sales plan outlining how resources and selling efforts should be allocated to achieve the sales forecast. The steps in systematic budget planning are (1) review and analyze the situation, (2) communicate sales goals and objectives, (3) identify specific market opportunities and problems, (4) develop a preliminary allocation of resources, (5) prepare a budget presentation, and (6) implement the budget and provide periodic feedback.

STUDY QUESTIONS

1. When salespeople are so busy doing their normal selling job, do you think there is a need for special training, compensation incentives, or motivational programs to encourage salespeople to collect information about the marketplace for headquarters sales planners and forecasters? Explain.

2. What kinds of assumptions might a sales manager make (almost subconsciously) about the marketplace in preparing the annual plan? How would you ensure that these assumptions are made explicit?

3. Do you agree or disagree with Apple Computer's strategy and tactics to sell its PCs? What would you do in competing with IBM and other PC manufacturers? Will the lower-cost foreign-made clones of IBM personal computers affect Apple? If so, how?

4. How might you use one of the business portfolio approaches to analyze the personal computer market for IBM?

5. Outline a strategic sales plan for IBM PCs, and then use dialectic planning to back up this strategic plan.

6. Discuss the relationship between strategic sales planning and budgeting.

7. What do you expect to learn from a sales environment audit? When or how often do you think this type of audit should be conducted?

8. Describe an SMIS. What will a sales management information system be like fifty years from now? Explain.

9. What important benefits does the sales department get from the use of objectives?

10. Give an example of companies that currently maintain products in the four growth strategies.

IN-BASKET EXERCISE

You are a sales manager for a consumer goods company that has just launched a new product. Although all the staff members are extremely excited about its potential, after only a few months on the market the product is generating disappointing responses from buyers. One of your salespeople recently heard a major wholesaler, serving over 500 supermarkets, say: "We've had this product three months, and it's not moving, so we're going to yank it from the stores!"

How do you respond to this? What do you tell your salespeople? What tools are available to help you in this rather gloomy situation?

CASE 3-1

C. T. ANTAEAN SERVICE COMPANY: SALES PLANNING IN AN UNCERTAIN ENVIRONMENT

C. T. Antaean is an oil-field service company which specializes in well cementing and acid and hydraulic fracturing treatments. The company was formed by two mergers; in 1983 Paquette Antaean merged with Formfrac to form Antaean Services, and in 1984 Antaean Services merged with C. T. Wilson to form C. T. Antaean. C. T. Antaean continues to report to two parent companies, Paquette Industries and Wilson Tool Company.

Oil Industry

Prior to 1981 the North American oil industry was experiencing a "boom." In the United States, Texas was a primary beneficiary of the boom, in Canada it was Alberta. Then in 1981 oil prices began to drop from the peak of $35 per barrel to a low of $10 per barrel in 1986. Since that time oil prices have increased and remained relatively stable at approximately $18 per barrel; however, prices increased dramatically in late 1990, peaking at $40 per barrel. Analysts have cited worldwide uncertainty of adequate supply as a result of the war in the Gulf as the primary cause of the dramatic price increase. The high oil price sparked increased oil-drilling interest in the United States.

The oil industry is expected to become more stabilized following the Gulf War, but analysts disagree on how stable the industry will become. Analysts cite the economic importance of energy resources as a stabilizing quality in that government energy policies are sure to guarantee stability. Others cite many different scenarios that could decrease stability. Exhibit 1 indicates the change in oil usage over the previous two decades. Exhibit 2 indicates the relative magnitude of world oil reserves (as of January 1, 1990, in billions of barrels).

Organization

In 1980 the premerger companies employed a total work force of 500 people, 20 of whom were salespeople. Sales were averaging $5 million per month in service calls. With the decline in oil prices came a drastic reduction in oil-field activity and a near halt in exploratory drilling. As a service company, CTA was at the mercy of the market and was powerless to prevent the reduction in the need for its services. Presently CTA employs a total of twenty-three people, three of whom are salespeople. Sales average $450,000 per month, partially boosted by the recent oil price increase.

Marketing Activities

Although its sales are down dramatically, CTA has managed to increase its market share in the Bryan district. In 1982 the premerger companies had a total market share of 15 percent in stimulation treatments and 5 percent in cementing. By 1991, CTA had increased its share to 30 percent of the stimulation market and 25 percent of the primary and secondary cementing market. The Bryan district market is shared by five major competitors. CTA has managed to increase its market share by adopting aggressive pursuit of new accounts and thorough follow-up of old or inactive accounts. In 1982, Paquette Antaean had 10 active accounts but has since increased that number

Case prepared by Robert Griffice, Texas A&M University. Used with permission.

EXHIBIT 1

U.S. Oil Use, 1970 and 1989

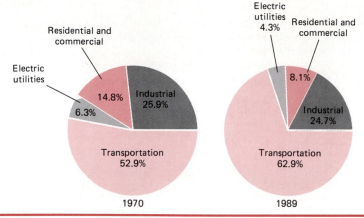

1970

1989

Source: Energy Information Administration.

EXHIBIT 2

Countries with Largest Crude-Oil Reserves

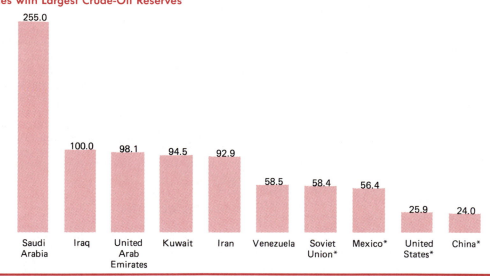

*Non-OPEC countries.
Source: Energy Information Administration.

to a total of 150 customers, 20 to 25 of whom are active at any given time. Since CTA is a service company with an intangible product, the company's reputation is perceived to be the most important factor in generating new and repeat business. CTA prides itself on the quality of the work it provides and is very concerned that the customer is presented with the "straight facts" about the work being performed. This concern was stressed by Rob Hill, district sales manager, because, as he admits, "errors on the job usually work out in the service company's favor." Hill maintains that job consistency and repetition of results are the keys to building CTA's reputation and, in turn, business.

The Sales Force

In 1981, during the boom, little sales management was needed because demand so far outpaced the supply of services that the entire service industry could offer. The CTA salespeople found themselves avoiding potential business because they could not commit any more of the company's resources. These salespeople, for the most part, had little formal training and, more often than not, were brought up through the ranks from the work crews. Since that time Hill has trimmed the sales staff down to the best and most experienced of the earlier sales group.

Eric Tyburec has a B.S. degree in chemistry and over eighteen years of experience in the oil-well service industry. He started with a competitor, working as a service crew supervisor in the Rocky Mountains for three years. Prior to the company mergers, he worked for Formfrac for six years, during which time he was promoted to district engineer/sales rep. Eric is considered an effective salesman, although his recent performance has been affected by the continued business slump. He has become somewhat disillusioned with the business, and this has translated to a diminished effort on his part.

Jeff Alexander is a highly motivated individual who has been with CTA for five years. He's worked his way up through the ranks from a service crew to his current sales position. Although he does not have a college degree, Jeff has an aptitude for technical sales and has learned engineering techniques through his own self-education. He has been very positive and enthusiastic about his work and tends to be very customer-oriented.

Marty Hardell has an M.B.A. and an undergraduate degree in business administration. After graduation he went to work for C. T. Wilson and participated in a company management training program. Upon completion of the training program, Marty decided to get into sales with CTA. To gain the necessary technical background, he participated in an optional oil-well service training program offered by CTA. He has been a sales rep with the company for six years and during that time has become CTA's top salesman.

Each sales rep is paid a straight salary ranging from $35,000 to $45,000 a year. There is no incentive plan, although the salesmen are provided with company cars. The reason no incentives are offered is that due to the nature of the oil business, one particular area (covered by one salesman) may be very active while there's little or no activity in other areas. This situation could lead to an inequity in bonuses not related to the performance of the salesmen.

With business down, the salesmen had to adopt an aggressive stance and begin actively pursuing accounts. The sales staff began to track drilling-rig activity by approaching the rig owners and not the current operators, who are the service company's customers. The salesmen would find out where the rig was to begin drilling next and who was taking out the contract for the rig. The CTA salesman would then approach the operator while the well was being drilled and become a familiar face so that he would be informed on which services might be needed. By the time the services were needed, the CTA sales rep was poised to offer immediate help in the form of consulting or the actual services themselves.

The Future

Since CTA and its competitors have no control over the demand for their services, there is a general feeling that the only true marketing strategy they can adopt is that which increases their share of the existing market. Hill states that as far as the immediate future is concerned, CTA's goal is to maintain the status quo in its services and try to expand its customer base. With $35 million in idle assets (service equipment) and an ample supply of experienced people in the area, Hill sees CTA in an excellent position, with its increased market share, to gain a majority of the market if the industry is to once again "boom."

Realizing that the industry is unlikely to experience another boom, Hill believes that CTA is long overdue for a reorientation in its sales objectives. CTA is still operating as if a boom will soon save the day. Hill states that CTA is operating with the goal of generating a positive cash flow (not necessarily profit) on each job. He notes that unlike other service companies, CTA has not taken on jobs in which there has been a loss on fixed expenses, although it has experienced a loss on variable costs in some cases, due to price-cost fluctuations.

Hill says that he, as sales manager, has no marketing strategy for the future except to weather the current situation until prices increase. He also says that since CTA is a subsidiary, there is little or no opportunity to diversify. The use of the equipment has been diversified, though. If it is not used for service work, CTA will lease the equipment to organizations outside the oil industry. Hill is optimistic that the recent surge in drilling will continue, but his optimism is guarded given that Middle East suppliers can strongly influence world oil prices. If activity does increase, the sales staff intends to maintain its aggressive tactics to increase business.

Questions

1. Could the service industry have planned for the current business slump? Explain why or why not.

2. What course of action do you think CTA should take to prepare for the future?

3. What precautions could the company take to avoid being caught overextended, as it was in 1981? In what ways could the company diversify?

4. Do you think CTA's passive acceptance of the market as unchangeable is justified? Why or why not?

5. What other tactics might the sales force use to increase its customer base? How would you, as sales manager, make the salespeople more effective? Would you institute training or bonus programs, for example? Explain.

6. Do you agree with Hill's contention that CTA was long overdue for a reorientation in its sales objectives?

7. What could CTA now do to improve its long-term planning capabilities? Can CTA avoid the negative impact of a continued sales decline yet be prepared to profit from future sales increases?

CASE 3-2

ARMSTRONG, INC., BUSINESS FORMS

Armstrong, Inc., Business Forms was once thought of as an office tradition. The company has been manufacturing and selling business forms and related products directly to industrial users for more than sixty years. The company has grown significantly over the past six decades and has seen considerable changes in customer demands. The last decade has been characterized as the "change decade" for businesses competing in this market. Kim Grant, general sales manager, stated: "We seemed to be altering our product line on a daily basis throughout the 1980s. Computer technology and increased competition from established competitors and new entrants into our market forced us to offer innovative products to our customers. Also, we noticed that our customers became much more demanding than they had ever been in the past. Prior to the 1980s, customers' expected delivery time (from time of order for custom forms) was six weeks; today we need to deliver custom forms within one week, or we can expect to lose a significant volume of sales."

Environmental Threats

Armstrong, Inc., can best be described as an organization that is faced with several environmental threats. Along with changing customer demands, printing equipment technology has been changing rapidly. Currently, Armstrong, Inc., has centralized printing facilities in Memphis, Tennessee. Centralization was made necessary by the decision to purchase high-technology printing equipment in the early 1980s. With this equipment it was possible to produce a high-quality product very quickly; however, it was necessary to centralize printing in order to create the volume required to make that equipment economical. Another threat is the changing nature of competitors' organizations. Most competitors have adopted a more recent technology that allows them to invest in smaller printing shops that can produce the same high-quality product, just as quickly, as Armstrong does. The smaller shops can be located in regional markets, thus reducing delivery time. Also, these smaller shops are less costly than comparable printing equipment was in the recent past; thus more entrepreneurs can now afford to enter the market and compete with large nationals such as Armstrong, Inc. Grant commented: "We are now finding that both regional and national competitors are able to deliver their products at less cost, and in many cases they can deliver more quickly than we can."

Organization

Armstrong, Inc., was organized along traditional lines, with each major product group having its own sales organization (see the accompanying exhibit). Decision making was centralized and rested in the hands of the general sales manager and the vice president of marketing. Armstrong could be characterized as formalized and inflexible.

With the product organization, sales representatives sell only one product line. Representatives quickly become familiar with their product lines, but buyers have complained of having more than one Armstrong, Inc., representative call upon them in a single day. Concerning those complaints, Grant stated: "I am very concerned that if that practice continues, we will lose

Case prepared by Debbie Boswell, Louisiana State University. Used with permission.

previous loyal customers. In many cases we are selling to small-business owners who do not have time for multiple sales calls from the same seller."

Currently, the sales force has little autonomy, authority, or accountability. Training has historically been in such areas as order taking and inventory control.

Marketing

Volume production, accompanied by a strong production orientation, has characterized the position of Armstrong, Inc. While marketing efforts have been on a national scale, promotions have been restricted primarily to promotional items distributed by sales representatives (e.g., calendars, pens, caps). Armstrong, Inc., was recently targeted by a lobbyist group against sexist advertising. The group cited Armstrong's use of women dressed (and in some cases not dressed) in provocative clothing as an unacceptable example of negative sex-role stereotyping. Grant commented: "I'm a woman, and I don't have a problem with our promotional items—customers don't have to accept them, and many customers demand them. The racier the promotion, the more demand we receive for it."

Competitors also use similar promotions, but Armstrong, Inc., is unaware of how racy their promotions tend to be or of how items are distributed. It is known, though, that an increasing number of competitors are using mail to market directly to both current and potential customers.

Another serious problem with Armstrong's promotional effort was that the company failed to direct promotions to potential new customers. Promotional items were distributed to representatives on the basis of the number of customers they historically sold to. This practice successfully controlled flagrant misuse of promotional items (e.g., distribution to friends and family), but it limited sales representatives' ability to distribute promotional items to new leads.

Current Situation

Of particular concern to Armstrong, Inc., are several problems:

- Demand for customized business forms has declined in recent years because of increased affordability and usage of desktop publishing.

- Armstrong's market share has been steadily shrinking over the past eight years.

- Armstrong's return on equity is approximately 5 percent less than the industry average.

- Future growth in sales and profit is not expected to come from business form sales.

Questions

Sales planning should be the primary function of sales managers, since it provides guidelines and direction for all other sales decisions and activities. On the basis of your understanding of sales planning, analysis, and operations at Armstrong, Inc., provide the following:

- An analysis of Armstrong's current situation. Your analysis should offer both a diagnosis and a prog-

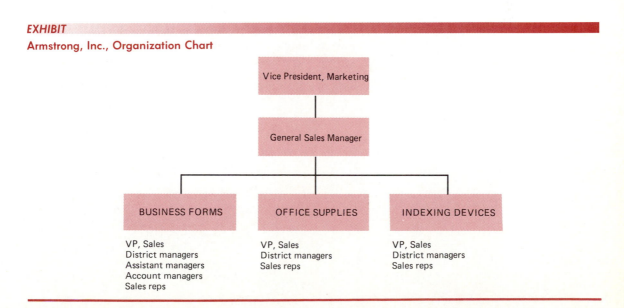

EXHIBIT

Armstrong, Inc., Organization Chart

Vice President, Marketing

General Sales Manager

BUSINESS FORMS	OFFICE SUPPLIES	INDEXING DEVICES
VP, Sales District managers Assistant managers Account managers Sales reps	VP, Sales District managers Sales reps	VP, Sales District managers Sales reps

nosis. Also, you should demonstrate your knowledge of objectives, strategy, tactics, and control of sales efforts at Armstrong.

• Suggested solutions for Armstrong, Inc.

Keep in mind the following questions:

1. What does the future hold for Armstrong, Inc.?

2. Are changes necessary at Armstrong, Inc.?

3. What specific actions need to be taken, by whom, and when?

4. What measures must be monitored?

5. Would you eliminate sales or sales management positions and/or dismiss particular individuals? Provide a specific response, and give reasons for your decision.

REFERENCES

1. Personal interview with James Kent, July 1990.
2. Steven Prokesch, "Xerox Halts Japanese March," *New York Times,* Nov. 7, 1985, pp. D1, D5; Thayer C. Taylor, "Xerox Sales Force Learns a New Game," *Sales & Marketing Management,* July 1, 1985, pp. 48–51.
3. Joseph W. Leonard, "Why MBO Fails So Often," *Training and Development Journal,* June 1986, p. 38.
4. Trish Baumann, "Coping with Information Overload," *Sales & Marketing Management,* April 1989, pp. 81–82.
5. Bob Francis, "Frito-Lay's, a New IS Bet," *Datamation,* Feb. 15, 1989, pp. 75–78.
6. Allan E. Alter, "A Customer Survey," *CIO,* June 1989, pp. 18–28.
7. Paul J. Solomon, "Strategic Planning for Marketers," *Business Horizons,* December 1978, pp. 65–73; Lester A. Neidell, *Strategic Marketing Management,* PennWell Books, Tulsa, 1983, p. 93; Lyndon E. Dawson, Jr., Timothy Paul Cronan, and Harold B. Teer, Jr., "Sales Force Planning, Implementation, and Control Using Artificial Intelligence," in Robert S. Franz, Robert M. Hopkins, and Alfred G. Toma (eds.), *Proceedings: Southern Marketing Association, 1979,* University of Southwestern Louisiana, Lafayette, 1979, pp. 398–401.
8. "Apple Peels Off the Unproductive," *Sales & Marketing Management,* May 1986, pp. 26–28; "Apple Gets Down to Business," *Management Technology,* January 1985, pp. 30–38; Felix Kessler, "Apple's Pitch to the *Fortune* 500," *Fortune,* Apr. 15, 1985, p. 54.
9. Rayna Skolnik, "The Birth of a Sales Force," *Sales & Marketing Management,* Mar. 10, 1986, pp. 42–44.

4

ESTIMATING MARKET POTENTIAL AND FORECASTING SALES

LEARNING OBJECTIVES

When you finish this chapter, you should understand:

▲ How sales forecasting, budgeting, and planning are interrelated
▲ The impact of an erroneous sales forecast on plans and budgets in various functional areas of the company
▲ How to estimate market potentials for consumer and industrial products
▲ How to use the most popular quantitative and qualitative sales forecasting tools
▲ The criteria on which to evaluate the various sales forecasting techniques

Tomorrow, tomorrow . . . everyone is fascinated with tomorrow because that is when dreams come true. Fortune-tellers, crystal balls, and tarôt cards are fun ways to deal with our curiosity about tomorrow. But knowing about tomorrow is serious business for strategic business unit (SBU) managers. Nearly all their strategic planning and decision making depends on estimates of market potential and predictions of future sales and income. Sales managers are especially interested in sales forecasts because they are responsible for achieving the forecasted sales that determine the company's income stream.

SALES FORECASTING AND OPERATIONAL PLANNING

Sales forecasting should be viewed as the central part of the strategic planning process, since the sales forecast becomes the keystone for overall company strategic planning. From giant multinational corporations to small entrepreneurs, the sales forecast directly or indirectly influences operational planning and budgeting for all functional areas. A sales forecast is the starting point for sales and marketing planning, production scheduling, cash-flow projections, financial planning, capital investment, procurement, inventory management, human resource planning, and budgeting. For example, before a production schedule can be developed, the company must know how much it expects to sell in the coming period. This production schedule, in turn, determines the material and labor inputs as well as the product outputs for the period.

An inaccurate sales forecast can mean an unfavorable inventory situation. The purchasing department must time purchases of supplies and materials according to sales forecasts. If the forecast is too high, the result may be a large inventory of unsold goods, plant shutdowns, layoffs, and deteriorating raw materials. On the other hand, too low a sales forecast can mean lost sales or even permanently lost customers. Sales managers must know how many new salespeople to hire and what their operating budget will be. Exhibit 4-1 illustrates the impact of erroneous sales forecasts on planning in various functional areas.

Unfortunately, sales forecasting is seldom simple because it relies on historical data to make predictions about the future. It is analogous to trying to

EXHIBIT 4-1

Impact of Erroneous Sales Forecasts

Functional Area	Forecast	
	Too High	Too Low
Production	Excess output, unsold products	Inadequate output to meet customer demand
Inventory	Overstock	Understock
Finance	Idle cash	Cash shortage
Promotion	Wasteful expenditures	Insufficient expenditures to cover the market
Distribution	Costly, insufficient to sell excess products	Inadequate to reach market
Pricing	Price reductions to sell excess products	Price increases to allocate scarce products
Sales force	Too many salespeople, high selling costs	Too few salespeople, market not covered
Customer relations	Money wasted on unneeded activities	Unsatisfactory due to out-of-stock products
Profits	Lower unit profits because expenses are high	Lower total profits because market not covered

drive an automobile forward with only a rear window to look through. Even though some problems and inaccuracies will accompany any forecast, the search for reliable and valid forecasting methods is worthwhile because it improves the efficiency and effectiveness of the manager's resource-allocation decisions.

Assessing the Forecasting Environment

Sales forecasts may be either short-run or long-run predictions. Short-run sales forecasts usually cover one year or less, and long-run forecasts typically cover five years, or perhaps ten. Before selecting the appropriate sales forecasting method, the sales manager must take into account all the possible factors that may affect sales volume. These various factors can be classified as either controllable or uncontrollable. *Controllable factors* are those elements of the internal business environment that the firm can manage. Basically, these include support for sales from within the company, for example, pricing policies, distribution channels, promotion campaigns, new-product development, and other marketing activities that affect future sales.

Uncontrollable factors include those elements of the environment over which the firm has little influence. For example, the state of the economy plays a major role in nearly all sales forecasts. What happens within the industry has an even more direct impact. Competitive conditions generally have the most direct impact, since new competitors in an industry may mean that there will be intense struggles for market shares.

Since the state of the economy and general business conditions play a major role in all sales forecasts, sales forecasters can better their understanding of the economic climate by keeping tabs on standard economic indexes. A *leading index* (one whose movement upward or downward leads the movement of the factor the sales manager is attempting to predict) is of greatest interest. Leading indicators are especially valuable in signaling turns in the economy several months in advance. Sales managers like to find an index that is highly correlated with company sales and available months ahead of the sales forecast. If, for instance, company sales are closely correlated with new orders for durable goods, then an 8 percent increase in durable-goods orders might predict a proportionate change in company sales. The leading indicators (reported by the National Bureau of Economic Research) that are most frequently used by business forecasters are:

- Prices of 500 common stocks
- New orders for durable goods
- Ratio of price to unit labor cost in manufacturing
- Nonagricultural placements
- Index of net business formation
- Corporate profits after taxes
- New building permits for private housing units
- Prices of industrial materials
- Average workweek in manufacturing
- Change in manufacturing and trade inventories
- Contracts and orders for plants and equipment
- Change in consumer installment debt

Identifying Levels of Forecasting

Sales managers are concerned with five distinct concepts in attempting to estimate demand and forecast sales, as Exhibit 4-2 shows. *Market capacity* is the number of units of a product or service that could be utilized by a market during a given period, regardless of product prices or the marketing strategies of competitors. In other words, market capacity is the demand for the product or service if it were free. *Market potential* is the highest possible expected industrywide sales of a product or service over a given period in a specified market. *Sales potential* is the maximum share of that market potential that a particular company could possibly hope to achieve. The *sales forecast* is the company's actual estimate of the dollar or unit sales that it will achieve during a given period under a proposed marketing plan. Finally, the *sales quota* is a specific sales goal assigned to a salesperson, sales region, or other subdivision of the sales organization. A sales quota is a motivational goal that is usually tied to incentive compensation for salespeople and sales managers.

EXHIBIT 4-2

Concepts in Demand Estimation and Sales Forecasting

Concept	Description	Example
Market capacity	Number of units of a product or service that would be taken by a market in a given period if the item were free	Number of electric razors people could use in the United States during fiscal year 1993
Market potential	Highest possible expected industry sales of a product or service during a set time period and specified market	Highest expected U.S. sales of electric razors during fiscal year 1993
Sales potential	Maximum market share that company or brand could possibly obtain during a given period	Schick's maximum U.S. market share for fiscal year 1993
Sales forecast	Expected actual sales for a company or brand during a given time period	Schick's sales forecast for fiscal year 1993
Sales quota	Sales volume goal for a salesperson or sales organization	Sales goal (quota) for a Schick salesperson for fiscal year 1993

These five levels of the forecasting process are illustrated in Exhibit 4-3. For example, the maximum possible sales, or market potential, for precision measuring tools (micrometers, calipers, and so forth) to the plumbing industry in the Pittsburgh primary metropolitan statistical area (PMSA) in 1993 will be about 350,000 units. This is the market potential. Swenson Tool Company, with sub-

EXHIBIT 4-3

Comparisons of Demand Estimation and Forecasting Concepts

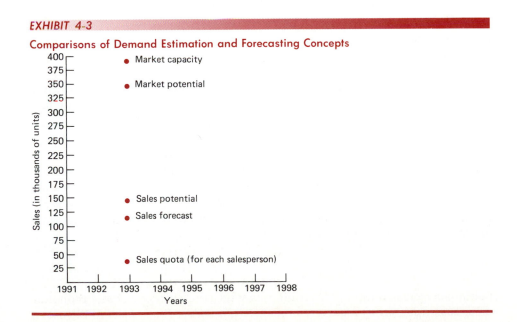

stantial marketing expenditures, could conceivably achieve a market share of 40 percent, or 140,000 units. This is the company's sales potential. On the basis of this sales forecast, Swenson has decided that it can achieve a sales volume of 120,000 units in 1993. There are three salespeople covering the Pittsburgh area, so Swenson's sales manager assigns each one a quota of 40,000 units.

Determining Market Potentials

In using the various demand-estimating approaches, the sales manager should distinguish between market potential and the company sales forecast that depends on its marketing effort. Some estimating approaches practically ignore the proposed marketing plan and expenditures and optimistically focus on the maximum quantity of the product or service that might be demanded by the target customer group. Estimates developed in this way are really measures of market potential for all competitors combined. The more weight given to the company's proposed marketing plan in developing a demand estimate, the more realistic the sales forecast will be.

The first question to ask in any demand analysis is: Who will use the product? Target markets may come from four basic categories:

- *Consumers,* or individuals and households who purchase for personal consumption
- *Producers,* or manufacturers, nonprofit organizations, and service industries that buy goods and services for use in producing other products or services that will be sold, rented, or supplied to others
- *Resellers,* or retailers and wholesalers that purchase products and services for resale or rent
- *Governments,* or federal, state, and local agencies that carry out the functions of government

Target markets are not always obvious. For instance, 45 percent of all razor blades are bought by women. But even though 66 million of the 120 million wet shavers are female, men still use more razor blades. So both the users and their usage rates must be identified to derive accurate estimates of demand.

A complicating factor in estimating demand for a product or service arises when the buyer and the user are different. For example, men's underwear is more often purchased by women than by the men who will wear it. Thus, the number of men who wear underwear and their expected rate of use will determine total sales potential, but the buying motivations of women are important in making actual sales forecasts.

Estimating Consumer Demand

Sales managers can estimate consumer market potentials from basic economic data. *Sales & Marketing Management* magazine's *Buying Power Index* (BPI) uses a weighted combination of population, income, and retail sales, expressed as a percentage of the national potential, to figure a given market's ability to buy. Weights are applied to reflect the relative importance of the three factors, as shown in the BPI formula below, where BPI_i = percentage of total national buying power in area i, I_i = percentage of U.S. disposable personal income, R_i = percentage of U.S. retail sales, and P_i = percentage of U.S. population.

$$BPI_i = \frac{5I_i + 3R_i + 2P_i}{10}$$

It is not necessary for the sales manager or sales rep to make any calculations, because *Sales & Marketing Management*'s annual survey of buying power reports the BPIs by metropolitan areas, counties, and cities. For example, the Philadelphia primary metropolitan statistical area had a BPI of 2.1747 in the 1989 survey, which means that potential sales for consumer goods in the Philadelphia area are about 2.2 percent of total U.S. sales. National sales managers can compare this figure with their company's actual sales in that market (as a percentage of total company sales) to determine whether present sales results seem adequate. Regional or district managers add the BPIs for each market in which they sell and then divide each separate market by this total BPI (since it is 100 percent of their market) to obtain an adjusted relative market potential. To illustrate, assume a regional sales manager has sales responsibility for five eastern metropolitan areas with the following BPIs: Baltimore (0.9923), Washington, D.C. (1.9756), Philadelphia (2.1747), New York (8.5369), and Boston (1.9099). The total BPI for this sales region is 15.5894. Dividing each metropolitan area's BPI by 15.5894 and multiplying by 100 gives adjusted BPIs, which the regional sales manager can use as an estimate of relative market potential, as shown in Exhibit 4-4. Now the sales manager sees that about 6 percent of regional sales ought to come from Baltimore, about 14 percent from Philadelphia, and over 54 percent from New York.

If there seems to be untapped potential in the market, the sales manager can develop more information about the specific market (such as the intensity of competitive efforts) before increasing sales efforts or selling expenditures. Poor estimates of market potential often lead to product failures and missed opportunities, as the cases that follow illustrate.

EXHIBIT 4-4

The Buying Power Index and Relative Market Potential

Metropolitan Area	Survey BPI	Adjusted BPI
Baltimore	0.9923	6.36
Washington, D.C.	1.9756	12.67
Philadelphia	2.1747	13.96
New York	8.5369	54.76
Boston	1.9099	12.25

Pepperidge Farm Cookies

In 1983, Pepperidge Farm (a subsidiary of Campbell Soup Company) saw an opportunity to piggyback on the *Star Wars* film series with a new cookie brand called Star Wars. Pepperidge Farm has long dominated the premium-priced end of the $2.5 billion retail cookie market. It used a less expensive method of making the Star Wars cookies but still charged a premium price of $1.39 a box. For the first three months, sales looked strong, and Pepperidge Farm was confident that it had a winner. But after an initial purchase at the insistence of their children, mothers were not willing to buy such expensive cookies the second time around. Star Wars cookies were not seen as a good value for the money, and one supermarket after another refused to stock the brand, so Pepperidge dropped the product after the first year. Fortunately for Pepperidge Farm's bottom line, Lucasfilm Company had not demanded any money up front, only 6 percent of cookie sales.[2]

Coca-Cola Company

In April 1985, Coca-Cola introduced New Coke with plans to phase out the old Coke formula. The $7.4 billion soft-drink maker had become frustrated because it had been steadily losing market share to its rival Pepsi-Cola. Pepsi had been outselling Coke in food stores since 1977, and Coke had been unable to effectively counter the ''Pepsi Challenge,'' which convinced many Americans that Pepsi tasted better than ''The Real Thing.'' Coke management had based its decision to change on taste tests with many thousands of people, who convinced the company that the new formula was preferred over old Coke. However, management had forgotten that a product is much more than a single dimension such as taste and that Coca-Cola was a vital part of the American culture and experience for millions of people. There was an angry uproar from Americans who deeply resented anybody daring to change something so traditional, so American, as Coke. It was almost like adding rhubarb to the recipe for apple pie or changing the shape of the hot dog or the rules for baseball. New Coke failed to switch the majority of people over from old Coke; the market potential for New Coke had obviously been badly overestimated. On July 11, 1985, old Coke came back as Coca-Cola Classic.[3]

3M Company

While trying to develop a superstrong adhesive, scientist Spencer Silver came up with something that wouldn't stick very well at all. No one could figure out a use for a weak adhesive, so the product went nowhere for about seven years. Then, one day, fellow 3M scientist Arthur Fry put some of the weak glue on a piece of paper to mark his place in a church hymnal. Eureka! Post-it notes, the yellow stick-on notepads, were created. Even when a use was identified, market potentials were substantially underestimated. Post-it notes took the office-supplies market by storm. 3M hasn't always been so lucky. For example, it developed disposable diapers years ahead of any other manufacturer but didn't find any consumer interest in the product.[4]

Estimating Industrial Demand

There are two typical approaches to estimating industrial demand. One utilizes the *standard industrial classification* (SIC), a uniform numbering system for categorizing nearly all industries according to their type of economic activity (that is, the product produced or the operation performed). The other approach involves surveys of buyer intentions. These surveys are conducted by the sales force, the in-house market research staff, or an outside research agency.

EXHIBIT 4-5

The Standard Industrial Classification System

Division	Two-Digit SIC Number	Major Industry Classified
A	01-09	Agriculture, forestry, fishing
B	10-14	Mining
C	15-17	Construction
D	20-39	Manufacturing
E	40-49	Transportation and other public utilities
F	50-51	Wholesale trade
G	52-59	Retail trade
H	60-67	Finance, insurance, and real estate
I	70-89	Services
J	91-97	Government
K	99	Nonclassifiable establishments

Standard industrial classification. The most widely used approach to estimating industrial demand relies on information provided in *The Standard Industrial Classification Manual,* published by the U.S. Office of Management and Budget (OMB) every five years. It classifies all industries into eleven divisions. Within each division, the major industrial groups are identified by two-digit numbers, as depicted in Exhibit 4-5.

All companies assigned the number 34 as the first two digits of their SIC code are manufacturers of fabricated metal products. Industry and product subgroups can be identified with increasing specificity by up to seven digits. As Exhibit 4-6 shows, SIC 3441121 describes manufacturers of fabricated structural iron and steel for buildings. If sales managers can classify current and potential

EXHIBIT 4-6

Detailed Breakdown of the SIC System

Classification	SIC Classification	Description
Division	D	Manufacturing
Major group	34	Manufacturers of fabricated metal products
Industry subgroup	344	Manufacturers of fabricated structural metal products
Specific industry	3441	Manufacturers of fabricated structural steel
Product class	34411	Manufacturers of fabricated structural metal for buildings
Product	3441121	Manufacturers of fabricated structural iron and steel for buildings

customers at least partially by the SIC numbers, they can locate prospective new customers, determine market potentials, and improve the accuracy of sales forecasts.

To compile a list of potential customers by SIC numbers, the sales manager can turn to the industrial directory for an individual state or to one of several other directories: *Survey of Industrial Purchasing Power, The Thomas Register of American Manufacturers, Dun & Bradstreet's Million Dollar Directory, Moody's Industrial Manual,* or *Standard & Poor's Register.* These reference sources will cite company names, addresses, and phone numbers; corporate officers; annual sales; number of employees; and products or services produced. If the sales manager does not have the time to compile such potential customer data, lists can be purchased from various organizations, including Dun & Bradstreet's marketing services division, which can provide the information desired on all the firms under a particular SIC code.

Other excellent sources for locating potential markets once the SIC codes have been identified are *Sales & Marketing Management*'s annual survey of industrial purchasing power and various government publications, including the *U.S. Census of Manufactures* (which uses the seven-digit SIC numbers), the *U.S. Survey of Manufactures* (which updates the *Census* but is less detailed), the *U.S. Industrial Outlook* (which categorizes by five-digit SIC numbers), and *County Business Patterns* (an annual publication of the Department of Commerce). Exhibit 4-7 shows some SIC-related sources of data for industrial markets.

Buyer intentions.   A direct approach to estimating industrial market potentials is to survey buyer intentions among the appropriate SIC codes. A company can send questionnaires to prospective customers listed under selected codes to find out what they intend to purchase over a given forecast period. The majority of buyers tend to be quite cooperative, and response rates are usually sufficiently high to develop a good estimate of the potential market. Surveys of buyer intentions will be discussed in more detail later in this chapter.

FORECASTING APPROACHES AND TECHNIQUES

Forecasts can be developed from the top down or the bottom up by using one of two basic methods: the breakdown approach or the buildup approach. The *breakdown approach* starts with a forecast of general economic conditions. Typically, this includes a forecast of gross national product (GNP) in constant dollars along with projections of the consumer and wholesale price indexes, interest rates, unemployment levels, and federal government expenditures. Then, in succession, an industry forecast, company forecast, and product forecast are made. These are the steps in conducting a sales forecast by using this top-down approach:

1. Start with a forecast of general economic conditions.
2. Estimate the industry's total market potential for a product category.

EXHIBIT 4-7

SIC-Based Sources of Data for Industrial Markets

Source	When Published	Digits of SIC Information	Type of Data
U.S. Census of Manufactures	Every five years (1987, 1992)	2-, 3-, 4-, 5-, and 7-digit data	Detailed industry information, product classes, etc.
U.S. Survey of Manufactures	Years other than when Census is published	2-, 3-, 4-, and 5-digit data	Data similar to that in Census of Manufactures but in less detail
U.S. Industrial Outlook	Annually	3-, 4-, and 5-digit data	Number of companies, where concentrated, industry trends
County Business Patterns	Annually	2-, 3-, and 4-digit data	Number of employees, taxable payrolls, totals by state and county
Sales & Marketing Management's "Survey of Industrial Purchasing Power"	Annually in Sales & Marketing Management	4-digit data	Number of plants, value of shipments, percentage of U.S. shipments by state and county
Private industrial directories	Annually	4-digit data	Company names, addresses, SICs, products produced, sales volumes, etc.
State/county/ municipality industrial directories	Varies—some annually, some every two years	4-digit data	Company names, addresses, SICs, products produced, sales volumes, etc.
Predicasts' "Basebook" and "Forecasts"	Quarterly	7-digit data	Industry forecasts and sources by SICs
Dun & Bradstreet's "Market Identifiers"	Not published— computerized data bank	4-digit data	Company names, addresses, SICs, sales volumes, net worth, line of business, etc.
Mailing-list companies	Not published— computerized data bank	4- and 5-digit data	Mailing labels—company names and addresses, more detailed company data on request

3. Determine the share of this market that the company currently holds and is likely to retain in view of competitive efforts.

4. Forecast sales for the product.

5. Use the sales forecast for operational planning and budgeting.

Coming from the opposite direction, the *buildup approach* simply asks individual salespeople what they expect to sell in the coming period or surveys customers about what they expect to buy and then sums their responses for a total forecast. Usually, a buying-intentions questionnaire is mailed to prospective customers or completed in telephone interviews. Most customers, especially industrial buyers, tend to be cooperative, and a response rate of 50 percent or higher from industrial customers is not rare. Even if nonprobability sampling techniques are used, the response rate is usually sufficiently high to develop a good estimate of the potential market. When nonprobability samples are used, however, profiles of respondents need to be examined to assess their representativeness.

Since there is no consensus on which approach is better, some companies prefer to use both the breakdown and the buildup approaches to increase their confidence in the sales forecast. In general, the breakdown approach is less expensive because it uses aggregate, publicly distributed forecasts from secondary sources such as universities or the federal government. It tends to be particularly useful and reliable for periods of six months or longer. But the buildup approach may be worth the extra effort and the cost for primary data collection because it is tailored specifically for the company and can be very accurate over the short run.

The common sales forecasting techniques can be classified as either nonquantitative or quantitative, as shown in Exhibit 4-8.[5] The *nonquantitative methods* rely primarily on judgment or opinion, whereas the *quantitative methods* use statistical techniques of varying degrees of difficulty.

Many companies utilize several methods to compare sales projections before settling on a particular sales forecast. Nonquantitative techniques are often called "subjective forecasts," but they are widely used and have proved very practical. At times, they can be superior to any sophisticated, quantitative technique. In fact, the jury of executive opinion and the sales force composite (both nonquantitative methods) are probably the techniques most often used for both consumer and industrial goods forecasts.

Nonquantitative Forecasting Techniques

Relatively nonquantitative forecasting techniques rely on executive experience, judgment, an intuitive feel for the market, and market surveys. Results can range

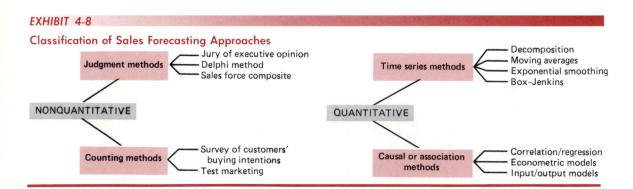

EXHIBIT 4-8

Classification of Sales Forecasting Approaches

Judgment methods
- Jury of executive opinion
- Delphi method
- Sales force composite

Counting methods
- Survey of customers' buying intentions
- Test marketing

NONQUANTITATIVE

Time series methods
- Decomposition
- Moving averages
- Exponential smoothing
- Box–Jenkins

Causal or association methods
- Correlation/regression
- Econometric models
- Input/output models

QUANTITATIVE

from very good to very poor. Two major categories of nonquantitative approaches to forecasting are judgment methods and counting methods.

Judgment methods. As shown in Exhibit 4-8, the three most common forecasting methods that use judgment are the jury of executive opinion, the Delphi method, and the sales force composite. The simplest forecasting technique of all is called the *naive forecast*. It assumes, usually naively, that next period's sales will be the same as they were in the past period or that mere extrapolation of last period's sales will give the best estimate of next period's sales. Although naive forecasts can occasionally be helpful, other judgment methods are more intuitively sound and accurate, especially when several are used to develop the final forecast.

The jury of executive opinion. Perhaps the oldest and simplest forecasting technique involves a poll of executive opinion. With this method the collective views of top company executives are pooled to develop the sales forecast. A jury may consist of the company president and several executives from different functional areas. Calculating a rough average of their opinions yields the sales forecast. Some executives' opinions may be supported by specific facts, while other officials may form their opinions on the basis of intuition alone. Nevertheless, the consensus of opinion is usually better than any one person's judgment. An obvious advantage of the jury of executive opinion is that a forecast can be developed easily and quickly. In industries characterized by rapid change, executive opinion may be the best method available because it is so flexible and fast. A final advantage of the executive-opinion approach is that information can generally be gathered at less expense than with other forecasting techniques.

Disadvantages attributed to the executive-opinion method are numerous. First, because it is highly subjective and relies on personal opinion often not backed up with facts, it may be viewed as unscientific and mere guesswork. Second, this technique adds to the workload of top executives by diverting them from problems in their functional areas. Also, many times these key executives are from functional areas that are not closely attuned to the marketplace. For example, what could a production manager or financial executive be expected to know about future sales?

Because the sales forecasts based on executive opinions typically are not based on facts about products, customers, or territories, it is difficult to break down the forecast for operating, budgeting, and controlling purposes in subunits of the organization. For this reason, some executives say that this technique should be used only when there is no external or internal data available on which to base the forecast. In such cases, executive opinion may be the only feasible way of forecasting sales.

Despite all the disadvantages and criticism, the executive-opinion approach is the most frequently used forecasting technique among small and medium-sized companies. Often, the owner-president and the sales manager get together, examine all the facts available to them, and come up with next year's sales forecast solely on the basis of their judgments, which are tempered by long experience.

The Delphi method.   A modified version of the executive-opinion approach to forecasting is the Delphi method. Developed during the late 1940s by the Rand Corporation, it depends on the advice of a group of experts. Results from experts in face-to-face panel discussions are often unsatisfactory because group opinion is highly influenced by dominant individuals, such as the higher-ranking executives. The Delphi method attempts to overcome this bias by asking expert panelists to make their forecasts anonymously and then send them to a group coordinator. The coordinator analyzes all the forecasts and sends each member an averaged forecast. Opinions, beliefs, expectations, and forecasts can be re-evaluated and changed but without the dominant influence of any one participant. Each expert is asked to submit another forecast and again receives feedback from the coordinator. This process continues until a near-consensus is reached. Such a procedure rests on the belief that an unpressured consensus forecast by experts will develop a good estimate of future sales.

Like the jury of executive opinion, the Delphi method depends on executive views instead of direct market factors. Its major disadvantage is the length of time needed to develop the consensus sales forecast, sometimes two months or more. Nevertheless, the Delphi method has been used with success. For example, after its first year of use at American Hoist & Derrick, the Delphi method reduced sales forecasting errors to less than 1 percent.

The sales force composite.   Among industrial manufacturers, the most popular sales forecasting technique is the sales force composite. This approach to forecasting combines each salesperson's estimate of future sales in his or her territory into a total company sales forecast. The total forecast is then analyzed, adjusted, and compared with forecasts from other sources. The advantages and disadvantages of the sales force composite are as follows:

Advantages

- Forecasting responsibility is assigned to those held responsible for making the sales.

- Specialized knowledge of salespeople in the marketplace is utilized.

- Salespeople have greater confidence in the individual sales quotas assigned to them because they participated in developing the sales forecast.

- Results tend to have greater reliability and accuracy because of the size of the sample.

- Estimates are developed by products, by customers, and by territories, so a final detailed forecast is readily available.

- Sales by individual territory and individual salespersons are emphasized.

Disadvantages

- Salespeople are not trained in forecasting, so forecasts are often too optimistic or too pessimistic.

- If estimates are used for setting sales quotas, salespeople often deliberately underestimate their forecast so that they can reach their quotas more easily.

- Salespeople often lack the perspective for future planning, so their forecasts are usually based on present rather than future conditions.

- Forecasting requires a considerable amount of sales force time that could otherwise be spent in the field attracting new customers.

- A salesperson, by nature, tends to be optimistic and tends to forecast higher sales than are possible.

- Most salespeople are not interested in forecasting, so they put little effort into their sales predictions.

Since salespeople know that sales forecasts are used to determine their individual sales quotas, they have a tendency to overestimate or underestimate sales in their territories. Comparing forecasts of individual salespeople with actual results over the years may indicate the need to use a weighting factor for those salespeople who are chronically wrong in one direction. A salesperson whose forecast is consistently 10 percent over actual sales should be assigned a 0.9 forecast weight, while someone who consistently forecasts 10 percent under should have a 1.1 weight. Some companies are using a bonus system to reward salespeople whose forecasts fall within a desired range of accuracy. But caution must be used in awarding such bonuses, because there are many things that salespeople can do to manipulate sales to match forecasts. The accompanying *Ethics* scenario gives a good example of how competitive salespeople can alter a sales forecast.

Counting methods.   Forecasting approaches that require little more than tabulating responses to questions on surveys or counting the number of buyers or purchases are called *counting methods.* One such method is a survey of consumer or industrial buyer intentions. Another makes use of test markets.

Survey of customers' buying intentions.   In this technique, customers are sampled and asked about their intentions to buy various products over a specified period. All the responses are then combined into one forecast. Forecasts are usually broken down by product, although many times a projection is made by customer or by territory. This method of forecasting sales is especially valuable

---

**ETHICS IN FORECASTING:
THE IMPACT OF ERRONEOUS SALES FORECASTS**

You are a sales manager for a privately owned business machine distributor. Each month your salespeople are required to submit a forecast of their sales for the coming month. The individual sales forecasts are posted on the office bulletin board to generate a competitive atmosphere among the salespeople as well as to give the company a visual indication of the inventory that will be needed each month. You are confident that most of your salespeople are honest with their estimates. However, you are a little suspicious that a few of your salespeople are deliberately giving low estimates of their sales in an attempt to "look good" at the end of each month when they equal or surpass their quotas.

What are the consequences of these low forecasts? How would you handle this situation?

for companies selling industrial goods because their customers tend to be (1) well identified and relatively few in number, (2) able to project their purchasing requirements well in advance of ordering, and (3) highly likely to follow through with their purchasing intentions, which are based on their past buying patterns.

Several surveys of consumer and organization buying intentions are available each year. The U.S. Department of Commerce and McGraw-Hill (*Business Week* magazine) survey businesses annually about capital equipment buying plans for the coming year. Consumer intentions to buy durable goods are surveyed by the U.S. Bureau of the Census and published in the *Quarterly Survey of Buying Intentions.* The University of Michigan's Survey Research Center, Institute for Social Research, publishes the *Index of Consumer Attitudes,* which reports on consumer attitudes toward personal finances and future purchases.

Even though a survey of buying intentions is classified as a nonquantitative technique, it can be quantitative and sophisticated when the survey is conducted as a true market research project, in which the selection of respondents is made by probability sampling techniques and analyzed with multivariate statistical tools.[6] The following list summarizes the advantages and disadvantages associated with a survey of customers' buying intentions:

Advantages

- The forecast is determined by the actual product users.
- The forecast is relatively fast and inexpensive when only a few customers are involved.
- Research gives the sales forecaster a good prediction of customers' buying intentions and some of the subjective reasoning behind their intentions.
- Research gives the forecaster a viable technique when all others may be inadequate or impossible to use, such as when there is a lack of historical data.

Disadvantages

- The technique becomes expensive and time-consuming in markets where users are numerous or not easily located.
- Buyer intentions can be inaccurate; for example, what people say they are going to buy and what they actually do buy may be two entirely different things.
- The forecast depends on the judgment and cooperation of the product users, some of whom may be uninformed and uncooperative.
- Buying intentions, especially for industrial goods, are often subject to multiple effects because the demand for industrial goods is derived from the demand for consumer products.

Test marketing.   Estimating sales for a new product is the most difficult type of forecast, since no historical sales data are available. It is particularly difficult when the product is sharply different from the company's current product lines. One of the most popular forecasting techniques for consumer packaged products is a counting method called *test marketing*. It is a ''full-dress rehearsal'' conducted in a limited market area to obtain consumer reaction prior to expanding to the regional or national market. By carefully selecting a few representative market areas (microcosms of the larger markets), marketing managers can observe the impact on sales of various combinations of the marketing mix. Measures of market share (based on trial and repeat purchase rates) in these small markets can be scaled up for forecasting sales in the total market. For example, if a company wins a market share of 10 percent in the small test markets, it may be assumed that approximately this share can be achieved in the expanded market. To minimize forecasting risks in introducing new products, many companies start in a small market and ''roll out'' gradually to the larger market as sales increase.

Some managers feel that test marketing takes too long (often a year or more depending on consumer repurchase cycles for the product), costs too much, and reveals too much to competitors, who often monitor the test markets and may even attempt to distort results. To avoid this visibility, some companies utilize their own ''laboratory'' methods or those of commercial firms such as Daniel Yankelovich or Elrick and Lavidge. The laboratory methods usually involve exposing a panel of consumers to different combinations of the marketing mix; then, in a private store or mock-up of the real-world buying environment, the panelists are free to choose among alternative products and brands, including the one being tested. Laboratory experiments provide more privacy, cost less, and result in quicker answers than does traditional test marketing; thus, they have gained increasing acceptance.

Quantitative Forecasting Techniques

Statistical techniques are increasingly being used by forecasters. They can be divided into two broad categories: time-series analyses and causal or association methods. *Time-series techniques* focus on historical data, while *causal models* are based on the relationships among various factors, both past and present, within the marketing environment. As shown in Exhibit 4-8, time-series methods include decomposition, moving averages, exponential smoothing, and Box-Jenkins. Causal or association methods include correlation-regression analysis, econometric models, and input-output models.

Time-series analysis. Time-series forecasting depends on analyzing past sales data to predict future sales. When any time-series analysis is used to forecast sales, there are four basic factors or types of movements to be taken into consideration:

- *Trend (T)*. Upward or downward movements in a time series as a result of basic developments in population, technology, or capital formation.

- *Periodic (P)*. Consistent pattern of sales movement within a given period, such as a year, generally called seasonal variations. Snow skis are an example of a product that has a seasonal sales pattern.

- *Cyclical (C).* Wavelike movement of sales that are longer in duration than a year and often irregular in occurrence, such as during business recessions. The housing market is especially affected by cyclical fluctuations.

- *Erratic (E).* One-time specific events such as wars, strikes, snowstorms, fires, or fads that are not predictable.

A sales forecaster needs to keep in mind that all four types of movements have an impact on sales—that is, $Y(\text{sales}) = f(T, P, C, E)$—and that their effects must be differentiated from random variation in forecasting to identify true trends in the data.

Decomposition methods. When the sales manager makes sales forecasts for each month or quarter of the year, he or she needs to use decomposition sales forecasting methods to isolate the four components of time-series data. First, the seasonal pattern is removed. Then, the cyclical element, if any, is estimated and removed. Finally, the forecaster considers the impact of erratic events before isolating any developing trends in the data.

Consider the set of actual sales data in Exhibit 4-9. To remove the seasonal fluctuations from the data to make them comparable to normal sales figures, multiply these historical sales figures by a seasonal index.

The deseasonalized sales data are shown in Exhibit 4-10. Sales increased from 98 to 150 between the second and third quarters of 1992, indicating a rising sales trend of 52 units per quarter. A simple line extension forecast for the fourth quarter would add 52 units to 150 for a sales forecast of 202 units. But, as illustrated in Exhibit 4-10, there was no significant increase in sales once the seasonal pattern of sales is removed.

To transform the deseasonalized sales figures in Exhibit 4-10 to a sales forecast for the coming year, multiply by the appropriate seasonal index. To illustrate: If seasonally adjusted sales in the second quarter of 1992 are 142, then estimated sales for the third quarter would be 142 times the seasonal index for the third quarter, or 155 (142 × 1.09). Since actual sales for the third period of 1992 were 150 (see Exhibit 4-9), our forecast missed by only 3.3 percent [(155 − 150) ÷ 150 = +3.3%]. If the sales data had not been deseasonalized,

---

EXHIBIT 4-9

Historical Sales*

Quarter	Year 1992	Year 1993	Year 1994	3-Year Quarterly Average	Seasonal Index†
1	110	113	120	114.33	0.85
2	98	83	99	93.33	0.69
3	150	142	149	147.00	1.09
4	190	168	193	183.67	1.36

*Sales are cited in units.
†First quarter seasonal index is 114.33 ÷ 134.58 = 0.85; second quarter is 93.33 ÷ 134.58 = 0.69; etc.
Note: Three years' total sales of 1,615 ÷ 12 quarters = 134.58 average sales per quarter.

EXHIBIT 4-10

Deseasonalized Sales*

Quarter	Year		
	1992	1993	1994
1	129	133	141
2	142	120	144
3	138	130	137
4	140	124	142

*Sales, in units, are computed by dividing actual sales (Exhibit 4-9) by the applicable seasonal index, e.g., 110 ÷ 0.85 = 129; 98 ÷ 0.69 = 142.

the forecast for the third quarter would have been off by 5.3 percent [(142 − 150) ÷ 150 = −5.3%].

Instead of relying on just one period to predict sales, as we have done here, time-series techniques frequently use several periods of historical sales, as the following paragraphs discuss.

Moving averages. This statistical approach is based on an average of several months' sales so that the high and low values are made less extreme. As each new period's sales data are added to the average, data from the oldest period are removed from the total. For each period a new average is computed, and this new average is, in essence, the moving average. Sales managers using this technique will have to decide the optimal number of periods to include. Moving averages of different lengths ought to be tried to find the most accurate predictor set. The more periods used, the less sensitive the average is to the movements in the data. In addition to reducing seasonal variations in the data, the moving-average approach tends to tone down the most recent sales figures, thereby leading to conservative forecasts during times of increasing sales. Another advantage of this approach is that it can often minimize the large random elements that frequently occur during short forecasting periods. A drawback of this method is that when a strong trend exists in the data, moving averages lag behind. The moving-average approach makes the assumption that the factors affecting past sales will also affect future sales. This technique used to be expensive, since it requires that all past data be stored for ready retrieval. But now that the prices of computer equipment are coming down so much, the cost is reasonable for many more firms. In fact, many firms now use desktop PC-based systems to develop moving averages. The formula for computing a moving average is

$$F_{t+1} = \frac{S_t + S_{t-1} \cdots S_{t-n+1}}{n}$$

where F_{t+1} = forecast for the next period
S_t = sales in the current period
S_{t-1} = sales in the previous period
n = number of periods in the moving average

Using data from Exhibit 4-11, we can compute a three-quarter moving-average forecast for sales in the month of April 1993 as follows:

$$F_4 = \frac{1{,}190 + 1{,}380 + 1{,}002}{3} = 1{,}190.7$$

Exponential smoothing.   Often used for short-range sales forecasting, exponential smoothing has gained increasing acceptance in recent years. Exponential smoothing overcomes one significant disadvantage of the moving-average method, namely, that the moving average is not sufficiently responsive to the most recent sales trends. Exponential smoothing modifies the moving-average method by systematically stressing recent sales results while deemphasizing old sales data. Exponential smoothing is a type of moving average that represents a weighted sum of all past numbers in a time series, with the heaviest weight placed on the most recent data. To illustrate, consider one of the most popular exponential smoothing formulas:

$$F_{t+1} = \alpha S_t + (1 - \alpha)F_t$$

where F_{t+1} = time period that is to be forecast
α = alpha, or the smoothing constant
S_t = current period's actual sales
F_t = current period's forecasted sales

The weight applied to the current period's actual sales represents the forecaster's estimate of their relative importance and is termed *alpha,* the smoothing

EXHIBIT 4-11

Sales Forecasts Using Moving Averages, 1993

		Forecasted Sales	
Month	Actual Sales*	3-Month Moving Average	6-Month Moving Average
January	1,002		
February	1,380		
March	1,190		
April	2,016	1,191	
May	1,842	1,528	
June	1,543	1,683	
July	1,328	1,800	1,496
August	1,276	1,571	1,550
September	1,762	1,382	1,533
October	1,981	1,455	1,628
November	1,490	1,673	1,622
December	1,206	1,744	1,563

*In units

EXHIBIT 4-12

Sales Forecasts Using Exponential Smoothing, 1993

Month	Actual Sales	Forecasted Sales		
		$\alpha = 0.2$	$\alpha = 0.4$	$\alpha = 0.8$
January	1,002*			
February	1,380	1,002	1,002	1,002
March	1,190	1,078	1,153	1,304
April	2,016	1,100	1,168	1,213
May	1,842	1,283	1,507	1,855
June	1,543	1,395	1,641	1,845
July	1,328	1,425	1,602	1,603
August	1,276	1,406	1,492	1,383
September	1,762	1,380	1,406	1,297
October	1,981	1,456	1,548	1,669
November	1,490	1,561	1,721	1,919
December	1,206	1,547	1,629	1,576

*There is no forecast for the first period when initiating this technique, so the first forecast is the same as the actual sales. Sales are cited in units.

constant. It is set at a value between 0.0 and 1.0. For example, if, as shown in Exhibit 4-12, actual sales for June 1993 were 1,543 units, the sales forecast for the current period is 1,395 units, and the smoothing constant is 0.2, then the forecast for the coming month's sales is $(0.2)(1,543) + (0.8)(1,395) = 1,425$.

The most critical decision in applying this technique is the value chosen for the smoothing constant. A smaller alpha value is used when actual sales are relatively stable. Higher values for alpha follow the actual sales figures more closely and should be used more often in fluctuating periods, although projections will still tend to lag behind actual sales. Thus, if the actual sales figures are changing rapidly, the alpha value should be large so that the forecast responds more to the actual figures. Exponential smoothing, like moving averages, has become increasingly feasible as a forecasting technique with the spread of low-cost, PC-based computing capabilities to even the smallest firms. In fact, lack of knowledge regarding these techniques is a considerably larger obstacle today than is cost.

A limitation of sales forecasts using exponential smoothing is that the estimates will lag behind trend movements. This is primarily due to the reliance on past data as the only factors considered in the forecast. Another disadvantage of this approach is that the smoothing constant is usually selected subjectively. Because the smoothing constant is the basis of this technique, some experimentation may be required before the forecaster selects a reliable constant. Representative sales figures can be used to measure errors with smoothing constants of different sizes. Finally, exponential smoothing, like moving averages, should be limited to short-run forecasts in industries characterized by mature and stable markets.

Box-Jenkins. A mathematical technique that uses computer analysis to select the model that best fits the time-series data, Box-Jenkins can provide an excellent forecast over a short-run period of three months or so. The results of this technique are generally fair in identifying significant turning points. However, it can be a very expensive procedure because of the high degree of expertise required. It requires a large number of historical data points for effective use, but it has proved to be no better than other, less mathematical, forecasting methods. Its most successful applications have been in production, inventory control, and financial forecasts.

Causal or association methods. Instead of predicting directly on the basis of judgment or historical data, causal-forecasting methods attempt to find the factors that affect sales and to determine the nature of that relationship. The correlation-regression method is one type of causal method.

Correlation-regression analyses. In *correlation analysis,* variables are studied simultaneously to see whether they are interrelated, or move together in some way. This technique tries to find correlations without implying cause and effect. *Regression analysis,* on the other hand, attempts to predict how one variable, such as sales, is affected by change in another variable, such as advertising expenditures. Both correlation and regression analyses usually start with a graph of paired data values, or a scatter diagram. When scatter diagrams are being constructed, the variable that is used to predict, referred to as the independent (X) variable, is scaled along the horizontal axis of the graph; the variable to be predicted, called the dependent (Y) variable, is scaled along the vertical axis. The scatter diagram is then plotted placing a mark at the intersection of each pair of X and Y scores. Scatter diagrams take different patterns, as shown in Exhibit 4-13. The exhibit illustrates a linear-positive relationship (*a*), a linear-negative relationship (*b*), no relationship (*c*), and a curvilinear relationship (*d*).

To show the relationship between the paired data (X, Y) of the scatter diagram, the simplest and most widely used technique is to fit a straight line to the plotted points. This line might be drawn with a ruler from visual inspection and individual judgment, but differing judgments could result in several such lines. To find the "best-fitting line," one needs to use the least-squares formula for a

EXHIBIT 4-13

Correlation Relationships

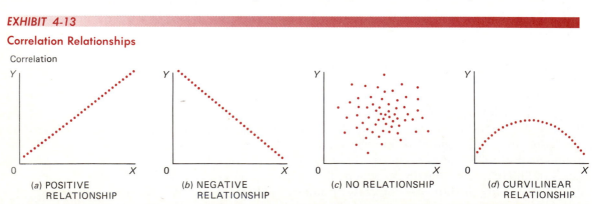

Correlation

(a) POSITIVE RELATIONSHIP   (b) NEGATIVE RELATIONSHIP   (c) NO RELATIONSHIP   (d) CURVILINEAR RELATIONSHIP

EXHIBIT 4-14

Simple Regression

Year X	Sales (Units) Y	XY	X²
1	43	43	1
2	52	104	4
3	73	219	9
4	71	284	16
Sum 10	239	650	30
Average 2.5	59.75		

$Y = a + bX$

$$b = \frac{n \Sigma XY - \Sigma X \Sigma Y}{n(\Sigma X^2) - (\Sigma X)^2}$$

$$= \frac{4(650) - 10(239)}{4(30) - (10)^2} \qquad a = Y - b\bar{X}$$

$$\qquad\qquad\qquad\qquad = 59.75 - 10.5(2.5)$$

$$= 10.5 \qquad\qquad\qquad = 33.5$$

$Y = 33.5 + 10.5X$

$\quad = 33.5 + 10.5(5) = 86$ units

straight line, $Y = a + bX$, where a is the intercept (intersecting with the vertical axis) and b is the slope or trend of the line. Least-squares estimates of the coefficients (a,b) minimize the squared differences between the actual plotted sales and the values predicted by the regression line. Exhibit 4-14 shows how a sales forecast can be developed by simple regression analysis. The regression equation $Y = 33.5 + 10.5X$ can be used to predict sales for year 5 by multiplying the trend of 10.5 by 5 and adding the constant term 33.5, yielding a forecast of 86. Simple regression describes the relationship between a single independent variable and a dependent variable. In our example, we have used time as the independent variable and sales as the dependent variable. More realistically, sales are probably associated with several independent variables (e.g., advertising expenditures, number of sales calls, prices, or interest rates). Multiple regression is a tool that can be employed to forecast the effect on sales of several independent variables.

Fortunately, there are a variety of prepackaged computer programs that can simplify the forecasting task by handling the complex mathematical calculations involved in multiple regression. Several computer software forecasting packages are available for PC-based systems. Two of the most popular are:

- *Statistical Analysis System (SAS)*. Anthony J. Barr et al.; SAS Institute, Inc.; Raleigh, NC 27605

- *Statistical Package for the Social Sciences (SPSS$_x$)*. Norman H. Nie et al.; McGraw-Hill Book Company; New York, NY 10020

If a multiple-regression program receives fifteen years of data on the dependent and three independent variables, the partial computer printout would provide the information in Exhibit 4-15. Using the constant term, or Y intercept, of -1.487 and the coefficients (weightings) for the three variables 0.364, 0.681, and -0.231, we come up with this forecasting equation:

$$Y = -1.487 + 0.364X_1 + 0.681X_2 - 0.231X_3$$

where Y = annual sales in thousands of dollars
X_1 = advertising expenditures in tens of thousands of dollars
X_2 = number of sales calls
X_3 = interest rate

The equation indicates that annual sales of the product increase with advertising expenditures and increase even more with the number of sales calls, but sales decline with an increase in interest rates.

In Exhibit 4-15, the *multiple R* of 0.833 is the correlation coefficient reflecting the degree of association of the dependent and independent variables. *Multiple R-square*, also called the coefficient of determination, indicates the percentage (69.4 percent) of total variation in Y (sales) explained by the three independent variables (X_1, advertising expenditures; X_2, number of sales calls; and X_3, interest rate). The *standard error of the estimate* is a measure of the accuracy of the prediction, that is, the range of error around the sales forecast. The standard error 0.872 means that there is a 68 percent chance (one standard deviation) that actual dollar sales will be within ±$872 of any forecast made with our

---

EXHIBIT 4-15

Multiple-Regression Example

Multiple R	0.833			
Multiple R-square	0.694			
Standard error of the estimate	0.872			

Analysis of Variance	Sum of Squares	DF	Mean Squares	F Ratio
Regression	118.3	3	39.43	50.08
Residual	21.1	11	1.92	

Variable		Coefficient	Standard Error of Regression Coefficient	F-Value
Y intercept	-1.487			
X_1		0.364	0.039	43.7
X_2		0.681	0.087	68.3
X_3		-0.231	0.073	2.4

derived equation. The forecasting ability of the prediction can also be evaluated by computing the standard errors of the coefficients for our three independent variables. These error coefficients show the expected dispersion (or scatter) around the coefficients. *F*-values indicate two highly significant variables and one (interest rate) that is less important in forecasting sales.

Among the advantages and disadvantages of multiple-regression analysis are the following:

Advantages

- One of the most objective methods used in sales forecasting, it forces the forecaster to consider multiple factors influencing sales and to quantify any assumptions being made.

- Causal relationships are determined between a company's sales and various independent factors influencing those sales.

- The method specifies the degree of reliability of relationships between the dependent and independent variables.

- When good leading indicators are used as independent variables, turning points for a company's sales can be estimated.

Disadvantages

- The sales forecast is often based on information that is derived from other estimates which may be of questionable validity.

- Some forecasters tend to readily accept results from sophisticated techniques without thinking about current market developments and trends.

- The complexity of this technique often leaves some managers skeptical and reluctant to accept the sales forecast.

- Multiple-regression analysis can be time-consuming and expensive; since it requires technical skill that is often not available within many smaller firms, outside consultants may be needed.

Econometric models. Econometric models can be thought of as a series of regression equations, often 1,000 or more. The major goal in using econometric models is to capture the complex interrelationships among the factors that affect either the total economy or an industry's or a company's sales. Organizations such as Chase Econometric Associates, Data Resources, and Wharton Econometric Forecasting Associates have developed macroeconomic models that trace the economic conditions in the United States by industries. Results of these models are published monthly and are available to the business community. Du Pont, General Motors, RCA, General Electric, and other giant companies have developed their own econometric models, custom-tailored to their unique needs. Exhibit 4-16 shows a flowchart of a multistage econometric sales forecasting model developed for Du Pont of Canada's Automotive Refinishes Division.

EXHIBIT 4-16

Flowchart of an Econometric Forecasting Model

This flowchart of the sales forecasting model, developed for du Pont of Canada's automotive refinishes division by Decision Science Corp., Jenkintown, Pa., illustrates the interactions that take place. The model produces three levels of forecasts—one each for the division, the product groups, and the individual products. As is true of most models, management can change the values of any of the indicators to assess the effects such changes would have on sales.

Model 1, an econometric one, uses those economic variables considered important to company sales, such as GNP, auto sales, auto accidents, and number of jobbers. Model 2 uses historical sales data as a forecast base and assigns weights to past sales results as well as seasonal factors. Model 3 takes the results of the first two models and gives each forecast appropriate weights depending upon their past predictive capabilities. Following this, the remaining models take the national sales forecast developed by model 3 and, with the same kind of interplay, break the forecast down into its monthly, product group, and individual product components.

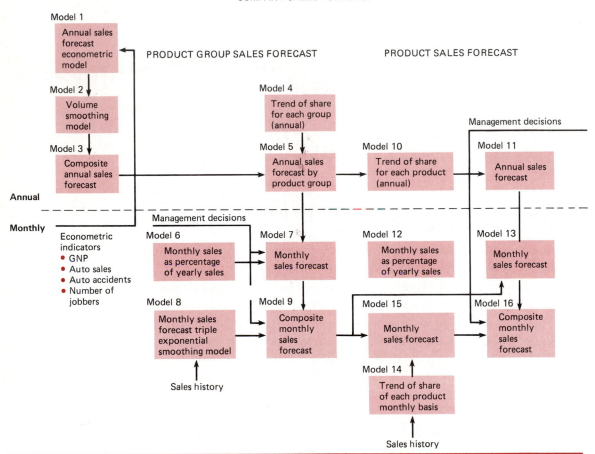

Source: Thayer C. Taylor, "Econometrics: A Formidable Weapon for GE, RCA, GM—or Nearly Anyone," *Sales & Marketing Management, Special Report on Forecasting for Higher Profits,* vol. 115, no. 17, November 1975, p. 37.

Building an econometric model is somewhat similar to building correlation-regression models. The sequential steps used in building an econometric model are these:

1. Identify factors that affect future sales.

2. Determine the correlation between sales and the causal factors.

3. Develop a series of equations that show the relationships between sales and the causal factors as well as the interrelationships of the causal factors.

4. Solve all the equations simultaneously by running them through a computer. On the basis of the results a new forecast can be created.

Advantages and disadvantages of econometric models for sales forecasting are as follows:

Advantages

• Utilization of all the interrelated equations yields causal relationships that can be expressed accurately.

• Uncertainties in the economy and the industry can be predicted.

• Econometric models can be used as a simulation of the entire economy. This can aid the sales forecaster in considering alternatives and in answering "what if" questions.

• Simple econometric models are increasingly possible because of the spread of low-cost PC-based systems to many firms that could not afford them in the past.

Disadvantages

• Forecasting with large, complex models can be expensive because much computer time is required and the forecaster needs great expertise.

• Econometric models are incapable of measuring all the impacts of all the possible forces affecting sales.

• A large amount of historical data is needed because of the great number of variables included in the model.

Econometric models are often used in conjunction with other forecasting techniques to project industry sales or general economic conditions. Perhaps the greatest value of econometric models is their potential for estimating future events.

Input-output models.   More appropriate for forecasting sales of industrial goods than consumer goods, *input-output models* are large matrices that show the amount of input required from each industry for a specified output of another industry. Input-output models are very tedious and expensive to develop, but they can provide good intermediate and long-range forecasts for industries such as metals, power utilities, and automobiles. Because of the difficulty in constructing large input-output models, companies usually turn to external experts for help.

Industrial goods sales managers with a good understanding of the SIC system can use national input-output analysis tables published by the Commerce Department's Office of Business Economics in its monthly *Survey of Current Business*. The Office of Business Economics' input-output table presents eighty-three basic industries in a matrix. Each row indicates how an industry's sales (outputs) are distributed among its customer industries. Since each sale is also a purchase, the columns show an industry's purchases (inputs) as a percentage of the seller's output. In another table, the percentages are converted to a dollar value of the flow of goods and services between industries. Still another table lists what the buying industry requires from direct suppliers for each dollar of output.

Exhibit 4-17 shows how input-output numbers could be used to identify potential customers for a manufacturer of farm machinery. Row 44 in the SIC table, as excerpted in the exhibit, defines the farm machinery and equipment industry. Thirty of the eighty-three industries in the table buy such equipment, and seven of these (2, 44, 45, 73, 69, 37, and 61) account for nearly 77 percent of the purchases in the farm equipment industry. The sales manager can see from the table whether his or her company is getting its relative share of the market. Specifically, if less than 23.8 percent of the company's products are being sold to the farm machinery industry, the company ought to consider strategies to better penetrate that market segment.

Having found out what industries purchase the types of goods and services

EXHIBIT 4-17

Converting Input-Output Data to SIC Codes

Major Customer Input-Output Number	Input-Output Industry Definition	Percentage of Total Intermediate Outputs	Appropriate SIC Numbers	Number of SIC Establishments in the U.S.
2	Other agricultural products	31.2	0112 Cotton growers	363
			0113 Cash grain growers	568
			0114 Tobacco growers	68
			0119 Field crops	664
			0123 Vegetable growers	889
			0141 General farms	2,263
44	Farm machinery and equipment	23.8	3522 Farm machinery and equipment	2,371
45	Construction, mining, and oil-field machinery	6.0	3531 Construction machinery	1,021
			3532 Mining machinery	335
			3533 Oil-field machinery	604
73	Business services	5.8	7394 Equipment rental and leasing services	11,232
69	Wholesale and retail trade	3.5	5083 Wholesale distributors of farm machinery	1,869
			5252 Farm-equipment dealers	21,801
37	Primary iron and steel manufacturing	3.4	In SIC's 331, 332, 339	Too broad to define
61	Other transportation equipment	3.2	3799 Transportation equipment, not elsewhere classified	917

produced by his or her company, the sales manager would need to locate specific customers. From Exhibit 4-17, the manager knows that 6 percent of sales are to the construction, mining, and oil-field machinery industries, which are classified by SIC codes 3531, 3532, and 3533.

EVALUATING QUANTITATIVE AND QUALITATIVE TECHNIQUES

Quantitative sales forecasting techniques employ an array of sophisticated mathematics and statistics, usually analyzed through high-speed computers. Many of these techniques—especially econometric models and multiple regression—are expensive and time-consuming and demand considerable forecaster expertise. Moreover, companies characterized by limited historical data or by a rapidly changing environment often must resort to less sophisticated techniques. The complexity of a forecast is no promise of predictive accuracy.

On the other hand, the nonquantitative techniques have been heavily criticized, particularly in regard to their inconsistency. How does one distinguish between shrewd, calculated opinions and mere hunches? The complications amplify when one is dealing with opinions from several people. Exhibit 4-18 provides a comparative analysis of the major forecasting techniques.

In selecting a forecasting method, several criteria ought to be considered:

- *Comprehensibility.* Managers must understand the basic methods by which the forecasts are developed if they are to have sufficient confidence in the estimates to use them. Highly complicated quantitative techniques that only statisticians understand may not have credibility among sales executives and other decision makers.

- *Accuracy.* The forecasting method must provide results that are sufficiently accurate for the purpose desired. Most forecasts contain inaccuracies but still furnish valuable information for managerial decision making. A projection within 10 percent accuracy would be considered acceptable by most sales forecasters.

- *Timeliness.* The forecasting method must generate forecasts in time to be useful to managers. Complex quantitative techniques or surveys can take weeks before good forecasts can be prepared. Thus, the sales manager who needs answers quickly may resort to quicker, perhaps less accurate, estimates.

- *Availability of information.* Any forecasting method is restricted by the amount and quality of information available to the organization. In forecasting as in other areas, a "garbage" input leads to a "garbage" output, that is, GIGO.

- *Qualified personnel.* It takes highly skilled people to develop an accurate forecast. Experts are needed to give their opinions in the qualitative methods like the jury of executive opinion or the Delphi method, and trained specialists are essential in forecasting with such techniques as multiple regression, Box-

EXHIBIT 4-18

Comparative Analysis of Forecasting Methods

Method	Cost	Accuracy	Weakness	Time to Develop	Resources Needed	Application
Judgment						
Executive opinion	Low	Fair over SR*	Subjective	Several weeks	Executive time, judgment; experience	Long- or short-run forecast; prediction of new-product success
Delphi	Low–medium	Good over LR*	Few experts available	2 months	Skilled coordinator; good questionnaire	Long-run forecasting
Sales force composite forecast	Medium	Fair to good	Salesperson bias	3 months	Salespeoples' time	Annual sales prediction of new-product success
Counting						
Survey of buyer intentions	Medium	Good	Weak for LR	3 months	Cooperative customers	Annual sales forecast; prediction of new-product success
Test marketing	High	Good	Competitive disruption	6–18 months	Tight control	New-product success; sales forecasts

Jenkins, or econometric models. Sales managers who will be hiring people to participate in any aspect of the sales forecast must take great care that the prospects are fully qualified for the job.

- *Flexibility.* The sales forecasting process should be flexible enough to adapt to changing conditions. Forecasting flexibility can be achieved by continually monitoring actual sales compared with forecasted sales for deviations that may indicate the need for revised sales forecasting tools and procedures.

- *Costs and benefits.* Benefits derived from the forecasting method must more than offset the costs of generating the sales forecasts. It is senseless to design an elaborate forecasting method that yields little information of value to management decision making.

In summary, any sales forecasting methods used should be comprehensible to managerial decision makers, timely, flexible, sufficiently accurate, and appropriate to the available data base; they should be developed by qualified people and evaluated on a cost-benefit basis.

Method	Cost	Accuracy	Weakness	Time to Develop	Resources Needed	Application
Time Series						
Moving averages	Low	Good over SR	Poor in spotting turning points	Hours	2 years of monthly data	Inventory control
Exponential smoothing	Low	Good	Poor in spotting turning points	Hours	2 years of monthly data	Inventory control
Decompo-sition	Low	Fair to good	Poor in spotting turning points	Hours	2 years of monthly data	SR forecasts
Box-Jenkins	High	Good over SR	Need expertise	Hours	50 or more historical data points	Production and inventory control
Causal or Association Methods						
Correlation-regression	Low	Good	Need computer expertise	Hours	2 years of monthly data	Company and SBU forecast
Econometric models	High	Good	Need great expertise	2–3 months	2 years of monthly data	Economy and company forecasts
Input-output models	High	Good medium-LR	Very costly	6 months	15–20 years of data	Sales forecast for company or SBU

*SR = short run; LR = long run

ORGANIZATION INVOLVEMENT

All functional areas of an organization should be involved in the forecasting and planning process. The sales force needs to be involved because it contributes directly to sales and is closest to the market. A lack of involvement in the forecasting process may negatively affect the overall direction and motivation of the company. For instance, if a functional area is left out of the process, the people working in that area may feel ignored, causing morale problems. When everyone participates and is involved in the forecasting process, each individual may take more interest in his or her job and in the direction of the organization.

Furthermore, any forecast ought to be reinforced by the general convergence of several estimates made with different forecasting techniques. If several methods are used in forecasting sales, then most functional areas of the organization will probably be participants.

PERSONAL COMPUTERS AND SALES FORECASTING

Computers are playing an increasingly important role in sales forecasting today. There was a time when only large organizations could afford computer systems. Things are quite different today: the cost of large-scale computers has dropped significantly, and the advent of personal computers has made computer technology available to anyone interested in using it. More and more companies are moving to microcomputers for sales forecasting. A survey of economists found that over 93 percent used a mainframe computer, a microcomputer, or both in developing sales forecasts. Of that number, less than 6 percent relied solely on a mainframe.[7] Another study of marketing professionals indicated that approximately 87 percent used computers in sales forecasting and only about 2 percent of those relied solely on mainframe computers.[8] Therefore, it is apparent that microcomputers are being used extensively in the preparation of sales forecasts.

Microcomputers, or PCs, have gained widespread acceptance for sales forecasting because they are very fast and capable of storing and processing large amounts of data. These technological advances in PCs have contributed to the use of many of the quantitative forecasting techniques that were discussed earlier. There are a number of software packages, at costs ranging from about $100 to several thousand dollars, that are currently being marketed for use in sales forecasting. Sales managers in all types and sizes of companies are increasingly utilizing these software packages because (1) they are user-friendly, (2) they allow the use of forecasting methods that could not be undertaken manually, and (3) they make the preparation of sales forecasts much less expensive than it would be with mainframe computers.

SUMMARY

Sales forecasting is the central part of the strategic planning process because the sales forecast becomes the keystone for all company planning, budgeting, and operational decision making. Sales managers are concerned with five levels in estimating demand. *Market capacity* is the maximum quantity of a product or service that the market could use regardless of price. *Market potential* is the highest possible industrywide sales of a product or service over a given period. *Sales potential* is the largest share of market potential that a given company could hope to achieve. *Sales forecast* is the company's best estimate of dollar or unit sales to be achieved during a given period under a proposed marketing plan. *Sales quotas* are the sales goals or targets assigned to individual salespeople or to the sales force as a whole. Consumer demand can be estimated with the help of the *Buying Power Index* (BPI), whereas industrial demand can be estimated with the aid of the *standard industrial classification* (SIC) system or surveys of buyer intentions. There are four categories of sales forecasting approaches: judgment methods, counting methods, time-series analyses, and causal or association methods. Forecasting techniques can also be grouped into quantitative and nonquantitative approaches. *Judgment methods* include the jury of executive opinion, the Delphi method, and the sales force composite. *Counting methods* include surveys of customers' buying intentions and test marketing. *Time-series* techniques include decomposition, moving averages, exponential smoothing, and Box-Jenkins. Finally, *causal methods* include correlation-regression analyses, econometric models, and input-output models. The most widely used methods are the judgment methods, but it is always wise to utilize more than one approach in forecasting to see whether there is general agreement on the forecast. In evaluating the forecasting technique, several criteria ought to be considered: comprehensibility, accuracy, timeliness, availability of required information, qualification of the people preparing the forecast, flexibility, and the trade-off between costs and benefits.

STUDY QUESTIONS

1. Why must organizations forecast sales? Are there any alternatives?

2. Why should sales forecasting be tied in with market planning?

3. Which of the forecasting techniques do you feel are most appropriate for small-business operations? Which for large corporations? Which for nonprofit organizations, such as museums or public libraries?

4. Assume that you are an entrepreneur who owns a small machine tool company with fourteen employees. Describe the kind of problems you will encounter if your sales forecast for the coming year is 25 percent too high. Describe the scenario if your sales forecast is 25 percent too low.

5. Try to think of some companies or industries that made poor estimates of market potentials for their products or services. What do you think caused the estimates of market potential to be so wrong?

6. Go to the library and ask the business reference librarian for *The Standard Industrial Classification Manual*. Then follow an SIC code from division to two-digit code and all the way through to seven digits. Write down the increasingly detailed descriptions that accompany each additional classification. Step by step, tell how you can use this information to identify potential customers.

7. What methods can you use to forecast sales for a new product?

8. If you were responsible for sales forecasting in your company, which of the forecasting techniques would you prefer to use? Why?

9. In evaluating forecasting methods, how would you rank the several comparison criteria in terms of decreasing importance? Would your ranking change for different industries or companies? Explain.

10. Do you think that sales forecasting is moving any closer to becoming a science? Explain.

IN-BASKET EXERCISE

You have just been hired as the national sales manager for a large industrial firm that makes and supplies products for the building materials industry. The marketing department wants your input for the 1993 sales forecast. Sales for the last six years are shown below:

Year	Sales (in millions)
1992	221.345
1991	200.176
1990	190.843
1989	196.284
1988	194.345
1987	200.250

Given the data, what would you recommend for the 1993 sales forecast? Why?

CASE 4-1

ZENON CORPORATION: DEVELOPING SALES FORECASTS

Zenon Corporation is a diversified producer of performance chemicals for the petroleum industry. Performance chemicals are designed to meet very rigid specifications in order to enhance the performance of a variety of end products. Zenon also produces high-technology chemicals, plastics, and aluminum products and has interests in oil, gas, and coal. Zenon, incorporated in the early 1930s, was originally founded as a gasoline-refining company. However, Charles Zenon, the founding entrepreneur, had a strong background in research and development of petroleum chemicals. This affected the strategic direction of the organization significantly over the years as the gasoline market became increasingly competitive. Today, the business has evolved into a very diversified corporation, with the Industrial Chemicals Group as the primary profit center.

Zenon's organizational structure is shown in Exhibit 1. Reporting to the CEO are five staff positions (senior vice presidents) and the senior vice president of operations, a line position. The corporation is structured as five major operating divisions. Each is directed by a vice president, who reports to the senior vice president of operations. The 1992 annual net sales (in

millions) of these divisions are shown in the following table:

Divisions	1992 Sales
Industrial Chemicals Group	$549.5
Petroleum Chemicals Group	$445.4
Plastics Group	$246.8
Aluminum Group	$252.6
Energy Group	$ 52.7

The company was founded in Houston, Texas, which is the site of corporate headquarters. The primary research and development center, as well as production facilities, is located in Baton Rouge, Louisiana.

The company's favorable 1992 performance stems from the successful implementation of the long-term strategy to enhance the value of Zenon to shareholders. This four-part plan includes:

1. Building on strong, established technology and market positions

2. Diversifying through selective acquisitions and research and development

Case prepared by Colleen Terro, Louisiana State University. Used with permission.

EXHIBIT 1

Zenon Organizational Structure

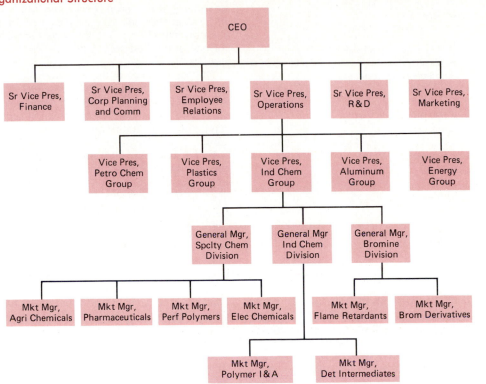

3. Maintaining a strong balance sheet while improving returns on equity

4. Maximizing cash flow from static or declining businesses

As the first step in this strategy, Zenon systematically analyzes each business unit to assess opportunities for expansion. As products and markets progress through cycles, Zenon's objective for many years has been to take advantage of strong business lines, reinvesting the cash from these products to extend the strength of its technology and market bases into promising new areas.

In describing the company's operating developments in 1992, one must consider the importance of product life cycles and their effective management. After a research breakthrough at Zenon, the new technology must be translated into a workable, salable product. There typically follows a period of rapid growth, then maturity, and eventually decline, at which time the product is replaced by new or improved technology and resultant products.

To maintain steady and profitable growth, Zenon manages its various product lines with the goal of maintaining a healthy mix of businesses in different life-cycle stages. It is essential to have a series of new products in development and commercial introduction ready to replace old ones in decline or withdrawal. Equally important is the successful management of growing and mature products to extend their lives and maximize cash flow to support new developments requiring substantial resources. The Industrial Chemicals Group has experienced dramatic growth and changing market conditions in the last three years, and Zenon has recently replaced the vice president of this group. Because of its importance to overall corporate profits, sales forecasts for the Industrial Chemicals Group over the next five years must be as accurate as possible.

The Industrial Chemicals Group is directed by David Stall, a newly appointed vice president, and is organized into three operating divisions with eight target markets or product groups (see Exhibit 2). The three divisions are guided by separate general managers who, in turn, have market managers for each product line.

EXHIBIT 2

Sales by Division and Product Line: Industrial Chemicals Group

		Percent of Sales
Industrial Chemicals Division		58
Polymer intermediates and additives	51	
Detergent intermediates	49	
	100	
Specialty Chemicals Division		40
Agricultural chemicals	19	
Pharmaceuticals	25	
Performance polymers	45	
Electronic chemicals	11	
	100	
Bromine Division		2
Flame retardants	71	
Bromine derivatives	29	
	100	
Total		100

In the Industrial Chemicals Division, total U.S. polymer sales rebounded dramatically during 1991 and 1992, increasing from 46 billion to 52 billion pounds. By 1993 sales are expected to reach 60 billion pounds. This represents a 30 percent increase over a two-year period. The market for detergent intermediates, on the other hand, is very mature and stable. The marketplace has become increasingly competitive, with an annual growth rate of only 2 percent. However, Zenon is a leading competitor and has recently made sizable gains in terms of market share.

The Specialty Chemicals Division is made up of a fairly diverse product mix. The performance polymer market is the primary revenue-producing unit and is highly dependent on current market conditions for crude oil. The agricultural chemicals and electronic chemicals are both growth markets but are also dependent on the oil market because price is a key marketing variable for these products, and it has a substantial effect on total sales volume. However, the pharmaceutical market is relatively stable and growing. Zenon also maintains a strong market position as the only domestic producer of the active ingredient for one of the best-selling new over-the-counter analgesics.

The performance of the Bromine Division is anticipated to be very good; Zenon's sales force has been successful in securing some very large accounts. This success has been achieved as a result of Zenon's strong reputation as a quality producer of industrial chemicals.

In the past, sales estimates have been prepared by the general manager of each division and were based on a percentage increase determined by the Industrial Chemicals Group's vice president. However, in approaching this task for the first time, Stall thinks that improvements are necessary in the sales forecasting method. Because the market conditions of each division are diverse, Stall believes that different methods of forecasting should be considered for each division.

Stall began his market analyses with a review of sales data for each division. Exhibit 2 provides the breakdown of sales by the three divisions of the Industrial Chemicals Group. In this manner, the contribution of each market to the total group is clearly defined.

Furthermore, Stall gathered sales data by year for each division to track the market trends of each. Exhibit 3 summarizes the sales of the Industrial Chemicals Division by quarter for a ten-year period from 1983 to 1992.

Pertinent sales data for the Specialty Chemicals Division encompass only a six-year period because the division is relatively new and experiences somewhat unstable market conditions. Quarterly sales data are outlined in Exhibit 4 for 1987 through 1992.

The Bromine Division is preparing to enter its second year of operation, so little sales history can be compiled for examination. Instead, Stall believes that input from the sales force as well as industry usage

EXHIBIT 3

Industrial Chemicals Division: Sales Summary

Quarter	1983	1984	1985	1986	1987	1988	1989	1990	1991	1992
1	53.2	55.3	57.0	58.8	62.4	65.0	68.4	66.3	70.4	78.8
2	54.2	56.0	58.0	62.5	64.8	67.6	71.1	75.0	89.6	100.2
3	54.3	55.1	58.0	60.0	62.4	65.0	68.4	75.0	86.4	96.7
4	53.3	54.1	57.1	58.7	59.9	62.4	65.7	72.1	73.6	82.3
Total	215.0	220.5	230.1	240.0	249.5	260.0	273.6	288.4	320.0	358.0

EXHIBIT 4

Specialty Chemicals Division: Sales Summary

Quarter	1987	1988	1989	1990	1991	1992
1	12.0	14.0	21.7	28.6	33.8	42.2
2	13.0	16.0	22.7	32.4	42.8	53.6
3	12.5	15.2	21.7	32.4	41.4	51.7
4	12.5	15.3	20.9	31.1	35.2	44.0
Total	50.0	60.5	87.0	124.5	153.2	191.5

data from trade publications will be the most useful information.

After reviewing the market conditions and sales data for each division, Stall outlined what he considers to be the key influencing factors for each division:

Industrial Chemicals Division

- Strong, stable, mature market for detergent intermediaries
- Recent increases for polymers
- Large number of competitors
- Large number of customers
- Recent strong gains in market share for polymers
- No foreseeable dramatic market changes for detergents
- Extensive historical sales data
- Accounts for 58 percent of Industrial Chemicals Group sales

Specialty Chemicals Division

- Growth market
- Uncertain market conditions
- Highly dependent on crude-oil market
- Accounts for 40 percent of Industrial Chemicals Group sales

Bromine Division

- New market
- No historical sales data
- Only a few key customers
- Small sales force with key sales reps
- Great need for accuracy by product
- Small number of products
- Few competitors

Questions

1. What recommendations for more precise forecasts would you give to Mr. Stall?

2. What forecasting methods would you use for each division? Why?

3. Prepare an actual sales forecast for the Specialty Chemicals Division.

4. Would any other information enable you to develop a more precise forecast for the Industrial Chemicals Division? If so, what?

CASE 4-2

INTERNATIONAL CONTAINER CORPORATION: FORECASTING SALES FOR NEW PRODUCTS IN NEW MARKETS

International Container (IC) is a large manufacturer and marketer of plastic containers, made for a variety of liquids from beverages to industrial fluids. It markets its product worldwide through a well-established channel of distributors. Recently, Mr. A. Jaye, director of new-product development for IC, returned from a vacation in the Bahamas with what he thought was a great new-product idea. It appears that after a week of lying on the beach and watching the sights, Jaye discovered something interesting about snorkelers. Most of them bring their snorkeling equipment to the beach

in a rather haphazard way. Either they attempt to carry their masks, fins, gauges, and so on, loosely—often dropping several of the items into the sand—or they put everything into a mesh bag. The divers' gear is a bit disorganized in the mesh bag, but the carrier appears to work well. The only problem is finding a place to put the bag once the gear is removed.

Jaye believes there is an unfulfilled need in the marketplace for a product that will help snorkelers carry their gear onto the beach. Therefore, he created the "Snork-All," a lightweight plastic device that could easily carry a diver's fins and mask, a knife, and various gauges or even an underwater camera if needed. Moreover, the Snork-All could easily snap on to any belt or bathing suit that the diver is wearing. Being an expert on plastics, Jaye believes this product represents an opportunity for IC to diversify its product portfolio and expand into new markets.

Once back in the states, Jaye presented his new product idea to a somewhat disenchanted board of directors. While the majority of company officials like the idea, they are uncertain about what action to take, since all the company's experience has been in an entirely different industry. The major concerns of the executives center around the potential sales of the proposed product. Without any knowledge of total market sales potential, and ultimately a sales forecast for Snork-All, the IC executives remain rather neutral on the backing of the product. While Jaye is a brilliant idea man, his expertise in marketing planning and forecasting is rather limited.

Questions

1. How would you estimate the total market potential for Snork-All? Can any kind of historical data help you with this?

2. Determine IC's sales potential for Snork-All.

3. What type of forecasting methods might work best in developing a sales forecast for Snork-All?

4. What would you recommend that Mr. A. Jaye do now? Is there any other information that could be used to help develop a better sales forecast for "Snork-All"?

REFERENCES

1. Douglas Newell, "Simple Methods Work for Candyman at Peter Paul Cadbury," *Journal of Business Forecasting*, Spring 1982, pp. 24–27.
2. "Pepperidge Farm's Fallow Ground," *Advertising Age*, Feb. 21, 1985, pp. 2–3.
3. "Coke's Man on the Spot," *Business Week*, July 29, 1985, pp. 56–61.
4. Ruth Hamel, "Wish You'd Thought of That? They Did," *USA Weekend*, Oct. 10–12, 1986, p. 14.
5. For a comprehensive overview of forecasting techniques, see David M. Georgoff and Robert G. Murdick, "Manager's Guide to Forecasting," *Harvard Business Review*, January–February 1986, pp. 110–120.
6. For a manager-oriented data analyst's understanding of multivariate statistics that can be used in forecasting, see Joseph F. Hair, Jr., Rolph E. Anderson, and Ronald L. Tatham, *Multivariate Data Analysis*, 2d ed., Macmillan, New York, 1987.
7. Barry Keating and J. Holton Wilson, "Forecasting: Practices and Teachings," *Journal of Business Forecasting*, Winter 1987–1988, p. 12.
8. J. Holton Wilson and Barry Keating, *Business Forecasting*, Irwin, Homewood, Ill., 1990, p. 6.

5

ORGANIZING THE SALES FORCE

LEARNING OBJECTIVES

When you finish this chapter, you should understand:

▲ Why organizational design is so significant to the achievement of organizational goals
▲ The difference between mechanistic and organic structures
▲ The development of sales departments
▲ What is meant by the "informal" organization
▲ What the sound guidelines are for a sales organization serving varying markets
▲ The dynamic nature of sales force organization

No sales organization can remain stagnant and expect long-run success. The sales success of organizations such as IBM, Coca-Cola, and National Cash Register (NCR) can be partially attributed to organizational design. Historically, IBM operated as a paternalistic dictatorship. Recently, this giant organization has been restructured into a decentralized democracy. This reorganization has improved the productivity of IBM. NCR has also been very successful by organizing its sales force according to market knowledge. Numerous other examples of the importance of organizational structure for sales managers' activities will be discussed in this chapter.

THE PURPOSE OF ORGANIZATION

Organizational structure plays an important role in bringing about the success or failure of marketing and sales activities. It determines how well activities are coordinated in serving customers profitably and how quickly the organization can adapt to changes in the marketing environment. The purpose of the marketing or sales organization is to facilitate the achievement of marketing and sales objectives and goals by:

1. *Responding to market needs.* A critical function of organization is to shorten the time a manager requires for evaluating a market situation and taking action. Flexibility and openness to change are important criteria for organizational structure.

2. *Arranging activities efficiently.* Efficiency is largely a result of specialization and routinization. The challenge is obtaining the required amount of flexibility while permitting the necessary bureaucracy.

3. *Establishing channels of communication.* The organizational structure must provide unclogged channels of communication with customers, employees, and concerned stakeholders. Without free-flowing feedback from the market and the workplace, an organization can become insensitive and unresponsive to the changing environments and thus endanger its survival.

THEORIES OF ORGANIZATION

Different degrees of flexibility are associated with various organizational structures. The term "mechanistic" describes rigid organizational structures, while "organic" describes the flexible types, as shown in Exhibit 5-1.

Mechanistic Organizational Structures

Classical or traditional organization theory usually distinguishes between *bureaucracy* and *administrative management*. Bureaucratic theorists tend to be sociologists or political scientists interested in developing a theory of organization based on a set of logical principles. Administrative-management theorists, on the other hand, tend to be managers who develop a set of principles based on their experiences in managing large organizations. Both approaches are largely mechanistic in that problems are resolved by structural changes in the organization. The "informal" organization, communication grapevines, group processes, individual conflicts, and human motivations are all but ignored by these theorists.

Bureaucracy.   Although today bureaucracy seems to symbolize inefficiency and red tape, Max Weber, the German sociologist, conceived of the bureaucratic model as the ideal organizational structure.[2] It was designed to increase the rationality of decision making by removing individual discretion so that everyone, customer and employee, could be treated efficiently and fairly. Government organizations are probably the most obvious examples of bureaucracies, since they must handle large numbers of people equitably. Characteristics of Weber's bureaucratic organization, which are still worthy of consideration by sales managers today, include:

- *Specialization of labor.* Goal-oriented tasks of the organization are divided into functional specialties, with individuals assigned responsibility for specific work. For instance, sales managers might assign segments of the sales force to such specialized functions as missionary sales, sales development, or national-account selling.

- *Well-defined hierarchy of authority.* Managers in the bureaucracy are arranged in a hierarchical order, with each succeeding level controlling the level below it.

EXHIBIT 5-1

Continuum of Organizational Structures

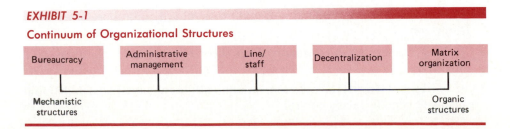

- *Clearly defined responsibility and authority.* Job descriptions detail each manager's sphere of responsibility and assign commensurate authority.

- *System of rules and procedures.* To ensure consistency in decision making, managers are guided by explicit policies and procedures. Decisions are first categorized by case. Then the applicable policy rule is applied.

- *Impersonality of relationships.* Emphasis is on logical analysis of situations—not emotions—so that all people are treated equally.

- *Promotions based on qualifications.* Jobs are always filled by qualified people because promotions are based on ability and performance, not friendships or loyalty.

- *Centralization of authority.* Coordination problems are minimized by concentrating authority in upper levels of the hierarchy.

- *Written records.* Consistent decisions and uniform actions are ensured by maintaining written files of previous decisions to serve as precedents for future situations.[3]

Although there is no purely bureaucratic organization in practice, enough experience has been obtained with organizations possessing different degrees of bureaucracy that some positive and negative aspects can be identified. While providing for equality of customer treatment and consistency in decision making, bureaucracies are often accused of being rigid and insensitive to individual problems, emphasizing quantity instead of quality of service to customers, identifying with unit subgoals instead of the larger organization goals, developing narrow technicians instead of broad managers, resisting change or innovation, avoiding responsibility, and accepting minimal employee performance. The degree of bureaucracy that an organization exhibits seems to vary inversely with its overall human orientation. That is, organizations that are more sensitive to the needs of individuals tend to be less bureaucratic.

Administrative management.   According to administrative-management theorists such as Fayol, Urwick, Mooney, and Reiley, the essential task of managers is to direct the use of scarce resources to achieve organization objectives. Several useful, empirically derived principles have been developed by the administrative-management theorists:

- *Coordination.* All activities must be arranged to ensure that all functional areas of the organization are working toward a common goal.

- *Unity of command.* Subordinates should report to only one superior to avoid confusion.

- *Unity of direction.* All organization efforts should be directed toward the same objectives.

- *Span of control.* There is an optimum number of subordinates that an individual manager can effectively control.

- *Specialization of labor.* Division of work into small components increases the efficiency and productivity of individuals and the organization.

- *Scalar chain of command.* All jobs in the organization should be connected from top to bottom by a hierarchy of authority that identifies channels of communication.[4]

The principles of administrative management are widely employed in contemporary organizations, but human beings tend to be regarded much like any other inanimate or animate resource—as something to be managed in an efficient, rational, and consistent way. Humans, of course, do not always behave in rational or consistent patterns, so the mechanistic administrative-management approach, like the bureaucratic design, tends to be of limited value in coping with the diversity of human problems that can arise in an organization of any size or type.

Organic Organizational Structures

Newer than the mechanistic theories of organization, organic structures evolved from the human relations movement of the 1940s and 1950s. Two types of organic structures are of particular relevance to sales management: decentralization and matrix organization.

Decentralization. Organizational decentralization first received wide attention in the 1920s with the successful reorganizations of General Motors and Du Pont. However, few companies followed their lead until several decades later, probably figuring that decentralization was something necessary only for giant corporations. Decentralization does not necessarily mean geographic separation of organization units as, say, with branches of a bank. In fact, an organization can retain centralized decision-making authority yet have widely scattered geographic units. IBM is an example of one such organization. IBM had long been known for its highly centralized, dictatorial management. Recently, in a major restructuring move, IBM has switched to a decentralized organizational structure, as discussed in the example that follows.

DECENTRALIZATION OF IBM

Towering over its competitors, International Business Machines Corporation (IBM) is the world's most profitable industrial company. It could also very easily be the most imitated and envied of all companies in the world. IBM doubled in size between 1980 and 1986, and analysts predict it could double again by the early 1990s. Since 1914, IBM's revenue has multiplied 12,514 times, from $4 million to $50.06 billion in 1985. For the same period, profits have grown by a factor of 13,110—from $500,000 to $6.56 billion. IBM collects 40 percent of the revenue and 70 percent of the profit in the industry worldwide. It holds 62 percent of the worldwide market share in "large systems."

IBM has recently instituted major changes and has opened up to outsiders, borrowing both their ideas and products. It has also changed its organizational structure.

Historically (for the majority of its first six decades), IBM has been operated as a dictatorship. Today, however, the company is run by a committee and is described as a vast, decentralized democracy. The result: IBM now performs with an agility that belies its size.

The process is termed "collegial." A management committee (MC), comprised of eight individuals, meets twice a week to make key decisions. A corporate management board, comprised of seventeen individuals, meets several times a year to formulate broad strategy guidelines.

These individual committee members are a close-knit group, cut from the same cloth, and most have spent their entire careers at IBM. They excel in IBM's politely combative "contention management" system, which defines the procedures by which corporate staff members must challenge the decisions they question.

Most of these executives have achieved their positions by starting in the sales force. They have a complete understanding of IBM's traditional attention to the needs of its markets. Without such an understanding, it would be hard to figure out what product and service to deliver, they explain.

That IBM is an unparalleled success is a well-accepted fact. That it has now adopted a successful organizational structure is also a fact. There is unanimous agreement that a muscle-bound bureaucracy would threaten IBM's progress. It is believed that the new decentralized organizational structure will foster the kind of visionary long-haul leadership that has long been the tradition at IBM.[5]

It is misleading to characterize an organization as decentralized or centralized, because different organizational functions may exhibit varying degrees of decentralization. A wholesale electronics chain, for instance, might have its purchasing function centralized for economies of scale, yet the pricing function might be decentralized to allow each wholesaling unit's salespeople to meet local market conditions or negotiate with individual customers. Organizations ought to be viewed as falling on a continuum ranging from total decentralization to total centralization, with all organizations being somewhere between the extremes.

A decentralized structure is more flexible than a mechanistic structure since it takes the limitations of individuals into account and increases the decision-making responsibilities of lower-level managers and employees. This freedom of action, combined with incentive plans such as team bonuses, can often motivate the entire selling organization to superior efforts. Another advantage of decentralization is that it develops potential managers with experience in accepting responsibility for decisions. Decentralization is generally thought to increase employee morale, although there are a few individuals who may not want the responsibility associated with this type of organizational structure.

However, centralization has certain advantages. Substantial economies are possible by centralizing certain functions, such as production, purchasing, advertising, and handling warehousing inventories, transportation, and accounting. Further, it can help ensure consistent managerial practices and similar treatment of customers served by widely scattered units of the organization. Two organizations, McDonald's and Holiday Inn, have convinced customers that product quality and service will be consistent in any of their outlets. Both these franchise operations retain centralization of marketing programs and managerial policies.

Many factors must be weighed in determining whether to decentralize the sales force organization.

Sales force size.   The smaller the size of the sales force, the more likely that it can be centralized. However, as the sales force grows, span-of-control problems may develop; more field supervisors and sales managers may be needed to recruit, train, and supervise salespeople. Although the optimum number of people that a manager can have reporting directly to him or her will vary with the talents of the individual concerned and the complexity of the work, the question of decentralization should probably be considered when the number exceeds eight.

Geographic dispersion of the market.   As the geographic size of the market expands, customer service tends to decline, sales expenses (travel, lodging, and food) generally increase, and supervision becomes more difficult. Decentralization, through the addition of branch sales offices with local sales managers, can usually restore organizational efficiency and customer satisfaction.

Relative role of personal selling.   The more important the role of personal selling in the promotional mix, the greater the need for field sales supervisors with local market responsibility and authority. Minnesota Mining and Manufacturing, better known as 3M Company, has always been highly decentralized, with a sales force specialized by product line. Its typical growth pattern has been based on developing a business to a certain level and then splitting it for sharper market focus. 3M's policy is to encourage local sales managers to tailor company programs to fit their markets. With forty-two U.S. divisions and $7.8 billion annual sales, however, the company became too fragmented, and many customers were unaware of all the 3M product lines that might serve their needs. Recently, 3M reorganized into four technologically related market sectors: Electronic and Information, Life Sciences, Graphic Technologies, and Industrial and Consumer. Although an executive vice president heads each market sector, all four heads report to the same chief executive officer. The market sectors structure is a means of uniting the company's domestic marketing efforts while allowing 3M to remain decentralized. Sales force organization is accomplished on a division basis. To tie the divisions together and to better serve the needs of the customer, 3M has instituted a program called Cooperating for Growth. Under this program, salespeople from different divisions meet monthly (on a local basis) to share ideas. The focus of the program is lead sharing and alertness to customer problems.[6]

Type of distribution channels.   The more direct the channels of distribution used (e.g., selling directly to retailers or manufacturers instead of through wholesalers or industrial suppliers), the more likely it is that decentralized product inventories will be required at branch locations near customers.

Customer service requirements.   The more presale (installation) and postsale (repair) services required by customers, the more need there will be for decentralized operations.

Overall costs. At different stages in organization growth, management may consider either decentralization or centralization of various activities, depending on the effect on total costs. A cost-benefit approach is necessary to determine whether benefits (if any) would be derived from further decentralization or centralization.

Matrix organization. One of the most recent structures is the matrix organization, developed in the aerospace industry to deal with rapid technological change and new-product development. In new-product development projects, it was discovered that creativity and flexibility were critical and that they could best be obtained in a structure designed around individual expertise instead of formal position. Many firms that must accomplish complex projects requiring technical expertise and specialized skills are now utilizing the matrix structure. Examples include General Motors, Shell Oil, Dow Chemical, General Foods, IBM, Alcoa, and Westinghouse.

Projects, not functions. Whereas traditional organizational structures tend to be designed around functions, matrix organizations revolve around projects. All organization efforts are focused on a specific project, and the functional areas are integrated into the project structure. Exhibit 5-2 shows the structure of a consumer products company organized by traditional functions. Even though the company markets several products, each functional unit makes an individual contribution to the entire product mix and the chain of command flows down through the functions.

By contrast, Exhibit 5-3 shows a matrix organization, in which the focus is on specific products or projects. The functional areas are still present, but they are secondary to the project structure. With the matrix structural design, project managers head a team of individuals from different functional areas and have responsibility for coordinating these functions toward project completion. Individual team members still have a functional superior (such as the sales man-

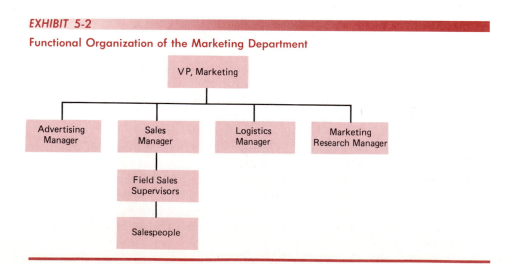

EXHIBIT 5-2

Functional Organization of the Marketing Department

EXHIBIT 5-3

Matrix Organization Focusing on Products or Projects

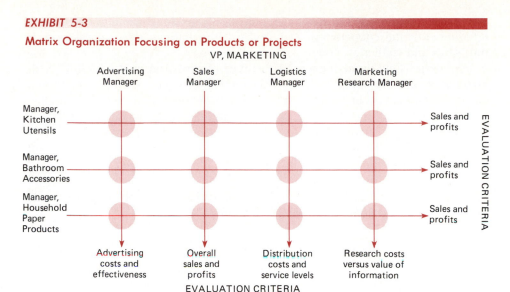

VP, MARKETING

ager), but they also report to their project managers. This, of course, violates the unity-of-command principle of administrative management because an individual has two bosses, a functional manager and a project manager. Salespeople who feel comfortable in the traditional authority-oriented organizational structure may suffer considerable anxiety in a matrix organization.

Teamwork.   Instead of relying on a traditional hierarchical arrangement, matrix organizations encourage the teamwork concept to maximize individual contributions. Team leaders are seen as coordinators of efforts rather than as bosses. Matrix organizations are most appropriate when the following conditions exist:

1. *Projects or products are unique,* so the activities to be accomplished are not routine.

2. *Team members are professional people* in terms of their expertise, skills, and attitudes toward the work to be done.

3. *Projects are of short duration,* as in the development and market introduction of a new product.

4. *Projects are of a ''crash'' nature,* where speed is more important than cost.

Advantages and disadvantages.   The matrix organizational structure is proving to be effective in today's rapidly changing market environment, and it is likely to receive even greater emphasis in the future than it has to date. This type of organization facilitates quick responses to changes in the environment and focuses attention on end results and goal accomplishment. A matrix organization also represents a recognition of the fact that programs comprise interacting systems and networks. The matrix organization provides flexibility, encourages interdepartmental cooperation, and develops the skills of the employees as it motivates and challenges them.

Some possible disadvantages of this type of organizational structure exist. There is always the potential for conflict (power struggles) between functional and project managers or between the professional experts. Another disadvantage is the possible additional cost of implementation. Finally, some critics believe that a matrix organization leads to more discussion and less action.

Despite the possible disadvantages, matrix organizational structures will probably become commonplace in the future. When organized properly, they provide a means for undertaking and accomplishing complex projects. One company that has recently moved toward a matrix organization is General Foods Corporation, as the following example explains.

GENERAL FOODS: A MAJOR REORGANIZATION

During the 1970s, General Foods was organized into separate strategic business units (SBUs). Each SBU concentrated on marketing families of products produced by separate process technologies but purchased by the same market segment. Since that time, General Foods has almost doubled in size and has made numerous acquisitions. One of the most successful companies in the United States (as well as abroad), General Foods has annual sales in excess of $9 billion.

While there remains a focus on marketing families of products, General Foods has evolved into a more sophisticated system that involves the integration of matrix management and strategic planning. The reorganization is a result of significant environmental changes and is an attempt to reflect the needs of the marketplace in the 1980s and 1990s.

Today, General Foods is organized on a sector basis. This is a distinct change from the former SBUs. There are three separate sectors, as described below.

Sector 1: Worldwide Coffee and International. This sector is made up of three divisions: Maxwell House (Sanka, Brim, and Yuban), Food Service Products (handling institutional accounts such as restaurants, hospitals, and airlines), and International (responsible for operations in Canada, Asia, and Europe).

To gain an understanding of the complexity and size of a sector, keep in mind that Maxwell House coffee alone accounts for the largest market share of coffee in the United States.

Sector 2: United States Grocery Business. This sector is made up of the following divisions:

• Beverages (Kool-Aid, Tang, Crystal Light)

• Baked Goods (Entenmann's, Orowheat)

• Desserts (Jell-O, Jell-O puddings, pudding pops, fruit bars)

• Breakfast (Post cereals, Log Cabin syrups)

• Meals (Birds Eye, Ronzoni pastas)

Additionally, Sector 2 includes support divisions, such as sales, information management, and operations.

Sector 3: Processed Meats. This sector is composed of the Oscar Mayer lines and Louis Rich meats.

Managers of these three separate sectors report directly to the president of General Foods as well as to other specialists in the organization. Titles of other specialists include group vice president for development and corporate marketing, chief research officer, chief planning officer, senior vice president for administration and public affairs, general counsel, and chief financial officer.

While this organizational structure may appear complex, it merely represents the complexity that pervades large multinational firms such as General Foods. The advantage of this matrix type of organization lies in its ability to foster cooperation between specialized departments and functions. It is an attempt to overcome the limitations of traditional hierarchical organizations.[7]

TYPES OF ORGANIZATIONS

Depending on its objectives, an organization can be structured in many ways. But most are one of three types: line, line and staff, or functional. Modifications of these types may develop as management sees the need to decentralize or to organize by product, customer, activity, territory, or a combination of these. In addition, every organization has an informal network.

Line Organization

The line organization is the simplest design and the one most often used by small firms. It usually consists of only a few managers, who exercise authority over specific functional areas of the business, such as production, finance, or sales. A simple line sales organization is shown in Exhibit 5-4.

EXHIBIT 5-4

Simple Line Sales Organization

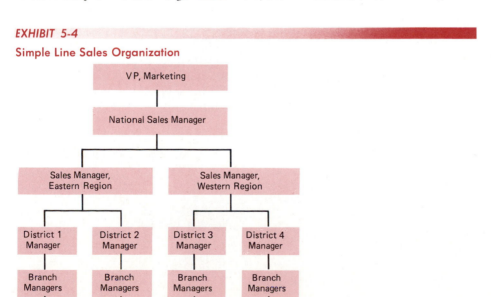

When a firm is small and the managers interact frequently, this basic line organization is efficient, effective, and flexible. But as a firm grows, the line organization tends to overburden managers, who become responsible for too many activities. Thus, decision making is slowed, and subordinates may become frustrated.

Line-and-Staff Organization

A line-and-staff structure creates more functional areas and adds staff assistants to accomplish many specialized support activities, such as sales forecasting or market research, for line managers. Typically, a vice president of marketing or a sales manager heads the department. Staff people provide the sales manager with specialized skills, allowing him or her to spend time working with the sales force. While line managers have direct authority over others in carrying out the operations of the organization, staff managers can only make recommendations or assist the line managers. Sometimes conflicts arise between line managers and staff executives, especially when staff people try to exercise control over line people or when line managers ignore staff advice. Of course, within each staff organization, there must be a line organization so that staff managers have line authority over their own staff people. An example of a line-and-staff organizational structure is provided in Exhibit 5-5.

Functional Organization

In the functional organization, the staff specialist is given line authority to control his or her function throughout the organization, as illustrated in Exhibit 5-6. The sales manager directs the salespeople through the district managers; the director of sales training has authority over the salespeople for all training; and the manager of technical services exercises line authority over the sales force in providing technical services. In the functional structure, each manager is a highly qualified specialist whose job is to make sure that his or her function is accomplished. Overall, the functional organization can be bewildering and frustrating for salespeople, who must respond to several bosses.

EXHIBIT 5-5

Line-and-Staff Sales Organization

EXHIBIT 5-6

EXHIBIT 5-6

Function-Oriented Sales Organization

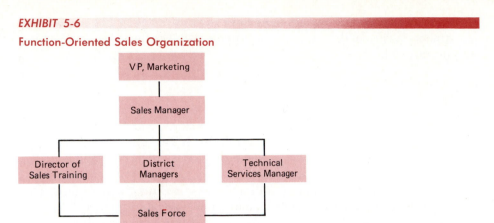

Informal Organization

In spite of organization charts, the informal organizational structure is the network by which things really get done. A healthy organization is dynamic and self-adjusting; it finds the most efficient methods for accomplishing jobs, with little regard to how these jobs are supposed to be done. Employees tend to adapt to how the organization actually works rather than to how the organization chart says it does. Real power and authority in an organization may belong to a strong staff manager or junior line manager who works with weaker or less competent senior managers. In one *Fortune* 500 consumer products company, the director of marketing services and the director of product management gained such influence with the president of the company that the three of them actually ran the company for a couple of years before each director was formally promoted to group vice president. Usually, the way an organization really functions is eventually reflected in the organization chart, but it can be a slow process, taking months or years.

EVOLUTION OF SALES DEPARTMENTS

All organizations have three functions. They must raise and manage money (finance), produce products or services (production), and sell them (sales). Organizational structure has an important bearing on the success of the sales and marketing activities—how well they are coordinated and how quickly they can be adapted to the changing marketing environment.

Marketing and sales department structures may be influenced by a number of factors, such as top-management philosophy and attitude toward marketing functions, company objectives, resources, competitive position, and the existing marketing environment. The overall purpose of marketing organization is to facilitate the achievement of organizational objectives, and this should be kept in mind when any organization is being designed.

Sales and marketing departments have evolved through five stages, and departments in each of the stages can be found today. The first stage is the simple sales department.

Simple Sales Department

In the simple sales department, the selling function is headed by a sales vice president or sales manager who directs the sales force and does some selling, too. In a small company, the sales manager normally has charge of all marketing activities. When the company needs some market research or advertising, the sales manager handles these duties as well.

The organization may develop informally. As the firm grows and the sales manager's duties multiply, subordinates are given special assignments, such as sales promotion, planning, and market research. Large firms usually have their own full-time sales managers and salespeople to sell their products, but small companies try to minimize costs by using independent salespeople, including brokers, manufacturers' representatives, selling agents, and commission agents. An example of a simple sales department is shown in Exhibit 5-7.

Sales Department with Ancillary Functions

As the organization continues to grow, it begins to require market research, advertising, new-product development, and customer services on a more regular basis. Eventually the company employs a few full-time specialists who can carry out this marketing service work, and often a permanent marketing service department is established. Exhibit 5-8 illustrates this level of organization by showing the hierarchy of a large food manufacturer in the late 1960s.

Separate Marketing Department

With sales growth, the importance and complexity of supporting marketing functions or services continue to increase. Because the sales vice president tends

EXHIBIT 5-7

Simple Sales Department

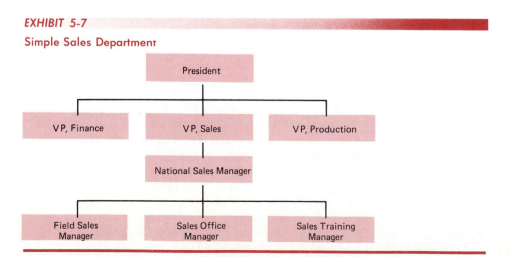

EXHIBIT 5-8

Sales Department with Ancillary Functions

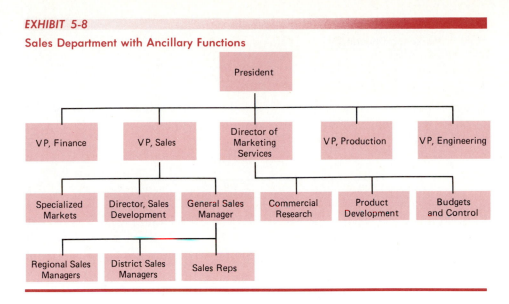

to focus on management of the sales force and to neglect the marketing support activities, the company president will create a separate marketing department. So the company now has both a sales vice president and a marketing vice president, as shown in Exhibit 5-9. If the sales vice president is qualified and capable of broadening his or her outlook, he or she may be promoted to the position of marketing vice president, with the assistant sales manager becoming sales manager. In other cases, however, the company will find it necessary to hire a marketing vice president from outside the company to obtain the expanded perspective and skills needed to direct the marketing functions.

EXHIBIT 5-9

Separate Marketing Department

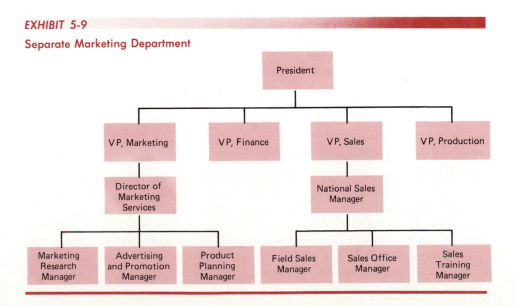

EXHIBIT 5-10
Modern Marketing Department

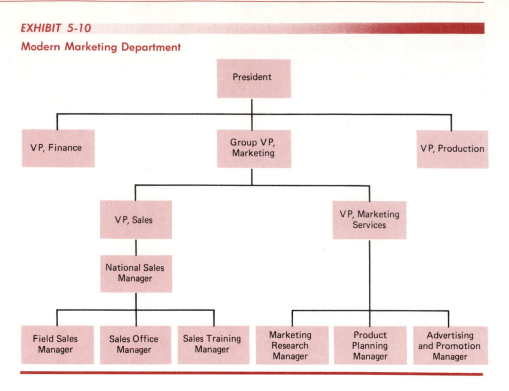

Modern Marketing Department

Unfortunately, the relationship between the sales vice president and the marketing vice president is often one of rivalry instead of cooperation. The marketing vice president tries to control all marketing functions affecting customer satisfaction, and the sales vice president perceives that the sales force has been downgraded until it is merely an important part of the company's marketing mix. The marketing vice president tends to take a long-range view, emphasizing new-product development and creative marketing strategy to satisfy customers profitably. Conversely, the sales vice president tends to stress sales volume through selling tactics. To resolve this conflict, another stage evolves in which the sales vice president reports directly to the marketing group vice president, as depicted in Exhibit 5-10.

Progressive Marketing Organization

Even though a company may have a modern marketing department, it still may not be a progressive marketing company unless marketing is seen by top management as the most crucial function, not merely as one of several equal functions in the company. Marketing's role is critical because it focuses on the one thing that the company must do to survive, that is, satisfy customers profitably. We are not advocating complete dominance of the company by marketing, for such a situation might lead to high inventory levels, minimal credit checks, abbreviated engineering design time, and short production runs. Other departments in the company should operate as checks and balances to marketing influence. With the marketing concept's emphasis on integrated company efforts to serve customers better, however, conflicts between marketing and other departments may arise along the lines suggested in Exhibit 5-11.

Understandably, other department vice presidents may initially resent and resist bending all the company's functions toward creating satisfied customers. Thus, full support from the chief executive officer is required to keep the company's goals in perspective.

EXHIBIT 5-11
Conflicts between Marketing and Other Departments

Other Departments	Their Emphasis	Marketing Emphasis
Engineering	Long design lead time	Short design lead time
	Functional features	Sales features
	Few models	Many models
	Standard components	Custom components
Purchasing	Standard parts	Nonstandard parts
	Price of material	Quality of material
	Economical lot sizes	Large lot sizes to avoid stockouts
	Purchasing at infrequent intervals	Immediate purchasing for customer needs
Production	Long production lead time	Short production lead time
	Long runs with few models	Short runs with many models
	No model changes	Frequent model changes
	Standard orders	Customer orders
	Ease of fabrication	Aesthetic appearance
	Average quality control	Tight quality control
Inventory	Fast-moving items, narrow product line	Broad product line
	Economical levels of stock	High levels of stock
Finance	Strict rationales for spending	Intuitive arguments for spending
	Hard-and-fast budgets	Flexible budgets to meet changing needs
	Pricing to cover costs	Pricing to further market development
Accounting	Standard transactions	Special terms and discounts
	Few reports	Many reports
	Expense-oriented reports	Functional cost-oriented reports
Credit	Full financial disclosures	Minimum credit examination of customers
	Lot credit risks	Medium credit risks
	Tough credit terms	Easy credit terms
	Tough collection procedures	Easy collection procedures

Source: Philip Kotler, *Marketing Management: Analysis, Planning, and Control,* 3d ed., Prentice-Hall, Englewood Cliffs, N.J., 1976, p. 415.

One possible solution for the conflicts and misunderstandings among departments is the encounter group. Real issues and concerns among different departments are obscured by unflatteringly stereotyping the work of other departments. In an attempt to reduce the strained relationships among departments, one company used an encounter-group approach. Executives from two departments, finance and marketing, met and were asked by a trained group leader to write down their candid impressions of the other department, their own image in the eyes of the other department, and the real nature of their department. Written comments were gathered and read to all participants. Marketing people saw the finance group as "rigid, penny-pinching, unimaginative," while the finance people saw the marketers as "bull artists and hucksters." Each group anticipated the impressions of their functions by the other group, but each group saw itself in a much more favorable light. Finance said it was "cost-conscious," not penny-pinching, and marketing said it was "customer-oriented," not a group of hucksters. After exploring these self-concepts, each group began to like the other group better, especially after the actual work of each group was openly discussed in a series of meetings. This approach increased the mutual appreciation of the groups and significantly improved their cooperative problem-solving orientation.

TYPES OF ORGANIZATION WITHIN THE SALES DEPARTMENT

All sales organization efforts tend to center around products, markets, and functions. These elements are blended together differently by various industries and by separate companies within the same industry. Sales departments have traditionally been organized into four types: geographic, product-oriented, function-oriented, and market-oriented. A more recent innovation is some combination of these four. A brief description of each type of organization follows.

Geographic Organizations

Geographic sales organizations are the most common, but they are usually used in combination with product-, function-, or market-oriented structures. Some examples of geographic organizations are banks with suburban branches, magazine publishers with regional editions, hotel chains with regional divisions, or companies with international and domestic sales divisions. Sales managers are typically called regional, division, or district sales managers, and large companies may have sales executives at three levels in the organization who carry one of these titles. A sales manager normally has complete authority over a specific geographic area; several salespeople, each assigned a separate part of the territory, report to him or her. The advantages of a geographic organization stem from its decentralized, line-authority structure, which ensures flexibility in adapting to the needs, problems, buying patterns, service requirements, and competitive conditions in the regional markets. Some disadvantages include the overhead costs of management as more levels of geographic executives are es-

EXHIBIT 5-12

Geographic Sales Department Organization

Appropriate when:
Customers are widely dispersed; customers in similar industries tend to be located near each other; regional differences in customer behavior are great; personal relationships are important in the marketing effort; geographic markets are large enough to justify special attention.

tablished and the problems in coordinating total company sales efforts when several sales divisions operate with considerable autonomy. The lack of functional specialists can also be a problem, since territorial managers are expected to operate as jacks-of-all-trades (e.g., advertising, sales analysis, billing, credit, and collection) in addition to managing the sales force. Exhibit 5-12 shows a simplified geographic sales organization.

Product-Oriented Organizations

Product-oriented sales organizations are applicable when product lines become sufficiently complex, distinct, or diversified to demand increased individualized attention. Under this setup, products compete among themselves for profit, market share, and company resources. Procter & Gamble, one of the world's most successful consumer products companies, makes extensive use of the product-oriented structure. Competition among P&G products, sometimes sold to overlapping market segments, is encouraged. If a company creates divisions to handle the different products, it is called a divisionalized product organization. But if all the products are managed within one companywide structural design, the company is called a consolidated product organization.

There are four variations of product-oriented organizations:

1. *Product divisions,* into which the entire company (not just sales operations) is subdivided by product. Automobile companies, such as General Motors, use this structure. Each product division (Chevrolet, Oldsmobile, or Cadillac) has separate sales outlets and engineering, production, finance, and marketing operations.

2. *Product marketing groups,* in which separate marketing strategies are carried out for each product but all other departments work with all products. Coca-Cola bottlers employ the same plant facilities to produce both Coke and Tab, but different marketing strategies are used.

3. *Product specialization within certain functions,* such as a separate sales force for each major product category. This structure is preferred when it is economically feasible to specialize throughout the entire marketing operation or when specialization is necessary for only a few functions, such as personal selling or advertising.

4. *Product managers,* who are like minipresidents within a company. They are responsible for developing plans and strategies for one or more product lines and for ensuring the success of the brand in the market. For instance, Quaker Oats Company has a product (or brand) manager for Ken-L-Ration dog foods, Puss 'n Boots cat foods, Aunt Jemima mixes, and each of its many other product lines. Lacking any formal line authority over other functional areas, product managers must exercise skillful persuasion to obtain cooperation and resources from other departments in the company. Procter & Gamble first used the product-manager system in 1927 to market a new hand soap, Camay.

When a sales organization takes on one of the various product structures, it increases sales force knowledge of company products and provides expertise in helping customers solve product-related problems. Two disadvantages of the product structure are the additional expense (increased specialization usually requires additional management) and the possible irritation of customers who lose time because more than one salesperson from the same company calls on them to present different products. Also, such multiple-salespeople calls tend to confuse the image of the seller because each salesperson comes across differently to the customer. A simple illustration of a sales force organized by product is provided in Exhibit 5-13.

Function-Oriented Organizations

Function-oriented sales organizations are structured by major functions, such as development of new accounts or maintenance of current customers. This structure offers specialization and efficiency in performing selling activities, and it is generally best for companies selling only a few or very similar products to comparatively few customer types. Generally, it is applied by medium- and large-sized companies that can afford the luxury of allowing salespeople to restrict their efforts to only one or a small number of activities. For example, a common problem among growth-oriented companies is motivating salespeople to call on potential new accounts. In contrast to the maintenance of present accounts, new-account development requires a different set of sales skills. Therefore, many companies assign these two functions to separate sales groups. Unlike the case in the pure line-and-staff organization, in the function-oriented structure the

EXHIBIT 5-13

Sales Department Organized by Product

Sales Manager

Computer Salespeople

Office Equipment Salespeople

Appropriate when:
Product complexities and differences are great; all aspects of the marketing program need to be coordinated at the customers' level; product introductions are frequent; there are large differences in locations of products on life cycles; products or product groups are sufficiently important to justify special attention.

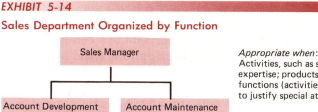

EXHIBIT 5-14

Sales Department Organized by Function

Sales Manager

Account Development Salespeople

Account Maintenance Salespeople

Appropriate when:
Activities, such as sales development, require special expertise; products are few in number and similar; functions (activities or jobs) are sufficiently important to justify special attention.

specialist has line authority over the salespeople handling his or her assigned function. Exhibit 5-14 depicts a simple sales department organized by function.

The cost effectiveness of a function-oriented organization for the sales department is questionable. Small companies would seldom find it practical to have such a high degree of labor specialization. In large organizations, however, it becomes extremely difficult to coordinate a function throughout the sales department because of the sheer size of the sales force. Furthermore, when several functional specialists have line authority over the salespeople, there is a strong likelihood of conflicts among the function managers plus confusion and frustration among members of the sales force. Nevertheless, International Minerals & Chemical Corporation successfully organized its agricultural business by marketing and production functions until it switched to a matrix structure a few years ago.

Market-Oriented Organizations

Market-oriented sales organizations are appropriate for companies whose products are purchased in multiple combinations by a variety of customer categories with unique needs. Aircraft manufacturers such as Boeing or Lockheed have different marketing efforts for their government and commercial markets. Similarly, electric utilities separate their markets into residential and commercial accounts.

Sales departments in many companies are organized by market or type of customer and are usually classified by industry, channel of distribution, or importance of the account (national or local). We have seen how different industries with unique needs can often be reached more successfully through a market-oriented sales structure, but the other two classifications—channel of distribution or account size—may be less obvious.

Organization by channel of distribution is appropriate when a company sells through several competing channels (such as drugstores, grocery stores, and discount houses) that apply distinct pricing strategies. Under these conditions, it may be advantageous to create separate sales units for each channel to reduce customer complaints and divided salesperson loyalties in dealing with such contrasting retail marketing philosophies.

Organization by national or key accounts is appropriate when a company's customers centralize buying at national or regional offices. Companies such as

grocery stores throughout the United States. Three regional sales managers report directly to Smith. Each region (western, central, and eastern) is composed of five districts headed by a district manager. The districts are divided into sales territories with size based on a consideration of sales potential and workload per salesperson (for example, New York City has only one territory, while the states of North Carolina, Georgia, and Florida are each separate territories). Each district manager is responsible for from one to eight territories composed of the independent brokers and their sales representatives. At the broker's level a total of 980 salespeople handle sales to the wholesale and retail clients for Hadley Foods, Inc. Wholesale salespeople call on the local offices of the major national and regional supermarket chains, with the retail salespeople calling on the independent grocery stores.

With the increased battle for shelf space in the grocery industry, a personal relationship between the sales representative and the buyer becomes significant. Not only is the sales representative competing for space with the other national brands, but he or she competes with the buyer's own private label and perhaps a generic brand, too. See Exhibit 2 for a detailed illustration of the sales organization for Hadley Foods, Inc.

This reliance on independent brokers to represent Hadley Foods follows a normally accepted recommendation for a small organization. It certainly allows for the sharing of costs of the sales force with other manufacturers, and with a straight 5 percent commission for sales, the variable expenses are directly related to sales. On the other hand, Hadley Foods has become dependent on brokers and the importance of the cheese line to each broker's profitability. In a highly competitive product environment great skill on the part of Hadley Foods managers and large resources in addition to commissions appear to be necessary to gain the broker sales representatives' attention to the cheese line. Hadley Foods views the sales increases in 1991 as due in part to an increased effort by the salespeople while the extra incentives were offered.

Looking to the Future

Mann calls in Smith to discuss the sales force. "Joe, with a year's experience as vice president you should have some opinion about the latest drop in sales. I need to know the positives you see in our current sales force setup, but I also hope you can evaluate it objectively. Headquarters wants me to get Hadley Foods on a sound financial footing. Could you work up a recommendation?"

"I've been waiting for six months to be asked to do just that," Smith responds. "It's obvious we have a product that is competitive provided it is priced right

---

EXHIBIT 3

Advertising and Promotion Expenditures

	Dollars (in millions)	As Percent of Sales
In 1992: Sales of $720 million		
Advertising	38,160	5.3
Promotion	23,040	3.2
Total	61,200	
In 1991: Sales of $1,220 million		
Advertising	87,840	7.2
Promotion	63,440	5.2
Total	151,280	

---

and has the necessary support from the promotion campaigns and the sales force. I'll leave the promotion and pricing problems alone except to emphasize that it is essential to have competitively priced products and an effective campaign to compete in this industry."

EXHIBIT 4

Cost of Sales

	Independent Reps	Company Sales Force
1992:		
Sales	$ 720,000,000	$ 720,000,000
Fixed costs	—	36,600,000*
Variable costs as percentage of sales (commissions)	6%	3%
Total variable costs	43,200,000	21,600,000
Total selling costs	43,200,000	58,200,000
1991:		
Sales	1,220,000,000	1,220,000,000
Fixed costs	—	36,600,000
Variable costs as percentage of sales (commissions)	6%	3%
Total variable costs (fixed and variable)	73,200,000	36,600,000
Total selling costs	73,200,000	73,200,000

*Includes managers' salaries, branch office expenses, base salaries of salespeople, and travel and entertainment expenses.

Now for the sales force—I'd like to meet with you again tomorrow with some figures."

Smith begins preparing the reports for the meeting. He projects that sales of $1.5 billion are needed to achieve an acceptable market share in the cheese industry. Advertising and promotion expenditures for the last two years are determined (Exhibit 3). Smith feels the percentage of sales spent for advertising and promotion in 1992 is appropriate for the food industry.

As he begins to compile the sales costs, Smith decides to contrast the costs of selling for the independent representatives with the costs of a company sales force (Exhibit 4). Switching to a new sales organization would be a dramatic step with a high degree of risk. But Smith sees it as a viable alternative, especially looking at the heavy campaign expenses that were required to generate the needed sales in 1991. "Could a company-owned sales force have accomplished those sales with the lower percentage of advertising and promotion expenditures in 1992?" he wonders. Smith's gut reaction is to change to a company-owned sales force, but he remembers Mann's emphasis on the need for objectivity.

Hadley Foods cannot survive with too many more years like 1992. Smith's recommendation, if accepted and successful, will ensure his success within Hadley Foods.

Questions

1. Prepare a chart for Smith's presentation that contrasts the two types of sales organizations. Show the advantages of each and the disadvantages of each.

2. Which of these two sales organizations would you recommend to Mann? Why?

3. If sales rise to $1.5 billion, which type of sales organization will have lower selling costs? If sales drop to $800 million, which type of sales organization will have lower selling costs?

4. Is there an optimal market share or sales volume Hadley Foods should strive for? Why or why not?

5. Comment on Hadley's current sales organization (Exhibit 2). Propose another alternative for the company. Defend your answer.

CASE 5-2

THE JERSEY PASTA COMPANY: IN NEED OF AN ORGANIZATIONAL STRUCTURE

The Jersey Pasta Company was started in 1979 by Anthony (Little Tony) Columbo in Hackensack, New Jersey. Little Tony had previously worked for Mama Corlini's restaurant for six years as an assistant to the chef and was made head chef in 1977. As head chef for Mama, Little Tony received many awards for his pasta and sauces and had several newspaper articles written about him. He became a celebrity in the restaurant business in the Hackensack area, and many of his friends and family members believed he should start a business to market his pasta and sauces. After much deliberation, Little Tony quit his job and put all his savings into the Jersey Pasta Company.

At first, Little Tony concentrated his efforts on establishing his business on a regional basis. He made all the pasta and sauces himself, while his brothers Vinnie and Franco called on grocery stores and supermarkets in the Jersey area. Sales of Little Tony's pasta and sauces were better than anyone expected. Many of the grocery store managers who purchased the pasta were quite taken by it and suggested that

Little Tony sell his products to national grocery store chains. Within two years after Little Tony started the company, his pasta and sauces were being sold in each of the forty-eight contiguous states.

Over the years, Little Tony added several new sauces and product lines to his menu of products. A line of pizzas, olive oil, spumoni, and spices soon carried the "Little Tony's" trade name. As the 1990s started, Little Tony was contemplating diversifying into nonfood products such as clothing, jewelry, and car-care products.

As owner of Jersey Pasta Company (JPC), Inc., Little Tony took great pride in closely managing the company himself. By the end of 1992, JPC had forty-two employees (whom Tony knew personally) and sales of $12 million. The company had twenty full-time sales personnel (four sales managers and sixteen salespeople), who were all from New Jersey. Each sales manager supervised approximately four salespeople and was responsible for selling all of JPC's products in a geographic area. While Little Tony was no longer

EXHIBIT

Jersey Pasta Company's Organization Chart

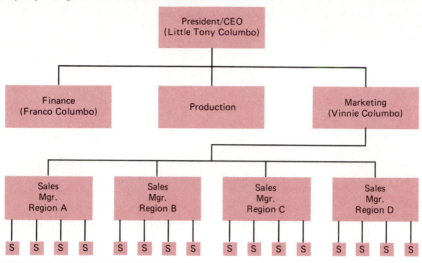

able to cook all the products, he closely supervised the production end of the business, as all products were made at the company headquarters in Hackensack.

Little Tony believes that quality control can be ensured only if he personally supervises the production of the products. While he remains active in the production, finance, and marketing areas of JPC, his brothers Vinnie and Franco have been put in charge of managing the financial and marketing activities of the company. A simplistic view of the organizational structure of JPC, Inc., is presented in the accompanying exhibit.

It is 1993, and as Little Tony takes a sip of Chianti, he once again ponders the thought of diversifying into nonfood products. His biggest question centers around his sales force. While the sales force does a good job now, he wonders what impact an additional product line or two in an unrelated area would have on the performance of his salespeople. Would hiring additional salespeople be the answer? What other prob-

lems might arise in attempting to market a line of Little Tony's clothing or car-care products? Several important sales force decisions must be made before the company can diversify into nonfood items.

Questions

1. How would you describe Little Tony's managerial philosophy?

2. Do you think a diversification strategy will work for JPC, given Little Tony's managerial style? Why or why not?

3. Comment on JPC's organizational structure for its sales force. Does it have any weaknesses? Any strengths?

4. Assume that JPC does diversify into nonfood products. Propose a new organizational structure (complete with organization chart) for the company. Thoroughly support your recommendation. Make Little Tony an offer he can't refuse!

REFERENCES

1. Personal interview with J. P. Downey, July 1990.
2. Max Weber, *The Theory of Social and Economic Organization,* A. M. Henderson and Talcott Parsons (trans.), Oxford University Press, New York, 1947.

3. H. H. Gerth and S. C. Wright Mills, "Characteristics of a Bureaucracy," in *From Max Weber*, Oxford University Press, London, 1946.

4. Henri Fayol, *General and Industrial Management*, Constance Storrs (trans.), Sir Isaac Pitman & Sons, London, 1949; Lyndall Urwick, *The Elements of Administration*, Sir Isaac Pitman & Sons, London, 1943; James D. Mooney and Alan C. Reiley, *The Principles of Organization*, Harper, New York, 1939.

5. Adapted from "Behind the Monolith: A Look at IBM," *Wall Street Journal*, Apr. 7, 1986, pp. 19–22.

6. Personal communication with Don Fisher, public affairs office, 3M Corporation, Sept. 7, 1986.

7. Personal communication with Jack Whiteman, public affairs manager, General Foods Corporation, Sept. 24, 1986.

8. Jerome A. Colletti and Gary S. Tubridy, "Effective Major Account Sales Management," *Journal of Personal Selling and Sales Management*, August 1987, pp. 1–10.

9. Richard L. Bencin, "Succeed in Telemarketing and Save Money," *Marketing Times*, January–February 1984, pp. 17–18. For more on telemarketing support of the sales force, see William C. Moncreif, Charles W. Lamb, Jr., and Terry Dielman, "Developing Telemarketing Support Systems," *Journal of Personal Selling and Sales Management*, August 1986, pp. 43–49.

10. John I. Coppett and Roy Dale Voorhees, "Telemarketing Supplement to Field Sales," *Industrial Marketing Management*, 1985, pp. 213–216.

11. "Industrial Newsletter," *Sales & Marketing Management*, Nov. 14, 1983, p. 32.

12. For various insights on determining the appropriate size and structure of the sales force, see C. D. Fogg and J. W. Rokus, "A Quantitative Method for Structuring a Profitable Sales Force," *Journal of Marketing*, July 1973, pp. 8–17; George N. Kagh, "Divide Your Sales Force to Multiply Sales," *Business Management*, October 1963, pp. 75–78; Leonard M. Lodish, "Vaguely Right Approach to Sales Force Allocations," *Harvard Business Review*, January–February 1974, pp. 119–134; A. Parasuraman and Ralph L. Day, "A Management-Oriented Model for Allocating Sales Effort," *Journal of Marketing Research*, February 1977, pp. 23–33; Robert F. Vizza, *Measuring the Value of the Field Sales Force*, Sales Executives Club of New York, New York, 1963, p. 25; Zarrel Lambert and Fred W. Kniffen, "Response Functions and Their Applications in Sales Force Management," *Southern Journal of Business*, January 1970, pp. 1–9; Zarrel V. Lambert, "Determining the Number of Salesmen to Employ: An Empirical Study," in Reed Moyer (ed.), *Changing Marketing Systems: Consumer, Corporate and Government Interfaces*, American Marketing Association, Chicago, 1967, pp. 338–341; Walter J. Semlow "How Many Salesmen Do You Need," *Harvard Business Review*, May–June 1959, pp. 126–132; Charles A. Beswick, "Allocating Selling Effort via Dynamic Programming," *Management Science*, March 1977, pp. 667–678; Ram C. Rao and Ronald E. Turner, "Organization and Effectiveness of the Multiple-Product Salesforce," *Journal of Personal Selling and Sales Management*, May 1984, pp. 24–30; Robert J. Zimmer and Paul S. Hugstad, "A Contingency Approach to Specializing an Industrial Sales Force," *Journal of Personal Selling and Sales Management*, Summer 1981, pp. 27–35.

13. Based on telephone conversation with Manufacturers' Agents National Association, June 1990.

PLANNING AND ORGANIZING THE CHEMCO SALES FORCE

Al Jorgenson, president of CHEMCO, has recently become quite concerned about the future of CHEMCO and, in particular, Division 2. While he is pleased that sales at CHEMCO have risen tremendously in the last several years, he recognizes that the rapid growth has brought with it a need for internal improvements. For example, the sales personnel have been so busy filling orders and servicing customers that they have had no time for planning.

Historically, on the rare occasions when planning or forecasting was done at CHEMCO, both sales divisions were treated as a single unit. Jorgenson had Dan Hager, vice president of sales, develop separate quarterly sales figures for each division. To the surprise of both men, Division 2 sales over the last several years have *not* increased to any great extent; in fact, they represent only a fraction of the company's total sales. Believing that it is time to start looking to the future, Jorgenson wants to develop some kind of planning framework for CHEMCO. He suggests that Dan Hager call a meeting of all regional and district sales managers to discuss strategic sales planning and forecasting.

As one of the regional sales managers for Division 2, you will be attending Hager's meeting next week. For this meeting, Hager wants you to give serious consideration to the lackluster sales at your division as well as to the future role Division 2 will play at CHEMCO.

This case was prepared by William Cunningham, University of South Alabama.

QUESTIONS

1. While overall company sales have risen sharply, Division 2 sales have been somewhat erratic. Suggest a sales planning approach that may help build stability for Division 2.

2. The diskette contains quarterly sales data for Division 2 from the first quarter of 1976 through the fourth quarter of 1992. (Sales data are given in thousands of dollars.)

   a. Using each of the three techniques—moving average, decomposition, and exponential smoothing—determine which technique is the best suited for use in forecasting sales. Discuss the pros and cons of each technique.

   b. Write a report in which you explain what a time-series decomposition analysis shows concerning sales. Be sure to include an explanation of seasonal, cyclical, and trend components. Plot the initial data, the deseasonalized data, and the long-term trend on a graph. Indicate the value of the seasonal indices. Also, plot the cycle factor projected through 1993.

   c. Use each of the three techniques to forecast for the four quarters of 1993 (or the next year). If actual values for each quarter were 1,898, 2,242, 2,247, and 2,231, which technique would have performed best?

   d. In light of Hager's request, can qualitative forecasting techniques be used for Division 2? Why or why not?

3. Could the lackluster performance of Division 2 be attributed to its organizational structure (see the Integrated Case for Part One)? Why or why not? What could some of the problems be?

   a. Suggest an alternative organizational structure for CHEMCO. Include both divisions in your recommendation.

   b. How will the sales force be organized in this organizational structure?

PART THREE

DEVELOPING THE SALES FORCE

6

RECRUITING THE SALES FORCE

LEARNING OBJECTIVES

When you finish this chapter, you should understand:

- ▲ The overall sales force recruiting process
- ▲ The legal rights of a sales applicant
- ▲ The difference between job analysis and job description
- ▲ The qualifications needed to fill a sales position
- ▲ Where organizations look to find qualified applicants

A DAY ON THE JOB

Edward A. Burch is a general agent for one of the most successful firms in the country—Northwestern Mutual Life. In fact, Northwestern Mutual agents are continually ranked among the most productive sales forces across all industries. Much of the success of Northwestern Mutual can be attributed to the company's recruiting system. "The professional sales manager in today's marketing environment must always be alert to the continuing necessity of recruiting and developing high-quality salespeople," says Burch. "In our industry we are particularly interested in someone becoming comfortable in a role as a counselor." Burch has had good success in recruiting by working with current clients and the college internship program. "We at Northwestern Mutual find that our greatest source of new recruits is referrals from our current clients and sales associates. They have had direct contact with the way we do business and know what it takes to be successful for the long-term career. Also, we have found that our college internship program has been particularly fruitful, as it has generated some of the top salespeople and sales managers in the company." When Burch is asked what's important in a new recruit, he lists "self-discipline, a desire to have ownership in a career, a need for continuing education, and the thrill of entrepreneurship."[1]

What do American Hospital Supply, AT&T, Penn State or Notre Dame football programs, and the Marine Corps have in common? They are all excellent recruiters. Their success is based primarily on the people they recruit and hire.

For many successful organizations it is the *people* who make the organization, and *recruiting* is the process of finding good people and ultimately selecting them for the organization. Recruiting is a critical activity for sales managers if they are to have a successful selling team.

New forces are reshaping the recruiting process in the 1990s. Recruiters in all functional areas of business will see the pool of qualified candidates shrinking throughout the decade because of changing demographics. The number of Americans between the ages of 18 and 24 is projected to decrease 17.5 percent by 1995. This statistic poses a very discouraging picture to recruiters, as historically this age group accounts for the largest number of college graduates. Moreover, the demand for college graduates is expected to increase dramatically during the 1990s. Therefore, sales managers will see greater competition for fewer qualified candidates.

THE IMPORTANCE OF RECRUITING

Sales force recruitment has always been one of the most important responsibilities of the sales manager because to most customers and prospects the salespeople are the company. What the salespeople say, how they handle themselves, and how they react in face-to-face interactions with customers definitely influence the firm's sales success.

Over the years sales force recruitment has become even more important. One reason is that the cost of hiring and training has increased dramatically. The other is that equal employment opportunity (EEO) legislation has made hiring and termination decisions more complicated and more difficult. Because of the critical importance of recruiting, sales managers should have an effective system for finding and selecting sales personnel.

An effective selection program cannot exist without a well-planned and well-operated system for recruiting applicants. A poor recruiting system may force an organization to hire people who do not actually meet its needs, because the recruiting system has not generated enough qualified applicants and a selection must be made immediately from the available applicants.

In many firms, recruiting must be continuous to combat the problem of high turnover. A recent survey of various industrial and retail organizations reported turnover rates from 11.6 to 45.8 percent, and the average turnover rate for all industry groups in this survey was 17.3 percent.[2]

The importance of planned recruiting is even more obvious when the costs associated with selecting and training salespeople are examined. Direct costs, such as maintaining recruiting teams and placing recruiting advertisements, are increasing rapidly. Exhibit 6-1 shows that 61 percent of all companies spend $1,500 or more on recruiting and hiring each new salesperson, and some firms spend as much as $25,000! James W. Kerley, a second vice president with New England Mutual Life Insurance, estimates that the loss of one salesperson because of a poor selection decision can cost a company $75,000 or more when the effort and expense of selecting, training, developing, and managing are calculated.[3] Management should view the recruitment and selection process as a subsystem of sales force management and evaluate it in terms of total cost. With this approach, the recruiting activities can be optimized to reduce the total cost of selecting and developing new salespeople to the point where their productivity is profitable.

Specific approaches and procedures that sales managers may use at various phases of the recruitment process are covered in this chapter. The focus is on "how to do it" from the sales manager's perspective. However, some of the material will be useful to you in learning what is expected when you apply for a sales position.

EXHIBIT 6-1

How Much Companies Spend on Recruiting and Hiring

Amount per Salesperson	Percentage of Companies
$500 or less	13.4
$501 to $1,500	25.8
$1,501 to $3,000	26.9
$3,001 to $5,000	18.3
$5,001 to $10,000	10.8
More than $10,000	4.8

Source: "Trends in Recruitment and Selection," Working Paper No. 87-2, Department of Marketing, Louisiana State University, January 1987.

Sales Jobs in the 1990s

The sales job of today is different from the sales job of the past. The old type of aggressive, hard-hitting salesperson is no longer typical, and the talents associated with this type are generally not sought after in the present economy. Instead, a new type of salesperson has emerged, one who is concerned with relaying customer wants back to the firm so that appropriate products can be developed. Contemporary salespeople engage in marketing, from missionary selling to training, and serve as very important sources of communication to the firm by feeding back marketing intelligence.

The salespeople of today have more responsibilities than ever before. They fill many roles, including territory manager, service supplier, information gatherer, persuader, expediter, problem definer, traveler, display arranger, and customer consultant. Their work is independent of the usual worker-boss relationship, and they often interact with groups that have different and conflicting expectations of the salesperson. In short, salespeople in the 1990s perform many functions that are similar to those of the marketing or sales manager. The major difference is that salespeople are responsible only for managing their own activities, not for managing the sales force.

Demand for Salespeople in the 1990s

Demand for salespeople increased substantially during the late 1980s. Today, many companies are not only maintaining the size of their sales forces but increasing them. The major reason for this trend, despite predictions that some areas of the economy may slow down, is that there is a shortage of young people who are interested in sales positions. This means not only a continued demand for qualified salespeople but an increase in the salaries being offered to persons entering the field of selling. The example that follows describes a few of the factors that organizations consider when they are hiring.

WHAT RECRUITERS LOOK FOR IN SALESPEOPLE

An applicant's attitude is a very important factor to recruiters. For example, the manager of training and recruiting for Xerox said: "We don't look at [recruits'] grades per se. More important to us is their capability, their demonstrated attitudes." Moreover, several psychologists have argued that recruiters err when they put intelligence ahead of personality in assessing a candidate for a sales position.[4]

The clothing an applicant wears is another important factor to recruiters. According to a Connecticut-based recruiter, "women have more leeway" than men when it comes to what they wear to a sales interview. However, "Man or woman, when it comes to clothing, discretion and understatement should be your guiding rule."[5]

Most recruiters claim they prefer candidates who have the confidence and maturity to "control" an interview, but some perceive assertiveness as being too dominant or pushy.

A recruiter at Korn Ferry International believes that while recruiters appreciate frankness, they back off when candidates discuss their work experience in emotional terms. "A lot of people are losing their jobs because of all the recent buyouts and mergers. But women [more often than men] take these matters too personally. When they come in, they tend to focus on negatives—the emotional side of things—instead of their background and achievements. It's best not to show your feelings during a professional situation."[6]

WHAT IS RECRUITMENT?

Recruitment is finding potential job applicants, telling them about the company, and getting them to apply. Recruiting efforts should not simply generate applicants; rather, it should find applicants who are potentially good employees. The entire sales organization ultimately depends on a successful recruiting approach.

The Law and Recruitment

Under civil rights law, certain groups of people are protected (blacks, those with Spanish surnames, Asians, native Americans, and women). Any questions asked of protected classes of people in recruitment must pass several tests:

1. Will the answers to a question tend to screen out minorities or women? They must not.

2. Is the inquiry really necessary to determine an applicant's competence or qualifications for the job at hand? It must be!

3. Does the question have the effect, directly or indirectly, of limiting job opportunity for protected people? If it does, it cannot be asked.

ETHICS IN SALES MANAGEMENT: PLAYING THE RECRUITING GAME

Your company uses a two-person team approach to recruit sales applicants. When visiting college campuses, two sales managers sit in on the initial employment interview and individually evaluate the applicant. You have been paired with a very successful veteran sales manager. After several interviews you noticed that he always brings up sports, in particular, golfing, during the interview. At first you assumed the sports questions were a form of "ice breaker" and a good way to build rapport with the college recruits. However, you've come to realize that your partner rates applicants poorly if they are not avid golfers and/or sports enthusiasts. This is particularly upsetting to you, as several of the recruits whom you evaluated very highly were rejected by the veteran sales manager. You feel that you really don't want to question his ability as a recruiter. However, you are concerned that if your evaluations of the recruits are continually different from those of the successful veteran, your own career may be jeopardized.

1. What do you do?
2. If you confront the veteran sales manager, could there be any negative outcomes? Any positive ones?
3. Are any legal ramifications possible as a result of the veteran sales manager's actions?

In addition, various other civil rights laws and regulations cover age, national origin, handicap, and religion. In fact, there are such a large number of laws and government agencies concerned with the area of equal employment opportunity that it is easy for sales managers or others involved in hiring to get into trouble unless they are very careful. Exhibit 6-2 provides a brief overview of what sales managers can and cannot do during the recruiting process. EEO laws and regulations are very important and must be observed throughout the entire hiring process.

While laws and regulations continue to play a major role in recruiting, ethical issues may also surface. The *Ethics* scenario on page 203 represents a possible ethical issue facing sales managers during the recruiting process.

Who Does the Recruiting?

There is no pat answer to this question. Actual practice will vary from one firm to another. Factors such as company size, departmental organization, and ex-

---

EXHIBIT 6-2

What Interviewers Can and Cannot Do

Subject	Can Do or Ask	Cannot Do or Ask
Sex	Notice appearance	Make comments or notes unless sex is a bona fide occupational qualification
Marital status	Ask status after hiring, for insurance purposes	Are you married? Single? Divorced? Engaged? Are you living with anyone? Do you see your ex-spouse?
Children	Ask numbers and ages of children after hiring, for insurance purposes	Do you have children at home? Who will look after your child while working? Do you plan to have more children?
Physical data	Explain manual labor, lifting, other requirements of the job; show how they are performed. Require physical exam.	How tall are you? How heavy?
Medical history	Consider applicants as they presently exist	Medical history of applicants in the past
Criminal record	If security clearance is necessary, can be done prior to employment	Have you ever been arrested, been convicted, or spent time in jail?
Military status	Are you a veteran? Any job-related experience?	What type of discharge do you have? What branch did you serve in?
Age	Ask age after hiring. Are you over 18?	How old are you? Estimate age.
Housing	If you have no phone, how can we reach you?	Do you own your home? Do you rent? Do you live in an apartment or a house?

Source: "Let's Not Shake on It," *Sales & Marketing Management*, May 14, 1984, pp. 47–51, and "Personnel Business," *Business Week*, May 26, 1975, p. 77.

EXHIBIT 6-3

Who Recruits and Hires Salespeople

Individual	Percentage of Companies
Regional or district manager	47.9
First-level sales manager	44.8
National sales manager	39.1
Campus recruiter	8.3
Personnel manager	4.2
Vice president of sales	4.2
Sales trainer	3.2
President or CEO	3.1
Outside agency	2.9
Other	5.7

Source: "Trends in Recruitment and Selection," *Working Paper No. 87-2*, Department of Marketing, Louisiana State University, January 1987.

ecutives' personalities will influence who does the recruiting. In some companies, such as Procter & Gamble and Burroughs, the sales manager is given the prime responsibility for recruitment of sales personnel. In others, such as American Hospital Supply, the personnel manager and the sales manager work jointly. As shown in Exhibit 6-3, the most common situation is for the sales manager—either at the local, regional, or national level—to be primarily responsible for recruiting and hiring salespeople. Exhibit 6-4, which shows who interviews potential recruits, indicates that personnel managers and higher-level sales executives are most involved in the interviewing process.

EXHIBIT 6-4

Who Interviews Potential Recruits

Individual	Percentage of Companies
Regional or district manager	59.4
First-level sales manager	50.5
National sales manager	48.4
Personnel manager	41.1
Sales trainer	22.9
Campus recruiter	11.5
Vice president of sales	9.4
Outside agency	6.8
President or CEO	5.8
General manager	1.6
Marketing manager	1.6
Store manager	1.6

Source: "Trends in Recruitment and Selection," *Working Paper No. 87-2*, Department of Marketing, Louisiana State University, January 1987.

A description of the recruiting process at Emery Worldwide follows.

RECRUITING SALESPEOPLE AT EMERY WORLDWIDE

Emery Worldwide has a unique recruiting process. Both the sales manager and the sales supervisor take part in recruiting salespeople. The sales supervisor does the initial screening of applicants by going through the résumés the company receives and pulling out the ones that have the most potential. The sales manager then does the same thing. Later, both the sales manager and the sales supervisor get together to discuss the applicants that each has chosen. Usually their choices are similar. After they discuss the applicants, the sales supervisor begins the screening process.

First, he or she looks at each applicant's background. Emery has certain requirements: past sales experience and a business degree. When applicants are selected and come in for the initial interview, their overall appearance and the way they conduct themselves are carefully scrutinized. Eye contact, self-control, and the like, are very important during the screening process. Emery also tries to get a general idea of applicants' organizational skills—how they organize themselves and how they would organize a sales week from their current position. Emery personnel ask applicants a lot of general questions to see how well they can communicate. An interviewer can usually tell within the first twenty minutes if the applicant will work well in the system.

Emery does most of its recruiting from advertising. Before it advertises an open position, Emery posts the position within the company so that current employees can apply first. Then it considers applications generated by advertisements. Emery may or may not consider applicants from competitors. Additionally, Emery does not do much recruiting from college campuses. Very few college graduates have the experience Emery is looking for. Emery does, however, have courier programs on college campuses. These programs combine sales and services at an entry-level position. All interviewing is done one-on-one; there are no group or panel interviews. After the sales manager interviews the applicants, a decision is made. References are rarely used until a job offer is about to be made.[7]

THE RECRUITMENT PROCESS

Previous research comparing sales aptitude and job performance with the sales recruit's personal characteristics has not identified any single set of characteristics or abilities that can be used by the sales manager in determining which recruits to hire for sales positions. Different activities must be performed for different types of sales positions. Therefore, each recruit's personality characteristics and abilities must be assessed to determine which type of sales job, if any, a particular recruit is suited for.

To ensure that new recruits have the aptitude necessary to be successful in a particular type of sales job, certain procedures should be followed in the recruitment process. The steps in this process are depicted in Exhibit 6-5.

Newly established firms or divisions will have to go through each of these steps. Existing firms should have completed the first three steps, but many have not. This is a major reason many firms are ineffective in recruitment and selection and ultimately suffer a turnover problem. Firms that have written job descriptions and qualifications need to review them from time to time to ensure that they

EXHIBIT 6-5

The Recruitment Process

accurately represent the current scope and activities of sales positions. Attracting recruits is usually an ongoing task of the sales manager, particularly in large or growing companies. The last step, evaluating and selecting recruits, will be discussed in detail in the next chapter.

Conducting a Job Analysis

Before a company can search for a particular type of salesperson, it must know something about the sales job to be filled. To aid in the process, a job analysis should be conducted to identify the duties, requirements, responsibilities, and conditions involved in the job. A proper job analysis involves these steps:

1. Analyze the environment in which the salesperson is to work. For example:
   a. What is the nature of the competition faced by the salesperson in this job?
   b. What is the nature of the customers to be contacted, and what kinds of problems do they have?
   c. What degree of knowledge, skill, and potential is needed for this particular position?

2. Determine the duties and responsibilities that are expected from the salesperson. In so doing, information should be obtained from (a) salespeople; (b) customers; (c) the sales manager; and (d) other marketing executives, including the advertising manager, marketing services manager, distribution manager, marketing research director, and credit manager

3. Spend time making calls with several salespeople, observing and recording the various tasks of the job as they are actually performed. This should be done for a variety of different types of customers and over a representative period of time.

Preparing a Job Description

The result of a formal job analysis is a job description. Since a job description is used in recruiting, selecting, training, compensating, and evaluating the sales force, the description should be in writing so that it can be referred to frequently. The written job description lets prospective job applicants, as well as current sales personnel, know exactly what the duties and responsibilities of the sales position are and on what basis the new employee will be evaluated.

The job description is probably the most important single tool used in managing the sales force. It is used not only in hiring but also in managing, and sometimes as a basis for firing, salespeople. It provides the sales trainer with a description of the salespeople's duties and enables him or her to develop training programs that will help salespeople perform their duties better. Job descriptions are also used in developing compensation plans. Often, the type of job determines the type of compensation plan that will be used. Job descriptions aid managers in supervision and motivation, and they are used as an official document that is part of the contract between management and a salesperson's union. Finally, a job description puts management in a position to determine whether each salesperson has a reasonable workload.

Since the job description is used in evaluating the salesperson's performance, many of the responsibilities listed in it must be stated in quantitative terms. For example, the number and frequency of sales calls by type of customer class, the number and types of reports to be turned in, and the number of sales promotion displays to be set up should all be included in the job description. In addition, since there are so many tasks competing for the salesperson's time, job priorities should be summarized in the job description.

Sales industry experts point out that many job descriptions are so brief and ambiguously written that they are of little use in the hiring process. Thus, it is very important that firms prepare job descriptions they can use effectively. Exhibit 6-6 shows a checklist that can be used by the sales manager in preparing a job description. It is organized into six major categories: sales activities, servicing functions, territory management, sales promotion, executive activities, and goodwill.

Job descriptions should be developed for sales managers, too. Their purpose is similar to that of job descriptions for salespeople; that is, they are used for recruiting, selecting, training, compensating, and evaluating sales managers. Exhibit 6-7 shows a checklist for preparing a sales manager's job description.

Developing a Set of Job Qualifications

The duties and responsibilities set forth in the job description should be converted into a set of qualifications that a recruit should have in order to perform the sales job satisfactorily. Determining these qualifications is probably the most difficult aspect of the entire recruitment process. One reason is that the manager is dealing with human beings; therefore, a multitude of subjective and very complex characteristics are involved. Specific qualifications such as education and experience should be included in the job description, thus making good candidates easier to identify. But most firms also try to identify personality traits that presumably make better salespersons, such as self-confidence, aggressiveness, and gregariousness.

Personality traits. Although many studies have attempted to determine which qualifications are most important for a sales position, none have developed an ideal list. A classic study by two industrial psychologists suggested that a successful salesperson needs only two personality traits: empathy and ego drive.[8] "Empathy" was defined as the ability to "feel as the other fellow does." Thus, empathic feeling provides feedback from the client, which enables the sales-

EXHIBIT 6-6

Checklist for Preparing a Salesperson's Job Description

Sales Activities

Make regular calls.

Sell the product or product line.

Handle questions and objections.

Check stock; identify possible product uses.

Interpret sales points or products to the customer.

Estimate customer's potential needs.

Emphasize quality.

Explain company policy on price, delivery, and credit.

Get the order.

Servicing Functions

Install the product or display.

Report product weaknesses and complaints.

Handle adjustments, returns, and allowances.

Handle requests for credit.

Handle special orders.

Establish priorities.

Analyze local conditions for customers.

Territory Management

Arrange route for best coverage.

Maintain sales portfolios, samples, kits, etc.

Balance effort with customers against the potential volume.

Sales Promotion

Develop new prospects and accounts.

Distribute literature, catalogs, etc.

Make calls with customer's salespeople.

Train personnel of wholesalers, jobbers, etc.

Present survey reports, layouts, and proposals.

Executive Activities

Develop monthly and weekly work plan.

Each night make a daily work plan for the next day.

Organize field activity for minimum travel and maximum calls.

Prepare and submit special reports on trends and competition.

Prepare and submit statistical data requested by home office.

Investigate lost sales and reason for loss.

Prepare reports on developments, trends, new objectives met, and new ideas on meeting objectives.

Attend sales meetings.

Build a prospect list.

Collect overdue accounts; report on faulty accounts.

Collect credit information.

Analyze work plans to determine which goals were not met and why.

Goodwill

Counsel customers on their problems.

Maintain loyalty and respect for the company.

Attend local sales meetings held by customers.

EXHIBIT 6-7

Checklist for Preparing a Sales Manager's Job Description

Executive Activities

Prepare annual sales budget (sales forecast).
Prepare annual sales expense budget.
Organize sales, service functions for productivity.
Recruit sales personnel.
Hire sales personnel.
Terminate sales personnel; conduct exit interviews.
Develop sales training programs.
Assign sales personnel to sales territories.
Recommend changes in the sales compensation package.

Analyze customers, sales territories, and total sales by:
  Total dollars of gross profit
  Percentage of gross profit
  Dollars of gross profit and percentage of gross profit for all product groups and by major account types (market segments)
Take action when analysis indicates negative variation from sales budget (forecast).
Prepare and submit written sales reports.

Areas of Information Exchange

Participate as a member of the marketing management team (or management team).
Direct the efforts of the sales team.
Develop the efforts of the sales team.
Develop product knowledge training programs.

Recommend personnel for promotion.
Assist in developing control procedures for other departments that interface with sales.
Share competitive price and quality information with other departments.

Interpersonal Relationships

Establish a productive working environment.
Set sales goals with sales personnel.
Counsel sales personnel and other immediate subordinates.

Evaluate salesperson performance.
Prepare qualified subordinates for promotion.
Report to marketing manager (branch manager, general manager, or owner).

Measurable Performance Standards

	Budgeted	Actual	Over/Under
Dollars of gross profit	_____	_____	_____
Percentages of gross profit	_____	_____	_____
Dollars of gross profit and percentage gross profit by major product group:			
Group 1	_____	_____	_____
Group 2	_____	_____	_____
Total sales volume by major account type:			
Type 1	_____	_____	_____
Type 2	_____	_____	_____
Sales expense budget:			
Amount	_____	_____	_____
As percentage of sales	_____	_____	_____
Credit expense budget:			
Amount	_____	_____	_____
As percentage of sales	_____	_____	_____

Self-Evaluation

Conduct a personal time analysis.
Attend training seminars.
Examine and revise job descriptions annually.

Keep current with new developments in field of sales management.

Source: Adapted from B. Robert Anderson, Professional Sales Management, Prentice-Hall, Englewood Cliffs, N.J., 1981, pp. 26–27.

person to adjust the selling message and to do whatever is necessary to close the sale. Ego drive makes the salesperson want and need to make the sale "in a personal or ego way, not merely for the money." The sale then becomes a conquest and a powerful means of enhancing the ego. As a result, the salesperson has the drive and need to make the sale, and empathy gives him or her the connecting tool with which to do it. These findings are consistent with the philosophy of Eastman Kodak of Rochester, New York, whose personnel manager indicates that they search for sales recruits with self-confidence, job commitment, persistence, and initiative in solving problems, gathering information, and asking direct questions.

One of the best-known studies of what it takes to be a successful salesperson was conducted by McMurry and Arnold.[9] They observed that "supersalespeople" have an inherent flair for winning the acceptance of others, but many have failed to grow up emotionally and are constantly attempting to gain acceptance and affection. Six attributes of successsful salespeople identified in their study were a high level of energy, self-confidence, a persistent hunger for money, ability to work hard without close supervision, a habit for perseverance, and a natural tendency to be competitive. Another study by Charles Garfield found that successful salespeople are goal-directed risktakers who identify strongly with their customers. Details of this study follow.

WHAT MAKES A SUPERSALESPERSON?

Charles Garfield, clinical professor of psychology at the University of California, San Francisco School of Medicine, claims his twenty-year analysis of more than 1,500 superachievers in every field of endeavor is the longest running to date. . . .Garfield says that the complexity and speed of change in today's business world means that to be a peak performer in sales requires greater mastery of different fields than to be one in science, sports, or the arts. The following are the most common characteristics he has found in peak sales performers:

- Supersalespeople are always taking risks and making innovations. Unlike most people, they stay out of the "comfort zone" and try to surpass their previous levels of performance.

- Supersalespeople have a powerful sense of mission and set the short-, intermediate-, and long-term goals necessary to fulfill that mission. Their personal goals are always higher than the sales quotas set by their managers, especially if the managers also are interested in peak performance.

- Supersalespeople are more interested in solving problems than in placing blame or bluffing their way out of situations. Because they view themselves as professionals in training, they are always upgrading their skills.

- Supersalespeople see themselves as partners with their customers, and as team players rather than adversaries. Peak performers believe their task is to communicate with people, while mediocre salespeople psychologically change their customers into objects and talk about the number of calls and closes they made as if it had nothing to do with human beings.

- Supersalespeople take each rejection as information they can learn from, whereas mediocre people personalize rejection.

> • The most surprising finding is that, like peak performers in sports and the arts, supersalespeople use mental rehearsal. Before every sale they review it in their mind's eye, from shaking the customer's hand when they walk in to discussing his problems and asking for the order.[10]

In a recent survey, sales executives of leading U.S. corporations were asked what they look for in new salespeople. One of the major conclusions of the survey was that "today's salesperson simply doesn't match the popular concept of a salesperson as a fast-talking, joke-telling, bundle of personality." The typical salesperson is likely to be an ambitious, enthusiastic, and well-organized person who is highly persuasive and has solid sales experience. Moreover, high-performing salespeople are those who:

1. Demonstrate a firm commitment to customer satisfaction

2. Maintain two-way advocacy, representing the interest of their companies and their clients

3. Bring added value to the sales task with their enthusiasm, sensitive interpersonal skills, and sense of professionalism

4. Tend to intellectualize the sales process, actively planning and developing strategies that will maximize their impact on the customer's time and provide efficient internal support relationships

5. Are committed to a "sales way of life"

6. Are highly time-conscious[11]

As would be expected, these are the qualities executives value most in sales applicants. Exhibit 6-8 shows the critical characteristics sought by a *Fortune* 500

EXHIBIT 6-8

Critical Characteristics and Behaviors of Sales Recruits

- *Intelligence.* Evident in verbal expression, depth of response, analytical thought process.
- *Decisiveness.* When asked, makes definite choices, lets you know where he or she stands on issues, is not tentative.
- *Energy and Enthusiasm.* Is animated, positive, spontaneous, fast-paced.
- *Results orientation.* Gets to the point, emphasizes achievement; responses are relevant to interview objectives.
- *Maturity.* Shows poise, self-confidence, and maturity in dress, general demeanor, and degree of relaxation.
- *Assertiveness.* Takes charge, is forceful, convincing, persuasive.
- *Sensitivity.* Is sincere, friendly, tactful, responsive, not aloof.
- *Openness.* Responses are not canned and superficial.
- *Tough-mindedness.* Discusses persons and events critically; doesn't allow emotions to cloud perceptions.

corporation in the health care industry. Using a three-point scale, the company evaluates candidates on college campuses in terms of these characteristics, and only those who score medium or higher are invited to follow-up interviews at the company.

Levels of qualification.   By knowing what the job really consists of, the sales manager has a good idea of the qualifications that a person should have to fill the position. A person who is overqualified will generally not be happy in a position that offers little challenge. On the other hand, a person who is in over his or her head usually will not succeed. In determining the type of person who will be sought for the sales position, the sales manager should keep in mind certain characteristics of selling and salespeople:

- *Travel, sometimes overnight.* Most sales positions involve some kind of travel, and many involve overnight trips. People who are to be successful in sales must have no major reservations about travel or overnight trips.

- *Supervision.* Few sales jobs involve close supervision. The salesperson is in the field, traveling from one account to another, and may have contact with the home office or sales manager only every two or three days. Salespersons are, in effect, their own boss, determining what time to get up in the morning and start work and what time to go home. To be successful, a salesperson must be a self-starter and have a great deal of self-discipline.

- *Little work experience.* People who enter sales generally have little or no work experience. Therefore, their success on the job is very hard to predict. Equally as difficult is the attempt to match the job description to the individual with no track record.

- *High turnover.* As a result of the above conditions, high employee turnover is typically found in sales. Many people change from job to job, while others exit from the sales profession after only a short period of time.

Job qualifications should specifically spell out the characteristics and abilities a person must have in order to carry out the requirements of the sales position. For example, a prospective salesperson might need any or all of the following qualifications: two years of college, at least four years of work experience, ability to make decisions under stress, specific product knowledge, and a car and the ability to travel.

The task of the sales manager (or job analyst) is to decide which qualifications are most important for a particular sales position. Since the sales manager will seldom find recruits with all the most important qualifications, some consideration must also be given to trade-offs among various qualifications. For instance, can enthusiasm and high ambition be substituted for relatively poor verbal skills? The answer to such questions will depend on the nature of the sales job and the extent to which the firm can train the recruit to overcome weaknesses.

There is no one satisfactory method for every company to use in determining the qualifications of sales recruits. The logical starting point, however, is the job description. If the sales position requires technical or analytical skills, then a specific educational background or work experience may be necessary. Also, sales positions that involve little supervision may necessitate hiring a mature, experienced person.

Models for success.   Companies that have been in business for several years and have a large sales force usually analyze personal histories of present and past salespeople to determine job qualifications. A comparison of the characteristics of good, average, and poor salespeople will suggest traits that can predict success in a sales career with the company. In the past this approach was used in a haphazard manner. The sales manager would audit a few personal histories, interject situations that he or she recalled, and develop a profile. Today, however, firms are beginning to organize this information into computerized data files and to develop statistical models to differentiate high performers from low performers. Sophisticated models incorporating the unique characteristics of salespeople who failed or were fired can also be developed.

In the future, sales managers will increasingly rely on these sophisticated computerized models because they improve the manager's ability to recruit qualified individuals. But equally important, they help the firm validate the selection criteria being used, and validation is required by government regulations on equal employment opportunity in hiring.

Scanner computer systems have now made it financially possible for new or small companies to use personal histories to determine important job qualifications. For some companies, an outside organization, such as a consulting firm specializing in personnel services or a similar but noncompeting firm, may help in establishing job qualifications.

Attracting a Pool of Applicants

The next major step in the recruitment and selection process is attracting a pool of applicants for the sales position to be filled. All large companies with a sales force have a continuous need to identify, locate, and attract potentially effective salespeople. The candidates recruited become the reserve pool of sales staff from which new salespeople will be chosen. The quality of this group will predict the future successes or problems of the sales organization.

The importance of starting with a large pool of applicants cannot be overemphasized. If there are too few applicants, the probability is high that a person with inferior selling abilities will be hired. When a large number of applicants are processed, the recruiting program serves as an automatic screening system. However, management must avoid bypassing potentially successful salespeople at the recruiting stage. Sales managers should be aware of this problem and be careful not to screen out good candidates. The interviewing process is one screening device; others are the recruiting sources used, such as the colleges visited or the newspapers in which ads are placed. An advertisement in the *Wall Street Journal,* for example, will attract a different type of recruit than would an ad in a daily newspaper.

Recruiting is not equally important in all firms. The quality of salespeople needed, the rate of turnover expected, and a firm's financial position are just a few of the factors that account for the difference. When higher-caliber salespeople are needed, a greater number of applicants must be screened before one is found who meets the hiring specifications. With firms that experience a high turnover in the sales force, a continuous recruiting program is required. Firms that are financially stable may be able to employ traveling recruiting teams, whereas financially troubled firms may rely heavily on advertisements.

SOURCES OF SALESPEOPLE

There are many places a sales manager can go to find recruits. Sales managers should analyze each potential source to determine which ones will produce the best recruits for the sales position to be filled. Once good sources are identified, sales managers should maintain a continuing relationship with them, even during periods when no hiring is being done. Good sources are hard to find, and goodwill must be established between the firm and the source to ensure good recruits in the future.

Some firms will use only one source; others will use several. The most frequently used sources are persons within the company, competitors, noncompeting companies, educational institutions, advertisements, and employment agencies.

Persons within the Company

Companies often recruit salespeople from other departments, such as production or engineering, and from the nonselling section of the sales department. The people are already familiar with company policies as well as the technical aspects of the product itself. The chance of finding good salespeople within the company should be excellent because sales managers know the people and are aware of their sales potential. In fact, most firms turn to nonsales personnel within the company as their first source of new sales recruits.

Hiring people from within the company can lift morale because a transfer to sales is often viewed as a promotion. But transferring outstanding workers from the plant or office into the sales department does not guarantee success. In some cases hostility can arise among plant and office supervisors, who feel their personnel are being taken by the sales department.

Recommendations from the present sales force and sales executives usually yield better prospects than those of other employees because the people in sales understand the needed qualifications.

Competitors

Salespeople recruited from a competitor are trained, have experience selling similar products to similar markets, and should be ready to sell almost immediately. But usually a premium must be paid in order to attract them from their present jobs.

Some sales managers are reluctant to hire competitors' salespeople because the practice is sometimes viewed as unethical. But is it? Is it really any different than attempting to take a competitor's customers or market share? No. But it is unethical if the salesperson uses valuable confidential information in competing against the former employer.

Recruiting competitors' salespeople may bring other problems. Although these people are highly trained and know the market and the product very well, it is often hard for them to unlearn old practices. They may not be compatible with the new organization and management. Also, recruits from a competitor usually are expected to switch their customers to the new business; if they are unable to do so, their new employer may be disappointed.

The potential for these problems to arise may be evaluated with one question: Why is this person leaving the present employer? A satisfactory answer to this question frequently clears up many doubts and usually leads to a valuable employee. The difficulty arises, however, in determining the real answer. Often, it is almost impossible to assess accurately why someone is looking for another job. Good sales managers must be able to evaluate effectively the information they get.

Noncompeting Companies

Noncompeting firms can provide a good source of trained and experienced salespeople, especially if they are selling similar products or selling to the same market. Even though some recruits may be unfamiliar with the recruiting firm's product line, they do have selling experience and require less training.

Companies that are either vendors or customers of the recruiting firm can also be an excellent source of candidates. Recruits from these sources already have some knowledge of the company from having sold to or purchased from it; their familiarity reduces the time it will take to make them productive employees. Another advantage of recruits from these sources is that they are already familiar with the industry.

Educational Institutions

High schools, adult evening classes, business colleges, vocational schools, junior colleges, and universities are all excellent sources of sales recruits. Large firms usually are successful in recruiting from universities, but small firms tend to be more successful in recruiting from small educational institutions or from other sources.

While most college graduates lack specific sales experience, they have the education and perspective that most employers seek in potential sales managers. College graduates tend to adapt more easily than experienced personnel. They have not yet developed any loyalties to a firm or an industry. As a rule, they have acquired certain social graces, are more mature than a person of the same age without college training, and have developed their ability to think logically and express themselves reasonably well.

A major problem in recruiting from college campuses used to be the unfavorable image of sales. Selling typically was associated with job insecurity, low status, and lack of creativity, but this situation has been changing in recent years.

College graduates are beginning to realize that selling provides challenge and a sense of accomplishment, that it is complex and exciting, that it allows them to be creative, that it rewards them well and in direct proportion to their level of achievement, and that it provides opportunity for rapid advancement. In short, many students today know that a sales career is a good use of a college education.

Small firms are less likely to recruit on college campuses because many graduates prefer large, well-known corporations with training programs and company benefits. College students tend to avoid small companies because these companies usually employ few college graduates, and students are afraid that people without college degrees will not understand or appreciate their needs and expectations.

Advertisements

Classified advertisements in newspapers and trade journals are another source of recruits. National newspapers such as the *Wall Street Journal* and various trade journals are used in recruiting for high-caliber sales and sales management positions. However, most firms that use advertising, especially in local newspapers, are recruiting for low-level sales positions. Many businesses use advertising only as a last resort.

While advertisements reach a large audience, the caliber of the average applicant is often second-rate. This places a burden on those doing the initial screening. The quality of applicants recruited by advertisements can be increased by carefully selecting the type of media and describing the job qualifications specifically in the ad. To be effective, a recruiting ad must attract attention and have credibility. The following elements should be included to ensure an ad's effectiveness: company name; product; territory; hiring qualifications; compensation plan, expense plan, and fringe benefits; and the way to contact the employer.

Employment Agencies

Employment agencies are among the best and the worst sources. Most of the time it depends on the relationship between the agency and the sales manager. The agency should be carefully selected, and a good working relationship must be developed. Sales managers should make sure that the agency clearly understands both the job description and the job qualifications for the position to be filled.

In recent years agencies have steadily improved and expanded their services. They can provide a highly useful service to sales managers by screening candidates so that recruiters may spend more time with those prospects who are most highly qualified for the job.

Factors to Consider in Evaluating Sources

The recruiting effort differs substantially from company to company. Some of the factors management should consider when deciding which recruiting sources to use are:

- *Nature of the product.* A highly technical product requires an experienced, knowledgeable person. The firm may look at persons in its own production department or at experienced persons from other companies.

- *Nature of the market.* Experienced salespeople may be needed to deal with well-informed purchasing agents or with high-level executives.

- *Policy on promoting from within.* If this policy is the rule, recruiters know where to look first.

- *Sales training provided by the company.* A company that has its own sales training program can recruit inexperienced people. But if a salesperson needs to be productive quickly, it may be necessary for the company to seek experienced recruits.

- *Personnel needs of the company.* If the company is seeking career salespeople, then colleges and universities are not good sources of recruits because many college graduates want to be managers.

- *Sources of successful recruits in the past.* These sources can be used again, as long as there have been no changes in the sales position.

- *Recruiting budget.* A small budget means a firm must limit its sources.

- *Legal considerations.* Civil rights laws and other regulations must be considered when a firm is deciding on sources of recruits.

Recruiters should recognize that a top-rated candidate can come from any source, and they must be careful not to overlook certain sources because of a few poor experiences in the past. However, with the cost of recruiting increasing so much in recent years, it is important to be selective. Increasingly, sales managers must analyze their sources and devote time to those that are most productive, while ensuring that EEO guidelines are satisfied.

SUMMARY

Recruiting applicants in today's business environment is a very important and challenging task for the sales manager. Sales managers must be aware of the legal rights of the candidate during the recruiting process. Moreover, the applicant's qualifications must be thoroughly assessed to determine if they match the organization's criteria for a salesperson. The area of sales is diverse, and different companies may use different criteria in the recruiting process. Some companies may not seek an experienced recruit for fear that the applicant has bad habits. Other companies may not be able to test an individual's sales skills thoroughly or train a recruit; in these cases, experience becomes a prime attribute in the recruiting process.

Companies use several sources to find qualified applicants. The search can begin within the company by surveying the sales force for possible recruits and then seeking individuals from other departments. Some of the external sources include competitive and noncompetitive firms, educational institutions, advertisements, and employment agencies. Recruiters must recognize that top-rated candidates can come from any source. However, with the increasing costs of recruiting, sales managers must be careful to devote their time to the most productive sources.

STUDY QUESTIONS

1. What are the steps involved in the recruiting process?

2. Why should sales managers conduct job analyses before recruiting salespeople?

3. How is the job description used in managing the sales force?

4. What are the characteristics of successful salespeople? If sales managers know these traits, how can they use them?

5. Why is it important to have a well-planned recruiting program?

6. What kinds of changes do you believe will occur in the recruiting process in the next few years?

7. What factors should sales managers consider when deciding which recruitment source to use? Explain.

8. What are the most frequently used sources of salespeople? Should a firm use only one or a few of these potential recruit sources?

9. What factors do you believe will influence the demand for salespeople in the 1990s? How have computer systems improved the recruitment process?

10. Why should sales managers develop a set of job qualifications? Is this a difficult process? Explain.

IN-BASKET EXERCISE

You have been working as a sales rep for an industrial firm for the last two years. Recently, you were asked to help out with this year's recruiting of entry-level salespeople. Your sales manager informs you that it is very difficult recruiting college students for industrial selling jobs: "You will spend time and money traveling to college campuses, and when you get there, you will have a difficult time getting students to sign up for interviews! In fact, those that do sign up will tell you that they're doing it for the practice of interviewing or that they're really interested in marketing mangement, not a sales job." You are asked to help improve the recruiting process for college students, in particular, the top students.

What are your suggestions? What can be done to attract top college graduates?

CASE 6-1

MURRAY BUSINESS PRODUCTS: RECRUITMENT POLICIES

Scott Parker, sales manager for Murray Business Products in Little Rock, Arkansas, was perplexed. Earlier in the week, he had received another resignation notice. This notice was especially surprising because it came from a salesperson whom Scott had predicted would be a career employee with Murray Business Products. For no apparent reason, Scott Parker was failing to recruit and keep good salespeople.

Background

Scott Parker was hired by Murray Business Products seven years ago and worked his way up the company ladder from sales trainee to sales associate to sales manager. With his last promotion, to sales manager, Scott was provided with extensive training in recruitment and selection policies, including sources of recruits, sample ads, interview formats, recruiting speeches, and EEO guidelines.

Furthermore, Scott was given a week's intensive training on recruitment and selection techniques during his initial management training, through role playing, discussion, videotapes, and lectures. Additionally, Murray Business Products held biannual meetings specifically to review each division's success or failure in recruiting. During these meetings, sessions were held to examine reasons why the last salesperson left the division and how the most recent salesperson was recruited and hired.

As a result of this training, Scott Parker was well aware of the company's position on recruitment of new salespeople. In short, a twofold concern of Murray Business Products was hiring quality salespeople and reducing turnover. The company sought to hire and subsequently to develop career salespeople who would be qualified to sell its highly technical products. To this end, the company offered a competitive compensation and fringe-benefit package. Murray Business Products prided itself on its relatively low turnover rate (18 percent). One of the company goals was to reduce this turnover rate from 18 to 10 percent, as indicated by the emphasis on recruitment in the management training programs. The company's basic attitude was that "the cost of lost revenue from turnover outweighed any recruitment costs."

While the company promoted certain recruitment policies and guidelines, it also allowed sales managers a great deal of flexibility in the administration of such policies and guidelines. With a decentralized organizational structure, Murray Business Products encouraged sales managers to develop their own unique approaches to decision making and personnel policies.

Present Situation

With the latest resignation letter, Scott Parker realized that he would have some explaining to do at the upcoming biannual company meeting. The situation bewildered him. Regardless of how hard he worked to recruit only the most promising salespeople, since he had assumed the position of sales manager two years ago, his turnover rate had slowly increased. It was now at the rather alarming rate of 30 percent. Scott

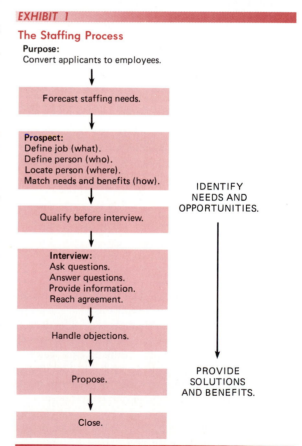

EXHIBIT 1

The Staffing Process

Purpose:
Convert applicants to employees.

↓

Forecast staffing needs.

↓

Prospect:
Define job (what).
Define person (who).
Locate person (where).
Match needs and benefits (how).

↓

Qualify before interview.

↓

Interview:
Ask questions.
Answer questions.
Provide information.
Reach agreement.

↓

Handle objections.

↓

Propose.

↓

Close.

IDENTIFY NEEDS AND OPPORTUNITIES.

PROVIDE SOLUTIONS AND BENEFITS.

Case prepared by Debbie Boswell, Louisiana State University. Used with permission.

EXHIBIT 2

The Murray Profile

Education:	Two years college.
Stability:	Three or less residential moves in five years. Attended no more than two schools after completion of high school. No more than three jobs in five years. Three full years' work history. Purchased home. Investments. No gaps in work or school history in last five years in excess of sixty days. Less than seven years unrelated field sales.
Success:	Objectives achieved. Increased earnings. Previous income level too low in comparison with desired earnings. Previous pay included commissions. Top 10 percent of commission scale or office. Increased responsibility from job to job. Independent, self-starter.
Automobile:	Late model (good condition). Two cars if married.
Appearance:	Weight proportional to height. Neat.
Family:	Married with children. Child care if spouse works.
Childhood:	Overcame a major problem, e.g., lost parents at an early age.
Work habits:	Worked during high school or college. Worked extra hours (20+/week).
Social:	Civic or social clubs.
Motivation:	Need to make more than $25,000 per year.
Energy level:	Excited and enthusiastic about self.
Maturity:	Style of living consistent with income. Persuasive selling credentials. Reputation solid. Good reason for leaving last job. Speaks well of company where last employed. Knows of Murray. Listens well. Reasonable financial and professional goals.
Sales personality:	Has or desires a competitive job. Makes statements such as "I like the challenge of getting people to buy."

---

found this situation especially puzzling, since he had attempted to strictly follow company policy with no deviations whatsoever.

Scott decided to evaluate the problem (and prepare for the upcoming meeting at the same time) by reviewing company guidelines on recruitment. Looking over his management training folder and notes, he first came across the handout that was used in class to illustrate the staffing process (Exhibit 1). Surely, there was no problem in this area, he reasoned. He was convinced that he had been properly following the simple flowchart.

Next in the folder was the Murray Profile (Exhibit 2). The profile listed minimum standards that applicants should meet in terms of education, employment stability, pattern of success, automobile ownership, appearance, work habits, motivation, maturity, sales personality, and energy level. Scott was convinced that he had hired only individuals who had met the standards described by the profile.

Also in the folder were the selection criteria (Exhibit 3). Scott rationalized that he had used these criteria

in every single interview with a new applicant. The problem must be elsewhere, he decided.

The next item in the folder was the sheet entitled "Finding Sources of Good People" (Exhibit 4). Scott recognized that he had not tapped all suggested sources

---

EXHIBIT 3

Selection Criteria

Successful salespeople for Murray Business Products are:

Analytical	Economically motivated
Athletic	Family-oriented
Competitive	Power-oriented
Empathetic	Status-oriented
Extroverted	Studious
High-energy	Team players
Independent	Technically oriented
Optimistic	Tenacious
Organized	Well-groomed
Punctual	

- Join and become involved with local organizations.

- Look where you buy other things (e.g., your clothes, video equipment, home computers).

- Speak to and interview students at vocational schools and community colleges.

- Announce upcoming interviews or be interviewed on college radio stations.

- Establish contact with heads of business departments at local universities.

- Become involved with hobby groups or clubs.

- Have an open house at fraternities or sororities.

- Run an ad in the sports programs of local universities.

- Develop a recruiting videotape.

he had said. "Honesty translates into providing the 'true' facts about the products being sold. By being honest, the salesperson will foster goodwill and, in turn, create loyal customers."

Coincidentally, Scott had also recently seen a *Wall Street Journal* article about employers giving job applicants "honesty" exams. The article stated that the tests were an excellent prescreening device and that sales for the tests were "booming."

As Scott reflected on the possibility of adding an honesty exam to his arsenal of tests, he realized that he didn't have much time to spare. The biannual meeting of Murray Business Products was fast approaching; he would soon be expected to provide an analysis of his recruitment and turnover situation.

of good people, but he didn't perceive this as a major detriment to his recruitment endeavors.

Next, Scott browsed through the assorted test instruments in the file. The file included tests of verbal abilities, sales comprehension, personality inventories, sales motivation, and electronics ability. Scott wondered if these tests were accurately assessing potential career salespeople. Could there be a gap somewhere?

Scott remembered a discussion he had recently had with a friend regarding the attributes of a good salesperson. The most valuable characteristic of a good salesperson, according to Scott's friend, was honesty. "An honest salesperson is a convincing salesperson,"

Questions

1. Do you agree with Scott Parker that there is no problem with the staffing process at Murray Business Products? Why or why not?

2. Do you see any weaknesses with the Murray Profile or the selection criteria used by Murray Business Products? If so, what are they?

3. Should Scott Parker add an honesty exam to the existing test instruments? Why or why not? What other tests might strengthen Murray's recruitment process?

4. How would you revise Scott Parker's recruitment policies?

5. Do you believe the relationship between recruitment and turnover is as strong as the company perceives it to be? Why or why not?

CASE 6-2

CELLULAR COMMUNICATIONS STRATEGIES: RECRUITING THE NEW SALES FORCE

Bill Dean has just been selected to manage a sales force for Cellular Communications Strategies (CCS) in the Tucson, Arizona, PMSA. CCS was awarded one of two licenses to operate a cellular telephone system in the Tucson PMSA by the Federal Communications Commission (FCC) and will operate with the other licensee, the existing telephone company.

Cellular Telephone Technology

Cellular telephone technology represents a significant advancement over traditional mobile telephone service in several ways. First, in most locations there are waiting lists for mobile service because of a restriction on the number of persons who can use traditional

Case prepared by Ronald F. Bush and Richard Sjolander, University of West Florida. Used with permission.

mobile telephone service. In contrast, cellular phones will be available to all applicants. Second, for those who have traditional mobile phones, there is usually a waiting period to get an open line (dial tone); sometimes the wait is as long as one-half hour. The reason for this situation is the limited number of airwave frequencies which the FCC makes available for conventional mobile telephone communications. On each of these frequencies a high-power radio transmission is beamed out over an entire market area by one central antenna. When a mobile telephone is in use, it occupies one of the frequencies allocated for mobile telephones and is not available to anyone else in the entire market area. Since there are only a few available frequencies, they are quickly occupied, making access to the mobile phone system's dial tone limited. This means that in any market, whether it is a large metropolitan market like Chicago or a small one like Bonifay, Florida, only twelve mobile phones could be used at one time.

Cellular technology does not use a single high-power antenna. Rather, many low-power antennas are placed all over the market, each transmitting a signal only in the immediately surrounding area. The low-power transmission around each antenna creates a circular range of transmission coverage; hence the name cellular. Since low-power transmissions are used, the same radio frequency being used in one cell may also be used simultaneously in another cell located only a few miles away without interrupting transmissions. This is the key advantage of cellular telephones. This means that in Chicago, for example, the hundreds of customers fighting for the use of twelve traditional mobile telephone "lines" could be expanded to over half a million satisfied cellular telephone customers in the next few years. This will be possible due to the availability of a large number of frequencies for cellular transmissions.

There are several other advantages to cellular telephone technology: clear, static-free communications; the ability to have two-way communication, as in conventional telephone service; and cost. An average monthly bill for a cellular telephone will probably be around $100 or more depending on usage. Prices are expected to decrease, however, in the years ahead.

What makes the cellular system workable is microcomputer technology. Each mobile telephone (most of which resemble today's Princess phones in size and shape) is itself a small computer, whose chips enable it to broadcast and receive on several hundred available frequencies. As one drives through a city using the mobile phone, the system's central computer will gauge the strength of an incoming signal and will switch automatically from a frequency of one cell to an available frequency of the next cell. This switch is accomplished in such an infinitesimal period of time that it is imperceptible to the persons on both ends of the telephone.

When the FCC set up the licensing requirements for each city, the commission decided that it would be in the public interest to have two independent systems for the sake of competition. One license would be awarded to the local telephone company (typically an AT&T company), and the other to another, newly established company. The local telephone company was referred to as the "wireline" company because it already had a phone system in operation in which the phones were connected by wires. On the other hand, the new phone company was referred to as the "nonwireline" company because its technology was based on transmission of messages (talking) over radio waves only. No wires would be necessary, except to make long-distance calls; these would be handled by an interface with the wireline competitor. Therefore, the FCC would license only two firms in a market area: the existing wireline company and a new firm formed to operate nonwireline cellular service.

CCS: Nonwireline Licensee for Tucson

CCS was awarded the nonwireline license for the Tucson PMSA. This gave CCS the right to build and operate a cellular system. It could market the service through a number of channels. It could use an agent to market the service and equipment directly to subscribers. Or it could use an agent to market to subscribers through other retailers. Finally, it could market service in bulk to a reseller who would in turn market the service through an agent.

CCS viewed the market as consisting of two major segments: business firms and consumer households. It decided to use the agent-retailer channel to reach consumer household subscribers. An agent was selected by CCS who agreed to locate CCS retail stores at various locations, such as selected shopping malls throughout the PMSA. CCS selected an agent, Bill Dean, to sell to and service the business accounts.

Dean's immediate task is to recruit and select a sales force. Since CCS, like all cellular companies, is brand new, there are few industry guidelines available to Dean to help in the process. However, Dean has had several years of sales experience. This experience, coupled with CCS's analysis of the Tucson market, should be helpful.

Market Analysis of the Tucson PMSA

The Tucson PMSA consists of Pima County in the south-central area of Arizona, which contains 9,187 square miles and may be thought of as two market areas: the metropolitan area of Tucson and the large

EXHIBIT 1

Business Establishments in Pima County

Industry Sector	Number
Agriculture	123
Mining	47
Construction	1,064
Manufacturing	406
Transportation, communications, and utilities	240
Wholesale trade	602
Retail trade	2,754
Finance, insurance, and real estate	1,113
Services	3,225
Other	552
Total	10,126

Source: Adapted from *County Business Patterns.*

"moderate" usage they could expect an additional usage charge of $50 per month. Revenues, therefore, were anticipated to be $149 per month per cellular phone unit. Because there are two competing firms in this market, it was assumed that CCS would have a 50 percent market share in developing the forecast.

When CCS conducted the surveys to estimate buying intentions, it utilized scientific surveying methodologies in order to ensure a representative sample on which valid statistical inferences could be made. As part of the survey data, CCS examined the likelihood of subscribing to cellular service by industry affiliation. This market information was developed for the Tucson PMSA. Dean is aware that it must be adjusted to reflect his estimated market share. He feels

rural area of the remainder of Pima County. Obviously, Dean knows that the new sales force needs to saturate metropolitan Tucson, since almost all of the larger businesses are in that area. Some coverage is needed to selected areas of rural Pima County.

Some additional information was provided by the CCS market analysis. Exhibit 1 displays the types and numbers of business firms located in Pima County.

Another significant set of data obtained by the CCS market analysis consists of sales forecasts for each of the next five years. Forecasts were based on surveys of buying intentions and were made for both the consumer market ($n = 400$) and the business market ($n = 400$). Dean is interested in the business market forecasts, which are shown in Exhibit 2. These forecasts were based on the following pricing information, which was given to respondents: The cost for the cellular service was to be $99 per month to cover leasing the cellular telephone unit itself and the basic service charge. Additionally, respondents were told that with

EXHIBIT 2

Sales Forecast for CCS's Business Market

Year	Number of Subscribers	Number of Phones
1	198	891
2	348	1,568
3	512	2,304
4	588	2,650
5	642	2,915

EXHIBIT 3

Profile of Cellular Phone Subscribers in Tucson PMSA

Industry	Total	Likely	Unlikely or Undecided
Agriculture	4 1.0%	2 3.8%	2 0.6%
Mining	2 0.5%		2 0.6%
Construction	33 8.2%	7 13.2%	26 7.5%
Manufacturing	13 3.2%	2 3.8%	11 3.2%
Transportation, communication, public utilities	6 1.5%	1 1.9%	5 1.4%
Wholesale trade	12 3.0%	2 3.8%	10 2.9%
Retail trade	60 15.0%	6 11.3%	5 15.6%
Finance, insurance, real estate	37 9.2%	4 7.5%	33 9.5%
Services	112 28.0%	12 22.6%	100 28.8%
Other	106 26.5%	14 26.4%	92 26.5%
Nonprofit	10 2.5%	2 3.8%	8 2.3%
No answer	5 1.2%	1 1.9%	4 1.2%
Total	400	53	347

EXHIBIT 4

Estimated Number of Cellular Phones per Company

				Units per Company						
	Total	1	2	3	4 to 7	8 to 10	11 to 20	21 or over	Don't know	Mean*
Total	53	13	22	6	3	1	2	3	3	4.54
	100.0%	24.5%	41.5%	11.5%	5.7%	1.9%	3.8%	5.7%	5.7%	
Agriculture	2	1	1	—	—	—	—	—	—	1.50
	100.0%	50.0%	50.0%							
Mining	—	—	—	—	—	—	—	—	—	—
Construction	7	2	3	—	1	—	1	—	—	3.43
	100.0%	29.6%	42.9%		14.3%		14.3%			
Manufacturing	2	—	1	1	—	—	—	—	—	2.50
	100.0%		50.0%	50.0%						
Transportation, communication, public utilities	1	—	—	—	1	—	—	—	—	4.00
	100.0%				100.0%					
Wholesale trade	2	—	2	—	—	—	—	—	—	2.00
	100.0%		100.0%							
Retail trade	6	1	2	1	—	—	—	1	1	6.40
	100.0%	16.7%	33.3%	16.7%				16.7%	16.7%	
Finance, insurance, real estate	4	—	2	2	—	—	—	—	—	2.50
	100.0%		50.0%	50.0%						
Service	12	5	4	1	—	—	—	2	—	8.17
	100.0%	41.7%	33.3%	8.3%				16.7%		
Other	14	4	6	1	1	1	—	—	1	2.54
	100.0%	28.6%	42.9%	7.1%	7.1%	7.1%			7.1%	
Nonprofit	2	—	—	—	—	—	1	—	1	12.00
	100.0%						50.0%		50.0%	
No answer	1	—	1	—	—	—	—	—	—	2.00
	100.0%		100.0%							

* This is an actual mean. The classes presented in the table were aggregated to create a better visual picture of the data.

the industry-specific data presented in Exhibits 3 and 4 will be particularly useful in targeting his market during the introductory period of cellular service.

The Recruiting and Selecting Decision

Dean is giving some thought to the sales job itself. He knows that it will be helpful for the salespeople to have good communications skills and to be able to analyze situations quickly. The reason for these required skills is that Dean believes that although a few customers will subscribe to cellular for prestige value, most clients will have to be convinced that the new cellular technology will actually improve their efficiency to the point that the service will at least pay for itself. Convincing the decision makers in these firms of cellular's ability to increase efficiency will require the salesperson to analyze the appropriate areas of need for cellular within a given industry, determine productivity increases, and value the cost savings. To aid in this task, Dean thinks that it will be beneficial to allocate salespeople by industry, within reason. Salespeople who are familiar with one or a few industries will be able to accurately project cellular efficiencies and savings within any given firm.

Dean concludes that to do a proper job, each salesperson probably should not be expected to make more than two calls per day. Furthermore, on the basis of his sales experience, Dean believes that sales calls should be made only Monday through Friday. The rationale for this decision is twofold: most of the businesses are closed on Saturdays, and those that are open on Saturday are normally so busy with their customers that they do not want to take time to visit with a salesperson.

Dean also expects the salespeople to select their prospects, determine the proper person to call on, and schedule sales calls themselves. Dean plans to require one weekly sales activity report of each salesperson. This report will allow him to determine which and how many accounts each salesperson has called on, the time allocated to each call, expenses, and the status of each potential account.

Dean feels that he should put salespeople on straight salary, at least in the beginning. He wants to ensure that he can attract the most appropriate salespeople and he is afraid any form of commission would be viewed as too risky by many recruits. Dean estimates that sales force salaries should represent approximately 20 percent of gross sales revenue.

Questions

1. What should Bill Dean do in the initial stages of recruiting and selecting a sales force?

2. When Dean does begin to recruit salespeople, what sources should be considered?

3. In determining the number of salespeople to employ, Dean perceives resources as the primary constraint; therefore, he must first determine the number of dollars available and the average cost per salesperson. With his knowledge of the market he assumes a cost of $22,000 plus 20 percent of this cost for fringe benefits per employee. Further, he assumes that new sales will be made at a constant rate each month and that existing customers will retain the mobile telephone service indefinitely. To simplify the calculation, he assumes that all phones installed during a month begin generating revenue from the first day of the month. Forecast revenue for each of the first five years. How many salespeople can Dean afford during the first two years? Discuss the implications of your findings.

4. Dean would like to allocate the sales force to maximize his probability of reaching the first-year sales goal. In his analysis he must make a number of assumptions and calculations based on the data.
   a. He assumes that all sectors of the economy will grow at the same rate. (Dean remembers making similar assumptions in his college economics courses.) How will this simplify his analysis?
   b. Given the information in the case, rank each industry from best to worst, using each of the following criteria: (1) probability of a market contact being a potential customer (defined by intent to purchase), (2) average size of sale in units of cellular telephones, and (3) market size in terms of cellular phone units. Highlight both consistencies and inconsistencies while interpreting the findings in terms of industry attractiveness.
   c. More than one sales call may be required to close a sale; Dean chooses three as a reasonable assumption for CCS. Why would he make such an assumption?
   d. The allocation of sales force efforts is of critical value to the firm. Dean is aware that good allocation will increase his chances of achieving the forecast sales. There are several ways of viewing the problem. He could use any of the criteria developed in question 4b to guide the allocation of sales effort. However, he feels there may be more he can do with the numbers he has at hand. Reviewing his analysis, he finds that he knows the probability of a positive response in each industry. He adjusts this to reflect the assumed CCS market share. Given this, he should be able to calculate the average number of sales calls required to reach a buyer in each industry. This figure needs to be further adjusted to reflect the additional sales efforts required to close a sale. This gives him an estimate of the number of sales calls required to make a sale in each industry. He also knows the average number of phones the sample respondents indicated that they would need. By combining these two numbers for each industry, he can derive estimates of average sales in units per sales call. Following the procedure outlined above, arrive at estimates of sales per sales call in each industry. Rank industry attractiveness and compare the results with your earlier rankings in 4b.
   e. Bill Dean thinks the rankings developed in 4d will provide an excellent guide for allocation. However, Dean is unsure of the sales effort required to cover the various industries. He reasons that this sales effort must be roughly equivalent to the effort required to call on everyone in the industry once and the number of firms in an industry that are likely to purchase from CCS (assuming 50 percent market share) times the number of additional sales calls required to close a sale within that industry. Briefly explain your long-term market strategy for sales force allocation. Allocate the sales force and justify your allocation in terms of the estimates derived above in 4d and 4e.

f. A lot of new information was derived from the analysis required for allocation of the sales force. Dean would like to check his original sales forecast using this data. Assume that each salesperson works 240 days per year. Calculate expected sales based on your allocation of the sales force. If the expected sales based on your allocation are not in agreement with the original sales forecast, what action (if any) should Dean take?

REFERENCES

1. Based on a personal interview with Edward A. Burch, October 1990.
2. "Compensation and Expenses," *Sales & Marketing Management*, Feb. 26, 1990, p. 78.
3. James W. Kerley and David W. Merrill, "New England Life Takes Steps to Insure Its Future," *Sales & Marketing Management*, Aug. 12, 1985, p. 74.
4. Based on an article from *Sales & Marketing Management*, Sept. 12, 1985.
5. Alice Shane, "Facing Up to a Recruiter," *Sales & Marketing Management*, May 1989, pp. 38–45.
6. Ibid.
7. Based on a telephone conversation with an Emery Worldwide sales manager, Apr. 16, 1986.
8. David Mayer and Herbert Greenberg, "What Makes a Good Salesman," *Harvard Business Review*, July–August 1974, pp. 119–125. Findings from other studies on personality are in G. A. Howells, "The Successful Salesman: A Personality Analysis," *British Journal of Marketing*, Spring 1968, pp. 13–23; Lawrence M. Lamont and William J. Lundstrom, "Identifying Successful Industrial Salesmen by Personality and Personal Characteristics," *Journal of Marketing Research*, November 1977, pp. 517–529; T. H. Mattheiss, Richard M. Durand, Jan P. Muczyk, and Myron Gable, "Personality and the Prediction of Salesmen's Success," in Ronald C. Curhan (ed.), *1974 Combined Proceedings, American Marketing Association*, American Marketing Association, Chicago, 1975, pp. 499–502; Henry O. Pruden and Robert A. Peterson, "Personality and Performance—Satisfaction of Industrial Salesmen," *Journal of Marketing Research*, November 1971, pp. 501–504.
9. Robert McMurry and James Arnold, *How to Build a Dynamic Sales Organization*, McGraw-Hill, New York, 1968, p. 3. Other interesting studies include James C. Cotham III, "Selecting Salesmen: Approaches and Problems," *MSU Business Topics*, Winter 1970, pp. 64–72; Robert J. Small and Larry J. Rosenberg, "Determining Job Performance in the Industrial Sales Force," *Industrial Marketing Management*, vol. 6, no. 2, 1977, pp. 99–102; James N. Mosel, "Prediction of Department Store Sales Performance from Personal Data," *Journal of Applied Psychology*, February 1952, pp. 8–10; E. James Randall, Ernest F. Cooke, and Richard J. Jefferies, "Can Assessment Centers Be Used to Improve the Salesperson Selection Process?" *Journal of Personal Selling and Sales Management*, Fall/Winter 1981/82, pp. 52–55; Wesley J. Johnson and Martha C. Cooper, "Industrial Sales Force Selection: Current Knowledge and Needed Research," *Journal of Personal Selling and Sales Management*, Spring/Summer 1981, pp. 49–57; E. James Randall, Ernest F. Cooke, and Lois Smith, "A Successful Application of the Assessment Center Concept to the Salesperson Selection Process," *Journal of Personal Selling and Sales Management*, May 1985, pp. 53–61.
10. "What Makes a Supersalesperson?" *Sales & Marketing Management*, Aug. 13, 1984, p. 86.
11. Thayer Taylor, "Anatomy of a Star Salesman," *Sales & Marketing Management*, May 1986, pp. 49–51. Other studies identifying key variables for selecting successful salespeople include Melany E. Baehr and Glenn B. Williams, "Predictions of Sales Success from Factorially Determined Dimensions of Personal Background Data,"

Journal of Applied Psychology, April 1968, pp. 98–103; David L. Kurtz, "Physical Appearance and Stature: Important Variables in Sales Recruiting," *Personnel Journal,* December 1967, pp. 981–983; Robert Tanofsky, Ronald R. Shepp, and Paul J. O'Neill, "Pattern Analysis of Biographical Predictions of Success as an Insurance Salesman," *Journal of Applied Psychology,* April 1969, pp. 136–139; Stan Moss, "What Sales Executives Look for in New Salespeople," *Sales & Marketing Management,* March 1978, pp. 46–48; Thomas Rollins, "A Blueprint for Salespeople Who Really Sell," *Training,* November 1989, pp. 51–55.

CHAPTER

7

SELECTING
THE SALES FORCE

LEARNING OBJECTIVES

When you finish this chapter, you should understand:

- ▲ The procedures and tools companies use to assist them in selecting sales applicants
- ▲ What sales managers look for in reviewing applicants
- ▲ Things that an applicant is responsible for in an interview
- ▲ The types of tests used and the problems surrounding tests during the interview process
- ▲ What sales managers consider when making the final selection decision
- ▲ Sales force socialization and its importance to the success of the sales organization

A DAY ON THE JOB

James Pappas, vice president of human resources for Engineering Resources, Inc. (ERI), gets actively involved in selecting the right salespeople to sell a proprietary steam-heat process. While Pappas feels it's important to assess a candidate's selling skills and technical background, he believes that the hiring decision is also based on intangibles. "Temperament, suitability to our culture, creativity, ambition" are important characteristics Pappas looks for in a recruit. "When we bring a person in, they talk to marketing, engineering, finance, all the departments—and everybody gets an appraisal sheet," says Pappas. "There are twenty different categories that they have to rank the person on from one to five, but only one category is for technical skills. The others are for integrity, creativity, people skills, etc." When Pappas is asked about the hiring philosophy at his firm, he states, "The company's hiring philosophy rests on less than scientific principles. What we sell is a concept, so we need someone with the ability to visualize. . . . We want to sell creativity and flexibility in our salespeople."[1]

The back-slapping, cigar-smoking, joke-telling salesman has become a relic in our society. There are many misconceptions about personal selling; perhaps the greatest one pertains to what sales managers should look for when selecting a salesperson. For example, sales managers often confuse aggressiveness with enthusiasm. This chapter should clear up many of the misconceptions about the selection process.

THE SELECTION PROCESS

The recruiting process furnishes the sales manager with a pool of applicants from which to choose. The *selection process* involves choosing the candidates who best meet the qualifications and have the greatest aptitude for the job. There are numerous tools, techniques, and procedures that can be used in the selection process. Companies typically use initial screening interviews, application forms, in-depth interviews, reference checks, physical examinations, and tests as selection tools.

None of these should be used alone. Each is designed to collect different information. While successful selection of sales applicants does not necessitate the use of all the tools and techniques, the more that are used, the higher the probability of selecting successful sales personnel. The following example describes the selection process of one company.

COMPUTER AID IN THE SELECTION PROCESS

Selecting the best recruit for a sales position is a very difficult, yet extremely important, task. When the sales manager selects a successful candidate, results in terms of added sales volume will follow. However, when the sales manager misses the mark, the results can be devastating. One authority in a consumer products company cites losses as high as $75,000 in recruiting, selecting, training, and the like, from losing one salesperson. To avoid these losses, many companies are using technological advances such as psychological prediction strategies and computerized data-base techniques in their selection process.

New England Mutual Life Insurance (NEL) is experimenting with several new technologies in its sales force selection process. Together with Tracom Corporation, an industrial psychology firm, NEL developed a computerized selection-oriented program called STEP (Selection, Training, Evaluation, Performance). This computer-based program provides summary reports to sales managers on thousands of candidates via IBM PCs. The process will assist sales managers in the recruiting, screening, processing, and hiring of candidates. Additionally, the program furnishes sales managers with activity and performance records from current employees that can be used as hiring guidelines for future recruits. NEL reports a much higher percentage of successful salespeople since it started the computerized STEP program.[2]

Selection tools and techniques are only aids to sound executive judgment. They can eliminate the obviously unqualified candidates and generally spot the more competent individuals. However, in regard to the majority of recruits who normally fall between these extremes, the current tools can only suggest which ones will be successful in sales. As a result, executive judgment is heavily relied on in selecting salespeople.

Initial Screening Interviews

The steps in the selection process vary from company to company, depending on the size of the company, the number of salespeople needed, and the importance of the position to be filled. The purpose of the initial screening interview is to eliminate, as soon as possible, the undesirable recruits. Initial screening may start with an application form, an interview, or some type of test. But no matter which tool is initially used, it should be brief. The shorter it is, the more it will cut down on costs. But it must not be so brief that it screens out good candidates.

Almost all companies make use of initial screening interviews. The interviews usually last from twenty to thirty minutes and are conducted by assistant personnel managers, assistant sales managers, sales personnel, and sometimes computers. The interviews that a recruiter conducts on campus with college students are initial screening interviews. Each recruiter can talk with eight or ten students in a day and select the best ones for follow-up interviews. Exhibit 7-1 is an example of a preemployment interview guide used by a *Fortune* 500 corporation. It should be of value to students in understanding what to expect in such a situation.

Computer interviewing is increasingly being used by personnel officers to screen job applicants. For example, personnel managers in a firm in Richardson, Texas, are using computer interviewing to question applicants about work attitudes, theft, and substance abuse. The computer interviewing procedure speeds the gathering and analysis of data, and some evidence suggests that people give more truthful answers to the machines than to flesh-and-blood interviewers. Bloomingdale's also uses computer interviewing and has found that it reduces employee turnover. The personnel manager notes that "the machine never forgets to ask a question and asks each question the same way. It covers all the bases."[3] The main drawbacks to computer screening are these: Computers cannot recognize fuzzy or superficial answers and prod interviewees to elaborate,

---

EXHIBIT 7-1

Preemployment Interview Guide

Effective interviewing requires active listening. The interview should not be aimless discussion: it should be a conversation with the purpose of exchanging knowledge to gain information. The following principles offer a brief guide for conducting an effective interview.

1. *Plan for the interview.* What do you want to find out (qualifications, attitudes, personality, effectiveness of communication skills, when available, relocation problems)?

2. *Be prepared.* What job do you have in mind for the candidate? If possible, review the applicant's résumé or application before the interview and identify four or five activities or accomplishments you want the candidate to elaborate on during the interview.

3. *Be interested.* Create the impression that the applicant is the most important thing on your mind. Remember that the purpose of the interview is to communicate.

4. *Encourage the applicant to talk about himself or herself.* Find out about interests, aspirations, and ambitions. What were the reasons for selecting his or her course of study at college? What electives did the applicant choose and why? What did the applicant like most and least about previous jobs and why? What does the applicant think are his or her strong points? weak points? Have the applicant talk freely about accomplishments and the way he or she achieved them. How does the applicant describe himself or herself?

5. Accurately describe the opportunities at our company and in your division. Be careful not to oversell, and avoid making any commitment about starting salary.

6. Send the applicant away with a positive feeling about our company whether or not you would recommend employment.

Remember to listen thoroughly and critically. Ask why; avoid questions that can be answered with a yes or no. Listen two-thirds of the time.

---

and they cannot ask follow-up questions of interviewees who drop unexpected leads.

Application Forms

Application forms are one of the two most widely used selection tools (the other is the personal interview). An application form is an easy means of collecting information necessary for determining an applicant's qualifications. Information requested on forms usually includes name, address, position applied for, physical condition, educational background, work experience, military service, participation in social organizations, outside interests and activities, and personal references. Other important questions on an application form relate directly to the sales position for which the application is made. For example:

- Why do you want this job?
- What minimum income do you require?
- Why do you want to change jobs?
- Are you willing to travel?

- Are you willing to be transferred?

- Are you willing to use your car for business?

- What do you want to be doing five years from now? Ten years from now?

Application forms will differ from company to company. On all forms, however, it is illegal to include questions that are not related to the job.

Some companies use a weighted application form that has been developed from the regular application form by analyzing the various items that help distinguish between good and poor salespeople. If companies can show that items such as educational level, personal indebtedness, and years of selling experience tend to be more related to success than are other items, then more weight (importance) can be placed on them in making hiring decisions. Thus, applicants who rate higher than an established minimum number of points on these items are considered, and those who fail to reach the cutoff point are usually rejected. Of course, sales managers must realize that weighted application forms must be validated for each sales position in the firm so that they reflect a position's unique requirements. Also, the validity of the weights must be reevaluated periodically because an item's importance may change over time.

An important function of application forms is to help sales managers prepare for personal interviews with candidates for sales positions. By looking over the application form before the interview, the sales manager can get an initial impression of the applicant and can prepare a list of questions to ask during the interview. Specific considerations are:

- Appearance of the application

- Missing information (Are there blank spots or shortcuts that seem inconsistent with the rest of the application? Interviewers will ask about these during the interview.)

- Indications of instability (Does the history include more than three jobs in five years, any job less than one year, more than two colleges, and the like?)

- Reason for job change

- Career progression (Do the job changes represent a growth in income and responsibility?)

- Health and energy

Sales managers look at the above items closely because past behavior patterns, as indicated by information on application forms, tend to be a major predictor of future behavior.

In-Depth Interviews

The interview is the most used and least scientific of the various tools for selecting employees. A salesperson is seldom hired without a personal interview. In fact, as many as three or four interviews are usually conducted with the most desirable candidates. No other selection tool can take the place of getting to know the applicants personally.

The personal interview is used to help determine if a person is right for the job. It can bring out personal characteristics that no other selection tool is capable of revealing. The interview also serves as a two-way channel of communication, which means both the company and the applicant can ask questions and learn about each other.

The questions asked during an interview should be aimed at finding out certain things: Is the candidate qualified for the job? Does the candidate really want the job? Will this sales job help the candidate fulfill personal goals? Will the candidate find this sales position challenging enough? These questions, like those on the application form, are directed at examining the applicant's past behavior, experiences, and motivation.

Every sales manager will use a different approach in attempting to elicit useful information. The approach used will depend on the sales manager's personality, training, and work experience. Exhibit 7-2 summarizes an interviewing guide prepared by one large corporation.

Types of interviews. Interviews differ, depending on the number of questions that are prepared in advance and the extent to which the interviewer guides the conversation. At one end is the totally structured, or guided, interview; at the other end is the informal, unstructured type. In the *structured interview*, the recruiter asks each candidate the same set of questions. These are standardized

---

EXHIBIT 7-2

Approaches Used by Interviewers to Obtain Useful Information

1. Build a rapport quickly.

2. Structure the interview so that the interviewee clearly understands what is expected.

3. Elicit desired behavior by not showing disapproval or disagreement, by using humor, by showing sympathy and understanding, and by interrupting infrequently only for clarification or redirection.

4. Use probing, open-ended questions and avoid yes or no questions. Examples of typical open-ended questions are:

   - Tell me about . . .
   - How would you compare . . .
   - Tell me about the people . . .
   - How would you describe . . .
   - How did you feel about . . .

   - What did you like . . .
   - Why did you decide to do that . . .
   - How did you find that experience . . .
   - What were the differences . . .

   Examples of probing techniques are phrases such as:

   - How so . . .
   - Because . . .
   - In what respect . . .

   - Use reflection and paraphrasing . . .
   - Use short phrases . . .

---

questions that have been designed to help determine the applicant's fitness for the sales position. Structured interviews can be used for initial screening but are not useful in probing for in-depth information. A structured approach is particularly useful for inexperienced interviewers, since it helps guide the interview and ensures that all factors relevant to the candidate's qualifications are covered.

At the other end of the continuum is the *unstructured interview,* which is informal and nondirected. The goal of the unstructured interviewing approach is to get the candidate to talk freely on a variety of topics. Frequently, the recruiter begins the interview by saying to the candidate, "Tell me about yourself," or by asking questions such as "Why did you decide to interview with our company?"

Several problems are associated with unstructured interviews. One is that they do not provide answers to standard questions that can be compared with other candidates' responses or with the company's past experiences. Also, considerable time may be spent on relatively unimportant topics. However, personnel experts say this technique is the best for probing an individual's personality and for gaining insight into the candidate's attitudes and opinions.

To administer and interpret unstructured interviews, interviewers must be well trained. Sales managers for most firms have had relatively little experience as interviewers, and only about one-half of them have ever had any special training in interviewing techniques. Therefore, many firms use a combination of structured and unstructured approaches, usually referred to as a *semistructured interview.* In semistructured interviews the interviewer has a preplanned list of major questions but allows time for interaction and discussion. This approach is flexible and can be tailored to meet the needs of different candidates as well as different interviewers. Exhibit 7-3 is an example of a questionnaire based on a semistructured approach. Note that the format includes structured and unstructured questions to ensure that the interviewer obtains all relevant information.

Applicants' responsibility in an interview. Applicants should prepare for interviews by learning about the company and trying to anticipate questions that may be asked. For some sales positions it may be helpful to practice answers ahead of time. After all, applicants are "selling" themselves to the interviewer, and the objective is to make a favorable impression. A review of Exhibit 7-3 will suggest some of the questions that applicants should be prepared to answer.

Applicants should also ask questions during the interview because this will help them decide whether they want the position if it is offered to them. Exhibit 7-4 lists questions candidates typically ask in the interview. While all these questions are important, some are more important than others. A recent survey showed that the major concerns of new salespeople are career path (45 percent); compensation (43 percent); relocation (6 percent); and other factors such as stability of company, time away from family, independence, and benefits (6 percent).[4] Sales managers need to be prepared to answer questions on these topics when they are asked by sales applicants.

Many recruits successfully pass screening interviews as well as appraisals of application forms. The in-depth personal interview is much more challenging,

EXHIBIT 7-3

Semistructured Questionnaire

Name _____ Position _____
Area/region/zone _____ Interviewer _____ Date _____

IMPRESSIONS
Appearance and dress _____ Manner _____ Speech _____

PRESENT POSITION: Company _____ From _____ To _____
How obtained _____
Job progression _____
Current job duties _____
Immediate superior _____ Title _____
_____ May _____ May not contact Relationship _____
Compensation at start _____ Currently _____
Job likes _____ Job dislikes _____
Reasons for leaving _____

PREVIOUS POSITION: Company _____ From _____ To _____
How obtained _____
Job progression _____
Current job duties _____
Immediate superior _____ Title _____
_____ May contact _____ May not contact Relationship _____
Compensation at start _____ Currently _____
Job likes _____ Job dislikes _____
Reasons for leaving _____

PLANS AND GOALS
Plans and goals for the future _____
Hope to be earning in five years _____ Ten years _____
Plans for self-development _____
Feelings about travel and relocation _____

SELF-APPRAISAL
(Everyone has strong points as well as some traits or characteristics they'd like to change. Could you describe for me the seven or eight personal traits and characteristics you consider your particular strong points and also the four or five personal traits or characteristics you'd like to change, improve, or eliminate.)

STRENGTHS	WEAKNESSES

What is your understanding of our job? _____
What are its appeals? _____
What are the negative considerations? _____

SUPPLEMENTARY/SALES EXPERIENCE

(For applicants with sales experience)

What is your strongest point as a salesperson? _____ Your greatest weakness? _____

Ever won any sales contests or awards? _____

What kinds of customers do you most enjoy selling to? _____

Least enjoy? _____

HIGH SCHOOL(s): _____ Graduated   Yes ____   No ____

Favorite subjects _____

Most difficult subjects _____ Grades _____

Extracurricular activities _____

Work _____

Early vocational plans _____

COLLEGE(s): _____ Degree(s) _____

Curriculum _____

Favorite subjects _____ GPA _____

Most difficult subjects _____

Career plans _____

How financed, work _____

OTHER TRAINING OR EDUCATION: _____

_____

HEALTH

Personal health _____ Hospitalized in past ten years ____ Willing to take physical? ____

Accidents and illnesses, past ten years _____ Days missed from work, past two years ____

What is your basic philosophy or approach to selling? _____

In what significant way do you think our job will differ from the selling you've done? _____

_____

OTHER INFORMATION

_____

_____

however, and many sales recruits have difficulty with it. Exhibit 7-5 lists negative factors, identified during employment interviews, that frequently lead to rejection of applicants. Sales applicants should be aware of these and avoid them whenever possible.

Reference Checks

A company cannot be sure it has all the information on an applicant until references have been thoroughly checked. Reference checks allow a company to secure information not available from other sources. References usually are

---

EXHIBIT 7-4

Questions Typically Asked by Candidates during Recruiting or Screening Interview

Where are the entry-level positions? (Start at the division level.)
What are those positions?
How is training done? How long? Formal or informal?
What is the likelihood of relocation?
What are the starting salaries for a particular position?
Where can I go in the company?
How long will it take?
What is the selection process like?
What is the compensation package?
What are the benefits?
How am I evaluated for promotion?
What are your selection criteria, or what do you look for in a candidate?
Does your company encourage furthering one's education?

---

checked while the application form is processed and before the final interview takes place.

In general, the quality of reference checks as a selection tool is questionable. Checking on the names supplied by a candidate is often seen as a waste of time because it is unlikely that serious problems will be uncovered. Therefore, many firms try to talk with people who know the applicant but were not listed on the application form. For reference checking to be a useful selection tool, the sales manager must be resourceful and pursue leads that are not directly given. If only one significant fact is uncovered, it usually makes the effort worthwhile.

References from teachers and former employers are generally more helpful than other types of references. Teachers can usually give an indication of intelligence, work habits, and personality traits. Former employers can be used to

---

ETHICS IN SALES MANAGEMENT: SELECTING THE RIGHT CANDIDATE

You just finished a series of three interviews with a person who you feel is an excellent candidate for your company. He has a 3.4 grade-point average and a marketing degree. The candidate has excellent communication skills, held a part-time sales job throughout college to put himself through school, and was an officer in the sales fraternity on campus. He will definitely make you and your organization look good. Your only concern is that another organization will offer him a job before you do!

Before any candidate is offered a job, your company requires that a few of the applicant's references be checked. During this process, you discover that your ideal candidate may have lied on his résumé. He was never an officer in the sales fraternity; he was only a member!

1. Given the difficulty in finding excellent candidates, what do you do with this person?

2. Would your decision change if you also find out that this candidate has several speeding tickets?

3. Can you ever trust someone who "stretches the truth"? Can this be an attribute of a supersalesperson?

EXHIBIT 7-5

Factors Identified during the Employment Interview That Frequently Lead to Rejection

- Poor appearance
- Overbearing, overaggressive, conceited attitude
- Inability to express self clearly; poor voice, diction, grammar
- Lack of career planning; no purpose or goals
- Lack of interest and enthusiasm; a passive, indifferent manner
- Lack of confidence and poise; nervousness
- Failure to participate in extracurricular activities
- Overemphasis on money, interest in "best dollar" offer
- Poor scholastic record
- Unwillingness to start at the bottom; the expectation of too much too soon
- Evasiveness; failure to be clear about unfavorable factors in record
- Lack of tact
- Lack of maturity
- Lack of courtesy
- Condemnation of past employers
- Lack of social understanding
- Marked dislike for schoolwork
- Lack of vitality
- Failure to look interviewer in the eye
- Limp, fishy handshake
- Indecision
- Unhappy married life
- Friction with parents
- Little sense of humor
- Sloppy, poorly prepared application
- Evidence of merely shopping around for a job
- Desires job for short time only
- Lack of knowledge in field of specialization
- No interest in company or industry
- Emphasis on whom the applicant knows
- Unwillingness to go where company may want to send him
- Cynical attitude
- Low moral standards
- Laziness
- Intolerance; strong prejudice
- Narrow interests
- Evidence of wasted time
- Poor handling of personal finances
- No interest in community activities
- Inability to take criticism
- Lack of appreciation of the value of experience
- Radical ideas
- Tardiness (to interview) without good reason
- Failure to express appreciation for interviewer's time
- Failure to ask questions about the job
- Indefinite responses to questions

find out why the person left the job and how well he or she got along with others. The question "Would you rehire the applicant again if you had the chance?" tends to bring out accurate responses. Exhibit 7-6 shows an evaluation form sent to a previous employer. A comparable form is typically sent to teachers or other knowledgeable persons (other than friends or personal references) who may be familiar with the candidate in a work situation.

Reference checks can uncover information about an applicant that may alter a sales manager's perceptions of the person's sales ability. The *Ethics* scenario on page 238 addresses such an issue.

EXHIBIT 7-6

Evaluation Form for Previous Employer

Please return to
XYZ Corporation.

**CONFIDENTIAL REPORT TO
XYZ CORPORATION**

We should like to give this applicant a prompt answer
so that he or she may formulate plans.
We ask your kind assistance in returning this
form to us today

CITY	STATE	ZIP

APPLICANT'S NAME AND SOCIAL SECURITY NO.	ADDRESS

Applicant named above claims employment with you as	Under (supervisor's name)	From	To

Is this information correct? ☐ Yes ☐ No	If not correct, please comment on discrepancy
Did Applicant resign voluntarily? ☐ Yes ☐ No	If no, please show reason
Are you willing to reemploy? ☐ Yes ☐ No	Comments

Applicant states that his/her rate of pay exclusive of travel expense was $	Is this correct? ☐ Yes ☐ No	If no, please show correct rate $

Please rate applicant on the following points:

	Exceptional	Very good	Satisfactory	Needs improvement	Unsatisfactory	Comments
Ability to sell a product (Even if applicant did not sell for you, please rate your opinion of potential)						
Leadership						
Character and integrity						
Industry and application to work						
Ability shown in learning your business						
Creative ability (resourcefulness)						
Dependability						
Ability to work with others						
Potential for advancement						

Additional comments:

Company name _____

Signature _____

Title _____

Date _____

Physical Examinations

Many sales jobs require a degree of physical activity and stamina. Poor physical condition can only hinder a salesperson's job performance; therefore, a company should insist on a thorough medical examination for all its sales recruits. The results from the examination should be interpreted by a doctor who is familiar with the demands of the sales job, and the sales manager should be notified of the results. Because of their expense, physical examinations usually are not given until a recruit has passed most of the steps in the selection process.

Tests

Tests are the most controversial tools used in the selection process. The need for application forms, reference checks, and personal interviews is seldom disputed, but there are differences of opinion about whether tests are necessary in the hiring of salespeople. Questions regarding the legality of testing have increased the complexity and the controversy surrounding the use of tests as a screening tool. But research has shown that test profile data can be useful to management in the process of selecting and classifying sales applicants who are likely to be high performers.[5]

There are seven basic tests used in the selection process of sales personnel:

- *Intelligence tests.* These tests measure raw intelligence and trainability. Recent research has indicated that a salesperson's cognitive ability or intelligence is the best indicator of future job performance. Thus, although once looked down upon, the intelligence test is slowly regaining status as the most effective tool for selecting salespeople.[6]

- *Knowledge tests.* These tests are designed to measure what the applicant knows about a certain product, service, market, and the like.

- *Sales aptitude tests.* These tests measure a person's innate or acquired social skills and selling know-how as well as tact and diplomacy.

- *Vocational interest tests.* These tests measure the applicant's vocational interest, the assumption being that a person is going to be more effective and stable if he or she has a strong interest in selling.

- *Personality tests.* These tests attempt to measure the behavioral traits believed necessary for success in selling, such as assertiveness, initiative, and extroversion.

- *Polygraph tests.* The polygraph test, sometimes called the "lie-detector test," measures blood pressure, respiration, heartbeat, and skin response as indicators of personal honesty. Because of questions about its validity, federal legislation now restricts the use of polygraph testing except in very few situations, such as those involving national security.

- *Attitude and lifestyle tests.* These tests became popular in the late 1980s because of the emergence of drug abuse as a major problem in the workplace and legislation that restricted the use of polygraph tests. Their primary purpose

EXHIBIT 7-7

Typical Attitude and Lifestyle Test Questions

1. How often do you drink alcoholic beverages?

2. How much attention do you pay to your personal appearance and grooming?

3. How often do you daydream?

4. Do you always tell the truth?

5. Would you agree that companies don't expect employees to always obey company rules and regulations?

6. Do you always tell the truth regardless of the circumstances?

7. How often, in recent years, have you simply thought about taking money without actually doing it?

8. Most people have tried drugs sometimes in their lives. An employer is basically interested in knowing if a job applicant falls into one of two categories:

   Category A is a person who is addicted to drugs. They are not dependable and may need some money to support their habit.

   Category B is the more average person who has tried some commonly used drugs out of curiosity or has used them socially. Many more people fall into this category.

   What kind of person are you? What are your feelings about drugs?

   _____

   _____

   _____

   _____

Questions 1 to 7 usually elicit applicant's responses in terms of a five- to seven-point rating scale, such as *Never* to *Very often*, or *Agree very much* to *Disagree very much*, or *Definitely yes* to *Definitely no*. Question 8 is an example of an open-ended question.

Source: Personnel Selection Inventory: PSI-7, London House, Inc., Park Ridge, Ill., 1986, pp. 3–7.

is to assess honesty and spot drug abusers. An example of several typical test items is provided in Exhibit 7-7.

- *Drug tests.* Drug testing programs are being used frequently in private industry. These tests are most commonly used to screen out applicants who are drug users. In the future, as drug testing spreads, many existing employees can expect to be ordered to submit to drug testing on a random basis at the directive of a suspicious manager or as part of a routine physical.

Proponents of drug testing claim that it will lead to a safer and more productive work environment. Critics argue that drug testing violates constitutional protection against unreasonable search and seizure and invades the individual's privacy. They also contend that such screening is an attempt by employers to regulate workers' behavior off the job and that the results may be used as a tool for harassment. Opponents also raise doubts about the validity of the most widely used tests because they are subject to large error rates. Thus, innocent persons may be falsely classified as drug abusers. Currently, the legal future of drug testing policies is uncertain; therefore, they must be used with extreme caution because of the threat that employees might file an expensive class-action lawsuit against the firm.[7]

Legal aspects of testing.   Testing provides an objective way to measure traits or characteristics of applicants for sales positions. The use of tests in the selection process was widespread up until the late 1960s. After the passage of the Civil Rights Act in 1964, companies tended to rely less on testing because of complaints filed under Title VII of the act. The complaints charged that tests had been used to discriminate against minority groups. As a result, some executives have the idea that it is illegal to use testing in the selection process. Testing is not illegal if done correctly; that is, the questions and procedures used in testing must be relevant to the job.

A company should use tests designed by a professional to meet the needs of a particular job. So job factors related to success must be identified; then valid and reliable tests that measure them must be designed specifically for the company, or appropriate standardized tests must be purchased.

Since tests can have a cultural bias and discriminate against certain groups, their use must be continually monitored. A test may be a valid predictor for one group of recruits but not for all groups. Also, different scores for different groups may be equally good indicators of success in a sales job. Therefore, the company should keep records showing that the tests and questions are relevant to the job and that the tests are not screening out a large proportion of women or minorities.

The use of testing as a selection tool began increasing again in the late 1970s as companies learned how to develop and use tests that would meet legal guidelines. In fact, two-thirds of all companies responding to one survey indicated they used psychological testing as a selection tool.[8]

Reasons for using tests.   Tests are used to increase the chances of selecting good salespeople. Tests can identify traits and qualifications (such as intelligence, aptitude, and personality) that cannot be measured by other selection tools. Another reason for using tests relates to the high cost of training and hiring the sales force. A selection tool that can reduce sales force turnover and increase sales productivity is definitely desirable. Tests also provide a basis for interviewing. Questionable points noted in the test results may be probed more deeply during the interview.

Considering the fact that a hiring mistake can cost a company between $40,000 and $50,000 today, any tool that will help firms make the right selection decision is welcomed. As one testing expert explained, "It all boils down to the importance attached to the hiring decision. Your people are what make your organization run, and because of that, you want to select your employees in the most cost-effective and timely way possible. Testing offers you a way to do that."[9]

Problems in testing.   A major problem involved with testing is that most tests are based on the concept that an average person is best suited for the job. This means that potentially successful salespeople may be screened out because they do not fit the stereotype.

Another problem is that tests may be used as the sole decision factor. Recruits may look good on the basis of interviews, application forms, and reference checks, but if their test scores are low, they may not be considered further. If the score is extremely low, rejection may be justified. But if the score is only slightly below the acceptable level, applicants should probably be retested. Test scores should not be the sole criterion used in making hiring decisions; rather, they should be one of several factors considered.

Tests are often misunderstood and misused, causing many sales managers to conclude that they are of little value as a screening tool. For example, management sometimes believes that the highest score on the test indicates the best prospect; however, all the applicants who fall within a certain range should be judged as equally qualified for the job. Many sales managers who do not understand tests use them only because the home office insists, and then they often ignore the results.

MAKING THE SELECTION

When all other steps have been completed in the selection process, the company must decide whether or not to hire each applicant. The company must review everything known about a particular applicant. The applicant's goals and ambitions must be matched against present and future opportunities, challenges, and other types of rewards that are offered by the job and the company.

The example that follows describes one selection process that is typical of many large firms.

SELECTING THE SALES FORCE AT NEW ENGLAND MUTUAL LIFE

As mentioned at the beginning of this chapter, New England Mutual Life Insurance (NEL) has a unique computer-based sales force selection process called STEP. This process consists of five steps:

1. *First interview.* This involves matching candidates against NEL's successful-agent profile. Next, candidates are screened by making observations about interpersonal skills. Finally, job-related information from a candidate's work, education, personal history, and test results is considered.

2. *Reference check.* Here, calls are made to verify candidate information by talking with several work-related and personal references.

3. *Second interview.* This step focuses on the candidate's qualifications in relation to the job position to determine the person's potential for success as an associate and the agency's potential for successfully training, marketing, and managing the person.

4. *Third interview.* This interview determines which candidates are most likely to succeed because they best match the job requirements.

5. *Performance follow-up.* This is a very important step. It involves checking the person's performance over time to determine how well the selection decision worked out in retention-production terms and deciding if changes should be made in the selection process.[10]

A seasoned sales executive should give consideration to intuitions as well as to facts. If any uneasy feelings about candidates exist, the candidate should be called back for another interview, and additional reference checking should be done. If a company follows the logical sequence of a well-planned recruiting and selection system, the executive's intuitions will soon be transformed into objective criteria that can be used to compare applicants and make decisions among them. Exhibit 7-8 emphasizes some key points for sales managers making a selection decision. Several important sales selection questions that sales managers should also consider are presented in the next example.

SELECTING THE BEST FOR YOUR SALES FORCE

Here are some common sales selection questions, with answers from Dr. David W. Merrill, chairman of Tracom:

Q: Sales managers know they've hired the best when a salesperson sells the most, but how do they know how to find this kind of person again?

A: You identify what you've learned that can apply the next time you hire a salesperson. That is, you need a system that keeps track of what it is about a person's background, experience, and abilities that is relevant to picking another like that. For example, what qualities does a person have before joining your organization that lead to success? You will not be able to find duplicate people, but you can find persons with approximately the same characteristics. In short, we're talking about the ability to identify specific qualities that contribute to success and to apply this information to your next selection decision. Obviously, everyone can't be the best. But you can expect the average performance per salesperson to get better if you have a system that tracks performance and constantly identifies success characteristics—and you use this information when hiring in the future. This approach translates into increased productivity and sales revenues.

Q: Can't psychologists simply provide a test that predicts sales success?

A: There is no single psychological test or set of characteristics that assures that you will get the best person for a position. And even if you could find one, it would not work across all companies or industries; there is no way to determine a single generic standard to pick what is best for all companies. Top performance in one company can't assure success in another. There is no single golden person who will perform best everyplace. Each organization must develop its own model of what is best based upon everything in its recruiting and selection process.

Q: Why can't sales success be defined generically?

A: It is vital for you to know what is best for your company, rather than in a generic sense, because sales success is much more dependent upon an individual's background and experience relevant to a company's products and services than it is upon personality types. It is true that some generalized characteristics are needed for all sales jobs. You need to find people who are willing to talk to prospects and to answer questions about the commodity they sell.[11]

EXHIBIT 7-8

Key Points to Cover when Hiring a Salesperson

Duties of the Salesperson

Exercise best efforts in representing the company and its products or services.

Make no representations, warranties, or commitments binding the company without the company's prior consent. The salesperson will be personally liable and required to reimburse the company in the event he exceeds this authority.

Forward all field inquiries or complaints in the field to the company immediately.

Must work full-time for the company without any sideline. Especially, he must not represent or form a competing business.

Must personally solicit the product and cannot hire an associate to represent the company without prior written approval.

Maintain minimum general and automobile liability coverage.

Attend sales meetings, both local and national.

Call on accounts periodically, service accounts, and maintain accurate selling records and lead sheets.

Assist in any collection efforts requested by the company.

Promise to protect all trade secrets, customer lists, and other forms of confidential information acquired while working for the company.

Compensation

1. *Salary (usually given to company-employed salespeople):*
   What is the amount and when is it payable?

2. *Draw (usually given to independent sales reps):*
   Is it applied against commission?
   What is the amount and when is it payable?
   The draw can be stopped by the company anytime without prior notice when commission earnings do not exceed draw.
   The sales rep is personally liable for repayment when draw exceeds commission earnings and the rep resigns or is fired from his or her job.
   The company has the right to sell off draw and reduce the amount of commission owed on termination of the employment relationship.

3. *Bonus (usually given to company-employed salespeople):*
   Is the bonus gratuitous or enforceable by contract?
   What is the amount and when is it payable?
   Specify that pro rata bonuses will not be given in the event the salesperson resigns or is fired prior to the date the bonus will be paid.
   Avoid basing the bonus on a determination of profits because this may give the salesperson the right to inspect your company's books and records.

4. *Commission:*
   Specify the commission rate and when it is payable.
   Avoid guaranteed shipping arrangements.
   Specify split-commission policies if applicable.
   Specify all deductions from commissions, how and when they are computed, e.g., returns, freight charges, unauthorized price concessions given by the salesperson, billing and advertising discounts, collection charges, failure of the customer to pay.
   Specify commission for large orders, special customers, off-price goods, and reorders.

5. *Expenses (usually for company-employed salespeople):*
   Specify the kind and amount of expenses that are reimbursable.
   Specify the kind of documentation the salesperson must supply in order to receive
   reimbursement.

Territory

Are you giving exclusive or nonexclusive territorial rights? Define the particular territory
and customers.
Be sure to discuss all house accounts and document these in writing.
What about products sold in one territory and shipped into another? Determine how this
will affect your split-commission policy.
Can the salesperson sell in other territories not solicited by other salespeople, e.g., at
trade shows?
If exclusive territorial rights are not involved, ensure that the salesperson will not receive
commission for orders not actually solicited by him or her.

Length of Employment Relationship

Date employment is to begin.
Length of employment. Is employment at will (the salesperson can be fired anytime) or for
a definite term, say, two years?
If employment is at will, is notice required? If so, how far in advance must it be sent for
the termination to be effective and how must it be sent (e.g., certified or regular mail)?
Never give assurances of job security if you are hiring a salesperson at will.
If employment is for a definite term, is the contract renewable under the same terms and
conditions after the expiration of the original term? Must notice be sent to confirm this?
Peg employment to a minimum sales quota if applicable.

Termination of Employment

Clarify when commissions stop; e.g., upon termination, upon shipment of order, upon
shipment with a cutoff date to eliminate the problem of reorders.
Avoid severance compensation arrangements.
Specify when a final accounting will be made.
Limit the right of the salesperson to sue for commissions within a specified period.
Specify the prompt return of all samples, customer lists, orders, field information, with a
penalty if not complied with.
Include a restrictive covenant for additional protection in writing.

Source: Steven M. Sack, "Let's Not Shake on It," *Sales & Marketing Management*, May 14, 1984, pp. 47–51.

A decision to hire is followed by a formal offer, with no unspecified details
or surprises; the terms should be in writing for the protection of both the recruit
and the firm. Many companies require that all new salespeople sign contracts
containing all important job-related information.

If a chosen candidate has lots of reservations about the job, sales managers
should not attempt persuasion. Such applicants are not likely to give the company their best efforts.

A factor that is becoming increasingly important in the sales force selection process is the entry of women into sales occupations. "Salesman" is an anachronistic word as more and more women enter what was once a male-dominated occupation. Approximately 23 percent of all individuals selling manufactured products are now women; a decade ago, the number was only 7 percent. Women currently make up over 39 percent of the sales force at Xerox Corporation.

SALES FORCE SELECTION IN MULTINATIONAL COMPANIES

A growing concern of many U.S. corporations is selecting qualified salespeople for their international markets. As U.S. companies go overseas to sell their products, they soon realize how different the selling environment and the markets are from those in the United States. Differences in ethnic compositions, religious orientations, social class, and education definitely complicate the sales force selection process for multinational corporations. A recent study of sales force recruiters at multinational companies discovered some differences between the ranking of various salesperson selection criteria for overseas markets and the ranking for U.S. markets. For example, education is more important in overseas markets, and selection criteria such as social class, religion, and ethnicity—which are seldom used in the United States—account for as much as 25 percent of the sales hirings abroad.[12] An important implication of this study is that the differences in the selling environments and cultures make the use of standardized selection criteria dangerous when salespeople are being selected for overseas markets.

SALES FORCE SOCIALIZATION

Once the process of recruiting and selecting the new salesperson is complete, that person must be integrated into the organization. The proper introduction of the recruit to company practices, procedures, and philosophy and to the social aspects of the job is crucial in achieving a return on the sizable investment made during the recruiting and selection process. The effective development of job skills, the adoption of appropriate role behaviors and organization values, and adaptation to the work group and its norms can influence a recruit's motivation, job satisfaction, and performance.[13] With large numbers of women and minorities entering the workplace as entry-level salespersons, the socialization process takes on an increasingly critical role in the future success of the firm.

A recent study of sales force socialization suggests that the firm's efforts in recruiting, selection, and training all play an important part in the socialization process.[14] One hundred eighty-nine of the "least experienced salespersons" from different companies were surveyed. The results of the survey imply that (1) if recruiters give the prospective employee a realistic picture of the sales job, the chances for job satisfaction are enhanced, (2) better training and initiation to

EXHIBIT 7-9

The Benefits of Formal Sales Force Socialization

Socialization Effort	Benefit to Recruit and Firm
Recruiting: Objective: To give recruit a realistic picture of the job	Greater job satisfaction Increased employee commitment Improved chance for survival
Selection: Objective: Compatibility of recruit's needs and skills with the work environment	Greater job satisfaction Better understanding of role as a salesperson in the firm Greater job involvement Greater chance for survival for new salespersons
Training: Objective: Better initiation to sales tasks	Greater job satisfaction Increased feeling of control by salesperson over how work is performed Greater task-specific self-esteem.

Source: Alan J. Dubinsky et al., "Salesforce Socialization," *Journal of Marketing*, October 1986, pp. 201–202.

the job lead to greater job satisfaction, and (3) sales recruits whose personal needs and skills are compatible with the firm and the job should be selected. The study also revealed that the socialization process begins when the potential sales candidate reads recruiting literature about the firm and attends the first interview with company representatives. Exhibit 7-9 lists some of the most important benefits of a formal sales force socialization program.

There are basically two levels of socialization. The first level is *initial socialization*. This preliminary exposure to the firm begins with the recruiting and selection process and ends with the initial orientation of the salesperson to the firm's procedures and policies. The second level, *extended socialization*, concerns making the new salesperson feel that he or she is an integral part of the company. This is achieved by exposing new recruits to the corporate culture (values, philosophy, group norms, different work groups, corporate officers, and so on) and aiding them in adopting and adapting to this new culture in as short a period of time as possible.

Initial Socialization

Initial socialization occurs during the recruiting, selecting, and introductory training efforts performed by the firm. Proper assimilation of the new salesperson into the organization is facilitated by attention to the socialization process at these early stages. Socialization at each of these stages is discussed in the following paragraphs.

Recruiting.   Most firms begin the socialization process by sending the sales candidate recruiting literature which details the company's philosophy and the role of the salesperson in the organization. Procter & Gamble's recruiting brochure addresses these points, as explained in the next example.

SOCIALIZATION AT PROCTER & GAMBLE

Corporate Philosophy

The key to our continued success will be our ability to attract the very best people to our organization and develop them to their fullest potential. Consequently, we believe in giving people early responsibility for important work. Within weeks of joining P&G you will be responsible for millions of dollars' worth of business. You will be backed up by personalized, on-the-job training and extensive resources. Because of the breadth of experience sales offers, because it demands creativity and resourcefulness, sales management is a proven route to corporate general management.

If you like a static environment offering few challenges and little adventure, you probably would not be happy in sales. But if you relish working with people, if you enjoy solving problems, if you crave the opportunity to establish high goals and work hard to exceed them—you're the kind of person who'll find excitement at P&G in sales management. Our organization is dedicated to encouraging initiative, diligence, and the acceptance of personal responsibility. We seek people ready to become a part of a world-class enterprise.

The following pages will tell you more about us, the nature of Sales, and what you can expect as an employee. Specifically it answers five basic questions:

1. Why Sales Management?
2. Why Procter & Gamble?
3. What is Sales Management's role at Procter & Gamble?
4. What can you expect from us?
5. What will we expect from you?

The Salesperson's Role at Procter & Gamble

From the beginning, salespersons have to be effective managers of people, good decision makers, creative problem solvers, and outstanding communicators. They also must work closely with other disciplines as part of the overall marketing team, helping to coordinate and focus the efforts of Product Development, Manufacturing, Market Research, and Advertising.

The challenge you face in sales is to become an acknowledged expert on your brands, categories, customers, and marketplace. Your personal responsibility is to develop and execute selling strategies needed to drive the business ahead. You must analyze the business, identify opportunities, and then develop specific plans to capitalize on them. Sometimes you work alone, but more often you must skillfully manage others to achieve your goals. As a member of P&G Sales, you also must be an "entrepreneur," and your own boss.

Obviously, as a member of P&G's Sales team you're no mere order taker. You must be a creative merchandiser with business-building ideas. As your knowledge increases, you'll develop creative solutions for the day-to-day problems and challenges that are an inevitable part of the business: a newspaper advertising theme tying in your brands; a unique promotion relating your brands with a topic in the national or local spotlight; an innovative selling idea specifically aimed at the demographics of your area; or a tailored solution to a warehouse-to-store distribution problem. This kind of creativity and results-oriented thinking is the hallmark of the P&G Salesperson.[15]

Selection.   The interview process can give both the candidate and the recruiter some idea of how the new salesperson will respond to the socialization efforts of the company. For example, sales representatives of Electronic Data Systems (EDS) are expected to dress conservatively. By conforming to this dress pattern, the recruiter signals the company's expectations to the recruit. In addition, this image may yield clues about the organization's philosophy and the structure of the company.

Many firms also schedule the sales candidate for multiple interviews at all levels of the company and in other functional departments. The purpose of this exercise is to expose the candidate to the organization culture and to get several opinions about how well the recruit will respond to socialization efforts. IBM requires that sales candidates go through five or six interviews in an effort to find those who will conform to the "IBM Way" of performing sales tasks.

Professional recruiting brochures and lengthy interview processes are typical of most large and many medium-sized firms. But small firms may not be able to afford the expense of such high-quality recruiting materials. When small firms recruit salespeople, a principal owner of the firm is often involved in the interviewing process. Thus, the candidate can get firsthand information about the owner's philosophy of running the business and the role of the sales force. Likewise, the owner may discern whether the candidate "fits" the characteristics the firm is seeking.

Once the salesperson has been selected by a small firm, he or she is likely to report directly to a principal in the firm. For example, EPI (an electronics company) hired two recent college graduates as salespeople. The recruits' offices were placed adjacent to the president's office, and they reported directly to the senior vice president (a founder of the firm). This enabled both the president and the senior vice president to socialize the new salespersons directly.

Introductory training.   After successfully completing the recruiting and selection process, the new recruit has some notion of the firm's corporate philosophy and the nature of the sales position. Some companies prepare a detailed human resources manual concerning the company's history, product line, organization, job descriptions, and various compensation and benefit packages. By receiving such a manual before they report for work, new salespeople can quickly find answers to many of their questions concerning the company's procedures and policies. IBM not only provides new salespeople with a manual but also requires that every salesperson read the book *The IBM Way* by the former executive vice president of marketing, F. G. "Buck" Rodgers. This book forms the basis for the first step in socializing the new salesperson at IBM.

When the salesperson reports to work for the first time, immediate placement into a field selling situation may result in improper socialization. New recruits should report first to the home or regional office so that they may be properly informed about the job, company procedures, policies, and the like. Recruits should also be encouraged to ask questions about information in the human resources manual or other materials given to them prior to reporting to work.

While at the home office, the sales recruit should be exposed to the actual operations of the firm. Payroll procedures, expense-account administration, office procedures and policies, and routine practices such as parking and dining facilities should be explained by members of the human resources department or sales training staff or by the sales manager.

Extended Socialization

Extended socialization programs involve long-term training, job rotation, and corporate social activities. The focus of extended socialization is on the long-term building of esprit de corps and camaraderie in the sales organization.

Long-term training.   Many large companies use long-term training programs to educate salespeople about the firm's products, customers, and competitors and to ensure that the new recruits are properly socialized. For example, IBM sales recruits go through an extensive fifteen-month training program before they are assigned to their own territory. The training involves classroom lectures, independent study, and actual field training under the direction of a veteran salesperson. All these efforts are undertaken to ensure superior product knowledge and an understanding of the IBM way of doing sales tasks.

Companies that engage in this type of extended socialization program are aiming for uniform adherence to company practices, procedures, and philosophy. In addition, they want to assist new salespeople in acquiring a high level of job skills and an understanding of appropriate role behaviors and work-group values. This standardization of values, behavior norms, and philosophy helps produce consistent sales performance results because salespeople become highly motivated team players.

There is, however, a negative side to this type of extended socialization. Some recruits may resent being asked to "fit the mold" and may leave the firm. Through proper selection methods and accurate presentation of company expectations, such individuals can be screened out before company resources are expended in training them.

Job rotation.   Both large and small firms use job rotation as a way to expose sales trainees to the corporate culture. Not only do the recruits learn the functional aspects of how different departments work, but they also make social contacts and are exposed to the overall organization. This broad exposure to the firm early in their sales career helps instill a sense of belonging and camaraderie in recruits.

One firm that practices job rotation with sales recruits is Apple Computer, Inc. New salespeople are first given introductory training on company procedures and policies. Before they are permanently assigned to a sales territory, they are expected to spend several weeks working in engineering, manufacturing, distribution, and customer and dealer service. This program has been successful in helping Apple's salespeople to better understand their role in the organization. It also establishes good resource contacts in these functional areas, should the salesperson need assistance with problems in the field.

Corporate social activity.   Many firms are beginning to recognize the value of informal ways of socializing new employees. Company picnics, sports teams, and sales meetings all provide an opportunity for the new salesperson to interact with experienced salespersons, sales managers, and company executives in a nonthreatening environment. In these types of settings, the new employee can ask questions and observe how everyone fits into the social structure of the firm. Often, the recruit's spouse or other special people may be included in the activity. This helps affirm the role of the new employee's partner in the successful performance of the sales job. The main problem with these kinds of activities is usually the distance between a salesperson's territory and the corporate headquarters.

Apple Computer, Inc., conducts informal corporate training sessions for new hires. The sessions are referred to as "Apple University." Spouses are invited to attend the three-day event, which is usually held at a resort or a company facility. New employees attend informal sessions with human resources personnel or outside consultants to learn about such things as "Apple values." Apple values are the company's social norms of behavior, which involve empathy for customers and users, quality and excellence, achievement and aggressiveness, individual reward, positive social contribution, team spirit, innovation and vision, individual performance, and good management. The employee's companion may attend these sessions or may spend the day engaging in a variety of leisure activities. After the informal socialization sessions are over, time is allocated for leisure activities with division managers and other executives of the company.

Corporate social activity aimed at socialization need not be so elaborate or expensive. Hallway conversations and softball teams can be effective means of socializing the new salesperson. Each of these various methods facilitates the major purpose of building esprit de corps within the sales organization.

SUMMARY

Selecting good applicants is an extremely important and challenging task for the sales manager. It is critical that the sales manager select the candidates who best meet the qualifications established by the company. Some of the tools companies use during the selection process include screening interviews, application forms, in-depth interviews, reference checks, physical examinations, and tests. Recently, companies have begun using psychological prediction strategies and computerized data bases in the selection process. Companies are putting more emphasis on the selection process as they realize the importance of selecting and keeping top-rated applicants.

Once the process of recruiting and selection is complete, the new salesperson must be integrated into the sales force. Socialization involves the formal introduction of the recruit to company practices, procedures, and philosophy as well as the social aspects of the job. Effective development of job skills, adoption of appropriate role behaviors and organization values, and adaptation to the work group and its norms can influence a recruit's motivation, job satisfaction, and performance. There are two levels in the socialization process. Initial socialization occurs during the recruiting, selection, and introductory training processes. Extended socialization is accomplished through long-term training, job rotation, and corporate social activities. In all firms new salespersons are socialized through both formal and informal methods.

STUDY QUESTIONS

1. What steps are involved in the selection process?

2. Why is it important to have a well-planned selection program?

3. What kind of changes do you believe will occur in the selection process in the next few years?

4. Which tool is more important in the selection process, application forms or personal interviews? Why?

5. What is the most important thing a sales recruit can do before going to an interview?

6. What is socialization? When does it occur?

7. Why is socialization of new salespersons important?

8. Will the socialization process change as more women and minorities begin sales careers?

9. What are the basic tests that can be used in the sales personnel selection process? Explain the purpose of each test.

10. Should sales managers give consideration to universities when making a selection decision? Why or why not? What are the positive and negative aspects of hiring college students?

IN-BASKET EXERCISE

You have just gone through a very challenging recruiting season, and you realize the mounting difficulty of finding good salespeople. However, you were particularly impressed by a very confident, intelligent individual with good communication skills. The only potential problem you foresee with this individual is his appearance—he is a very sloppy dresser and is a bit overweight. Your company does not have a formal policy about employee appearance, but you know that sloppy and overweight candidates have been rejected in the past because "they didn't show the energy and effort required for a sales position." Although you want to hire this person, you know that your company employs only salespeople who "fit the corporate image."

1. What do you do?

2. Are there any legal ramifications associated with this decision?

3. Should companies today work with individuals to help them lose weight or dress more professionally?

CASE 7-1

SELECTING A SALESPERSON AT JAK PHARMACEUTICAL

JAK Pharmaceutical is rearranging sales territories. The sales manager must begin the process of selecting a salesperson qualified to develop a new territory so that it will perform at the same profit level as present territories.

Rather than approach this selection process in the traditional manner, JAK Pharmaceutical has decided to use an analytical approach. This approach consists of separating a job into its two major components—(1) the sales activity needed by the company so profit is realized and (2) the qualifications of the recruit—and then analyzing each component individually, without influence by the other. Matching sales activity with the person whose qualifications are best suited to perform that *sales activity in the marketplace* (SAM) fits a round peg into a round hole rather than a round peg into a square hole. Since company revenue is obtained by performing its SAM effectively, primary emphasis is on profit. Once SAM has been defined by the company, then all management functions—hiring, paying, training, and evaluating—are shaped for the purpose of motivating salespeople to perform that SAM better. Profit continues as the number-one priority throughout. Exhibit 1 outlines the SAM chosen as the most profitable means of directing JAK Pharmaceutical's sales force efforts.

JAK Pharmaceutical is a four-year-old pharmaceutical firm that markets over-the-counter ophthalmic products west of the Mississippi River by concentrating sales force efforts on selected retail drugstores.

The primary promotional thrust is toward trade advertising, point-of-purchase display materials, and co-op advertising with local pharmacists. Although the retail price is competitive with similar products available in the marketplace, the retail margin for the drugstores is slightly higher than on other brands. Package design and color are contemporary, and product quality meets or exceeds competitive offerings. By providing an extensive array of in-store promotional materials, JAK Pharmaceutical relies on the local pharmacists to recommend its products. This strategy's success relies on the salesperson's suggesting to the pharmacists how JAK products can be merchandised profitably.

An opening in the sales force has resulted because the company is reducing the size of each territory, enabling present salespeople to provide closer merchandising help by increasing the frequency of callbacks. This strategy encourages each account to purchase more goods more often from JAK, offsetting the higher cost of sales incurred. In this new territory structure, salespeople must balance their time effectively between serving established accounts, serving newer accounts in varying stages of development, and hunting for new accounts. Critically important for successful sales performance is the ability to manage one's time prudently because bonus levels and raises are dependent on territory profitability. Five candidates are being considered for the sales force opening. Brief backgrounds for each are provided in Exhibit 2.

A territory contains approximately 1,000 potential accounts. A company car is furnished; compensation is salary and bonus with an excellent potential

---

EXHIBIT 1

JAK Pharmaceutical's Sales Activity in the Marketplace

1. Primarily, JAK sells directly to retail drugstores with minor emphasis on drug wholesalers.

2. The training program requires the trainee to be flexible and adaptable because the development stage of accounts varies.

3. The salesperson will handle customer complaints and returned goods; full discretionary authority is delegated accordingly.

4. The salesperson must have sufficient talent to help retailer merchandise goods profitably.

5. JAK's products are not offered to grocery stores or other competing outlets, so the firm doesn't scramble their channels of distribution.

6. The salesperson must spend whatever time is needed to service present accounts properly so that they show steady sales increases; the remaining time should be spent developing certain potentially important accounts and prospecting for new accounts.

7. The salesperson must diversify routing so time is maximized for higher-volume accounts and minimized for lesser-volume accounts.

8. The salesperson must sell the complete product line rather than push personal favorites.

9. The annual bonus depends on volume increases over last year and this year's territory profitability versus last year's.

Case prepared by Jack Degan, Texas Wesleyan University. Used with permission.

for an override that depends on increasing profitability from last year's operating costs. Salespeople are required to make daily reports and furnish the home office with bimonthly itineraries. Product knowledge is heavily emphasized by JAK during the extensive training program; a recruit can easily lose his or her position if educational level or abilities are not satisfactorily demonstrated.

EXHIBIT 2

Background of Applicants

Applicant A:

No full-time experience selling; worked part-time in retail sales throughout college
Age 22, single
Annual income: midteens through school, income derived from part-time retail sales and lawn-care business
Hobbies: tennis, golf, racketball
Started own lawn-care business in high school

Applicant B:

One year of experience selling insurance; compensated totally by commission
Age 23, married, wife works, no children
Annual income: upper teens last year
Hobbies: fishing, gardening, do-it-yourself projects around house

Applicant C:

Three years of selling health and beauty products for a national firm
Age 28, married, husband is a schoolteacher, no children
M.B.A. degree
Annual income: upper 30s
Hobbies: plays golf, active in church club

Applicant D:

Twenty years of sales experience in insurance and financial-services industries; worked for six different companies, all in sales
Age 45, single
High school graduate
Annual income: ranged from low 20s to low 50s
Hobbies: travel, sports

Applicant E:

Seven years of experience selling medical products to hospitals; two years of sales management experience
Age 34, married, two children
Degree in biology
Annual income: ranged from low 20s to upper 40s
Invests in real estate

EXHIBIT 3

Personal Qualifications

1. Seeks challenge, enjoys being creative, is able to work as an individual developing and building market share

2. Demonstrates communication skills

3. Is multitalented with a penchant for improving

4. Demonstrates ability to generate ideas by explaining to pharmacists how greater profit can be realized by featuring JAK Pharmaceutical's products

5. Possesses the maturity to plan time judiciously so that maximum potential can be realized from sales effort

6. Commands thorough understanding of JAK Pharmaceutical products so that new uses and users' ideas can be conveyed to retail consumers

7. Shows personality traits considered most desirable for success in performing JAK Pharmaceutical's SAM profitably: extroverted, resourceful, confident, adaptable, imaginative and shows initiative as a self-starter

Traditional business attire is required when salespeople are calling on the trade, so the company's professional image is maintained. Detailed job descriptions are presented along with the initial application form. The job description includes expected sales volume standards (quotas) for each territory. Each salesperson is given wide authoritative latitude in in-

EXHIBIT 4

Candidate Compatibility with SAM Requirements

On the criteria below, indicate how you would rate each applicant according to JAK Pharmaceutical's SAM needs. Rate each as: *Match, Mismatch, Not Applicable.*

Type of product sold
Services provided accounts
Type of accounts called on (drugstores, wholesale, notions, etc.)
Level of accounts called on (retail, wholesale, agent, manufacturing)
Frequency of sales calls
Number of calls per day
Extent of market penetration enjoyed by former employers
Authority/responsibility relationship between salesperson and boss
Competitive intensity of marketplace
Type of calls (service, new accounts, development)
Primary purpose of previous sales calls
Personality fit of previous sales jobs
Personality fit for JAK

terpreting how these sales figures will be achieved. Management reflects a modern approach to working conditions, delegating authority and freedom in proportion to each salesperson's maturity.

The sales environment at JAK is a mixture of strictness and liberalism almost to the point that each salesperson seems to be in business individually. JAK Pharmaceutical's salary ranks in the lower range of competitive salaries in this field; the liberal bonus and override must be realized for this job to rank as toppaying. Exhibit 3 shows the personal qualities sought by JAK in hiring new salespeople. To determine which sales candidates best fit SAM requirements, JAK uses the checklist provided in Exhibit 4.

Competitive intensity is moderate because the many firms marketing goods in this field have taken a ho-

hum approach to the marketplace. The aggressive posture of JAK Pharmaceutical should awaken some sleeping giants in the field.

Questions

1. Which applicant would you hire? Support your answer.

2. Which applicant's qualifications best fit JAK Pharmaceutical's needs? Which person would best fit JAK's SAM requirements?

3. If a second sales position opened up, whom would you hire? Why?

4. Recommend ways to improve JAK Pharmaceutical's salesperson slection process. Be specific.

CASE 7-2

BELCO, INC.: SALES FORCE SELECTION

Belco, Inc., is a U.S.-based supplier of electronic components for radios, television sets, videocassette recorders, and numerous other electronic products. In the past, components have primarily been sold to U.S. companies such as Zenith and Magnavox. But recently Belco has expanded its market to include companies in Canada. The components range in price from $25 to $450, depending on the complexity and capabilities of the individual components. Belco contracts with manufacturers in Taiwan and Korea for the supply of all components. The company chose manufacturers in these countries because cheap labor enables them to supply components at prices considerably lower than manufacturers in other countries.

William Simmons, national sales manager of Belco, Inc., is faced with three major problems: sales force performance that is below potential, a high turnover of salespeople, and the need to hire more salespeople in order to cover the expanded market area. In total, there are 1,032 manufacturers who purchase approximately $2.5 billion of electronic components annually. These manufacturers are in seventeen states across the United States, with the majority of the plants in the northeast and south. However, the state with the largest number of manufacturers is California, which has 272. Belco has approximately 5 percent of the total market.

Belco employs twenty-five salespeople—twenty men and five women. Each salesperson is assigned a spe-

cific geographic territory; each territory represents approximately 4 percent of Belco's total market. Each salesperson is responsible for the maintenance of approximately twenty accounts, and the development of additional accounts depending on the number of manufacturers in the given region.

There are five regional sales managers responsible for supervising and hiring salespeople. In hiring, the regional sales managers are guided by the job description shown in Exhibit 1.

The current selection procedure for new salespeople is basically the same within all regions. Simmons described the selection procedure as follows:

1. All applicants complete application forms.

2. Applications are initially screened by the regional sales manager's secretary.

3. After initial screening by secretaries, applicants are selected for interviews by regional sales managers.

4. A brief interview is conducted by the regional sales manager.

5. The selection is made by the regional sales manager on the basis of the application, the interview, and the sales manager's personal opinions.

Reference checks are made on applicants if there are any concerns about whether or not the person should be hired.

Case prepared by Suzanne Desonier, Louisiana State University. Used with permission.

Job Description: Salesperson

Position: District sales representative
Reports to: Regional sales manager

Purpose of position: To sell electronic component parts in the assigned territory to assigned customers and assist on national account promotions and sales.

Position responsibilities:

1. Manage territory in order to create and maintain an attractive purchasing environment for customers and potential customers.

2. Call regularly on major customers and potential customers.

3. Make sales presentations, determine customers' needs, and sell product line.

4. Maintain healthy relationship with all accounts and potential accounts.

5. Work with other departments within the company to ensure prompt delivery of parts and continued customer satisfaction.

6. Keep updated on all customer complaints and report these to the regional sales manager.

7. Aggressively support product line and cooperate with company promotional programs.

8. Manage time and utilize resources in the most efficient manner in order to provide above-average coverage to customers.

9. Aid management in preparing sales forecasts by accumulating and analyzing statistical data.

10. Prepare monthly work plan.

Position requirements:

1. Two years experience

2. B.S. degree in business or engineering

3. Willingness to travel

After examining the files of the twenty-five salespeople, Simmons decided that they could be divided into three groups: low-, middle-, and high-level performers. The division was based on the factors Simmons believes are important in evaluating a salesperson: sales volume, customer satisfaction, and the evaluation of the salespeople by the regional sales manager. He noted that the turnover rate for those classified as low- or middle-level performers was significantly higher (approximately 20 percent annually) than the turnover rate for those classified as high-level

performers (approximately 2 percent annually). Simmons also noted that only 44 percent of the sales force (eleven salespeople) could be classified as high-level performers under the current criteria. He also decided that the turnover rate was excessive and that it was costing the company about $7,500 per person annually (the cost to hire and train new recruits).

Simmons concluded that there was a need to revise the selection process and sought the aid of a local management consulting firm. The firm was asked to investigate the alternatives available and the advantages and disadvantages associated with each alternative. After reviewing the situation, the consulting firm concluded that Belco had several alternatives.

In-Depth Personal Interview

The first alternative dealt with the addition of an in-depth personal interview. The consulting firm concluded that a structured interview would be beneficial to Belco. The rationale for this addition to the procedure is that only through an in-depth interview can sales managers gather sufficient data to be able to predict whether a salesperson will be successful in the position. Guidelines for the interview would be set as follows:

1. Interviewer explains the basic structure of the organization and how the sales position fits into the overall structure of the company.

2. Review résumé information with applicant.

3. Discuss applicant's educational achievements and extracurricular activities.

4. Review previous job experience and ask why the applicant chose past jobs and the reasons for leaving those jobs.

5. Review job performance and responsibilities in most recent jobs.

6. Present a typical problem the applicant may face in the sales position, and ask how he or she would handle it.

7. Discuss the applicant's career plans and aspirations.

8. Ask about the applicant's personal assessment of his or her strengths and developmental needs.

9. Wrap up the interview with an open-ended question which will give the applicant the opportunity to gather more information about the company and the position and to bring up issues not already discussed.

The consulting firm assured Belco that the addition of a structured interview such as this one would increase the reliability and effectiveness of the selection process. If implemented properly, this addition to the procedure should reduce turnover, increase customer satisfaction, and improve performance because of a better match between the person chosen and the position. However, there were drawbacks to the inclusion of this type of interview. The regional sales managers would have to be trained in the implementation and interpretation of the new interview, and may be reluctant to comply because of the amount of time they would have to invest. The effective implementation of this addition to the selection procedure would depend heavily on Simmons's presentation of the new interview to the regional sales managers.

Development of Test

The second alternative for Belco is the development of a test which will identify successful (high-performing) salespeople. Results of the test would aid sales managers in the classification of applicants into low-, middle-, and high-level performers. The first step in the development of such a test is determination of characteristics which typify each performance group. For example, Simmons felt that high self-esteem, internal motivation, self-confidence, and being goal-directed were characteristics typical of high performers. However, consideration would have to be given to the fact that some salespeople may get favorable evaluations but not be high-level performers. Belco would have to be careful in the development of the test because EEO legislation allows personnel tests only if the tests have proven ability to predict performance for the job in question. Therefore, the consulting firm advised Belco to hire a firm that could aid in the development and validation of the test.

The advantages of developing a test to identify successful salespeople include the reduction of turnover and the increase in sales volume. Also, the test data could be extremely useful to Belco in the process of selection and classification of applicants as well as current salespeople. Finally, the consulting firm believed that the percentage of high-level performers hired would substantially increase with the inclusion of the test.

Addition of this selection tool also has disadvantages. The process of development would be time-consuming and costly. It would probably take six months and cost around $30,000 to develop and validate. After a period of time, sales managers may begin to rely solely on test results in the selection of salespeople rather than on other tools. The test would have to be constantly updated and monitored for it to continue to accurately predict what it is intended to predict.

System for Testing and Evaluation of Potential (STEP)

The third alternative recommended was to utilize an in-depth interview and to purchase a standardized selection tool. The consulting firm suggested that Belco management evaluate the System for Testing and Evaluation of Potential (STEP), which was developed by London House, Inc., and which was especially designed to evaluate higher-level personnel. STEP enables management to measure the Potential for Successful Performance (PSP) and the level of job skills for any of twelve positions. These twelve key positions are based on four managerial hierarchies (line, professional, sales, and financial) and on three occupational levels. The Level III positions within the hierarchy include sales representatives. The Level II positions are held by the middle-level managers (regional sales managers). Level I positions are held by general managers and executive vice presidents. Therefore, STEP could be used for the evaluation of regional sales managers as well as for salespeople.

The STEP program consists of three parts: job analysis, test battery, and skills assessment. A job analysis is recommended for each position for which applicants are being considered. Since the test is based on the job analysis, London House also suggests the purchase of a job analysis kit. The kit includes instructions for preparing a managerial and professional job function inventory and provides computerized scoring and assessment of individual and composite profiles of current employees by an industrial psychologist. After development of the job analysis, London House uses computerized procedures to determine the congruency between the job analysis and the job profile. The job profile is based on a national sample of employees.

The second step of the standardized testing procedure is the actual testing of applicants. On the basis of the hierarchy (in this case, sales), a test battery is given (sample test questions can be seen in Exhibit 2). The entire test battery consists of eleven tests; however, only seven or eight tests are given to each candidate depending on which are appropriate for the position. The tests are selected from five general areas, including personal background, mental abilities, aptitudes, temperament, and emotional adjustment.

The third step, skills assessment, involves the determination of each individual's level of competency. Competency levels are assessed in four job function areas: organizational abilities, leadership, human resources, and community relations.

The importance of an applicant's competency score in any area varies with different positions. National norms are supplied for those functions that have been identified as important for the occupational levels. For example, the assessment of an applicant for a sales position (Level III) may show the person is ready to operate at this level, but the person may clearly require improvement in one of the job function areas before becoming a regional sales manager (Level II).

London House then provides a computer report on each person tested. The report indicates scores on the test measure, relevant norms with which the scores can be compared, and PSP estimates for each of the three levels in the hierarchy.

Numerous advantages exist with the purchase of the STEP program. The test allows management to assess individuals currently with the organization as well as individuals applying for positions. The STEP

EXHIBIT 2

Sample STEP Test Questions

1. EXPERIENCE AND BACKGROUND INVENTORY
   Between the time you left your last job, and the time you applied for this job, how long were you not employed? (Check "Does Not Apply" if you are currently not applying for a job.)
   a. _____ My first application for a job
   b. _____ Was employed when I applied
   c. _____ Less than 1 month
   d. _____ 1 month–1 year
   e. _____ 1–5 years
   f. _____ 6 years or more
   g. _____ Does Not Apply

2. SPECIAL APTITUDES QUESTIONS
   Would you enjoy being the toastmaster at a banquet?   Y   N
   Do you often tell stories to entertain others?   Y   N

3. SALES INVENTORY

	Most	Least
I enjoy phone conversation	_____	_____
I am empathetic to a customer's feelings	_____	_____
I am an effective negotiator	_____	_____
I set priorities well	_____	_____

4. VOCABULARY TEST (MENTAL ABILITIES)
   Squander: (1) gamble, (2) confuse, (3) dissipate, (4) tinkle
   Vat: (1) lump, (2) craft, (3) vessel, (4) adiposity

Source: Used with permission from *Personnel Selection Inventory: PSI-7,* London House, Inc., Park Ridge, Ill., 1986.

EXHIBIT 3

Sample Personnel Selection Inventory Questions

1. Do you always tell the truth regardless of the circumstances? _____

2. Do you always tell the truth? _____

3. Would you agree that most companies don't expect employees to always obey company rules and regulations? _____

---

1. How often, in recent years, have you simply thought about taking money without actually doing it? _____

2. How often have you personally known people who have taken money from their company without getting caught? _____

3. Realistically, how often in the next few years do you think you'll be forced to quit a job without giving notice? ___

Most people have tried drugs sometime in their lives. An employer is basically interested in knowing if a job applicant falls into one of two categories:

Category A is a person who is addicted to drugs. They are not dependable and may need some money to support their habits.

Category B is the more average person who has tried some commonly used drugs out of curiosity or has used them socially. Many more people fall into this category.

What kind of person are you? What are your feelings about drugs? _____

_____

_____

Source: Personnel Selection Inventory: PS1-7, London House, Inc., Park Ridge, Ill., 1986, pp. 3–7.

---

program also provides relevant norms with which scores can be compared, whereas the development of a test by Belco would not provide any norms with which to compare until a significant number of applicants could be tested. In the opinion of a well-known law firm, use of the STEP battery is not likely to precipitate any inquiry on the basis of EEO legislation. In the event of a court case, London House will also provide, at no extra charge, expert testimony concerning the construction, validity, fairness, and use of STEP.

The only disadvantage of the STEP procedure is cost. The test price depends on the quantity of STEP batteries purchased as the following table shows.

Quantity of STEP Batteries	Price per Battery
1–5	$225
6–24	$200
25–49	$175
50–99	$150
100–249	$125
250 +	$100

While the test represents an additional cost, its use should result in considerable savings from reduction in turnover as well as increased revenues from hiring better salespeople. To evaluate this alternative adequately, Belco management must compare the cost versus the savings and anticipated additional revenues.

The management consulting firm also suggested that Belco consider the purchase of a test to determine honesty and the use of drugs by applicants. London House provides this type of test as well, which is referred to as a Personnel Selection Inventory (PSI). The PSI test contains 108 questions; examples of the questions can be seen in Exhibit 3. The majority of questions provide a scale to base answers on; however, there are some open-ended questions.

The PSI is a viable alternative to the lie-detector test in instances where an applicant's honesty and use of drugs is in question. Drug abuse costs millions annually, and although Belco does not know of any problems presently, the company may want to adopt the test as a preventive measure. Disadvantages of the honesty and drug test include the cost of the test and the fact that, although it is highly reliable, some persons could be labeled incorrectly.

Belco management is having difficulty determining what action will be most beneficial to the company.

Questions

1. Do you see any problems with Belco's current sales force selection procedure? If so, what are they?

2. Critically evaluate the recommendations of the management consulting firm. Has the consulting firm omitted any alternatives? If so, what are they?

3. Develop a chart showing each of Belco's sales force selection alternatives along with the strengths and weaknesses of each. Include on the chart your personal alternative along with its corresponding strengths and weaknesses.

4. Which sales force selection procedure would you recommend to Belco? Why?

REFERENCES

1. Craig Mellow, "Who Really Got That Job?" *Sales & Marketing Management,* July 1989, pp. 41–47.
2. James W. Kerley and David W. Merrill, "New England Life Takes Steps to Insure Its Future," *Sales & Marketing Management,* Aug. 12, 1985.
3. S. Feinstein, "Computers Replacing Interviewers for Personnel and Marketing Tasks," *Wall Street Journal,* Oct. 9, 1986, sec. 2, p. 31.
4. A. Bragg, "Recruiting and Hiring without Surprises," *Sales & Marketing Management,* 1981 Portfolio, 1980, p. 66.
5. William Perreault, Warren French, and Clyde Harris, Jr., "Use of Multiple Discriminant Analysis to Improve the Salesman Selection Process," *Journal of Business,* January 1977, p. 59.
6. Richard Kern, "IQ Tests for Salesmen Make a Comeback," *Sales & Marketing Management,* April 1988, pp. 42–46.
7. Henry Weinstein, "Drug Tests: Use, Conflict Growing Fast," *Los Angeles Times,* 1986, as reported in *Sunday Advocate,* Baton Rouge, La., Sept. 21, 1986, pp. 16A–17A.
8. Bragg, op. cit.
9. Kern, op. cit.
10. Kerley and Merrill, op. cit.

11. Ibid.
12. John S. Hill and Meg Birdseye, "Salesperson Selection in Multinational Corporations: An Empirical Study," *Journal of Personal Selling and Sales Management,* Summer 1989, pp. 39–47.
13. D. C. Feldman, "A Socialization Process That Helps Recruits Succeed," *Personnel,* March–April 1980, pp. 11–23.
14. Alan J. Dubinsky et al., "Salesforce Socialization," *Journal of Marketing,* October 1986, pp. 201–203.
15. Procter & Gamble Company, *Sales Management,* Cincinnati, Ohio, 1986.

8

TRAINING THE SALES FORCE

263

A DAY ON THE JOB

Glen Boucher, the marketing and services education training manager at British Columbia Telephone Company, believes sales training is becoming increasingly more important to businesses today. Companies are not only conducting more training but becoming more progressive in the content of their training programs. "Involved is far more than the traditional list of selling skills and interview roleplays," says Boucher. "We are in the process of changing our entire training grid. We've started by helping our salespeople understand business in general, as well as our customers' specific businesses. It is very clear to me that the sales professional must be equipped to build strong relationships with customers and develop a partnering environment." According to Boucher, "The customer is now saying, 'Stop pitching products and help me solve my problems.'" When asked what role sales trainers will play in the future, Boucher states that they will have "greater involvement in a broader range of activities than ever before. The sales trainer is now a part of the sales team."[1]

A famous opera star was once asked by a tourist how to get to the Metropolitan Opera. The opera star answered somewhat facetiously: "Proper training and practice, lots of practice!" The same reply can be given to students when they ask how to develop the skills and qualities necessary to become a successful salesperson or sales manager. It is important for sales managers to develop the proper training program in order to assist their people in becoming the best salespeople they can be.

THE IMPORTANCE OF SALES TRAINING

Developing effective sales training programs for both new and experienced salespeople is rapidly becoming one of the most important parts of a sales manager's job. This renewed importance in sales training stems from a host of environmental changes in the past decade that have influenced the sales encounter. These changes include better-trained purchasing people who interact with salespeople, increased competition from overseas companies, and customers' recent emphasis on product and service quality.[2] These changes mirror what seems to be the theme of the new sales environment for the 1990s: partnership. The training an organization offers its sales force can greatly influence the partnership it builds with its customers and ultimately the health of the organization.

Sales training programs strive to take human inputs—salespeople who were recruited and selected—and develop them into a successful, productive part of the marketing team. According to Ed Flanagan, president of the Sales Executives Club of New York, "It may be one of those summary statements, but it's true: Sales and increased sales will always go to the better trained people."[3]

Sales training and sales force development should be thought of as a long-term, ongoing process because they ensure the continual growth and increasing productivity of salespeople. In other words, sales training and development programs should continually help salespeople grow in knowledge, selling habits, and selling techniques and develop good attitudes about themselves and their jobs, companies, and customers. Thus, sales training should be thought of as a specific program, formal or informal, designed for sales force development in order to achieve the overall, long-run goal of a marketing organization.

THE EVOLUTION OF SALES TRAINING PROGRAMS

In the past, specifically designed sales training programs often were not viewed by top-level management as an important element of the selling function. Many people involved in top and middle management felt that the development of a productive sales force resulted from recruiting and selection efforts. In other words, the overriding view was that "good salespeople are born, not made," and it was up to the organization to recruit and select top sales producers. Once selected, these "good" salespeople were usually trained through the "sink or swim principle." That is, they were thrown right into the selling field, with only meager instructions, and told to do their best and to learn from experience.

This was the approach used by CMC Corporation, the fifth-largest consumer electronics specialty retailer in the nation. Mike Maglione, director of sales training, comments: "When salespeople become frustrated, it's generally because they don't have the answers. You need to know about products, sales techniques, administrative procedures and technical aspects of the job." Maglione adds that prior to establishing a formal sales training program at CMC in 1981, "We never taught employees what they were getting paid to do. Now we try to give them the tools they need to go out to the stores, close deals and make money."[4]

Another popular sales training method used in the past (and still used occasionally today) is the "buddy system." It involves assigning a sales trainee to a senior sales representative to learn by observation and imitation. The rationale for buddy-system training is that good salespeople have a natural way with people and a natural knack for selling and, thus, need only to be taught the basics (the product line and the way to fill out orders). Too often, this type of training led to wasted recruiting and selection efforts, poor sales force morale, bad selling habits, high turnover rates, and poor customer relations—all of which have a negative impact on an organization's profits. Maglione of CMC contends that on-the-job training has its place but that salespersons may be "lost in the shuffle" during the process.[5]

Today, organizations are realizing the importance of developing and implementing specifically designed sales training programs for their sales forces. Even firms that have not traditionally thought of their customer or client interactions as "selling"—such as banks, hospitals, and nonprofit organizations—are implementing sales training programs. Such programs were once thought to be cost-effective only for full-time direct salespeople employed by the company. Now firms that employ contract manufacturer's representatives, distributors, and lower-skilled or temporary salespeople understand the value of sales training. For example, in a recent nationwide ten-day campaign promoting

AT&T Long-Distance Service on college campuses, AT&T invested eight hours of sales training for each student representative who was involved in the campaign.

AT&T and other companies have realized that salespeople generally yield a geometric return on the training dollars invested in them. While this return grows larger for every year the salesperson stays with the organization, sales training efforts for short-term assignments also tend to have returns in excess of their cost. Some companies—Xerox, for example—have even found that they get a better return on investment through sales training than they get from other marketing activities.[6] For this reason Xerox has been intensifying the focus on sales training programs in recent years.

Another company that has put increased effort into its training programs and benefited is Roche Laboratories. Like other pharmaceutical companies, Roche has been blamed for overpromoting its products and undertraining the salespeople it sends to call on doctors. Roche responded by sending nearly eighty salespeople to a two-week training program at Jackson Memorial Hospital in Miami. The salespeople were subjected to the same regimen as interns and resident doctors. After the salespeople returned to their territories, Roche asked every doctor its people called on whether the salespeople's additional training aided in their selling. The doctors overwhelmingly stated that Roche's additional training was worthwhile.[7]

SALES TRAINING AND THE CORPORATE MISSION

When designing sales training programs, sales managers must be guided by corporate goals and objectives. Jack Wilner, director of marketing and sales training for Blue Bell (manufacturer of Jantzen and Wrangler products), identified seven major concerns in designing the sales training program at Wrangler. These concerns form a framework that can guide the development of a sales training program:

1. *Identifying the sales mission.* The mission for the sales force and its relationship to the corporate mission must be clearly identified.

2. *Establishing criteria for training objectives.* These include setting specific, measurable, attainable, realistic, and time-bounded (SMART) objectives for the training program.

3. *Understanding the sales force.* In order to involve the sales personnel in selling by objectives and training them to do so, the sales training program must comprehend their needs, desires, aspirations, interests, and personal and career goals.

4. *Sharing organization information.* To understand the logic behind the company's goals and strategies and contribute to their attainment, employees must be presented with a clear understanding of the company's strengths, weaknesses, problems, and potentials during sales training.

5. *Setting short-range objectives.* If objectives for the sales training program are long-term (in terms of annual goals, for example), sales trainees can become frustrated because of lack of feedback.

6. *Enlisting sales force participation.* The sales force should participate in setting goals for the sales training program.

7. *Controlling objectives for results.* The results of the sales training program should be monitored by the sales manager and trainer to assess the attainment of the corporate mission via the objectives spelled out in the sales training program.[8]

   Recent annual surveys of sales managers in most industries have shown a pattern that indicates that the top 20 percent of the sales force produces about 40 percent of the sales, the middle 60 percent of the sales force produces nearly 50 percent of the sales, and the bottom 20 percent of the sales force produces about 10 percent of total sales. Since sales managers can identify the poor and average sales producers, they can design training programs to help poor sales producers develop into average producers, and average producers develop into top sales producers. Given the high costs of salespeople and the ever-changing marketing environment, it can be expected that sales training programs will become more important in the future. But this does not mean that they will be any easier to design. As shown by the checklist in Exhibit 8-1, there are many questions of varying degrees of complexity to be answered in designing sales training programs. While these are important questions, the initial stages of training design must be guided by the overall mission and goals of the organization.

RESPONSIBILITY FOR TRAINING

In order to develop and successfully implement a sales training program, it is very important for management to decide who is to do the actual training. The responsibility of training can be delegated to line executives, staff trainers, or outside training specialists. The specific situation determines whether one or more types of trainers should be used.

Line Sales Executives

Whether the company is large or small, line executives (sales managers, senior sales representatives, field supervisors, and division managers) are often chosen to train new trainees as well as experienced salespeople. There are several advantages in having line executives train a sales force. First, line sales executives are usually highly respected by sales trainees, and the executives' words tend to carry much more authority than those of staff executives or outside training specialists. Because trainees look up to line sales executives, the trainees will try harder to determine exactly what is expected of them and should more easily

EXHIBIT 8-1

Checklist for Developing Sales Training Programs

Needs Analysis

Who needs to be trained?   How can the deficiency be corrected?
What can't they do?   When should the training be done?
Why can't they do it?   Where should the training be done?

Education Evaluation

Who do we send?   What benefits can we expect?
How do we determine the outcome?   What kind of follow-up is expected?

Sales Training Objectives

What role will sales training play in the organization?
Can we define the objectives of the sales training department?
Will the sales training development solve our existing problems?
Who will we find to run the sales training department?

Sales Training Program Content

List a profile of salespeople who will be trained.
List qualifications of training staff.
Will outside speakers be necessary?
Can demonstrations be used?
Can measurements for training performance be developed?

Location of Training

What will be the class size?
Do we have the available space?
What will be the cost per individual?
How long will the training program last?
How flexible can the program be to the different types of salespeople who will attend?

Source: Adapted from Mary E. Boylen, "The ABC's of Training," Data Management, December 1980, pp. 32–35.

learn to sell the way the executives want them to sell. Also, since line sales executives were once trainees themselves, they can often establish a rapport that creates a very positive learning environment. In addition, line sales executives who train their own sales forces are in a better position to evaluate each trainee's ability and performance than are administrators who do not participate in training.

Using line sales executives to train does have some disadvantages. One of the major disadvantages is the line executives' lack of time. The responsibilities sales executives and managers have often do not allow them to pay enough attention to the training function, and this can be harmful to trainee morale and enthusiasm. To overcome the problem of time, the training function should be

a specific duty with a proper time allotment. Training should not be a responsibility added as an afterthought to the sales executive's other duties. State Farm
Insurance has explicitly included sales training in the sales manager's job description. Donald W. Frischman, vice president for agency relations, comments:
''We did some research on what the managers were doing and what we want
them to do. As a result, we have defined five management performance criteria:
(1) recruiting, (2) sales training, (3) agent-manager relations, (4) sales leadership, and (5) business management.''[9] Thus, sales training is a clearly defined
objective for sales managers at State Farm Insurance.

Another major disadvantage of using line sales executives is that they may
know a great deal about selling and be very successful at it, yet be unable to
teach others about it. Frequently, the lack of teaching skills can be overcome,
however, since line executives can be trained to teach just as sales trainees can
be taught to sell. Nabisco Brands' Biscuit Group has set up a system for teaching
managers how to implement sales training into regular sales strategy meetings.[10]

Even though sales executives may not be entirely responsible for training,
they should always be used in planning sales training programs and in selecting
the training situations. Sales executives are most familiar with the needs of the
entire sales force and the selling resources of the firm, and they can effectively
design such programs. Large organizations typically hire training specialists or
staff assistants. But in small organizations, which often cannot afford to hire
outside training specialists, the line sales executives usually perform the entire
training function, if there is one. Unfortunately, line sales executives in small
companies frequently feel they are too busy to design training programs, and
salespeople are left to manage as best they can.

Staff Trainers

Staff trainers are either persons within the organization who hold jobs in personnel, production, or office management or else company employees hired
specifically to conduct sales training programs. People from elsewhere in the
organization are best used in combination with other trainers, such as line sales
executives or outside specialists. Because they are not salespeople, they may be
unable to relate their experience effectively to the selling function, even if they
have good teaching skills and expertise in their own field. Also, because these
people have other responsibilities within the organization, sales training programs conducted solely by persons from other areas may suffer; time that can
be allocated to any one training program may be limited.

If a company wishes to use staff trainers, often the best strategy is to maintain
trainers for the specific purpose of conducting the sales training program, in
other words, to set up a training department. Staff trainers have the time and
teaching skills necessary for sales training. Hired to handle the details of the
training program, they can give trainees the attention they need and usually are
good communicators who have an understanding of the problems of educating
people. In addition, staff sales trainers can conduct training programs for a firm's
dealers and distributors in order to teach them how to sell the firm's product

effectively. Sometimes, staff sales trainers also design training programs, prepare training materials, and train the line executives (or others who perform the training) in the teaching and communication skills necessary to conduct training programs.

Staff trainers hired specifically for training purposes do have a few disadvantages. To some extent staff trainers lack control over the trainees, who often do not look up to them in the same way as they look up to line sales executives. But this can be overcome by establishing the fact that the sales trainers are supported by the boss. Another problem is that the cost of hiring and maintaining staff trainers is often high. Depending on personal qualifications, the trainer's salary can be over $45,000 per year. Obviously, small companies cannot afford to hire staff trainers. One other problem is a tendency on the part of the staff trainers to overdo training programs by scheduling far more training than is required. Close supervision of staff trainers should minimize this problem. CMC Corporation addressed these problem areas by recruiting the top salesperson as the company's first training director in charge of developing a structured training curriculum.[11]

Outside Training Specialists

Manville Building Materials successfully utilized the services of Personnel Prediction & Research, a Denver consulting firm, to develop its sales training program materials for corporate staff and sales managers. The purpose of the training was to teach the managers to train salespersons in interpersonal skills. Once the program was developed, the implementation was turned over to Performance Training Corporation, which actually conducted the training session. Measures of performance in the field showed great improvement after training, and the program became a mandatory part of the Manville Sales Development Program.[12]

Outside training specialists include firms that specialize in sales training and individual experts, such as college professors, who consult on training programs and problems. Outside training specialists help many small businesses that cannot afford to have their own sales training departments. They also help large companies by implementing refresher training programs and special-purpose training sessions. Outside training specialists offer great flexibility because they can conduct the entire training program or handle only the particular part that a firm feels it needs the most help with. Because much of their livelihood depends on the satisfaction of their clients, outside trainers usually are knowledgeable, interesting, and inspiring in conducting their sales training programs.

DESIGNING THE SALES TRAINING PROGRAM

The major point to remember about designing training is that programs should be developed on the basis of the skills and experience of the salespeople. This involves first identifying the gaps between the sales force's skills and the firm's objectives and then developing programs to fill these gaps. Sales training programs may weed out individuals who slipped through the selection process but are not actually fit for the job. Usually, however, training programs serve to identify the skills needed by the sales force and then to develop these skills.

Basically, there are two types of sales training programs. One is the *initial sales training program*, designed for the newly recruited salesperson. This program usually lasts three to six months and is comprehensive. The second type is the *continuing sales training program*, often called "refresher training." This type of program is for experienced salespeople and is normally shorter and more intensive in its coverage of specialized topics than the initial sales training program.

Delta Airlines offers such a two-tiered approach to training for its nearly 100 marketing representatives. These salespeople, who are brought up from ticket sales or office positions, are first trained to be familiar with the company's functions: air freight, ticketing, computer operations, and the full range of travel services offered by Delta. The second level of training involves continuing reinforcement of selling skills by Delta managers at regular training sessions.[13]

Whether the sales manager is designing initial or continuing sales training programs, several planning decisions must be made. These planning decisions cover the following major areas: training objectives, content of programs, methods of training, implementation, and evaluation. Each of these major areas will be examined in the following sections.

Training Objectives

The first step in designing an effective sales training program is to decide what you want to accomplish with the program. The objectives should be stated in realistic, quantifiable terms with respect to a specific time period. They should also be stated in written form so that they can be used later in evaluating the program's effectiveness.

Specific aims of different types of sales training programs vary. For instance, the objective of the initial sales training program is usually to assimilate new salespeople into the organization and then to develop them into top sales producers. But refresher training programs are designed to keep the entire sales force informed of changes in products, markets, competition, company policies, marketing strategies, and industry trends. In addition, refresher programs may seek to retrain salespeople for new duties or responsibilities, such as managing the sales force.

Generally, the overall objective of the sales training program is to increase the sales force's performance. However, more specific goals and objectives should be developed. For example, a specific objective of an initial sales training program could be to train new salespeople to sell at least 75 percent of what experienced salespeople sell within one year after they are hired.

A primary objective of many training programs is to teach the sales force how to be more productive. Usually, a salesperson's productivity will increase with experience. But if sales training can substitute for some of the needed experience, higher productivity levels should be reached earlier. Also, sales training not only helps the sales force to increase productivity faster but aids in decreasing sales force turnover rates, which means total hiring and training costs should fall. Both initial and refresher sales training programs are designed to increase sales force performance.

Another aim common to both types of sales training programs is to instill pride and to show the importance of the selling function to the individual, the firm, and the economy as a whole. In order to achieve high morale, which is a major key to success, the sales force must realize the value of the selling profession. Specifically, sales trainees need to be taught the importance of the role they play in introducing innovations to markets, conveying information to customers, facilitating the consumption of goods and services, serving as a channel of communication between the company and its markets, and—most important for a marketing-oriented sales organization—solving problems for customers. The overriding philosophy is that professional salespeople should be taught to be advisers or consultants, not mere product pushers. Exhibit 8-2 contrasts the two types of salespeople.

In addition to instilling pride in sales trainees, training programs must stress the idea that a professional salesperson can never achieve perfection. That is, sales trainees must be taught to continually seek self-improvement. For example, trainees should learn that it pays to be an avid reader of materials concerning selling techniques, new products in their field, new uses for old products, and upcoming changes and emerging problems in their industry.

Initial sales training.   Objectives of initial sales training programs should be determined by examining the requirements of the sales job, the trainees' backgrounds and past experiences, and the company's marketing policies. Management should first study the formal job description to determine areas in which

---

EXHIBIT 8-2

New versus Old Salesperson Concepts

Sales Adviser or Consultant	Product Pusher
Develops a long-term relationship with clients.	Interested in making an immediate sale. Shows little concern for the long term.
Identifies the client's problems and suggests solutions.	Emphasizes a particular product's benefits regardless of a client's need.
Depends on providing helpful information and service to secure business.	Uses high-pressure, sometimes unethical, tactics to close a sale.
Often works as a member of a team of specialists.	Works alone and has little special product knowledge.
Uses the computer to back up the sales effort and follows through to ensure customer satisfaction.	Handles all the paperwork and often neglects the follow-up.
Works closely with headquarters marketing support staff.	Ignores headquarters marketing people; thinks they are a nuisance or hindrance to field sales.

the new trainees are most likely to require training. In addition, other elements should be considered, such as how salespeople allocate their time, the sales duties that require the greatest proportion of selling time, the duties that are often neglected by salespeople, and why they are neglected.

Trainees' backgrounds and past experiences should be reviewed to identify the gaps between the trainees' qualifications and the specific job activities. By tailoring the initial sales training program to the individuals, management can increase trainee satisfaction and program effectiveness. However, in many large organizations, this is not possible because of time and costs. In such cases all trainees must be put through identical training programs. The main point to be remembered is that all organizations, large and small, must first determine the new trainees' actual training needs and then fill the gap in order to get the optimum benefit of the sales training program.

A company's marketing policies with regard to products and markets, promotion, price, and distribution should have a large impact on the objectives of the initial training program. For example, programs for training the new sales force to sell a line of highly technical products, such as computers, should stress product knowledge and customer applications along with selling techniques. In contrast, training programs for teaching the sales force to sell simple, nontechnical products should stress only selling techniques.

Refresher training.   Objectives of refresher, or continuing, sales training programs also should be based on the needs of the sales force, as seen by management. Management, as well as the sales force, must realize that training is an ongoing process. Top graduates of excellent initial sales training programs may often slide into careless, nonproductive selling habits, which can be corrected through the use of refresher training programs. Also, refresher training courses are needed to convey to the sales force complex information about changes in the company's policies, products, marketing strategies, and the like. Refresher training can help the sales force understand and adapt to changes quickly, thereby increasing the sales force's overall selling effectiveness. Refresher training is covered in more depth later in the chapter.

Content of the Training Programs

The scope of initial sales training programs is usually broader than that of refresher training programs because initial training must cover all aspects of the new salesperson's job. Five basic elements should be included in the program: company knowledge, product knowledge, knowledge of competitors and the overall industry, customer and market knowledge, and knowledge of the selling process.

The content of salesperson and sales manager training programs is presented in Exhibit 8-3. As would be expected, the content of salesperson training programs is primarily product knowledge, sales techniques and the selling process, and market and industry knowledge. In contrast, sales manager training programs place much more emphasis on supervisory skills and interpersonal skills and spend relatively less time on product knowledge, the sales process, and

EXHIBIT 8-3

Content of Salesperson and Sales Manager Training Programs

	Percent of Formal Training	
Content Area	Salesperson	Sales Manager
Company knowledge	8	12
Product knowledge	34	18
Sales techniques and selling process	25	16
Interpersonal skills	11	19
Market and industry knowledge	22	8
Supervisory skills	0	27

Source: R. Erffmeyer and J. Hair, "Training Programs for Salespersons and Sales Managers: An Assessment," *Proceedings*, American Educational Research Association, San Francisco, May 1986, p. 176.

market and industry knowledge. Thus, salespeople are trained to sell effectively and sales managers are trained to manage effectively.

Company knowledge. New recruits should be taught about the organization's policies in general as well as the company's specific selling policies. Some of the basics to be learned involve parking privileges, eating facilities, office practices, the paycheck, the expense account, and channels of communication. Trainees must also be taught the organization's specific policies concerning selling practices, such as how many sales calls to make per day, how to handle returns, and how to write up orders. In general, company knowledge is not hard to teach. Usually, lectures and printed materials are used to explain policies and procedures and the rationale for them. Once company policies are covered, however, the training program should move to other topics. Too often, sales trainers overdo discussions of policy, and the results are boredom and a decrease in morale and enthusiasm.

Product knowledge. A major portion of the initial sales training program should be devoted to teaching the new trainee about the products or services that the company offers for sale. Not only should trainees learn about the products and how they are used by customers, but they should also believe in the products' merits and the products' usefulness in solving customers' problems. After trainees are told about the products and their uses, they should be allowed to see or use the products in order to gain as much technical understanding of them as possible. Beyond this, it is highly beneficial for salespeople to learn about and use competitive products. Salespeople can compete more successfully when they can communicate to the customer the advantages of their product over competitors' products.

Lincoln Electric, a manufacturer of arc-welding equipment and supplies, recruits engineers for its field sales positions. During their eight-week training program, the engineers are required to attend welding school and become certified welders. Before the new recruits are promoted to a field sales position, each must demonstrate the ability to find a welding-related cost reduction at the company's manufacturing plant. These salespeople possess superior product knowledge and an edge on competitors because of the rigorous product-related training they receive.[14]

Knowledge of competitors and the industry. Sales trainees need to be made aware of industry trends and competitive tactics and must understand how these may affect the demand for the company's products. Trainees should know almost as much about competitors' products as they know about their own. It is only through this knowledge that salespeople can compare brands and overcome customer objections concerning the purchase of one brand over another. Detailed knowledge of competitors' products can also aid salespeople in designing sales presentations to highlight the advantages of their company's products.

Customer and market knowledge. Sales trainers today are emphasizing the customer more than ever in their training programs. In the new selling environment of the 1990s, customers are highly knowledgeable and professional, and they have greater demands and expectations than they did in the past. Consequently, an effective sales training program must go beyond the basics. It is no longer enough merely to teach salespeople to overcome customer objections; salespeople must be trained to create cooperative partnerships with their customers. The importance of building such partnerships must be emphasized, since many U.S. businesses now prefer this type of relationship.[15] Exhibit 8-4

EXHIBIT 8-4

Training to Build Partnerships

The following points can assist sales trainees in building customer knowledge:

1. *Understand your company's products thoroughly*. Purchasing agents today expect salespeople to know how the products they sell are made, packaged, shipped, installed, etc.

2. *Understand your customers' buying organizations*. Salespeople need training on how to find and communicate with the decision makers in their customers' organizations.

3. *Understand your customers' products*. Customers today want solutions to problems, not sales pitches.

4. *Understand your customers' requirements*. Salespeople need training on customers' requirements concerning inventory control and how they can best meet these requirements.

5. *Understand your customers' markets*. Successful partnerships are created when salespeople understand the problems that their customers have with *their* customers.

6. *Be able to make professional sales calls*. Training programs must emphasize the importance of *listening*. In today's selling environment, listening has overtaken presenting in importance.

7. *Learn to become "team" coordinators*. Salespeople must participate in or be aware of all communication that takes place between the company and the customer.

8. *Stay in close contact with customers*. Salespeople today must realize that making a sale is merely the first step in a long relationship with the customer.

Source: Based on William Atkinson, "A New Approach to Sales Training," *Training*, March 1989, pp. 57–60.

highlights eight important components that should be included in a sales training program to assist sales trainees in creating partnerships.

Knowledge of the selling process.
Sales trainees must learn the steps involved in selling as well as various selling techniques that can be applied in different situations. The basic steps of the selling process are prospecting, planning the call, approaching the prospect, making the sales presentation, meeting objections, closing the sale, and following up. (For in-depth discussions of the selling process, see Appendix A.)

Prospecting. Sales trainees must learn to seek out potential customers who need the product and are able to buy it. These potential customers are called *prospects.* Sales trainees quickly learn the value of prospecting because it keeps them from wasting time trying to sell products to people who don't need or cannot afford them. Often, new salespeople are given a list of prospects from the sales manager. But during the training period trainees should be taught the system that experienced salespeople use to generate prospects. In general, prospecting systems are based on acquiring leads from customers, competitors, and publications with relevant information. Sales trainees must learn to recognize and to use any sources that might lead them to good prospects.

Planning the call (the preapproach). Sales trainees need to learn how to plan sales calls to make sure the actual presentation will be effective. Trainees should learn to gather information so that they can answer the following questions: What are the objectives of the sales call? What are the customer's needs? How can my company's products satisfy these needs? How do my competitors' products satisfy the customer's needs? What objections might be raised, and how can these objections be handled? What kinds of audiovisual aids or support materials will be needed? The planning process helps the salesperson qualify prospects and provides information that can be used in tailoring the sales presentation to the prospect.

Approaching the prospect. Depending on the particular selling situation, there are several effective ways to approach prospects, ranging from being referred by a mutual acquaintance to sending a gift to the prospect. Few prospects are eager to talk to a salesperson even if they may need the product or service, so it is essential that the approach offer some incentive or provide reassurance that the sales presentation will be beneficial.

Making the sales presentation. Sales presentations typically consist of two major phases: the *opening* and the actual *presentation*. Trainees must understand each of these to become effective salespeople.

The opening phase of the sales presentation represents only a small percentage of the total presentation time, but it is very important. The salesperson generally will be given about thirty seconds to secure the prospect's attention and interest. Unless the opening is effective, the rest of the sales presentation will probably fail.

The opening generally begins with preliminary chitchat designed to establish rapport. This is particularly important if the salesperson and the prospect have not met before. Sales trainees must learn to move quickly from the chitchat to a discussion of their product's benefits. The benefits should be specific, quantifiable, and highly desired by the prospect. By presenting benefits early, the salesperson will stimulate interest and begin to develop desire for the product.

The actual presentation is the heart of the sale. A good presentation is built around a forceful demonstration that illustrates all selling points and buying motives in such a manner as to arouse the prospect's interest and desire to purchase.

Sales trainees should be taught how to employ trial closes throughout the sales presentation in order to determine if the prospect is ready to buy. Many times, they can prevent the salesperson from losing the sale through overselling. The trial close consists of asking questions such as "Which color do you prefer?" or "Would you like to pay for this by cash or charge?" Prospects who are ready to purchase will answer such questions favorably. Prospects who are not ready to purchase will avoid the questions or deny having an interest in purchasing. If the trial close gets a favorable response, the salesperson closes the sale immediately.

Meeting objections. Sales trainees should understand that objections raised by the prospect are a good sign; they signify that the prospect has some interest in the product. If the objections can be met successfully, the prospect will normally purchase. Objections can be stated or hidden and may be related to the product itself, its price, or the timing of the purchase. The salesperson must learn to identify the actual objection. Once the objection is determined, the salesperson can then work to overcome it by pointing out the advantages that offset what is seen by the prospect as a disadvantage. For example, if the prospect raises an objection concerning price, the salesperson can point out the quality involved and the long life the product should have.

Closing the sale. The closing occurs when the salesperson asks for the order. Trainees often feel that the closing is the easiest part of selling to remember. However, many salespeople fail to ask for the order because they assume the prospect will automatically purchase the product after completing the earlier stages of the selling process. If they do not ask for the order, they may not get it, and the entire effort of the salesperson is wasted.

There are several popular closing strategies. The *assumptive close* implies that the prospect will purchase by asking questions such as "To what address do you want this delivered?" or "When can we deliver this, today or tomorrow morning?" In the *physical-action close* the salesperson suggests to the prospect through a physical action, such as handing the prospect a pen to sign the contract, that the time has come to place the order. The *trap close* occurs when the prospect's objection is used to close the sale. For example, when a prospect states that he or she would not pay a penny over $4,000 for a car having a sticker price of $4,600, the salesperson quickly springs the trap by saying: "I'll write up the order for $4,000 and ask the boss's approval." The *special-offer close* moves the prospect to purchase immediately in order to take advantage of a special offer, such as a 20 percent discount if ordered today. This close can be effective in overcoming the prospect's objections concerning the timing of the purchase.

Following up. It is very important for trainees to learn that the sale is not complete once the order is obtained. A good salesperson follows up the sale with a call to make sure that all questions have been answered, the product was delivered at the specified time and in good condition, and the customer is satisfied. Following up the sale serves to reassure the customer that a wise decision was made, and the customer usually appreciates being served by salespeople who strive to satisfy. A good follow-up leads to loyal clientele, which can substantially increase the salesperson's and the organization's future sales. Finally, in following up with customers, salespeople can often generate sales of complementary items or referrals to new prospects.

Methods of Group Training

The methods employed to train the sales force depend not only on the objectives and content of the training program but also on whether a group or an individual is being trained. When there is a group of trainees, the training methods typically used are lectures, group discussions, role playing, teletraining, videotapes, audiocassettes, slide presentations, and simulation games.

Lectures. Lectures are often employed because they can present more information to a large number of students in a short period of time than any of the other teaching methods. However, only a limited amount of lecturing should be used in sales training programs because lectures usually do not generate active participation on the part of the trainees; this typically leads to boredom and a lack of enthusiasm. When lecturing is used, it should be thoughtfully planned, and the lecture sessions should be short and interspersed with other activities.

Storytelling, a form of lecturing, is beginning to be used as a sales training technique by some companies. The following example illustrates how Porsche has used storytelling to successfully train its sales force.

STORYTELLING AS SALES TRAINING AT PORSCHE

Storytelling has long been an important teaching medium. Putting information into story form to pass along from person to person is a natural and easy way for people to transfer ideas, information, and concepts.

Storytelling has been incorporated into the sales training program at Porsche Cars of North America. The idea began when three people—John Storm, manager of sales and management training for Porsche; a technical writer; and a sales trainer—decided to transfer their own love of storytelling to the selling of cars. What resulted was an innovative selling technique that differed significantly from the standard features-and-benefits approach.

The technique involved the identification of seven locations on a car at which a salesperson could pause during a "walkaround" with a customer. Each location was illustrated with a story. For example, the salesperson would pause by the brakes and explain: "The Porsche 944 Turbo has the same brakes that were used on the Porsche 917 that raced at LeMans. At the end of the Mulsanne straightaway, the cars had to slow down from a maximum speed of 240 mph to about 38 mph. The brakes would glow white-hot at night during the 24-hour race."

In order to introduce storytelling into the training process at Porsche, a workbook that includes anecdotes for each of the Porsche line of cars was developed. Training seminars were held for the 600 salespeople in 290 dealerships around the country. Salespeople studied the workbook first and then practiced walkarounds on real cars.

A videotape was produced that included footage of salespersons' walkarounds. The videotape was then sent to each dealership for use in training new salespeople. The response from salespeople has been enthusiastic. Storm believes this information helps salespeople build value for the Porsche product.[16]

Group discussions. Several forms of group discussion can be employed in sales training programs. The simplest form is one in which the trainer leads and stimulates talk and participation on the part of the trainees. Case studies have been used widely as a tool to stimulate group discussion. Trainees are given cases to study, and then the trainer leads a class discussion to analyze and solve the problems involved in the case.

Group discussions should play a large role in sales training programs because they give trainees a chance to discuss their own selling problems. Group discussions also encourage two-way communication. However, group discussions are not useful if the trainees are so inexperienced that they cannot contribute.

Role playing. If experience is the best teacher, then a good role-playing session is the next best teacher because role playing is learning by doing. In role playing the trainee tries to sell a product to a hypothetical prospect (usually the trainer or another trainee). Role playing can help trainees learn to handle unforeseen developments that often arise in selling situations. It also gives the trainer a chance to work with trainees on voice, poise, mannerisms, speech, and movements. Through role playing, trainees can be made aware of weak points. They also learn the importance of being knowledgeable about the product, company, competition, customers, and industry. All in all, role playing impresses on trainees that knowing what to do in a selling situation is one thing but doing it is another.

Teletraining. With the rise in travel costs and the increasing burdens on managerial time, teletraining has become a viable alternative for sales training. *Teletraining* involves linking remote locations (sales offices) to the home office or another facility with a telephone line and a video link via satellite. Participants in different locations may talk with and see each other as well as the trainer in the central location. Many large companies have realized the benefits of teletraining for their sales force, including Honeywell Information Systems, Century 21 Real Estate, The Travelers Insurance Company, and Roche Laboratories. Because many hotel chains, such as Holiday Inn, offer teleconferencing facilities at selected locations (usually in metropolitan areas near airports), even small and medium-sized firms without in-house teleconferencing facilities can take advantage of this sales training method.

Teletraining is most appropriate when an outside consultant or a member of senior management wishes to address a large group of geographically dispersed salespeople. Since the speaker's time is at a premium, transporting him or her all over the country is not very efficient. Likewise, fatigue due to travel may dampen the speaker's enthusiasm for the training exercise; this can lead to a lack of enthusiasm on the part of the trainees. The use of teletraining avoids these problems.

Teletraining has several other advantages over traditional training. It can increase productivity because the nonproductive time spent in traveling to remote training sites can become workdays. Also, the number of trainees is not limited by the size of the training room. Teletraining can also accommodate key people from the firm or outside consultants who may not have time to travel; with teletraining they can respond to trainees right from their offices. Finally, teletraining can reduce training expenses. Companies in the United States collectively spend over $45 billion annually on training; more than one-quarter of that is for airfare, lodging, and meals for traveling trainees. With teletraining much of this travel expense can be either saved or redirected toward other training.

Studies conducted by AT&T Communications, the University of Wisconsin, and Johns Hopkins University confirm teletraining's effectiveness. Both pretest and posttest scores of trainees show no significant difference in learning when trainees take courses via teletraining or with an in-class instructor. According to Johns Hopkins researchers, "The tasks that most frequently occur in educational settings—giving and receiving information, asking questions, exchanging opinions and problem solving—are tasks for which telecommunications are as effective as face-to-face meeting." Moreover, questionnaire responses confirm favorable trainee reaction. Studies show that 85 percent of participants find teletraining to be an effective approach and would take future courses via teletraining.[17]

Some negative aspects of teletraining include the impersonal nature of the interaction. One of the motivating dynamics of many sales training seminars conducted at the home office is getting to personally shake hands with the CEO or another high-ranking manager. This is not possible with teletraining. Therefore, it is advisable to use teleconferencing in conjunction with a live training exercise at the sales office or hotel, where a regional sales manager can be present. The presence of a member of management serves to let the trainees know that training is very important to the company. A second limitation to this method is technological: poor video or audio transmission owing to bad weather or faulty equipment may destroy a well-planned training exercise. The training staff should have a backup "manual" program in place in case these types of difficulties occur.

Videotapes.   Videotapes serve a function similar to teletraining. They allow outside consultants and senior management to prerecord training messages. Videotaped lectures minimize travel and time-loss expenses because the tapes may be easily mailed to remote sales offices for training seminars. As with teletraining, the use of videotapes may be impersonal. In addition, the interaction is one-way, from presenter to trainee. Since no questions may be asked directly of the trainer, a sales manager or other knowledgeable individual should be available to address trainee questions. One note of caution: Videotape lectures should be used sparingly. While effective on a limited basis, a full day of videotaped training would be extremely boring and not likely to be effective in meeting training objectives.

Video tape recorders have become standard equipment for role playing at training sessions because they enable trainees to see themselves and others in action. As one sales trainee stated after attending role-playing sessions in which videotapes were employed, "I learned more about effective sales presentations than in a classic training situation. It was a 'backdoor way,' since I had to prepare myself for each role, then review the video-tapes and analyze my own role . . . as well as those of other salespeople. Through such reinforcement, you cannot help but learn about the sales presentation strengths and weaknesses of yourself as well as others."[18] Videotape playback usually allows trainees to spot their own selling weaknesses rather than having to be told about them by observers or trainers.

Audiocassettes.   Many companies are discovering that audiocassettes can be effective tools for teaching salespeople. There are virtually thousands of audio-cassette programs available today that can assist salespeople in anything from selling skills to personal development. Companies such as Pfizer Labs, Scott Paper, Johnson & Johnson, and Gillette use audiocassettes to help train their salespeople. These companies believe that this is a worthwhile method of sales training because it uses unproductive driving time for training and professional development.[19]

Slide presentations.   Slide presentations are an effective way to present graphics and material in outline form. The major advantage of slide presentations is that they are easy to put together and execute. They also help the trainer stay on schedule by pacing the training program. The movement and color provided by a slide show are also visually pleasing to the trainees. The major application of this method of sales training is in the presentation of technical data or information that would require a large amount of time to write on a chalkboard. Slide presentations are particularly useful in training sessions on company policies, product knowledge, and industry or market knowledge.

Simulation games.   Simulation games can aid in learning by allowing the train-ees to assume the roles of decision makers in either their own or customers' organizations. In simulation games, which are highly structured and based on reality, trainees must make decisions about the timing and size of orders, sales forecasts, advertising, pricing, and the like. Then the trainees are given feedback concerning the outcomes of their decisions. Simulation games have advantages in that they generate enthusiasm through competitive game playing, aid trainees in developing skills to correctly perceive key factors that influence customers' decisions, and show the uses and value of planning techniques. Some disad-vantages should also be weighed when considering the use of simulation games. First, simulation games are very time-consuming: it usually takes three to four hours for trainees to generate decisions, and several rounds of decisions are needed for the learning process. Also, because simulation games are in the form of preprogrammed computer packages, decisions that are novel or unique seldom receive the payoff to which they are entitled.

Methods of Individual Training

Several methods can be used to train persons individually, including on-the-job training, personal conferences, correspondence courses, and interactive video.

On-the-job training.   On-the-job, or buddy-system, training occurs when an experienced salesperson is assigned to a trainee to teach him or her about the job and how to sell. Normally, the experienced salesperson goes along on sales calls the trainee makes. After the trainee's presentation, the experienced salesperson and the trainee evaluate and analyze the call. The major advantage of on-the-job training is that trainees can learn firsthand how actual sales calls are conducted. However, for on-the-job training to be effective, the experienced salesperson must be highly qualified to train and influence the trainee. An important disadvantage of on-the-job training is that it is very time-consuming and costly for both the experienced salesperson and the trainee.

Mentoring, a form of on-the-job training, is gaining popularity among many sales organizations. The following example illustrates how the mentor program is being used at Pathfinder Software.

SALES TRAINING AND MENTORING AT PATHFINDER SOFTWARE

It has been estimated that up to one-third of the nation's major companies now have a formal mentoring program, which pairs senior managers with younger salespeople as part of one-on-one training. The goal of mentoring programs is to make new employees feel at home in their new jobs, to teach them the corporate culture, and to provide them with a source of advice.

Coworker mentoring is commonly used by sales forces as part of their formal training or as a substitute for formal training. Although many major companies are using mentoring programs, smaller companies have been less likely to adopt such programs. One exception is Pathfinder Software, a small, Vancouver-based company. Pathfinder adopted its coworker mentor program three years ago, when the company had only eight employees. At the time, Pathfinder was faced with the problem of having to train its people to use a new programming language so that they could help sell the firm's products. A mentoring consultant, William A. Gray, taught the company's employees how to teach their expertise (marketing, product, and so on) to one another. For example, the salesperson taught the other employees the new programming language and how it would help them conduct a sale.

According to Gray, the mentoring program worked well for Pathfinder. He reports that the employees learned faster from each other than they would have from seminars. More importantly, though, he reports that the teaching and coaching skills the mentors learned were also employed in teaching Pathfinder's clients how to use software. This reduced the number of callbacks that Pathfinder had to make in order to help clients through the process of learning new systems.[20]

Personal conferences.   Training can take place in personal conferences in which the trainer and the trainee discuss and analyze problems in selling. Often, managers and trainers hesitate to use personal conferences because they assume that learning cannot take place in an unstructured situation. However, experience has shown that learning can occur in structured or unstructured situations. The personal conference can be a very effective learning tool, and it can establish good rapport between the trainee and the sales executive or trainer. But the trainer must be careful to avoid idle chitchat during conference time.

Correspondence courses.   Correspondence courses alone are not very effective. But when combined with other training methods, they can be a helpful learning tool. Correspondence courses can effectively explain the basic duties of the sales job and teach selling concepts, but they do not necessarily teach how to sell. Correspondence courses have been used successfully to teach product data, company policies, and competitor knowledge. However, there are several disadvantages. First, it is hard for management to motivate trainees to get their course work completed on schedule. One company even pastes dollar bills on random pages in its correspondence course to encourage sales trainees to do the work. Second, unless face-to-face meetings are arranged, trainees' questions often go unanswered. Last, feedback concerning grades and errors is often slow.

Interactive videodiscs.   This method of sales training allows the trainee to control a videodisc learning program by using a computer. The interactive videodisc combines the technologies of a videodisc player with a microcomputer so that video segments may be mixed with computer menus and programs. One useful application of this approach to sales training is that it teaches salespeople how to use a personal computer. Manufacturers, such as IBM, have coupled videodisc instructions with hands-on exercises that enable the trainee to learn how to use a microcomputer in a few hours. The trainee watches video demonstrations interspersed with exercises on the computer's video display. As each task is successfully completed, more complicated tasks are presented to the trainee.

Combination Methods

In order to achieve an optimal level of effectiveness in teaching, combinations of both group and individual training methods should be used. Usually, group training methods are used in formal training programs, and individual training methods are used in informal training programs (specifically, in field training). For example, lectures and role playing are usually effective with groups of trainees in a formal sales training program, whereas personal conferences and on-the-job training are better for individual trainees once they are in the field.

Companies must decide when to use group rather than individual training. Most firms want trainees to go through formal group training before they are allowed into the field. However, some firms—for example, many insurance companies—use field training and selling first to see if the trainee's selling ability justifies the cost of formal training. Also, many organizations do not hire enough salespeople to justify formal programs of group training.

Not only is the type of method chosen impacted by the type of training program selected (for example, informal versus formal training), but recent evidence suggests that certain training methods are more effective than others in their ability to achieve specific objectives. The results of a survey of 125 sales training managers are presented in Exhibit 8-5. The managers were asked to rate the effectiveness of particular training methods in achieving six objectives. The rating scale ranged from 1, indicating that the method was judged "not effective," to 5, "highly effective." Role playing was the most highly rated method. Methods such as correspondence study received much lower ratings.

EXHIBIT 8-5

Effectiveness of Sales Training Methods*

Training Method	Training Objective					
	Knowledge Acquisition	Knowledge Retention	Attitude Change	Inter-personal Skills	Problem-Solving Skills	Trainee Acceptance
Lectures	3.0	2.4	2.2	2.0	2.2	2.5
Group discussion	3.7	3.2	3.0	2.9	3.0	3.6
Role playing	4.0	4.2	4.1	4.3	4.0	3.7
Simulations	3.2	3.2	3.0	2.5	3.3	3.3
Correspondence courses	2.8	2.6	2.1	1.8	2.3	2.0
Computer-assisted instruction	3.3	3.2	2.7	2.1	3.1	3.0

*Mean ratings by sales training managers on a five-point scale with 5.0 as highly effective.
Source: R. Erffmeyer and J. Hair, "Training Programs for Salespersons and Sales Managers: An Assessment," *Proceedings*, American Educational Research Association, San Francisco, May 1986, p. 178.

High-Tech Sales Training

High-tech equipment has had a major impact on all aspects of business in recent years. This impact is beginning to be felt in training programs and will be much more significant in the future. Computer-based systems are the most popular means of high-tech training, and the use of the systems will increase substantially during the 1990s.[21] In contrast, teletraining and interactive video are used by relatively few companies today, and their use is expected to decline during the 1990s.

The advent of technology in the area of sales training has resulted in three major benefits: an increase in the availability of sales training to small and medium-sized firms, a reduction in the cost of developing and distributing many training aids, and an improvement in existing methods.

Many sales training programs produced by independent consulting companies are now distributed on videotape or videodisc. Prior to the availability of such programs, small businesses had difficulty providing suitable training for their employees. Usually, they cannot afford to hire an individual consultant to conduct training, nor can they afford to produce quality materials in-house. Now, the availability of recorded training programs has made high-quality materials affordable for even small firms. For example, Xerox Learning Systems recently introduced an extensive revision of its selling-skills training program on videodisc. The three-day seminar is recorded on seven discs and is the first sales training system to use videodisc technology. The fact that tape and disc players are now sold at relatively low prices also contributes to the availability of training programs for firms that might otherwise have to do without them.

Declining costs for satellite transmission and long-distance service have made teletraining a viable approach to sales training. For example, during the introduction of the Macintosh computer system in 1984, Apple Computer rented satellite transmission capability to broadcast an eight-hour program containing new-product information and speeches by Apple executives. Originating in San Francisco, the program was beamed to retail dealers and distribution centers in several locations throughout the United States and Canada. While this program is thought to have cost Apple Computer several hundred thousand dollars, the cost would have been much greater had Apple chosen to fly more than 2,000 dealers to California for the program.

Even critics of high-technology training aids, who claim that one can never remove the human element from the training process, may find solace in an innovative copier offered by both Sharp Electronics and Xerox Corporation. This new copier allows a lecturer to simply press a button in order to copy all the notes that have been written on a special board. This technology overcomes one of the negative aspects of the lecture method: trainee fatigue from note taking. With this type of innovation, technology contributes to the improvement of existing training methods.

IMPLEMENTING TRAINING PROGRAMS

Several common mistakes can occur in implementing training programs. The greatest mistake is not giving enough time and attention to planning. Often, sales managers feel they only need to visit briefly and informally with trainees in order to pass along their knowledge and experiences of selling. Other mistakes are using unrealistic demonstrations that oversimplify the selling situation, having boring speakers, or overwhelming trainees by trying to teach too much in training sessions. With average per-salesperson training costs ranging from $22,500 for consumer products companies to $30,000 for service firms, special efforts to avoid training-program mistakes should be considered worthwhile investments.

Implementation of sales training programs requires extensive planning concerning location, timing, training aids and instructional materials, and various routine details, such as food, lodging, parking, and recreation.

Location

The location of the training program is determined by the extent to which it should be centralized. *Centralized training* programs usually involve organized training schools, periodic conventions, or seminars held in a central location such as the home office. In small firms, where sales territories are in proximity, it is convenient and logical for training activities to be centralized. Also, organizations that hire large numbers of salespeople each year typically use centralized training. Centralized programs have advantages in that trainees can quickly get acquainted with each other, top managers, and key home-office personnel. Beyond this, many experts feel that removing trainees from the distractions of their daily home life is conducive to learning. The major disadvantages of centralized training are that it usually is expensive and requires a great

EXHIBIT 8-6

Sites Most Frequently Used for Sales Training

Location	Percentage of Companies Conducting Training at This Location		
	Industrial Products	Consumer Products	Services*
Home office	75	60	67
Field office	88	80	89
Regional office	13	20	44
Central training facility (away from home office)	38	0	33
Noncompany site (resort, hotel)	0	0	22

*Includes insurance, financial, utilities, transportation, retail stores, etc.
Source: Sales & Marketing Management, Feb. 22, 1988, p. 49.

deal of organizational effort. As shown in Exhibit 8-6, the field office is the site most often used for sales training in industrial, consumer, and service-oriented companies.

Decentralized training can involve one or more different types of training, such as office instruction, use of experienced salespeople, on-the-job training, or traveling sales clinics. Decentralized training usually takes place while the trainee is actually working in the field; this gives trainees the chance to learn and be productive at the same time. Thus, the cost of supporting nonproductive trainees while they are trained in centralized programs is avoided. Also, the branch manager or an assistant is usually responsible for decentralized training, thereby permitting sales managers to directly evaluate the trainees. The major drawback of decentralized training is that the branch manager may be ineffective in performing the training function.

Almost all selling organizations, even those with highly centralized training programs, use some form of decentralized training. This is because sales training should be a continual process, which means that some portion of training must always be decentralized to local levels.

Timing of Training Programs

Although training should be a continual process, management must decide when training should be stressed. Basically, there are two philosophies concerning the timing of sales training programs. Some executives believe that no one should be placed in the selling field until he or she is thoroughly trained to sell. That is, the salespeople must develop a thorough knowledge of the product, company, customers, competitors, and selling techniques before they are allowed in the field. The other philosophy suggests evaluating the new salesperson's desire and ability to sell before spending money and time on actual training. Thus, recruits are placed in the field with minimum information concerning selling and are then evaluated on the basis of how well they do, considering their lack of actual training.

Both philosophies have advantages and disadvantages. Insisting that salespeople be thoroughly trained before they enter the field means they should be top sales producers once they begin selling. But this policy is costly in terms of money and time, and it may lower the new salesperson's morale and enthusiasm because he or she may resent feeling nonproductive for the length of time it takes to become thoroughly knowledgeable. The strategy of placing new salespeople into the field first and then training them has major advantages. It can weed out people not suited for selling, and those who are selected for training are easier and quicker to train because they have had previous selling experience. However, customers can be lost and the organization can be seriously injured by sending untrained salespeople into the field.

The training period for new salespeople has lengthened dramatically over the last several years. As shown in Exhibit 8-7, the average training period has increased from about nineteen weeks to nearly twenty-four weeks.

Training Aids and Instructional Materials

To successfully carry out a sales training program, trainers should give much consideration to training aids and instructional materials. The most widely used training aids are manuals, other printed materials, and sight or sound equipment. Manuals or workbooks are used most in formal training programs for groups. The manual should supplement the training program by being a study guide for the trainee. Good manuals contain outlines of the presentations that will be made throughout the training program, lists of related reading materials, learning objectives of each training session, and thought-provoking questions, cases, and problems. Other printed materials used in sales training programs are company

EXHIBIT 8-7

Length of Training Period for New Salespeople

Time Period	Industrial Products (%)		Consumer Products (%)		Services (%)*	
	1987	1983	1987	1983	1987	1983
0 to 6 weeks	13	42	20	22	11	17
6 weeks to 3 months	0	8	10	33	11	0
3 to 6 months	74	33	50	45	22	50
6 to 12 months	13	8	10	0	11	33
Over 12 months	0	9	10	0	45	0
Median training period (weeks)	22	20	22	18	27	20

*Includes insurance, financial, utilities, transportation, retail stores, etc.
Source: Sales & Marketing Management, Feb. 22, 1988, p. 52.

bulletins, sales and product handbooks, standard texts, and technical and trade publications. Any or all of these can be used to supplement the training methods and content.

Training aids that appeal to the senses are increasingly being used in sales training programs. Blackboards, posters, motion-picture projectors, tape recorders, video tape recorders, and other playback equipment can be tremendous aids in training programs. For example, the approach being used by American Poclain Corporation in Fredericksburg, Virginia, involves role playing and video feedback. First, selling skills for a complete sales call are illustrated. Next, in a workshop session sales trainees prepare themselves for a series of sales calls, each of which deals with a specific selling problem. Trainees are then recorded making their presentations. Seeing this playback exposes weaknesses in selling skills and product knowledge.[22] Sales training programs such as this portend the future, in which interactive computer terminals will simulate different selling situations and trainees will respond on videotapes and through the terminals.

EVALUATING TRAINING PROGRAMS

Once a sales training program has been carried out, it is essential that the program's effectiveness be evaluated. That is, the sales manager must determine how well overall objectives and specific goals have been met.

An important aspect of the sales manager's job is determining how a sales training program is to be evaluated. Exhibit 8-8 illustrates four levels at which training programs can be evaluated. First, at the reaction level the trainees' attitudes and feelings toward the training program are measured. Second, evaluation at the knowledge level assesses how well the trainees learned basic principles, facts, and so on, during the training program. Third, attitude-level

EXHIBIT 8-8

Training Evaluation Levels

Levels	Measures	Methods
Reaction	Attitudes and feelings	Survey, comment sheets, exit interview, and discussion
Knowledge	Principles, facts, and techniques	Tests
Attitude	Changes in behavior	Questionnaires and observation
Results	Changes in performance	Change in sales, profits, expenses, etc.

Source: Earl D. Honeycutt and Thomas H. Stevenson, "Evaluating Sales Training Programs," *Industrial Marketing Management*, 18, 1989, p. 217.

EXHIBIT 8-9

Training Program Evaluation Form

	Strongly Agree	Agree	Neutral	Disagree	Strongly Disagree
The instructor was well prepared.	_____	_____	_____	_____	_____
The material was relevant.	_____	_____	_____	_____	_____
The instructor's objectives were made clear.	_____	_____	_____	_____	_____
Visual aids were effectively used.	_____	_____	_____	_____	_____

evaluation measures changes in behavior as a result of the training. This is usually accomplished by collecting questionnaires from supervisors, subordinates, and even customers; however, such assessments are often subjective because of the personal relationships that frequently develop during training. Finally, at the results level changes in performance are measured. This is done by plotting salespeople's performance before and after training and comparing the results against training program objectives.

Exhibit 8-9 is an example of an evaluation form that would be distributed to trainees in order to assess their reaction to the sales training program. The sample evaluation form in Exhibit 8-10 would be used by trainers to assess trainees' changes in attitudes and behaviors throughout the training program.

As companies spend more and more money on sales training each year, they are becoming more interested in evaluating their training programs. A recent survey of industrial marketers indicated that a majority of companies today use some form of evaluation for their sales training programs. As Exhibit 8-11 shows, only 2 percent of large companies (sales of $50 million or more per year) and 16 percent of small companies (sales of less than $50 million per year) do not evaluate the effectiveness of their sales training programs. Furthermore, large companies are relatively more interested in assessing reaction and knowledge during sales training, while small companies put more emphasis on results and attitudes in evaluating their training programs.[23]

THE BENEFITS OF SALES TRAINING PROGRAMS

As one would expect, the long-term aim of sales training is to increase profits. In so doing, management also hopes to improve customer relations, lower sales force turnover, increase earnings for sales reps, and achieve better sales force

EXHIBIT 8-10

Field Evaluation and Career Development Report

CONFIDENTIAL

4	Superior	1	Satisfactory
3	Excellent	0	Needs
2	Average		improvement

Date_____

Salesperson_____ Regional manager_____

Date report discussed with salesperson_____

1. *Sales profile*   0 1 2 3 4
   Knowledge of product
   Product-line representation and stock balance
   Opening new accounts and follow-up of leads
   Knowledge of advertising and sales promotion procedures
   Sales conference preparation and participation
   Creative selling techniques
   Ability to meet assigned goals

2. *Time and territory management*
   Account analysis
   Workload analysis
   Allocating time for maximum productivity
   Customer sales planning
   Territory coverage
   Territorial control

3. *Customer relations*
   Familiar with all company policies and procedures
   Creates confidence with accounts
   Handles complaints locally where possible
   Rapport with customers
   Control of credit problems

4. *Personal traits*
   Appearance
   Reliability
   Attitudes, job and company

5. *Growth development*
   Potential for advancement
   Motivation level
   Desire for advancement

control. The immediate benefits of sales training are faster development of the sales force, greater role clarity, improved morale, and higher job satisfaction. The long-run benefits of sales training are outlined in Exhibit 8-12.

Training teaches the sales force the most effective ways to plan, sell, serve customers, and implement company procedures. Thus sales training programs develop efficient salespeople more quickly than would be the case if the sales-

EXHIBIT 8-11

Evaluating Effectiveness of Sales Training Programs

Method	Large Companies (%)	Small Companies (%)
No evaluation conducted	2	16
Reaction (written critique of content)	76	29
Knowledge test	53	28
Attitude	35	45
Results	49	65

Source: Earl D. Honeycutt and Thomas H. Stevenson, "Evaluating Sales Training Programs," *Industrial Marketing Management,* 18, 1989, p. 218.

people had to learn through their own time-consuming experiences. Because training accelerates development, the sales force's confidence and enthusiasm are enhanced. Training programs also promote role clarity and thereby encourage greater job satisfaction. Improved sales force morale and higher job satisfaction translate into better customer relations (as salespeople confidently and enthusiastically try to solve customer problems) and reduced turnover rates (because salespeople face less discouragement after training and are usually more successful). These benefits reinforce the position of sales managers and enable them to maintain better control of the sales force. Thus, it is in the best interests of sales managers to help decide what the training program will include, how it will be approached, and who the trainers will be.

Sales training programs can definitely improve the sales force and help an organization accomplish its objectives. However, sales managers must be aware of possible ethical issues that can surface during training programs. The *Ethics* scenario on page 292 illustrates a few such issues.

EXHIBIT 8-12

Benefits of Training Programs

Training Program Inputs	Anticipated Changes due to Training	Long-run Training Program Outputs
Initial training	Faster development	More sales force control
Continuous training	Better role clarity	Better customer relations
	Improved morale	Lower turnover
	Higher job satisfaction	Increased sales
		Higher company profits

REFRESHER TRAINING

Up to this point most of the discussion of sales training has focused on initial sales training programs. There are three other types of training the sales manager must be concerned about. Two of these, continuous training and retraining, involve upgrading the present sales force. The third, managerial training, focuses on the sales managers, who need to ensure that they maintain and sharpen their skills so that they can remain effective and efficient.

Continuous Training and Retraining

Nothing is constant except change, and nowhere is this more true than in selling. Thus, there is a constant need to train the sales force, keeping it abreast of changes in products, markets, and company objectives. Also, today's emphasis on productivity creates a constant need to upgrade the sales force and to maximize the value of each salesperson. Rare is the successful company that assigns salespeople to territories without first training them; rarer still is the company that believes that once salespeople are in the field, experience is the only teacher they will ever need. Sterling Drug holds training seminars for salespeople who have been on the job for only three months; Kellogg schedules sales management meetings every two to three months to make certain that new products and selling techniques are completely understood.[24] These are only two examples of the trend toward increased emphasis on continuous training and retraining.

The purpose of continuous training is to help salespeople do their jobs better. Initial training of salespeople is usually restricted by time, budget, and the limited experience of the trainee. After the salesperson has been in the field for a while,

---

EXHIBIT 8-13

A Checklist for Upgrading the Sales Force

Individual Training

On-the-job coaching by sales supervisor
Courses for self-instruction prepared by the training department
Commercial self-instruction courses (example: cassette tape course in selling skills)
Attendance at workshops, clinics, or seminars
Courses in local schools for special skills (accounting, computer science, drafting, design, etc.)
Senior salesperson (example: goes with trainee to witness special kind of sales presentation)

Group Training

Sales meetings
Presentation by specialists in the firm (engineer, accountant, purchasing agent, etc.)
Presentations by other salespeople (example: how he or she landed a good account)
Workshops and seminars developed by the firm's training department
Commercial training aids (example: films on selling skills and motivation)
Subscriptions to journals relating to the industry
Journals relating to the industries of key accounts
General business magazines (*Business Week, Dun's Review, Forbes, Nation's Business*, etc.)
Marketing magazines (example: *Sales & Marketing Management*)
National newsmagazines (*Time, U.S. News & World Report, Newsweek*, etc.)
Business newspapers (*The Wall Street Journal, The New York Times*, etc.)

---

deficiencies in knowledge, skills, and work habits usually become evident. These deficiencies are identified from observations by the sales supervisor or manager, call reports, sales results, customer complaints, and other sources. Then training programs are designed to overcome the deficiencies.

Continuous training may be done either individually or in groups. The nature of the salesperson's deficiencies determines which approach is most appropriate. Exhibit 8-13 shows a checklist of ways to overcome deficiencies and thereby upgrade the sales force.

When a salesperson's job requirements change, then retraining is needed. A salesperson's job requirements may change because the company has added new products or services, revised sales territories, or developed new policies. Changes in customer markets may also require retraining of salespeople who must serve the needs of new customers. When a salesperson is promoted into a management or supervisory position, retraining is also necessary.

Retraining uses many of the same approaches as initial training because both are training for a new experience. In designing programs to retrain salespeople, the following steps should be taken:

1. *Determine which aspects of the new job are the most important.* All aspects must be understood, but to design the proper retraining program, the sales manager must know what is most essential and teach that first.

2. *Determine which aspects of the new job are the most difficult.* Some new information can be learned quickly; some takes longer. Retraining programs must devote more time to difficult areas of a new position or responsibility.

3. *Determine which aspects of the new job are the most prevalent.* Tasks that the salesperson will do most often or spend more time on should be emphasized.

An often-neglected aspect of retraining is the importance of the job-related attitudes of the salespeople. Recent research has discovered that salespeoples' attitudes toward the organization have a major influence on their retention behavior.[25] Therefore, in their retraining programs, sales managers should consider including methods to foster positive attitudes toward the job itself, the other salespeople, and themselves. Salespeople who are satisfied with their jobs and the organization can ultimately lead to a more loyal and productive sales force.

While retraining is vital to the health of a sales force, sales managers must be prepared to deal with individuals who have an emotional barrier toward retraining. Established salespeople may feel that management is trying to "change them"; there are many individuals who will resist anything that hints of change. Moreover, the emotional barrier may be greater when the retraining is done by outside trainers. In this case, sales managers should be aware of the contents of the retraining and support it wholeheartedly once the salespeople are back on the job. Therefore, the challenge facing those involved in retraining the sales force is not only to design the right kind of retraining program but also to anticipate and dissolve any type of resistance.[26]

Managerial Training

Sales managers must participate in training programs to ensure that they are aware of new developments. Training programs for sales managers are usually sponsored by the company itself or by professional associations, universities, training companies, or private consultants. Training programs for sales managers should cover all aspects of the sales manager's job, not just the training function. The purpose of the programs is to introduce new approaches to organization, planning, motivation, compensation, supervision, evaluation, and control over the areas the sales manager is responsible for. It is only through attending these refresher training programs that the sales manager can be confident that the most effective means of managing the sales force are being used. Two examples of companies that regularly train their sales managers are Ford Motor Company and Cheesebrough-Pond. Ford Marketing Institute, which oversees the training of all Ford personnel, provides dealer and sales manager training programs to Ford Division and Lincoln Mercury Division personnel on typical dealership problems. At Cheesebrough-Pond, the Health and Beauty Aids Division recently completed a training program for regional sales managers; it was designed to improve their effectiveness in training salespeople. But beyond ensuring effectiveness in training, managerial refresher programs should train sales managers in controlling the sales force through skillful planning, goal setting, motivation, performance evaluations, and profitability analysis.

Whether training programs are for sales managers or the sales force, the purpose of the training must be clear. Otherwise, the training program is not likely to achieve its objectives and valuable resources (both time and money) will be wasted.

SUMMARY

Developing an effective sales training program is increasingly becoming a critical part of the sales manager's job. With the rapidly rising costs of training and the vast amount of new and high-technology products, sales training is gaining more respect among upper-level executives. The responsibility of training the sales force is usually delegated to line executives, staff trainers, or outside training specialists. Many times the specific selling situation dictates who actually does the training. Once this decision has been made, the company is then ready to design and implement an effective sales training program. The training program should be based on the requirements of the company and on the skills and experience of the company's salespeople. The methods used to train the sales force depend on the objectives and content of the training program as well as on whether a group or an individual is being trained. When there is a group of trainees, the training methods typically used are lectures, group discussions, role playing, and simulation games. When training is on an individual basis, on-the-job training, personal conferences, correspondence courses, and programmed instruction are used. The proper implementation of a sales training program is important because costly mistakes can often occur without it. Implementing a sales training program requires extensive planning concerning the location of the training, the timing, and the training aids and instructional materials, as well as routine details, such as food, lodging, parking, and recreation. Once a training program has been carried out, it is important that sales managers know how well overall objectives have been met. This is done via an effective training evaluation program. Finally, all organizations must realize the importance of continuous training, retraining, and managerial training because these are critical components in the long-term success of the sales force.

STUDY QUESTIONS

1. Why should sales training and sales force development be thought of as a long-term, ongoing process?

2. "Good salespeople are born, not made." Do you agree or disagree?

3. Do you think sales training programs will become more or less important in the future? Why?

4. What are some of the problems that can arise when delegating the responsibility of the sales training program to line executives? To staff trainers? To outside training specialists?

5. Briefly discuss the planning decisions that must be made by sales managers in designing sales training programs.

6. Name and discuss the five basic elements that all initial sales training programs must cover. Are these elements any different from elements of refresher training programs?

7. What factors should sales managers consider before deciding on implementing group training rather than individual training for their sales force?

8. Why is the implementation of sales training programs such a critical task for sales managers? What are some of the areas that require considerable planning during the implementation process?

9. What are some of the benefits a company can expect from a well-developed sales training program? Do these benefits outweigh the costs? Why or why not?

10. Why must organizations constantly give attention to continuous training, retraining, and managerial training programs? Won't these types of training programs cause resentment among top salespeople?

IN-BASKET EXERCISE

You are a sales manager for a large consumer goods company, and you have just gone through your best recruiting and selection process in years. You hired six great people from college campuses around the country, and you believe that one of these recruits has the potential to be a top salesperson. Out of the hundreds of college students you interviewed, he scored the highest on the intelligence and sales aptitude tests.

This morning you received a surprising memo from the sales trainer. She reports that your superstar recruit is doing terribly in training; in fact, he constantly finishes last on all the exams. Furthermore, he isn't interested in the training, and he has indicated that since the trainer has "never been in the field, there's no point listening to her!" She has labeled your top recruit a "know-it-all" who won't respond to sales training.

1. The sales trainer wants your help in this matter. She is at the point where she is considering firing your top recruit. Is this a wise decision? Why or why not?

2. What can you do to help train this person without showing favoritism and possibly alienating the other five trainees?

CASE 8-1

CYCIL C. MARTIN COMPANY: DEVELOPING AND EVALUATING SALES FORCE TRAINING

The year was 1980 and the U.S. economy was experiencing a sharp recession as GNP showed an annualized decline of almost 10 percent in the second quarter. The unemployment rate was about 8 percent, while the CPI (consumer price index) showed an increase of 13 percent. The prime rate rose to 20 percent in April and was to be volatile in the next few months. New housing starts dropped to the lowest point in five years, and the auto industry was experiencing layoffs. Corporate profits were down 10 percent.

Case prepared by Joyce L. Grahn, University of Minnesota–Duluth. Used with permission.

Cycil C. Martin, owner of the sales and distribution company carrying his name, was sitting in his office. In front of him was a unique piece of medical equipment: a bed to provide rest and promote healing of decubitus ulcers or orthopedic problems by lessening pressure on the skin. The bed had a unique support device which supported the patient above the typical hard bed surface. The bed had an interesting history. It was originally designed by an Australian company and then sold to a foreign company, Super Bed, Ltd. Martin had recently paid $250,000 for the rights to manufacture and distribute the bed in the southern United States. Under the agreement, each bed would sell for $6,500, with royalties paid on a graduated scale: Martin paid no royalty for gross sales up to $100,000 and a 2 percent royalty on gross sales over $100,000.

Opportunities and Problems

As Martin viewed the situation, he saw great opportunities and several small problems. (Martin was known for his opportunistic personality.) First, the bed had originally sold for $12,000 to $18,000 to hospitals, but there had been few takers. The principal purchasers had been veterans' hospitals. Second, there was a problem with federal reimbursement. Medicaid and medicare would not pay for air-flotation beds. An initial survey had been conducted before purchase to analyze market acceptance of the bed. The results were dismal. Because the beds often failed to operate properly and because of the lack of federal reimbursement, few hospitals were interested in acquiring the beds. But Martin had assured the other potential investors that they were not to worry; this was an innovative, exciting concept. He proceeded to purchase the rights to the bed and named it The Martin Bed, Model A.

Martin decided the best way to market the bed was through manufacturers' agents. However, despite many improvements to the bed, the results were disappointing. There were alternative ways to treat burn patients, and these had greater market acceptance. Not only that, every improvement in design in the bed was quickly incorporated into the licenser's product distributed in the nothern United States at no R&D cost to the licenser.

At this point Martin called his investors together to discuss what they had learned. One of his investors with knowledge of the hospital equipment industry said that the decision makers, those who decided whether or not the beds would be purchased, were the head nurses on the floor. "It seems to me we should be working with them to improve the product. We should also be dealing directly with the head nurses for sales. The manufacturers' agents have been working with the doctors, and they have little or no idea of the working conditions on the floor. They don't understand the frustrations of working with nonperforming equipment."

Joe Stiles, director of manufacturing operations, said: "I'm sick and tired of spending my time on design improvements and then watching the northern U.S. licenser incorporate them into their products. We do the work and they benefit with no effort."

Peter Jablownski, vice president and long-time friend of Cy Martin, added to the complaints. "The manufacturer has been causing us some other problems. They don't deliver parts when they say they will. I think it's a deliberate slowdown. We need to do something different, and we need to do it now. The manufacturer must agree to supply the component parts we purchase from them on time with minimum defects, or we will buy from another vendor."

Nurses as Sales Reps

Martin said, "OK, let's get started on some new plans. If the agents don't sell well for us and the nurses are the decision makers, why not have nurses sell our product? Nurse sales representatives would understand the problems of hospital nurses. Furthermore, since we are dissatisfied with our supplier, let's put the bed out on bids and see what happens."

That weekend the following ad appeared in a Kansas City, Missouri, paper which had a circulation of about 500,000:

OPPORTUNITY FOR RN

Medical Sales

TO EARN $50,000 or more per year

Represent a growing, dynamic medical-device company to hospitals. Experience in ER or CCU a plus. Salary plus commission. Send resume to:

Jean Johnson
Personnel director
Cycil C. Martin Company
P.O. Box 251132-B
Kansas City, MO 64118

Within a week there were almost 200 responses to the ad. Jean Johnson, head of personnel, began an intense, time-consuming selection process among the applicants. Finally, after several tests and a series of personal interviews, thirty candidates remained. All were hired. All the applicants had one thing in common: They were highly qualified, talented people who were willing to give up the security of the nursing profession to move into the nontraditional role of an industrial sales representative, which offered opportunities for high pay. They were creative, hard-driving, ambitious, *underpaid* women who wanted something more, something better, and they were eager to accept the challenge.

Because the company had urgent needs for sales, the nurses were sent into the field to sell soon after they were hired. The job required that they both sell and service the product. Fortunately, most had mechanical aptitude and were fast learners.

Training and Development

Their training was minimal and primarily product-related. Peter Jablownski conducted a one-day seminar on the bed and how it worked. He encouraged them to rely on their instincts and to tell him when they had problems. "When you don't know what to do, don't sit back and worry; do something. Call me if you have a problem you can't handle. Remember the law of holes: If you find yourself in one, stop digging. Otherwise, use your own judgment." He was always accessible for support.

The nurses received 10 percent commission plus a base salary and travel expenses. They did not receive a car, however, because it was decided that the nurses should have some investment in their job. At the end of the three years the range of earnings for the nurses was expected to be from $40,000 to $200,000. This compared with an average pay in the hospital of about $15,000.

Bids for manufacturing the bed were solicited from four companies. The bid from one of the companies was selected, and within two months that company was producing the Martin Model C Bed. Distribution began in Missouri, and sales mushroomed quickly. Within one year, Martin Company purchased all its beds from the new vendor, and the former nurses continued to have excellent success in selling them.

By the end of the first two years, the bed was substantially improved. Several models were available that rented from $64.50 per day for a basic bed (Model C) to $99 per day for the deluxe model (Model D). There also were long-term lease arrangements available. Given these new alternatives, medicare reimbursement was possible.

Martin then moved to a roll-out program which involved selling and leasing the bed in new markets. There were three new offices opening per month, each one in a major city. The nurse–sales representatives were given the jobs of opening up the new territories. New offices were established in Atlanta, Phoenix, Orlando, Jacksonville, St. Louis, Dallas, Houston, and New Orleans.

Several of the salespeople had been promoted to sales managers. On promotion they received only minimum training for their new jobs. Martin Company used training as a reward. Twice a year the new sales managers were called together for a grand meeting. It was held in elegant settings where they were all treated very well. They all understood they were there because of superb performance.

Questions

1. Evaluate the sales training philosophy at Cycil C. Martin Company. Do you agree or disagree with this philosophy? Why?

2. Why do you think sales training played such a small role at Cycil C. Martin Company?

3. Develop an alternative sales training program for Cycil C. Martin Company. What part or parts of a sales training program would be most important for the nurses? Why?

4. Develop a formal evaluation program for your proposed sales training program. What do you think is the most important aspect of a sales training evaluation program? Why?

CASE 8-2

TENNESSEE CARBURETOR COMPANY:
RETRAINING IN A CHANGING SELLING ENVIRONMENT

Tennessee Carburetor Company was started in the late 1950s by Phillip Octeen. The company rebuilt truck and automobile carburetors for transport companies around the Memphis area. As Memphis grew as a distribution center, so did Tennessee Carburetor. The company quickly built a good reputation as a quality rebuilder of carburetion systems, and it grew tremendously throughout the 1960s and 1970s as it added major regional and even national clients.

As the company became profitable in the 1980s,

Octeen decided to develop a research and development facility. In changing with the times, the company added new product lines such as alternators, brake systems, and fuel pumps. As the auto industry moved more toward fuel-injection systems, the company decided to build on its reputation as a fuel systems company and began to increase research and development in this area.

Phillip Octeen, as president of Tennessee Carburetor, took an active role in the manufacturing and marketing side of the business. He had started out as an auto mechanic in Memphis, and at the age of 21 he invented a component part for a carburetor that resulted in better fuel economy. This invention enabled him to start his own business in 1958, when he was 22. His orientation, therefore, had always been on the production, or manufacturing, side of the business. Even as sales escalated during the 1960s and 1970s, little attention was given to marketing. In fact, Octeen hired many of his mechanic friends as salespeople during those growth years.

During the 1980s, attention was still given to the production side of the business. The company's focus was on developing an effective fuel-injection system that could be marketed to automakers. While the system was being perfected, the majority of sales were coming in from transportation firms that were purchasing the rebuilt carburetion systems. Most of these sales were basically reorders from clients the sales force had been working with for years.

The sales force at Tennessee Carburetor consisted of fourteen salespeople and two sales managers. All the sales personnel were very close friends of Octeen, and many of them started with him when the company was formed in the late 1950s. The salespeople were organized by specific geographic locations, and they called on garages or trucking firms within those locations. There was a great deal of customer loyalty and repeat business, which consistently translated into very good salaries and commissions for all the salespeople. Sales force turnover at the company has been

relatively nonexistent; the majority of salespeople who started with the company are still there. Several salespeople were added throughout the years, and only one of them subsequently left the company. The sales training at Tennessee Carburetor focuses exclusively on product knowledge. Since many of the salespeople were formerly automobile mechanics, Octeen believes he has a very skilled sales force.

During the last several years, Octeen has noticed a gradual decline in the company's sales volume. Since many transportation firms are switching to smaller trucks and vans, carburetors are becoming obsolete. Octeen has expected this trend for some time, which is why he invested in research and development for fuel-injection systems. He feels that he now has a superior fuel-injection system for automobiles and that carburetor rebuilding is a thing of the past. He is at a very critical transition point with his business: he is convinced he should slowly harvest the dying carburetor business and concentrate on marketing his superior fuel-injection system to automobile manufacturers. In fact, he believes his company is in a prime position to market this fuel-injection system to the ultramodern and efficient new-car plant that is just a few hundred miles east in Tennessee.

While Octeen feels confident about his new product, he is unsure about how his sales force will market it. Although the sales force has been very loyal throughout the years, can the salespeople handle the new, progressive companies that emerged in the automotive market in the early 1990s?

Questions

1. What are Octeen's options at this point?

2. Give positive and negative aspects of (a) retraining his old sales force and (b) hiring a new one.

3. What should be the major emphasis in a retraining program for the salespeople at Tennessee Carburetor Company?

REFERENCES

1. Jim Rapp, "Team Selling Is Changing the Sales Trainer's Role," *Sales Training*, May 1989, pp. 6–10.
2. William Atkinson, "A New Approach to Sales Training," *Training*, March 1989, pp. 57–60.
3. "They Manage to Train, Too," *Sales & Marketing Management*, Aug. 13, 1984, p. 70.
4. "CMC Corporation: When OTJ Training Isn't Enough," *Training*, February 1985, p. 73.

5. Ibid.
6. See *Xerox Sales Training Marketing Case History*, Intercollegiate Video Clearinghouse, Miami, 1976.
7. *Sales & Marketing Management*, January 1976, p. 36.
8. Jack Wilner, "Tending Goals for Sales Management," *Training and Development Journal*, November 1985, pp. 46–47.
9. "They Manage to Train, Too," op. cit.
10. Ibid., p. 72.
11. "CMC Corporation: When OTJ Training Isn't Enough," op. cit.
12. John B. Dorsey, "Manville Trains with Style," *Sales & Marketing Management*, Aug. 15, 1983, pp. 66–67.
13. "They Manage to Train, Too," op. cit.
14. James A. Narus and James C. Anderson, "Turn Your Industrial Distributors into Partners," *Harvard Business Review*, March–April 1986, p. 70.
15. Atkinson, op. cit.
16. Ron Zemke, "Storytelling: Back to a Basic," *Training*, March 1990, pp. 44–50.
17. *AT&T Teletraining*, AT&T Communications, 1985.
18. Gerhard Gschwandter, "Videotape Demonstrations and Sales Training Effectiveness," *Industrial Marketing*, December 1977, p. 42.
19. Jack Falvey, "The Most Neglected Training Tool," *Sales & Marketing Management*, January 1990, pp. 51–54.
20. Arthur Bragg, "Is a Mentor Program in Your Future?" *Sales & Marketing Management*, September 1989, pp. 54–63.
21. Robert H. Collins, "Sales Training: A Microcomputer-Based Approach," *Journal of Personal Selling and Sales Management*, May 1986, pp. 71–76.
22. Ibid., p. 43.
23. Earl D. Honeycutt and Thomas H. Stevenson, "Evaluating Sales Training Programs," *Industrial Marketing Management*, 18, 1989, pp. 215–222.
24. "Training to Reach New Heights," *Sales & Marketing Management*, August 1978, p. 43.
25. Jeffrey K. Sager, "How to Retrain Salespeople," *Industrial Marketing Management*, 19, 1990, pp. 155–166.
26. Phil Anderson, "Refresher Sales Training," *Sales Training*, May 1989, pp. 19–22.

DEVELOPING THE SALES FORCE AT CHEMCO

Larry Ebert, the regional sales manager of CHEMCO (see the Part One case for company information) is preparing to hire a new salesperson for the St. Louis sales territory. The territory was left without a sales rep after the sudden departure of the salesperson assigned to the area. Ebert is reviewing a list of applicants from which he feels confident that he can select a new salesperson.

THE ST. LOUIS SALES TERRITORY

The sales territory that Ebert is attempting to fill is based in St. Louis, Missouri. It consists of the state of Missouri and the southern half of Illinois, from Peoria south. The territory is large enough that overnight travel is usually required to properly manage the business. The last salesperson averaged two nights out per week. Most of the accounts are located in or near the larger cities in the territory: St. Louis, Kansas City, Peoria, Springfield, Columbia, Decatur, and St. Joseph. However, there are also several good accounts located in a variety of smaller cities. Ebert feels that there is more business than the previous salesperson was able to tap; thus, he believes that a new salesperson should be able to earn more

Case prepared by Philip Nitse, Memphis State University.

than the $31,000 in commissions that the previous salesperson averaged over the last couple of years.

THE TRAINING OF A SALESPERSON

All new salespeople are required to spend seven weeks in training before being left on their own. The training consists of four parts. First, each trainee is given a one-week orientation to the territory; during this time, he or she rides with a manager or other designated trainer. (One week is usually long enough to ensure that new employees have an understanding of the job involved and that they are happy with their decision to work for CHEMCO.) Second, the trainee spends two weeks at the home office learning about the company and its people, products, customers, and selling techniques. Third, the trainee has a two-week period of on-the-job training; while riding with a senior salesperson, usually in that salesperson's territory, the trainee is able to apply much of the information he or she has already learned. Fourth, the trainee spends two weeks riding with a district manager in the assigned territory to ensure that the trainee is capable and to introduce him or her to the key accounts in the territory.

CHEMCO uses this approach, together with consistent supervision and periodic follow-up training programs, regardless of the amount of sales experience a new employee had before joining the organization. Ebert wishes that he could shorten the time during which the St. Louis territory must go without a regular salesperson, but he was at a loss regarding how to restructure the training program. He decided that his first order of business is to hire a new salesperson; then he can work on reducing the time during which the territory is left uncovered.

THE RECRUITMENT AND SELECTION PROCESS

The company's policy on recruiting is to advertise the job in the local and regional newspapers, review all inquiries and résumés, send applications to persons who seem to qualify, review returned applications, and set up interview appointments for prospective employees. For the St. Louis sales position, this procedure narrowed the choice to six applicants who came in for personal interviews. Notes from these interviews (Exhibit 1) are what Ebert is reviewing in his attempt to select the new salesperson.

EBERT'S SELECTION PROCESS

Ebert can simply select the candidate who he feels is the best choice on the basis of intuition and experience, or he can use modern technology to aid him in the selection process. He decides that since information is available on the salespeople in the company, he will use that information as a guide to selection. He

EXHIBIT 1

Applicants' Background

1. *Karen Larsen:*

Eight years of selling health and beauty aids to local food stores

Age 30, divorced, one child

College graduate, degree in history

Annual income: high 20s

Owns home

Hobbies: cooking, tennis, political activities

Comments: well groomed, reasonably intelligent, very personable, good experience

2. *Charles Morgan:*

Two years of selling insurance on straight commission

Age 36, married, no children

College graduate

Twelve years of military service in Army; highest rank, captain

Annual income: low 20s

Rents apartment

Hobbies: photography

Comments: not career salesperson, likes structure, willing to relocate

3. *Douglas Simpson:*

No direct selling experience

Age 24, not married, no children

M.B.A. in marketing

Annual income: below $10,000, from campus jobs

Hobbies: basketball, dating

Comments: good appearance, moderately aggressive, may be slightly immature

4. *Adam Youngblood:*

Twenty years of selling and sales management experience; sold both products and services for national and local companies

Age 42, married, two children

College graduate

Annual income: high 30s

Owns home

Active in various organizations; has held offices in several

Hobbies: jogging, tennis, golf

Comments: solid experience, possible managment potential, aggressive, intelligent

5. *Christina Popper:*

Six years of bookkeeping experience; seven different jobs

Age 31, married, three children

College graduate

Annual household income: mid-20s to high 30s; husband in construction work

Rents home

No hobbies

Comments: not very aggressive, not tied to area, personable, good appearance, reasonably intelligent

6. *Ivan Peskopos:*

Fifteen years of direct selling experience; sells chemical products for a small West Coast company, is looking for new position because company is closing

Age 40, divorced, no children at home

High school degree

Annual income: low 40s

Rents condo

Hobbies: reading, acting, church activities

Comments: well recommended by his employer, good appearance, reasonably intelligent

---

must first profile the typical CHEMCO saleperson by using demographic information. Ebert feels that if he selects a candidate who is very similar to the typical salesperson, the new employee's socialization into the company will be quicker.

The information that Ebert has available includes marital status, spouse employment, gender, education level, household income, and sales experience in months. Using his portable computer, Ebert develops a profile of the typical CHEMCO salesperson and then compares each of the candidates to this profile.

After reviewing the information from this comparison, he remembers that the head of personnel sent him copies of tests that have been accepted as relevant to the employment of salespeople. Ebert had administered the tests to the can-

EXHIBIT 2

Test Results

	(1)	(2)	(3)	(4)	(5)	(6)
comm	2.00	3.87	2.67	2.53	3.27	3.27
inv	2.17	3.83	3.17	2.83	3.00	3.50
al	4.50	1.50	4.00	3.50	4.00	2.00
tsse	1.90	3.10	2.50	2.80	2.20	2.40
satsg	2.21	4.21	2.36	2.43	2.50	3.14
spay	2.29	3.79	2.64	2.79	2.71	2.86
satsd	2.43	4.00	2.29	1.64	3.21	3.21
satsr	2.36	3.36	2.29	4.29	3.00	3.07
pcs	2.00	4.00	2.50	3.00	1.50	3.00
ijs	2.38	3.38	2.61	2.08	3.23	2.62
satc	2.67	3.27	2.40	2.13	3.13	3.27
satpro	2.63	3.88	2.75	3.38	2.88	2.88
satcw	2.17	3.92	1.92	2.08	2.25	3.33
pcp	4.00	1.33	3.33	3.33	4.00	3.67

didates at the end of the interviews. The results of the tests (Exhibit 2) provide additional information about the candidates. Ebert again uses his computer to access the information about the company's current salespeople and to compare the candidates to them. He still believes that a new employee should match the existing personnel to ensure rapid socialization into the company. After reviewing his notes from the interviews, and his two attempts to match the candidates to the existing salespeople, Ebert feels that he is ready to make his selection to fill the sales position for the St. Louis territory.

QUESTIONS

1. Basing your decision on only the notes from the interviews, which candidate would you select? Support your answer.

2. How did the candidates compare with the company's typical salesperson? Should anyone be eliminated from the list of possible candidates? If so, why? If not, why not?

3. Using this new information, which candidate would you select? Again, support your answer.

4. On the basis of the test results, which of the six candidates should Ebert hire? Why? Which of the candidates should not be hired? Explain.

5. If the person selected after the interviews, the person selected after the current-employee matching profile, and the person selected after the employment tests are different individuals, explain the disparity.

6. On the basis of the information presented in this case, discuss the positive and negative points of each of the six candidates with regard to the position that is available.

7. Review the information on the training program, and discuss the changes, if any, that you would recommend to the division manager at the next meeting.

8. Review the recruitment process, and either make recommendations on how you would change it or discuss why you would leave it the way it is.

PART FOUR

DIRECTING THE SALES FORCE

9

SALES FORCE PERFORMANCE: AN OVERVIEW

LEARNING OBJECTIVES

When you finish this chapter, you should understand:

- ▲ The many factors that influence a salesperson's performance
- ▲ The role that planning, organizing, recruiting, selecting, and training play in overall sales force performance
- ▲ How motivation and sales performance are related
- ▲ The relationship between motivation, aptitude, and skill level
- ▲ The importance of such external factors as the environment and the organization to an individual's performance level
- ▲ The dimensions that make up the role perceptions of a salesperson and how they affect performance
- ▲ The role communication plays in sales force performance

A DAY ON THE JOB

Leo B. Kelly, a sales executive for the Business Systems Group of Xerox Corporation, is definitely a top sales performer. During his twenty years with Xerox, Kelly has reached the top of the company in sales seventeen times, often surpassing his sales plan by 200 percent or more! Leo Kelly is a star performer who takes his job very seriously. "Any assignment I'm given, whether it's geographic or by industry," says Kelly, "I run as though it's my own business and try to maximize the potential." Being prepared and gaining respect is also an important part of Kelly's philosophy. "For every hour I spend in front of a customer, I probably spend five hours getting ready," he explains. "When I get in front of that decision maker, I'd better be ready, I'd better not be looking for something, I'd better know what he's going to be asking me." When Kelly is asked what it takes to be a top-performing salesperson, he sums it up this way: "The performers—the people who succeed—have tremendous discipline. There's always a reason not to call on someone. There's always a reason to go home early. Sales is a matter of being in the right place at the right time, and the only way you're going to be in the right place at the right time is if you're in a lot of places a lot of times! If you do that, you're going to be successful."[1]

How do sales managers get optimal performance from a sales force? Should they motivate the sales force with expensive gifts and trips to the Caribbean? Is the monetary reward system important? Or is hiring the right people going to lead to the best-performing sales force? All these factors and more play an important part in sales force performance. This chapter presents an overview of the many interrelated factors that influence sales force performance and identifies what sales managers can do to achieve optimal performance from their salespeople. Beyond this, the chapter provides a conceptional framework for better understanding the remainder of the book.

The sales manager's job involves many interrelated tasks: planning, organizing, developing, directing, controlling, and evaluating. The first half of the book concentrated on planning, organizing, and developing; the second half concentrates on implementing—that is, directing, controlling, and evaluating—the sales program and its impact on sales force performance.

Effective implementation of a sales program requires that sales managers gain a thorough understanding of how to motivate and direct the sales force. Sales managers, therefore, must understand the behavioral patterns of the sales force. Once this is accomplished, sales managers can better direct and motivate their people, and this should ultimately lead to better sales force performance. This chapter offers an overview of sales force performance by examining the factors that have an impact on an individual's behavior.

DETERMINANTS OF SALES FORCE PERFORMANCE

For many U.S. companies, improving the performance of the sales force represents both a challenge and an enormous opportunity during the extremely competitive 1990s. While more and more companies see limited potential for further gains from manufacturing, many companies are in agreement that significant gains can be realized by improving sales force performance. Therefore, it is critical that sales managers understand the determinants of sales force performance. Once sales managers understand these determinants, they can do a great deal to assist their sales force in achieving optimal performance. Although researchers have studied various assumed determinants during the past seventy-five years, the studies do not report consistent results with respect to which factors affect sales performance.[2] However, they do provide sales managers with a broad, overall perspective on what influences sales force performance, and this chapter will enhance your understanding of these factors.

A salesperson's job performance can be thought of as being a function of two basic types of factors: internal, or individual, factors and external factors. Exhibit 9-1 presents this conceptualization of a salesperson's performance as well as the determinants that make up the two categories of factors.

The determinants that influence sales force performance are highly interrelated. Even with a simplified model, it is not possible to show all the interactions among these variables. Much of the literature on industrial and organizational

EXHIBIT 9-1

Determinants of Sales Force Performance

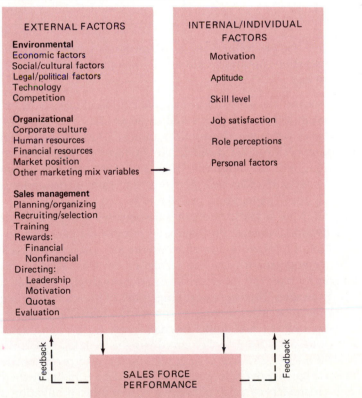

EXTERNAL FACTORS

Environmental
Economic factors
Social/cultural factors
Legal/political factors
Technology
Competition

Organizational
Corporate culture
Human resources
Financial resources
Market position
Other marketing mix variables

Sales management
Planning/organizing
Recruiting/selection
Training
Rewards:
   Financial
   Nonfinancial
Directing:
   Leadership
   Motivation
   Quotas
Evaluation

INTERNAL/INDIVIDUAL FACTORS

Motivation

Aptitude

Skill level

Job satisfaction

Role perceptions

Personal factors

Feedback

SALES FORCE PERFORMANCE

Feedback

psychology indicates that many of these factors combine to influence job performance. The literature further suggests that if an individual is lacking in any one of the influences, he or she would be expected to have a lower performance than someone who has all the influences. For example, salespeople who have the required skill level and an accurate understanding of the sales job but lack motivation can be expected to be low performers. Similarly, individuals who have the necessary aptitude and are highly motivated but lack an understanding of the sales job can be expected to perform poorly. Therefore, it is important to realize that the major influences on an individual's performance are not independent of each other.

The model presented in Exhibit 9-1 indicates that a salesperson's performance is affected by the sales manager's planning, organizing, developing, directing, controlling, and evaluating. How well sales managers carry out these tasks can have a strong impact on both internal and external factors. For example, poor organization of a territory or product line by a sales manager can lead to confusion among the sales reps, which could ultimately lead to poor performance. Similarly, a poorly implemented training program could discourage a highly motivated individual, leading again to poor job performance. Therefore, it is important that a sales manager understand the critical interaction of these activities in determining sales force performance.

Internal Factors

The internal, or individual, factors influencing a salesperson's performance include the following: motivation, aptitude, skill level, job satisfaction, role perception, and personal factors.

Motivation.   Motivation is the basis behind all behavior: individuals act or behave in a certain way because they are motivated to do so. Since all behavior starts with motivation, sales managers must gain a thorough understanding of this important influence on performance. From a sales management perspective, motivation can be thought of as the amount of time and effort salespeople put into their job. This includes such activities as developing sales presentations, calling on new accounts, doing paperwork, and the like.

Many things can motivate a salesperson. A salesperson's inner values or drives can act as a motivational device. For example, salespeople can be motivated if they feel that a lot of hard work and effort on the job will lead to better performance, with better performance leading to higher rewards. While sales managers have little control over the inner drives of an individual, they play a large role in motivating the sales force by controlling many of the more tangible motivational tools. For instance, sales managers control the financial compensation programs that help motivate and guide the sales force. Additionally, sales managers can help motivate sales personnel by providing up-to-date knowledge about the company, customers, products, selling techniques, and performance expectations. This knowledge can give salespeople self-confidence and raise their career aspirations. Sales managers can also consider a host of other motivational tools, such as sales contests, sales meetings, and special recognition, to enhance the performance of the sales force.

Since sales managers directly influence sales force motivation, they must be extremely sensitive to how the various motivational tools can influence sales force performance. These motivational factors are discussed more fully in Chapter 13.

Aptitude.   A salesperson's job performance will definitely be a function of his or her aptitude, or special ability. For example, two individuals with equal motivation and the same skills might perform at entirely different levels because one has more innate aptitude than the other.

It has generally been assumed that sales success is a function of various personal and psychological characteristics, for example, physical characteristics (height and physical attractiveness), mental abilities (verbal intelligence, mathematical ability, and educational attainment), and personality traits (empathy, ego strength, aggressiveness, and sociability). Recently, however, several studies have shown that significant relationships also exist between aptitude variables and performance.[3]

Skill level.   While aptitude focuses on the individual's innate abilities, skill concerns with how well an individual can learn and perform necessary tasks. Therefore, skill level and aptitude are related concepts. The major difference between the two is that aptitude consists of enduring personal abilities while skills can change with learning and experience.

An individual should possess several skills to become a high-performing salesperson. First, sales skills are a must. Knowing how to make a sales presentation or how to close a sale will definitely improve the salesperson's performance. Second, interpersonal skills in communicating with clients or resolving problems are critical for a salesperson. Third, technical skills, such as knowing the product, market, competition, and customers, are also important in becoming a successful salesperson.

Which of these skills is most important is often a function of the selling situation. For instance, the degree of technical skills needed would vary according to the type of product the salesperson is selling. Nevertheless, a high-performing salesperson is one who is proficient in sales, interpersonal, and technical skills.

Interpersonal, problem-solving skills often vary considerably among salespeople. Unfortunately, these differences can lead to lower morale in the sales force. The *Ethics* scenario on page 314 illustrates such a situation.

Job satisfaction.   Sales force performance can be affected by how satisfied individuals are with their jobs. The level of satisfaction can depend on how rewarding, fulfilling, challenging, or frustrating the salesperson feels his or her job is. Seven different factors of sales job satisfaction have been identified: the job itself, coworkers, supervision, company policies and support, pay, promotion and advancement opportunities, and customers.[4]

The seven dimensions of job satisfaction are grouped into two major components: intrinsic and extrinsic. *Intrinsic satisfaction* is related to the job's internal rewards. For example, salespeople who derive enjoyment from talking to clients, learning more about their company's products, and the like, are intrinsically motivated. *Extrinsic satisfaction* is derived from the job's external rewards. For instance, salespeople who are concerned about money, promotions, and recognition are extrinsically motivated.

A salesperson's job satisfaction can affect other determinants of sales performance. For example, an individual's satisfaction on the job can influence his or her motivation to perform. Although the relationship between satisfaction and motivation is not completely understood, it would appear that more highly motivated salespeople are often relatively more satisfied with their sales jobs and vice versa. Finally, job satisfaction can be influenced by how well salespeople understand what is expected of them on their jobs. A clear understanding is referred to as *role clarity*. Salespeople who experience great uncertainty about what is expected from them on the job tend to be less satisfied than those who have a good understanding of what is expected from them.

Role perception. *Role perception* is an individual's understanding of the demands, expectations, and pressures communicated to salespeople by the individuals around them. These people can include top management, the sales manager, customers, other salespeople both within and outside the firm, and family members—in other words, anyone who has a vested interest in the salesperson's performance or whom the salesperson might look to for guidance. It is the salesperson's perceptions of their expectations that ultimately influence behavior and job performance. How the sales manager communicates expectations and demands will definitely have an enormous impact on the sales force and its performance.

Sales managers should be aware of three problems that may arise in regard to a salesperson's role perception. The first concerns the *accuracy* of a salesperson's perceptions of his or her superiors. Are the perceptions of the sales force regarding job expectations the same as the superior's actual expectations and demands? If not, difficulties will result. The second problem occurs when the salesperson perceives that the expectations of two or more of his or her role partners are inconsistent. For example, the sales manager may believe that the salesperson should be doing paperwork at home in the evenings and on weekends, whereas the spouse believes that time at home should be spent with the family. In such instances, salespeople experience a great deal of *conflict* because they cannot adequately satisfy the expectations of both role partners. Role perceptions can be affected if salespeople believe that they are not getting the necessary information to perform their job adequately. In this case, *role ambiguity* occurs because salespeople may be uncertain about what is actually expected of them in their selling roles. Therefore, it is critical that sales managers work closely and communicate effectively with their salespeople so that everyone has a clear understanding of demands and expectations.

Personal factors. Personal factors can be thought of as individual characteristics that might be related to sales force performance but are not part of aptitude, skill level, motivation, and role perception. Such personal factors as the salesperson's age, height, education, and family situation have been included in past studies that test the variables that influence sales. Some research has suggested that these factors tend to be good predictors of sales force performance. However, many of the personal characteristics found to be related to sales performance were specific to certain situations in particular industries or products.[5]

External Factors

External factors can influence a salesperson's performance in several ways. They can directly assist or constrain performance. Competition or the lack of it, size of the sales territory, and market share of the company can all influence a salesperson's performance. External factors can also affect performance by interacting with other influencing factors, such as motivation or role perception.

A great deal of research has been conducted that identifies the influence of external factors.[6] The research indicates that the following variables can cause differences in sales force performance:

- Regional differences in the amount of money spent on the firm's marketing and promotional elements
- Differences in the firm's past experience or market position in different markets
- Differences in the number of salespeople a sales manager supervises
- Intensity of competition across markets
- Market potential across markets
- Concentration of customers within markets
- Geographic dispersion of customers

The impact each of these external factors has on sales performance is summarized in Exhibit 9-2. All these external factors can be classified into three groups of factors: environment, organization, and sales management.

Environment. A salesperson's performance can be affected by factors in the environment that are often beyond his or her control. Variables in the environ-

---

EXHIBIT 9-2

External Factors Influencing Sales Performance

- Relatively high expenditures on marketing and promotional efforts: *positive impact*

- A relatively high market share in recent years: *positive impact*

- An increasing market share in recent years: *positive impact*

- Sales manager and each field supervisor controls a relatively large number of salespeople: *negative impact*

- Relatively intense competitive activity: *negative impact*

- Relatively high total market potential: *positive impact*

- Concentration of relatively large proportion of big and potential customers: *positive impact*

- Relatively large distances between customers: *negative impact*

Source: Based on a summary of research findings presented in Adrian B. Ryans and Charles B. Weinberg, "Sales Productivity: A Multiple Company Study," in Richard P. Bagozzi (ed.), *Sales Management: New Developments from Behavioral and Decision Model Research*, Marketing Science Institute, Cambridge, Mass., 1979, pp. 92–129.

---

ment that can impact sales force performance include the economy; developments in society, culture, law, and politics; technology; and competition.

The sales of a product are definitely influenced by the *economic conditions* of a particular region, state, or country. Individuals and organizations cannot purchase products and services unless they have purchasing power. An individual's total purchasing power is a function of current income, prices, savings, and credit availability. Sales managers should follow trends in each of these four areas because a change in any one of these can have an immediate impact on sales performance.

The social environment can affect sales force performance in several ways. As society and individuals change over time, so do market opportunities. Changes in *social values and lifestyles* will influence what people buy as well as how they react to various marketing activities. Over the last several years social changes have drastically affected sales activities. For example, high-pressure selling tactics are less prevalent than they were and, in fact, may now have a negative effect on sales performance. Another social trend that can influence sales performance involves society's concerns about *ethical issues.* Consumers and salespeople alike are not comfortable in situations that involve unethical practices. More and more salespeople today want explicit guidelines from management to help them resolve ethical issues. These guidelines can do a great deal to reduce any ambiguity a salesperson may experience, and the result is likely to be better job performance. These are just a few examples of how social variables can influence sales force performance; to perform effectively, sales managers need to be familiar with many of the social changes occurring in the marketplace.

New *laws and regulations* can ultimately affect sales force performance. The number of laws regulating business and selling has increased dramatically during the past several decades. The laws that have been of particular importance to sales managers in recent years are those concerning antitrust and consumer protection. The antitrust laws restrict marketing practices that tend to hinder competition. Consumer protection legislation attempts to ensure that consumers are provided with accurate information for use in making purchase decisions. Since many of these laws deal with the disclosure of information to consumers, they have a direct impact on selling activities. It is up to sales managers to stay current on this legislation and to be sure the activities of their sales force, as well as the competitor's sales force, are within the law. Deviations from these regulations can cause dissatisfaction among salespeople and consumers and ultimately affect sales performance.

One of the most dramatic external factors affecting sales performance is technology. *Changes in technology* can result in new products and new sales opportunities. In many companies, new products account for most of the growth and profits. Sales managers should work closely with research and development people to encourage more market-oriented research and to keep up with many of the changes in technology that could ultimately influence sales force performance. Another area where technology is impacting sales force performance is productivity. Increasingly, new technology—laptop PCs, cellular mobile telephones, facsimile machines, teleconference equipment, and low-cost software—is making today's sales forces more productive. Sales managers must keep abreast of these developments so that they can ensure that their salespeople do too.

Competition represents an environmental variable that can greatly influence sales. The number of competitors a firm has can drastically alter performance. If a new company enters the market or a current competitor launches a new product, the additional competition can have dramatic effects on company sales. Therefore, it is critical that sales managers identify all competitors and monitor the market for new competition. It is also extremely helpful to identify the relative strengths of each competitor in the marketplace. Ideally, a company's sales program should be developed with the goals of understanding the competition and achieving a differential advantage over it.

A close monitoring of external factors by sales managers is often not enough to ensure gains in sales performance, however. Many times, sales managers adapt their sales programs to the external environment without a great deal of success. In many instances, sales programs are adapted to the external environment for all sales territories in the same manner. Problems often arise, however, because some external environmental factors affect different parts of the market to different degrees. Therefore, adjusting sales plans for certain external trends may help sales performance for one salesperson but not for another in a different territory. A company can have two similar salespeople with relatively equal aptitudes, skill levels, and motivation, yet one's sales performance can be much better than the other's simply because the external factors have a different impact from one territory to another.

According to research, many of the external factors that impact sales performance are due to regional differences. In fact, one study indicates that regional variations can account for as much as 80 percent of the variation in the sales volume of a sales force.[7] It is therefore critical that sales managers take these differences into account when evaluating sales performance. Additionally, many of the other sales management activities—such as time and territory management, sales forecasting, and quota setting—must be implemented with regional variations in mind. These external environmental differences make some sales representatives less productive than others; thus, it becomes very difficult to evaluate salesperson performance solely on the basis of sales volume. It is evident that other types of evaluation become necessary to keep the morale and motivation level of the sales force high. These issues will be discussed in more detail in Chapter 16.

Organization.   The organization a salesperson works for can play a major role in that person's sales performance. All companies are unique to some extent, and it is the uniqueness of each company that can alter a salesperson's performance. Organization variables that can have a direct impact on sales force performance include corporate culture, personnel, finances, and market position and other marketing-mix variables.

The *culture,* or *personality,* of a corporation tends to extend into every aspect of the organization, including its sales activities. The top management of a firm has various values and beliefs that overlay the organization. These values and beliefs lead to a corporate culture that will ultimately shape the marketing and sales plans of an organization, as can be seen in successful companies such as IBM, Xerox, and NCR. These organizations are committed to better serving the needs of their customers, and this commitment is emphasized in their sales training and reward systems. Thus, a company's personality, or culture, can do a great deal to influence sales force commitment and performance.

Many believe that it is *personnel,* or *people,* who separate the successful companies from the not-so-successful companies. One of the most difficult tasks for the sales manager is recruiting and selecting highly qualified people for today's increasingly complex sales positions. Good salespeople are hard to find. Yet it is good personnel that ultimately lead to excellent sales performance.

An organization's *financial strength* can influence sales force performance too. Firms with limited financial resources may be at a disadvantage in their ability to develop new products or increase the size of their sales force to adequately cover the market. Struggling companies often are forced into selling out to larger firms in order to realize their full marketing potential. Thus, good financial resources can lead to good sales force performance.

A firm's *market position* can do a great deal to influence sales performance. Firms with strong market positions provide their sales forces with a competitive advantage that enhances sales force performance. Some companies have strong market positions in some geographic areas but not in others. This scenario can be true for some or all of the firm's competitors. Therefore, salespeople in different markets tend to face different levels of competition. Salespeople who are in a market with aggressive competitors may have a much more difficult time reaching sales goals than salespeople in less competitive markets. Similarly, since some markets are more heavily populated than others, sales potential will depend on the population density of the assigned market. For example, there is a heavy concentration of oil companies in Houston and auto manufacturers in Detroit;

consequently, these territories contain greater sales potential for suppliers to these industries than markets that are more sparsely populated. It is important that sales managers make sure the right salespeople are assigned to the proper market, since this can change sales force performance dramatically.

Finally, sales force performance can be affected by an organization's *commitment to the other marketing-mix variables*. When the intensity of one firm's marketing efforts is much greater than that of another firm, salespeople in the marketing-oriented firm will definitely have a sales edge over the other firm's salespeople. Organizations must realize that personal selling is only one element of the marketing mix. A commitment to the other elements can significantly enhance sales performance.

Sales management. Understanding the many factors that influence sales force performance is critical for successful sales management because almost everything the sales manager does can affect the performance of his or her salespeople. It should now be evident that the way sales managers plan and organize sales force activities can have an important impact on how well the sales force understands what is required and how well it performs. In particular, selection and training decisions made by sales managers can greatly influence the aptitude and skill level of the sales force. The importance of time and territory management is discussed in Chapter 10. Sales quotas and their impact on performance are considered in Chapter 11. Compensation, an extremely important influence on sales force performance, is discussed in Chapter 12.

The relationship between compensation and performance is very complex. There are many different ways that sales managers can reward their sales force, and choosing the right method can dramatically affect performance. Rewards can be divided into two broad categories: extrinsic and intrinsic. *Extrinsic rewards* are rewards controlled by managers and customers. Such things as pay, bonuses, and promotions are external to the individual and thus are considered extrinsic rewards. *Intrinsic rewards* are rewards that salespeople achieve for themselves. Such things as personal growth and self-esteem are internal to the person and thus are considered intrinsic rewards. It is extremely important that sales managers understand these types of rewards, since they influence motivation and ultimately performance.

Motivating the sales force is discussed in Chapter 13. In addition to motivational theories, the various *nonfinancial* methods available to sales managers are presented. For example, recognition, plaques, trips, and various "perks"—personal parking spaces, special club memberships, and other privileges—can be used by sales managers to help increase the performance of the sales force. Leader behavior and the different leadership styles are presented in Chapter 14. Sales managers are, in essence, leaders, so they must understand what makes an effective leader. Sales managers who are perceived as good leaders will have more success in motivating their sales force to perform than those who are perceived as weak leaders. Chapters 15 and 16 explain how the controlling and evaluating tasks of the sales manager can influence performance. For example, a company can evaluate its salespeople on quantitative and objective measures (sales volume, quota attainment, and new accounts generated) or on more subjective, qualitative criteria (customer relations, quality of sales presentations, cooperation, and resourcefulness). Sales managers must decide which methods of evaluation are best for their sales force, since the evaluation criteria can also affect satisfaction, motivation, and—ultimately—sales force performance.

COMMUNICATION AND SALES FORCE PERFORMANCE

The two broad categories of influences on sales force performance, internal and external influences, are either indirectly or directly affected by the sales manager. Therefore, it becomes critical that the sales manager and the sales force maintain channels of communication between each other.

Although not included in Exhibit 9-1, communication has a pervasive impact on a salesperson's performance. Communication plays a key part in the recruiting, selecting, and training of the sales force. A great deal of role ambiguity can result if communication does not occur in these development stages. Similarly, the planning and organizing done by a sales manager will be meaningless unless the results are communicated properly to the sales force. Communication is equally important in eliminating any role conflict or ambiguity that may arise from the interaction between the internal and external aspects of the selling role. Therefore, the ability of sales managers to communicate effectively with their sales reps can definitely impact how well the sales force understands its role in the organization.

In a recent survey, over 500 salespeople and sales managers were asked whether they agreed with a number of job-related statements. As the table below shows, the opinions of the two groups were quite different:

Statement	Percentage Agreeing	
	Salespeople	Sales Managers
Salespeople are happy with company recognition program.	57	31
Salespeople are happy with company compensation policies.	57	36
Salespeople in company are under too much pressure to produce.	44	60

The study indicates that failure to communicate can lead to serious discrepancies between the perceptions of salespeople and those of their managers.[8] Effective communication is critical in eliminating conflict and ambiguity from the sales force. Communication and the role it plays in sales management will be explored more fully in Chapter 14.

SUMMARY

A salesperson's performance is a function of internal and external factors. Internal factors include motivation, aptitude, skill, job satisfaction, role perception, and other personal factors. External factors that affect performance include the environment, the organization, and sales management.

Regional differences in economy, law, society, and competition play a large role in determining a salesperson's success. Technology is also a significant environmental factor. Sales managers must carefully consider the effect of environmental differences when planning and evaluating; if they do not, their basis for decision making will be invalid. A firm's financial strength and corporate philosophy are external factors that relate to the organization. The ability of sales management to establish extrinsic and intrinsic rewards that motivate salespeople and maintain their morale is also an external factor that affects performance.

A role perception is a person's understanding of what is expected of him or her. Role conflict arises when the expectations of role partners differ. Communication between the sales manager and the salesperson in regard to planning, sales activity, and evaluation is the key to avoiding role conflict and ambiguity and enhancing sales performance.

STUDY QUESTIONS

1. How can activities of the sales manager (such as planning, recruiting, and selecting) affect sales force performance?

2. Explain the relationship between motivation, role perception, and performance. Which causes which?

3. How are aptitude and skill level related?

4. Is it possible for a salesperson to perform well when he or she is deficient in only one of the three aspects of internal influences (motivation, aptitude, and skill level)? Why or why not?

5. Why is it so important for a salesperson to understand the sales job thoroughly? What problems can occur if salespeople misperceive their roles? How do these misperceptions occur?

6. Is it possible for a sales manager to have a sales plan which is well adapted to the external environment but which results in inconsistent sales force performance across markets? Explain.

7. Explain the importance of communication to salesperson performance.

8. Why is it so important for sales managers to understand the many factors that influence salesperson performance?

IN-BASKET EXERCISE

You are a district sales manager for one of the oldest and most productive appliance manufacturers in the United States, and you just received the annual sales report for last year. Owing to increased foreign competition, as well as a slumping economy, overall sales for your company declined by approximately 5 percent. However, sales volume declined by as much as 20 percent for several of the salespeople in your own district. Economic projections indicate that things will get worse before they get better.

1. What can you do as a sales manager to keep morale high during this difficult period?

2. Which determinants of sales force performance are most important here? Why?

CASE 9-1

RAMBOR MACHINE TOOL COMPANY: DETERMINANTS OF SALES FORCE PERFORMANCE

It was a beautiful autumn day in downtown Detroit, and the three sales managers were enjoying a hearty breakfast in the hotel restaurant. While sipping their second cup of coffee, Jerry Kline, Frank Gallo, and Paul Swenson were discussing the events of the first day in the three-day sales management seminar that Rambor Machine Tool Company now required all its sales managers to attend.

Jerry Kline: I wonder why we spent so much time talking about the determinants of sales force performance this morning. They're making a big deal about what determines salesperson success. All that stuff about external and internal factors and performance determinants is textbook garbage that has absolutely nothing to do with the real world of selling. No matter the fancy talk, the salesperson's job is to sell the product. I'm kept running like a deer on the opening day of hunting season just pushing my people to make sales quotas. Working with my salespeople in the field and helping them make sales presentations and handle complaints keeps me from even making it into the office some weeks to do all the paperwork headquarters keeps demanding. I sure don't have any extra time to worry about the subtle factors like role perceptions that affect sales force performance. In my opinion, there's only one factor that really counts and that is M-O-N-E-Y. You make the carrot big enough and any donkey will get the job done.

Frank Gallo: Yeah, I know what you mean. Seems like the sales training manager is trying to impress the big boss by bringing in these ivory tower academic types to tell us in fancy terms what we're doing.

Today, the schedule says we're going to discuss how environment, organization, and sales management determine sales performance. I don't know about those first two factors, but my people sure know that I'm one of the big determinants of their performance. They know what they have to do if they want their commissions and bonuses: sell. If my people make their quotas, I leave them alone. If they don't, I come down hard on them and motivate them the one sure way that works; I just tell them, "Nobody's forcing you to stay." With salespeople, you're always going to have 20 to 40 percent turnover a year because a lot of people just can't cut the mustard.

Paul Swenson: I have to admit that I've learned some things I'm going to try when I get back to the office next week. My first boss when I started in sales was a fatherly type of guy who really helped me get over some rough spots that first year. I remember that he would call me into his office to talk about my perceptions of my sales job, my opinions on the reward system in place, my feelings about different aspects of the job, and even how my personal life was going. He really gave me the feeling that he cared and that he was pulling for me to do well. You should have seen his beaming face when I made the "million sales club" my second year. I think he was happier than I was. If it hadn't been for him, I know I would have quit sales forever that first year. My wife was really pushing me to get into something that didn't put so much pressure on me to perform. Now she knows how right sales is for me.

You know, I've got a couple of people in my sales

force right now who are probably at the same decision point I was at during that first year. I think I'm going to use some of the performance factors we've been talking about in the seminar to see if I can help them like I was helped. It can't hurt.

Frank Gallo: Hey, it's almost 8:00! We'd better get over to the seminar room.

Questions

1. On the basis of the brief conversation between Jerry Kline, Frank Gallo, and Paul Swenson, what kind of sales manager do you think each is? What do you think is the level of performance of the sales force that each heads? How do you think each will benefit from the sales management training seminar?

2. If you were a top executive for a company, how would you go about selecting your new sales managers? What specific criteria and objectives would you use? How would you determine whether your candidates had the qualities desired?

3. Do you think that outstanding salespeople newly appointed to the position of sales manager need any special training? If so, what should the training cover? Why?

4. Do you think that sales managers can have much impact on the performance of individual salespeople? Specifically, what might a new sales manager do to increase the performance of his or her sales force?

5. How might a sales manager use an understanding of the internal factors affecting salesperson performance to help each salesperson achieve his or her full potential?

CASE 9-2

THE HIGH-PERFORMANCE CLUB AT MORTIMER FOODS: A BOOST OR BUST FOR SALES FORCE?

Mortimer Foods Corporation distributes a line of consumer food items to grocery stores throughout the United States. The company has been in business for over twenty years and has achieved small but steady increases in sales every year. Ten years ago Mortimer started the High-Performance Club for its salespeople as a means of identifying potential stars of the company who may ultimately become future corporate leaders. Top corporate officials are the only ones who know which individuals have been designated as fast-track salespeople in the High-Performance Club. The top 20 percent of each incoming group of sales trainees are identified by top management as fast-track trainees and are usually given special assignments and premium sales territories. Moreover, these fast-track sales trainees are transferred to new territories very frequently to give them a broad exposure to various markets and regional offices of the company. These high performers are usually promoted to management within eighteen to twenty-four months. Since the top company officials are the only ones who know which trainees have been designated as high performers, or fast-track recruits, the sales trainees have to guess which of their peers have been put into this elite group. They

draw conclusions by observing who is transferred most rapidly and who gets the prime sales territories. The frequency of change in assignments is often used as an index of a sales trainee's success and potential.

Questions

1. Are there any potential company problems that may arise because of Mortimer's High-Performance Club?

2. What are some of the negative effects of the High-Performance Club on the 80 percent of the sales trainees who are not members?

3. Which determinants of sales force performance may have been overlooked when Mortimer executives developed this program?

4. Should the sales trainees be told whether they have been designated as fast-track salespeople? Why or why not?

5. Should the High-Performance Club be eliminated entirely? Why or why not? Are there ways to improve this program?

REFERENCES

1. Leslie Brennan, "Sales Secrets of the Incentive Stars," *Sales & Marketing Management*, April 1990, pp. 92–100.

2. Orville C. Walker, Jr., Gilbert A. Churchill, Jr., and Neil M. Ford, "Motivation and Performance in Industrial Selling: Present Knowledge and Needed Research," *Journal of Marketing*, May 1977, pp. 156–168; Gilbert A. Churchill, Jr., Neil M. Ford, Steven W. Hartley, and Orville C. Walker, Jr., "The Determinants of Salesperson Performance: A Meta-Analysis," *Journal of Marketing Research*, May 1985, pp. 103–118; Alan J. Dubinsky and Steven W. Hartley, "A Path-Analytic Study of a Model of Salesperson Performance," *Journal of the Academy of Marketing Science*, Spring 1986, pp. 36–46.

3. Ibid. Also see Jeffrey K. Sager and Gerald R. Ferris, "Personality and Salesforce Selection in the Pharmaceutical Industry," *Industrial Marketing Management*, November 1986, pp. 319–324; David T. Wilson and J. David Lichtenthal, "Testing for Deterministic Salesperson Attributes in Mature Markets," *Journal of Personal Selling and Sales Management*, May 1985, pp. 23–30; S. J. Lyonski and E. M. Johnson, "The Sales Manager as a Boundary Spanner: A Role Theory Analysis," *Journal of Personal Selling and Sales Management*, November 1983, pp. 8–21; R. K. Teas, "Supervisory Behavior, Role Stress, and the Job Satisfaction of Industrial Salespeople," *Journal of Marketing Research*, February 1983, pp. 84–91; C. Kendrick Gibson and John E. Swan, "Sex Roles and the Desirability of Job Rewards, Expectations, and Aspirations of Male versus Female Salespeople," *Journal of Personal Selling and Sales Management*, Fall/Winter 1981/82, pp. 39–45; John Hafer and Barbara A. McCuen, "Antecedents of Performance and Satisfaction in a Service Sales Force as Compared to an Industrial Sales Force," *Journal of Personal Selling and Sales Management*, November 1985, pp. 7–17.

4. Richard P. Bagozzi, "Salesforce Performance and Satisfaction as a Function of Individual Difference, Interpersonal, and Situation Factors," *Journal of Marketing Research*, November 1978, pp. 517–531; Gilbert A. Churchill, Jr., Neil M. Ford, and Orville C. Walker, Jr., "Measuring the Job Satisfaction of Industrial Salesmen," *Journal of Marketing Research*, August 1974, pp. 254–260; John M. Gwin, Douglas N. Behrman, and William D. Perreault, Jr., "A Canonical Rotation Analysis of Relations among Aspects of Salesforce Performance and Satisfaction," in Terrence A. Shimp, George John, Meryl P. Gardner, John H. Lindgren, Jr., Subhash Sharma, John A. Quelch, William Dillon, and Robert F. Dyer (eds.), *1986 AMA Educators' Proceedings*, American Marketing Association, Chicago, pp. 224–228; D. N. Behrman and W. D. Perreault, "A Role Stress Model of the Performance and Satisfaction of Industrial Salespersons," *Journal of Marketing*, Fall 1984, pp. 9–21.

5. Gilbert A. Churchill, Jr., Neil M. Ford, and Orville C. Walker, Jr., "The Determinants of Salesperson Performance: A Meta-Analysis," *Journal of Marketing Research*, May 1985, pp. 103–118; Barton A. Weitz, Harish Sujan, and Mita Sujan, *Knowledge, Motivation, and Adaptive Behavior: A Framework for Improving Selling Effectiveness*, Marketing Science Institute, Cambridge, Mass., 1986; Ramon Avila, "Predicting Salesperson Success Using Personal and Personality Characteristics: A Theoretical Framework," in Naresh K. Malhotra (ed.), *Developments in Marketing Science*, Academy of Marketing Science, Atlanta, 1986, pp. 242–246; Ajay K. Kohli, "Effects of Supervisory Behavior: The Role of Individual Differences among Salespeople," *Journal of Marketing*, October 1989, pp. 40–50; Thomas N. Ingram, Keun S. Lee, and Steven J. Skinner, "An Empirical Assessment of Salesperson Motivation, Commitment, and Job Outcomes," *Journal of Personal Selling and Sales Management*, Fall 1989, pp. 25–33; Kenneth R. Bartkus, Mark F. Peterson, and Danny N. Bellenger, "Type A Behavior, Experience, and Salesperson Performance," *Journal of Personal Selling and Sales Management*, Summer 1989, pp. 11–18.

6. For example, see David W. Cravens, Robert B. Woodruff, and Joe Stamper, ''An Analytical Approach for Evaluating Sales Territory Performance,'' *Journal of Applied Psychology*, June 1973, pp. 242–247; Henry C. Lucas, Charles B. Weinberg, and Kenneth W. Clowes, ''Sales Response as a Function of Territorial Potential and Sales Representative Workload,'' *Journal of Marketing Research*, May 1977; Adrian B. Ryans and Charles B. Weinberg, ''Sales Productivity: A Multiple Company Study,'' in Richard P. Bagozzi (ed.), *Sales Management: New Developments from Behavioral and Decision Model Research*, Marketing Science Institute, Cambridge, Mass., 1979, pp. 92–129.

7. See the summary of the results in Ryans and Weinberg, ''Sales Productivity,'' op. cit.

8. ''High Turnover? Maybe You Just Aren't Listening,'' *Sales & Marketing Management*, December 1989, p. 21.

10

TIME AND TERRITORY MANAGEMENT

LEARNING OBJECTIVES

When you finish this chapter, you should understand:

- ▲ The importance of time and territory management in achieving sales objectives
- ▲ The basic reasons for establishing sales territories
- ▲ The procedures for setting up sales territories
- ▲ Why sales territories are revised and how the revision can affect the sales force
- ▲ The many new technologies being used in time and territory management
- ▲ The impact of these new technologies on the sales manager and salesperson
- ▲ The impact of scheduling and routing plans on the salesperson's success

What harm can a two-martini lunch or a Friday afternoon golf game do to salesperson performance? With the rapidly rising costs associated with selling activities, these "time traps" can have serious ramifications for a salesperson's productivity. Sales managers are increasingly looking for ways to make selling time more effective, and efficient time and territory management can assist them in making their sales force more productive.

Time and territory management is a key function in any company with a field sales force. It involves determining which accounts are called on, when these accounts are called on, and how often. Management of time and territory has become an increasingly important function because of the skyrocketing cost of sales calls. Increasing fuel prices during the early 1990s greatly affected the prices of many other products. As a result, the costs of sales calls escalated continuously throughout that period. Companies are now, more than ever, searching for less expensive ways to sell their products. With the cost of an industrial sales call averaging over $225, sales managers are turning to the use of computers, telemarketing, industrial stores, demonstration centers, and the like, in an effort to hold the line on selling costs.[2] Territory and time management will continue to be an essential part of the sales manager's job throughout the 1990s.

ESTABLISHING SALES TERRITORIES

An important task in time and territory management is the effective assignment of sales personnel to territories. A *sales territory* is usually thought of as a geographic area that contains customer accounts. These accounts may consist of both present and potential customers who are assigned to a particular salesperson. Customers and prospects are grouped in such a way that the salesperson serving these accounts can call on them as conveniently and economically as possible.

Assigning sales territories helps the sales manager achieve a match between sales efforts and sales opportunities. The total market of most companies is usually too large to manage efficiently, so territories are established to facilitate the sales manager's task of directing, evaluating, and controlling the sales force.

Even though most companies establish territories on a geographic basis, sales managers should not be overly concerned with geographic considerations. The major emphasis should be on the customers and prospects because a market is made up of people and customers, not geographic areas. Markets are not measured in square miles but in number of customers and their purchasing power.

Reasons for Establishing Sales Territories

The primary reason for establishing sales territories is to facilitate the planning and controlling of the selling function. But sales managers typically have more specific reasons for establishing territories.

To enhance market coverage. A salesperson's calling time must be planned as efficiently as possible in order to ensure proper coverage of present as well as potential customers. Coverage is likely to be more thorough when each salesperson is assigned to a properly designed sales territory rather than when all sales personnel are allowed to sell anywhere. A sales territory should not be so large that the salesperson either spends an extreme amount of time traveling or has time to call on only a few of the best customers. On the other hand, a sales territory should not be so small that a salesperson is calling on customers too often. The sales territory should be big enough to represent a reasonable workload for the salesperson but small enough to ensure that all potential customers can be visited as often as needed.

To keep selling costs at a minimum. Inflation has definitely affected the prices of food, lodging, transportation, and other elements included in the cost of selling. Even when adjusted for inflation, the cost of a sales call has been rising tremendously over the past decade. In 1989 the average cost per sales call, $224.87, was 25.6 percent higher than the cost in 1986.[3] This increase means that sales managers must put more effort into establishing cost-effective territories, for example, by eliminating or minimizing overnight travel and by finding alternate methods of reaching customers.

A selling method that is rapidly becoming an important alternative to face-to-face selling is *telemarketing*, that is, using the telephone in conjunction with traditional marketing methods and techniques. If used properly, telemarketing can be the most cost-efficient, flexible, and statistically accountable medium available to sales managers.[4] The findings of a recent survey illustrate the growing acceptance of telemarketing: over 70 percent of the firms that responded to the survey use telemarketing. Sales managers are increasingly using telemarketing as a means of soliciting accounts, qualifying sales leads, setting appointments, and maintaining good customer relations. Furthermore, many sales managers are discovering the efficiency of telemarketing. For example, Bioproducts for Medicine, a pharmaceutical company, accomplished the same level of sales in three months by phone as it had in fifteen months with its outside sales force.[5] Transamerica Life Insurance Group, a major writer of property and casualty coverage, sells through independent agents, not Transamerica employees. Transamerica's telemarketing center supports hundreds of these independent sales agents by providing them with qualified sales leads. The agents can spend their time productively by doing what they do best, selling.[6]

Another tool that can be used to inform prospects and customers and generate sales is a *facsimile machine*. Rather than mailing a flier to a customer, the salesperson can put it in a facsimile, or "fax," machine and have a reproduction copied on the customer's machine. This method is much faster and cheaper than mail. How does the salesperson know who has a fax machine? The solution is *The Fax Directory*, which lists thousands of companies from around the world that are using fax machines. This directory includes a company's address and special fax number. Fax machines have become a standard tool for most sales managers.

To strengthen customer relations.   Properly designed sales territories allow salespeople to spend more time with present and potential customers and less time on the road. The more salespeople can learn about their customers, the better they can understand the customers' problems and the more comfortable their relationship becomes. Well-designed sales territories should result in regularly scheduled sales calls on customers. In some cases, a telephone call can replace a personal visit. For example, a customer who purchases regularly but is too busy to see a salesperson may prefer placing an order over the phone. Or the customer can receive updated pricing information and place an order on the fax machine.

Another convenient way of eliminating the need for a personal visit is through the use of *voice mail*. A computer system with voice-mail capabilities takes an oral message and translates it into digital computer language. The message is sent to another computer, which reads the message and translates it back into the oral message. This allows a customer who is more comfortable communicating in the verbal mode to place an order even though the salesperson is not present. Of course, both the buyer and the seller have to have computer systems with voice-mail capabilities.

These new technologies save the customer's and the salesperson's time as well as save the company the cost of a visit. Also, they promote a comfortable working relationship between the salesperson and the customer. Regularly scheduled sales calls are very important in cases where the customer is an infrequent or potential buyer; the persistence of the salesperson can turn infrequent buyers into regular buyers and prospects into customers. However, where the cost of a sales call is too high, the telephone, voice mail, or a fax machine can be used.

To build a more effective sales force.   Well-designed sales territories can stimulate and motivate sales personnel, improve morale, increase interest, and build a more effective sales force. Establishing territories defines jobs concretely, gives each salesperson a reasonable workload, and encourages the sales force to do a good job. When a salesperson is assigned a territory and given responsibility for it, that person becomes manager of the territory and tends to take pride in his or her accomplishments. Clearly defined responsibility can be a powerful motivator for many people. Moreover, when territories are distributed equitably among the sales personnel, with specific accounts given to each salesperson, fewer conflicts arise from calling on someone else's customer.

To evaluate the sales force better. Assigning salespeople to certain geographic areas assists the sales manager in evaluating performance. Salespeople can be evaluated on the basis of their performance compared with the territory's potential. By keeping past performance figures on a PC disk, the sales manager can use the PC to access the past information and compare it with current figures for each territory. By examining sales performance territory by territory, the sales manager can spot changing market conditions and make needed adjustments in sales tactics. Restricting a salesperson to a specific geographic area allows for efficient routing, helps establish a strong customer base by building rapport with each customer, and aids in determining the best call frequency for each customer. (Evaluation of the sales force will be discussed in depth in Chapter 16.)

To coordinate selling with other marketing functions. A well-designed sales territory can aid management in performing other marketing functions. Sales and cost analyses can be done more easily on a territory basis than for the entire market. Market research on a territory basis can be used more effectively for setting quotas and establishing sales and expense budgets. If salespeople are to aid customers in launching advertising campaigns, distributing point-of-purchase displays, selling dealers on cooperative advertising, or performing work related to sales promotions, the results are usually more satisfactory when the work is assigned and managed on a territory-by-territory basis rather than for the market as a whole. Finally, if the company is using telemarketers to support the field sales force, territory assignments enable them to pinpoint whose territory the customer or potential customer is in rather than just randomly assigning a salesperson to the account. In this way salespeople can respond to customers quickly.

Reasons for Not Establishing Sales Territories

Despite the advantages related to establishing sales territories, there are certain situations in which they are not needed. For example, small companies with only a few people selling in a local market do not need territories. Assigning sales territories in this case would only slow down decision making by sales managers. Territory assignments generally become necessary only as a company's sales force increases in size.

Individuals are not assigned to sales territories when the available sales coverage is far below the sales potential of the market, that is, when there is more than enough business for every salesperson. This is often the case with small companies, with companies introducing a new product, or with products that everyone needs (such as insurance). However, not assigning sales territories in such situations could mean that a potential segment of the market is being neglected, thereby inviting competition into the market. If this is the case, consideration should be given to hiring additional sales personnel as soon as possible.

Other reasons have been used to justify not establishing territories. For example, sales territories may not be added when sales are made primarily on the basis of social contacts or personal friendships. Also, many managers fail to establish territories because they feel that eventually the territories will have to be revised, thus causing disagreement in the sales force.

SETTING UP SALES TERRITORIES

Whether a company is setting up sales territories for the first time or revising ones that are already in existence, the same general procedure applies: (1) select a geographic control unit, (2) make an account analysis, (3) develop a salesperson workload analysis, (4) combine geographic control units into territories, and (5) assign sales personnel to territories.

Selecting a Geographic Control Unit

The starting point in establishing territories is the selection of a geographic control unit. The most often used units are states, counties, zip-code areas, cities, metropolitan areas, and trading areas. Management should strive for as small a control unit as possible for two major reasons. One is that a small unit will aid management in pinpointing the exact geographic location of sales potential. The second reason is that the use of small geographic areas will make management's task of adjusting the territories much easier. For example, if a company wants to add to one salesperson's territory and reduce another's, the adjustment can be accomplished more easily if the control unit is a county rather than a state.

Political units (state, county, or city) are presently used quite often as geographic control units. These units are commonly used because they are the basis of a great deal of government census data and other market information. Along with political units, other market factors like buying habits and patterns of trade flow can be used. For example, a sales territory may be based on a trading area that lies within specific county lines. This is done so that data can easily be collected for this particular trading area.

States.   Many companies have used state boundaries in establishing territory boundaries. A state may be an adequate control unit if used by a company with a small sales force that is covering the market selectively rather than intensively. The use of states as territory boundaries may also work well for a company that is seeking nationwide distribution for the first time. In fact, in these situations salespeople may be assigned to territories that consist of more than one state. This may be done on a temporary basis until the market develops, at which time a change can be made to a smaller control unit.

State sales territories are simple, convenient, and fairly inexpensive. But most companies do not use them for several reasons. Many customers from one state often cross boundaries into another state to do their purchasing. For example, hundreds of thousands of shoppers a year cross from New York into northern New Jersey to make their purchases because shopping malls are centrally located and easy to get to, there is less traffic, and there is a lower sales tax. In the same vein, the tourist appeal of New York draws millions of shoppers from around the country to the city's stores.

Another reason for not dividing territories by state is that some states are just too large. Obviously, for most companies, it would take more than one person to handle the state of New York. If one person did cover New York, another salesperson would have to cover a dozen or more Rocky Mountain states to have a territory equal to New York in sales potential. Finally, a state may be too large for management to control adequately and to evaluate its sales force.

Counties and zip codes.

The county is a much smaller unit than the state and acts as a better focal point for dividing territories. There are almost 3,100 counties in the United States but only 50 states. A smaller control unit makes management's job of designing territories of equal sales potential a lot easier.

There are several other advantages in using counties as control units. The county is usually the smallest unit for which government data are available. Several other sources report market data (population, retail sales, income, employment, and manufacturing information) by counties. Also, counties are usually small enough that management can better pinpoint problems. Finally, the small size of counties can offer flexibility in shifting from one territory to another.

Counties tend to have the same drawbacks as states; that is, not all counties are similar in size, sales potential, or ease of market coverage. Also, for some companies even the county may be too large a control unit. For example, Cook County (Chicago) may require several people to cover the market adequately. In this case, a company may want to divide one county into several territories; thus, a control unit smaller than a county is needed.

Zip-code areas can also be used as geographic control units. The first three digits refer to a section of the country (there are approximately 600, each of which is larger than a county but smaller than a state). The last two digits identify a specific post office within a section. Territories based on zip codes have the advantage of being very flexible, and they typically reflect the economic and demographic characteristics of the individual areas, whereas political subdivisions, such as states and counties, do not.

Cities and metropolitan areas.

In the past, the city was used as a control unit for establishing sales territories. This was because most customers were within city limits. After World War II, however, many Americans began to migrate to the suburbs, and the market shifted outside the central city limits. Thus, for many companies, cities were no longer adequate as control units. Companies that experienced problems because of these changes were helped when the Bureau of the Budget established standard metropolitan statistical areas (SMSAs).

These SMSAs were boundaries that included the city as well as the surrounding suburban and satellite cities. On June 30, 1983, the U.S. Office of Management and Budget changed the term from SMSA to MSA (metropolitan statistical area) and, in doing so, revised the geographic definitions of many metropolitan areas.

Current standards provide that each MSA must include at least:

- One city with 50,000 inhabitants or more, or
- A Census Bureau–defined urbanized area of at least 50,000 inhabitants *and* a total MSA population of at least 100,000 (75,000 in New England)

The 1983 revision designates some of these areas as consolidated metropolitan statistical areas (CMSAs) and others as primary metropolitan statistical areas (PMSAs). A PMSA is a metropolitan complex with a population of 1 million or more. Any area containing PMSAs is designated as a CMSA. As of June 30, 1989, there were 255 MSAs, 80 PMSAs, and 23 CMSAs in the United States, including Puerto Rico.[7]

Trading areas.   Another control unit used for establishing sales territories is the trading area. The trading area is perhaps the most logical control unit, since it is based mainly on the natural flow of goods and services rather than on political or economic boundaries. Firms that sell through wholesalers or retailers often use the trading area as a control unit.

The *trading area* is a geographic region that consists of a city and the surrounding areas that serve as the dominant retail or wholesale center for the region. Usually, customers in one trading area will not go outside its boundaries to buy merchandise; nor will a customer from outside enter the trading area to purchase a product. This is not always the case, however, because sometimes trading areas overlap, and buyers in the overlapping areas make purchases in one or both areas.

The trading area as a geographic control unit has several advantages. Since trading areas are based on economic considerations, they are representative of customer buying habits and patterns of trade. Also, the use of trading areas aids management in planning and control. For example, the same salesperson usually calls on all wholesalers in a trading area; thus, the possibility that salespeople will take each other's accounts is reduced.

Several disadvantages are associated with using trading areas as control units. Two of the main problems are defining trading areas and obtaining statistical information to use in forecasting the sales potential in each area. The difficulty of defining trading areas has been reduced by companies such as Rand-McNally, which publishes a trading-area map of the United States that delineates 494 basic trading areas and 50 major trading areas. *Sales & Marketing Management* also publishes maps relating to trading areas; one provides consumer market information by counties, while the other shows industrial market data on a county basis. The lack of statistical data on trading areas can be overcome by adapting the dimensions of the trading areas to the counties that are partially or wholly included. While the county market information may not fit the trading area exactly, it is probably the best and most readily accessible data available.

Making an Account Analysis

After a company selects the geographic control unit, the next step is to conduct an audit of each geographic unit. The purpose of this audit is to identify customers and prospects and determine how much sales potential exists for each account.

First, accounts must be identified by name. Many sources containing this information are available. For example, the Yellow Pages have become computerized, and they represent one of the most effective sources for identifying customers quickly. One such service, the *Instant Yellow Pages Service,* contains a data base of over 6 million U.S. businesses. This service can, for example, tell the sales rep how many doctors there are in any city in the United States, complete with names, mailing addresses, and phone numbers.[8] Other sources include company records of past sales; trade directories; professional association membership lists; directories of corporations; publishers of mailing lists; trade books and periodicals; chambers of commerce; federal, state, and local governments; and personal observation by the salesperson.

After potential accounts are identified, the next step is to estimate the total sales potential for all accounts in each geographic control unit. The sales manager estimates the total market potential by using one of the methods discussed in Chapter 4 and then determines how much of this total the company can expect to get. The estimated sales potential for a company in a particular territory is often a judgmental decision. It is based on the company's existing sales in that territory, the level of competition, any differential advantages enjoyed by the company or its competitors, and the relationships with existing accounts.

The personal computer has become a tremendous management aid in analyzing the sales potential in a territory. The information gathered on potential and existing accounts can be stored and organized in a variety of ways: by name, by zip code, by account size, or by primary business. Once stored, this information can be retrieved in a matter of seconds. The PC can also calculate the estimated sales potential based on the predetermined criteria much faster than the sales manager can.

Once the sales potential estimates have been made, the PC can classify each account according to its annual buying potential. One commonly used approach is to employ an ABC classification. The computer identifies all those accounts whose sales potential is greater than a predetermined amount and classify them as A accounts. Next, the accounts that are considered to be of average potential are classified as B accounts. Finally, accounts whose potential is less than a certain amount are classified as C accounts. This type of classification provides some of the information needed to determine the salesperson's call patterns, and it can be done by the PC in a fraction of the time it would take to do it by hand.

Developing a Salesperson Workload Analysis

A *salesperson workload analysis* is an estimate of the time and effort required to cover each geographic control unit. This estimate is based on an analysis of the number of accounts to be called on, the frequency of the calls, the length of each call, the travel time required, and the nonselling time. The result of the workload analysis estimate is the establishment of a sales call pattern for each geographic control unit.

Several factors affect the number of accounts that can be called on in each geographic control unit. The most basic factor is the length of time required to call on each account. This is influenced by the number of people to be seen during each call, the amount of account servicing needed, and the length of the waiting time. Information about these factors can be determined by examining company records or by talking with salespeople.

One factor that affects the number of accounts that can be called on is the travel time between accounts. Travel time will vary considerably from one region to another, depending on factors such as available transportation, conditions of highways, the weather, and the density of present and potential accounts. In carrying out the workload analysis, the sales manager seeks ways to minimize travel time and thereby to increase the number of accounts that can be called on.

The frequency of sales calls is influenced by a number of factors. Accounts are generally grouped into several categories according to sales potential. Group A accounts are called on most frequently, group B accounts less frequently, and group C accounts the least of all. Other factors that influence the call frequency are the nature of the product and the level of the competition. For example, grocery stores purchasing canned food products require frequent calls because of the high turnover rate, whereas high schools purchasing textbooks require only two or three calls a year. Of course, if there is strong competition within the market, more frequent sales calls may be needed.

The level of nonselling activities influences the time and effort required to cover a geographic control unit; therefore, nonselling time must also be included in a workload analysis. Nonselling activities include preparing for sales calls as well as processing orders and servicing accounts after the sale. A step-by-step explanation of workload analysis for the sales force is provided in Chapter 6.

Combining Geographic Control Units into Sales Territories

Up to this point the sales manager has been working with the geographic control unit selected in the first phase of the procedure for setting up sales territories. The unit may be a state, county, MSA, or some other geographic area. The sales manager is now ready to group adjacent control units into territories of roughly equal sales potential.

In the past the sales manager developed a list of tentative territories by manually combining adjacent control units. However, this was a long procedure that, in most cases, resulted in split control units and territories with uneven sales potential. Today, computers are handling this task in a much shorter time period. A number of territory-mapping software packages are available that can align territories quickly and evenly. One of these packages is described in the example that follows on the next page.

Sometimes, territories that have been mapped out will have equal sales potential, but each territory will have its own level of coverage difficulty. Therefore, the sales manager must revise the tentative territories accordingly. This typically is not a problem, though, because in minutes the PC can produce several alignments from which the sales managers can select the best. The result of the realignment is that some compromises must be made, and some territories may have a higher sales potential than others.

Territories with unequal sales potential are not necessarily bad. Salespeople vary in ability and experience as well as initiative, and some can be assigned heavier workloads than others. The sales manager should assign the best salespeople to territories with a high sales potential and the newer, less effective salespeople to the second- and third-rate territories. Of course, some adjustment in sales quotas and commission levels may be necessary, depending on the relative sales potential of a specific area and the types of selling or nonselling tasks assigned to the sales reps.[10]

Assigning Sales Personnel to Territories

When an optimal territory alignment has been devised, the sales manager is ready to assign salespeople to territories. Salespeople vary in physical condition, as well as ability, initiative, and effectiveness. A reasonable and desirable workload for one salesperson may overload another and cause frustration. In addition, interactions of an individual salesperson with customers and prospects will be affected by environmental factors such as customer characteristics, traditions, and other social influences. The result is that a salesperson may be outstanding in one territory and terrible in another, even though sales potential and workload for the two territories are the same.

In assigning sales personnel to territories, the sales manager must first rank the salespeople according to relative ability. When assessing a salesperson's relative ability, the sales manager should look at such factors as product and industry knowledge, persuasiveness, and verbal ability. All good salespeople rate high on these factors, though some are better than others. What will determine the salesperson's assignment to a territory, however, is his or her potential sales effectiveness within that territory. In order to judge a salesperson's effectiveness within a territory, the sales manager must look at the salesperson's physical, social, and cultural characteristics and compare them to those of the territory. For instance, the salesperson raised on a farm in Iowa is likely to be more effective with rural clients than with urban customers because he or she speaks the same language and shares the same values as the rural clients. The goal of the sales manager in matching salespeople to territories in this manner is to maximize the territory's sales potential by making the salesperson comfortable with the territory and the customer comfortable with the salesperson.

REVISING SALES TERRITORIES

Two major factors may cause a firm to consider revising established territories. A firm just starting in business usually does not design territories very carefully. Often, it is unaware of the problems inherent in covering a certain territory, and sometimes it overestimates or underestimates the territory's sales potential and required workload. But as the company grows and gains in experience, the sales manager recognizes that some territory revision is needed. In other situations, a well-designed territory structure may become outdated because of changing market conditions or other factors beyond the control of management.

With the aid of a PC and one of the mapping programs mentioned earlier in this chapter, the sales manager can produce several revised territory alignments in minutes. Without a computer this task would consume days. Before embarking on the revision, the sales manager should determine whether the problems with the original alignment are due to poor territory design, market changes, or faulty management in other areas. For example, it would be a serious mistake for management to revise sales territories if the problems are really due to a poor compensation plan.

Signs That Justify Territory Revision

As a company grows, it usually needs a larger sales force to cover the market adequately. If the company does not hire additional sales personnel, the sales force will probably only skim the territory instead of covering it intensely. If sales potential has been estimated in an inadequate manner, the performance of the sales force may be very misleading. For instance, territory M's 100 percent sales increase for the past year was the best in the company; however, the territory's potential could have been underestimated, or perhaps sales could have grown at an even higher rate. The former case could cause disenchantment among the sales force, since M's salesperson probably earned a larger commission and greater recognition than the other salespeople because of the error. If sales growth could have been higher, the firm could actually be losing market share because the territory has not been properly reduced to encourage the sales force to do a better job of covering the market.

Territories may also need revision because of an overestimation of sales potential. For instance, a territory may be too small for a good salesperson to earn an adequate income. Certain environmental changes could also warrant the revision of a sales territory. For example, the Iraqi invasion of Kuwait during the summer of 1990 dramatically increased the price per barrel of oil. This in turn led many consumers to be more cautious with their purchasing decisions.

Sales fell in many markets, causing companies to revise sales territories accordingly.

Overlapping territories are another reason for revision. This problem usually occurs when territories are split, and it can cause a tremendous amount of friction in the sales force. Salespeople are very reluctant to have their territories divided because that means handing over accounts they have built up and nurtured. The mere thought that another salesperson is reaping the benefits of their hard work can lead to much bitterness. The organization should immediately correct this problem in a way that will benefit the existing rep, the new rep, and the company.

Territorial overlap should be minimized or eliminated for other reasons, too. The primary reason is that overlapping territories mean higher traveling costs and wasted selling time. These are severe problems, considering the escalating rate of selling expenses.

Territory revisions may be necessary when one salesperson jumps into another salesperson's territory in search of business. This is an unethical practice, and it will cause problems within the sales force. If territories have been designed properly, there should be no need for jumping. Territory jumping is usually a sign that a salesperson is not developing his or her territory satisfactorily. However, it can also indicate that the sales potential in one territory is greater than that in another. If a salesperson is doing a good job covering his or her market but the contiguous market has more potential, the rep may be forced to enter the adjacent market. If this is the case, the territory alignments may need to be revised. But before revisions are made, the sales manager should evaluate whether closer personal supervision or the refusal to pay commissions on orders outside a rep's territory is a better solution to the problem.

Territory jumping may also be a sign of poor management. Some salespeople are interested only in quick and easy sales. Instead of developing their own territories, they will jump into another area unless management stops them. Obviously, territory jumping leads to higher costs, selling inefficiencies, bitterness, and low morale in the sales force.

In the accompanying *Ethics* scenario, you face a situation of territory jumping and must decide how to handle it.

ETHICS IN SALES MANAGEMENT: ESTABLISHING BOUNDARIES FOR SALES TERRITORIES

You have recently received complaints from several of your salespeople concerning one of your newer sales reps. It appears that although this person is familiar with the assigned sales territories, he has gone into another sales territory several times to make a sale. It's important to note that he recently landed a new account that you have been trying to get for years. When you question him about leaving his territory to make a sale, he claims that the prospect was a ''referral from the new, important client,'' who wanted him ''to call on a friend of his across town.''

1. How do you handle this situation without insulting the new client?
2. What do you do about the salespeople in the territory that is being invaded by this new sales rep?
3. Are there any alternatives regarding realignment of sales territories?

The Effects of Revision

Salespeople, like most others, dislike change—probably because of the uncertainty that accompanies it. Management must make a decision either to avoid territory revisions for fear of damaging sales force morale or to revise the territories in order to eliminate problems. When a territory is reduced, a salesperson might face a reduction in potential income and the loss of key accounts that he or she has developed over the years. Both of these can result in low morale. Therefore, before revisions are made, the sales manager should ask the sales force for ideas and suggestions that might alleviate such problems.

Compensation adjustments sometimes must be made to avoid low morale. The salesperson whose territory is being reduced should be shown that a smaller territory can be covered more intensely, thereby offering a higher volume for the same travel time. Many firms will talk with the sales rep before making a change but make no salary adjustments until the territory develops. The problem here is that developing the territory may take some time, and the salesperson's income could suffer. During this transition period a special means of compensation or an increased commission may be needed to preserve morale and loyalty.

One approach to compensating the salesperson during the transition period is to guarantee the previous level of income. For instance, a sales rep who is covering the whole state of Texas may be earning an excellent commission, even though he or she is only skimming the territory. The sales rep will probably balk at the idea of having the territory split in two in order to attain a more penetrating coverage. Thus, the company may guarantee the salesperson's level of commission until he or she has had reasonable time to penetrate the territory and achieve a satisfactory level of commission. This approach may preserve morale and loyalty, but it may also hamper the salesperson's aggressiveness in gaining new accounts.

Another solution used by many firms is to work out a compromise. For example, if the transition period is three years, the company could guarantee a portion of the salesperson's income but the guaranteed portion could decline in the last two years. As the salary guarantee declines, the salesperson's incentive to develop the territory to its full potential increases.

USE OF COMPUTERS IN TERRITORY MANAGEMENT

This chapter has already discussed how computers have taken over the time-consuming task of aligning territories. PCs have made it easy for sales managers to map and remap territories, several times if necessary, in a few minutes. Many sales managers have become familiar with computer hardware, but still there are some who are not computer-literate. These managers must be educated on the benefits that can be gained from using computers because it is obvious that future management will rely heavily on computer technology.

A sales manager's education and training should stress the knowledge and understanding of computer software. Computer software is constantly changing, enabling the sales manager to become more efficient and productive. Recently, great advances have been made in creating software that assists sales managers in designing sales territories. The recent development of TIGER and its related software is one example.

USING A TIGER TO PLAN SALES TERRITORIES

TIGER (Topologically Integrated Geographically Encoded Records) is a computerized mapping data base that can be used to plan sales territories, pinpoint direct marketing prospects, or design routes for door-to-door sellers. Originally developed by the government for use with the 1990 census, TIGER contains digital cartographic data for the entire country, including streets, roads, waterways, railroads, and up-to-date boundaries for cities, post office zones, and census tracks. Recently, private companies have been acquiring the TIGER data base and have developed new software so that the TIGER files can be applied to sales territory management, pin-mapping, logistics management, and so on. Many are predicting that "the whole area of computerized strategic mapping is going to explode." As more and more companies develop software to use with the TIGER files, designing and revising sales territories will become easier and much more precise.[11]

Electronic spreadsheet programs are widely used for sales analysis, planning, and control; other programs allow sales managers to keep track of prospects, leads, and product inquiries all the way through to the after-sale follow-up. Software can evaluate the quality and cost of leads according to the various media that produced them or the performance of individual sales reps.[12] At one time, the cost of high-tech equipment and sophisticated software excluded all but the large companies from enjoying their benefits, but in recent years competition and the spread of technological knowledge have made them affordable and profitable for most companies.

TIME MANAGEMENT

After sales managers have established the sales territories and assigned salespeople to them, they should turn their attention to scheduling and routing the sales force within territories. Scheduling and routing are vital in order to keep productivity high and sales costs low; however, many companies ignore these tasks. In many instances, the salesperson is told either to call on as many accounts as possible or to call on only those whose potential is above a specified level. Some companies will not take the time to route or schedule a salesperson, especially if the salesperson's sales figures are good. However, a good record can be misleading because even if sales are high, the cost of the sales may also be high. One salesperson may be spending more time and money than necessary on overnight sales calls or wasting time on the road by taking inefficient routes. Another could be spending too much money in entertaining clients or even entertaining the wrong clients. In order to accomplish the sales objectives set for the sales force and each individual territory, the sales manager must properly route and schedule each sales rep.

EXHIBIT 10-1

Common Time Traps

Poor planning of the day's activities	Putting in a short day's work
Calling on unqualified prospects	Taking off early on Friday afternoon
Following a haphazard travel schedule	Too much chatting
Insufficient use of the telephone	Too many coffee breaks
Taking long lunch hours	Inefficient use of waiting time
Drinking a lunchtime cocktail	Too much entertaining of customers
Inefficiency in paperwork	Walking in without an appointment

Staying out of touch too long with the home office so important messages are delayed

Scheduling the Salesperson

The use of the salesperson's time should be thought of as a resource-allocation problem, intended to eliminate wasted time, increase efficiency, and maximize productivity. Examples of time allocation problems are (1) deciding which accounts to call on; (2) dividing time between selling and paperwork; (3) allocating time between present customers, prospective customers, and service calls; and (4) allocating time to be spent with the overly demanding customer or prospect. To overcome these problems and to maximize productive time, that spent in face-to-face selling, salespeople must learn to be good time managers.

How can salespeople maximize their productive time? The obvious solution is by consistently using time well.

Avoid time traps.   Good time use requires that salespeople always be aware of the "time traps" (see Exhibit 10-1) that can erode their effectiveness.

Along with avoiding time traps, salespeople need to have a system or procedure to help them plan how to use their time effectively. Different selling

EXHIBIT 10-2

How Salespeople Spend Their Time

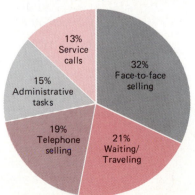

Source: "How Salespeople Spend Their Time," Sales & Marketing Management, *Feb. 26, 1990, p. 81.*

situations will require different approaches to time management. The sales manager must work with the salespeople to develop an effective time management procedure.

Allocate time.   The first step is to decide on the principal tasks or activities the salesperson must do and then determine the amount of time that should be allocated to each. Although tasks will vary, in general they may be classified into five areas: waiting and traveling, face-to-face selling, service calls, administrative tasks, and telephone selling. Exhibit 10-2 indicates how salespeople are spending their time. Note that nearly one-fifth (19 percent) of a salesperson's time is spent on the telephone. Many companies are using telephone selling in order to curb the costs of personal selling.

In order to decide on the amount of time to allocate to each task, the sales manager and the salesperson must first determine how much time is at present being spent on each activity. The most widely used approach is to have the salesperson carry out an activity analysis for several representative days—usually five, but no more than ten. The analysis should include different days of the week as well as days in different parts of the territory. The salesperson records time use on an activity analysis sheet such as that shown in Exhibit 10-3. Once

---

EXHIBIT 10-3

Daily Activity Analysis Report

Sales Rep: John Doe   Date: May 23
Territory: Northern New Jersey   Day: Wednesday

Call 1, 9:00, Phil Piper at XYZ Co. in Clifton.   Travel: 20 min.
  Reorder, and try to sell him on new products   Wait: 10 min.
                                                      Contact: 35 min.

Call 2, 10:00, Carolyn Crawford at BTW Co. in   Travel: 10 min.
  Clifton. New prospect, just opened last month   Wait: 5 min.
                                                      Contact: 75 min.

Call 3, 12:00, luncheon presentation with A&R Industries   Travel: 20 min.
  in Passaic. Group of 17, including VP Bill Dole   Set-up: 20 min.
                                                      Contact: 60 min.

Call 4, 1:30, Bob Joyce at Acme Co. in Wallington.   Travel: 10 min.
  Service visit   Wait: 20 min.
                                                        Contact: 45 min.

Call 5, 2:30, Sid Green at Pinnacle Industries in   Travel: 5 min.
  Wallington. Reorder and service visit. Will try to sell   Wait: 10 min.
  him on the new products   Contact: 30 min.

Call 6, 3:30, Laura Smith at Smith & Assoc. in Lodi.   Travel: 15 min.
  New prospect; saw ad in newspaper   Wait: 15 min.
                                                        Contact: 75 min.

To office: 15 min. Travel
Paperwork: 30 min.

EXHIBIT 10-4

Sales Call Plan

Sales Rep:
Territory: Week ending:

Planned Itinerary	Completed Itinerary
Number of sales calls _____	Number of sales calls _____
Number of demonstrations _____	Number of demonstrations _____
Number of A account calls _____	Number of A account calls _____
Number of B account calls _____	Number of B account calls _____
Number of C account calls _____	Number of C account calls _____

Detailed Sales Itinerary

Company	City & State	Rating	Purpose
Smith Co.	Baton Rouge, La.	A	Reorder

the information is gathered, the sales manager works with the salesperson to increase the amount of time spent on productive activities.

Set weekly and daily goals.   The salesperson and the sales manager should work together to develop a weekly action plan. Weekly sales goals set targets for planned days, number of sales calls, number of demonstrations, and type of customer coverage. The sales call plan is used to set the course of action for the week as well as for each day. Exhibit 10-4 is an example of a sales call planning sheet.

Probably the most important aspect of the sales call planning sheet is the attention placed on the type of customer coverage. This target area is extremely important because it involves ranking customers by the volume of business generated. It allows the salesperson to focus on important accounts and minimize the time spent with unimportant ones. Exhibit 10-5 demonstrates the ranking. It shows that 15 percent of the accounts usually produce 65 percent of the volume; these are labeled "A accounts." The next 20 percent, referred to as "B accounts," represent 20 percent of the volume. And the rest of the accounts, 65 percent, provide only 15 percent of the volume; these are "C accounts."[13] Ranking is essential in planning the correct frequency for sales calls.

In addition to developing a sales call plan, the sales manager and the salesperson must properly allocate time to selling and nonselling activities. Selling and servicing should be planned for the hours in the day when customers and prospects are available. Nonselling activities—traveling, waiting, handling paperwork and correspondence—should be done in nonprime hours, when customers are not available.

Manage time during sales calls.   An often-neglected aspect of time management for salespeople is how they manage their time *during* a sales call. A recent study

Customer Ranking Based on Sales Volume

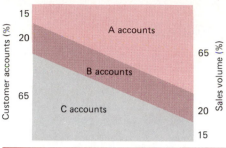

reported that the amount of time salespeople spend with customers does not appear to influence a salesperson's performance. The authors of this study explain that sales success is related more to specific events that take place during the customer-salesperson interaction than it is to time management.[14] Therefore, salespeople and sales managers alike should not expect that spending extra time with customers is always going to lead to additional sales. Customers may be more appreciative and more likely to develop partnerships with salespeople when the sales call is efficient rather than long.

Evaluate. As the week progresses, salespeople keep records on their planned activities. At the end of the week, the salesperson meets with the sales manager to review the week's activities. Efficiency in selling activities is measured from the sales call plan. Time devoted to nonselling activities is also evaluated. In this manner time-allocation problems are detected quickly, and corrective actions are taken. Information on time usage should be monitored over time so that trends can be identified and necessary actions taken to improve the salesperson's efficiency and productivity.

Time Management Tools

There are many aids available to help salespeople manage their time more efficiently and be more productive. The telephone, for example, is a tremendous tool. Even if the company does not have the resources for a telemarketing department to support the sales rep, the salesperson can utilize the telephone to set and confirm appointments, to inform the client of a delay, and to relay and receive vital information quickly.

Telephone use by salespeople is not new. In the past, however, it was not employed as much as it should have been, probably because of the inconvenience of having to find a telephone booth while driving. Today, however, the inconvenience has been eliminated by *mobile communications equipment,* such as pagers, cellular telephones, and airfones.

Pagers are battery packs that beep to let the salesperson know that he or she should call the office. (Beepers have been used for years by doctors for the same reason.) Pagers have the capability of reaching someone on a regional, national, or international basis and allow the sales manager to speak to sales-people when they are needed, not when they feel like calling the office. For example, with the PageCanada system, business travelers carry only one pager and use it in a number of cities throughout Canada. Salespeople must keep the home office aware of which city they are in; then they simply notify Page-Canada's local office that they want to use the pager while in the area.[15] Similar service is available throughout the United States.

Cellular telephones, have become very popular because they can reach almost all metropolitan areas and major interstate corridors. According to a study prepared by AT&T, sales reps using cellular phones increased their sales by 9 percent during the seven-month study period.[16] Cellular phones allow the salesperson to place or receive calls from the car. A network of antennas divides the service area into cells, and a switching office shifts the call from one cell to the next until the call has been connected. This lets salespeople talk while they drive; thus, no time is lost. Because of the tremendous competition within the cellular phone industry, prices have dropped rapidly and companies are adding incentives like three-way calling, call forwarding, and expanded service areas. Some companies are offering telecomputing devices that plug into the cellular phone unit and allow the salesperson to work off the home office's computer.

Airfones are another new technology; they allow people to make phone calls while in an airplane. A phone unit is built into the wall of the airplane, and it contains a slot for a credit card. The caller puts a credit card in the slot, and if the card is valid, a portable phone will detach from the wall. The caller can take the phone to his or her seat and make calls. Airfones enable salespeople to be fully informed on all events relating to a sales call while they are still in the air.

The chapter has already discussed how computers help management map territory alignments. The salesperson can also benefit from PCs, and the use of these computers by the sales force is already widespread. Today, increasing emphasis is being placed on laptop computers, whose share of the PC market is about 15 percent, with strong future increases projected.[17] Salespeople can take laptops on the road with them to keep apprised of up-to-the-minute changes in prices and inventory and to track the progress of shipments. Also, they can access a customer's file to refresh themselves on past purchases and any problems the customer has had in the past with the product, service, or delivery before they make the sales call. The computer enables the sales rep to be fully informed on all facets of the company's relationship with each individual account in the territory, so there are no surprises when the salesperson walks in the door.[18]

The PC allows salespeople to send and receive messages, no matter where they are, through its electronic-mail function. With electronic mail the sales-person can type out a message and send it through a computer to another person. That person accesses the message by typing in his or her code. Thus, the sales-person is always in close contact with both the sales manager and the customer.

There are several other PC functions that can increase the salesperson's efficiency and lead to greater productivity. While the salesperson is making a presentation, he or she can use a PC to calculate quickly all the numbers and variables needed to answer any "what if" questions the customer might have concerning financing terms, operating costs, or tax benefits. Without a PC, the sale would be slowed by time-consuming paperwork. Even worse, the salesperson might have to leave a "hot" prospect in order to use the home office computer; upon returning, he or she might find that the customer has "cooled down" significantly. The PC, in this instance, saves time and travel costs. It can also lead to additional sales by eliminating situations in which the customer would have become frustrated and ended negotiations. Also, a PC with graphics capabilities will serve as a "catalog in motion," with its screen showing the products as well as the cost benefits.[19]

After a sales call, the salesperson can use the PC to handle any record-keeping tasks quickly; if multiple visits are required for the sale, the computer can keep track of where each customer is within the sales cycle. A portable PC can hold a whole cabinet of files on a few easy-to-handle floppy disks or tape cassettes. This information will help salespeople schedule visits and will give them access to a customer's file in minutes. The PC can also process an order immediately after the sales call and update the salesperson on the inventory remaining for the next customer.

Computers also enable the salesperson to exchange electronic messages with the sales manager when both are away from their computers. This can even be done from across the country while one party is sleeping. For example, Raytheon Semiconductor Division in Mountain View, California, keeps its terminal online twenty-four hours a day so that when the sales rep in New York closes an order at 9 A.M. eastern time, it will be on the computer at the home office to be processed when work starts at 9 A.M. Pacific time. This eliminates any communication problems associated with time zone differences.

Raytheon also is using a system that allows salespeople to communicate with the main office via voice or text. Because salespeople are considered to be predominantly "verbal communicators," the firm believes that this will increase their efficiency and productivity by making them more comfortable.[20]

These new technological advances have had a tremendous effect on sales-people's ability to manage their time efficiently. The sales manager has also benefited from these aids. However, the underlying challenge of sales is constant improvement. No matter what was done this year in terms of sales figures, the sales manager's job is to encourage and assist the sales force to do better next year. Thus, keeping abreast of new technology and finding new methods of scheduling are constant concerns of the sales manager.

Time Management for the Sales Manager

Just as salespeople need a system to help them make effective use of their time, so sales managers must have a system. The approach to designing both systems is similar. The sales manager needs to identify the tasks that must be carried out and allocate time accordingly. The sales manager's tasks will differ from company to company. For example, some managers will manage a group of salespeople and also cover a territory; others will sell to a limited number of major accounts while managing a sales force; still others will only manage.

The sales manager must set daily and weekly objectives. He or she will make an itinerary of the things that should be done in a particular week and rank them in the order of their importance. Examples might be to set up recruiting visits to two universities, to work out the details for a training program for new salespeople, to hire a training consultant to present a motivational seminar to the sales force, and to evaluate the sales call reports for each salesperson.

As the week progresses, sales managers, like salespeople, will review and evaluate their performance to determine how successful they have been in accomplishing their objectives. If planned tasks are not complete, then the sales manager must examine the planned time allocation for the various tasks and make adjustments where necessary. Sales managers must be effective managers of their own time in order to plan and control the activities of the sales force so that sales goals and objectives can be realized.

ROUTING

We have discussed how technological advances are helping sales reps and sales managers utilize time more effectively. Another vital tool for time management is the planning of efficient routes. *Routing* is formally setting a pattern for a salesperson to use when making calls. Routing systems may be complex, but a basic pattern can be developed simply by finding the accounts on a map and then deciding the optimal order for visiting them and the fastest route to take. As simple as this sounds, waste of time on the road is due mostly to having poor directions and getting lost. The salesperson who gets lost runs the risk of being late for an appointment, and customers do not look favorably on tardiness. Indeed, some customers will refuse to see the latecomer. At a minimum, tardiness will create an atmosphere that makes it harder to close the sale.

During the training period, routing is usually done jointly by the sales rep and the sales manager. After training, routing becomes the primary responsibility of the salesperson. Routing is not a difficult task for most salespeople, especially if they are familiar with the territory. However, being unprepared can mean the difference between closing the sale and losing it.

A properly designed system has three primary advantages:

1. *Reduced travel time and selling costs.* Perhaps the greatest advantage of a careful routing plan is that it can reduce travel time and costs, thereby giving the salesperson more time to spend productively with customers. The main objective is to eliminate much of the backtracking and nonselling time involved in completing a sales call. Various studies reveal that approximately one-third of the salesperson's daily working time is spent traveling; this means that the average sales rep spends about four months of the year out on the road. Obviously, anything that can reduce travel time and increase the salesperson's productive selling time is highly desirable.

2. *Improved territory coverage.* A routing plan should also help improve the coverage of territory. Detailed information must be available on the numbers and locations of the customers, the methods of transportation available within a territory, and the call frequencies of all classes of customers. This type of information is essential in developing a routing plan that will ensure an orderly, thorough coverage of the market.

3. *Improved communication.* When the sales manager always knows where the salespeople are, it is easier to give them last-minute information or instructions. With a planned call schedule, the sales manager can better monitor individual salespeople. A well-designed routing plan can definitely improve communication, resulting in more effective control over the sales force.

The major disadvantage of routing is that it reduces the salesperson's initiative and places him or her in a pattern of relatively inflexible design. Many sales executives believe that it is the salesperson in the field who is best able to determine the order in which customers should be called on. Many times, an important prospect can be won over with just a little more time and effort, something a formalized routing plan may not allow. Also, in times of erratic market conditions, a strict routing plan prevents a salesperson from making changes in order to adapt to a new situation.

These disadvantages can be reduced by using a PC-based system that allows for continuous updating of the routing pattern. After sales reps have completed a sales visit, they can phone the next customer to reconfirm their appointment or adjust the routing pattern accordingly. As already mentioned, the TIGER data base, along with the appropriate software, not only assists sales managers with territory assignment but also helps establish efficient routing patterns.

Routing is recommended for all companies, but some must be more flexible in its implementation. For instance, the novice firm entering a new area may not know the number and location of potential customers, and so a strict routing schedule is impractical. Such companies should have a routing plan that structures their sales calls yet is flexible enough to allow the sales rep to pursue a previously unknown prospect. Also, high-caliber salespeople and independent salespeople such as manufacturers' reps require a more flexible routing guide than do other types of salespeople. These rather individualistic salespeople will resent a strict routing schedule that tends to make them ineffective.

In general, the extent to which routing is adopted depends on two components: the nature of the product and the nature of the job. If the nature of the product warrants regular calls and frequent servicing, routing is definitely necessary. Driver-salespeople who sell soft drinks, tobacco, and grocery items are usually routed. In fact, routing is so important to these salespeople that an irregular call can often lead to losing the account.

The nature of the job also determines whether routing is favorable. Routing is definitely needed if the job is very routinized, but situations that involve creative selling techniques and a high-caliber sales force may require a more flexible routing schedule. Finally, established companies are more apt to use a routing plan than a new company just entering a new geographic area.

Setting Up a Routing Plan

In order to develop a routing plan, the salesperson and the sales manager must gather the necessary information. This includes the number of calls to be made each day by the salesperson, the call frequency for each class of customer, the distance to each account, and the method of transportation to be used. With this information the salesperson and the sales manager will locate present and potential customers on a map of the territory. In the past, an easy way to classify these accounts on the map was to mark their location with felt-tip pens or round-headed pins, distinguishing each class of accounts and potential customers by using a different color. Once this was done, the routing path could be determined. Today, the salesperson and the sales manager just feed the necessary information into a PC, and the computer maps out a routing plan in minutes. The objective in developing a routing path is to minimize backtracking and crisscrossing, thereby enabling the salesperson to use time in the most efficient manner.

Routing patterns are commonly either straight or circular. With a *straight-line route* the salesperson starts at the office and makes calls in one direction until he or she reaches the end of the territory. *Circular patterns* involve starting at the office and moving in a circle of stops until the salesperson ends up back at the office. Two less common and more complex routing patterns are the cloverleaf and the hopscotch. A *cloverleaf route* is similar to a circular pattern, but rather than covering an entire territory, the route circles a part of a territory. The next trip is an adjacent circle, and the pattern continues until it covers the entire territory. With *hopscotch patterns* the salesperson starts at the farthest point from the office and makes calls on the way back to the office. The salesperson would typically fly to the outer limits of the territory and drive back. On the next trip the salesperson would go in another direction in the territory. Both cloverleaf and hopscotch patterns are shown in Exhibit 10-6. The basic advantage of these two routing patterns is that they enable the salesperson to make sales trips from the home office while minimizing travel time.

EXHIBIT 10-6

Complex Routing Patterns

HOPSCOTCH   CLOVERLEAF

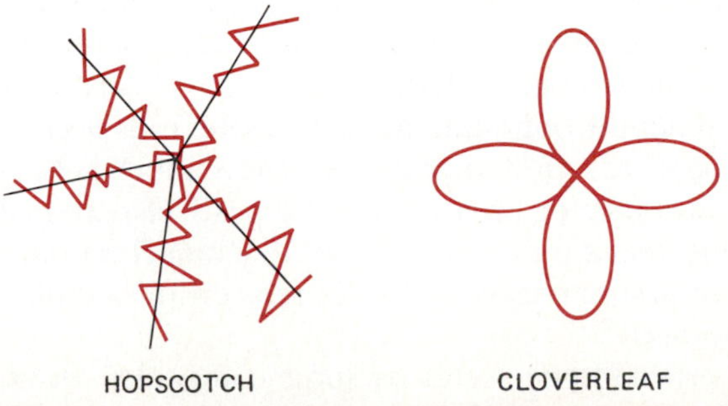

Another routing pattern that can be used along with those already discussed is a *skip-stop routing pattern*. A skip-stop routing pattern is usually used when call frequencies are different among customers. With a skip-stop pattern salespeople will make one trip in which every customer is called on, but on alternate trips they will call on only the more profitable accounts.

In some companies, the territories are so big that routing can become a time-consuming task that leads to an expensive problem. Consider the planning required of the salesperson who has to make a call in ten different cities in the eastern part of the country. One solution is to have a computer route the ten cities in every possible combination, add up the total mileage, and choose the route with the lowest number of total miles. This is easy for a mainframe computer, even though the number of possible routes is 181,440. However, what happens if the salesperson must visit thirty cities? The number of possible routes comes to 1 trillion billion billion (a 1 followed by thirty zeros). This is a heavy job even for a mainframe, and it requires a neural-network computer designed to react like the neurons in the human brain.[21] The result is an immediate answer that may not be the best answer, but it is a very good one. In some situations it is better to get a good answer fast than to wait for the best one.

Using Mathematical Models in Routing

Computerized mathematical models can also be used in solving routing problems. Several different models have been developed to determine the route that will maximize selling time or minimize travel cost. For example, Bayesian decision-making models have been developed that not only account for normal time restrictions in setting up a salesperson's route but also are profit-oriented. Linear programming models are also regularly used for routing.[22]

Three computer-based interactive models have been successfully applied to sales force routing and territory management. CALLPLAN asks sales managers or salespeople to estimate how customers will respond to various sales call frequencies. With this input sales territories can be realigned into more manageable account groupings and sales reps routed on the basis of call frequencies, travel time, length of call, and customer profitability potential. In an extension of the CALLPLAN model, sales managers calculate the relative effectiveness of matching different sales reps' characteristics (personality, education, training, and experience) to customer or buying-center characteristics (size, composition, technical expertise, or industry affiliation).[23] Another model, called SCHEDULE, also requires data inputs from salespeople on each customer's sales potential, call lengths, profit contribution, and estimated share penetration. Given sales and profit goals, the model determines the optimum number of sales calls needed to achieve them.[24] The third model, ALLOCATE, estimates how much selling effort should be allocated to a customer or prospect on the basis of potential sales and current share of the customer's purchases. Use of this model requires historical data or estimates from sales managers and sales reps on the number of sales calls made on each customer.[25]

Mathematical models have proved to be useful for some companies. However, many sales organizations have not accepted them because they are so

EXHIBIT 10-7

Sales Call Allocation Grid

Strength of Position

	Strong	Weak
High Account Opportunity **Low**	*Segment 1* *Attractiveness:* Accounts are very attractive since they offer high opportunity and sales organization has strong position *Sales call strategy:* Accounts should receive a high level of sales calls since they are the sales organization's most attractive accounts	*Segment 2* *Attractiveness:* Accounts are potentially attractive since they offer high opportunity, but sales organization currently has weak position with accounts *Sales call strategy:* Accounts should receive a high level of sales calls to strengthen the sales organization's position
	Segment 3 *Attractiveness:* Accounts are somewhat attractive, since sales organization has strong position, but future opportunity is limited *Sales call strategy:* Accounts should receive a moderate level of sales calls to maintain the current strength of the sales organization's position	*Segment 4* *Attractiveness:* Accounts are very unattractive since they offer low opportunity and sales organization has weak position *Sales call strategy:* Accounts should receive minimal level of sales calls and efforts should be made to selectively eliminate or replace personal sales calls with telephone calls, direct mail, etc.

Source: Raymond W. LeForge, Clifford E. Young, and B. Curtis Hamm, "Increasing Sales Productivity through Improved Sales Call Allocation Strategies," Journal of Personal Selling and Sales Management, November 1983, pp. 53–59.

complex; also, not every sales call can be accurately programmed, since diverse variables affect success and failure. The Sales Call Grid Analysis Approach seeks to reduce some of the analytical rigor of the mathematical models.[26] In this approach, a sales call strategy is based on the account's attractiveness. Exhibit 10-7 shows this grid relationship. Segment 1 represents what most companies call a key account; Segment 2 would be considered a potential customer or prospect; Segment 3 is a stable account; and Segment 4 represents a weak account.

While the Sales Call Grid Analysis Approach is logical and easy for sales managers to understand, it is limited by the fact that all the accounts are divided into only four segments. Thus, the results are an averaged description of the accounts and may not hold true for every account.

Sales managers should recognize these routing methods as tools that can assist them in making territory management decisions. However, the final decision on which pattern to use and how much flexibility to allow should be based on the sales manager's judgment.

TRENDS IN ROUTING AND SCHEDULING

Effective and efficient routing and scheduling plans will be essential for maintaining profits during the 1990s. Each company will devise its own plans based on its own circumstances. But several trends that emerged in recent years will probably continue well into the 1990s:

1. Routing and scheduling will continue to be developed primarily by the field salespeople, since typically they know the territory best.

2. The primary role of the sales manager will be to monitor the sales force and make sure that key accounts are not neglected and that profits meet projected goals.

3. Use of computers by salespeople and sales managers will increase tremendously, and applications will become even more sophisticated.

4. Use of mobile communications, especially cellular phones and beepers, will increase substantially. These devices, along with laptop computers, will make salespeople a more productive and effective force within the organization.

SUMMARY

The escalating cost of making a personal sales visit has caused sales managers to seek more efficient and less expensive means of reaching customers. This is done through effective time and territory management with the aid of innovative ideas and new technology.

Managing sales territories includes establishing the territories, analyzing accounts, analyzing each salesperson's workload, assigning personnel to territories, and—if necessary—revising territories. Effective territory management is needed to provide salespeople with evenly divided sales territories, estimate a territory's potential correctly, formulate a strategy for achieving that potential, and properly consider each individual salesperson's strengths and weaknesses.

Telemarketing is rapidly becoming a vital tool in the sales manager's arsenal because it provides quick and inexpensive personal contact between customer and company. Telemarketing is being used to prospect for new accounts, qualify sales leads, set appointments, and maintain good customer relations. It allows salespeople to spend their time in the field wisely by calling on qualified customers with preset appointments. Also, it allows them to reach more people in a shorter amount of time and at less expense.

New technology is aiding sales managers in making their sales forces more efficient. Computers are being used by sales managers to evenly align territories, and PCs are being used by sales reps to manage their time efficiently. Cellular phones, pagers, and airfones allow salespeople to maintain contact with customers and the home office and thus save time while traveling. Facsimile machines, electronic mail, and voice mail can reproduce original documents and written and verbal messages even though both parties may be miles apart.

Effective methods of scheduling maximize the salesperson's productive selling time. Scheduling seeks optimal allocation of time through the use of today's time-saving technologies, goal setting, and evaluation. Efficient routing is necessary in order to reduce travel time and costs. Many computerized mathematical models have been designed with the specific intention of routing salespeople so that their selling time is maximized and their travel costs are minimized.

Professional sales managers will have to utilize all the tools available to them in order to design sales territories effectively and route salespeople efficiently. Emphasis on these functions is needed to maintain control over rapidly escalating sales costs.

STUDY QUESTIONS

1. Why is it necessary to establish sales territories that are equal?
2. "Telemarketing is used only by small companies who are seeking to make a fast buck." Do you agree or disagree? Why?
3. Why is it important to match the right salesperson with the right territory?
4. If you were a sales manager, what would you tell your salespeople concerning the value of using personal computers?
5. How would you, the sales manager, use the computer?
6. Why are goals necessary for both the salesperson and the sales manager?
7. What are some advantages and disadvantages of routing?
8. Describe the Sales Call Grid Analysis Approach.
9. What are some of the most commonly used time management tools?
10. Is it important for a salesperson to be worried about time management during a sales call? Why or why not?

IN-BASKET EXERCISE

You were recently promoted to sales manager of one of your company's most productive regions. After several weeks on the job you are becoming concerned about the time management of one of your veteran salespeople. Although he is quite successful as a salesperson, he seems to have a problem dealing with time. On several occasions you received reports from him that read "Chicago Monday, Detroit Tuesday, and Chicago Wednesday." Moreover, his paperwork is late—if turned in at all. When you questioned him on these issues, he replied: "I just want to hit the road and sell. I don't have time for all this paperwork! Plus, I've always had the impression it's sales volume that counts with this company. In sixteen years with the company, I've always surpassed my quota!"

1. Should this really be a concern of yours? Why or why not?
2. Should sales managers put up barriers and tell top salespeople to change?
3. Do you think more effective time management will truly improve this person's performance?

CASE 10-1

DATACOR SOFTWARE, INC.: TIME AND TERRITORY MANAGEMENT

Datacor Software, Inc. (DSI) is a small computer software company located in Lexington, Massachusetts. DSI develops and markets innovative software packages. Currently, DSI has only one marketable product, but the future looks promising; two innovative packages that appear to have significant market potential should be market-ready within twenty-four months.

The partners of DSI include Ralph Heath, who is considered a software development whiz; Bob Booth, who is a former IBM sales representative; and Bill Grant, an independently wealthy entrepreneur who provided most of the capital necessary to finance DSI's rapid growth.

DSI has experienced rapid growth since its formation in January 1990, but sales have not reached expectations. Average yearly sales have not been increasing and are averaging 4,000 units per year. The partners are unable to explain why sales have not materialized as expected. In 1989, a business plan was prepared by a consultant who had been recommended by a Harvard business professor. The professor recommended him because she knew of the consultant's extensive industry knowledge and small-business development expertise. The business plan projected that sales would be at least 10,000 units by 1991 (see Exhibit 1).

The Product

The software package that is being sold is called HURRY-SELL. This package was developed in 1989 by Ralph Heath as part of his senior project for the computer science degree he was completing at a university in eastern Canada. A truly innovative software package,

it was designed to allow sales organizations to train sales representatives at their own pace and also at a reasonable cost. Several trade journal product reviewers have highly recommended HURRY-SELL as a good investment for any sales firm concerned about sales force training. The package has been designed to be compatible with the most popular computer systems that sales organizations tend to use.

Selling

DSI's primary method of selling has been to use telemarketing to sell directly to end users (who tend to be companies) and to dealers throughout the United States and Canada. This method of selling evolved naturally as a result of a lack of cash flow that restricted DSI's ability to establish a more extensive sales force. The partners' primary objective was to retain complete control over distribution of DSI products; telemarketing was viewed as an affordable means of accomplishing that objective.

EXHIBIT 1

Business Plan Sales Projections (in units)

	1990	1991	1992*	1993	1994
Optimistic	10,000	14,000	21,000	35,000	42,000
Likely	8,000	12,000	18,000	26,000	35,000
Pessimistic	6,000	10,000	12,000	20,000	29,000

*Significant sales increases were anticipated after 1991 because of planned new-product introductions.

Case prepared by E. Stephen Grant, Memphis State University. Used with permission.

DSI's sales force is organized geographically so that each of the five sales reps has sole responsibility for a defined territory (see Exhibit 2). With the exception of sales to dealer accounts, reps are expected to move the HURRY-SELL package exclusively by telephone and mailed brochure. All reps are expected to visit dealer-account purchasing executives at least twice each year. Concerning this expectation, Bob Booth commented: "Dealers are in a position to move a lot of product for us; therefore, I do not want my reps to be strangers to these organizations. There is no substitute for personal contact."

Consultant's Report

Unable to explain DSI's less-than-expected sales performance, the partners retained a consultant to assess both the market situation and DSI operations. Like the consultant who prepared the business plan, this consultant is highly respected within his profession. He is a partner with an international accounting and management consulting firm. This enables him to solicit knowledge and support from a network of over 4,000 professionals. The appendix on page 356 includes excerpts from the consultant's report.

Planning Session

Following a review of the consultant's report, the partners had a planning session in order to reach some decisions about future operations at DSI. The session proved successful in that many issues were debated and minor policy issues were resolved; however, several critical issues identified in the consultant's report were left unresolved. The following comments reflect each partner's opinion concerning some of the critical issues:

Ralph Heath: The ideas concerning revision of our sales territories are super.

We will have to fire John Parker for cheating. If we allow him to remain with us, other reps will learn of his activity and take our lack of punishment as a signal that his behavior was acceptable.

Bob Booth: The reorganization of our sales organization looks good, but I believe we will lose at least 50 percent of our current sales force if we attempt to implement these changes.

We can't fire John Parker; he is our best rep. I don't think he has really harmed anyone.

Bill Grant: I'm not at all concerned about losing 50 percent of our people; sales force turnover can have positive benefits. My real concern is that the revised sales territories will result in dealer confusion and perhaps frustration if they do not receive the quick order delivery time that they have come to expect. My point is that reorganization could really slow our response times while we are attempting to implement these changes.

Unable to reach a consensus on what to do, the partners decided that it would be necessary to take a few more days before making these important decisions. Before leaving their planning session, they decided to

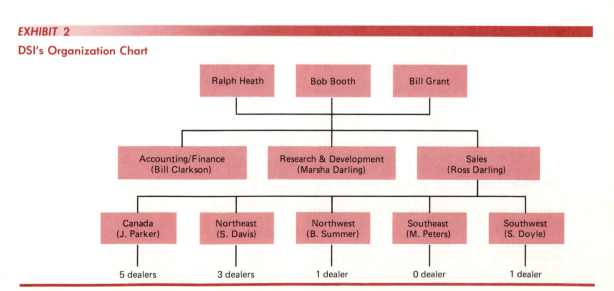

EXHIBIT 2

DSI's Organization Chart

EXHIBIT 1

Example of Mary Clark's File Sheet

Front of File

PATERSON EASTSIDE HS	555-3434
37 PARK AVE	rt 80 to exit 59
PATERSON 07644	follow ramp to the end
	make right onto Park Ave

English: Tom Snyder (Free 1st two periods of the day 8–9:40)
9/84 Left copy GRAM, COMP. 5/85 Left copies of LIT SERIES. He's going to order COMP for 11th grade honors class. 9/85 Not available; left copy of new SAT-PREP with a note. 5/86 Reviewed new SAT-PREP. Has 400 students in their SAT prep program and plans to have students purchase it every year from the bookstore.

Foreign Languages: Eduardo Lopez (Free 8:45–10:15)
9/84 Not available. 5/85 Left copy SPAN-1-RDR. 9/85 Ordered SPAN-1-RDR. 5/86 Not available. 9/86 Left copy of new ITAL-4-WB and ITAL-4-RDR. Small ITAL class. 5/87 Left copy FREN, SPAN, ITAL. He likes these dictionaries very much. May have kids buy them. 9/87 Not available. 9/88 Not available.

Social Studies: Pam Coffey (Free 1st two periods 8–9:40)
9/84 Left copy of AHIST, WHIST. 5/85 Went with Ginn for both Amer. & World History. Does not like our stuff. 9/85 NEW DEPT HEAD. Left copy of PSY, WCIV. 5/86 Likes the PSY and is going to order. No money now for WCIV, maybe next year. 9/86 Ordered PSY. 5/87 Got the money in budget to order WCIV. 9/87 Left copy SOC. 9/89 Left copy FREN.

Clark keeps all the information concerning submission rules and dates on each school district on her file sheets. She has discovered that this practice has become a burden. She finds that she can carry only so many files with her on the road, and they are very awkward to deal with. She often must flip through hundreds of sheets just to find the one she is interested in. On more than one occasion she has lost one or more files, and she is finding it increasingly tiresome to update these files daily.

Clark also finds problems in the amount of material she has to carry with her on sales calls. This includes a large book bag filled with texts she is to present, a notebook filled with her file sheets for the day, price lists, catalogs she is to hand out during her presentations, her daily report pad, and company stationery she carries in case she has to write a note to those she attempts to meet with. All these materials make it very difficult for her to move around through the school's

EXHIBIT 2

Example of Mary Clark's File Sheet

Back of File

7-17-84	7-3-87
275 BIOL(10TM)	225 SPAN-1-WB(9TM)
135 CHEM(4TM)	225 SPAN-2-WB(9TM)
530 ALG-1(15TM)	110 SPAN-3-WB(4TM)
8-23-84	175 FREN-1-WB(7TM)
200 SPAN-1-WB(8TM)	175 FREN-2-WB(7TM)
200 SPAN-2-WB(8TM)	50 FREN-3-WB(2TM)
100 SPAN-3-WB(4TM)	400 GEOM(16TM)
30 SPAN-1-RDR	200 ALG2/TRIG(8TM)

halls, especially when the students are changing classrooms. Consequently, Clark has been looking for a way to condense her files and to reduce the amount of material she carries with her while making sales calls.

Portable PC Purchase?

Clark has been giving consideration to the purchase of a portable personal computer. She has heard favorable reports about portable PCs and has priced them at several computer stores. She has also spent time discussing the use of a PC with Bill Staples, the New York sales rep, who purchased a system a year earlier. Bill told her that the PC has allowed him to gain increased control because it enables him to organize his days much more effectively than he could without the PC. Bill is one of the company's better salespeople; he went over his sales quota last year by more than $100,000. Bill credits his success to the PC.

EXHIBIT 3

Example of Textbook Submitting Procedure

TO: Textbook vendors
FROM: City of Newark Board of Education
RE: Submission of textbooks for committee approval

1. All samples must be submitted to the Textbook Committee by September 15.
2. Two copies of each title to be considered must be submitted along with any ancillary materials that accompany the text.
3. All catalogs, price lists, and company promotions must also be submitted at this time.
4. All materials must be boxed with labels to properly identify the vendor's shipping address and all contents.

Clark figured she could carry the PC in her briefcase and take it along with her book bag on her sales calls. All the file sheets could be put onto disks and could be accessed very quickly. Also, she could establish an electronic calendar to keep track of when she is to call on each school district and when each district has its budget meetings. Clark could also keep track of trade shows that she is supposed to attend.

Clark also thinks she could computerize her daily reports and thus take care of her reports and her file updating at the same time. Another benefit of the portable PC is that Clark could have instant access to a brief synopsis of each of the features and benefits of all 250 Gillis Books titles, including suggested grade and competency levels and prices. This would allow her to improve her presentations because she would be able to quickly retrieve an answer for almost any question.

The most important benefit of the PC is that it would help Clark manage her time much more efficiently. Whereas in the past she was able to make a second visit per year only to very large accounts, the PC would allow her to make a second visit to almost all her accounts and, more importantly, to do so at the time they need to see her.

Clark could find only two disadvantages associated with the portable PC. It would cost at least $2,000 to get all the hardware and software that she would need, and she would need time and assistance to learn how to use the system. She had never used a PC before and did not consider herself to be technically oriented. Gillis Books would not reimburse her for buying the PC, so Clark would have to make the outlay from her own personal funds.

Questions

1. What advice would you give Clark about being an effective time manager?

2. Given each of the following scenarios, when do you recommend that Clark buy the PC:
   a. Suppose Clark has decided to buy the portable PC now. It will cost her $2,000. School starts next week, so Clark will have to learn the PC's operations and convert all her files in her spare time. For the first few months, her operations will be slow and awkward, so she estimates her increase in sales to be only 5 percent in the first year. In subsequent years, however, she expects a 15 percent increase.
   b. Suppose Clark has decided to postpone her purchase until July. In July, the cost will be only $1,500, and she will have her vacation months (July and August) to learn operations and to convert all her files. However, by waiting, she will lose the expected 5 percent increase from this year. Also, she will be without the full year's experience with everyday usage of the PC that she would gain if she purchases it in September. Consequently, she expects only a 10 percent increase in subsequent years. Assume that Clark's quota will stay the same and be surpassed in each year regardless of the increases. Her bonus is subject to a 25 percent tax rate.

3. Explain how the executives of Gillis Books could help the sales reps improve their time management skills. Be specific.

REFERENCES

1. Bill Kelley, "How Much Help Does a Salesperson Need?" *Sales & Marketing Management,* May 1989, pp. 32–35.
2. William C. Moncrief, Shannon H. Shipp, Charles W. Lamb, Jr., and David W. Cravens, "Examining the Role of Telemarketing in Selling Strategy," *Journal of Personal Selling and Sales Management,* Fall 1989, pp. 1–12.
3. "1990 Survey of Selling Costs," *Sales & Marketing Management,* Feb. 26, 1990, p. 75.
4. Robert J. McHatton, *Total Telemarketing,* Wiley, New York, 1988.
5. "Telemarketing Seen as Speedy Alternative to Hundreds of Filing-Cabinet Records," *Marketing News,* June 6, 1986.
6. John I. Coppett and Roy D. Vorhees, "Telemarketing: Supplement to Field Sales," *Industrial Marketing Management,* vol. 14, 1985, pp. 213–216.
7. "Statistical Abstract of the United States," U.S. Bureau of the Census, 106th ed., 1989.

8. "Computerized Yellow Pages Seen as Aid to Sales," *Marketing News*, May 24, 1985, p. 43.

9. "Merrell Dow Gives Territories a Better Balance," *Sales & Marketing Management*, Dec. 9, 1985, pp. 67–68.

10. See Harry D. Wolfe and Gerald Albaum, "Inequality in Products, Orders, Customers, Salesmen, and Sales Territories," in Robert F. Givinner and Edward M. Smith (eds.), *Sales Strategy, Cases and Readings*, Appleton-Century-Crofts, New York, 1969; Spencer S. Meilstrup, *Allocating Field Sales Resources*, Experiences in Marketing Management, The Conference Board, New York, 1970; Lawrence M. Lamont and William G. Lundstrom, "Defining Industrial Sales Behavior: A Factor Analytic Study," *1974 Combined Proceedings*, American Marketing Association, Chicago, 1974, pp. 493–498; O. A. Davis and J. D. Farley, "Allocating Sales Force Effort with Commissions and Quotas," *Management Science*, 18 (December 1971), pp. 55–63; Gary M. Armstrong, "The Schedule Model and the Salesman's Effort Allocation," *California Management Review*, 18 (Summer 1976), pp. 43–51.

11. "Computerized Street Maps of Entire United States," *American Salesman*, May 1990, pp. 27–28.

12. Robert Collins, "JPSSM Introduces New Section," *Journal of Personal Selling and Sales Management*," May 1984, pp. 56–57.

13. Henry Porter, "The Important Few—The Unimportant Many," *Sales & Marketing Management, 1978 Portfolio*, 1977, pp. 31–34.

14. William A. Weeks and Lynn R. Kahle, "Salespeople's Time Use and Performance," *Journal of Personal Selling and Sales Management*, February 1990, pp. 29–37.

15. Stephen Harris, "Nationwide Paging," *Debuts*, July 1986, p. 34.

16. "Case Study Demonstrates Cellular Telephones Enhance Sales Revenues," *AT&T*, AT&T, Basking Ridge, N.J., 1986.

17. Thayer C. Taylor, "More Software, but Higher Prices," *Sales & Marketing Management*, April 1989, pp. 86–89.

18. Charles C. Smith, "Selling in the Age of Silicon," *Infoworld Special Report #2*, Sept. 24, 1984, p. A40–A47.

19. Smith, "Selling in the Age of Silicon," p. A42.

20. Thayer C. Taylor, "How Raytheon Plugs In the Sales Force," *Sales & Marketing Management*, Dec. 3, 1984, pp. 62–63.

21. "Computers That Come Awfully Close to Thinking," *Sales & Marketing Management*, June 2, 1986, pp. 92–94.

22. For examples see William Lazer, Richard T. Hise, and Jay A. Smith, "Computer Routing: Putting Salesmen in Their Places," *Sales Management*, Mar. 15, 1970, p. 29; M. Bellnore and G. L. Nembauser, "The Traveling Salesman Problem: A Survey," *Operations Research*, May–June 1969, pp. 538–558; Andres A. Zoltners, "Integer Programming Models for Sales Territory Alignment to Maximize Profit," *Journal of Marketing Research*, November 1976, pp. 426–430; R. Buzzell, *Mathematical Models and Marketing Management*, School of Business Administration, Harvard University, Boston, 1964; D. Montgomery, A. Silk, and C. Zaragoza, "A Multiple-Product Sales Force Allocation Model," *Management Science*, 18 (December 1971), pp. 3–24; Adrian B. Ryans and Charles B. Weinberg, "Managerial Implications of Models of Territory Sales Response," in Neil Beckwith, Michael Houston, Robert Mittelstaedt, Kent B. Monroe, and Scott Ward (eds.), *1979 Educators' Conference Proceedings*, American Marketing Association, Chicago, 1979, pp. 426–430; H. C. Lucas, Jr., C. B. Weinberg, and K. Clowes, "Sales Response as a Function of Territorial Potential Sales Representative Workload," *Journal of Marketing Research*, August 1975, pp. 298–305.

23. For more explanation of CALLPLAN, see Leonard M. Lodish, "CALLPLAN: An Interactive Salesman's Call Planning System," *Management Science*, December 1971, pp. P25–P40; Leonard M. Lodish, " 'Vaguely Right' Approach to Sales Force Allocations," *Harvard Business Review*, January–February 1974, pp. 119–124; Leonard M. Lodish, "Sales Territory Alignment to Maximize Profits," *Journal of Marketing*

Research, February 1975, pp. 30–36; Leonard M. Lodish, "Assigning Salesmen to Accounts to Maximize Profits," *Journal of Marketing Research,* November 1976, pp. 440–444.

24. Gary M. Armstrong, "The SCHEDULE Model and the Salesman's Effort Allocation," *California Management Review,* Summer 1976, pp. 43–51.

25. James H. Comer, "ALLOCATE: A Computer Model for Sales Territory Planning," *Decision Sciences,* July 1974, pp. 323–338.

26. Raymond W. Laforge, Clifford E. Young, and B. Curtis Hamm, "Increasing Sales Productivity through Improved Sales Call Allocation Strategies," *Journal of Personal Selling and Sales Management,* November 1983, pp. 53–59.

11

SALES QUOTAS

LEARNING OBJECTIVES

When you finish this chapter, you should understand:

- ▲ What sales quotas are and how they are developed
- ▲ The basic reasons for establishing sales quotas
- ▲ The procedures for setting sales quotas
- ▲ Why and how sales quotas are adjusted
- ▲ The need for proper administration of a quota system

A DAY ON THE JOB

Kevin Neels, of Charles River Associates, believes that sales managers should give a great deal of thought to setting sales quotas. "Sales quotas must motivate people while being neither too easy nor too difficult to attain," says Neels. Furthermore, Neels states that "sales quotas involve a policy decision about how a company wants to treat its people." According to Neels, many factors—such as the company's marketing objectives, the industry climate, regional economies, and the individual salespersons themselves—must be considered before sales quotas are set. Neels suggests that "a quota system should target the middle 60% of the salesforce, based on existing performance," and that "salespeople should be consulted and allowed to provide input in setting quotas." When setting sales quotas, sales managers must remember that all salespeople are not alike. Having one sales quota system, whether it be too high or too low, aimed at the entire sales force may be self-defeating. Neels recommends that a sales quota plan should be designed so that salespeople compete against themselves, not against each other."[1]

Lawrence Taylor, the all-pro linebacker for the New York Giants, receives extra compensation each time he sacks a quarterback; he also receives a bonus for making the pro-bowl team. Most of today's professional athletes, whether in baseball, basketball, football, or hockey, have contractual incentives to motivate them to strive for superior performance. Not unlike athletes, professional salespeople also usually have special incentives for top performance. These sales incentives, or motivational targets, are called *quotas* and they may take a variety of forms. Successful sales managers who skillfully make use of sales force quotas can stimulate their salespeople to achieve exceptional individual and team performances.

After the sales forecast and sales budget have been prepared, the next step is to establish specific quantitative goals, or quotas, for each marketing unit (e.g., sales representatives) and to plan the activities that are necessary to achieve these quotas. Quotas are usually established in terms of sales volume; however, they can also be established for profits or gross margin, expenses, activities, or some combination of these. Quotas are used as standards to specify a desired level of performance for a specified marketing unit. A *marketing unit* may be defined as an individual sales representative, a sales territory, a branch office, a region, a dealer or distributor, or a district. Quotas that are set for regional offices are usually broken down and assigned to the individual territories that make up a region. All quotas are guided by a certain time element within which management feels the quota should be attained.

Sales quotas are an important device in the strategic planning, control, and evaluation of a marketing unit's sales activities.[2] The effectiveness of quotas depends on both the information used in setting them up and management's administration of the system. Quotas are based on the company's sales forecasts and cost estimates and on the market's sales potential. Therefore accurate data, as well as administrative expertise, are needed for a quota system to be effective.

THE PURPOSE OF QUOTAS

Quotas serve several purposes. They provide goals and incentives for salespeople. They are also used to evaluate the salesperson's performance, control the salesperson's activities, uncover strengths and weaknesses in the selling structure, improve the compensation plan's effectiveness, control selling expenses, and enhance sales contests.

Providing Goals and Incentives

All people need some sort of feedback on where they stand in life in general, whether in relation to a member of the opposite sex, a competitive sporting event, or school or business. This is especially true for salespeople, who are usually very competitive by nature. Telling a salesperson that he or she is doing well will have little impact. Salespeople want to know how well in relation to a benchmark figure that distinguishes success and failure.

A quota provides salespeople with a standardized measure of their sales ability. It provides a goal for them to shoot for—a given dollar sales volume or the number of new accounts to be opened within a specified period of time—and it inspires them to reach that goal. One of the problems in establishing quotas is that inaccurate information can lead to unrealistic quotas, which in turn can lead to unhappy, uninspired salespeople. For a quota to be motivational, it must be realistic and attainable. The salespeople must feel very positive about their ability to attain the quota so that they will not give up when times get tough. Also, they must feel that attainment of the quota is imperative to maintaining their position with the company and that performance above and beyond the quota will be well recognized. In many companies, salespeople who surpass the quota receive increased compensation through commissions or bonuses and/or are recognized for superior performance.

Evaluating Performance

Just as a quota provides the salesperson with a goal to shoot for, it also provides management with a tool to use in measuring the salesperson's performance. If a salesperson falls far short of the quota, a problem exists with the individual or territory or the quota was overstated and unrealistic. On the other hand, if a sales rep goes way beyond the quota, he or she is doing a superhuman job or the quota was understated. In either case, the use of a quota can point out problems that the company can work on in order to improve the sales force's performance and motivation. Sales performance in relation to the quota is also used for decisions on promotions and salary increases.

Controlling the Salesperson's Activities

Quotas enable management to direct and control the activities of the sales force. Salespeople are responsible for certain activities, including, for example, calling on a minimum number of accounts per day, calling on new accounts, and giving a minimum number of demonstrations. These activity quotas are designed to ensure that the salespeople perform their duties and stress those duties that are most important to the company. If the sales rep does not attain these quotas, then the company can take corrective action immediately before the situation becomes a major problem.

Uncovering Strengths and Weaknesses in the Selling Structure

If sales fall significantly short of the quota in a particular territory, the cause must be determined. It may be that atypical environmental or market conditions exist only in that territory. If the quota is easily surpassed, the reasons for this must also be analyzed. Thus, by using a quota system, the company can spot certain strengths and weaknesses within its selling structure and work toward enhancing the one and rectifying the other.

Improving the Compensation Plan's Effectiveness

Quotas can play an important role in the company's sales compensation plan. In some companies, salespeople must exceed the quota before they start to receive any commission. For example, a salesperson may be given a quota of $250,000 in sales per year, with an 8 percent commission being paid on any sales above that quota. On sales of $270,000 per year, the salesperson would receive a commission of $1,600 (270,000 − 250,000 = 20,000 × 0.08). In this case, the commission is unlimited, and this acts as a strong incentive for the sales rep. Other companies will use a quota as the basis for calculating the bonus. In this case, the quota is set very high, and the maximum bonus awarded only for 100 percent quota attainment. If the salesperson did not reach the full quota, the bonus is set in proportion to the percentage of the quota that the salesperson did attain. For instance, the salesperson may have the opportunity to make a $3,000 bonus at the end of the year for attaining the $250,000 sales quota. If the salesperson reached only $225,000 (90 percent) in sales, then the bonus would be 90 percent of the $3,000 bonus, or $2,700.

Companies know that a bonus or commission is a powerful incentive that can be used to motivate salespeople to increase their level of performance, and quotas are used as the basis for this incentive. At the same time, salespeople know that the attainment of quotas can not only increase their short-term compensation but also enhance their chances of receiving raises and promotions.

However, a poorly constructed or unrealistic quota can demoralize a sales representative. If quotas are too high and attainment is not possible, the sales force will become irritated and performance will suffer. This frustration may lead the sales force to cheat in order to meet the quotas.[3] This situation is illustrated in the *Ethics* scenario on page 366.

Controlling the Selling Expenses

Quotas are also designed to keep selling costs at a minimum. By restricting the amount of money that may be spent on meals, lodging, and entertaining, man-

> **ETHICS IN SALES MANAGEMENT: MAKING THE QUOTA**
>
> You are a sales manager for a company that markets large engines for a variety of uses and in a variety of markets. Your salespeople are evaluated on how close they come to meeting their monthly quota of engines sold. Recently, your business has been in a slump, and only one of your salespeople reached her quota during the last two months. Since compensation is tied to quotas, you decided to check on this salesperson's activity. To your surprise, you discovered that she has been very creative with her paperwork. It appears that occasionally, during months in which she met her quota, she informed customers that there were no engines available and that an engine would be sent to them in the following month. Although your company always has plenty of engines in inventory, this sales rep kept customers waiting so that she could apply the sales to her next month's quota. Moreover, when customers bought more than one engine, she frequently billed the engines to them over several months (i.e., one engine per month) so that her sales would appear to be more constant throughout the year. This, too, enhances her chances of reaching her quota each month. She is a very successful salesperson, and you're not sure what to do about her at this point.
>
> **1.** Is there anything "wrong" with what this salesperson is doing?
> **2.** Should she be reprimanded? Why or why not?
> **3.** What possible ramifications can her actions have for your customers?

agement can control the costs of selling. This results in increased profits. The company can also tie expenses to the salesperson's compensation in an effort to curb wasteful spending. For example, the company may allow only a certain number of samples to be given away before charging the salesperson a fee for each. This forces salespeople to do a better job of qualifying their accounts and to restrict their sampling to "hot prospects" only. Other companies may use the amount of the salesperson's expenses in evaluating the salesperson's overall effectiveness and in giving salary raises.

Enhancing Sales Contests

Sales contests can be powerful incentives and motivating forces for salespeople. Generally, quotas used for sales contests are specific only to the contest and are usually adjusted for the short-term duration of the contest so that all salespeople have an equal opportunity of winning. This is designed to stimulate extra effort from the salespeople, causing them to turn in outstanding performances.

TYPES OF QUOTAS

There are four basic types of quotas: sales volume, financial, activities, and combination. The company can use any one or several of these quotas, depending on the nature of the product and the industry.

Sales Volume Quotas

The most commonly used quotas are those that are based on sales volume. Most of these quotas use dollar sales as their basis, but some stress unit sales, sales of new products, or sales of neglected products or product sizes. Management regards these quotas as important standards in evaluating salespeople and other marketing units. They signify management's expectations of the minimum level of performance for a given period of time.

While sales volume quotas can be measured as a dollar unit, or point amount, they are generally established on the basis of a geographic area, a product line, or a customer type for a specific period of time. In establishing the basis for the volume quota, it is wise to use the smallest marketing unit possible in order to provide for tight control. For instance, if the company is basing its sales volume quota on geographic regions, it would be better to establish a quota for each territory in the region than for the region as a whole.

Some quotas can be established to evaluate how well the salesperson is selling the company's new products. New products are the lifeblood of any company. When sales of existing products have matured, the company must be prepared to introduce and sell new products; otherwise, when competition, new technology, or obsolescence forces existing products to die, the company will be left with nothing. Thus, all managers know the importance of pushing new products into the forefront, so they establish new-product sales quotas to make the salesperson equally aware of the importance of these products. If left to their own devices, salespeople may tend to concern themselves only with existing products because these are the products they know and feel most comfortable with.

Management can also use a sales volume quota to ensure that certain slower-moving products are not being neglected by the salesperson. By placing a quota on these products, management will make salespeople more conscientious in presenting *all* the company's products.

Salespeople in larger companies often sell to only one or two types of customers. For example, some Unisys sales reps call only on banks or financial institutions; Motorola salespeople may call only on industrial accounts or chemical plants. Specific quotas for each of these types of customers are then set to ensure a balance in coverage. But in smaller companies the sales reps typically are responsible for selling to five or six different types of customers. They may sell to industrial customers, wholesalers, retailers, and final consumers all at the same time and may be responsible for meeting sales quotas for each.

Finally, the sales quota is generally established for a certain time period. Again, the shorter the time period, the more effective the quota. For this reason many companies establish quotas on a monthly or quarterly basis. However, if sales are seasonal, an annual quota may be necessary. For example, textbook salespeople are guided by an annual quota because even though they work when school is in session (September to June), the bulk of their orders do not come in until July and August, when schools are closed for summer vacation.

Dollar sales volume.   Sales volume quotas expressed in terms of dollars provide the convenience of being easily understood by the salesperson and commonly recognized as a measure for all products. The salespeople are fully aware of what is expected in the way of sales and can gauge their performance directly against a dollar figure. Dollar quotas are also a lot easier to manage when the salesperson is responsible for selling many products. In this case, it would be impractical to have a dollar quota for each of, say, thirty products. Instead, the salesperson would be responsible for one total figure governing either groups of products or all products. However, if sales reps have PCs, they can easily manage a separate dollar volume for each product that they sell.

Dollar volumes also allow for a more direct analysis of the ratio of selling costs to quota. Individual expense-to-sales ratios can then be calculated, and comparisons can be made using these ratios. Finally, dollar volume quotas are frequently used because they can be calculated and adjusted quickly and easily from year to year.

Unit sales volume. Unit sales quotas are useful when the salesperson is responsible for selling only a few products. Thus, a quota may be set in terms of the number of gallons of chemicals or the number of personal computers sold. Unit sales volumes are also attractive when prices fluctuate rapidly. With the price of oil skyrocketing during the early 1990s, a dollar volume quota based on sales in recent years would allow salespeople to reach the quota much easier than in the past. The use of a dollar quota could perhaps even backfire and lower overall performance; in essence, a salesperson could work less and still make the quota. In this case, a per-barrel quota would be a much better indicator of how well the sales force is attaining its quota.

A per-unit quota is also advisable when big-ticket items are being sold. For example, a quota of $1 million may look frightening to a sales rep even though each unit is $50,000. But if the quota is set on a per-unit basis, say, twenty units, it is much easier to understand and accept.

Point sales volume. Some companies will combine dollar or unit sales or both into "points" and use this measure as the basis of a sales volume quota. Companies typically award points according to the level of sales. For example, $100 might equal 1 point, $200 could equal 2 points, and so on. At the same time, the company may award 3 points for unit sales of product A and 2 points for product B. Companies generally use this type of approach because they are having problems trying to implement either a dollar or a unit volume quota. It also helps companies balance the need to emphasize a particular sales volume and the need to promote sales of specific products.

Basis for Setting Sales Volume Quotas

Past sales experience. Setting quotas on the basis of past territorial sales is by far the easiest method of establishing quotas. The procedure in this case would be to determine the percentage by which the market is expected to increase and then add this onto last year's quota. Hence, if the company expects an increase of 10 percent this year, then the new quota for each marketing unit would be last year's quota plus 10 percent, or 110 percent of last year's quota. Generally, companies that use this method are small and cannot afford or understand sophisticated analysis.

Some companies believe that the preceding year's actual performance is more reliable than its quota because the quota could have been underestimated or overestimated. Other companies try to reduce the margin of error by averaging the sales results of the previous three or five years to account for any trends. Still some companies evaluate this year's performance on the basis of whether or not it surpassed last year's results.

Companies that use past sales records to establish future quotas are making the assumption that future sales are related to past sales. This assumption should not be made blindly because it ensures that past mistakes will go on uncorrected. If past results were achieved through lazy work habits, future quotas based on these results will perpetuate these habits. If last year's results account for only 50 percent of the territory's potential and next year's quota is based upon those results, the sales reps will be unaware of the missed opportunities. They may surpass that quota and be very proud of themselves, yet they will not have tapped that territory's potential. Past sales should be regarded as only one of the factors to be considered in establishing sales volume quotas.

Territorial sales potentials. A sales volume quota is management's evaluation of the sales effort that must be put forth by a marketing unit, while the sales potential is the maximum amount of opportunity available to that marketing unit. Many sales managers use this relationship to derive their sales volume quotas. For example, the company may use a computer program to set up fifty sales territories of equal sales potential. Each sales representative is then responsible for 2 percent of the total company sales potential of $10 million, or $200,000. This method holds that the sum of all territorial sales volume quotas should equal the total company sales potential. This seems logical. However, it assumes that each representative is working under perfect selling conditions. A quota should be directly related to the company's sales forecast, not its sales potential. The difference is that the sales forecast takes into account somewhat less-than-perfect selling conditions to estimate what management feels it can reasonably attain.

Another way of deriving sales volume quotas from territorial sales potential is through bottom-up planning. This method incorporates the input of the sales rep, who is closest to the market, as well as past sales, competition, market trends, and the salesperson's ability. First, the salesperson is asked to estimate his or her territory's sales potential. Second, the field sales manager is asked to adjust this estimate according to the factors mentioned above. In making these adjustments, the sales manager will consider salesperson factors such as age, energy, initiative, experience, knowledge of territory, and physical condition. Realistically, these factors will be different for each salesperson; they must be considered, since they will affect the probability of each salesperson's attaining the assigned quota. For example, an older representative who has served the company well over the years may not be as physically capable as he or she once was. Thus, the sales manager must adjust the quota downward in order to compensate. In the same way, a new rep may not know all the ins and outs of the territory or customers. The quota should start out low and increase over the first two or three periods as the sales rep gains experience. Third, each territory's revised sales estimate is sent up to the sales manager, who adjusts it according to the company's plans for future changes in price, products, and promotion.

Finally, the sales manager converts these revised estimates of sales potential into sales quotas, the sum of which equals the company's total sales forecast.

Total market estimates.   Some companies are too small or too young to have territorial sales statistics based on potentials or sales force estimates. These companies rely on market estimates, from which they forecast a company's sales estimate. Top management sets the quotas and filters them down to the sales reps. There are two methods for doing this:

1. Break down the total company sales estimate into territorial estimates, and then adjust accordingly.

2. Take the company estimate, adjust it according to expected company changes in price, product, and promotion, and then break down the adjusted estimate into territorial estimates, and adjust accordingly.

These methods are very similar, the difference being that the second method recognizes that adjustments made at the corporate level are distinct from those that are made at the territorial level.

When ITT's Information Systems Division was first being established, management had very little information to work with in setting quotas. Since the division was new and the industry was young, there was virtually no past experience to draw upon. Therefore, the managers took the market potential and estimated what portion of the market they could attain in the first year. This gave them their company sales forecast. The forecast was then adjusted at the corporate level and broken down by territory. Because this was a recently established industry, ITT utilized a six-month rolling forecast. They would establish a six-month sales forecast and each month would update it and adjust it accordingly for the next six months. This gave managers tight control over performance in relation to the sales forecast.

Quotas established by salespeople.   Some companies allow the sales representatives to establish their own quotas because salespeople are closest to the market and are therefore thought to be the ones who know the most about its potential. Although salespeople should have some input in the quota-setting process, assigning total responsibility to the salesperson is merely a cop-out on the part of management. Salespeople cannot be expected to establish responsible, realistic quotas on their own. Optimistic sales reps will tend to overestimate their ability and set excessively high quotas for themselves. When these salespeople realize that they cannot meet their quotas, their morale is damaged.[4] On the other hand, some sales reps may set ridiculously low quotas for themselves so that they can attain them easily and earn high commissions or large bonuses. When salespeople feel that the quota is easily attainable, their motivation to put forth a maximum selling effort is greatly reduced.[5] Management should have better information than the sales rep for making quota decisions, especially information concerning future corporate strategies on price, product, and promotion.

Financial Quotas

Financial quotas are established to control gross margin and net profit or expenses for the various marketing units. Like volume quotas, these quotas can be applied to salespeople, regions, and product lines.

Gross-margin or net-profit quotas.
Companies use these quotas to emphasize to the salesperson that the company would prefer making a large profit to selling a large volume. High-volume salespeople may not always be the best sales reps for achieving the company's goals. For example, Joe sells the highest volume in XYZ Company; however, he stresses the easy-to-sell, low-margin products. Jane, on the other hand, sells a somewhat lower volume, but her sales involve larger, more expensive items that carry a greater profit margin. As shown in Exhibit 11-1, although Joe sold $15,000 more than Jane, his profit margin was almost $8,000 less than Jane's margin because of the type of product that each one emphasized.

This illustration is important to management because it points out the need to control the salesperson's selling emphasis. Salespeople receive an emotional boost every time they make a sale, so naturally they are going to try to make as many sales as possible, and in order to do this they may emphasize the easy-to-sell items. In essence, by spending so much time on less profitable products, the sales reps are limiting the company's opportunity to earn higher profits from its high-margin products. Granted, it may take a salesperson longer to sell higher-priced products, but the higher profits are well worth it to the company.

Salespeople also have a tendency to spend more time calling on customers whom they feel more comfortable with. These customers, however, may not purchase in large quantity or may require numerous services. Thus, they can be far less profitable than the salesperson's other customers.

Management's job is to ensure that salespeople spend the majority of their selling time on the more profitable products and with the more profitable customers. Management can do this by placing a quota on net profits, thus encouraging the sale of the high-margin products and deemphasizing the low-margin products.

While profit quotas are very desirable to some companies, there are some disadvantages. First of all, gross-margin or net-profit quotas are the hardest for

EXHIBIT 11-1

Ratio of Sales Volume to Net Profit

	Sales Price per Unit	Profit Margin per Unit (%)	Volume per Month		Net Profit per Month	
			Joe	Jane	Joe	Jane
Product A	$20	$15.00 (75%)	$ 5,000	$30,000	$ 3,750	$22,500
Product B	5	3.00 (66%)	5,000	2,500	3,000	1,500
Product C	2	.50 (25%)	40,000	2,500	10,000	625
			$50,000	$35,000	$16,750	$24,625

salespeople to understand. The net profit depends on the range of products they sell and the margin for each of these products. Thus, it is more difficult for them to determine how well they are doing at any given time, and they can get frustrated. This can cause them to lose their motivation. Second, the salesperson's net profit is affected by external factors, such as competition and economic conditions, and internal factors, such as the ability to negotiate on price. There are those who feel that it is unfair to subject the salesperson to this type of evaluation because of the many uncontrollable forces. Finally, it is very time-consuming to calculate net profit from the company's normal accounting records, and this will lead to additional clerical and administrative costs. However, many companies are alleviating these extra costs through the use of PCs.

Expense quotas. Expense quotas are designed to make salespeople aware of the costs involved in their selling efforts. Companies are trying many ways to control the escalating costs of travel, food, and lodging. One method is to tie reimbursement for expenses directly to the sales volume or compensation plan. For example, salespeople may be allowed to spend 5 percent of their sales for expenses. If they surpass this quota, the difference comes out of their salary or commissions. This method is also used to control a salesperson's use of samples. Some companies limit their salespeople to a certain dollar amount that they can spend per day on food and hotels. Other companies use expense-to-sales ratios in determining the amount of the salesperson's raises. By comparing how much it costs each representative to bring in a dollar's worth of sales, management has another standard for evaluating the salesperson's overall effectiveness.

Although it is advantageous to have salespeople be aware of costs and responsible for controlling expenses, this approach does have drawbacks. The company can hinder the sales reps' performance by causing them to alter otherwise effective methods in order to reduce their costs. The salespeople's job is to sell, and they can't do this effectively if they are preoccupied with finding shortcuts in order to save money. Also, there are variations in territories that can cause one sales rep's expenses to be significantly higher than another's. For example, someone covering northern New Jersey would have fewer expenses than someone covering Arizona, New Mexico, and Nevada, even though total sales volume may be about the same. Because of the high concentration of people and businesses in northern New Jersey, the sales rep would not need to travel more than 60 miles in any direction to make a sales call and would probably spend very few nights in hotels. The other rep, however, would be required to travel great distances and spend many nights in hotels. Obviously, each salesperson's expense quota must be based on a realistic assessment of the territories; management cannot just automatically assign expense quotas as a percentage of sales volume.

Activity Quotas

Salespeople, especially outside representatives, generally have the freedom to plan and conduct their daily activities by themselves. In an effort to ensure that salespeople are conducting their activities conscientiously, many companies require that their salespeople meet activity quotas. These quotas are designed to control the many different activities the salesperson is responsible for. Activity quotas also serve as guidelines for younger, inexperienced sales reps, who may tend to place emphasis on the wrong activities.

The first step in setting an activity quota is to determine what the salesperson's most important activities are; these include making sales calls on customers and prospects, demonstrating products, establishing new accounts, and building displays. Before setting activity quotas, management should do research on how long it takes to perform these duties, how long it takes to travel throughout each territory, which activities should be given priority, and how much priority each activity should be given. Finally, management must set a target level of performance, usually expressed as a frequency (see Exhibit 11-2).

Activity quotas can be advantageous to both the salesperson and management. Salespeople control their activity quotas through daily planning, routing, and efficient use of time; if they plan their work carefully, they should have no trouble in meeting their daily activity obligations. Salespeople do not have such control over their sales volume quotas because external factors, such as economic conditions and competitive forces, have a strong effect on a company's sales.

Activity quotas allow management to control the salesperson's selling efforts; this should result in a more efficient and more effective sales force. They also allow management to give recognition to sales reps for performing non-selling activities and maintaining contact with infrequent customers who buy in large quantities. Finally, they serve to quickly point out lazy and time-wasting salespeople so that corrective action can be taken immediately.

One problem with activity quotas is that salespeople may not be motivated to perform their activities effectively; they may just go through the motions and not do a quality job. It is wise to use activity quotas in conjunction with sales volume quotas. Any slouching on the part of the salesperson that is not revealed by the activity quota is sure to be indicated by the sales volume quota. However, salespeople may become so preoccupied with the sales volume quota that they acquire bad habits, such as pressing for a quick sale, covering only large or existing accounts, and trying to bypass necessary stages in the selling process. For example, the salesperson may make the presentation before the prospect has been qualified; thus, the salesperson may waste time trying to sell to a person who does not have the ability to buy. Certain products may require several sales calls before a sale can be made, yet because the salesperson is anxious to reach the sales volume quota, the buyer is made to feel uncomfortable and the ne-

---

EXHIBIT 11-2

Common Types of Activity Quotas

- Number of prospects called on
- Number of demonstrations made
- Number of displays set up

- Number of service calls made
- Number of new accounts established
- Number of dealer training sessions given

gotiations are cut off early. It is for these reasons that activity quotas are generally used with salespeople who provide numerous nonselling functions.

Combination Quotas

Combination quotas are used when management wants to control the performance of both the selling and nonselling activities of the sales force. These quotas generally use points as a common measuring tool to overcome the difficulty of evaluating the different units used by the other quotas. For example, dollars are used to measure sales volume, and the number of prospects called on is used to measure activities; by converting each unit to points, the sales manager can easily measure the salesperson's overall performance. This is done by computing the percentage of quota attained for a specific quota and then multiplying this by a weight designed to show the importance management places on achieving that quota. This results in a point total for the quota. The calculation is repeated for each quota being used, and all the point totals are added together to provide a total point score for the salesperson.

This method is shown in Exhibit 11-3. The three sales reps are being evaluated on their attainment of three separate quotas: net profit, sales volume, and the number of new accounts established. Joe Freedman has the highest point

---

EXHIBIT 11-3

Combination Quotas

	Quota	Actual	% of Quota	Weight	Quota × Weight
		Salesperson: Joe Freedman			
Net profit	$ 50,000	$48,000	96	4	384
Sales volume	$100,000	$75,000	75	3	225
Number of new accounts	25	22	88	$\frac{1}{8}$	$\frac{88}{697}$
		Total score = 697/8 = 87.125			
		Salesperson: Julie Cangelosi			
Net profit	$ 80,000	$ 52,000	65	4	260
Sales volume	$125,000	$105,000	84	3	252
Number of new accounts	25	25	100	$\frac{1}{8}$	$\frac{100}{612}$
		Total score = 612/8 = 76.5			
		Salesperson: Terri Spencer			
Net profit	$50,000	$38,000	76	4	304
Sales volume	$75,000	$73,000	97	3	291
Number of new accounts	15	9	60	$\frac{1}{8}$	$\frac{60}{655}$
		Total score = 655/8 = 81.875			

total even though he had the lowest sales volume percentage of the three reps. A major reason for this is that he attained an extremely high percentage of his net-profit quota. Obviously, Freedman stressed the company's high-margin products. Julie Cangelosi did an excellent job establishing new accounts; however, the company did not assign as much importance to this quota as it did to the others. Terri Spencer came very close to attaining her full quota, but she did not do well in setting up new accounts.

This illustration points out some of the problems of combination quotas. First, combination quotas are difficult for salespeople to understand. Sales reps easily get confused about which aspects are more important than others and often put more emphasis on the less important activities. Second, salespeople have a hard time assessing their own performance and thus do not know what needs to be improved. However, by using a personal computer, salespeople can easily monitor their performance; by hooking into the company's main computer, they can get up-to-the-minute information on new orders, accounts, and prospects.

The combination quota system can also be used to evaluate the salesperson's performance in selling individual products. The salesperson may have a separate quota for each product. Management calculates the percentage of quota attainment achieved for each product, multiplies each percentage by an assigned weight (usually higher for products that have just been introduced or that have high-profit margins), and adds the points together to obtain a total point score.

ADMINISTRATION OF SALES QUOTAS

A well-thought-out quota system is ineffective unless it is properly and skillfully administered. In order for the quota system to effectively plan, control, and evaluate the sales effort, the sales force must be willing to cooperate with the system. There are salespeople who welcome the challenge of having their performance strictly monitored and measured; however, they are few and far between. Most salespeople dislike quotas. They become anxious and nervous when they are being evaluated so closely. They become very conscious of the factors and conditions that go into setting quotas, and they question anything that suggests the quotas may be unfair, inaccurate, or unattainable. Thus, management must "sell" the salespeople on the fairness and accuracy of their quotas and assure them that the quotas are reasonably attainable provided the salespeople willingly accept them and expend an honest effort.

Setting Realistic Quotas

Much of the success of a quota system, as well as the selling effort in general, is determined by motivation. The salesperson must be motivated in order to sell effectively. Proper motivation to reach a quota is determined by the attainability of that quota and the recognition or incentives that are gained from its attainment. If salespeople feel that the quota is unrealistic, they will not be motivated to attain it. And if recognition, compensation, or job security is not dependent on the quota, then the sales force is less likely to be concerned about attaining it.

In setting quotas, different companies have different theories of attainability and motivation in mind. For example, 3M believes in setting an average quota; however, the company rewards salespeople according to the percentage of quota earned. It believes that this type of system, in which rewards are given for average work, motivates the salesperson to continually work hard. Xerox, on the other hand, sets quotas very high and rewards salespeople only for performance above and beyond their quotas. Xerox believes that rewards are for those who put forth an excellent performance and that this attitude will motivate the salesperson to strive for recognition. Xerox's base salaries are much higher than those at 3M; however, 3M salespeople have a good chance to make up the difference through bonuses, whereas only the very top Xerox salespeople receive bonuses.

All quotas, in order to be accurate, must be closely related to territorial potentials. However, sound, objective executive judgment is also required. Market data must be analyzed, adjustments made wisely (both at the territorial level and the corporate level), and personnel capabilities appraised objectively in order to arrive at an accurate quota. The quota must be fair and based on market facts if the sales force is to willingly accept it. Sales managers are becoming more accurate in setting quotas with the help of computer programs like the one discussed in the following example.

PCs USED FOR SETTING QUOTAS

Developing fair and equitable quotas is an idea that has been laughed at for years. Differences between the field sales manager and the home office have always been considered to be the root of the problem.

Boardroom Planning and Consulting Group (BPCG), however, has developed a computerized sales forecasting program that allows regional sales managers to develop customized sales goals based on their corporate environment. This forecast then becomes the foundation for setting goals.

The Centerport, New York, firm bases its program on these computer-based models:

1. A set of fifty-five businesses and economic variables that can be weighted to reflect the user company's sales trends

2. A forecast of the user company's industry, adjusted by factors affecting the company

3. A set of regional models that represent the relative importance of the user company's three largest customers in each local market

One of the advantages of the program is that it allows these regional managers to do "what if" type exercises on their PCs. They can juggle different variables exclusive to their particular regions and see what the effect of each scenario is on their sales.

After the forecasts and quotas have been set, adjustments by field sales managers and corporate executives can be negotiated with the regional sales manager. The regional managers can justify their results with the figures they used, and adjustments can be made from there.

The prime benefit of this program is that it puts more quota-setting responsibility on the regional sales managers. Thus, they put a greater effort into setting their quotas. Also, it allows the regional managers to set quotas that are related to their "penetration and growth potential in local markets."[6]

Creating Understandable Quotas

The quota plan must be fully understood by the salespeople if management is to gain their cooperation and acceptance. So the quota-setting procedure must be carefully explained to them, or else they may feel that management is trying to coerce them into giving more effort without reward for it. This can lead to resentment and suspicious feelings on the part of the sales force toward management. Also, if the quota system is fully understood by the sales reps, it is more likely that they will view it as fair, accurate, and attainable. There are several ways management can help the sales force understand the quotas.

Including the salesperson in quota setting.   Management can ease the sales reps' understanding of quotas by allowing salespeople to participate in the quota-setting procedure. This not only enhances understanding but also significantly reduces questions of inaccuracy, unfairness, and unattainability. The amount of input the sales reps should have depends on their experience, the amount of information available, and the company's management philosophy.

Keeping the sales force updated.   It is important that management keep the sales force updated on its performance relative to the quotas. This reinforces the significance of the quota and allows salespeople to analyze what they are doing right and what they are doing wrong so that they can improve their performance. Supervisors must keep in close personal contact with the sales reps, for the reps often need advice and encouragement in attaining their quotas.

Maintaining control.   Management needs to maintain a maximum level of control in administering the quota system. Performance must be monitored continuously, and up-to-the-minute information gathered and analyzed. Companies are increasingly producing periodic charts to show each salesperson's progress toward his or her quota. These charts may be done weekly or monthly, and they sometimes include a ranking of the entire sales force on the basis of actual performance compared with the quota. Some managers feel this ranking creates a competitive atmosphere that will cause the poorly ranked salespeople to try harder so as not to be embarrassed. Others feel this type of approach can produce more harm than good, and they prefer to provide each sales rep with a chart monitoring his or her own progress toward the quota. One of these charts is shown in Exhibit 11-4.

EXHIBIT 11-4

Performance Evaluation Sheet

Sales Rep: *Timothy Hawkins*
Territory: *Florida*

Sales Period	Actual	Quota	% of Quota
October 1992	$ 22,765	$ 25,000	91.1
October 1991	$ 21,050	$ 19,500	107.9
Year to date: 1992	$267,567	$300,000	89.2
Projection: 1992	$321,081	$300,000	107.0

SUMMARY

A sales quota is a quantitative goal that is assigned to a marketing unit. A marketing unit may be a salesperson, territory, branch office, region, distributor, or district. Sales quotas are used to plan, control, and evaluate sales activities. More specifically, they provide goals and incentives for salespeople, evaluate their performance and control their activities, uncover the strengths and weaknesses in the selling structure, improve the compensation plan's effectiveness, control selling expenses, and enhance sales contests.

The sales volume quota is the most commonly used type of quota. Sales volume can be measured in terms of dollars or physical units. Other types of quotas set goals for net profit or gross margin, sales expenses, sales activities, or a combination of these.

There are three basic procedures for setting sales volume quotas. The simplest method is based on the marketing unit's past sales results. The quota can be established by taking last year's actual sales, or an average of several past years' sales, and adjusting the figure according to expected trends in the market.

The second method uses territorial sales potentials as its basis. The sales potential is the maximum amount that can be attained with perfect selling conditions. Since perfect selling conditions are impossible to achieve, the territorial sales potential is adjusted first by the district or branch sales manager and then by the national sales manager. The district or branch sales manager adjusts the quota to reflect the salesperson's ability, experience, and physical condition and the difficulty of covering that territory. The national sales manager adjusts the quota according to future price changes, sales promotions, and new-product offerings.

The third procedure uses an estimate of the total market to determine the company's sales potential; then individual quotas are set on the basis of this potential. There are two ways of doing this: by taking the company estimate and adjusting it or by breaking the company estimate down into territorial estimates and then adjusting them. Some companies allow the salesperson to have an input in setting his or her individual quota. The theory is that salespeople are the best judges of a territory's potential because they are closest to the market.

In order for the quota system to be successful, the quota must be realistically attainable and significance must be placed on its attainment. Also, the quota must be fairly and objectively determined. Finally, it must be easily administered and understood. This is achieved by including the salespeople in quota setting, keeping them updated periodically on their performance vis-à-vis their quota, and maintaining tight control over the entire quota system.

STUDY QUESTIONS

1. A computer, with the help of a software program, can be used to establish territories of equal potential. Is it necessary to establish equal quotas for these territories? Why or why not?

2. Can you establish a quota without a sales forecast? A sales budget? An estimate of the territory's potential?

3. A company may set two sales volume quotas. Salespeople would receive a 4 percent commission when they surpassed the "temporary quota" and an 8 percent commission when they surpassed the "assigned quota." The temporary quota would be set at 75 percent of the assigned quota. Why would a company use such an approach? Can you think of any advantages or disadvantages of this type of approach?

4. James R. Lofton Company manufactures and distributes consumer goods to all the grocery chains, small independent grocery stores, and convenience shops in the Baton Rouge, Louisiana, area. The company employs six sales reps who report to one manager in this district. Each representative has the opportunity of earning a maximum year-end bonus of $3,000 if the entire district attains 100 percent of its quota. In order to attain any bonus at all, the district must achieve at least 75 percent of quota. If 75 percent or more is reached, the percentage of quota achieved becomes the percentage earned of the maximum $3,000 bonus. For example, if the Baton Rouge district attained 96 percent of its quota, then each of the six sales reps would be entitled to a bonus of $2,880. What is your opinion of this type of arrangement? Are you in favor of a salesperson's being evaluated and rewarded on the basis of a district quota? What are the advantages or disadvantages of setting a maximum bonus level?

IN-BASKET EXERCISE

You just received a memo from your boss concerning your company's current position in the market. Over the last several years your company has slowly been losing market share, and your boss feels that your sales force has become complacent and has not been aggressive enough in the market. In fact, his remedy for the declining market share is that your salespeople should become more aggressive. Furthermore, he believes this can be accomplished by raising the quota (and compensation) for each of your salespeople!

1. How do you respond to your boss?

2. Do you agree or disagree with his remedy? Why or why not?

3. What are the positive and negative outcomes of raising quotas for your salespeople?

CASE 11-1

STYLER CHEMICAL COMPANY: TYING QUOTA AND COMPENSATION PLANS TOGETHER

In 1988, Darrell Styler left the West Star Chemical Company to start his own business in Oakland, California. Styler had been a regional sales representative for West Star in the Oakland area for more than twelve years. West Star was a major manufacturer's distributor of chemicals with three divisions: industrial, agricultural, and institutional chemicals. The primary products included herbicides, insecticides, greases, specialized lubricants, solvents, and disinfectants.

Market Opportunity

During his time as a sales rep, Styler noticed that all of his major competitors were also large-volume man-

Case prepared by Frank Notturno, Louisiana State University. Used with permission.

ufacturers' distributors and that they all competed intensely for the same large accounts. The sales representatives for these companies all maintained a few small accounts ($200 per order); however, these accounts were not aggressively marketed and were considered to be more trouble than they were worth. This attitude was common among these sales reps, even though the profit margins on both the small and large accounts were approximately the same, and the difference in selling costs was negligible.

Styler recognized these small accounts as a niche in the highly competitive consumer chemicals industry and decided to establish his own chemical distributorship in order to take advantage of the opportunity. Styler Chemical's strategy was to target the small customer (annual sales of less than $6 million) and place heavy emphasis on service. Styler felt that service was critically important, since most customers were dependent upon chemical products in their operations. Failure to provide the right product in a timely manner would result in lost sales and lost customers, as there were many substitutes and alternative sources of supply.

Implementation

In order to implement this strategy, Styler needed a supplier who would be willing to provide relatively small quantities of product on a very reliable basis. Subsequent conversations with the six major manufacturers proved unsuccessful, however, as they were unable or unwilling to carry a new distributor who would effectively be competing against their own existing distributors. Styler was able to convince four of these manufacturers to supply product on a specific-order basis at a price approximately 5 percent above the price to other distributors. This arrangement was allowed under a direct-manufacturer-distribution clause in the franchise distribution agreement.

This arrangement allowed Styler to expand product lines, as he could now offer products from four different suppliers. Furthermore, product availability was no longer a problem, since substitutions could now be made between suppliers. Styler agreed to carry a small level of inventory from each supplier which consisted primarily of samples from all product lines. Limited amounts of frequently ordered items were also inventoried. The total initial investment was $35,000. Specific customer orders were placed directly with the manufacturers, and delivery was made directly to the customer.

Trudy Watson, who had worked for West Star as a secretary, left West Star in the spring of 1989 too. She was to become Styler Chemical's office manager. Styler also convinced fifty-three of his larger accounts to come along with him. These accounts, with an average order value of approximately $1,600, included four schools, two hospitals, six banks, eight farms, and a manufacturer of plastic valves. A local bank provided the working capital for start-up expenses and initial inventory. The team rented a small office with warehouse space, and Styler Chemical Company was open for business. Watson ran the office, handling the telephone and processing orders; Styler was in the field, making customer calls and selling.

Customers

During the first year of operation, the fifty-three original customers provided the bulk of Styler's sales and were very cooperative and supportive of the new venture. Although these customers accepted increased risk by deviating from traditional sources of supply, they were very satisfied, as product selection and availability improved. Styler also offered these customers deep discounts on large-volume orders so that the final unit cost was significantly less, although doing so required that he reduce an already slim profit margin.

In Styler Chemical's first three years it grew from its original 53 customers to over 200 accounts. The original customers remain the largest-volume customers, representing almost 40 percent of annual sales. The balance of the customers are, according to plan, small, independent businesses and farmers. The standard procedure is for Styler to visit or telephone each of these customers at least once each month to estimate their needs, then order and ship the products directly to the customer. Although the terms of sale are 2/10, n/30, most customers take around 60 days to pay. Only 2 to 3 percent of all sales go past 120 days, at which time they are considered to be uncollectible. Styler has found that of his 200 active accounts, approximately 30 will place an order every week with an average order price of roughly $300.

Styler estimates that, exclusive of his large accounts, approximately 60 percent of his remaining sales originate from the commercial sector and the remaining 40 percent is split evenly between the industrial and agricultural lines. Although margins are the same across product lines and suppliers, orders generated from the industrial and agricultural segments are nearly 50 percent larger than the average order derived from the commercial segment. Although there are no specific boundaries, Styler generally considers Oakland and a 50-mile radius to be the primary market area for Styler Chemical.

Expanding the Sales Forces

Near the end of the 1990 operating year, Styler and Watson were reviewing the estimated performance of the company over the past year (see the exhibit). Business had been good, but both were tired and neither had taken a vacation since beginning the company almost three years earlier. Styler noted that the company had reached its capacity without expanding its staff in either the office or the field.

They had already planned to hire an assistant on a part-time basis to help in the office, but hiring another salesperson would be more complicated. If Styler Chemical hired someone new, it would have to decide on whether to compensate the new salesperson on a commission, straight salary, or bonus basis or combine these methods into a customized plan. Styler and Watson believed they would also have to devise some type of quota system in order to direct and evaluate the salesperson.

Styler examined the company's income statement and the industry's salary averages. He recognized that he would have to provide a recent college graduate with a compensation package totaling at least $35,000 per year in order to be competitive with the industry. This compensation package had to include either a travel allowance or a company car. In order to afford this kind of compensation, Styler figured that the new salesperson had to bring in more than $50,000 in new sales in the first year just to break even. This meant the person had to open at least ten *new* accounts per week at an average of $100 per order. Although not impossible, it certainly represented a huge challenge to an inexperienced salesperson—one that would require many hours of training and orientation between Styler and the new salesperson.

It was now up to Styler and Watson to devise a compensation plan and quota system that would best suit their needs. They agreed that Styler would devise a plan and then Watson would review it and make any necessary adjustments or devise her own plan.

Styler's plan was to pay the new salesperson a straight salary of $25,000, plus a bonus of $5,000 for attaining 100 percent of his or her annual quota. Each annual quota would be to set up 500 new accounts of at least $100 per order. The bonus allowed the new salesperson to earn $10 per new account, up to a maximum of $5,000. However, at least 350 accounts (or 70 percent of quota) must be set up in order to earn any bonus at all. Also, the new salesperson would be given a car allowance of $300 per month. Styler based these plans on his analysis of the industry's salary averages and the company's income statement.

Questions

1. What is your opinion of the way Styler devised Styler Chemical's compensation and quota plans? What do you think of his sources?

EXHIBIT

Styler Chemical Company: Financial Information 1991 (estimated)

	Amount	% of Sales
Sales	$250,000	100.0
Cost of goods sold	87,500	35.0
Gross income	162,500	65.0
Sales and administrative expenses	136,250	54.5
Earnings before interest and taxes	26,250	10.5
Interest expense	18,500	7.2
Taxable income	7,750	3.3
Tax	1,200	0.5
Net income	6,550	2.8
Depreciation	10,000	4.0
Cash flow	16,550	6.8
Sales and administrative expenses:		
Salaries: Darrell Styler	60,000	24.0
Salaries: Trudy Watson	25,000	10.0
Advertising	12,000	4.8
Rent	10,000	4.0
Depreciation	10,000	4.0
Bad debts	6,250	2.5
Insurance	5,000	2.0
Shipping	5,000	2.0
Utilities	1,500	0.6
Telephone	1,500	0.6
Total	$136,250	54.5

2. What is Styler Chemical's market potential?
3. Shouldn't he devise a quota system separate from the compensation plan, and *then* tie them together?
4. Does it make sense to pay a new salesperson $35,000 for bringing in only $50,000 in new business?
5. Is it wise for Styler to be responsible for $250,000 of business, while the new salesperson is responsible for only $50,000?
6. Should more emphasis be placed on performance by guaranteeing less money and offering a larger bonus or commission?
7. The market potential for Styler Chemical's area is $2.5 million, and its current market share is 10 percent. With the right salesperson, it should be possible to increase market share by about 6 to 8 percent! Devise your own quota system and compensation plan.
8. Styler and Watson believe they need some form of quota system to direct and evaluate the salesperson. What is your opinion on this issue?

CASE 11-2

HARRIS UNIFORMS, INC.: ESTABLISHING QUOTAS

Harris Uniforms is a privately owned sales agency specializing in athletic uniforms and supplies. The company was started in 1980 by two brothers, Ray and Bob Harris, as the exclusive representative of Star Athletic Wear in Pennsylvania and Ohio. Ray serves as president and is responsible for selling Star's athletic uniforms to retail sporting goods outlets, colleges, junior and senior high schools, middle schools, and elementary schools in eastern and central Pennsylvania. Bob is the vice president and handles western Pennsylvania and Ohio.

The company started out in the basement of Ray's home in Elizabethtown, Pennsylvania, but by the end of the first year it had moved 20 miles west to a rented office in Harrisburg. Ray's wife, Betty, handles the office duties and helps to set up sales appointments.

Star Athletic Wear manufactures uniforms for a variety of men's and women's sports, with the bulk of its sales coming from softball. Other products include hats, sweatpants and sweatshirts, coaching wear, and referees' uniforms. The sales agent's job is to promote and sell Star's products to retail outlets and schools in its specific area. Star's products are sold nationally through seventeen different sales agencies. Some of these agencies handle only Star's products and thus receive 25 percent of what they sell. Those agencies that handle several manufacturers receive only a 13 percent commission on what they sell.

Sales Cycle

Harris Uniforms' business runs in cycles. From January through March, Ray and Bob spend the vast majority of their time promoting Star's softball lines to the local retail establishments. Recreational softball is their big money-maker, considering there are approximately 16,500 such teams in Pennsylvania and Ohio and they generally buy new uniforms every year or two. Many of these retail establishments sponsor uniform "shows," where several manufacturers display their uniforms for the local teams to look at. These shows are usually put on at night during the week, and Ray and Bob must be there to answer questions the teams might have. Thus, they spend many nights away from home in motels and travel and set up displays during the day. If there is any time left, they may try to fit in a call or two at the local schools to promote their baseball and softball uniforms. However, the schools generally buy a higher grade of uniforms and use them for five to ten years.

Ray and Bob spend most of April and May in the office processing and shipping the orders from the retail outlets for softball uniforms. The ordering process itself is a cycle. The teams place their uniform orders with the retail outlet. The retail outlet usually sends several orders at a time to Harris. Harris then takes all the orders that it receives and sends a bulk order to Star Athletic Wear. Star fills the bulk order, Harris breaks it down to individual orders, and the retail outlets do any printing or silk-screening that is necessary.

Business is light for Harris Uniforms during June. Ray and Bob handle any complaints or damages that may arise, and then go back on the road in July, August, and September. During these three months, the emphasis shifts more toward the junior and senior high schools and colleges who are looking for new football, cross-country, soccer, and field hockey uniforms. Calls are still made to the retail outlets to promote uniforms for the recreational football and soccer seasons. The last three months of the year, October, November, and December, are spent in all the different schools promoting basketball uniforms. Because the schools are looking for uniforms that will last a long time, all printing for these uniforms is done by Star Athletic Wear.

Over the last several years, Ray and Bob have done quite well as representatives for Star Athletic Wear. They have gained a reputation for giving a better discount than their competitors, and Star's durability and selection have been praised by both the schools and the retail outlets. Financially, the company has done so well that Betty was able to stop working in 1989 and the in-house staff had grown to four people by May 1992.

New Markets

The Harris brothers were pleasantly surprised in October 1992, when Star Athletic Wear asked them to expand their operations to include Delaware, Maryland, Washington, D.C., Virginia, and West Virginia. Apparently, Star had had problems with Mid-Atlantic Outfitters, which represented them in those states and which had a reputation for providing poor service and not showing up for softball demonstrations and other sales appointments. Included in the deal was a $100,000 bonus and a promise that Star would provide marketing assistance if needed.

The offer appealed to Harris Uniforms because Vir-

Case prepared by Frank Notturno, Louisiana State University. Used with permission.

EXHIBIT 1

Customer Prospect Base

	Del., Md., D.C.	Ohio	Pa.	Va.	W.V.†
No. public schools	1,363	3,824	3,362	1,763	1,095
No. private schools	185	843	1,495	317	82
No. adult softball teams*	3,080	6,650	7,400	3,500	1,210
No. youth softball teams*	610	1,320	1,465	695	240

*Numbers are approximated on the basis of Star Athletic's marketing research.
†Includes western Pennsylvania.

ginia and Maryland were noted for being strong recreational softball states and because these states also contained major metropolitan areas with plenty of schools to call on. Ray and Bob accepted the offer. They then broke the total area down into five territories, as shown in Exhibit 1. Bob wanted to spend more time in the office and less time on the road, so his territory was changed to consist of western Pennsylvania and West Virginia. Ed Lynch was hired to handle Ohio, Bill McDougall was hired to cover Virginia, and Ray's son, Mark, a recent college graduate, was hired to handle Maryland, Delaware, and Washington, D.C. These new people were to be trained in the field during the month of December; Mark would be trained by Ray in eastern Pennsylvania, and Bob would train the other two reps in Ohio. Ray and Bob wanted the new reps to be fully trained and able to go out in the field on their own when the expansion took place in January 1993. They also realized that they would need an experienced marketing director to support and coordinate all the activities in the field, especially for the new reps, so they hired Tom Cerrina, who had had three years' experience in a similar capacity with another sales agency.

Quotas

One of the problems Harris Uniforms would confront was establishing quotas. Ray and Bob never used a quota system when they were the only two sales reps because they both knew that the other was giving a maximum effort. However, now that the company was about to expand and more reps had been hired, they knew that a quota system was necessary to maintain control over these sales reps and to evaluate each rep's performance.

The Harris brothers had never kept a sophisticated account of which states their sales were coming from or what type of customer was responsible for sales. Using 1991's sales figure of $1.52 million and 1992's prorated sales figure of $1.7 million (see Exhibit 2), they reasoned that Pennsylvania and Ohio should each account for approximately $1 million in 1993. They

had received a sales estimate of $2.4 million from Star Athletic Wear that represented the four additional states. This figure was derived from the projected industry sales in these states of $12 million and the expectation that Star would increase its market share from 11 percent to 20 percent under Harris Uniforms' representation. After a lengthy discussion, Ray and Bob established the quotas in the following manner: They took the $2.4 million estimate and split it evenly over the three new territories. Since western Pennsylvania was taken away from the Ohio territory and added to the West Virginia territory, Ray and Bob reasoned that approximately $200,000 should be shifted from the old Ohio–western Pennsylvania territory and added to the new western Pennsylvania–West Virginia territory. Thus, the following quotas were set:

EXHIBIT 2

Harris Uniforms, Inc.:
Financial Information, 1991–1993

	1991	1992	1993 (estimated)
Sales	$1.52M	$1.7M	$4.4M
Commissions (25%)	380,000	425,000	1.1M
Bonus	—	100,000	—
Total income	380,000	525,000	1,100,000
Sales and administrative expenses	325,000	458,200	851,000
Earnings before interest and taxes	55,000	66,800	249,000
Interest expense	18,000	22,000	44,000
Taxable income	37,000	44,800	205,000
Taxes (33.3%)	12,210	14,920	68,265
Net income	24,790	29,880	136,735

- Eastern Pennsylvania, $1 million
- Western Pennsylvania, West Virginia, $1 million
- Ohio, $800,000
- Virginia, $800,000
- Maryland, Delaware, Washington, D.C., $800,000

Ray and Bob also developed some activity quotas based on their past experience in order to provide the sales reps with the incentive of earning more money. These activity quotas were established to induce maximum effort during Harris Uniforms' heavy quarters and to offer an even distribution of incentives so that the sales reps' motivation would be high throughout the year. Since the second quarter is when the bulk of ordering is done, most of the commissions would be paid at this time. And during the fourth quarter, schools are closed for holidays and the weather makes for difficult traveling. Thus, Ray and Bob provided activity quotas specifically targeted to provide incentives for the first and third quarters. To further motivate the salespeople, Ray and Bob put themselves on the same quota system. Of course, their income was greatly boosted by the $150,000 they took as salary for being the president and vice president of the company.

Sales Contest

While on their own, Ray and Bob never established sales contests between themselves because they never realized a need to provide such an incentive. Now that they had expanded, they thought it would be necessary to introduce a sales contest as a means of providing performance incentives. They decided to offer an escape weekend for two (cost not to exceed $400) that could be won by any rep at the end of each quarter. To win, a rep had to increase the dollar level of his current-quarter sales by 5 percent over the sales of the previous quarter.

Compensation Plan

The next problem confronting Ray and Bob was establishing an effective compensation plan. They wanted the sales reps' compensation to depend directly on performance, so they decided upon a commission structure. The sales reps would be paid 18 percent of Harris Uniforms' 25 percent commission for sales in their territory. To provide a guaranteed level of income for each month, each rep was allowed to draw $2,500 per month, with excess commissions being paid quarterly. The level of excess commissions was determined by dividing the salesperson's total quota by the four quarters. Thus, Mark's quarterly quota would be $200,000 (25 percent of $800,000), of which Harris

EXHIBIT 3
Compensation Plan

Salesperson	Sales	Harris Commission*	Rep's Commission†
Mark, Ed, Bill	$ 800,000	$200,000	$36,000
Ray, Bob	$1,000,000	$250,000	$45,000
Additional bonus for 100 percent attainment (all reps)			$ 6,000
First-quarter activity quota: 60 softball demonstrations			$ 1,500
Third-quarter activity quota: 15 new school accounts			$ 1,500
Minimum compensation (Mark, Ed, Bill) for 100% attainment of all quotas = $45,000; (Ray, Bob) = $54,000			

*25% of total sales.
†18% of Harris commission.

Uniforms would receive $50,000 (25 percent of $200,000) if attained in full. Mark's commission for the quarter would amount to $9,000 (18 percent of $50,000), of which he would have already received $7,500 (3 months × $2,500) in draw. Thus, Mark's excess commission would equal $1,500 ($9,000 − $7,500) and would be paid at the end of the quarter. Exhibit 3 details the compensation for each rep for the year.

Questions

1. Ray and Bob "guesstimated" the quotas for Pennsylvania and Ohio on the basis of past experience. Where could they have found more accurate information?

2. What is your opinion of their quota system considering that they used full attainment of Star's expected sales as their measure?

3. Would you split the expected sales for the three new territories evenly without regard for population or the number of retail outlets, schools, and softball teams? What suggestions would you make to correct this practice?

4. How do you feel about having the incentives evenly distributed throughout the year?

5. Is Ray and Bob's compensation plan a good one? Would you want to work under this plan?

6. Is their sales contest plan an appropriate one? If you do not believe it is, offer suggestions for a revised plan.

7. What other recommendations would you make?

REFERENCES

1. Regina Eisman, "Setting Fair Sales Quotas," *Incentive,* September 1989, pp. 192–196.
2. Philip Kotler, *Marketing Management: Analysis, Planning, and Control,* Prentice-Hall, Englewood Cliffs, N.J., 1986.
3. "Incentive Plans for Salesmen," *Studies in Personnel Policy, No. 217,* National Industrial Conference Board, New York, 1970, pp. 27–29.
4. Thomas R. Wotruba and Michael L. Thurlow, "Sales Force Participation in Quota Setting and Sales Forecasts," *Journal of Marketing,* April 1976, pp. 11–16.
5. Leon Winer, "The Effect of Product Sales Quotas on Sales Force Productivity," *Journal of Marketing Research,* May 1973, pp. 180–183.
6. "Haworth Pegs Quotas to Local Markets," *Sales & Marketing Management,* Dec. 9, 1985, pp. 68–69.

12

COMPENSATION

LEARNING OBJECTIVES

When you finish this chapter, you should understand:

- ▲ Why many companies are unhappy with their sales force compensation programs
- ▲ Why the combination method of compensation is preferred by most sales organizations
- ▲ Different methods for controlling expense accounts
- ▲ Why selling costs are rising so rapidly
- ▲ Some of the alternatives to making personal sales calls on customers
- ▲ The major advantages and disadvantages of the different methods of sales compensation

A DAY ON THE JOB

Edwin Lewis, a sales management consultant, views compensation planning as one of the sales manager's toughest jobs. "Even seasoned managers make mistakes in setting commission rates and bonus thresholds," says Lewis. Recently, he identified several universal mistakes sales managers routinely make when developing compensation plans. "Sales managers often fail to develop or maintain a balance between salary and incentives. . . . If there's too much of a comfort level in the salary, the salesperson doesn't need to stretch to make a difficult sale," explains Lewis. Another mistake sales managers commonly make is to design the compensation plan so that it favors top producers. "Managers should try to motivate their average producers," according to Lewis. "The stars will overachieve regardless of the compensation plan. It's the average salespeople, who make up 60% of the typical sales force, who can make a real difference." Finally, Lewis believes that sales managers "often assign quotas or goals that are too high. A goal that is set too high does nothing for sales volume, because the reps don't even try to make the unrealistic goals." According to Lewis, "To succeed, a compensation program must make participants want to play and allow them to meet their objectives." Sales managers should remember, when developing a compensation plan, that salespeople like to succeed![1]

A top salesperson is usually among the highest-paid people in an organization, sometimes earning more than the president or the chief executive officer. How important are monetary rewards to a sales force? Which forms of monetary compensation can get optimal performance from a salesperson? These and other issues will be addressed in this chapter.

Successful sales managers have three primary concerns in managing the sales force: attracting outstanding salespeople, motivating them to work both effectively and efficiently, and holding on to good salespeople. Among the most important tools for accomplishing these three objectives is the organization's compensation plan. Organizations use two basic types of compensation: financial and psychological (e.g., recognition and opportunities for growth). This chapter focuses on financial compensation, including salary, incentives, and fringe benefits. Nonfinancial incentives will be discussed in Chapter 13.

THE IMPORTANCE OF FINANCIAL COMPENSATION PLANS

Despite its disparagement by some researchers,[2] monetary compensation is one of the most direct, least ambiguous ways of communicating to salespeople about their performance. Sales compensation plans can be the "steering wheel" that enables management to guide the activities of salespeople. Sales force compensation is by far the largest component of direct selling costs. In industries like construction, for example, compensation can be as high as 91 percent of total selling expenses. While compensation does vary considerably across industries, on the average compensation represents approximately 79 percent of selling costs, with travel and entertainment accounting for about 11 percent and automobile outlays about 10 percent.[3] There are three basic methods of financial compensation:

1. *Straight salary.* The person receives a fixed amount of money at fixed intervals, such as weekly or monthly.

2. *Straight commission.* The person receives an amount that varies with results, usually sales or profits.

3. *Combination.* The person receives a mix of salary, commission, and/or bonus.

Depending upon the situation, any of the above methods may be appropriate.

    Compared with other occupations, it could very well be that salespeople respond in a unique way to monetary rewards. Companies have found that in order to retain top performers, they must provide a competitive compensation package. This is indicated by a recent survey that asked participants, "What are the most effective factors in encouraging a valuable employee to stay with your company?" The participants were vice presidents and personnel directors of 100 of the largest 1,000 corporations in the nation. The answer to this important question? Fully 42 percent of the participants replied, "More money."[4] Nick DiBari feels that salespeople do respond uniquely to financial rewards. DiBari maintains an impressive track record in sales; he has been the number-one earner for five consecutive annual compensation surveys conducted by *Sales & Marketing Management.* (In a recent year, his annual compensation exceeded $1.5 million.) According to DiBari, most salespeople are "crusaders, builders, and competitors." They want and need to make a difference in whatever they are involved in. These people see financial compensation as a way of "keeping score" among their peers. They are, understandably, highly motivated by their "scorecard" (the paycheck).[5] Realistically, it can be concluded that money is an effective incentive for some people at different earning levels but perhaps is not very effective for other people.

    In investigating the effect of various compensation plans on company profits, Darmon identified several types of salespeople. There are those who are:

- *Creatures of habit.* They try to maintain their standard of living by earning a predetermined amount of money.

- *Goal-oriented individuals.* They prefer recognition as achievers by peers and by superiors and tend to be sales quota–oriented, with money serving mainly as a by-product of achievement.

- *Satisfiers.* They perform just well enough to keep their jobs.

- *Trade-offers.* They allocate their time according to a personally determined ratio of work and leisure that is not influenced by opportunities for increased earnings.

- *Money-oriented individuals.* They seek to maximize their earnings. These people may sacrifice family relationships, personal pleasures, and even health to increase their income.[6]

Although this classic study was conducted during the late 1970s, discussions with numerous sales managers and salespeople in the field suggest that these classifications still hold true in today's sales environment.[7]

The sales manager must identify these basic types of salespeople and design a compensation package that will maximize total sales force efforts. Salespeople may be viewed as "internal consumers" of management's compensation package, and the relationship between profits and sales force satisfaction is analogous to that between profits and buyer satisfaction.

Developing a compensation plan that will satisfy all salespeople is next to impossible. Research indicates that there is no one best plan for any one organization or industry. Perhaps, then, the best that can be hoped for is to develop a plan that will satisfy the majority of the sales force while not totally alienating the remainder.

If people are not satisfied with a compensation plan, why aren't they changing it? There are several reasons for this inaction:

- The plan is entrenched in industry tradition.
- It is often difficult to assign credit when various salespeople, sales offices, or departments participate in the sale.
- There are complex financial or product-line considerations.
- There may be a failure to recognize that an appropriate compensation plan can improve profits.
- Sales managers may fear that the new plan will be worse than the present one.

However, many firms do change their compensation plans. Also, new firms must devise compensation plans before hiring salespeople. When new plans are developed or existing ones revised, a logical process should be followed. A proposed approach is discussed in the next section.

DEVELOPING THE COMPENSATION PLAN

There are seven distinct steps in the process of developing a compensation plan:

1. Prepare job descriptions.
2. Establish specific objectives.
3. Determine general levels of compensation.
4. Develop the compensation mix.
5. Pretest the plan.
6. Administer the plan.
7. Evaluate the plan.

If any of these steps is skipped or poorly executed, the compensation plan has little hope of being as effective as it should be in motivating the sales force.

Preparing Job Descriptions

Detailed, meaningful job descriptions are needed before a compensation plan can be adequately developed. Responsibilities and performance criteria are required for every sales position. These job descriptions should be systematically compared to other sales positions in terms of their importance to the organization. Jobs of approximately equal value are assigned to a particular grade or level. For example, in the federal government, all jobs under civil service have been described, evaluated, and categorized vertically into grades ranging from GS-1, the lowest, to GS-18, the highest. On a horizontal basis, at any one civil service grade, say, GS-14, there are different jobs, such as contract administrator or accounting supervisor. The U.S. Bureau of Labor Statistics conducts national surveys every March to adjust the GS pay levels relative to private industry. Many companies also classify their sales positions by levels of responsibility.

Sales positions typically vary on both vertical and horizontal levels. Vertical positions may be sales trainee, sales representative, and senior sales representative. Horizontal jobs may be missionary salespeople or regular salespeople. Each position, on both the vertical and horizontal scales, needs a separate job description for assignment of a minimum starting salary and a maximum salary, often determined by surveys of what other organizations are paying.

Establishing Specific Objectives

Compensation plans are designed to achieve certain organizational objectives, for example, improving market share, increasing profit margins, introducing new products or services, winning new accounts, or reducing selling costs. Surprisingly, an "extraordinary number of American companies use sales compensation plans that are inconsistent with their marketing goals," according to the results of a recently published survey. Forty-eight percent of the companies surveyed reported that their sales compensation plans are revised annually, even though their corporate goals and objectives stay the same for several years. From these findings, it is obvious that sales managers are having a very difficult time trying to bring their compensation plans in line with organizational objectives. In fact, more than 50 percent of the companies surveyed expressed this difficulty.[8]

The results of the survey are dramatic because they belie the vaunted U.S. reputation for the application of highly sophisticated sales and marketing techniques. Furthermore, the findings are rather puzzling, since it appears that the procedure for establishing organizational goals that are consistent with compensation goals is relatively straightforward. Ready availability of sales data means that the productivity of salespeople is more easily measured than that of most other types of employees. Moreover, achievement of organizational objectives may also be measured, even when few sales are being made. For example, the number of sales presentations made to customers may be an important objective for making potential buyers aware of company offerings. Another

objective might be the conversion ratio (orders as a percentage of sales presentations). Low conversion rates may indicate a large number of permanently
turned-off potential buyers; hence, sales to these customers may be even more
difficult for future sales reps. This perspective sees potential customers as scarce
resources that can be irretrievably lost if not properly cultivated.

Any compensation plan may have several objectives, depending upon the
needs of the specific company, sales manager, or salesperson. From the company's vantage point, the plan should stress:

- *Control.* Sales managers prefer a plan that allows maximum control over how
  salespeople allocate their time.

- *Economy.* Sales managers want a plan that offers a desirable balance between
  sales costs and sales results.

- *Motivation.* Sales managers want a plan that can motivate their salespeople
  to optimal performance.

- *Simplicity.* Sales managers like a plan that is simple to administer, easily
  explainable to salespeople, and sufficiently flexible to ensure timely adjustments to changing market conditions and organizational goals.

From the standpoint of sales representatives, the compensation plan should offer:

- *Income regularity.* Salespeople want to be protected from drastic fluctuations
  in income so that regular monthly expenses for home mortgage, food, and
  utilities can be paid without hardship.

- *Reward for superior performance.* Salespeople like compensation in direct relation to the amount of effort expended and the results obtained. Superior
  performance should reap superior rewards.

- *Fairness.* Salespeople want their earnings to be equitable in terms of their
  experience and ability, the pay of coworkers, competitor's sales reps, and the
  cost of living.[9]

It is not easy for a single compensation plan to achieve all these objectives,
especially since some objectives, such as economy and income regularity, tend
to conflict.

Because of the diversity of marketing situations and objectives among organizations, a wide variety of compensation plans are used across industries,
ranging from simplistic to complex. Regardless of the sophistication of the plan,
it is important for sales force morale that sales reps be able to calculate their
own expected earnings over a given pay period to facilitate their personal financial planning.

Determining General Levels of Compensation

It is generally agreed that companies and industries with low average levels of
compensation tend to suffer high turnover rates. Therefore, it is necessary that

the general level of compensation be sufficiently competitive to attract and retain competent salespeople.

Several factors determine the basic level of pay for a sales force. The most significant ones are (1) the skills, experience, and education required to do the work successfully; (2) the level of income for comparable jobs in the company; and (3) the level of income for comparable jobs in the industry (that is, the competitive environment). The importance of each of these factors will vary from one situation to another.

One approach to establishing general pay levels for sales positions is to assign numerical values to each job requirement. For instance, previous experience in sales might be rated high for a particular sales job (say, 8 on a scale of 1 to 10), and a college major in marketing may receive a value of 6. For another selling job, past experience may be worth only 4. Point values for all requirements can be summed to compare the importance of different sales jobs within and outside the organization. From this analysis, a rank order of jobs may be obtained and a range of basic income assigned to each level, as shown in the simple example in Exhibit 12-1.

Usually, there is some overlap in salaries among the different job rankings in order to allow for growth within each position on the basis of the individual's experience, skills, and performance. In civil service positions, a GS-14 may be paid anywhere from $44,430 to $57,759 (1986 figures), depending upon the individual's position in that grade level. Similarly, in one sample of seven firms salaries of sales representatives with three to five years' experience and a college degree ranged from $27,000 to $62,700 annually.

Living costs.   Beyond the general level of compensation, any plan should be sufficiently flexible to adjust to area living costs. *Sales & Marketing Management* publishes an annual "Survey of Selling Costs," which identifies living costs by selected metropolitan area. Sales managers can use this to help establish the level of compensation for particular areas.

EXHIBIT 12-1

Sales Position Analysis

Job requirements Total numerical values	Experience 10	Education 6	Test scores 10	Total possible score 26
	Minimum Scores Required			
Sales Position	**Experience**	**Education**	**Test Scores**	**Position Totals**	**Pay Range**
Sales trainee	4	3	3	10	$20,000–$26,000
Sales representative	6	4	6	16	$24,000–$40,000
Senior sales representative	8	4	8	20	$36,000–$60,000

Earnings ceilings.   Should there be a ceiling on what an outstanding sales representative can earn? More specifically, should salespeople be able to earn more than their bosses? Although there are arguments on both sides of the issue, the answer depends on circumstances and management philosophies. Where ceilings are placed on earnings, management must set reasonable sales quotas to avoid discouraging the sales force. In many progressive companies, no limits are placed on a salesperson's earnings as long as selling costs are kept within acceptable limits. For example, James B. Horton, president and chief executive officer of Hall Publications, Inc., is a strong advocate of no ceilings on the salaries of sales representatives. When Horton was publisher of *Psychology Today,* an ad salesman made the most money in the company, the sales manager made the second most, and Horton made the third most. Horton thought this was excellent. "All I wished was that I had five more salesmen like that. . . . As the guy sells more, he gets more commission. Because of the salary component of the structure, my sales cost per page came down."[10]

Developing the Compensation Mix

Most contemporary sales organizations have found that a compensation mix of salary, commission, and/or bonus is more effective in achieving objectives and goals than salary or commission alone. Essential in this mix is the relationship between the regular salary and incentive pay.

Costs for alternative compensation mixes.   Sales managers need to consider the costs of alternative compensation mixes before drawing up a compensation plan. Generally, it can be said that straight-commission plans are most efficient at lower levels of sales volume, while the straight-salary plan is least expensive at higher levels. Recognizing this, companies often shift from commissioned sales agents to salaried salespeople once sales volume has reached the critical level.

Exhibit 12-2 illustrates, by means of a hypothetical example, the impact on costs of alternative compensation mixes for three salespeople. At the lower sales volumes, the straight-commission plan is the most cost-efficient. At the highest sales volume, however, straight salary is preferable. Salary plus commission is most efficient at a slightly lower sales volume. Each compensation plan ought to be evaluated in view of the alternatives at different sales levels.

In considering the breakdown of salary and incentives, sales managers must decide what degree of control is needed over the sales force activities, what amount of incentive is required to reach objectives and goals, and what total costs will be with different compensation mixes. After answering these questions, managers must decide what proportion of each salesperson's total income should be earned through incentives and whether the incentive pay schedule should be fixed, regressive, or progressive.

Proportion for salary.   Salaries should enable salespeople to meet everyday living expenses while encouraging them to perform tasks that are not directly measurable by sales, such as servicing customer accounts. However, the salary should not be so high as to make the salesperson complacent or content with it alone. In most plans, about 70 to 80 percent of the salesperson's total income is fixed.

EXHIBIT 12-2

Comparison of Costs for Alternative Compensation Mixes

Salespeople	Compensation Method
Andrews	Straight commission (10%) of $ sales
Baker	Straight salary ($2,500/month)
Cunningham	Salary plus commission ($1,200/month + 5% of $ sales)

Sales Volumes	Compensation Costs		Cost to Sales Ratio, %
$10,000	Andrews	$1,000	10.0
	Baker	2,500	25.0
	Cunningham	1,700	17.0
15,000	Andrews	$1,500	10.0
	Baker	2,500	16.7
	Cunningham	1,950	13.0
20,000	Andrews	$2,000	10.0
	Baker	2,500	12.5
	Cunningham	2,200	11.0
25,000	Andrews	$2,500	10.0
	Baker	2,500	10.0
	Cunningham	2,450	9.8
30,000	Andrews	$3,000	10.0
	Baker	2,500	8.3
	Cunningham	2,700	9.0

Proportion for incentives.   Commission and bonus are the incentive parts of the compensation plan, and they typically depend upon the salesperson's attaining some predetermined sales quota. A recent survey indicated that incentives were about 15 to 20 percent of base salary for salespeople at consumer products companies and about 20 to 25 percent of base for reps at industrial products companies. However, for salespeople in business services, incentive pay was as high as 50 to 70 percent over base.[11]

Fixed, progressive, or regressive incentives.   Fixed commission or bonus rates are the easiest to compute, but they do not offer salespeople much incentive for seeking higher, increasingly more difficult levels of sales. Progressive rates, which increase the percentage of commission or bonus awarded as sales volume rises, are best when profit margins climb significantly after the break-even point is reached. Conversely, regressive incentives decline as sales increase: for example, 6 percent for all sales up to 1,000 units, 4 percent for all sales from 1,000 to 1,500 units, and 2 percent for all sales over 1,500 units. Regressive commission rates are usually used if there is a high probability of windfall sales and a propensity to overload customer inventories. In choosing among fixed, progressive, or regressive commission plans, sales managers need to estimate the effect on overall profits under the separate proposals.

Splitting commissions.   A special administrative problem for sales managers is how to split commissions when two or more people are involved in a sale. For example, a key-account sales rep may call on the customer's headquarters, while other salespeople call on the customer's branch offices. Because disagreements may develop afterward as to who is most responsible for the sale, management should decide in advance how commissions will be divided.

Types of incentives.   There are a host of fringe benefits that companies may consider using to reward high-performing executives (see Exhibit 12-3). Although most are reserved for top-level management, fringes such as a company car and stock options are frequently made available to the sales force.[12] Others such as club memberships are often given to salespeople to entertain customers. In 1978, Congress limited some tax deductions that companies could claim for "entertainment facilities," such as yachts, resorts, and hunting lodges, but business-related entertainment expenses are still legitimate tax deductions, no matter where the function is held.

   Stock options.   To retain top-quality people, sales organizations may offer stock options in proportion to the salesperson's productivity. A *stock option* is simply a chance (option) to purchase stock in the company at some future date at a preset price—usually lower than the prevailing market value. If the shares rise in price, the individual may buy them at the lower, preset price, sell them at a profit, and pay tax on the profit. When the price of the firm's stock is climbing, salespeople and managers may be reluctant to leave without exercising the options available at some future date. If stock options are awarded according to productivity, the company's hold on top performers increases. Some com-

EXHIBIT 12-3

Types of Fringe Benefits

Fringe Benefit	Percentage of Companies Offering	
	CEO	COO
Company car	77	69
Supplemental life insurance	54	49
Tax-return preparation	46	32
Supplemental medical insurance	34	32
Personal-tax and financial planning	28	14
Low- or no-interest loans	17	14
Deferred compensation	15	13
Supplemental retirement benefits	13	12
First-class air travel	9	6
Relocation allowance	5	6

Source: Jill Andresky Frazer, "1990 Executive-Compensation Survey," *Inc.*, November 1990, p. 64.

panies allow salespeople to make contributions, which the companies match, to a special equity fund for each sales order. When salespeople leave, their own contributions are returned but they forfeit the company's contributions. These types of incentives are called "golden handcuffs," since they tend to hold people to a company. The following example explains how stock options work.

> Ruth Bronsen, a top-notch sales manager for an office equipment manufacturer, earns approximately $80,000 annually in salary and bonus. In an effort to secure her services, a competitor offers the same salary plus a stock option. If Bronsen accepts the competitor's offer, she will receive an official statement granting her the right to buy 3,000 shares of the company's stock at $10 at some future date (when the market price is expected to be higher), usually two or three years hence so that management can evaluate her performance before she obtains windfall profits on the stock option. Because some companies have terminated an executive prior to the required waiting time for exercising the stock option, many executives now insist upon an employment contract that extends beyond the exercise date of the stock option.

Alternative stock plans.   When the stock market is not performing well, companies try other approaches, such as stock-appreciation rights or performance-unit plans. Under the stock-appreciation approach, the executive receives cash or stock equal to the gain possible by exercising a stock option without having to come up with the money to purchase the stock. Top-performing individuals, such as Lee Iacocca (Chrysler Corporation), John Sculley (Apple Computer), and Ochs Sulzberger (*The New York Times*) have been known to make nearly $1 million in a single year from stock-appreciation rights alone.

Performance-unit plans give managers cash or stock when they achieve long-range goals, such as increasing company profits by a certain annual percentage. Again, top-performing individuals are able to supplement their salaries greatly with this type of plan. Sales managers must work closely with corporate personnel experts to discover new ways of attracting and keeping top-performing salespeople.

Pretesting the Plan

Any compensation plan must be pretested and evaluated before being adopted. To identify the probable impact on profits, the sales and potential earnings (under the new plan) for each salesperson over the past several years should be computed. Pretesting the proposed compensation plan can be carried out in one or more sales divisions for a time sufficiently long to evaluate its effect on achievement of organizational objectives. If the limited trial is successful, then the plan can be implemented throughout the sales force. Finally, because people often resist change, it is critical that any proposed new plan be developed, approved, and implemented through committees of key affected employees.

Administering the Plan

A compensation plan should be fair, easy to understand, simple to calculate, and flexible. As market conditions and organizational objectives change, the compensation plan may need to be altered.

Sales are not always a fair or adequate measure of a salesperson's contribution. In times of product and service shortages, for example, equitable allocation of available supplies to satisfy customers may become the company's major short-run objective. In general, the increasing demands on salespeople to perform nonselling activities have required reevaluation of basic compensation plans. The fact that only 32 percent of the salesperson's time is spent on face-to-face selling clearly demonstrates the need for planning and time management and a compensation plan that reinforces this need.

In administering the compensation plan, most sales managers feel that peer pay should not be disclosed to the sales force. Pay experts generally fear that greater salary disclosure would lead salespeople to demand justification for pay changes and would increase friction and jealousy among employees. So, most firms limit information to expected scheduling of raises and, perhaps, the likely range of pay in certain job categories. But it is also possible that lack of pay information may have a negative effect on employee performance and satisfaction. This occurs because pay secrecy prevents people from judging their progress in relative terms. Research has supported the position that greater disclosure can have a positive impact on performance, satisfaction with pay, and acceptance of company promotional policies. One warning, though: Salespeople seem to become less satisfied (at least initially) with their superiors after implementation of open pay policies. Also, organizations not capable of objectively measuring performance are likely to have difficulty with an open pay system.

Evaluating the Plan

Before being set in concrete, even for a relatively short period, the compensation plan should be thoroughly evaluated with regard to the sales managers' goals of attracting desirable people, keeping them, and motivating them to achieve organizational goals. Once established, the compensation plan must be continually reviewed and evaluated to determine its ongoing effectiveness. Such a review can be conducted on a quarterly, semiannual, or annual basis.

ADVANTAGES AND DISADVANTAGES OF DIFFERENT COMPENSATION METHODS

In the next several pages, we review the advantages and disadvantages of various compensation methods under changing market conditions and different sales objectives.

Straight Salary

Even though sales recruits will often claim that compensation level is far more important to them than compensation method, many will reject any plan that creates wide variability in their income. These security-oriented people prefer a base salary or drawing account so that they can depend on some regular income to meet basic living expenses. This becomes even more important when sales are infrequent and seasonal.

Straight salary is most appropriate in the following situations:

- *Team selling situations.* Several people—for example, a coordinating salesperson, a technical engineer, a marketing service representative, and a member of marketing management—cooperate as a team in making a sale. IBM incorporates this approach in selling computer systems.

- *Long negotiating periods.* A year or more may be needed to make a complex sale of a system of products and services. This could also apply to big-ticket items, such as private-jet sales.

- *Mixed promotional situations.* Advertising sometimes plays a vital role in selling, and the relationship between a salesperson's efforts and advertising may be difficult to evaluate. This situation would also apply to "inside-outside" sales forces.

- *Learning periods.* During the first year, a salary is usually required to attract new recruits into selling and to compensate the trainee at least until commissions are large enough to provide an adequate living standard.

- *Missionary selling.* These are nonselling jobs, such as developing goodwill among customers by providing them with advice, service, and assistance in merchandising (setting up displays or developing local advertisements). Other examples would be public relations efforts conducted by not-for-profit organizations such as hospitals, museums, or government agencies.

- *Special conditions.* Special activities include introducing a new line of products, opening up new territories, calling on new customer accounts, or selling in unusual market conditions. The rapidly rising gasoline prices during the 1990s would be an example of an unusual market condition.

At Xerox Corporation, district managers are expected to be in tune with any unusual conditions in the marketplace in order to make adjustments in the compensation plan for sales force personnel. For instance, individuals within the sales force (who are directly affected by an unusual market condition) have the option of switching from a combination compensation plan to a 100 percent straight-salary plan. This plan is offered to sales force personnel to avoid instability of income and to promote satisfaction with the compensation plan in general. Additionally, Xerox Corporation conducts evaluations of its compensation plans on a quarterly basis to ensure timely responses to the needs of the sales force and to monitor any changes in the environment.[13]

Since earnings under a straight-salary method are independent of any productivity measures such as sales, profits, sales calls, or presentations, this method provides salespeople with the security of a precise income. From the managerial perspective, the chief advantage of the straight-salary plan is that the salespeople's activities can be directed toward company objectives. Many successful companies pay their salespeople on a straight-salary basis. Generally, a professional and technical, rather than a marketing, orientation underlies the company's value system.[14] For this reason, straight-salary plans are widespread in the aerospace, petroleum, and chemical industries, where service and engineering skills are particularly important to customers. In these industries, salespeople are more likely to think of themselves as consultants or engineers and often do not even carry the title "sales representative." Under a straight-salary plan, high productivity can be rewarded by annual salary increases. Overall, the straight-salary method of compensation has these advantages and disadvantages:

Advantages

- Provides security to salespeople, since they know their basic living expenses will be covered.
- Helps develop a sense of loyalty to the company.
- Increases flexibility in territorial assignments because salespeople are less likely to become attached to certain sales territories and customers.
- Gives a higher degree of control over salespeople's activities.
- Permits rapid adaptation of sales force efforts to changing market demands and company objectives.
- Is simple to administer.

Disadvantages

- Provides no financial incentive to put forth extra effort.
- May increase selling costs because salaries go on when sales are not being made.
- Often leads to income inequities, since the least productive salespeople tend to be overpaid, and the most productive underpaid.
- Leads to adequate, but not superior, performance.

Straight Commission

Straight-commission plans provide strong incentives rather than security, and they tend to result in higher productivity and earning levels for salespeople than do salary-based commission plans in similar organizations. Straight-commission plans are likely to be used in industries such as real estate, furniture sales, door-to-door sales, or party-based sales (such as Mary Kay Cosmetics or Tupperware).

Commissions are paid only for measurable achievements (usually sales volume), so straight-commission plans offer rewards and risks much like those assumed by independent entrepreneurs. When compensated by straight commissions, less productive salespeople eventually resign, whereas under a guaranteed salary the sales manager would usually have to fire them.

Application of commission plans requires the sales manager to decide:

1. The base, or unit, upon which the commissions will be paid (dollar sales, units sold, or gross profits)

2. The rate to be paid per unit (usually expressed as a percentage of sales or gross profit)

3. The point at which commissions start (after selling the first unit or after reaching a sales quota)

4. The time when the commissions are paid (when the order is obtained, when it is shipped, or when it is paid for)

If salespeople are not paid their commission until the order is shipped, they will likely pressure plant managers to ship promptly. This means customer relations are being improved at the same time that salespeople are looking out for themselves.

Companies without large working capital often use commissions as a method of keeping selling costs directly related to sales. Some companies prefer to use part-time salespeople or independent manufacturers' reps on straight commissions to avoid the administrative costs associated with collecting federal social security taxes, unemployment taxes, and income taxes. Whenever the company is not very concerned about service or the development of long-term customer relationships, commissions are an effective way to obtain high sales. High commissions on sales are often criticized for promoting unethical selling practices, as illustrated by the *Ethics* scenario below.

Profitability.   Though commissions ought to be related to profits, management is often reluctant to reveal profit margins to salespeople for fear that they may quit and take the information to competitors. Yet it is desirable for salespeople to be able to compute their expected income. One approach to solving this dilemma is to divide products into profit groups and assign a different commission rate to each group.

Drawing accounts.   Commission plans may include a *draw*, which is a sum of money paid against future commissions. A *guaranteed draw* is one that does not

---

ETHICS IN SALES MANAGEMENT: THE COMMISSION OR THE CONSUMER?

You were recently hired as a sales manager for a successful financial-services firm, and you are beginning to question the company's compensation plan. The salespeople are compensated on a salary-plus-commission basis. However, after a salesperson reaches a certain level of sales, commissions can be as high as 60 percent of annual income. This high rate of commission, along with the fact that your company offers over 100 different services to its customers, may be creating a situation that is a little unfair to your customers. In fact, after only a month on the job, you've already received several calls from customers who've said that "your salespeople tend to be a little aggressive" and that the sales reps confuse them into "buying more services than are needed." You discuss this with one of your top salespeople, and he basically downplays the issue, stating: "With our compensation system, selling only a little extra service to each customer can mean the difference between earning $100,000 and $50,000 a year. And selling our customers a little extra service isn't really hurting them at all. In fact, everyone benefits!"

1. Is this salesperson acting in an unethical manner? Why or why not?
2. Should your company's compensation plan be changed? Why or why not?

have to be repaid by the salesperson if insufficient commissions are earned. Thus, it acts like a salary but is lower than a straight salary would be. Commissions may be paid under varying conditions and times. Salespeople may receive commissions on all orders written, accepted, shipped, or paid for during a given period.

A draw, or advance, against future commissions is one way of giving salespeople the security of a fixed income while providing them with an incentive for greater productivity. As indicated in Exhibit 12-4, a salesperson may receive a weekly draw of $300, with 10 percent commission on all sales. Note that this sales rep's balance was negative until the seventh week, when sales volume reached a high enough level for total commissions earned to exceed the total draw against commissions. Throughout these first seven weeks, however, the sales rep enjoyed the security of a fixed $300 income. With the high positive balance, the salesperson might reasonably request an increase in the draw. Generally, management's objective is to set the draw high enough to offer the needed security but low enough to prevent large overdraws. Some sales managers put upper limits on permissible draws.

If a salesperson's balance is negative at the end of the quarter, it is usually carried over to the next quarter. If such a situation continues, however, the company should consider reducing the draw amount or switching the sales rep to straight commission. In cases in which a salesperson leaves with a negative balance on the statement, legal precedence does not call for the terminated employee to repay the draw. Some companies use a negative commission system to control a sales rep's efforts. For example, if a customer terminated a machine lease, the sales rep assigned to that particular account would lose the original commission paid when the machine was placed. This type of policy helps ensure

EXHIBIT 12-4

Salesperson's Earnings Statement for a Weekly $300 Draw with 10 Percent Commission

Week	Sales Volume	Earned Commissions	Weekly Draw	Balance
1	0	0	$ 300	− $ 300
2	$ 1,000	$ 100	300	− 500
3	2,000	200	300	− 600
4	4,000	400	300	− 500
5	6,000	600	300	− 200
6	3,000	300	300	− 200
7	8,000	800	300	+ 300
8	5,500	550	300	+ 550
9	7,000	700	300	+ 950
10	2,500	250	300	+ 900
11	6,000	600	300	+ 1,200
12	5,000	500	300	+ 1,400
13	2,000	200	300	+ 1,300
Totals	$52,000	$5,200	$3,900	+ $1,300

that sales reps do not neglect present or long-term customers. Many experts believe that if a sales manager has a sales force with a large amount of pay at risk and more than 20 percent variation in pay from month to month, he or she should very seriously consider whether the benefits of the draw program outweigh its negative points.[15]

Advantages and disadvantages of straight-commission plans include these:

Advantages

- Income is directly related to productivity.
- Commission is easy to calculate, so salespeople may keep track of their earnings.
- There is no ceiling on potential earnings.
- Money is not tied up in salaries, because commissions are paid only when revenues are generated.
- Costs are proportional to sales.
- Salespeople have maximum work freedom.
- Poorly performing salespeople eliminate themselves by quitting.
- Income is based strictly on accomplishments, not on subjective evaluations by sales managers.

Disadvantages

- Excessive emphasis may be placed on sales volume rather than profitable sales.
- Salespeople have little loyalty to the company.
- Because of extreme fluctuations in earnings, such plans create uncertainty for many salespeople about meeting daily living expenses for their families.
- There may be high sales force turnover rates when business conditions are slow.
- Nonselling activities (service, missionary sales, displays, etc.) are neglected.
- Salespeople may overload customers with inventory, thereby straining long-term customer relationships.
- Windfall earnings may come about under good business conditions, which may be disturbing to sales management.
- Flexibility to split territories or transfer salespeople is diminished because of limited means of control over the sales force.
- Sales managers may become perfunctory in recruiting, selecting, and supervising, since they may consider marginal salespeople acceptable under this compensation plan.

Bonus compensation plans. These plans provide a lump sum of money or stock for some exceptional performance, such as making quota, obtaining a new customer account, or selling a desired product mix. Bonuses may be paid for individual performances or group achievements, and they can be given in the current period, distributed over several time periods, or deferred until after retirement, when the executive is earning less money and will pay less tax. In general, most companies pay salespeople incentive earnings annually. However, there are some companies that pay incentive earnings on a semiannual, quarterly, or monthly basis. It is usually best for bonuses to be paid as soon as possible after being earned so that there is positive reinforcement of the desired salesperson behavior. If paid annually or semiannually, a bonus tends to lose its effectiveness in stimulating superior performance. Additionally, bonuses should not routinely be allocated on an equal basis to all members of a team that achieve a certain goal. They should be allocated according to individual contributions to the goal achievement so that marginal contributors are not rewarded equally with high producers. Probably the major advantage of bonus plans is their flexibility in quickly adapting individual and group efforts toward changing organizational objectives.

Combination Compensation Plans

Combination compensation plans combine two or three of the basic compensation methods. Commissions and bonuses are usually employed to achieve volume or profit goals, while salary helps attain less quantifiable goals, such as customer service, expense control, and long-run sales development. Combination plans are the most widely used of all compensation methods. A recent study revealed that 92 percent of the companies surveyed used a combination compensation plan: 46 percent paid a salary and a bonus, and another 46 percent paid a salary and a commission; 3 percent paid on a commission-only basis, and 5 percent paid only on a salary basis.[16]

The critical factor in a combination compensation plan is the selection of a target salary-and-incentive mix. The process is not an aribtrary one. What is needed is a salary that is high enough to attract talent and an incentive sufficient to motivate. The sales manager needs to be familiar with the competitive compensation environment and the amount of incentive that will motivate the sales force, given the nature of the sales job. The compensation leverage ratio varies widely; but it is generally somewhere between 70 to 80 percent salary and 20 to 30 percent incentive.[17]

No compensation plan will fit all situations. Combination compensation plans, however, are the most flexible of all approaches. These are some combination compensation plans that fit a variety of conditions:

- *Salary plus commissions.* This is best when management wants to get high sales without sacrificing customer service. It is good for new salespeople, since it provides more security than straight commission.
- *Salary plus bonus.* This combination is best for achieving long-run objectives, such as selling large installations or product systems or achieving a desired customer mix.

- *Salary plus commission plus bonus.* This is best for seasonal sales, when there are frequent inventory imbalances and when management wants to focus on certain products or customers.

- *Commission plus bonus.* This is usually applied to group efforts, in which some salespeople call on central buyers or buying committees while others call on store managers.

The main advantages and disadvantages of a combination compensation plan are as follows:

Advantages

- Provides the greatest flexibility and control over salespeople, in that all desirable activities can be rewarded
- Provides security plus incentive
- Allows frequent, immediate reinforcement of desired sales behavior

Disadvantages

- Can be complex and misunderstood
- Can be expensive to administer, particularly if not computerized
- May fail to achieve management objectives if not carefully conceived

TRENDS IN SALES COMPENSATION

Many changes have occurred recently concerning salesperson compensation, and these changes are expected to continue throughout the 1990s. The recent trends in sales compensation include:

- Signs of sales compensation compression
- An increase in flexible compensation plans
- An increased emphasis on international sales compensation

Sales Compensation Compression

A great deal of attention has recently focused on the range of salaries across industries. Not all salespeople are alike. Every company has top performers as well as a host of average performers. Yet a recent survey of over 120 companies concluded that there are definite signs of sales compensation compression in consumer and industrial products companies. The range of compensation is growing narrower as the compensation levels of top performers are being kept closer to the overall average. The survey also suggested that while companies may pay lip service to the idea of pay for performance, compensation levels for salespeople are becoming more alike, more homogeneous, whether the salesperson is a star performer or just an average one.[18] The real issue here is how compression might affect the top sales performers. Sales managers should consider the implications of this trend and determine how it may influence the motivations of the sales force.

Flexible Compensation Plans

Companies are definitely adopting more and more flexible compensation plans for their salespeople. Many sales compensation plans fail because they do not simultaneously address sales force concerns and the business objectives of management.[19] Many firms today are attempting to work more with their salespeople regarding compensation and, at the same time, to meet the firm's business objectives of not increasing costs, losing control, and so on. For example, a Canadian company recently offered its salespeople an annual choice of four different compensation mix options, ranging from 100 percent commission to 25 percent commission and 75 percent salary. Other companies are working with salespeople to establish certain quota levels that the salesperson is comfortable with. Compensation is then tied to the quota level selected. By offering the salespeople a choice of salary and incentive mixes, firms can better reach their goals of reducing turnover and keeping morale high. This approach also meets the sales force's needs by offering alternative plans for different experience levels and personalities.

International Sales Compensation

As more and more U.S. firms enter international markets, they are being confronted with a range of circumstances that require them to adjust their sales compensation plans.[20] For example, in the Far East, sales volume is the primary indicator of success. Therefore, compensation is tied almost exclusively to this factor. In this instance, less weight should be placed on nonselling activities when developing a compensation plan. With such extreme cultural differences throughout the world, U.S. companies today must carefully assess each market's culture before tailoring a sales compensation plan for that market.

COMMISSION FOR SALES MANAGERS

While we have focused on methods of compensating salespeople, we should not overlook the obvious fact that sales managers are concerned about their own compensation, too. Logically, the sales manager's compensation ought to be closely tied to the performance of the sales force.

Developing a sales manager's compensation plan, however, isn't an easy task. First, the responsibilities of a sales manager are not purely sales or management. Good sales managers strike a balance between these two distinct goals: they continually strive for short-term sales, yet must also meet long-term corporate goals. Therefore, developing a sales manager's compensation plan solely on the basis of yearly sales performance may not be appropriate. Second, designing a sales manager's compensation plan is further complicated by the expectations of other functional areas of the organization. For example, financial executives may expect sales managers to control selling costs and compensate accordingly, while marketing executives may want to reward a sales manager for emphasizing new products or the long-term image of the company. So organizations should consider a blend of sales-oriented goals as well as organizational goals when developing a compensation plan for sales managers.[21]

EXPENSE ACCOUNTS AND FRINGE BENEFITS

Expense accounts enable sales representatives to carry out necessary selling activities, while fringe benefits help provide them with personal security and job satisfaction. Although expense allowances and fringe benefits should not be used as a means of augmenting the income of salespeople, they are often perceived by salespeople as important parts of the total compensation package. Therefore, it is appropriate that both expense accounts and fringe benefits be discussed in this chapter. Sales contests and other indirect monetary incentives used as motivational devices are dealt with in Chapter 13.

Acknowledging the Importance of Selling Expenses

The costs associated with supporting salespeople in the field have been rapidly increasing and are expected to continue increasing well into the 1990s. The major sales expense categories—other than salary, commissions, and bonuses—include meals and entertainment, air travel, automobile rentals, and lodging. The increasing cost of lodging during the late 1980s single-handedly pushed the selling cost index to an all-time high. More recently, sales managers are beginning to voice concern over automobile expenses because the costs of new cars and ongoing maintenance have also driven up the price of putting salespeople on the road.[22] To make matters even worse, the skyrocketing gasoline prices during the early 1990s not only increased the costs associated with automobiles but also dramatically increased the costs associated with air travel.

While selling costs have increased, they do represent expenses that are necessary and important in order for salespeople to carry out their jobs. In fact, sales managers have been known to consider travel and entertainment expenses as both "a tool and a curse." Firms must continue budgeting for these expenses, as they are often very important for the company's image. Many U.S. companies seem to have found that "entertainment is to the businessman what fertilizer is to the farmer . . . it increases the yield." Some firms take business expenditures one step further, as the following example demonstrates.

CORPORATIONS TOE THE PARTY LINE

With the passing of the 1986 Tax Reform Act, the amount of entertainment expenses that can be written off was reduced from 100 percent to 80 percent, and the days of "scandalous" entertaining may be over. Nonetheless, many multinational firms continue to lavishly entertain their most "beloved" customers and probably will continue to do so, even "if they [the expenditures] were not deductible at all." In fact, entertainment was "business as usual" at the 1987 Super Bowl, where 50-yard-line tickets were sold out at $1,500 each.

One of the most sought-after events on the corporate calendar is the Lawn Tennis Championships at the All England Lawn Tennis and Croquet Club—better known as Wimbledon. Seagram's is among the hundreds of multinational corporations that shell out $5,000 a day to entertain guests at Wimbledon each year. (This figure does not include the caterer's fees.) Competition for space is tremendous, but Merrill Lynch, IBM, British Petroleum, and Avis were among the fortunate few to fête prized clients with traditional tournament fare of champagne, cold salmon, strawberries and cream.

Another advocate of this type of entertainment for customers is Jim Beightol, president of Wexford International. Recently, he put on a golf tournament for 60 of his customers at a country club in New Jersey, where his firm is based. The 2-day affair cost Wexford about $10,000, but Beightol says such events help build a network of people he does business with. "We have our suppliers playing with our customers. . . . I'm sure that will translate into dollars somehow."

Some companies who depend a great deal upon their distributors devote a large part of their entertainment budget to these individuals. For example, Coca-Cola invited 20 of its bottlers to view the 1986 Statue of Liberty celebration from the choice vantage point of the Staten Island Ferry. Chrysler Corporation topped that act by treating 700 dealers and their guests to a view from the *Queen Elizabeth 2*.

These companies obviously value great company-client relationships. They appear to believe that the customer and client who play together, stay together.[23]

Every effective sales force must incur expenses in order to accomplish sales objectives. However, it is probably more realistic to see the expenditures related to selling not as expenses but as investments that will yield future dividends (as in the vignette above). Because salespeople usually spend their own money for daily expenses, it is especially important to their morale that these outlays be quickly reimbursed. Most firms reimburse salespeople for items such as meals, lodging, auto expenses, personal phone calls home, drinks, and laundry costs while on the road.

Designing the Expense Plan

Any well-designed expense plan requires several building blocks. These are flexibility, equitability, legitimacy, simplicity, and affordability of administration.

Flexibility. A plan that tries to relate selling expenses only to sales may discourage longer-run profitable sales activities, such as prospecting for new customers or providing special services. Thus, expense plans need to be designed to accommodate these other objectives.

Equitability. An expense plan should be sufficiently flexible to ensure equal treatment of all salespeople regardless of their territory or sales assignment. Thus, regional cost differences for food, lodging, and travel, as well as expense variations for handling different types of customers or for doing different sales tasks, need to be taken into account. Each year *Sales & Marketing Management* calculates a selling cost index (SCI) for a typical five-day week for a salesperson working in each of eighty metropolitan markets. This index is used by many firms to determine appropriate reimbursement levels.

Legitimacy.   The plan should simply reimburse legitimate expenses, with neither profits nor losses for salespeople on the road or at the home office. Expense allowances should never be used in lieu of compensation. This would weaken the sales manager's control via the basic compensation plan, encourage expense padding, and violate federal income tax laws. Only expense accounts that reimburse salespeople for legitimate business expenses are nontaxable.

Simplicity.   Expense-account reimbursement policies must avoid legalistic language. Salespeople should easily understand which expenses are reimbursable so that they have clear guidelines for making expenditures.

Affordability.   Too many organizations require excessive, redundant paperwork for reimbursement of expenses. An efficient expense control plan should minimize the clerical burdens of both the reps and the sales office staff.

Controlling Expenses through Reimbursement

Although salespeople on straight commission often pay their own expenses out of commissions, most companies reimburse their salespeople for legitimate selling expenses. Three basic reimbursement plans are widely used: unlimited, limited, and combination.

Unlimited reimbursement plans.   By far the most popular method of expense control, unlimited reimbursement allows salespeople to be reimbursed for all their necessary selling and travel expenses. No limit is put on total expenses, but sales reps must regularly submit itemized records of their expenditures. With the flexibility provided by unlimited payment plans, the expense variations involved in serving different customer types and territories or in performing diverse selling tasks are easily handled. This unlimited aspect may tempt some salespeople to be extravagant or to pad their expense accounts. While its flexibility allows sales managers some control in directing sales force activities, an unlimited payment plan tends to make forecasts of selling costs more difficult.

Limited reimbursement plans.   Under limited payment plans, expense reimbursement is restricted either to a flat dollar amount for a given time period (usually a day or week) or to an allowable cost per item (such as for a motel room, daily meals, or each mile of travel). To develop a limited payment plan, past company records need to be studied to learn what the costs of meals, lodging, and travel have been over the years (using dollars adjusted for inflation). With limited payment plans, expenses can be predicted and budgeted more accurately, expense-account padding reduced, and unequivocal guidelines established for spending by salespeople. There are disadvantages, however. Salespeople may feel that these plans indicate management's lack of trust. Such plans restrict those unusual (perhaps unallowable) expenses that might win or save a customer. And they make salespeople too expense-conscious, to the possible detriment of sales and profits. They also tempt salespeople to switch reporting of expenditures from one time period to another to avoid going over expense ceilings. Finally, they require frequent revision of expense ceilings during inflationary periods; this may lead to confusion among salespeople as to what the current ceiling is.

Combination reimbursement plans.   Sales managers may consider a combination of the unlimited and limited expense reimbursement programs in order to secure the advantages of both. One approach sets limits on certain items such as food and lodging but not on transportation. Another variation of the combination plan relates expenses to sales. For example, the salesperson may be reimbursed for expenses up to 5 percent of net sales or be awarded a bonus for keeping expenses below 5 percent of net sales. Probably the greatest advantage of this approach is that it ensures that expenses do not get out of line in relation to sales. The major disadvantage is that it diverts some of the sales rep's attention from obtaining profitable sales to worrying about expense ratios.

Curbing Abuses of Expense Reimbursement Plans

Since few salespeople can afford frequent company travel on their personal funds, some means of immediate funding must be available to them. Unfortunately, travel advances have been a source of much waste and abuse by salespeople. It is a temptation for salespeople to draw a larger advance than needed for a trip and to spend the full amount. Some companies have resorted to credit cards for salespeople, but these have proved so painless to use that travel expenses have been known to jump as much as 25 percent as the salespeople upgrade their out-of-town lifestyle.

An approach designed to overcome some of the problems associated with expense reimbursement has recently been offered by the Traveletter System, implemented by Gelco Payment systems, as seen in the following example.

With Traveletter, an employee is funded for a year at a time. He or she is given drafts that can be cashed at a bank weekly, up to a preset limit. The draft can be cashed only after expenses have been incurred. The employee is also given a letter of credit to present to the bank that identifies him or her and states the weekly limit of the draft. Traveletter has advantages for both the company and the employees, says Gelco president, Joseph M. Dale. ''Without this system,'' he says, ''there is no limit on what an employee spends. With it, there is a limit, and if an individual draws beyond the limit, the company rejects the draft.'' Also, control is decentralized, rather than handled through field offices. And the employee is pleased because he or she knows that funds will be promptly reimbursed.

Implementing the Traveletter System costs less than $1 per week per employee for a small company. Digital Equipment Corporation, for instance, has more than 14,000 people on the system and pays less than $12 per person per year to administer the system.[24]

Adjusting to Rising Selling Costs

As the costs of sales calls climb, many companies are being forced to rethink their selling strategies and tactics. A recent survey indicated that approximately

62 percent of its responding companies take steps to make sure they are getting the best deals on all their travel arrangements.[25] More companies today are taking such measures as planning well in advance to get better airfares and shopping airlines, hotels, and car rental agencies to ensure they are getting the lowest possible prices. One of the most interesting responses to rising travel and entertainment expenses comes from a manufacturing company that recently developed a video to use in place of face-to-face sales calls. This firm's sales force does about two-thirds less traveling now that it uses the video. According to the marketing manager of the firm, the use of the video saves the company about $30,000 to $40,000 per year in travel and lodging costs alone.

SUMMARY

While generally accepted as the most important concern of the sales force, compensation packages may elicit different responses from different types of salespeople. For example, salespeople tend to be either creatures of habit, satisfiers, trade-offers, goal-oriented, or money-oriented. It is up to sales managers to identify the basic types of salespeople in their sales forces and to design compensation plans that will elicit top performance from the total sales force.

Basic steps in developing a compensation plan are (1) prepare job descriptions, (2) establish specific objectives, (3) determine general levels of compensation, (4) develop the compensation mix, (5) pretest the plan, (6) administer the plan, and (7) evaluate the plan. If any of these steps is poorly executed, the compensation plan will probably not be very effective in steering and motivating sales force efforts.

There are three major types of compensation plans: straight salary, commission only, and a combination of the two. Each plan has its unique advantages and disadvantages in different sales situations.

Runaway selling costs and sales force morale make it imperative that expense reimbursement options and fringe-benefit packages be carefully analyzed, well planned, and skillfully implemented. Any of the three basic expense reimbursement plans (unlimited, limited, or combination) may be appropriate depending upon the sales situation. Successful expense reimbursement plans are generally flexible, equitable, legitimate, simple, and affordable to administer.

In adjusting to rising sales costs, other options to consider include telemarketing, computer-aided selling, and videoconferences.

STUDY QUESTIONS

1. Do you believe that most salespeople can be effectively "steered" by financial compensation? Explain.

2. If so many companies are unhappy with their compensation programs, why don't they change them?

3. What compensation mix do you think is best for creative selling of intangible goods, like estate planning advice? What mix would be best for a drug detail person calling on physicians? A salesperson for large factory machines? A rep for office equipment?

4. How is the future of the salesperson threatened by the increasing cost of sales calls?

5. What would you suggest to reduce selling costs? Do you think selling costs are like profitable investments and thus should not necessarily be reduced? Explain your answer.

6. What method of reimbursing sales expenses would be best for a life insurance salesperson, a computer hardware sales rep, or an account executive who sells commercial time for a television station?

7. What are the essential criteria for designing and implementing a sound bonus incentive program?

8. What would be the ideal compensation package for the type of sales career you would consider? Would this ''ideal'' package change over the course of your career?

IN-BASKET EXERCISE

You are the national sales manager for a large medical products company that sells a broad line of products to hospitals. After several years of fine-tuning your compensation plan, you feel you've finally got it right. The plan will achieve corporate goals while maximizing sales force performance. The details are as follows: Salespeople are paid a salary, a bonus for making quota, another bonus for signing up new accounts, and a commission on certain medical equipment that the product managers want emphasized. Your salespeople are very happy with the plan, and sales are steadily growing. In fact, it looks as if your division is going to reach sales volume goals for the first time in years.

You received a memo today from the new financial vice president of the company. In it, she informed you that a detailed financial analysis of the company has revealed that your division is *losing* money! Furthermore, she has scheduled a meeting with the top-ranking officials of the company for next week, and you are to attend to discuss this problem.

1. What kind of information should you bring to the meeting?

2. What might have gone wrong with your compensation plan?

3. Should you develop an alternative compensation plan for next week's meeting? Why or why not?

CASE 12-1

HABCO, INC.:
DEVELOPING A COMPENSATION PLAN AT A TIME OF TRANSITION

Background

HABCO, Inc., is an established domestic manufacturer of industrial air compressors and other related prod- ucts. The company worked with major retail chains such as Sears and Montgomery Ward during the 1970s to develop a small, efficient air compressor for the industrial and commercial market. In turn, these large retailers marketed the compressors under their own brand names to painters, carpenters, bricklayers, and other people in small businesses. Additionally, HAB-CO's own brand was introduced and developed by other merchandisers during the same time period. HABCO, Inc., had a good image among both the companies and the customers it served as experts in air compressor manufacturing.

During the 1970s, HABCO and many of the companies that purchased its air compressors recognized the growing trend in the do-it-yourself market. Many consumers at this time were taking an active interest in doing home-improvement projects and automotive repairs themselves. This led to a tremendous market for do-it-yourself products. During this time, the marketing vice president and sales manager of HABCO, Inc., took an especially active interest in the demand for the company's smaller commercial line of air compressors. Close monitoring of the sales of small air compressors revealed that as consumers became more involved in do-it-yourself projects, more and more of them discovered the benefits of using small air compressors for home and automotive projects.

The In-Home Consumer Market

As a result of the tremendous growth of this market during the 1970s, HABCO, Inc., seriously considered manufacturing a small, lightweight air compressor. After conducting several marketing research projects, HABCO decided to develop a prototype of the product for further consumer testing and possible commercialization. The prototype had the following characteristics: It had a $\frac{1}{2}$-horsepower motor and a portable air compressor; it did not require lubricating and was virtually maintenance-free; it could do more than fifty tasks around the house; and it weighed 18 pounds and came with a 12-foot cord and a kit of accessories.

Once the prototype had been developed, HABCO conducted additional research on the product in the consumer market. Market research revealed that consumers liked its portability, its regulator dial, its ability to be attached to a wall in the garage or workshop, and its attractive design. Overall, it was viewed as a useful and versatile product. As a result of these research findings, HABCO, Inc., decided to enter the in-home consumer market with its new lightweight air compressor.

The HABCO Sales Force

In attempting to develop the in-home air compressor market, HABCO faced the traditional problems of bringing a new product to market; it also faced the problem of an inadequate sales force. Historically, the firm had produced private-label air compressors for

mass merchandisers. HABCO also sold to major accounts such as Tru-Value Hardware, Ace Hardware, and large independent distributors. The unit sales were large, but there was a very limited number of customers. The company had six full-time salespeople and a sales manager. In order to gain national distribution as quickly as possible, the firm contracted with a large number of manufacturers' representatives who collectively covered the United States. They called on smaller accounts and/or accounts that HABCO could not cover owing to the small size of the internal sales force. The manufacturers' representatives were compensated through commissions. They could elect to have their commissions computed on either a per-unit basis or a sliding-scale percentage of their invoice totals. Initially, both HABCO and the reps benefited. As the product became more accepted in the channels of distribution, the reps began to "cherry-pick" their accounts and ignored the smaller accounts in their territories. Recognizing this, HABCO decided to enlarge the size of its internal sales force; it hired sixteen new salespeople. Their compensation was salary plus benefits. Their role in the sales organization was to call on the accounts the reps were bypassing. At the time of the decision to hire the "junior salespeople," the original six internal salespeople were promoted to national-account managers, handling only Sears, K-Mart, and the like. Their compensation would be salary and benefits in addition to a year-end bonus on volume and profitability.

After a few years of having three different groups of salespeople (junior, national account, and manufacturers' reps), HABCO faced a serious problem with its junior salespeople. The junior salespeople pointed out that the manufacturers' reps continued to pick the large accounts in their territories, thus earning large commissions, while they had to make three times the sales calls for a minimal salary. In addition, the junior salespeople felt that the old guard had an unfair advantage with the national accounts. Not only were they making considerably more, but they had much less responsibility in addition to their bonus opportunity. A summary of the annual compensation for each category of salesperson is shown in the accompanying exhibit.

The Small Contractor Market?

Despite the unusual makeup of HABCO's sales force, sales increased rapidly during the 1980s. The do-it-yourself market grew faster than HABCO officials had anticipated. With the growth, however, came a great deal of competition. Although HABCO's sales force strategy had weaknesses, company officials felt they were doing an adequate job in the in-home consumer market. Turnover remained high (50 percent or more

Compensation and Turnover for HABCO's Sales Force

Type of Salesperson	Commission	Compensation		Benefits	Turnover (%)
		Average Yearly Salary	Year-End Bonus		
Old reps (6)	None	$40,000–$50,000	$11,000–$20,000	$5,000–$7,000	0
Manufacturers' reps	$35,000–$40,000	None	None	None	0
New reps (26)	None	$28,000	None	$5,000–$7,000	50 +

in some years) for new sales reps, but there was never any problem hiring additional new salespeople. By 1990, HABCO's sales force had grown to thirty-two sales reps (six senior national-accounts reps and twenty-six new reps).

As competition in the in-home market slowed the growth rate at HABCO, Inc., the company president began thinking about separately targeting the small-contractor segment of the market. It appears that as the consumer market grew, the small-contractor segment was virtually forgotten or was assumed to be part of the consumer market segment. Experts were projecting that the home-improvement market would surpass $175 billion by the mid-1990s. Many of the products aimed at the home-improvement market were actually purchased by the thousands of small contractors throughout the United States.

While the tremendous growth during the 1980s left many unsolved problems within HABCO's sales force, the company president wants to get a jump on the competition in the relatively neglected small-contractor market.

Questions

1. Should HABCO enter the small-contractor segment with its product? Why or why not?

2. Give some suggestions on how the turnover problem among HABCO's new salespeople may be solved.

3. What are the major questions that must be answered before HABCO makes the decision to enter the small-contractor market? Should its sales force structure remain the same? Why or why not?

4. Assuming HABCO enters the small-contractor market while remaining in the in-home consumer market, recommend a compensation program for the entire sales force. Be very specific in your recommendation. Include each of the seven steps of developing a compensation plan, as listed in the chapter, in your recommendation.

CASE 12-2

SUN-SWEET CITRUS SUPPLY, INC.: CONTROLLING DIRECT SELLING EXPENSES

Sun-Sweet Citrus Supply (SCS), Inc., located in Orlando, Florida, is a wholesaler of citrus farming supplies and equipment, particularly heavy-duty equipment such as pickers, forklifts, fruit washers and driers, and crating machines. In the company's thirty-year existence, SCS has become a well-known industry name, earning a reputation without parallel.

Ed Bell assumed the position of sales manager for SCS less than two weeks ago. He was recruited from a large wholesaler of mining supplies in Louisville, Kentucky. When Ed's secretary presented him with

the sales force expense accounts for the past week, he almost fainted. He quickly asked her to double-check the figures, but she assured him that they were correct. Ed had been in sales too long not to recognize padded expense accounts.

After checking the expense-account records of the eight SCS salespeople for the past six months, Ed realized that last week's expenses were not unusual for the salespeople but were way out of line when compared with industry norms. He quickly picked up the phone and summoned to his office any salesperson

EXHIBIT

Sales Force Compensation and Selling Expenses

	SCS	Industry Average
Compensation:		
Salary	$28,000–$35,000	$30,000–$45,000
Commission	$8,000–$12,000	$8,000–$15,000
Year-end bonus	None	$3,000–$5,000
Selling expenses as a percentage of sales:		
Meals and entertainment	8–12%	2–4%
Air travel	2–3%	3–4%
Lodging	6–8%	5–6%
Total expenses as a percentage of sales	16–23%	10–14%

who happened to be in the office on that particular day. Mary White happened to be that most unlucky person.

When initially questioned about her expense account, Mary was a bit uncomfortable. After a few minutes, Mary suggested to Ed that he check with the boss on this matter, stating that the boss must have forgotten to mention how the expense accounts were handled. Upon Ed's insistence, Mary finally remarked that this was the way the salespeople get part of their pay each month, insisting that in this fashion the sales force made up for the low pay scales SCS used. Ed thanked Mary for informing him about this, but he was still quite outraged at the figures.

The next morning Ed immediately took the matter up with his boss and found that Mary had indeed told the truth concerning the institutionalized nature of padded expense accounts at SCS. Ed was very distressed, as he did not approve of the practice. Not only was it illegal, but Ed thought it also reflected poor management.

After several days' thought on the matter, Ed confronted his boss again. He told him he very much disapproved of the way the expense accounts were being handled and requested permission to change the procedure so that it would be more in line with industry norms. Ed received the go-ahead from his boss to take whatever measures he deemed appropriate.

That afternoon Ed sat in his office pondering the situation and how best to resolve it. He wanted honest expense reporting, but wondered if it should be an open expense system or one with limits on the various types of expenditures the salespeople were allowed to make? He also wondered how he would adjust the sales force's salaries to compensate for the tighter restrictions on the expense accounts.

To help SCS better address this problem, Ed researched the industry and came up with the information that is presented in the accompanying exhibit. The information revealed exactly what Ed knew all along—the SCS sales force was taking advantage of the tradition of padding the expense account.

Questions

1. How should Ed approach the matter to ensure that management and administration do not frown upon his actions and to keep from creating a morale problem within the sales team?

2. What type of expense budgeting should Ed initiate at SCS? Why?

3. Should any changes be made to the compensation plan at SCS? Why or why not?

4. Recommend an alternative compensation and selling expense plan for SCS. Support your recommendation.

REFERENCES

1. Kate Bertrand, "The 12 Cardinal Sins of Compensation," *Business Marketing*, September 1989, p. 51.
2. For example, see Frederick Herzberg, Bernard Mausner, and Barbara Block Sunderman, *The Motivation to Work*, 2d ed., Wiley, New York, 1959; Edward E. Lawler III, *Pay and Organizational Effectiveness: A Psychological View*, McGraw-Hill, New York, 1971; R. L. Opsahl and M. D. Dunnett, "The Role of Financial Compensation in Industrial Motivation," *Psychological Bulletin*, vol. 66, 1966, pp. 94–118; William L. Buron, "There's More to Motivating Salesmen Than Money," in Taylor W. Meloan and John M. Rathmell (eds.), *Selling: Its Broader Dimensions*, Macmillan, New York, 1960, pp. 62–65; Henry O. Pruden, William H. Cunningham, and Wilke D. English, "Non-Financial Incentives for Salesmen," *Journal of Marketing*, October 1972, pp. 55–59; William J. Paul, Jr., Keith B. Robinson, and Frederick Herzberg, "Job Enrichment Pays Off," *Harvard Business Review*, March–April 1969, pp. 61–78.
3. "1990 Survey of Selling Costs," *Sales & Marketing Management*, Feb. 26, 1990, p. 40.
4. *Compensation and Benefits Review*, September–October 1986, p. 6.
5. Nick DiBari, "Straight Talk," *Sales & Marketing Management*, October 1984, p. 48.
6. Rene Y. Darmon, "Salesmen's Response to Financial Incentives: An Empirical Study," *Journal of Marketing Research*, November 1974, pp. 418–426.
7. Based on personal interviews with sales managers between August and October 1990.
8. *Marketing News*, Nov. 7, 1986, p. 1.
9. Philip Kotler, *Marketing Management*, 4th ed., Prentice-Hall, Englewood Cliffs, N.J., 1980, p. 562. Additional perspectives on objectives for a compensation plan can be found in John W. Barry, "A Guide to Better Methods of Sales Compensation," *Industrial Marketing*, May 1963, pp. 97–101; Paul D. Berger, "Optimal Compensation Plans: The Effects of Uncertainty and Attitude toward Risk on the Salesman Effort Allocation Decision," in E. M. Mazze (ed.), *Marketing in Turbulent Times, 1975 Combined Proceedings*, American Marketing Association, Chicago, 1975, pp. 517–520; James F. Carey, "Paying the Sales Trainee," *Sales & Marketing Management*, Aug. 23, 1976, pp. 43–49; Jack R. Dauner, "A Comparative Analysis of Salesmen's Compensation Plans, Policies, and Trends," in D. C. Sparks (ed.), *Broadening the Concepts of Marketing, 1970 Educators' Proceedings*, American Marketing Association, Chicago, 1970, p. 70; John P. Steinbrink, "How to Pay Your Sales Force," *Harvard Business Review*, July–August 1978, pp. 116–117; Richard C. Smyth, "Financial Incentives for Salesmen," *Harvard Business Review*, January–February 1968, p. 111; Leon Winer and Leon Schiffman, "Developing Optimum Sales Compensation Plans with the Aid of a Simulation Model," in Ronald C. Curham, *1974 Combined Proceedings: New Marketing for Social and Economic Progress and Marketing's Contributions to the Firm and to the Society*, American Marketing Association, Chicago, 1974, pp. 509–514; Alan J. Dubinsky and Eric N. Berkowitz, "The Frequency of Monetary Compensation for Salesmen," *Industrial Marketing Management*, January 1979, pp. 12–23; William Strahle and Rosann L. Spiro, "Linking Market Share Strategies to Salesforce Objectives, Activities, and Compensation Policies," *Journal of Personal Selling and Sales Management*, August 1986, pp. 11–18.
10. Barbara Love (ed.), "Does Your Compensation Plan Inspire Sales?" *Folio*, March 1985, pp. 74–85.
11. William Keenan, Jr., "Is Your Sales Pay Plan Putting the Squeeze on Top Performers?" *Sales & Marketing Management*, September 1988, pp. 58–65.
12. Jill Andresky Frazer, "1990 Executive-Compensation Survey," *Inc.*, November 1990, p. 64.
13. Based on phone call to Jerry Johnson, Xerox Corporation, December 1986.

14. "Straight Salary Has Many Angles," *Sales & Marketing Management*, Mar. 10, 1986, p. 76.

15. Rick Dogen, "Don't Be Too Quick on the Draw," *Sales & Marketing Management*, September 1988, pp. 58–65.

16. *Marketing News*, Nov. 7, 1986, p. 1.

17. Ibid.

18. Keenan, op. cit.

19. Dean Walsh and Joanne Dahm, "Going Flex—Four Adjustable Comp Plans That Work," *Sales & Marketing Management*, September 1989, pp. 16–19.

20. Frank Zaret, "Adapting Distribution and Compensation to Cultural Needs," *Market Facts*, September–October 1989, pp. 26–27 ff.

21. Thomas Mott, "Hot Ticket: Incentive Pay for Field Sales Managers," *Sales & Marketing Management*, March 1989, pp. 21–22.

22. William Keenan, Jr., "Are You Getting Your Money's Worth?" *Sales & Marketing Management*, May 1989, pp. 46–52.

23. *U.S. News & World Report*, July 14, 1986, p. 42.

24. "Corporate Travel," *Sales & Marketing Management*, July 1, 1985, p. 36.

25. Keenan, op. cit.

13

MOTIVATING THE SALES FORCE

LEARNING OBJECTIVES

When you finish this chapter, you should understand:

▲ The importance as well as the complexity of sales force motivation
▲ The basic needs that motivate salespeople to perform on the job
▲ The various theories of motivation
▲ How nonfinancial rewards such as recognition can motivate salespeople
▲ The various motivational tools available to sales managers
▲ The fact that all salespeople are different and each of them may require different motivational techniques

A DAY ON THE JOB

Jim Anglin, vice president of sales and sales operations for Kraft Food Ingredients, believes motivation is something that's within an individual. "I believe that virtually 100 percent of the salespeople who begin a career want to contribute to the growth of the company," says Anglin. "The new salesperson wants to make a difference—a positive impact—and be a valued employee." Anglin thinks that salespeople are self-motivated and will do well until something happens to demotivate them. Therefore, "A good sales manager is one who minimizes any motivational barriers that can arise during a salesperson's career," states Anglin. "With the barriers eliminated, the sales manager can then stimulate individuals via rewards such as cash, new challenges, growth opportunities, recognition, or 'at-a-boys.'" Anglin's unique view of motivation stems from the key philosophy that rewards stimulate the self-motivation of the individual. If someone is not truly self-motivated, rewards will not have a great impact. According to Anglin, sales managers' key task in motivating salespeople is "to provide an environment in which subordinates can be or will remain highly motivated."[1]

A Rolex watch, a Caribbean cruise, a Cadillac, a mink coat, applause, or a spotlight can all act as motivational factors for the sales force. Each of these may motivate salespeople to put out that extra effort needed to dramatically increase sales performance. But which motivational technique works best?

Pacific Northwest Bell recently introduced a program called "Club 20" to motivate its sales force. This program honors people who reach the top 20 percent of sales for the group for two consecutive quarters. Those who do so are brought into the club and given a ring. Each ring is designed with a place for eight diamonds. For each additional period in which a salesperson reaches the top 20 percent sales figure, he or she is given a diamond for the ring.

Zeigler Tools hopes to motivate its sales force by offering trips to a resort area each winter. There, over a two-day period, awards are presented to the best of its salespeople. Believing that recognition of achievement is the key to sales force motivation, Zeigler makes sure that the leading salespeople are singled out with special appreciation for their extra effort.

Many companies are starting to realize that it is not always money that motivates the sales force. Odetics, a high-technology company in California, believes that recognition and the work environment are keys to motivation. Keith Brush, personnel manager for Odetics, has said, "To get the most bang for your buck in terms of motivation, you make it so comfortable that they [the salespeople] *want* to contribute. They don't do it for pins."[2] The rapport the sales reps have with each other and the sales manager as well as recognition for performance are major motivating factors for today's sales force. Exhibit 13-1 shows how senior sales and marketing executives rank the effectiveness of various sales force motivators.

There is no single motivating force that will work in all situations. Yet it is extremely important that the sales manager gain a thorough understanding of the various motivating factors and how they influence sales performance. This chapter will discuss the concept of motivation and its implications to sales management.

WHAT IS MOTIVATION?

"Motivation" is derived from the Latin term *movere,* meaning "to move." Motivation stimulates the movement of an individual. On the basis of this definition, *human motivation* can be defined as a dynamic process set in motion by creating or arousing internal needs that activate goal-directed efforts and determine their intensity and persistence.

It has been estimated that roughly 85 percent of the work force is weakly motivated, yet effective motivation of people offers one of the most direct and powerful means for increasing organizational performance. Many companies spend large amounts of time and money researching the behavior of potential customers while neglecting to study the motivation and behavior of their own salespeople. As a result, sales managers have generally had to develop their own approaches to motivating the sales force, based on a mixture of intuition, folklore, industrial traditions, managerial role models, and their own experiences.

Compounding the problem of motivation is the fact that sales managers frequently do not understand the relative value placed on different incentives

EXHIBIT 13-1

Sales Force Motivators in Order of Average Rated Effectiveness

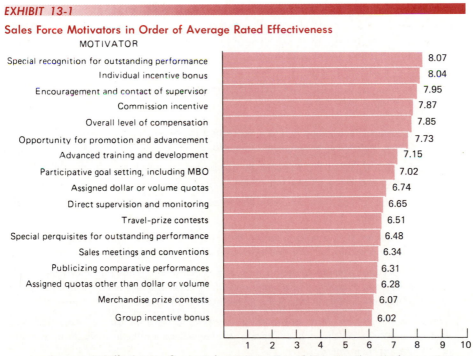

MOTIVATOR	
Special recognition for outstanding performance	8.07
Individual incentive bonus	8.04
Encouragement and contact of supervisor	7.95
Commission incentive	7.87
Overall level of compensation	7.85
Opportunity for promotion and advancement	7.73
Advanced training and development	7.15
Participative goal setting, including MBO	7.02
Assigned dollar or volume quotas	6.74
Direct supervision and monitoring	6.65
Travel-prize contests	6.51
Special perquisites for outstanding performance	6.48
Sales meetings and conventions	6.34
Publicizing comparative performances	6.31
Assigned quotas other than dollar or volume	6.28
Merchandise prize contests	6.07
Group incentive bonus	6.02

Average rated effectiveness: On a scale from 1 ("poor") to 10 ("excellent") as sales force motivators.

Source: Based on a mail survey of 192 senior sales and marketing executives of Fortune 500 companies, M. Johnston, J. Boles, and J. Hair, "Motivation and Supervision of the Sales Force," *Working Paper No. 87-3,* Department of Marketing, Louisiana State University, January 1987.

by their salespeople. Traditionally, studies on sales force motivation have assumed that financial rewards are the most important motivators of sales efforts and that proper design of the compensation package is the best approach to motivating salespeople.[3] However, research findings with other occupational groups consistently show that money is not necessarily the prime motivator of work efforts. Instead of supporting the contention that salespeople are a distinct breed who respond uniquely to financial rewards, the evidence indicates that sales forces tend to be a composite of personality types, motivated by nonfinancial as well as financial incentives.[4] Moreover, it is becoming more common to hear that increased pay is not always the most desired reward among salespeople. A recent study indicated that high-order rewards (e.g., promotions or opportunities for growth) are very attractive to salespeople in the early stages of their careers. That is, while monetary rewards are important to individuals under 35 years of age, the opportunity for advancement and promotion also are strong motivators for them.[5] Exhibit 13-2, based on a study of several thousand salespeople, shows the variety of factors that motivate top sales performers.[6]

Sales managers must realize that all motivation is self-motivation. Salespeople cannot be motivated unless they decide to let themselves be motivated. In other words, motivation is personal and must take place within the individual before it becomes apparent to others. Individuals will become motivated only if they find something in the sales job that is a source of personal motivation for them. Sales managers have the responsibility of creating the type of environment and incentives that encourage salespeople to want to motivate themselves.

EXHIBIT 13-2

What Motivates Top Sales Performers?

1. *Need for status.* Recognition is a key motivating factor for top salespeople. This group seeks power, authority, image, and reputation.

2. *Need for control.* While top salespeople like being with other people, they also like to be in control and enjoy influencing others.

3. *Need for respect.* Top sales achievers like to be seen as experts who are willing to help and advise others.

4. *Need for routine.* It is a misconception that successful sellers thrive on freedom. Most like to follow a routine strictly and are upset when it is interrupted.

5. *Need for accomplishment.* Money is only one of the many things that motivate the top sales performers. In addition to a big house, fancy cars, and nice clothes, they constantly go after new challenges in their jobs to maintain enthusiasm.

6. *Need for stimulation.* Most outstanding salespeople have an abundance of physical energy and thrive on challenges. Therefore, they welcome outside stimulation as a way of channeling their energy.

7. *Need for honesty.* Top sales achievers have a strong need to believe in the product that they are selling. If they have doubts about the company or a new product line, they are apt to switch jobs.

Monetary rewards for job performance are considered *financial incentives.* These include the salesperson's salary, commission, bonuses, stock options, and fringe benefits such as a company car, medical and dental coverage, life insurance, or educational aid. In contrast, *nonfinancial incentives* are less tangible, psychological rewards that relate to the individual salesperson's intrinsic needs in that they are internally experienced payoffs. Examples are job security, relationships with superiors and coworkers, working conditions, challenging sales assignments, increasing responsibility, and recognition for special achievements such as reaching sales quotas or winning sales contests. Financial incentives were discussed in Chapter 12, so only nonfinancial incentives will be dealt with in this chapter. Both have a role to play in motivating salespeople.

MOTIVATION THEORIES

Researchers in the behavioral sciences have shown that all human activity is directed toward satisfying certain needs and reaching certain goals. How salespeople behave on the job is directly related to their individual needs and goals. Thus, some individuals will behave differently and will be more successful because of different motivational patterns. Many people feel that individual motivation is dependent upon whether or not salespersons find something in the job that is personally motivating for them. Therefore, the job of the sales manager must be redefined, with greater emphasis placed upon understanding and accepting the idea of how motivation works. The sales manager is responsible not only for motivating the sales force per se but also for counseling each salesperson individually to find the source of that person's self-motivation.[7] Ten of the most common errors managers make when counseling the sales force in the goal-setting process are presented in Exhibit 13-3.[8] Avoiding these errors will not necessarily guarantee success for sales managers, but it can do a great deal in helping them understand the very complicated and extremely important area of sales force motivation. Several contemporary theories of motivation will now be discussed to further assist sales managers in their understanding of needs and motivation.

Maslow's Need Theory

Maslow's well-known theory contends that people are motivated by a "hierarchy" of psychological growth needs.[9] Relative gratification of the needs at one level activates the next-higher order of needs. The hierarchy-of-needs theory implies that salespeople come to their jobs already motivated and that they only need the opportunity to respond to the challenges of higher-order needs. Exhibit 13-4 presents the order of priority of the needs individuals seek to fulfill and the needs sales managers must consider. Sales managers applying need theory should keep in mind its two major premises:

The Importance of Goal Setting to Tap Self-Motivation

The ten most common errors in the goal-setting process are:

1. Failure to involve the salesperson actively and openly in the goal-setting process

2. Failure to set realistic goals

3. Failure to meet and reset goals when conditions beyond the control of either party change, or when they prove to be unattainable because of unrealistic assumptions

4. Failure to fix goals that can be measured in tangible ways, such as time or dollar volume

5. Failure to incorporate the development of the measurement system into the goal-setting process

6. Failure to consider the measurement system in terms of real-time feedback

7. Failure to meet promptly with personnel to determine the reasons for a goal shortfall

8. Failure to provide positive feedback on how to correct shortfalls

9. Failure to develop goals and a measurement system for the new corrective plan of action

10. Failure to provide timely public recognition for goal achievement

- The greater the deprivation of a given need, the greater its importance and strength.

- Gratification of needs at one level in the hierarchy activates needs at the next-higher level.

Sales managers must keep track of the level of needs most important to each salesperson, from the beginning trainee to the senior sales representative. Before salespeople become stagnated at one level, they must be given opportunities to activate and satisfy higher-level needs if they are to be successfully motivated toward superior performances. Since various salespeople are at different need levels at any one time, sales managers have to retain their sensitivity to the evolving needs of individual reps through close personal contact with each member of the sales force.

Motivator-Hygiene Theory

Herzberg's classic research studies found two types of factors associated with the satisfaction or dissatisfaction of employees. Sources of satisfaction are called *motivators* because they are necessary to stimulate individuals to superior efforts. They relate to the nature or content of the job itself and include responsibility, achievement, recognition, and opportunities for growth and advancement. Sources of dissatisfaction are called *hygiene factors* because they are necessary to keep employee performance from dropping or becoming unhealthy. They comprise the environment, include salary, company policies and administration, supervision, and working conditions.[10]

EXHIBIT 13-4

Hierarchy of Human Needs and Their Implications for Sales Managers

Maslow's Hierarchy	Salesperson's Needs	Sales Manager's Task
Self-actualization needs	Self-development Creativity Self-fulfillment	Provide greater job control, freedom, self-development workshop
Esteem needs	Recognition Status	Provide greater job responsibilities, promotion opportunities, public recognition for achievements
Social needs	Social interaction Friendship Acceptance among peers and superiors	Maintain close relationships with sales force Sales meetings Newsletters, memoranda, etc.
Safety needs	Freedom from worry about security of jobs, incomes, medical expenses, etc.	Provide a balanced package of fringe benefits
Physiological needs	Food, shelter, overall health, etc.	Be aware of general health and living conditions of sales force

According to Herzberg's theories, to improve productivity, sales managers must maintain hygiene factors (pleasant work environment) while providing motivators (job enrichment) for the sales force. Here are some examples of job enrichment:

- Give salespeople a *complete natural unit of work responsibility and accountability* (e.g., specific customer category assignments in a designated area).

- Grant *greater authority and job freedom* to the salespeople in accomplishing assignments (e.g., let salespeople schedule their time in their own unique way as long as organizational goals are met).

- Introduce salespeople to *new and more difficult tasks and to challenges not previously handled* (e.g., opening new accounts, selling a new product category, or being assigned a large national account).

- Assign salespeople specific or specialized *tasks enabling them to become experts* (e.g., training new salespeople on ''how to close a sale'').

- Send *periodic reports and communications directly to the salesperson* instead of forwarding everything via the sales supervisor. (Of course, the supervisor must be informed about what information the salespeople are receiving.)[11]

Expectancy Theory

As developed by Vroom and his colleagues, expectancy theory contends that people are motivated to work toward a goal when they expect their efforts will pay off—that is, when achievement of the goal is both profitable and desirable. Each of us estimates (if only subjectively) the probability of success in our work endeavors and the relative value of the payoff if we do succeed. Although it can be interpreted in several ways, the central idea of the expectancy theory of motivation is as follows:

> Needs alone cannot explain behavior. In order to be motivated to work harder, people must expect that if they try, they can actually accomplish the task before them, and if they do complete the task, the rewards will be worth the efforts expended.[12]

Expectancy-valence calculations.   One aspect of expectancy theory is that the force or effort to do something depends on the *valence* (anticipated satisfaction) in accomplishing it and the *expectancy* (probability) that an action will yield the expected result. In equation form,

$$\text{Effort} = \text{expectancy} \times \text{valence}$$

where effort = the person's motivation to perform
  expectancy = the degree to which one believes that certain performance levels will lead to certain outcomes (scaled from 0 to 1)
  valence = the value placed on each outcome (scaled -1 to $+1$, with extremes indicating strong displeasure or pleasure and 0 meaning indifference)

Suppose, for example, that a sales manager wants to stimulate sales of a new product and asks all the salespeople to make extra calls to earn a special double commission. If the salespeople believe that extra calls will very likely result in more sales, their personal expectancy rating may be 0.7. The double-commission reward for selling each new product may be highly valued, say 0.9 for valence. Then the likely increase in effort would be 0.63 (0.7×0.9). Sales managers should devise incentive plans that will maximize the product of expectancy and valence for their salespeople.

Expectations of salespeople.   According to expectancy theory, sales managers must create the expectation in salespeople that their efforts will be more than adequately rewarded. To become motivated in most situations, salespeople must expect that the rewards for extra efforts will be greater than the costs so that they will profit personally. Therefore, in any attempt to motivate salespeople to greater efforts, the alert sales manager will remember that salespeople are going to ask (usually only internally): "What is in it for me—that is, what is my payoff, what is required from me (my costs or efforts expended), and what is the probability of success?" Unless the sales manager can satisfactorily anticipate and answer these questions, his or her salespeople won't be motivated to greater effort.

Achievement Theory

Research by McClelland and his associates confirmed that some people have higher achievement needs than others; they labeled such persons "achievement-oriented."[13] Children who are given greater responsibilities and trusted from youth to do things on their own are more likely to have achievement-oriented profiles. *Achievement-oriented* people readily accept individual responsibility, seek challenging tasks, and are willing to take risks doing tasks that may serve as stepping stones to future rewards. These individuals receive more satisfaction from accomplishing goals and more frustration from failure or unfinished tasks than the average person. Any achievement-related step on the "success path" may include rewards (positive incentives) or threats (negative incentives). A path is *contingent* if the individual feels that immediate success is required in order to have the opportunity to continue toward further successes and that immediate failure causes loss of the opportunity to continue on the path. If immediate success or failure has no effect on the opportunity to continue on the path toward future success or failure, the path is *noncontingent*.

Sales managers need to identify the achievement-motivated salespeople and then give them personal responsibility for solving definable problems or achieving certain goals. Frequent, specific feedback is also essential so that these salespeople can know whether they are successful or not. Managers may have to temper negative feedback because achievement-motivated people may resign if they feel that they are going to be unsuccessful. Finally, competition among such salespeople can become cutthroat and damaging to the organization unless carefully monitored and controlled.

Contrasted with these achievement-oriented individuals, *affiliative* people are not as competitive nor are they as anxious about uncompleted tasks; they require only general feedback regarding goal achievement. Affiliative types like to work in groups and want to be accepted by others.[14] They are less self-centered, usually help bind the group together, and are less able to tolerate traveling jobs involving long periods of solitude.

Although salespeople generally exhibit traits of both task achievement and group affiliation, it is up to the sales manager to learn the dominant needs of individual salespeople in order to devise specific strategies for motivating them.

Inequity Theory

According to the inequity theory of motivation, people compare their relative work contributions and rewards with those of other individuals in similar situations. As "positive-thinking" minister and author Robert Schuller says: "Many people hear through their peers, not their ears." Inequity is experienced when a person feels either underrewarded or overrewarded for his or her contribution relative to that of others. The stronger the feeling of inequity, the stronger the drive to reduce tension. Although individuals may respond in unique ways to inequity, most people who feel underpaid or underrewarded, relative to others making similar contributions, tend to decrease their work efforts; people who feel overpaid tend to increase their efforts. People may also reduce their inequity tensions by distorting their perceptions of their rewards and contributions versus those of others. Finally, individuals may leave a perceived inequitable situation by quitting the job or changing the comparison group.[15]

According to inequity theory, it is important that sales managers learn how individual sales representatives feel about the equity of their contributions and rewards compared with those of others. If inequity is perceived by some of the salespeople, the sales manager needs to correct the situation if inequity really does exist or help the salespeople reduce tensions by altering their perceptions of the comparison group's relative contributions and rewards.

Role Clarity

Donnelly and Ivancevich contend that one of the most important needs of salespeople is *role clarity,* or a concept of exactly what their job entails.[16] Because salespeople often lack sufficient job knowledge, must deal across departmental boundaries, and are challenged by complex problems requiring innovative solutions, precisely defined goals and clear role expectations can be motivational. Empirical research with salespeople correlates increased role clarity with greater job interest, more opportunity for job innovation, less work tension, more job satisfaction, and a lower propensity to leave.[17] Salespeople usually want and need more information about what is expected of them and how they will be evaluated.

Clearly written job descriptions and management-by-objectives (MBO) conferences that set precise goals (mutually agreed upon by the salesperson and sales manager) can have important motivational effects and stimulate job satisfaction. Clarifying the role expectations for salespeople by individualizing achievement plans and providing a continuous flow of helpful information will consume significant amounts of sales management time. But this seems to be one of the least complicated, least expensive, and surest ways of obtaining higher sales force productivity.

Attribution Theory of Motivation

Recently, Sujan has suggested a theory of motivation based on the psychological theory of attribution.[18] Attribution theory holds that people are motivated not only to maximize their own rewards but also to understand their environment or surroundings. That is, people are motivated to know why an event occurred and why they succeeded or failed at a certain task. The explanations for success and failure lead individuals to make *causal attributions* for the outcomes that they experience. The causal attributions (or perceived causes of success and failure) usually include ability, effort, strategy, luck, and the difficulty of the tasks. These attributions, or perceptions, influence motivation. For example, a successful salesperson may be motivated to continue a certain selling activity if he or she attributes the success to that activity or behavior. Similarly, an individual who attributes failure to a certain selling activity or strategy is likely to be motivated to change that work habit so that he or she has a better chance of succeeding the next time.

The outcome of the attribution process is that salespeople can choose either to *work harder* or to *work smarter.* The difference between working harder and working smarter and the implications for motivation and performance have been discussed in recent sales literature.[19] Motivation to increase the amount of effort on the job pertains to working harder. For example, calling on more accounts or putting in more hours is working harder. On the other hand, motivation to change the type or direction of effort involves working smarter. Learning new sales skills or altering a sales presentation to match the customer is a way to be more effective on the job, or a way to work smarter. For certain selling situations, working smarter may produce greater benefits than working harder. Sales managers can do a great deal to motivate their sales forces by understanding which of these two approaches their salespeople should follow.

Traditionally, sales managers have attempted to motivate their sales forces to work harder by increasing the extent of each salesperson's activity. Working longer hours and contacting more clients have long been among the primary objectives of sales managers. Yet the work of Sujan suggests that sales managers should concentrate on motivating the salespeople to make better choices concerning activities they perform—in other words, to work *smarter*. Sales managers can do this by helping the sales reps direct their efforts better in terms of searching for new clients, making different presentations for different types of clients, deciding which clients to visit more often, and other strategies. By getting a better understanding of the causal attributions salespeople make, as well as the outcomes of those attributions, sales managers can add much to their understanding of the motivation of the sales force.

EMERGING PERSPECTIVES ON MOTIVATION

In addition to the established theories of motivation, other perspectives are emerging that can assist sales managers. Two of the most promising are goal-setting theory and the Japanese style of management.

Goal-Setting Theory

Goal-setting theory attempts to increase motivation by linking rewards directly to individuals' goals. Sales managers and subordinates should set specific goals for the individual salesperson on a regular basis. These goals should be moderately difficult to achieve, but they should be the type of goals that the salesperson will want to accomplish. Unlike the traditional quota system, goal-setting theory integrates other motivational theories in an attempt to develop a reward system tailored to individual needs. Because it helps sales managers develop individualized reward systems, goal-setting theory provides a means of clarifying any role ambiguities or conflicts that may arise. Many experts are predicting that this approach to motivation will increasingly gain popularity in many organizations.[20]

Japanese Style

Another perspective on motivation that has recently gained popularity is the Japanese style of management.[21] This approach attempts to increase motivation by bringing management and workers together. In Japan, managers and workers see themselves as one group; as a result, everyone is highly committed and motivated. Japanese salespeople in the United States adhere to this philosophy, and to the dismay of U.S. competitors, it appears to be working well. Under this approach, the salesperson, engineer, sales manager, and so on, are members of a team and are rewarded accordingly.[22] The emphasis in the United States has traditionally been on individual performance, but a number of U.S. companies are beginning to stress the team approach in motivating their sales forces. Xerox, a leader of this trend, recently introduced its Partnership Excellence incentive program, in which its salespeople, service reps, and business operations managers are all eligible for the incentives. The goal of the program is to build partnerships and promote teamwork within the company by rewarding gains in regional or district profit rather than individual performance.[23] Like goal-setting theory, Japanese-style motivation is likely to become more common among sales organizations in the United States.

MOTIVATION AND PRODUCTIVITY

Despite the popularity of productivity improvement approaches such as job enrichment and incentive programs, most dramatic productivity gains are short-lived. Although consultants tend to feel that companies that do not succeed in improving productivity have failed to implement their programs correctly and wholeheartedly, the evidence suggests that few companywide performance improvement programs can succeed because employee motivation depends on too many diverse, individualized factors. Moreover, performance improvement is not easily measured, especially at successively higher organizational levels. While the productivity of salespeople can be reasonably accurately measured, sales managers most often are evaluated on basic performance criteria that are less quantifiable. Sales managers know that their responsibilities include a variety of tasks, but they are often unsure what priority to assign to each. Job descriptions, because they tend to be too broad, seldom provide much assistance. Even task-oriented descriptions usually fail to give guidance about the relative productivity trade-off of, say, revising sales territories versus conducting additional sales training to improve closing techniques and "hit ratios."

Sales managers tend to take for granted the relationship between motivation and productivity. But even within categories of motivators, individual perceptions can vary. One salesperson may see a pay raise in terms of what the money can buy, while another may value it as recognition of superior performance. Moreover, senior salespeople may be more productive (motivated) as a result of commission-based motivators, whereas junior salespeople are likely to be motivated by opportunity for advancement.

Inpsych, a psychological consulting firm in California, surveyed 1,335 employees and their supervisors at three companies—an electronics company, a national bank, and a laser manufacturer. No specific patterns of productivity-related factors were found that applied across different companies or even across departments in the same company. The study did find that employees generally have the same perceptions of their own productivity as do their supervisors, but it revealed almost no correlation between job satisfaction and productivity. In the words of one Inpsych psychologist, "Things are different at a batch industry, a process industry, or a cottage industry, and within a company you need different methods to motivate people."[24] In sum, individual sales managers can identify means for motivating individual salespeople or perhaps even particular groups, but it is counterproductive to use blanket approaches to increase the productivity of a large number of salespeople who are involved in diverse activities.

If blanket motivational approaches are unworkable and attempts to motivate each individual separately are inefficient, what is a sales manager to do? Perhaps a blend of goal-setting theory and the Japanese philosophy can help sales managers properly motivate their salespeople. In applying goal-setting theory, sales managers must assess individual needs in order to properly motivate each person. Then, to encourage teamwork within the company, rewards could also be tied to overall district or regional goals, as advocated by the Japanese style of management.

MOTIVATION AND RECOGNITION

For years, the majority of sales managers assumed that monetary rewards were most valued and therefore most motivating to salespeople. Recently, however, sales managers across all industries are beginning to realize that while monetary rewards are initially motivating to salespeople, it is nonfinancial rewards that are critical in getting the most performance from the sales force. As indicated throughout this chapter, one nonfinancial motivational tool that is quickly gaining popularity among sales managers is *recognition*. Most sales managers are beginning to realize that to get peak performance from salespeople today, they must pay more attention to the individual's higher-order needs (e.g., appreciation, admiration, and recognition). All levels of salespeople appreciate some form of public recognition.

There are many ways to give recognition to a salesperson. Several companies believe that creating a "fun" working environment in which everyone is aware of others' accomplishments is an excellent form of motivation. Intertic Components, an electronics distributor in Longwood, Florida, adheres to the philosophy that fun and accessibility to management are keys to employee motivation.[25] Tom Ferrante, president of Intertic, believes in talking to anyone in his company who is willing to listen. At Fel-Pro, a gasket manufacturer in Skokie, Illinois, all compliments the home office receives from customers are immediately relayed to the sales force. The corporate office believes it is important that the salespeople learn of these compliments directly from their superior.[26] Other forms of recognition used at Fel-Pro are listed below.

INCENTIVES TO MOTIVATE THE SALES FORCE AT FEL-PRO

Fel-Pro, a gasket manufacturer in Skokie, Illinois, offers its employees some unique incentives to keep motivation high:

- Candy is given out on Valentine's Day, turkeys at Christmas, and hams for Easter.

- When employees get married, they receive $100 from the company. When a child is born, $1,000 is awarded. When the child graduates from high school, there is an additional $100.

- The company provides a day-care center, tutorial assistance for dependent children, and a summer day camp.

- For employees who like to garden, the company has minifarms that are plowed so that the employee can plant things and watch them grow.

- The company even stocks a lake for those employees who like to fish.[27]

More and more companies today are realizing that giving salespeople symbolic motivators, such as plaques, rings, and memberships into elite sales clubs, can instill a certain pride in an individual that a paycheck or free trip cannot. Recognition is earned; it cannot be bought with money. Money and other incentives are spent or consumed, but recognition acts as a constant reminder of a salesperson's accomplishment. Xerox Corporation has a President's Club for its top sales achievers. As one of Xerox's top salespeople states, "The President's Club is what we all strive for because it's how our success is measured within Xerox."[28] While a free trip accompanies membership in the President's Club, for many salespeople the real motivator is being recognized as a member of that elite group. Many top-performing salespeople win company incentives year after year. What eventually becomes important is being recognized as a top salesperson. As one salesperson put it, "If the top guys are there [in the spotlight], you want to be there. The individual's ego becomes much more important than an incentive can ever be."[29] Seattle-based Nordstrom, Inc., one of the most successful retailers in the country, attributes much of its success to its recognition program, which is described in the following example.

RECOGNIZING THE NORDIES

Analysts claim that the key to Nordstrom's success lies in the firm's approach to motivating the sales force. At Nordstrom they don't rely on discount pricing or substantial product distinctions; they rely on a sales force that drives itself. A variety of motivational techniques are used to create this "driven" sales force. At Nordstrom the salary component of the compensation plan is 10 percent as compared with 90 percent in the typical department store. Therefore, commissions are extremely important to the sales force. Also, Nordstrom sales clerks, who call themselves "Nordies," are subjected to no rules or guidelines. Nordies report that this environment offers them the opportunity to make decisions and to handle their own situations. Another significant motivator is Nordstrom's policy of recognizing the top-five pacesetters at each store. On a monthly basis these pacesetters, who are crowned the "Fabulous Five," win recognition at monthly banquets, plus a 33 percent discount on personal purchases at the store. Nordies do appear driven, as they are known to carry notebooks filled with customer names and it's not unusual for them to send thank-you notes to customers.[30]

EXHIBIT 13-5

Developing a Recognition Program

- The program should be *objective* and based on *performance* only. It must be clear to everyone how an individual won. No subjective judgments should be in the program.

- Everyone must have a chance to win. The program should be neither so difficult that no one will try nor so easy that the program is meaningless.

- The award should be presented in public. Much of the recognition is lost if there is no ceremony or if awards and plaques are distributed in the mail.

- The ceremony must be in good taste. A poorly done recognition program can leave employees uninspired and take away any motivation they may have had.

- The program must be highly publicized. If no one knows about it or if it is poorly communicated so that no one understands it, the program will lack involvement. It must be promoted in company publications as an important and prominent endeavor.

Source: Bill Kelley, "Recognition Reaps Rewards," *Sales & Marketing Management*, June 1986, p. 104.

While recognition is an excellent motivator, there is no single form of recognition that works for everyone. A good recognition program starts by finding a person's "start center,"[31] which is activated by higher-order needs, such as appreciation and admiration, that everyone values. Finding a person's start center is not easy, because it is as unique as the individual. Yet it is the sales manager's duty to work with each person individually and to recognize and develop those talents that are unique to each salesperson. Recognition of salespeople is becoming a major part of a sales manager's job. The factors sales managers should consider in developing a recognition program for their sales forces are presented in Exhibit 13-5.

MOTIVATIONAL TOOLS

Sales managers can choose from several motivational devices to implement their general theory of, or approach to, motivating the sales force. First, the compensation plan must be designed (as explained in Chapter 12) to focus the desired emphasis on organizational goals. If, however, as Herzberg contends, compensation plans are merely hygienic or if salespeople have come to take a relatively stable plan for granted, other tools are needed. Sales training programs (discussed in Chapter 8) can also help motivate sales personnel by providing up-to-date knowledge about the company, customers, products, selling techniques, and performance expectations that can give salespeople more self-confidence, instill enthusiasm, and raise career aspirations. Beyond offering attractive financial compensation and well-designed training programs, sales managers can consider a host of motivational tools. Four of the most important are sales contests, sales meetings, promotion opportunities, and incentive programs.

EXHIBIT 13-6

Sales Contest Objectives and Rewards

- *Increase dollar volume.*
  Prize to salespeople who increase sales (based on percentage of dollar increase over previous period).
  Two quotas with prize to salesperson who reaches first quota, and prize for husband or wife if second quota is reached.
  Several prizes, with top producers awarded most expensive prize. Runners-up receive less expensive prizes. Points for each $1 of sales. Prizes won by fixed number who have most points.

- *Stimulate more orders.*
  Prize for all salespeople who pass quota of orders.
  Points for each order, with fixed number of prizes to those with most points.

- *Increase sales orders.*
  Prizes to those who make most demonstrations and/or complete most call reports.
  Prizes to all who make quota of calls and demonstrations.
  Additional prize for meeting a second quota.

- *Build higher unit sales.* Points for higher dollar or unit volume (based on past averages), with prizes for those who make best showing.

- *Add customers.*
  Reach quota of new customers to earn prize. Sellers who add most customers earn prize. Several prizes, with best prizes to top producers.
  Points toward prize for each new customer, with bonus points for target accounts.

- *Secure prospects.* Points toward prize for each new prospect, with additional points for each prospect that becomes a customer within a specified period.

Sales Contests

As a motivational device, the sales contest has the potential for undesirable as well as desirable results. Therefore, it is important that sales managers understand the goals that can be accomplished through sales contests, the essential decision areas in planning contests, and the potential pitfalls associated with them.

Contest goals.   Contests can be used to focus sales force attention on any particular goal area for short periods of time. They can motivate salespeople to sell new products, to give attention to problem products, to provide more customer service, to sell new accounts, or to make more demonstrations. Contests can be used to clear an overstocked condition, to keep production lines running, to smooth out seasonal variations, and to train salespersons in selling the whole line. Sometimes, contests simply encourage salespersons to sell more volume within a given period of time. At other times, they are designed to achieve complex multiple goals. Some of the many reasons contests are used, in addition to simply providing periodic challenges to the sales force to reinstitute good work procedures, are set forth in Exhibit 13-6.

Contest decision areas.   Contest themes, rules, prizes, participation, duration, and publicity are important specifics associated with the planning and imple-

- *Build off-season business.* Dollar or unit-volume quota to earn prize during slow months. Two quotas: first for salesperson, second for spouse (if trip).

- *Push slow items.* Points awarded for sales of slow-moving stocks, with prizes for biggest point getters.

- *Stimulate balanced selling.* Prizes to those who maintain best sales record for selling entire line during specified time.

- *Introduce new product.*
  Points toward prize for best sales record with new product.
  Prize to salespeople who reach quota of customers who buy new product.

- *Increase use of displays.* Prize to salespeople for placing quota of displays.

- *Stimulate dealer tie-ins.* Prizes to salespeople who get most dealers to tie in with national advertising campaign.

- *Revive dead accounts.*
  Prizes to salespeople who reactivate most old accounts.
  Prizes for greatest sales volume from formerly dead accounts.

- *Switch users to your brand.* Points toward prize for salespeople who switch users or owners of competitive product to yours.

- *Improve sales abilities.* Prizes to salespeople who score best when graded by professional shopper.

- *Intensify training.* Prizes to salespeople who score best on examinations after training period.

- *Reduce costs.* Prize to salespeople and managers who set best record of sales-to-costs ratio.

- *Build multiple sales.* Prizes to salespeople with best carload or multiple-sales record.

mentation of this motivational tool. All planning must begin with the specific purposes of the contest; then plans are developed in light of these goals.

Themes.   Sales managers should ensure that contest themes are creative, novel, timely, implementable, promotable, visibly measurable, and self-image reinforcing. Variations of sports and games in season are frequently used as a theme, as are travel routes, mock battles, races, building construction, and clothing contests (in which the salesperson can wear to meetings what he or she wins). There must be some easily understood way to measure milestones of progress. Contest themes that create great difficulties in implementation or involve complex measurement processes should be avoided. Above all, salespeople should be able to identify psychologically with the theme, and it must not be so juvenile or silly that mature salespeople feel childish when playing "the game."

Contests can be designed for the entire sales force, for those with different levels of experience (such as junior or senior salespersons), or for horizontal business segments (such as different customer classes or territorial zones). Grouping salespeople for contest purposes is consistent with the hierarchical segmentation approach to motivation, and it recognizes that different levels of salespeople tend to have different needs. Contests should be customized to each separate group of participants, with goals, themes, and awards reflecting their different drive levels. For example, junior salespeople might be motivated by the expectation of glamorous prizes, while senior salespeople might prefer a vacation trip with top officials of the company.

In planning contests, caution should be taken to ensure that territorial differences do not preclude some sales representatives from having an equal chance to win. Otherwise, the effect will be demotivational. Suppose, for example, that banks and savings and loan institutional buyers are the best prospects for products included in the contest scope and that some salespeople have few of these institutions in their sales territories. Such salespeople would likely resent those responsible for planning the contest and become cynical about the whole thing.

Rules. It is important that contest rules be carefully formulated to clarify goals and prevent abuses. Obsolete or deficient products as well as all unethical tactics must be deemed outside the ground rules of the contest. Rules should also be phrased so that they discourage salespeople from holding back orders before the contest, applying undue pressure on buyers during the period, or suggesting that buyers can cancel the orders after the contest. However, the rules can be used to orient the contest toward obtaining specific organization goals. For instance, restricting the contest to accounts not reported on call sheets for two months preceding the contest period might channel contest efforts more toward selling newly developed prospects. Finally, rules must clearly define the contest time period, the action that actually constitutes a sale for contest purposes (order, delivery, payment), and the exact basis for accumulating points for prizes.

Prizes. Unless contest prizes include items that the majority of participants want, the desired motivational effects will not be created. While many salespeople will say they prefer cash, more unusual and visible awards that the winners could conspicuously enjoy (and that could be bought at wholesale prices), such as glamorous trips, luxurious boats, cars, sporting equipment, or home entertainment systems, serve as long-lasting incentives for all participants. Consideration of the salesperson's family support is important in selecting incentives. Awards ought to be something the whole family would enjoy, ensuring their participation in cheering on their prospective winner. Exhibit 13-7 shows the use of various incentives and their relative popularity as judged by sales managers.

Many corporations are turning to productive travel as incentives—for example, inspirational training in exotic settings. Control Data Corporation has been scheduling sales meetings abroad for almost twenty years to reward salespeople who make the company's "100 Percent Club."[32] Sales meetings have the advantage of being easily justified to top management, since they combine business and pleasure, family participation, highly visible recognition, and nontaxability while giving salespeople the chance to share spirited interaction with other high producers in the company. Sales meetings also allow salespeople to feel less guilty about leaving their territories and accounts than would a vacation trip.

Participation. Sometimes, only upper-level salespersons have the opportunity to compete for the chance to go to national sales conventions or to be

EXHIBIT 13-7

Usage and Popularity of Sales Force Recognition Methods

Method	Percentage Who Use	Popularity Rating by Users		
		Very Popular	Popular	Not Very Popular
Wall plaques	72.5	43.2	51.3	5.5
Trophies	39.2	45.0	50.0	5.0
Publicity—company	33.3	52.9	35.3	11.8
Membership in special sales club	25.5	38.5	61.5	0.0
Jewelry	23.5	50.0	33.3	16.7
Special meetings with top executives	21.6	63.6	27.3	9.1
Publicity—trade	19.6	60.0	30.0	10.0
Publicity—hometown	17.6	55.6	11.1	33.3
Special business cards	17.6	22.2	55.6	22.2
Other*	15.7	100.0	0.0	0.0

*Personalized gifts, cash, trips, nonpersonal merchandise clothing.
Source: Mail survey of 192 senior sales and marketing executives of Fortune 500 companies, 1986. M. Johnston, J. Boles, and J. Hair, "Motivation and Supervision of the Sales Force," *Working Paper No. 87-3,* Department of Marketing, Louisiana State University, January 1987.

awarded membership in an elite group such as the President's Club or the Million Dollar Sales Club. Junior salespersons are more likely to have their own contests with awards such as a trophy and a letter of praise signed by a top company official. An example of a creative incentive with probable high-level appeal for senior-level salespeople is the family-roots trace in the "Hermitage Hunt" contest of Armour Food Service. Winners receive a trip to the homeland of their earliest traceable ancestor and a professional five-generation genealogy.[33]

Most contests do not pit one salesperson against another but award prizes for accomplishing certain individual standards of performance. There is disagreement over whether it is better to have lesser prizes that nearly everyone can win or to have expensive prizes that only a few can win. Prizes must be at least attractive enough to motivate because token prizes with little recognition value may kill the motivational effects of the contest. On the other hand, excessively expensive prizes may overemphasize competition and hurt sales force cohesiveness.

Duration. Contests usually last more than one month and less than five months. In general, salespeople should have enough time in the contest to make at least one complete pass through their territories. Extra-effort pressures can be maintained for only a limited time before participant interest begins to lag. Contests that occur too regularly (at the same time each year) may be looked upon as routine and lose their incentive value, while contests that are unexpected should generate more enthusiasm.

Publicity. Contests should be introduced in a surprise announcement followed by a publicity blitz. It is important that the exact nature and rules of the contest be announced to all salespeople at the same time in a dramatic fashion. Explanatory posters should be put up after the contest is announced, and some device showing everyone's relative progress should be prominently exhibited. If the contest involves a race, for example, model cars could show the leaders by their relative position on a track. Detailed, official feedback should be given to all participants at frequent intervals unless the contest is not competitive, in which case each person's progress can be conveyed confidentially.

Potential pitfalls. While well-devised contests can accomplish multiple organizational and individual salesperson's goals, the sales manager ought to recognize and avoid certain negative side effects. Contests can become so routine that they are expected and the value of awards is thought of as part of yearly compensation. Moreover, contests can become like addictive pills, providing only temporary benefits and a short-run cover for managerial deficiencies. Like any overused incentive, the contest award eventually tends to lose its motivational effects. Professional salespeople may look on even well-designed contests as beneath their image, and it is always difficult to devise themes that are simultaneously fun and image-enhancing. Some sales managers even feel that the money put into contests would provide a continuous incentive if it were instead spread to high performers as pay increases. This approach would be likely to increase costs, and there is little to substantiate its relative benefits compared with those of contests.

While the major purpose of sales contests is to enhance motivation, many times they can end up demotivating the sales force. An improperly implemented sales contest can destroy morale among salespeople as well as negatively affect sales. For example, if the sales contest rewards one person each year and the same person tends to win the contest year after year, some negative side effects are bound to occur. With only one winner per contest, everyone else feels like a loser. And if the company has a real top performer who continually wins the contest, this can only serve to reinforce the loser attitude among the sales force. Finally, the top performer and winner of the contest usually does not need the reward as much as some of the other salespeople do. Therefore, when the same person continually wins the award, this can create jealousy among the sales force as well as make the winner unpopular with his or her colleagues.

After sales contests end, some salespeople fall into a motivational valley, resulting in sales slumps. Sales managers need to provide positive encouragement to perk them up. The zeal to win contests can also lead to pressure-selling tactics, inventory overloading, outright cheating, and neglect of other customer relationships. Despite shortcomings, contests can provide a flexible and valuable managerial tool if themes, rules, prizes, participation, duration, and publicity are tailored to organizational and salespersons' goals. Some general guidelines concerning what not to do with sales contests are presented in Exhibit 13-8.

Sales Meetings

One of the most popular means of enhancing motivation as well as continuous training of salespeople is the sales meeting, be it national, regional, or local.

EXHIBIT 13-8

What *Not* to Do with a Sales Contest

1. *Do not reward just one person.* One or only a few winners can serve to demotivate the losers. A contest which no one has a chance of winning can often cause salespeople to sell less than before the contest started.

2. *Do not set goals too high.* Do not alienate the bulk of salespeople with goals that are too high. Motivate everyone, because the bulk of sales does not come from a top performer. There should be as many winners as possible.

3. *Do not start contests toward the end of the year.* Many salespeople perceive a year-end contest as a way to make up for poor planning and a bad sales year.

4. *Do not use sales volume as the only goal of every contest.* There are many marketing goals other than sales. Other goals can also increase motivation of salespeople who achieve less than others.

5. *Do not use the same prizes for every contest.* The same prize can lose impact very quickly.

6. *Do not include only salespeople in the contest.* A good opportunity to involve other people within the company is to make them part of the sales contest. The nonselling staff can do a great deal to help push their salespeople to perform better.

7. *Do not let the sales contest become a guessing game.* Everyone should clearly understand the purpose of the contest; otherwise lost sales are bound to occur. A sales contest is not an intelligence test.

8. *Do not look for a "fair" or a "just" contest.* Sales contests have specific goals to accomplish, and unfortunately some goals will be easier to accomplish for some than for others.

Source: Adapted from Heinz Godlmann, "Unrewarding Rewards," *Sales & Marketing Management,* April 1986, pp. 136–138.

Instead of utilizing the normal one-way communication from management to salespeople, sales meetings provide opportunities for two-way communication and interaction among all members of the marketing team—field and head-quarters. The company comes alive at sales meetings, and names become people as sales representatives, sales managers, marketing managers, and top company executives interact. Salespeople are able to see how their role as the field marketing arm of the company blends with headquarters marketing activities. Sales meetings may be viewed as the strategic "halftimes" in the selling game for communicating about new-product introductions, price changes, upcoming promotional campaigns, new policies, and overall company goals. They can help motivate salespeople to greater productivity through renewed consciousness of total company support efforts.[34]

National, regional, or local meetings. Usually held once a year, *national meetings* may include the entire sales force or only a select group of top performers. Travel and lodging expenses for sending salespeople to national meetings are considerable, and territorial opportunities or problems must go unattended while salespeople are away. National-meeting benefits, however, may overbalance these costs. Sales representatives get the chance to exchange ideas with company management, experience a pleasant change of environment and a break in their normal routine, and even hear motivational talks by experts and/or celebrities so that they return to their territories with renewed enthusiasm. Especially when the sales force is relatively small and scattered, national conferences can be an important unifying device. *Regional conferences,* planned with a work-oriented agenda, can be less expensive for large corporations whose sales forces have more localized selling problems. *Local meetings* and seminars are the backbone of the communication system and usually give salespersons the greatest support. These regularly held meetings are important for bestowing timely recognition on salespeople, providing group interaction, and focusing sales training on solving territorial problems and creating selling opportunities.

Planning.   Detailed advanced planning is required for effective sales meetings. Regional or local meetings are generally held monthly or weekly in the regional or branch sales office, and success depends upon developing a strong agenda. Planning for national conferences, however, is much more demanding. National-conference facilities must be reserved many months in advance, and goals, dates, programs, participants, and publicity must be arranged early on, often starting a year or more ahead of time. Usually, national sales conferences are held away from the immediate work environment, either at a resort area, if the purpose of the meeting is largely motivational, or a hotel close to company headquarters, if work is the primary objective. In planning sales meetings, there are several tasks:

- Establish meeting goals (from both the company's and the sales representatives' perspectives).

- Select a theme that integrates goals and communicates the overall purpose of the meeting.

- Develop a tentative agenda or program for the meeting and work up a preliminary budget.

- Finalize the program and budget, and send copies of the program to all attendees.

- Coordinate closely with all participants in the program to ensure they know their roles.

- Provide handouts summarizing the main points of the meeting for salespeople to take home for further review.

- Evaluate the meeting in terms of goal achievement.

Videoconferences.   An efficient way to link several different locations together for one sales meeting is by having a videoconference. Rather than bringing the entire sales force of an organization together under one roof, everyone can be linked together via satellite and/or interactive video. Recently, Avon celebrated its one-hundredth anniversary by connecting over 2,000 district sales managers in five cities for a videoconference. "We held a videoconference for the first time because we wanted every member of the Avon sales management family to be together simultaneously and share the excitement coming out of the celebration," says Linda Livingston-Mugnos, creative manager, sales meetings and conferences for Avon.[35] Many companies are realizing the benefits of videoconferences and are beginning to use them. A videoconference is an excellent way to inform and motivate the entire sales force of a company at one time. More important, it enables top management to provide consistent information to the entire sales force. Moreover, a teleconference to several locations enables top management not only to speak to each location simultaneously but also to tailor the content of each of the locations' meetings without having to hold separate regional meetings. Finally, as a spokesperson for Avon put it, "We could have brought all 2,000 sales managers to a central location for one big meeting, but we wouldn't have had the same feeling that we got with only 400 people in the room."[36] With the success Avon and others are experiencing with videoconferences, it is likely that videoconferences will become a big part of sales meetings in the future.

Promotion Opportunities

An attractive career path with "promotion decision" stages coming at regular intervals (at least every three to five years) can keep many individuals motivated throughout most of their careers.[37] People tend to become ego-involved with succeeding on the "fast track," and they continue to strive for the next promotion. To maximize motivational benefits from a career development plan, the sales manager must provide periodic feedback—at least yearly but more frequently in the early stages of career development. This feedback ought to come to salespeople through a comprehensive performance evaluation. Small sales units may find informal evaluations practical, but larger sales organizations need more formalized performance evaluation systems, supported by rating forms and written narratives maintained in the employee's personnel file.

In a simplified career path, sales trainees have an introductory or trial period of up to three years. By that time, the salesperson must either be promoted to the sales development stage or be terminated. Then, no later than his or her seventh anniversary with the sales force, the individual must be promoted to senior salesperson or let go. At this level, the individual may continue on a *career sales path* or switch to a *sales/marketing management career path.* Although the decision to remain on the sales path is largely up to the individual salesperson, the opportunity to move into management depends upon performance evaluations, which are discussed in Chapter 16.

Incentive Programs

Many companies feel that the most effective way to motivate the sales force is through an incentive program. Incentive spending is continually increasing and becoming a bigger part of many firms' budgets because incentives are viewed as tools with tremendous motivating power.[38] A recent survey indicated that approximately one-half of the responding companies considered incentive programs as essential to the success of their overall marketing plans. Moreover, 83 percent of the sample indicated that they use and will continue using incentive programs for their sales forces.[39]

Among the more important motivators in incentive programs are cash, travel, and merchandise. When salespeople achieve or surpass a specified sales quota, they are often given a certain monetary bonus to reward them for their performance as well as to motivate them to continue this behavior. Travel is also used in the same way to help motivate the sales force. Some of the more popular destinations for travel incentives are Europe and the Mediterranean, Hawaii, the Caribbean, Bermuda, Mexico, and South America. The most common items of merchandise used as a sales force incentive include award plaques and trophies, consumer electronics, household goods, clothing, sporting goods, and travel accessories. See the following example of a unique incentive currently being used by Timex.

A "DRESS-FOR-SUCCESS" SALES FORCE AT TIMEX

One indirect motivation for the sales force is the use of "percs"—additional perquisites like autos and office furniture. Timex attempts to perk up its sales force by reimbursing its Watch Division salespeople for 67 percent of their clothing purchases each year. As long as the new clothing conforms to corporate standards, Timex allows annual payout limits of $1,500 for salespeople, $2,000 for middle managers, and $2,500 for senior sales management. New or entry-level salespeople are given an additional $500 to $1,000 allowance to help build a basic wardrobe. Timex gives its sales force a list of recommended stores and brands, including Brooks Brothers, Paul Stuart, and Hickey-Freeman. Additionally, all salespeople are given the dress-for-success paperback by Jacoby to assist them in their purchases. Timex feels this program is an excellent investment in the company's image and worth every penny of the $75,000 it spends each year on clothing for the sales force. Moreover, this program may act as an excellent incentive to make the sales force much more professional and efficient and, in essence, to motivate the sales force to *work smarter!*[40]

In some cases, cars, jewelry, and mink coats have been awarded to top achievers. Many companies will select one of these and use it as the primary tool of their incentive program. Recently, however, a study reported that 15 percent of the companies it surveyed preferred a three-tiered approach using cash, travel, and merchandise because they found it to be their most cost-effective and productive tool.[41]

An effective sales incentive program can accomplish several important goals. Perhaps the main reason for using an incentive program is to increase sales per salesperson. Many companies find that incentives help boost the individual sales productivity of the sales force. Additionally, sales incentive programs can help increase the number of new accounts brought into a company. Other benefits of sales incentive programs include helping launch new products, boosting morale, and reviving old products. Exhibit 13-9 presents some additional reasons why companies offer sales incentives to their sales forces.

Sales incentive programs can be a very inexpensive way to increase sales. The Incentive Marketing Association reports that in 1989 the typical sales in-

EXHIBIT 13-9

Why Companies Offer Sales Incentives

Reason	Percent
Boost morale.	12.0
Provide sales training.	2.0
Increase dollar sales per salesperson.	17.0
Increase units sold per salesperson.	10.0
Increase average dollar sales per account.	8.5
Upgrade existing accounts to high-ticket products.	4.0
Open new accounts.	15.0
Promote dealer activity.	6.5
Launch new products.	10.0
Revive old products.	4.0
Boost recession-period sales.	5.0
Increase awareness of company name.	3.0
Match competition's program.	2.0
Other*	1.0

*Other (equal precentage for): Boost effort to switch from customer to us. Increase salary level. Maintain flow of information on competitors. Increase gross margin sales per salesperson. Get rid of slow-moving equipment. Match industry's total compensation package. Assist long-range goal setting/planning.
Source: Adapted from a study reported in *Business Marketing*, April 1985, p. 42.

centive program increased sales by an average of 19 percent. Moreover, the cost of the incentive program as a percentage of increased sales was only 8 percent. Since 40 percent of all participating salespeople earned awards, it is obvious that the incentive programs were not only cost-efficient tools but also strong motivators.[42]

It is clear that more and more sales managers are finding incentives to be of considerable value in helping them achieve their goals. Incentives are excellent motivational tools as well as morale-building activities. The important implication for sales managers is that salespeople are willing to extend themselves if there is a carrot dangling in front of them.

While travel and expense accounts can build morale as well as sales, sales managers must deal with unique situations that often arise concerning these matters. The *Ethics* scenario on page 442 presents such a situation.

MOTIVATING SALESPEOPLE OVER TIME

Just as salespeople change over time, so may their job performance and motivation. Recently, researchers have identified four distinct stages in a sales career and possible motivators at each corresponding stage; Exhibit 13-10 summarizes this research. Sales managers must realize, for instance, that what motivates

---

ETHICS IN SALES MANAGEMENT: LOWER EXPENSES OR MORALE?

You are the national sales manager for a large consumer goods company with a liberal travel and expense program for its salespeople. Many of your reps have large territories requiring a great deal of air travel. Your company always reimburses all travel expenses, but does suggest that reps "search for the best possible airfares whenever traveling." Because of rising fares, your boss has asked you to do whatever you can to hold down air travel expenses. From a preliminary investigation of your reps' travel patterns, you discovered that the majority fly with only *one* airline. When you confronted them about this issue, most gave the same explanation: "All airlines charge about the same fares, so I stick with one airline so I can take advantage of the frequent-flyer programs!" Some of your reps travel so frequently that they can accumulate five to ten *free* tickets a year!

1. Are the reps behaving ethically by flying with only one airline? Why or why not?
2. Should any or all of the sales force's free airline tickets be given back to the company to be used for future business travel?
3. What can be done to hold down air travel costs in this situation?

---

top-performing salespeople in the maintenance stage of their selling career may not work for younger salespeople in the exploration stage; the latter may need more personal mentoring as part of their motivation. Therefore, sales managers should consider which career stages their salespeople are in before developing a motivational program for the sales force.

EXHIBIT 13-10

Motivating Salespeople throughout Their Career

Career Stage	Characteristics of Salesperson	Sales Force Motivator
Exploration	Is in early phase of career Is searching for comfortable position Is likely to change occupation	Use communication to build self-confidence and lower uncertainties
Establishment	Seeks stabilization in occupation Sees career as very important Strives for professional success and promotion	Widen criteria for success Introduce rewards for meeting challenges
Maintenance	Is concerned with retaining current position Shows greater commitment to firm; is less likely to switch jobs Adapts to changes to keep performance at current level	Reward creativity and self-reliance Emphasize techniques for working smarter
Disengagement	Exhibits declining performance Psychologically disengages from work Is preparing for retirement	Help reduce number of work hours

Source: Based on William L. Cron, Alan J. Dubinsky, and Ronald E. Michaels, "The Influence of Career Stages on Components of Salesperson Motivation," *Journal of Marketing,* January 1988, pp. 78–92.

SUMMARY

Motivation plays a major role in a salesperson's performance, yet it is a difficult and complex concept to understand. Each person can be motivated by different factors. Traditionally, monetary rewards have been thought of as the primary motivating force among salespeople. Recently, however, sales managers have begun to consider nonfinancial rewards as major motivating factors.

There are several theories of motivation that can be used to assist sales managers in their understanding of what motivates the sales force. Maslow's theory is based on the assumption that people are motivated by a hierarchy of psychological growth needs. As one level of needs is satisfied, individuals move up to fulfill higher-level needs. Sales managers should be aware of which level the sales reps are on and help their people accomplish the corresponding needs. Herzberg's motivator-hygiene theory contends that managers must be aware of sources of satisfaction, or motivators, that are related to the job as well as sources of dissatisfaction, or hygiene factors, that are part of the worker's environment. Expectancy theory is based on the fact that people are motivated to work toward a goal when they expect their efforts will pay off. Achievement theory contends that people are motivated on the basis of their achievement needs and that some individuals have greater achievement needs than others. Inequity theory says that people compare their relative work contributions and rewards with those of other individuals in similar situations. People are motivated if they feel that there is an inequitable situation—one in which they feel that they are under-rewarded or overrewarded for their contribution. Finally, attribution theory contends that people are motivated on the basis of their perceptions of why an event occurred. For example, if individuals feel they failed because of a lack of effort on their part, they may be motivated to work harder. In short, there are many theories that can provide insight to sales managers and help them better motivate the sales force.

Sales managers have several motivational tools at their disposal to implement their general theory of, or approach to, motivating the sales force. Beyond offering the financial compensation rewards discussed earlier in the text, sales managers can consider such motivational tools as sales contests, sales meetings, promotion opportunities, and incentive programs for their salespeople. All these tools are important; they can significantly enhance the performance of each salesperson if implemented correctly.

STUDY QUESTIONS

1. Define motivation. Discuss how motivation affects performance.

2. Which of the contemporary theories of motivation would you use to help motivate your sales force? Why?

3. "The best way to motivate a sales force is by monetary incentives." Comment.

4. Discuss the reasons for using sales contests. What makes a good sales contest?

5. Many sales managers face the problem of motivating top-performing salespeople who no longer respond to the incentive of more money. How would you motivate these people?

6. What is the difference between working harder and working smarter? How can sales managers use these concepts in increasing sales force performance?

7. What advantages do videoconferences have over the traditional sales meeting? When might a videoconference be more appropriate than a sales meeting?

IN-BASKET EXERCISE

Several months ago you hired one of the most energetic, highly motivated, achievement-oriented college recruits in years. This person had a 3.2 grade-point average, was an officer in the business fraternity, and supported herself through school with a part-time sales job. However, you just finished her first quarterly performance review, and things do not look too good. She finished last in your region in sales volume and in generating new customer leads. You are very confident that she has the brains, communication skills, and product knowledge to succeed, so you are very surprised with her performance.

1. What should you do in this situation? Should you do nothing and give the salesperson time to prove herself?

2. Do you think the situation indicates a motivational problem? If so, what motivational tools do you think might be important here?

CASE 13-1

WESTERN RAIL: MOTIVATING INSIDE AND OUTSIDE SALESPEOPLE

Western Rail (WR) has merged with several smaller railroads in the past two decades to become one of the leading railroads in the nation. The railway serves thirty-five states primarily in the western and southern sections of the country. The deregulation of the rail industry has made pricing a major marketing variable and caused the rail industry to reevaluate the role of its sales forces. Although transporting raw materials is still an important customer base for the railroad industry, the real profit is being derived from a relatively new division known as intermodal (piggybacking trucks on rails). The ironic aspect is that this has made truckers (a primary competitor) potential customers. Prior to deregulation, convenience and service were the only way to differentiate carriers. Now, mar-

keting has become a necessity in the strategic programs of the railroad. Previously, the sales and marketing departments were the same. Now, sales has been reorganized as a separate division.

History of the WR Sales Forces

Prior to 1980 there was only one sales force comprised of 256 salespeople. The salespeople sold transportation and concentrated their sales by business units (BU). The basic divisions or units consisted of forestry, auto, commodities, grains, coal, international, and industrial. The salespeople were headquartered in twenty-eight area offices across the west and south. Each office was composed of a sales manager and four to twelve

Case prepared by William Moncrief, Texas Christian University. Used with permission.

salespeople. Each office may or may not have contained a national-account manager. The account manager was responsible for the very large accounts, and the accounts were serviced by a number of WR salespeople. An account might have had as many as twelve salespeople calling upon it from different area offices around the country. The account manager, however, had the ultimate responsibility for the account.

By 1985, company sales were in excess of $1 billion annually. The number of customers that each salesperson called on varied widely. A salesperson might have anywhere from 16 to 260 active accounts (an active account is one that made a purchase in the past year). Therefore, the number of actual in-person calls also could vary widely, ranging from 20 to 120 sales calls per month. Management was concerned that there was considerable business being lost because of wasted salesperson time spent on small accounts, and the neglect of larger potential accounts. In 1986, after much research and discussion, management decided to create a telemarketing division. Telemarketing, although not widely used in the railroad business, had proved to be very effective in other industries. The telemarketing division's responsibility would be to sell to all customers that produced $50,000 dollars or less in a year.

Telemarketing

The telemarketing division was headquartered in a large southern city with forty telemarketers working in a single partitioned room. The telemarketing organization used a computerized data base consisting of information on 20,000 accounts that were considered to be too small to justify field sales force attention. Only 14,000 of the accounts were active. Management estimated that half of the inactive accounts had the potential to become active. The telemarketing department was divided into four selling groups consisting of a manager and ten account representatives.

Each telemarketing salesperson has a variety of responsibilities. First, the salesperson has specific accounts for which he or she has responsibility. Incoming calls are dispatched to the account manager for that particular account. The telemarketer has full account responsibility for the account unless the account surpasses $50,000 dollars, in which case it is supposed to be transferred to a field salesperson. In reality, this occurs only about 50 percent of the time. Second, the salesperson is responsible for maintaining contact with both the active and the inactive accounts and for prospecting for new accounts. Third, the telemarketer conducts surveys and market intelligence for the business units, sets up appointments, and coordinates activities. Fourth, the telemarketer answers inquiries from a toll-free number in response to direct-mail and magazine advertisements. Last, the telemarketer handles complaints about lost, delayed, or problem shipments.

Reorganization

The creation of a telemarketing unit required some degree of reorganization. One question that management wrestled with was "Where will we obtain the telemarketers?" Previously, management had determined that there were too many salespeople in the field, but the company had never had to lay off any salespeople in the past. This was a record that it did not want to break. Therefore, management decided to move some salespeople from the field into the telemarketing center. This naturally required a relocation on the part of the salesperson. Several salespeople refused to move, and quit. Sixteen salespeople did move, although with a great deal of resistance and some resentment. The other twenty-four telemarketers were hired from outside the company or primarily from the ranks of the salesclerks.

In 1988, two years after the creation of the telemarketing unit, the field salespeople were again reorganized. Marketing research indicated that the field sales force was improperly deployed and that there were still too many people in the field. As the company acquired smaller railroads, it also acquired their salespeople. With very little turnover occurring, streamlined procedures, and the acquired salespeople, WR had too many people in the field sales force. The reorganization forced some people to relocate; others were terminated. Meanwhile, the telemarketing unit was performing better than expected. The telemarketers were producing over $3 million a week, and the field salespeople were becoming apprehensive about their jobs. The last straw was a consulting company that was brought in to examine the deployment of the salespeople. Rumors started among the sales force that many would be moved to telemarketing, others would be fired, and still others again forced to relocate. Although the rumors were not totally accurate, there was some basis for the fear and anxiety. The telemarketers were performing exceptionally well at considerably less cost, and management still felt that there were too many field salespeople. The result of the rumors and recent changes was a loss of morale among the field sales force.

Meanwhile, everything was not running as smoothly with the telemarketers as management would have liked. Sales and contacts were definitely up, but there was not a positive attitude in the telemarketing unit. Consultants were hired to examine the telemarketing unit and offer an assessment of the organization. The consultants found that the former field salespeople were bored with making all their contacts by phone. They missed the relative freedom they possessed as field representatives. The former field telemarketers also felt some resentment because of a perceived or actual demotion to telemarketing. The former sales-clerks were basically happy with the job but resented the second-class citizenship they felt from the field salespeople and some managers. The telemarketers as a whole were unhappy that they were not allowed to maintain large accounts and that they were "sup-posed" to give up accounts once they exceeded the $50,000 limit. The telemarketers also complained about their working conditions. They felt that the forty cu-bicles, which were only 5 feet high, did not allow much privacy. The consultants also noted that the telemarketers spent an inordinate amount of time in the coffee room, as much as two hours a day.

After examining the telemarketing operation the consultants went to the field salespeople to determine their attitudes toward the telemarketers. The consul-tants were particularly interested in the field sales-people's views as to whether they thought that a team concept (a telemarketer and a field representative) would be helpful in the selling process. Some cus-tomers had complained that the field salespeople were difficult to contact because of their travel and time spent out of the office. The consultants felt that the account-knowledgeable telemarketer might make an effective team with the field salesperson. The field peo-ple were asked, "How effective would you and a te-lemarketer be as a team?" The results were:

Very effective	10.5%
Effective	42.1%
Uncertain	15.8%
Somewhat effective	10.5%
Not at all effective	21.1%

The field salespeople were then asked, "How useful would a telemarketer be as a backup?" The results were as follows:

Very useful	31.6%
Useful	21.1%
Uncertain	21.1%
Somewhat useful	15.8%
Not at all useful	10.5%

The consultants concluded that there was still a feeling of fear and resentment toward the telemarketers. Many of the field salespeople still feel that their jobs will be taken by telemarketers or that they will someday have to become telemarketers.

Salesperson Description

The typical WR field salesperson has been with the company 15.8 years and is 43 years old. The field salesperson is paid by straight salary. The pay is very good and above industry averages. The salespeople, when questioned, indicated an unusually high degree of satisfaction with pay. The company wanted straight salary to be able to better control the day-to-day ac-tivities of the sales force. Currently, WR does not use a bonus system although the concept is under study.

The telemarketers are also paid by straight salary. The salary is not as high as that of the field sales force but is higher than the standard telemarketing job. The former field salespeople are paid at the rate that they were making in the field. The consultants recom-mended a salary plus commission for the telemar-keters to give them more incentive, but management has problems with this approach because of potential confrontations with the field salespeople.

The many changes that have occurred at WR have increased sales and profit. However, they have also created problems. Morale is lower than it has ever been. Management is seeking a way to motivate the two sales forces and decrease the competitiveness and resentment among them. The railroad industry had changed very little in the previous century, until the past few years. Now, deregulation and modernization have caused the railroad to look to new ways of selling and marketing. Unfortunately, changes have resulted in motivation problems for the sales force.

Questions

1. What would you do to motivate the field sales force and to rebuild morale? How would your solution affect the telemarketers?

2. Would any of the theories of motivation that were presented in the chapter help WR gain a better understanding of its morale problem? If so, which one or ones?

3. Do you believe the compensation plan is the root of the morale problem among the sales force? Why or why not? Recommend an alternative compen-sation plan for WR.

4. Would any type of recognition program help re-build morale for the WR sales force? If so, what type?

5. The nonintermodal sales force was historically the backbone of the company. Now, the intermodal division is the "darling" of the company. How would you remotivate the nonintermodal salespeople.

6. The consultants suggest that a team effort be de-veloped between the telemarketers and the field sales force. How would you motivate the two groups to work together in a team effort?

CASE 13-2

MOTIVATIONAL PROBLEMS AT MEDCO PHARMACEUTICALS

Ralph Starr, vice president of marketing at MEDCO Pharmaceuticals, is beginning to question his company's various methods of motivating the sales force. Over the last year or so he has noticed a gradual decline in sales force morale. Sales among his top salespeople have been relatively flat, and from various conversations he has heard around the office, Starr believes his salespeople have become somewhat complacent and could use a good dose of motivation. The motivational techniques currently used at the company include a generous commission system, a promotion plan, sales contests, and sales meetings. In an attempt to determine if the motivational tools at MEDCO are inadequate, Starr critically evaluated them.

Commissions on Sales

MEDCO believes that the compensation package at the firm can do a great deal to motivate the salespeople to work harder. All salespeople are paid a fixed salary of $28,000 a year plus commissions on sales volume. The commission system is set up so that the higher the sales volume, the higher the commission. Commissions for the sales force range from 6 to as high as 18 percent.

Starr believes that this is a generous compensation plan and that "the sky's the limit" when it comes to salespeoples' earnings at MEDCO. According to Starr, who believes that "salespeople are, to a great extent, motivated by money," there are very few problems with the compensation package at MEDCO.

Promotion within the Company

Another means of motivating the salespeople is MEDCO's promotion-from-within program. MEDCO is very proud of the fact that the majority of company executives started their careers in entry-level positions within the firm. Furthermore, all the marketing management personnel started in sales. The promotion-from-within program for the salespeople is set up so that the promotion is tied almost exclusively to sales performance. Salespeople who were top performers over the last several years are the ones that are promoted.

Starr believes the promotion-from-within program is an excellent way to motivate the sales force. "Each person knows exactly where he or she stands and what it will take to move up the corporate ladder. If a salesperson wants to become part of the management group at MEDCO, all it takes is a little hard work!" Starr's first job was as a sales rep for MEDCO sixteen years ago.

Sales Contests

MEDCO constantly uses sales contests as a motivator for its sales force. Despite the fact that MEDCO's sales force is well compensated, management feels that individuals can be motivated to reach their peak sales performance with sales contests. The company conducts a sales contest every year and is very careful to make the contest a fair one. The contest is set up to reward individual performance rather than the top performers. Themes of the contest are changed yearly, as are prizes. While the prizes are usually trips to exotic locations, expensive gifts such as new cars and Rolex watches are given on occasion.

Once again, Starr has a difficult time finding fault with the yearly sales contests. "We have thoroughly done our homework concerning how to run sales contests, and I feel we are doing an excellent job of motivating our salespeople with these contests," says Starr. "When I was a salesperson, I couldn't wait for the chance to reach my next year's sales goal. By reaching this goal, I was assured of a free vacation to Jamaica or Tahiti or even a gold watch. These things motivated me to sell my heart out!"

Sales Meetings

MEDCO's Atlanta, Georgia, headquarters has annually held a national sales meeting and five regional sales meetings. The national sales meeting is held at exclusive resort areas, usually in early June. The last six years' meetings were held at Knots Berry Farm, near Los Angeles, California; Colonial Manor, Williamsburg, Virginia; Kennedy Flight Center, Florida; French Quarter, New Orleans, Louisiana; Harrah's Club, Lake Tahoe, Nevada; and Disney World, Orlando, Florida. The meetings start on a Tuesday, last three days, and are considered an excellent means for announcing new-product lines. All of MEDCO's top management and the board of directors attend, with the daytime devoted to business discussions and the nighttime set aside for recreation for management, employees, and their families. The national meetings are attended by approximately 100 to 150 people. Each year, the total attendance has increased by 10 percent. The national meetings have become extremely expensive and time-consuming to prepare. On the other hand, the regional meetings have proved to be more productive and far less expensive, primarily because of the lower transportation and lodging costs.

The effectiveness of both the national and regional meetings is being evaluated. When the regional meetings are held, MEDCO sends eight top executives. The format is geared to seminars and workshops. Although the regional meetings appear to be better for technical instruction, they are not thought to be as valuable in strengthening total company morale. Starr has reviewed the major cost factors associated with the meetings and has listed several alternatives. They are as follows.

1. Change the format of the national meeting to include technical instruction, thus eliminating the need for the regional meetings.

2. Exclude the nighttime recreational activities.

3. Hold meetings at less expensive locations.

4. Send fewer top management personnel.

5. Discourage relatives from attending the national meetings.

While the meetings are expensive, Starr believes they are great at building morale and improving communication between the salespeople and management. "It is important for all employees of a company to get together once a year in order to lift spirits and increase camaraderie," says Starr.

Nonfinancial Factors?

After evaluating the motivational tools that MEDCO employs, Starr was having difficulty finding any problems. However, many of the other MEDCO executives felt that these motivators were a bit excessive given the recent lackluster sales performance from the sales force. These other executives are continually pressur-

ing Starr to control some of the costs associated with the motivators, since it is very difficult for them to see how such motivators as sales contests and sales meetings contribute to the overall success of the company, especially during years of very marginal sales increases. Recently, Starr has read about nonfinancial motivators for the sales force. However, he foresees the following problems with them:

1. Will nonfinancial motivators actually keep his salespeople happy and enthusiastic?

2. Can a sales force that is accustomed to high financial and tangible incentives be motivated with intangible things?

3. How can he actually measure the return generated by nonfinancial rewards?

Questions

1. Do you agree with Starr's evaluation of MEDCO's motivational tools? Why or why not?

2. Do you perceive MEDCO's philosophy regarding sales force motivation as working harder or working smarter? Why? Why do you think this philosophy is used? Should it be changed?

3. Do you think Starr is justified in believing that nonfinancial incentives will cause problems at MEDCO? Comment on the three problems Starr foresees.

4. Recommend a totally new motivational program for MEDCO. Support your recommendations.

REFERENCES

1. Personal interview with Jim Anglin, October 1990.
2. Jane Templeton, "Carving Out True Recognition," *Sales & Marketing Management*, June 1986, pp. 106–114; Bill Kelley, "Recognition Reaps Rewards," *Sales & Marketing Management*, June 1986, pp. 100–104.
3. See R. C. Smyth and M. J. Murphy, *Compensating and Motivating Salesmen*, American Management Association, New York, 1969; A. Haring and M. L. Morris, *Contests, Prizes, Awards for Sales Motivation*, Sales and Marketing Executives International, New York, 1968; D. A. Welks, *Incentive Plans for Salesmen*, The National Industrial Conference Board, New York, 1970.
4. See C. P. Alderfer, "An Empirical Test of a New Theory of Human Needs," *Organizational Behavior and Human Performance*, vol. 4, 1969, pp. 142–175; Frederick Herzberg, Bernard Mausner, and Barbara Snyderman, *The Motivation to Work*, 2d ed., Wiley, New York, 1959; Edward E. Lawler III, *Pay and Organizational Effectiveness: A Psychological View*, McGraw-Hill, New York, 1971; R. L. Opsahl and M. D. Dunnette, "The Role of Financial Compensation in Industrial Motivation," *Psychological Bulletin*, vol. 66, 1966, pp. 94–118.

5. N. Ford, O. Walker, Jr., and G. Churchill, Jr., "Differences in Attractiveness of Alternative Rewards among Industrial Salespeople: Additional Evidence," *Journal of Business Research,* April 1985, pp. 123–138.

6. "What Motivates Top Salespeople," *Psychology Today,* March 1984.

7. Robert A. Weaver, "Set Goals to Tap Self-Motivation," *Business Marketing,* December 1985, p. 54.

8. Ibid., p. 55.

9. Abraham H. Maslow, *Motivation and Personality,* Harper & Row, New York, 1954.

10. Frederick Herzberg, "One More Time: How Do You Motivate Employees?" *Harvard Business Review,* vol. 46, 1968, pp. 53–62.

11. Ibid., p. 60.

12. Victor H. Vroom, *Work and Motivation,* Wiley, New York, 1964; David C. McClelland, *The Achieving Society,* Van Nostrand, New York, 1964; John W. Atkinson, *An Introduction to Motivation,* Van Nostrand, New York, 1964. For other insights on expectancy theory, see Richard L. Oliver, "Expectancy Theory Predictions of Salesmen's Performance," *Journal of Marketing Research,* August 1974, pp. 243–253; Arnold K. Korman, "Expectancies as Determinants of Performance," *Journal of Applied Psychology,* vol. 55, 1971, pp. 218–222.

13. David C. McClelland, John W. Atkinson, Russell A. Clark, and Edgar L. Lowell, *The Achievement Motive,* Appleton-Century-Crofts, New York, 1953, pp. 275–318.

14. Saul W. Gellerman, *Motivation and Productivity,* American Management Association, Stanford, Calif., 1978, pp. 115–141, reviewing Stanley Schacter, *The Psychology of Affiliation,* Stanford University Press, Stanford, Calif., 1959.

15. P. S. Goodman and A. Friedman, "An Examination of Adams' Theory of Inequity," *Administrative Science Quarterly,* vol. 16, 1971, pp. 271–288.

16. James H. Donnelley, Jr., and John M. Ivancevich, "Role Clarity and the Salesman," *Journal of Marketing,* January 1975, pp. 71–74.

17. For perspectives on managing sales force turnover, see Allen C. Bluedorn, "Managing Turnover Strategically," *Business Horizons,* March–April 1982, pp. 6–12.

18. See Harish Sujan, "Smarter versus Harder: An Exploratory Attributional Analysis of Salespeoples' Motivations," *Journal of Marketing Research,* February 1986, pp. 41–49.

19. Harish Sujan and Barton A. Weitz, "The Psychology of Motivation," *Marketing Communications,* January 1986, pp. 24–28.

20. Dov Eden, "Pygmalion, Goal Setting and Expectancy: Compatible Ways to Boost Productivity," *Academy of Management Review,* October 1988, pp. 639–652; Gary P. Yatham, Miriam Erez, and Edwin A. Locke, "Resolving Scientific Disputes by the Joint Design of Crucial Experiments by the Erez-Yatham Dispute Regarding Participation in Goal-Setting," *Journal of Applied Psychology,* November 1988, pp. 753–772.

21. Ricky Griffin, *Management,* Houghton Mifflin, Boston, 1990.

22. George Leslie, "U.S. Reps Should Learn to Sell Japanese," *Marketing News,* Oct. 29, 1990, p. 6.

23. Kate Bertrand, "Incentives Reward Teamwork," *Business Marketing,* December 1989, p. 29.

24. Templeton, op. cit.

25. Kelley, op. cit.

26. Ibid., p. 103.

27. Adapted from Templeton, op. cit.

28. Leslie Brennan, "Sales Secrets of the Incentive Stars," *Sales & Marketing Management,* April 1990, pp. 92–100.

29. Ibid.

30. Stephanie Della Cogna, "The Invasion of the Nordies," *New England Business,* January 1990, pp. 24–25.

31. Herzberg, op. cit.

32. Rayna Skolnik, "Who Gets What—and Why," *Sales & Marketing Management,* Apr. 9, 1979, pp. 39–42.

33. Robert Patty, *Managing Salespeople*, Reston Publishing, Reston, Va., 1979, p. 261.
34. For a detailed discussion of sales meetings, see Rolph Anderson and Bert Rosenbloom, ''Conducting Successful Sales Meetings,'' in John L. DiGaetani (ed.), *The Handbook of Executive Communication*, Dow Jones-Irwin, Homewood, Ill., 1986, pp. 611–632.
35. ''How Avon Rings Their Chimes,'' *Sales & Marketing Management*, November 1986, pp. 117–118.
36. Ibid., p. 118.
37. Marvin A. Jolson, ''The Salesman's Career Cycle,'' *Journal of Marketing*, July 1974, pp. 39–46.
38. ''Survey Facts 1989,'' *Incentive*, December 1989, pp. 21–37.
39. John Couretas, ''Most Plan to Boost Spending; Cash Tops List,'' *Business Marketing*, April 1985, pp. 40–48.
40. Adapted from ''Timex Subsidizes Suits and Ties,'' *Sales & Marketing Management*, November 1986, pp. 26–27.
41. Couretas, op. cit., p. 42.
42. ''Survey Facts 1989,'' op. cit.

14

LEADING THE SALES FORCE

LEARNING OBJECTIVES

When you finish this chapter, you should understand:

▲ How leadership and motivation are related
▲ The dynamics of leadership
▲ The basics underlying the major theories of leadership
▲ The sources of power leaders tend to possess
▲ The general styles leaders use
▲ The importance communication plays in effective leadership
▲ The barriers to communication and the ways to overcome them

A DAY ON THE JOB

Marilynn Davis, divisional vice president at American Express, has a unique leadership style that may become very popular in the 1990s. "It only takes a few minutes to do small things that will keep employees motivated and caring about the company," says Davis. "Simple acts of recognition," she says, "accomplish more than the crack of a whip any day." Davis is a very concerned and empathetic leader when it comes to her subordinates. For example, when she took over the division, she started a tradition of "cake and bull" sessions for employees' birthdays. "People are your biggest component," says Davis, and "you can't expect them to be machines." According to anyone familiar with Davis's division, her leadership style inspires loyalty and trust among all her subordinates. Davis's leadership style can be summarized as one that builds team spirit and morale by tempering business with pleasure. This is a philosophy that works well for this leader at American Express Corporation.[1]

What do Lee Iacocca, Admiral "Bull" Halsey, Vince Lombardi, and Joan of Arc have in common? They are all great leaders. What makes a great leader? Most people equate a leader with the military or with sports. Generals and coaches are people who provide direction, goals, tools, and tactics and are generally believed to be leaders. Leaders are organized thinkers who have a long-term perspective and a plan to get there. A leader must be able to work with people. General Dwight D. Eisenhower explained leadership to his men this way: He would lay a piece of string on the table and pull one end. He'd then say, "Pull it, and it will follow you anywhere, push it and it goes nowhere at all."[2]

The 1980s may be remembered by many employees as the decade of the "big bad boss." The intense competition from foreign companies forced many U.S. firms to become lean and mean, which meant cutting costs, laying off workers, and closing down factories. Many experts are now questioning whether these extreme tactics will work in the 1990s. Several of the tough-guy leaders of the eighties, like Texas Air's Frank Lorenzo or Helmsley Hotel's Leona Helmsley, were not always that successful. Leaders today must realize that U.S. business is facing its first labor shortage in twenty years. Therefore, good employees will be harder and harder to find.

The study of leadership is not only timely but important as well. In Chapter 13, motivation was described as a concept meaning "to move." But in moving, one needs a direction or something to move toward—and this is where leadership comes in. Motivation stimulates the movement, while leadership provides the direction that simultaneously achieves both the sales organization's and the individual salesperson's goals. Leadership can be thought of as motivation theory in action. This chapter presents an analysis of leadership as well as various workable concepts and applications that will help sales managers keep the sales force enthusiastic, goal-directed, and achievement-oriented.

Successful sales organizations usually have one critical asset that significantly differentiates them from unsuccessful organizations. That asset is *effective leadership*. One recent study postulated that all companies are basically alike and that only 20 percent of what a company does is unique. But it is that 20 percent which enables a company to distinguish itself in the marketplace. Moreover, the key to uniqueness or success is *people!*[3]

Plenty of people will put themselves up for leadership positions, but few of these people are really capable of providing the leadership needed by the organization. Sales managers occupy positions that call for strong leadership, but it is often not provided because too few sales managers understand the role of leadership or its proper application. *How* sales managers lead frequently determines organizational success or failure as much as, or more than, *what* they attempt to accomplish. It is important that sales managers study leadership theories and the appropriate application of different leadership styles because leadership is vital to organizational success.

WHAT IS LEADERSHIP?

Leadership can be many things. An effective leader is one who motivates, influences, provides a good example, and gives direction. Leadership can be associated with a person's inner traits. A person who has leadership qualities is also one who is achievement-oriented, assertive, and decisive. Leadership can be seen as the ability to set goals and to communicate as needed in order to direct people toward those goals. With these perceptions in mind, one can define the basics of leadership as *people, influence, goals,* and *communication.* Leadership involves communication between people and the use of power or influence, and its major purpose is to achieve a goal. These four elements are the basis of the formal definition of leadership. According to Tannenbaum and his coauthors, "Leadership is a behavioral process in which one person attempts to influence other people's behavior toward the accomplishment of goals."[4]

In a sales management context, leadership focuses mainly on the qualities of the sales manager and the organizational situation. Specifically, leadership deals with the relationship between a sales manager or sales supervisor and the salespeople. The dynamics of leadership are presented in Exhibit 14-1 and include the sales manager (leader), the salespeople (followers), and the specific

EXHIBIT 14-1

The Dynamics of Sales Management Leadership

situation. As shown, leadership is an ongoing process that cannot be studied in a vacuum. The organizational setting, human needs and power, and the specific situation have an important influence on leadership ability.

To further clarify the nature of leadership, one must understand the relationship between administration, supervision, and leadership—all different but somewhat overlapping functions of sales managers. Briefly, *administration* tends to be identified with the largely nonpeople, policy-making functions of management, whereas *supervision* pertains to responsibilities that closely focus on interpersonal relationships and monitor the daily work of a group of people. Nearly all managers perform some supervisory duties, but direct supervision becomes less evident at higher levels in the organization. Most important, *leadership* is the process of exercising social influence or inspirational power over people's behavior toward goal achievement. It is the ability to get people to do willingly what they would not do on their own. Leaders influence people's *willingness* to act rather than force compliance.

LEADERSHIP AND MANAGEMENT

Sales managers must understand that although leadership and management are related, they are also very different. Management is primarily a *learned* process whereby subordinates are guided in the performance of formally prescribed duties toward the achievement of organizational goals. By contrast, leadership is more of an *emotional* process whereby people are moved in some direction through noncoercive means. Thus, a person can be a manager, a leader, both, or neither. People said that Steven Jobs had charisma and could inspire motivation; however, he failed as a manager at Apple Computer because he lacked managerial ability. On the other hand Harold Geneen, former CEO of ITT, was considered a very good manager, yet he lost his position because he alienated his subordinates—he was thought to lack leadership ability.[5] An effective manager is one who has both management skills and leadership ability. A sales organization is a reflection of its leader. Shortcomings in salespeople or in their performance can usually be traced to inadequacy in sales management, while superior performance is generally the result of outstanding leadership.

Leader Influence and Power

Tannenbaum and his coauthors have described leadership as involving "interpersonal influence, exercised in situations and directed, through the communication process, toward the attainment of goals."[6] Central to understanding leader influence over an organization is the concept of power. Leaders may draw upon power from a variety of sources: legitimate power, reward power, coercive power, referent power, and expert power.[7]

Legitimate power derives from formally delegated authority and is recognized by others as necessary in achieving organizational objectives. It is based on a person's position in a hierarchy. *Reward power* involves the ability to provide subordinates with various benefits, including money, praise, or promotion. *Coercive power* comes from the ability to punish or withhold rewards. It is based on obtaining compliance through fear of punishment. *Referent power* depends upon the leader's ability to inspire and to connect with other influential people. Finally, *expert power* is based on the leader's skills, knowledge, and special abilities. Most sales managers have access to all these power sources, and they attempt to use each at the appropriate time and situation to influence salespeople to achieve desired goals. Top management can help create an organizational climate in which leadership thrives by encouraging, recognizing, and rewarding skillful, innovative leadership.

Sales managers can influence the behavior of their salespeople by using the various sources of power. The major behaviors that can be affected include commitment, compliance, and resistance.[8] *Commitment* occurs when salespeople are enthusiastic about carrying out the sales manager's request and make a maximum effort to do so. They are committed to their sales manager's objectives. With *compliance,* salespersons are not as enthusiastic about their sales manager's plans and will go along with them without necessarily accepting them. *Resistance* is the most undesirable of the three behaviors. It occurs when the sales force rejects the sales manager's plans and in some cases deliberately delays, pretends to comply with, or sabotages the plans. Exhibit 14-2 presents the likelihood of eliciting each type of behavior by using the various sources of power. Sales managers who exercise expert and referent power are likely to achieve commitment, while those using legitimate and reward power are likely to get compliance from their salespeople. Sales managers displaying coercive power tend to get resistance from their salespeople.

The performance of the sales force tends to be better when the sales manager relies on expert and referent power.[9] These two types of power tend to increase the motivational level of salespeople as well. If salespeople are highly motivated by monetary rewards, a sales manager may exercise reward power to increase performance. Good sales managers are likely to utilize all five sources of power at one time or another. The key is for the sales manager to know the appropriate source of power to use for each salesperson and in each situation. Using the wrong source of power can lead to dissatisfaction among the sales force, as illustrated in the *Ethics* scenario on page 456.

EXHIBIT 14-2

Sources of Sales Manager Power and Their Effect on Salesperson Behavior

Power Source	Commitment	Compliance	Resistance
Legitimate	Possible	Likely	Possible
Reward	Possible	Likely	Possible
Coercive	Unlikely	Possible	Likely
Referent	Likely	Possible	Possible
Expert	Likely	Possible	Possible

ETHICS IN SALES MANAGEMENT:
SOURCES OF POWER AND RESISTANCE AMONG THE SALES FORCE

You are the national sales manager for a large financial-services firm, and one of your regional sales managers has asked you for some advice. She is having problems in one of her districts primarily because of the leadership style of one of her district sales managers. He is a highly successful veteran who believes in gaining compliance from his salespeople through fear and punishment. He makes it very clear to his salespeople that if they don't perform up to his standards, they *will not* receive bonuses and might even be fired. He firmly believes every salesperson can be replaced. This district sales manager has never given your company any problems before. In fact, his sales district is one of the most profitable in the company. However, the regional sales manager believes that the salespeople in his district are becoming a bit disenchanted with his management style. She has heard rumors that one of the salespeople in the district has deliberately ignored the sales manager's suggestions and, when given the chance, will do anything he can to make his sales manager look bad in front of customers or other salespeople. The regional sales manager believes there is potential for big problems in this district. How do you advise her?

1. Is the salesperson practicing unethical behavior? Why or why not?

2. Should anything be done about the district manager in regard to his leadership philosophy?

3. Whom should the regional sales manager back in this case? Why?

Formal versus Informal Leadership

Formal leadership is the exercise of influence over others by someone in an official position of authority. *Informal leadership* is the unofficial exercise of influence over others through competence, trust, and respect. Informal leaders are the "people's choice"; they may influence people's behavior even more than persons assigned formal leadership positions. In some situations, the formal and the informal leader may be the same individual. If so, the formal leader has gained the confidence, respect, and support of the group. When the formal and informal leader are two different people, there is the potential for conflict. An astute formal leader can make his or her job easier by gaining the cooperation of the informal leader.

WHAT MAKES A SUCCESSFUL LEADER?

Mortimer Adler, the well-known American philosopher, says a good leader must have ethos, pathos, and logos. *Ethos* is moral character, the source of one's ability to persuade. *Pathos* is the ability to stir feelings, to move people emotionally. *Logos* is the ability to explain one's actions, to move people intellectually.[10]

Psychoanalyst Jules Masserman says, "Leaders must fulfill three functions—provide for the well-being of the led, provide a social organization in which people feel relatively secure, and provide them with one set of beliefs."[11]

Robert McMurry defines leadership as "the capacity of an individual to inspire confidence, admiration and trust in others so that they will turn to him for help and guidance; i.e., establish a dependent relationship upon him."[12]

According to British author C. P. Snow, "I don't believe much in great leaders. Great leaders emerge from circumstances and normally don't create them. Very occasionally one or two produce a difference."[13]

Former Secretary of State Henry Kissinger comments:

> In my studies of great leaders, I have often thought: what are the differences between them and the idols who fail? I am certain it is not I.Q. It is clear vision and self-confidence to act on the basis of that vision. One asks what is the most important thing a national leader can do, whether he has charisma or not? In my judgment, there are two things. One, to make only those decisions that only he can make and not to become so obsessed with the technical process of decision making that he does the work of subordinates and therefore, overloads himself and demoralizes them. Secondly, the most important thing the head of any large organization can do is to bring out in his subordinates the conviction that they can do things that they did not know they were capable of doing—that is, make them work at the absolute top of their capacity.[14]

Leadership Theories

A great deal of research has been conducted over the years to find out what makes a person an effective leader. The earliest such research, conducted hundreds of years ago, was based on the "great man" approach to leadership. This research concluded that great leaders are born, not made. People such as Alexander the Great, Joan of Arc, and George Washington were believed to be "natural" leaders, persons who were born with leadership qualities and thus were destined to lead others. The emergence of large businesses during the industrial revolution initiated a reassessment of leadership theories, since so many people were suddenly in leadership positions.

Since the start of the twentieth century, much more research has been done on leadership. The three major categories of leadership research are trait theory, behavioral theory, and contingency theory. As Exhibit 14-3 indicates, each of

EXHIBIT 14-3

Major Theories of Sales Manager Leadership

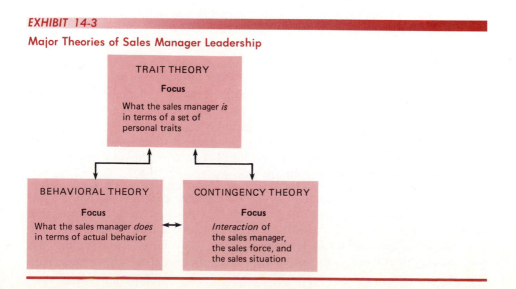

these categories, or theories, uses a different set of characteristics to assess different styles of leadership.

Trait theory.   Early studies assumed that certain inherited personal traits, such as honesty, ambition, initiative, and drive, determine successful leadership. Later, it was thought that leadership traits were not completely inborn but could be developed through experience and learning. So the search began for universal traits of leaders. Various traits, or characteristics, were found to have a positive correlation with successful leadership, including height, weight, intelligence, appearance, academic performance, dominance, initiative, persistence, self-confidence, socioeconomic status, sociability, and dependability in exercising responsibilities. However, it was observed that many good leaders did not possess the expected traits and that possession of the traits failed to predict leadership success reliably.

Trait theory has been widely criticized because of the infrequent occurrence of the same traits across different studies and the failure to consider the situational context of leadership. Moreover, a "chicken and egg" controversy revolved around trait theory. For example, was George Washington a leader because he was self-confident, or was he self-confident because leadership responsibilities were thrust upon him at a young age? Other weaknesses of trait theory include the following: (1) Lists of traits seldom distinguish which traits are most or least important; (2) traits often overlap—for example, intelligence, judgment, and common sense; (3) trait studies do not differentiate between traits needed for *acquiring* leadership and traits necessary for *maintaining* it; (4) trait studies describe but do not analyze behavior patterns; and (5) trait theory sees the leader personality as a mere collection of traits instead of as a complex whole.[15]

In 1948 Stogdill completed a comprehensive review of over 100 trait theory studies, and he found that only 5 percent of the traits appeared in four or more studies.[16] More recently, Stogdill reported a review of 163 additional trait studies, from which he concluded that the leader characteristics identified were similar to those found in previous research.[17] However, because of the many weaknesses associated with trait theory, it has lost popularity. Research efforts have turned to the relationship between leader behavior and desired goals, such as job performance and employee morale.

Implications for sales management.   While no single profile of traits can identify an effective sales force leader, many researchers believe that certain traits, or characteristics, are needed to become an effective sales manager. For example, some hold that an effective sales force leader must be a hard worker and be people-oriented. Others feel a sales manager must have the innate ability to take risks and be a decision maker. Exhibit 14-4 presents the personal qualities needed to be a successful leader in any endeavor.

Behaviorial theory.   From the late 1940s through the early 1960s, many leadership studies focused on patterns of leader behavior, or "style." During that period emphasis shifted from who the leader *is* to what the leader *does*. The research did not identify a standardized profile of traits for effective leaders. But some leadership *behaviors* were found to be more effective than others. Moreover,

EXHIBIT 14-4

The Twelve Qualities of Leadership

1. *Courageous.* Leaders set courageous examples for others to follow. They have what it takes to hold on. As General Patton once said, "Courage is fear holding on another minute."

2. *A big thinker.* Leaders have the ability to see things in a larger perspective than others. They can help others to expand their thinking and imagination.

3. *A change master.* Leaders have the ability to create change, to accept it, handle it, and to move people in directions which are more beneficial to everyone.

4. *Ethical.* Leaders are fair and just individuals who are loyal and conscientious in their work while expecting the same from others.

5. *Persistent and realistic.* Leaders set realistic goals and maintain commitment to those goals until they are accomplished.

6. *Gifted with a sense of humor.* Having a sense of humor can turn routine tasks into enjoyable experiences. Leaders are spontaneous and express their feelings.

7. *A risk taker.* Leaders take the initiative, are independent, and are willing to fail in order to succeed.

8. *Positive and hopefilled.* Leaders have the ability to see good in a bad situation and to have faith when others do not. They tend to be optimistic and elicit that from others.

9. *Morally strong.* Leaders value the power of truth, yet they are not judgmental in their morality.

10. *A decision maker.* Leaders know that not deciding is a decision, and that indecision wastes time, energy, money, and opportunity.

11. *Able to accept and use power wisely.* Leaders know that power can intimidate others, so they use it wisely. Power is used to help others achieve their full potential.

12. *Committed.* The key to successful leaders is their commitment. Without commitment one cannot be a good leader. Leaders are committed to their goals, their employees, and their company.

Source: Sheila Murray Bethel, "The Twelve Qualities of Leadership," *Marketing Times,* September–October, 1985, pp. 12–13.

behavioral theories of leadership provided a way to distinguish effective from ineffective leaders by their different behavior patterns.

Studies conducted at Ohio State University identified two composite dimensions of leader behavior: *consideration* (i.e., friendship, mutual trust, respect, and warmth)—sometimes called the "human relations" approach—and *initiating structure* (i.e., the extent to which leaders organize and define the relationship between themselves and their followers)—sometimes called a "task orientation."[18] These dimensions were investigated in terms of their degree of presence; the resulting four leadership styles are depicted in Exhibit 14-5. Research focused on determining the association of these styles with job performance and employee satisfaction. Although "high consideration, high initiating structure" (quadrant 2) tended to yield high employee satisfaction and performance, no

EXHIBIT 14-5

Dimensions of Leadership Style: Ohio State Leadership Studies

HIGH	**1** High consideration / Low structure / Leader focuses on achieving group harmony and individual need satisfaction.	**2** High consideration / High structure / Leader strives to accomplish the job while maintaining a harmonious work group.
	3 Low consideration / Low structure / Leader becomes largely passive and allows the situation to take care of itself.	**4** Low consideration / High structure / Leader focuses on getting the job done.

Consideration (vertical axis), Initiating structure (horizontal axis: LOW to HIGH)

Source: Adapted from Ohio State Leadership Studies, "Dimensions of Leadership Style," in Edwin A. Fleishman and James G. Hunt (eds.), *Current Developments in the Study of Leadership,* Southern Illinois University Press, Carbondale, Ill., 1973. Reprinted by permission of Southern Illinois University Press.

single leader behavior surfaced as best for all situations. Moreover, few managers can be both task- and human relations–oriented. In examining the research evidence, Korman found few studies that substantiated a significant relationship between the two dimensions of leader behavior and productivity. Furthermore, the impact of situational variables was all but ignored in the studies.[19] Nevertheless, the leader behavior approach continues to appeal to managers because it is understandable and there is widespread belief that specific leader behaviors can be learned and put into practice.

Implications for sales management. A number of behavior styles may be effective for sales managers in different situations. Exhibit 14-6 utilizes the four basic leadership styles identified by the Ohio State researchers to show how certain leadership styles can work for sales managers.

EXHIBIT 14-6

Behavioral Styles for Various Sales Management Tasks

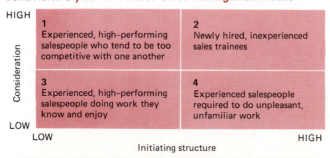

HIGH	**1** Experienced, high–performing salespeople who tend to be too competitive with one another	**2** Newly hired, inexperienced sales trainees
	3 Experienced, high–performing salespeople doing work they know and enjoy	**4** Experienced salespeople required to do unpleasant, unfamiliar work
LOW		

Consideration (vertical axis), Initiating structure (horizontal axis: LOW to HIGH)

- *Quadrant 1.* A high-consideration, low-structure style is appropriate if the sales force consists of highly motivated individuals who are dedicated to the task at hand but require social support from superiors. Example: experienced, high-performing salespeople who tend to be too competitive with one another.

- *Quadrant 2.* A high-consideration, high-structure style is appropriate if the sales force consists of individuals who require social support from superiors, are not cohesive, and lack a strong identity with the task at hand. Example: newly hired, inexperienced sales trainees.

- *Quadrant 3.* A low-consideration, low-structure leader style is appropriate if the sales force consists of highly motivated individuals who are socially mature and dedicated to the task at hand. Example: experienced, high-performing sales representatives doing work they know and enjoy.

- *Quadrant 4.* A low-consideration, high-structure leader style is appropriate if the sales force consists of individuals who are socially mature and highly cohesive but who do not understand or identify with the task at hand. Example: an experienced sales force that is required to do unpleasant, unfamiliar work such as collecting payments on overdue customer accounts.

Like trait theories, the behavioral theories by themselves may not be adequate to explain leadership. Gouldner believes that a theory of leadership should combine traits and situations. Some traits may be unique to certain leaders, while other traits may be common to all leaders.[20]

Contingency theory.   The first two leadership theories—trait and behavioral—focus primarily on the leader. The third leadership theory emphasizes the contingencies among the leader, followers, and situation. Exhibit 14-7 illustrates

EXHIBIT 14-7

A Contingency Approach to Sales Force Leadership

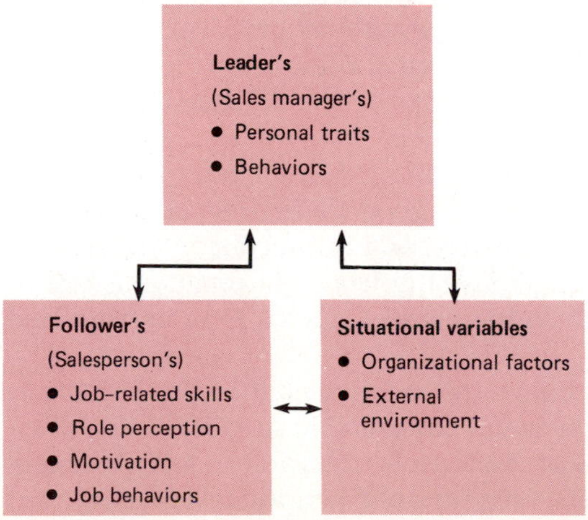

how this contingency theory may apply to the sales manager. This theory assumes that successful leadership is dependent (or contingent) on various factors related to the salesperson (or follower) and the situation. Therefore, the sales manager's traits and behavior can directly influence both the sales force and the situation. Moreover, the double-headed arrows used in the exhibit indicate that salespeople and the situation can also influence the leader (or sales manager). For example, a supervisor who has been constantly unsuccessful in trying to get an employee to improve his or her performance will eventually decrease efforts to work with that employee.

Fred Fiedler developed the first and perhaps best-known contingency model of leadership. The model incorporates both leadership style and the nature of the leadership situation. Since 1951, Fiedler has been conducting research on the relationship between organizational performance and leader attitudes.[21] He believes that a leader's performance depends on two interrelated factors: (1) the degree to which the situation gives the leader control and influence and (2) the leader's basic motivation—whether toward accomplishing the task or toward having close, supportive relations with others. Leaders are either task-motivated or relationship-motivated. These two orientations are roughly equivalent to *initiating structure* and *consideration* from the Ohio State studies mentioned under behavioral theory.

Specifically, Fiedler has tried to discover which leaders are most likely to develop high-producing groups: leaders who are very lenient or those who are highly demanding and discriminating in evaluating subordinates. His results indicate that the most effective type of leadership depends upon three situational variables:

- The quality of the leader's personal relationships with members of the group
- The formal power or authority provided by the leader's position
- The degree to which the group's task is structured

Situations high on all three components are considered "favorable" because (1) leaders can usually expect support from group members; (2) leaders can enforce their will with the legitimate power or formal authority of their positions; and (3) more structured tasks can be more clearly defined, delegated, controlled, and evaluated by all members of the organization.

The most favorable situation (cell I in Exhibit 14-8) for a leader is one in which he or she is well liked by the members (good leader-member relations), has a powerful position (high position power), and is directing a well-defined job (high task structure). Conversely, the most unfavorable situation is one in which the leader is disliked, has little position power, and faces an unstructured task (cell III).

Fiedler discovered that a discriminating, task-oriented leader attitude is effective in either highly favorable or highly unfavorable situations. But when the situation is moderately favorable or moderately unfavorable, a more lenient and considerate leader attitude is best for higher group performance, as suggested in cell II of Exhibit 14-8. When relations with group members are moderately

EXHIBIT 14-8

EXHIBIT 14-8

Fiedler's Contingency Theory

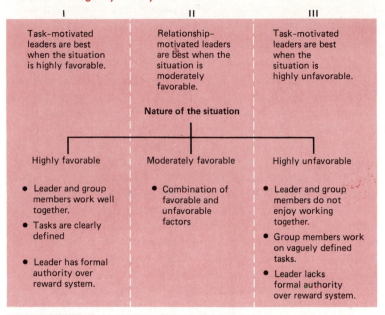

Source: Robert Kreitner, *Management: A Problem-Solving Process,* Houghton Mifflin, Boston, p. 396.

poor, position power is low, and a highly structured task is at hand, the leader should be permissive and accepting in behavior and attitude.

Fiedler's contingency model of leadership effectiveness suggests that group performance can be improved either by modifying the leader's style or by modifying the group's task and situation. However, he believes that most organizations cannot afford expensive selection techniques to find talented leaders who fit specific job requirements.[22] Nor does training provide adequate answers to the problems of leadership.[23] The most reasonable approach is to tailor the job to fit the manager. Since the type of leadership called for depends on the favorableness of the situation, the organization can more easily alter the job than transfer managers or train them in different styles of interaction with group members. Such factors as the power associated with the leader's position, the task assigned to the group, or the composition of the group's membership can be changed.[24]

Implications for sales management.   Fiedler's contingency theory offers several important implications to sales managers. Most important, it should be understood that both relationship-oriented and task-oriented sales managers can perform well under some situations but not others. For example, a high-performing salesperson who is promoted to sales manager may fail because his or her task-oriented leadership style does not match the demands of the situation. In the past this person may have had very clearly defined performance goals (e.g., to increase sales revenue by 15 percent) and may have known exactly how to achieve them. In the new situation as sales manager, this person may face tasks that are more complex and nonroutine, such as motivating an older sales representative or building confidence in younger salespeople. Thus, the new task-oriented sales manager will not be an effective leader unless he or she adopts a more relationship-oriented style.

Substitutes for leadership.   A new perspective on leadership that has recently attracted a great deal of attention is the concept of substitutes for leadership. It was developed because existing leadership models and theories do *not* account for situations in which leadership is not needed.[25] The concept pertains to situations in which leadership is neutralized or replaced by characteristics of the subordinate, the task, and the organization. First, such characteristics of the subordinate such as experience, need for independence, and professional orientation may serve to neutralize leadership behavior. For example, productive employees with a high level of professionalism may not have to be told what to do. Second, characteristics of the task itself may substitute for leadership. For example, individuals whose tasks are challenging or intrinsically satisfying may not need or want direction from a leader. Finally, organizational characteristics that may serve as substitutes for leadership include formalization, group cohesion, inflexibility, and a rigid reward structure. For example, leadership may not be needed when company policies and practices are formal and inflexible. Preliminary research on substitutes for leadership has provided support for this concept as a viable leadership perspective.[26]

Implications for sales management.   The substitutes-for-leadership perspective offers several important insights to sales managers. Most important, it points out that there are many instances in which leadership may not be needed. In many selling situations leader behaviors are neutralized or replaced by characteristics of the individual salesperson, the selling task being performed, and the organization itself. For example, salespeople with a great deal of experience or a great need for independence may not require as much direction as younger, less confident salespeople. Additionally, many individuals go into sales as a career because of the challenge and flexibility it offers them. Thus, it appears that the personal selling environment is very applicable to the concept of substitutes for leadership. According to this concept, sales managers, in some situations, can be better leaders if they know when *not* to lead.

SALES MANAGEMENT LEADERSHIP IN PRACTICE

The leadership role for sales managers is a multifaceted one that must result in accomplishing organizational goals. Perhaps the most critical facet of the leadership role revolves around staffing—ensuring that recruiting, selecting, and training are done well. An organization's ultimate success or failure depends largely upon the quality of the people it hires and retains.

The demands of sales management call for leadership in a variety of situations—from reassuring a struggling salesperson to standing up for the sales team before superiors. Motivating salespeople through integration of their personal goals with those of the organization continuously challenges the sales manager's leadership. Another critical leadership responsibility is evaluating and controlling the activities of salespeople in order to take timely corrective action where and when needed. Sometimes the role may be unpleasant, as, for example, when it is necessary to reprimand or terminate a salesperson. The sales manager must not yield to the temptation to shirk any of the leadership roles—even the extremely unpleasant ones. Finally, the leadership role requires that the sales manager represent the selling organization through interaction in a complex network of contacts with superiors, peers, subordinates, and external parties such as customers and suppliers.

Leadership Styles

Sales managers are nearly always looked to by their subordinates for leadership. The critical question is not *if* a sales manager is going to lead but *how.* All sales managers exhibit a leadership style, whether they are conscious of it or not. No one style of leadership is appropriate for all situations. Effective leaders match their style with the maturity and duties of the sales force. A range of leadership styles from task-oriented to human relations–oriented can be successful as long as the style is matched correctly with the situation. Experienced salespeople, used to operating largely independently, may resent a sales manager who exercises tight supervision and control over their activities. Conversely, an experienced sales force used to close supervision may feel anxiety about the abilities of a sales manager who allows too much freedom of action. One way of visualizing leadership styles is to diagram them as the parts of a four-speed automobile gearshift or the capital letter "H," as shown in Exhibit 14-9.[27] A sales manager may need to *shift* leadership style as the composition and responsibilities of the sales force change. Xerox's Information Systems Group, which is responsible for copier and duplicator products, became one of the first companies to teach "situational leadership" to each middle-level and new first-level manager.[28]

Continuing the analogy of the gearshift, we can say that the sales manager exercises strong pulling power in first (autocratic) and second (paternalistic) gear, with the sales force largely dependent on the sales manager for rewards and punishments. In neutral (consultative), the sales manager exerts little push

EXHIBIT 14-9

Leadership Styles

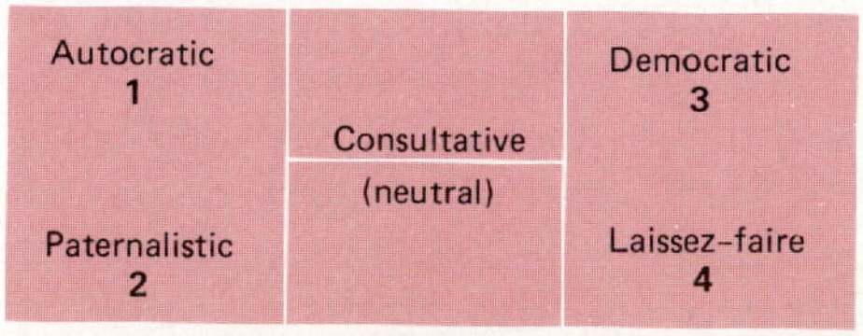

Autocratic 1		Democratic 3
	Consultative (neutral)	
Paternalistic 2		Laissez–faire 4

or pull and allows the salespeople to influence management decisions. In third (democratic) and fourth (laissez-faire) gear, the sales manager functions in a largely passive manner as salespeople operate quite independently. The real task of the successful sales manager is to select the style of leadership most appropriate for the individual salesperson, for the sales force as a whole, and for the particular sales situation.

No one leadership style fits all situations, and research indicates that about three-fourths of sales managers use two different styles to handle various members of the sales force. Effective leadership seems to call for flexibility and modification of style to match the changing sales situations. However, the sales manager must take care to be fairly consistent in handling each salesperson and group. Studies have indicated that the lowest morale usually comes about when a sales manager's style vacillates between an authoritarian approach at one time and a permissive approach at another. Capsule views of the five leadership styles are provided in Exhibit 14-10.

There seems to be a relationship between the size and type of organization and the style of leadership required. In a huge government bureaucracy or a research organization, the leader may need to be more low-keyed and methodical, whereas in a private small business, innovative, action-oriented leadership may be needed. Miles and Petty found that the initiating structure, or task orientation, of the leader is more effective in small organizations than in large ones and that the effectiveness of a leader's consideration or human relations orientation does not appear to vary with organizational size.[29]

Development of Leaders by Mentors

One of the proven ways to develop leaders is by using mentors. A *mentor* is someone who systematically helps develop a subordinate's abilities through careful tutoring, personal guidance, and example. Mentors are typically strong, self-confident people who do not fear an aggressive young subordinate. They take risks in betting on perceived talent in subordinates, but mentors are an important source and stimulus for development of leaders. A young sales manager would do well to spot a potential mentor from whom to learn and gain support.

Sales managers can also be effective mentors by working closely with their salespeople. A form of mentoring that has recently gained popularity among sales managers is "curbstone coaching." In this practice, the sales manager remains with a salesperson during a sales call and then counsels the rep immediately after the call. Many experts feel that tremendous improvements can be made if a sales manager can properly coach a salesperson about a sales call while the call is still fresh in their minds.[30] Sales managers must realize the importance of setting aside a few minutes after the sales call—either over a cup of coffee or on the way to the next appointment—to analyze what did or did not happen and what improvements can be made. If sales managers can provide instant feedback that is truly helpful and acceptable to the salesperson, the payoffs can be almost instantaneous. A few minutes of concern can do a lot to boost a mentor's leadership ability.

EXHIBIT 14-10

Leadership Styles and Sales Force Situations

Authoritarian	Paternalistic	Consultative	Democratic	Laissez-faire
Characteristics of Leadership Style				
Tight control and rigid authority Clearly defined tasks Downward communication from sales manager	"Kindly father knows best" Authority is centralized with sales manager	Two-way communication with sales force Right to make final decision retained by sales manager	Much authority delegated but sales manager retains the right to determine group consensus Participatory decision making and division of work	Leader responsibility abdicated and authority given to sales force Primarily horizontal communication between sales force peers
Appropriate Situation for Leadership Style				
New or inexperienced salespeople Disciplinary action needed Emergencies Complacent sales force	Weak sales supervisors Immature or inexperienced salespeople Informal sales force leaders expressing discontent	Well-trained, experienced sales force Sales force works well as a team	Small, well-informed sales force Cooperative salespeople Lots of time to make decisions	Salespeople have expert knowledge Nature of work guides salespeople
Inappropriate Situation for Leadership Style				
Mature, experienced salespeople Teamwork and cooperation needed	Mature, independent salespeople Strong, competent sales force	Inexperienced, poorly trained sales force Sales force does not work well as a team	Larger groups of salespeople Decisions must be made quickly Salespeople are not sufficiently informed	Salespeople are reluctant to make decisions Nature of work is similar

Can leaders be created? Many people feel that they can. Mentors or senior sales managers can create better leaders by helping young sales managers with various aspects of their careers.[31] For example, mentors can equip individuals with the skills, tools, and techniques that will bring out their natural leadership talents. Additionally, young managers must be exposed to any concepts or theories that will assist them in making critical decisions. A good, solid background of information can also give young sales managers the confidence needed to make those decisions. Finally, a senior member of a company can do a great deal for an entry-level employee by instilling the values of curiosity, idealism, entrepreneurism, and commitment in him or her, as these are in the hearts of

EXHIBIT 14-11

Developing Leadership Characteristics

Handling Change

- Leaders realize that nothing in this world is permanent except change.
- Leaders don't have to like change, just understand it.
- Leaders understand that people as well as events change.
- Leaders must be able to cope with and handle the uncertainty that goes with change.
- For leaders, one key to success is finding the opportunity in change.
- Leaders must change themselves with change.
- For leaders, change is exciting and inevitable, and should be welcomed.

Risking Failure

- Leadership is the willingness to fail in order to succeed.
- Leaders must be able to take risks.
- Leaders develop alternate plans in case of failure.
- Leaders remember the law of averages.

Source: Adapted from Sheila Murray Bethel, "Eagles Don't Flock," *Marketing Times,* September–October 1985, pp. 10–13.

most leaders. While implementing these strategies will not necessarily guarantee a leader, they can do a great deal to bring out natural leadership talents that may be latent in an individual. For some additional points on the development of leaders, see Exhibit 14-11.

Leadership Stereotypes

All organizations need to be on guard against prejudiced categorization of people into stereotypes. Such stereotypes are undoubtedly one reason for the low representation of women and minorities in leadership positions. Researchers in the late 1960s and early 1970s found that both male and female college students associated leadership qualities with males and not females. Men were seen as aggressive, independent, unemotional, objective, dominant, and competitive. Women were described as talkative, tactful, gentle, neat, and security-conscious.[32] Furthermore, successful male middle managers associated "male" characteristics with the managerial role.[33]

Things are definitely changing in the 1990s, as more and more women are taking leadership roles in industry as well as government. In fact, in their book, *Megatrends 2000,* John Naisbitt and Patricia Aburdene call the nineties the "decade of women in leadership." While research on leadership has either ignored women or focused on sex differences, researchers are beginning to investigate the sex-role orientation rather than sex differences associated with women in leadership roles.[34] As more and more women become successful sales managers, the archaic negative effects of sex stereotypes will continue to fade.

COMMUNICATION

Earlier in this chapter, the basics of leadership were given as people, influence, goals, and *communication*. At its most basic level, leadership is communication between people. Communication is a way of transferring ideas, facts, thoughts, and values from one person to another. Thus, it is an essential component of leadership.

Without effective communication, strong leadership is impossible. Setting objectives and goals, organizing, staffing, forecasting, supervising, compensating, motivating, evaluating, and controlling the sales force—nearly all sales management functions—involve communication. Open channels of communication are especially critical when the sales organization must quickly adapt to changing corporate objectives in a dynamic marketing environment. The typical manager spends more time communicating than doing anything else. Most of a manager's day involves some form of communication: 75 percent in face-to-face listening or speaking, 9 percent in writing, and 16 percent in reading.[35]

Defining Communication

Communication is a process whereby information is transferred and understood between two or more people. It is a two-way process involving listening or reading as well as speaking or writing. In fact, some of the best communicators practice sage advice: "Always use your ears and mouth according to the number you have of each." Successful sales managers and salespeople are usually exceptionally good listeners. Many studies support the conclusion that good communication improves the productivity of an organization.[36] Exhibit 14-12 presents some helpful guidelines that sales managers can use to improve their own communication skills.

Listening

Perhaps one of the most important and often overlooked qualities of a good communicator and, thus, a good leader is listening. Typical business executives

---

EXHIBIT 14-12

Guidelines for Effective Communication

- Clarify your ideas before communicating.
- Examine the purpose of your communication.
- Consider the situation in which the communication will take place.
- Consult with others in planning the communication.
- Be aware of nonverbal messages you send.
- Convey something that will help the salesperson.
- Follow up the communication.
- Be sure your actions support your communication.

spend over half their communication time listening. Most business executives place listening at the top of the list of essential managerial skills, as it provides managers with the bulk of the information they need to do their jobs. However, research shows that the average person is a poor listener, remembering only half of what is said during a ten-minute conversation and forgetting half of that within forty-eight hours.[37] Listening has become such a vital part of business today that a number of companies now train their employees in listening.[38]

The way individuals listen and the listening skills they use will vary according to the situation. There are four basic types of listening, and they differ not only in purpose but also in the amount of feedback or interaction that occurs:

1. *Content listening.* The receiver's goal is to understand and retain information. The receiver's task is to identify key points and create an outline of the speaker's remarks. The receiver asks questions, takes notes, and so on, as the information is flowing primarily in one direction—from speaker to receiver.

2. *Critical listening.* The receiver's goal is to critically evaluate the message by looking at the logic of the argument, strength of the evidence, and validity of the conclusions. A great deal of interaction is involved, as the receiver is attempting to uncover the speaker's point of view.

3. *Empathic listening.* The receiver's goal is to understand the speaker's feelings, needs, and wants in order to solve a problem. Less interaction is involved, as the receiver is attempting to gain insights into the speaker's psyche.

4. *Active listening.* This listening technique attempts to help people resolve their differences. Before replying to the speaker's comment, the receiver must restate the ideas and feelings behind the comment to the speaker's satisfaction. The goal here is to appreciate the other person's point of view, whether or not you agree.

All four types of listening can be used by sales managers to become better leaders as well as by salespeople to build relationships with their customers. For example, sales managers can help alleviate any role ambiguities among their salespeople by honing their active listening skills. On the other hand, salespeople can learn a great deal about their customers by engaging in more empathic listening. Regardless of whether the sales management situation calls for content, critical, empathic, or active listening, sales managers can improve their listening ability by following the basic guidelines presented in Exhibit 14-13.

Understanding Nonverbal Communication

People communicate their ideas, attitudes, desires, and feelings verbally and nonverbally. Many feel that nonverbal communication has more impact than verbal communication, as nonverbal cues account for as much as 93 percent of the emotional meaning that is exchanged in any interaction.[39] Nonverbal communication takes place largely through body language: facial expressions, gestures, or body postures. Facial expressions (such as smiles, frowns, clenched

EXHIBIT 14-13

Ten Keys to Effective Listening

To Listen Effectively	The Bad Listener	The Good Listener
1. Find areas of interest.	Tunes out dry subjects.	Opportunizes. Asks, "What's in it for me?"
2. Judge content, not delivery.	Tunes out if delivery is poor.	Judges content. Skips over delivery errors.
3. Hold your fire.	Tends to enter into argument.	Doesn't judge until comprehension is complete. Interrupts only to clarify.
4. Listen for ideas.	Listens for facts.	Listens for central themes.
5. Be flexible.	Takes intensive notes using only one system.	Takes fewer notes. Uses four or five different systems, depending on speaker.
6. Work at listening.	Shows no energy output. Fakes attention.	Works hard. Exhibits active body state.
7. Resist distractions.	Is distracted easily.	Fights or avoids distractions. Tolerates bad habits. Knows how to concentrate.
8. Exercise your mind.	Resists difficult expository material. Seeks light, recreational material.	Uses heavier material as exercise for the mind.
9. Keep your mind open.	Reacts to emotional words.	Interprets emotional words. Does not get hung up on them.
10. Capitalize on the fact that thought is faster than speech.	Tends to daydream with slow speakers.	Challenges, anticipates, mentally summarizes, weighs the evidence. Listens between the lines to tone of voice.

Source: Courtland L. Bovée and John V. Thill, *Business Communication Today,* Random House, New York, 1989, p. 538.

teeth, or wrinkled brows) convey a myriad of messages from approval to disapproval, from understanding to confusion. Gestures (such as nodding the head or shrugging the shoulders) can signal agreement, understanding, or indifference. Body postures (bowing, slouching, or standing rigidly) assumed by superiors can significantly affect subordinates' behavior. A timely smile, wink, or pat on the back can give salespeople positive feedback that is often more powerful than words. Sales managers and salespeople ought to familiarize themselves with the psychological dimensions of nonverbal communications summarized in Exhibit 14-14.

Of the many forms of nonverbal communication, three of the most important to sales managers are communication with space, communication through dress, and communication with our bodies. For example, the distance between individuals when they talk or sit can have an impact on communication. Some clients may feel threatened if a salesperson is too close to them during the sales presentation. Additionally, how a person dresses can definitely communicate something to others. Dress can affect perceptions that others have not only toward an individual but also toward the company that employs the individual.

EXHIBIT 14-14

The Psychological Dimensions of Nonverbal Communications

High Status	Low Status	Positive Evaluation	Negative Evaluation
Direct eye contact while speaking	Looking away before speaking	Head nods	Reclining position
Moderate eye contact while listening	Steady eye contact while listening	Uh-huh	Backward lean
Relaxed posture	Hesitations	Rhythmic following	Avoiding or shifting eye contact
Arm-position asymmetry	Halting speech with shifting eye contact	Close proximity	Avoidance of close proximity
Sideways lean	High speech error rate	Touching	Closed arrangement of arms
Hand relaxation	Inactive communication activity range	Eye contact	Torso orientation away from addressee
Neck relaxation	Depressed posture	Forward lean	Finger tapping
Head nodding	Forward lean	Higher speech rate	n.d.
Gesticulation	Bowed head	Lengthier communication	n.d.
Increased facial activity	Drooping shoulders	Frequent verbal reinforcer	n.d.
Low speech error rate	Sunken chest	Gesticulation	n.d.
Halting speech with eye contact	Shifting body orientation	Smiling	n.d.
Active speech rate	n.d.	Less frequent self-references	n.d.
Strong speech volume	n.d.	Open arrangement of arms	n.d.
Chest expanded	n.d.	n.d.	n.d.
Backward lean	n.d.	n.d.	n.d.
Direct body orientation	n.d.	n.d.	n.d.

n.d. = no data.

Source: Thomas V. Bonoma and Leonard C. Felder, "Nonverbal Communication in Marketing: Toward a Communicational Analysis," *Journal of Marketing Research,* vol. 14, May 1977, p. 176.

Therefore, how salespeople dress will affect their image, the company's image, and the persuasiveness of their presentation. Finally, the body and its movements can communicate a lot about a person. The ability of salespeople to interpret the facial expressions of their clients is extremely helpful in the communication process. Responding to expressions of confusion, anger, or interest can help salespeople in altering their presentations.

Sales managers can utilize the principles of nonverbal communication in two ways. First, they can instruct the sales force on the use of nonverbal cues for improving the sales presentation. For example, the proper handshake, eye contact, and attire can assist the salesperson during visits with clients. Second, nonverbal cues can enhance the leadership qualities of sales managers. For example, the confidence sales managers exude or the way they dress may help boost their referent power among the sales force.

Breaking Down Communication Barriers

Perhaps the first step in enhancing communication is to identify the barriers that stand in the way. There are many communication barriers in a sales organization. For simplicity, they have been divided into organizational and individual barriers.

Organizational barriers. Communication problems are likely to occur between an employee and a supervisor because of the hierarchy of most organization structures. If the company objectives are not filtered down correctly to a salesperson, problems are sure to arise. A barrier to communication in this case may cause role perception problems for the salesperson and affect the salesperson's performance.

Individual barriers. The sales manager must be an effective communicator to help overcome many of the communication barriers that are due to organizational structure. More important, however, sales managers must be able to send clear and effective messages that the entire sales force can understand. What may be clear to some salespeople may be confusing to others. Some of the individual barriers to communication that sales managers should be aware of are conflicting assumptions, semantics, emotions, and communication skills.

Two individuals can state the same message yet have *conflicting assumptions* about the meaning of that message. For example, a client telephones a sales representative and asks her to ship an order "as soon as possible." The client receives the order five days later and never orders from that salesperson again. In this case, the conflicting assumption occurred between the salesperson and the company's shipping department. To the salesperson, "as soon as possible" meant today. To the shipping department, it meant something totally different!

Semantics, or the meaning of words, can cause communication failure. Most words have multiple meanings; some common words can have as many as fifteen to eighteen meanings. Communication barriers are sure to exist when two people attribute different meanings to the same words and do not know it.

Feelings, or *emotions,* can also create communication barriers between individuals. All communication is influenced by emotions. When a person sends a message, feelings are attached to it; if the receiver of the message is unaware of or misinterprets those feelings, the intent of the message may be lost or misconstrued.

Finally, the *communication skills* of the communicator can greatly affect the communication process. Since the ability to communicate varies greatly, some people will be better communicators and thus better leaders than others. Some differences in communication skills are due to education and training, while others may be due to more innate personality traits. No matter what its origin, effective communication is essential for effective leadership.

Overcoming barriers. Sales managers can overcome the barriers to communication if they acknowledge their existence and are willing to take the time necessary to work them out. Some of the ways sales managers can overcome these barriers are outlined in Exhibit 14-15.

Information flow. Too much information can cause anyone to experience information overload. Sales managers can improve their leadership qualities by establishing a system to regulate the amount of information that reaches the sales force. Important points to consider regarding messages are as follows: First, a system should be established that allows priority messages to receive immediate attention. Second, all messages should be short; in fact, Procter & Gamble believes that all messages should be limited to one page.

EXHIBIT 14-15

Overcoming Barriers to Communication

- Encourage feedback.
- Use simple, direct language.
- Listen effectively.
- Restrain emotions.

- Regulate the flow of information.
- Watch for and use nonverbal cues.
- Be aware of and use the grapevine.

Feedback.   Feedback should be encouraged at all times. Good sales managers will follow up whenever any nonroutine messages have been received. Sales managers need feedback to be assured that the sales force has understood the message. When addressing a group, sales managers should closely watch for nonverbal feedback to make sure their message is getting across.

Simple language.   Sales managers must use words that *everyone* can understand. Jargon or technical language should be avoided unless absolutely necessary. Sales managers should select words carefully, especially if addressing a group of salespeople. The larger the group one is addressing, the greater the chance of miscommunication.

Effective listening.   As discussed previously, effective listening is an important component of effective communication and, thus, leadership. Sales managers can become better listeners by becoming familiar with the four types of listening and knowing when to apply them.

Emotional restraint.   Emotions are in all communications, and they sometimes can distort the content of the message. A highly emotional sales manager can easily convey the wrong emotional feeling in a message. For example, if a sales manager is emotionally upset, he or she may transmit (or interpret) the message in a more negative way.

Nonverbal cues.   Nonverbal cues can help sales managers emphasize major points and express feelings. Most important, sales managers must make sure that their nonverbal codes reinforce their words so that they do not send out mixed messages.

The grapevine.   Sales managers should not be afraid to use the grapevine in their organizations, since it can be useful in several ways. It can help sales managers send information rapidly without having to go through formal channels. Also, it can be an excellent way to obtain feedback from the sales force. Finally, it can be used to test salespeoples' reactions before making any final decisions. The major concern in using the grapevine is to make sure that all information conveyed by it is accurate and meaningful.

PROMOTION OF A SALES REPRESENTATIVE TO SALES MANAGER

One of the most difficult problems confronting a sales manager who has recently been promoted from salesperson is changing from "one of the gang" to "the boss." After sharing gripes, personal dreams, ambitions, and weaknesses with other sales representatives over months or years, the new sales manager can find it very awkward to be suddenly exercising authority over former close friends. To minimize potential problems stemming from previous social relationships, many companies have a standard policy of transferring new sales managers to new territories.

If transfer is not desirable, it is essential that the new sales manager be given adequate training in his or her new responsibilities. Unfortunately, too few companies provide more than superficial preparation to persons making the switch from sales representative to manager. Thus, many newly appointed sales managers feel unprepared and unsure in taking on their new duties. An organization can avoid this dilemma by properly training managers—not only in basic managerial functions but in leadership and communication skills—and by using appropriate criteria to select managers, as discussed in Chapter 1.

CONTINUING SALES MANAGEMENT CHALLENGE

Although scholars have been researching motivation, leadership, and communication for many years without coming to definitive answers, sales managers must still strive to develop a personal blend of these human relations variables that will maximize sales force productivity. To ignore the linkage between motivation, leadership, communication, and productivity or to allow the blend to become incompatible with the situation and the needs of the sales force invites failure. All sales managers *must* try to motivate, lead, and communicate with their salespeople. The only question is whether they will be successful in their attempt.

SUMMARY

Successful sales organizations usually have one critical asset that significantly differentiates them from unsuccessful organizations. That asset is effective leadership. Leadership occurs in a sales organization when the sales manager attempts to influence the sales force's behavior toward the accomplishment of the organization's goals. Much research has been conducted in an effort to find out what makes a person an effective leader. The three major categories of research have focused on trait theory, behavioral theory, and contingency theory. Each of these theories uses a different set of characteristics to assess leadership styles.

One of the basic elements of leadership is communication. At its most basic level leadership is two-way communication between people. Communication is a way of transferring ideas, facts, thoughts, and values from one person to another. Thus, it is an essential component of leadership. People, including salespeople and sales managers, communicate both verbally and nonverbally. Sales managers and salespeople must understand the dimensions of both verbal and nonverbal expression and work to overcome barriers to communication. Effective sales managers will skillfully use the linkage between motivation, communication, and leadership to increase sales force productivity.

STUDY QUESTIONS

1. What theory of leadership do you think is most sound? Which, if any, do you think you might apply in your career?

2. Explain the distinction between sales management and sales leadership.

3. Think of some interactions you have had with people today. What kind of nonverbal communication took place? Were you conscious of your own nonverbal communication?

4. What are the common causes of communication barriers? How can a sales manager overcome these barriers?

5. Define communication. How may sales managers improve their own communication skills?

6. Leaders may draw upon power from a variety of sources. What are these sources? Briefly explain each source of power.

7. Define leadership. What are the qualities of good leaders (i.e., what is it they do)?

8. Explain your understanding of Fiedler's contingency model of leadership. Does this model offer implications to sales managers? If so, what are the implications?

9. When a sales representative is promoted to sales manager, what should be done to facilitate a smooth transition from being "one of the gang" to being "the boss"?

IN-BASKET EXERCISE

You were recently hired as sales manager for a large industrial products firm. You just received your first memo, and it addresses a very serious issue that's facing not only your company but your overall industry: "salesperson burnout." Upper-level management at your firm believes that many of the salespeople in the organization have plateaued and are no longer improving. Your boss would like your input regarding this issue at next week's regional sales meeting.

1. What are you going to recommend at the upcoming meeting?

2. Is there such a thing as a "plateaued" or "burned-out" salesperson?

3. What specific things can sales managers do as leaders to revitalize their salespeople?

CASE 14-1

LEADING A DIVERSE SALES FORCE AT SCHOOL SUPPLIERS, INC.

School Suppliers, Inc. (SSI), is a national distributor of elementary and secondary school supplies. The company has fifty salespeople located in eight regional offices throughout the United States. The salespeople call on purchasing agents or principals at elementary and secondary schools in their assigned regions. Over the past decade, the southeastern region has been one of the fastest growing regions within the company.

Primarily because of the increasing population in Florida, SSI's southeastern region has led the company in sales and is projected to be the strongest region for the next several years.

Howard Larsen, one of the top sales reps for SSI over the past several years, was recently promoted to sales manager of the premier southeastern region. Howard, age 28, was at first very pleased and excited to be able to manage one of the most promising regions within the company. After only four months as the sales manager of this region, however, he began to question his ability as a sales manager. Howard believes that he is having problems managing his salespeople.

The Southeastern Region's Sales Force

Howard recently met with his close friend John—who manages a large resort in the Orlando area—to discuss his problems with the sales force. He gave John a brief rundown of the situation: "Well, my problem concerns the way I'm leading my salespeople. Things seem to be going fine with five of my seven salespeople. Melissa and Jeff, who I just hired six months ago, are going great. They are both young and eager to learn. Both have been progressing well, with slight increases in sales volume over the last two months. They both have very little sales experience, so they do make a few mistakes now and then. However, both will take constructive criticism very well, as they continually want to improve their selling skills. Melissa's and Jeff's ages are both very close to mine. Therefore, they relate to me very well. I have no problems with my two new salespeople.

"Rhonda is perhaps one of my best salespeople. Everyone enjoys being around her. Rhonda can give the other reps a lift when they are down. Her own sales performance is exceptional. Rhonda continually surpasses her quotas and actively seeks out new customers. Rhonda accepts my leadership as if I were the V.P. of marketing. I wish all my salespeople were like Rhonda.

"Robert is also a fun salesperson to manage. He's been out of college for only about two years. He's young and wants to do well in the company. He reminds me a lot of myself when I first started with SSI. Robert is very competitive. So he readily accepts my criticism, since he constantly wants to improve. I made a few sales calls with him last week, and he must have asked over twenty questions dealing with selling activities. He sort of looks on me as a big brother and that makes him very easy to manage. To be honest with you, Robert is good for my ego.

"George is about my age, and if he has a problem, it's that he likes to goof off too much. George is good at bringing life and laughter into the job. He is well liked by everyone. However, he does spend too much time bull-shooting! Every so often I have to get after him. When I do, George does pick up his pace and is a very good salesperson. Managing George always keeps me busy. I don't think he really minds being supervised. Actually, I think he realizes that a little bit of leadership now and then will help his sales performance."

"It sounds like things are going pretty well for you, Howard," interrupted John. "Five of your seven salespeople seem to be doing fine. Is it the other two salespeople who are causing you all this grief? I can't wait to hear about these two!"

Problem Salespeople

"Well, Freddie is my biggest problem. He's a veteran salesperson who has been with the company for over thirty years. Freddie started out by selling the liberal arts textbooks. In fact, Freddie has been the top salesperson in the company many times. Freddie *does* have superstar qualities. However, since he's been working for me, his performance has been terrible. His performance is not quite bad enough for me to recommend that SSI fire him. However, if it gets any worse, I'm going to have to do something.

"The biggest problem with Freddie is that he doesn't listen to me. He is very hardheaded and seemingly feels insulted every time I tell him to do something. For example, the other day I told Freddie that he wasn't spending enough time with several of his customers. He then told me that he was selling textbooks before I was born and that he has forgotten more about selling than I ever learned from textbooks.

"Recently, I've been going out of my way to try to work with Freddie. I've asked him to go on recruiting trips with me, and I've tried to help make his job easier by trying to get him familiar with a personal computer. In both instances, he rejected me by making up some silly excuse. Freddie refuses to listen to me, no matter how hard I try to win him over.

"Freddie also shows me very little respect. He will often address me as 'the college boy' in sales meetings. Last week, in front of one of our largest accounts, he called me 'sonny.' I don't know how much more I can take from him.

"Warren is my other problem. Warren is about 48 and has been with the company for over ten years. He is a hard worker and continually achieves his quota. I have the feeling, however, that Warren wants to be a sales manager. Also, I think he resents me for having this job at such a young age. I don't want to sound paranoid, but I have the feeling that he wants my job and will do anything he can to get it. Warren is very competitive and is seemingly using his experience to show people that he can do a better job managing the sales force than I can. Given this circumstance, I have a very difficult time being a leader to Warren.

"The way I look at it, I am an effective leader with most of my salespeople. Five of my seven people are doing well and accept my leadership. However, it really disturbs me that I can't do a better job with Freddie and Warren. These two guys have the potential of being the best two salespeople in the company. If they would improve just a little, I could have the best sales district in the company. I just don't know what to do to be a more effective leader to these guys!"

"I personally feel that you have nothing to worry about," said John. "You definitely have the ability to manage this sales force, or your company would never have promoted you. Howard, you need to build up your self-confidence so that these old guys don't bother you. Don't be afraid to boss them around. Remember, the future of your company is with the younger and currently more successful people. I didn't become a

manager of a resort hotel by being afraid to boss people around."

Questions

1. Comment on Howard's leadership style. What kind of leader is he?

2. Do you agree with John's advice? Why or why not? Is John's leadership style different from Howard's? If so, how?

3. Should Howard take John's advice? Why or why not?

4. Should Howard change his leadership style in an attempt to be a more effective leader to Freddie? To Warren? Why or why not?

5. What would your advice be to Howard? Do you think Howard is management material? Why or why not?

CASE 14-2

COMMUNICATION BARRIERS AT SK CHEMICAL CORPORATION

Brian Morris has been a junior salesperson for three years at SK Chemical Corporation, a national distributor of industrial chemicals and solvents. SK Chemicals had built quite a reputation for itself over the last fifty years in the chemical industry, growing large enough to be listed among the Fortune 500 companies. Three years ago, the company decided to widen its product mix and enter the textile and institutional markets. Acquisition of several independent supply houses across the middle and southern United States was accomplished, and a new division emerged within the SK corporate structure—the Textile and Institutional Products Division (TEX-INT). Twenty-four sales districts were set up to accommodate sales of the new line of products, with two salespeople per district. Brian Morris was selected as one of those salespersons.

TEX-INT Sales Structure

SK's textile and institutional sales force was a separate entity from the industrial chemicals sales force. Although both shared district offices, warehousing, and delivery facilities, management of the sales force was handled differently. At each district office a separate district manager was in charge of the industrial chemicals salespeople and the textile and institutional sales-

people. However, SK had created a national sales manager for the textile and institutional products to oversee the forty-eight salespeople for the new-product line. Mike Bonn, a highly productive salesperson who had been with SK for ten years, was selected to fill this position, which reports directly to the executive vice president.

Although Brian considered Mike Bonn to be his immediate supervisor, he also came under the management of Joan Fleming, the district manager at his office, on a day-to-day basis. Brian, fresh out of college when he began his job at SK, was eager to "set the world on fire." A highly motivated salesperson, he had many of the qualities needed to be very successful in his chosen field.

And successful he was—at first, anyhow. During his second year at SK, Brian was one of the top-five salespeople in the TEX-INT Division. In addition, he was ranked number eight in a national sales contest for Evershine, a group of products within the institutional line.

SK's upper management was eager to push the Evershine product group. All the products in the TEX-INT line were bought from suppliers and sold under their brand names, but Evershine, a group of institutional cleaning products, was a departure from the usual, as it was purchased in bulk from suppliers and then packaged and branded under the SK Evershine name.

Brian Morris's territory included three medium-sized cities in the southern United States within a 50-mile radius. He averaged about seven calls a day, and his accounts were divided into priority classes based on sales potential. Competition was stiff in Brian's territory, with three major competitors after his accounts. Brian had few problems for the first two years, since he was very successful at opening new accounts and did his very best to service his current accounts as well as new accounts. SK had a good reputation, and most of the products performed well.

Developing Problems

Brian began to notice deterioration in his customers' attitudes during his third year at SK. Upper managers were so eager to push the Evershine line that they became blind to many serious problems emerging with the product that were increasingly obvious to Brian.

At first the products moved well, and Brian took many orders for Evershine. Then distribution and warehousing problems began to prevent customers from receiving their orders on time. This soon created distrust toward SK and brought frustration and disappointment from customers that Brian had to work with on a day-to-day basis.

These were not the only problems for Brian. He worked on a straight-salary basis, and since SK was a distributor and did not manufacture its TEX-INT products, there was added cost that competitors who were producers did not have. SK's upper management had decided on a 30 percent gross profit figure for the TEX-INT products, and had established a rigid price book for the salespeople.

Brian knew that he was being undercut by his competitors. All three of the competitors' salespeople were compensated on either a straight-commission or a salary-plus-commission basis. These salespersons also were allowed price flexibility, which meant lowering prices if necessary to make a sale. Brian's customers could not understand why he could not do the same, and as a result he was starting to lose accounts.

Besides the problems with Evershine and the price inflexibilities, Brian began to become disgusted with the outdated inventory system he had to use. Salespeople from competing companies worked with personal computers that allowed them to see suggested retail prices at different quantities, as well as quantities in the warehouse and other information that was helpful in making a sale. Brian was forced to work with a fixed-price book, and he often had no idea of what was in the SK warehouse.

Communicating with Managers about Problems

Brian was a perceptive, intelligent, and extremely company-oriented employee, and because he was, he could see serious problems emerging for SK and decided to do something about them. SK supposedly welcomed suggestions from employees, so Brian began to turn in "suggestions" to the district manager, Joan Fleming, about the problems. Brian also expressed his views to Clyde Peters, western TEX-INT sales manager. (Eastern and western sales manager positions had been created, and they reported to Mike Bonn, the national sales manager for TEX-INT.) Clyde had previously been a top salesperson for TEX-INT products in an area with little competition and could not understand the problems so obvious to Brian. He had never faced the problems of being undercut in price. Clyde's attitude was that the problem was strictly sales effort. He told Brian, "Face it—you're being outsold." This statement infuriated Brian, since he knew his sales ability and efforts were of the highest caliber.

Brian spoke to several other salespeople for the TEX-INT line who expressed similar misgivings. As a final resort, he wrote a detailed letter expressing the serious problems he saw and gave suggestions about solving them. Specifically, he noted the inventory and distribution problems, inadequate sales incentives, lack of personal computers, price inflexibilities that were resulting in lost accounts, and what he termed "marriage of SK to a few suppliers," who often caused problems in distribution. Brian had several suggestions that would spur sales: (1) develop some sort of incentive or commission plan; (2) consider the idea of vertical integration for SK production of the TEX-INT products, which Brian felt would help lessen the price problems and result in less "undercutting" by competitors, most of whom owned their own production facilities; and (3) modernize inventory systems so that customers could have confidence in receiving their orders on time. Brian knew that his suggestions might be inconsistent with SK's present structure and goals. But he felt that some changes were necessary and that he must do something.

Although these problems were in fact realized later by management to be the true "culprits" in the decline of sales, it was too late to retain Brian, one of the most effective salespersons SK employed. He was fed up with the frustrations in his third year and quit. SK lost not only Brian, but several other top salespeople as well before its problems were cleared up.

Questions

1. How would you rate the leadership and communication skills of SK management? Why?

2. What suggestions do you have for improving the leadership and communication activities of SK sales managers?

3. What do you think SK's management could have done to keep Brian Morris from leaving, even if all his suggestions could not be implemented?

REFERENCES

1. Lorraine Calvacca, "Leader for the '90's: The One-Minute Motivator," *Working Woman,* March 1990, p. 76.
2. Sheila Murray Bethel, "Eagles Don't Flock: How to Create a Leader," *Marketing Times,* September–October 1985, pp. 10–13.
3. Joel Whitfield, "Leadership, Power, Productivity and You!" *Marketing Times,* September–October 1985, pp. 7–8.
4. R. Tannenbaum, I. R. Weschler, and F. Massarik, *Leadership and Organization,* McGraw-Hill, New York, 1961, p. 24.
5. Ricky Grithin, *Management,* Houghton Mifflin, Boston, 1990.
6. Tannenbaum, Weschler, and Massarik, op. cit.
7. John R. R. French and Bertram Raven, "The Bases of Social Power," in Dorwin Cartwright (ed.), *Studies in Social Power,* University of Michigan, Ann Arbor, 1959, pp. 612–613; Paul Busch, "The Sales Manager's Bases of Social Power and Influence upon the Sales Force," *Journal of Marketing,* Summer 1980, pp. 91–101. For other perspectives on sources of power, see Louis W. Stern and Adel I. El-Ansary, *Marketing Channels,* Prentice-Hall, Englewood Cliffs, N.J., 1977, pp. 286–292; Robert Lusch, "Sources of Power: Their Impact on Intra-Channel Conflict," *Journal of Marketing Research,* November 1976, pp. 382–390; Paul Busch and David Wilson, "An Experimental Analysis of a Salesman's Expert and Referent Bases of Social Power in the Buyer-Seller Dyad," *Journal of Marketing Research,* February 1976, pp. 3–11.
8. G. Yukl and T. Tabor, "The Effective Use of Managerial Power," *Personnel,* March–April 1983, pp. 37–44.
9. Don Helbriegel and John W. Slocum, Jr., *Management,* Addison-Wesley, Reading, Mass., 1986, p. 447.
10. *Time,* July 15, 1974, pp. 26–28.
11. Ibid.
12. Robert N. McMurry, *How to Recruit, Select, and Place Salesmen,* Dartnell Corporation, Chicago, 1964, as reprinted in Marvin A. Jolson (ed.), *Contemporary Readings in Sales Management,* Petrocilli/Charter, New York, 1977, p. 181.
13. *Time,* July 15, 1974, pp. 26–28.
14. *Management Review,* December 1979, p. 19.
15. Alvin W. Gouldner (ed.), *Studies in Leadership,* Harper, New York, 1950, pp. 23–24, 31–35.
16. Ralph M. Stogdill, "Personal Factors Associated with Leadership: A Survey of the Literature," *Journal of Psychology,* vol. 25, 1948, p. 63.
17. See Ralph M. Stogdill, *Handbook of Leadership,* Free Press, New York, 1974, for summaries of over 3,000 leadership studies.
18. Ralph M. Stogdill and A. E. Cooms (eds.), *Leader Behavior: Its Description and Measurement, Research Monograph No. 88,* Bureau of Business Research, Ohio State University, Columbus, 1957.
19. Abraham K. Korman, "Consideration, Initiating, Structure, and Organization Criteria—A Review," *Personal Psychology,* Winter 1966, pp. 349–361.
20. Gouldner, op cit.
21. Fred E. Fiedler, *A Theory of Leadership Effectiveness,* McGraw-Hill, New York, 1967.
22. Fred E. Fiedler, "The Leadership Game: Matching the Man to the Situation," *Organizational Dynamics,* Winter 1976, pp. 6–16.

23. Fred E. Fiedler, "The Trouble with Leadership Is That It Doesn't Train Leaders," *Psychology Today*, February 1973, pp. 23–30.

24. Orlando Behling and Chester Schriesheim, *Organizational Behavior: Theory, Research and Application*, Allyn and Bacon, Boston, 1976.

25. Steven Kerr and John M. Jermier, "Substitutes for Leadership: Their Meaning and Measurement," *Organizational Behavior and Human Performance*, December 1978, pp. 375–403.

26. Charles C. Mang and Henry P. Sims, Jr., "Leading Workers to Lead Themselves: The External Leadership of Self-Managing Work Teams," *Administrative Science Quarterly*, March 1987, pp. 106–129.

27. Discussion of "theory H" is largely based on Thomas F. Stroh, *Effective Psychology for Sales Managers*, Parker Publishing, West Nyack, N.Y., 1974, pp. 59–70.

28. Raymond A. Gumpert and Ronald K. Hambleton, "Situational Leadership: How Xerox Managers Fine-Tune Managerial Styles to Employee Maturity and Task Needs," *Management Review*, December 1979, pp. 8–12.

29. Robert E. Miles and M. M. Petty, "Leader Effectiveness in Small Bureaucracies," *Academy of Management Journal*, June 1977, pp. 238–250.

30. Thomas L. Quick, "Curbstone Coaching," *Sales & Marketing Management*, July 1990, pp. 100–101.

31. Bethel, op. cit.

32. Paul Rosenkrantz, Susan Vogel, Helen Bee, Inge Broverman, and Donald Broverman, "Sex-Role Stereotypes and Self-Concepts in College Students," *Journal of Consulting and Clinical Psychology*, June 1968, pp. 287–295.

33. Virginia E. Schein, "The Relationship between Sex Role Stereotypes and Requisite Management Characteristics," *Journal of Applied Psychology*, April 1973, p. 99.

34. Karen Korabik, "Androgyny and Leadership Style," *Journal of Business Ethics*, April–May 1990, pp. 283–292.

35. Courtland L. Bovée and John V. Thill, *Business Communication Today*, Random House, New York, 1989, p. 37.

36. E. Rogers and R. Rogers, *Communications in Organizations*, Free Press, New York, 1976.

37. Philip Morgan and H. Kent Baker, "Building a Professional Image: Improving Listening Behavior," *Supervisory Management*, November 1985, pp. 35–36.

38. Bovée and Thill, op. cit.

39. Mark L. Hickson III and Don W. Stacks, *Nonverbal Communications: Studies and Applications*, Wm. C. Brown, Dubuque, Iowa, 1985.

DIRECTING THE SALES FORCE AT CHEMCO: A TURNOVER PROBLEM

Dan Hager, vice president of sales at CHEMCO, was preparing for the upcoming two-day quarterly meeting with the division, regional, and district sales managers. He was reviewing some of the findings from a university research project that focused on CHEMCO sales personnel. The study was a pet project of CHEMCO president, Al Jorgenson, who believes management has lost touch with the sales force because of rapid expansion. Dan thought the study was more of a bother than it was worth, but he had to admit that he was surprised by some of the findings. Maybe Al was right. Sales force turnover was higher than they had expected. Perhaps they were assuming everything was all right in the ranks when it wasn't. Al had told him to brief the sales managers and to give them direction in using the study's data base to combat this problem. It had been a busy, sometimes frustrating week, but all he had left to do was organize his notes and figures. Then he'd be ready for the meeting.

DEVELOPMENT OF THREE GENERAL SCALES FROM THE DATA BASE

Dan had requested that personnel send him a list of the persons who left the company since the completion of the sales force study. He found that there had

Case prepared by Steve Remington, Memphis State University.

been a 15 percent turnover in Division 1 and more than a 30 percent turnover in Division 2 during the past year. The adoption of more aggressive marketing strategies by CHEMCO had led to a rapid expansion of the sales force, and Dan attributed some of the turnover to the normal shakeout of new reps. But the loss of several reps who had been with the firm for more than ten years and the noticeable exit of many of the female sales reps from Division 1 were troublesome and unexplainable.

A discussion between Dan and Al Jorgenson concerning sales force turnover had centered on three figures drawn from the university research report. Each added clues as to what problems might be causing the turnover but did not provide a clear picture of the cause. Although overall the sales force's propensity to quit (Exhibit 1) was low, it was high for a few reps in each division. This might be partially explained by the higher role ambiguity (Exhibit 2) reported by Division 1 and the obviously higher role conflict (Exhibit 3) identified in Division 2. Both men realized that either problem might stem from a wide range of causes. Further examination of the report proved frustrating because it was highly detailed and provided little broad analysis. It was decided that an analysis with a wider perspective than that provided by the report was needed. Dan made an appointment to meet with Sandy Spotts, the manager of the data processing department, to see if she could help.

At the meeting Dan explained his problem. The research report included eight satisfaction scales, six job performance scales, and four scales measuring perceived organizational climate. What he wanted was a single measurement for each area. Sandy assured Dan that it would not be difficult to provide the information he requested. Using the study's data base, she developed an overall measurement of satisfaction, job performance, and perceived organizational climate by taking the average of each participant's scores for that particular section.

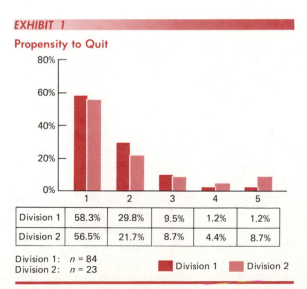

EXHIBIT 1

Propensity to Quit

	1	2	3	4	5
Division 1	58.3%	29.8%	9.5%	1.2%	1.2%
Division 2	56.5%	21.7%	8.7%	4.4%	8.7%

Division 1: n = 84
Division 2: n = 23

■ Division 1　■ Division 2

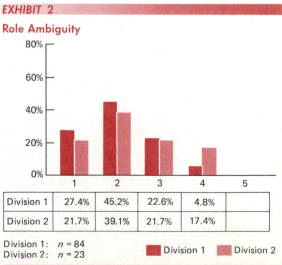

EXHIBIT 2

Role Ambiguity

	1	2	3	4	5
Division 1	27.4%	45.2%	22.6%	4.8%	
Division 2	21.7%	39.1%	21.7%	17.4%	

Division 1: n = 84
Division 2: n = 23

■ Division 1　■ Division 2

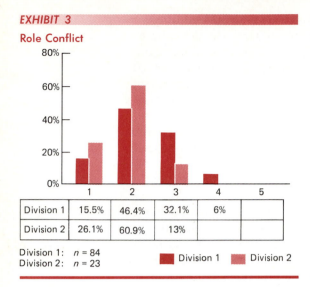

EXHIBIT 3

Role Conflict

	1	2	3	4	5
Division 1	15.5%	46.4%	32.1%	6%	
Division 2	26.1%	60.9%	13%		

Division 1: *n* = 84
Division 2: *n* = 23

■ Division 1   ■ Division 2

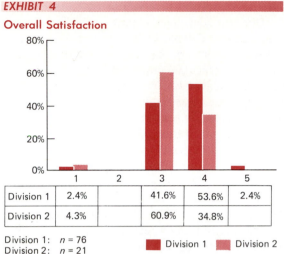

EXHIBIT 4

Overall Satisfaction

	1	2	3	4	5
Division 1	2.4%		41.6%	53.6%	2.4%
Division 2	4.3%		60.9%	34.8%	

Division 1: *n* = 76
Division 2: *n* = 21

■ Division 1   ■ Division 2

She explained that this average could be computed for each individual, region, or division or for the entire sales force. Dan decided that he wanted to make a comparison between divisions, as had been done in the study's report. Sandy provided him with a set of figures similar to those found in the report. Dan left feeling that now he would be able to get a better grasp of the problem at hand.

DAN'S ANALYSIS

Gathering together his copy of the research report and the figures Sandy had provided, Dan began his analysis. His first impression of the figures he'd requested was that there was nothing unusual about them. The majority of the salespeople were satisfied in their positions, felt they were doing an above-average job, and thought CHEMCO was a good place to work. There were groups in each division that were below-average, but these groups didn't seem to be large enough to account for the turnover rate.

Upon closer examination of the overall satisfaction scale (Exhibit 4), Dan noted that a small percentage of the salespeople in each division were very dissatisfied in their positions. Also, the overall satisfaction of the members of Division 1 seemed to be a little higher than that of the members of Division 2. Still, eleven salespeople had left Division 1 and eight had left Division 2 during the past year. Why, then, did only two Division 1 reps (2.4 percent of seventy-six) and one Division 2 rep (4.3 percent of twenty-one) report that they were dissatisfied? Perhaps the others were dissatisfied with only one or two of the factors measured. The researchers had noted a general dissatisfaction with pay, but Dan considered it simply part of human nature to want more money. So which of the eight factors of satisfaction should be examined?

Referring to the report, Dan divided the eight satisfaction scales into three categories according to how much influence CHEMCO had over the factors they measured. Satisfaction with pay and general policies seemed to be highly influenced by the company. Both factors were controlled at the corporate level, but input from the reps through the sales managers was obviously needed. Next, Dan decided that CHEMCO moderately influenced satisfaction with promotional opportunities, coworkers, district and regional sales managers, and the job itself. Satisfaction with these factors might be increased through new motivational methods or additional training, and Dan decided that this category should be a focus of the quarterly sales meeting. Finally, Dan believed that CHEMCO had only limited influence over the sales rep's satisfaction with customers, but he'd ask for input on this from the sales managers.

The overall job performance scale (Exhibit 5) added more pieces to the turnover puzzle. It showed that 9.2 percent of the salespeople in Division 1 and 23.8 percent of those in Division 2 felt their performance was below-average. Dan believed that these findings were closer to the true feelings of the sales force than were the satisfaction findings. He remembered the comments of a management trainer at a recent "skunk camp": Dissatisfied salespeople would most likely feel they were not performing up to their potential. They would, the trainer had noted, be more likely to blame elements of their work environment, rather than acknowledge personal weaknesses, for their inability to reach their perceived potential.

Reviewing the six scales that Sandy had combined to create the overall job performance scale, Dan noted that each seemed to be directly related to CHEMCO training programs. Sessions reviewing selling skills, technical knowledge, customer relations, and territory management were always included in the annual sales meeting. Perhaps CHEMCO needed to schedule a skunk camp training session—an activity Al Jorgenson was usually quick to fund—focused on one

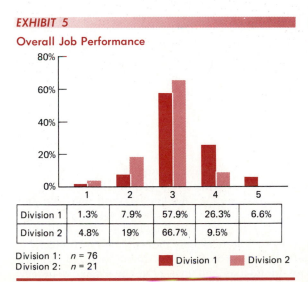

EXHIBIT 5

Overall Job Performance

	1	2	3	4	5
Division 1	1.3%	7.9%	57.9%	26.3%	6.6%
Division 2	4.8%	19%	66.7%	9.5%	

Division 1: $n = 76$
Division 2: $n = 21$

Division 1   Division 2

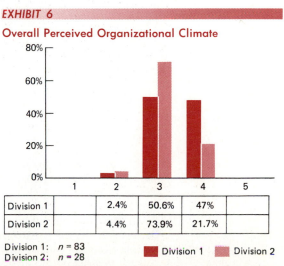

EXHIBIT 6

Overall Perceived Organizational Climate

	1	2	3	4	5
Division 1		2.4%	50.6%	47%	
Division 2		4.4%	73.9%	21.7%	

Division 1: $n = 83$
Division 2: $n = 28$

Division 1   Division 2

of these topics. But Dan would rather handle such problems in house, so he decided that he would ask the sales managers to concentrate on these factors during the upcoming sales force evaluations.

The last scale developed for Dan gave him a ballpark measure of the sales force's perception of the working conditions at CHEMCO. The overall organizational climate scale (Exhibit 6) included measures of corporate status, quality of coworkers, fairness of rewards and punishments, and ability to meet personal goals. That the reported perception of the overall organizational climate at CHEMCO was lower for Division 2 than for Division 1 did not surprise Dan. Glancing at the research report, he compared the averages of the two divisions and noted that Division 2 scored noticeably lower on all the factors except perceived quality of coworkers. Dan mentally noted that he would need to meet with George Parker, the Division 2 sales manager, to talk about the general atmosphere in his division. For the time being, Dan believed the perceived organizational climate would improve if the factors he had already noted were worked on.

DAN'S PLAN FOR THE QUARTERLY SALES MANAGERS' MEETING

Dan knew that the sales managers had each received a copy of the research report that focused on their division. He had requested that they bring their copies along with them to the meeting. He would provide copies of the overall scales Sandy Spotts had created. To prevent the direct comparison of the overall scales by the managers, he had asked Sandy to break the scales down by division.

Several sessions dedicated to developing a strategy to improve the turnover problem were scheduled during each of the meeting's two days. During the opening session, Al Jorgenson would make a few general comments about the research project and its results. Dan would then outline the turnover problem and establish the general goals for their individual sessions. Dan and Al had agreed that they wanted this exercise to initiate what they believed should be an ongoing process. The managers would then separate for division meetings. Dan had scheduled time with each of the divisions during the first morning in order to present a more detailed account of his findings. At the end of the second day Dan would meet with each of the division managers and review the beginnings of a strategy to lessen turnover.

QUESTIONS

1. Assume the role of division sales manager. You have just listened to Dan Hager make his presentation to your division. He has requested that you develop a strategy to lessen turnover. He feels you should focus on the sales force's satisfaction with promotional opportunities, coworkers, district and regional sales managers, and the job itself. Outline the procedure you believe your division should take in developing this strategy. Using the research report's data base, identify the information you feel you would need to complete the task. Do not limit yourself to the factors Dan included on his list. Gather the necessary information and analyze it. Outline your strategy, and support your major points quantitatively as well as qualitatively.

2. Assume the role of regional sales manager. Complete the activity in question 1.

3. Assume the role of district sales manager. Complete the activity in question 1.

4. Turnover among the female sales reps in Division 1 has been higher than expected. Analyze the situation by developing information from the data base. List what you consider the major causes of this turnover. What motivational techniques might you use to lessen this problem.

5. Compensation was singled out by the university research team as a specific problem for CHEMCO. Some sales managers believe it is the only valid motivational tool. Further explore CHEMCO's turnover problem, and pay special attention to the sales force's satisfaction with pay and perception of the use of rewards and punishments (perceived climate). What methods, other than modifying the compensation plan, might be used to improve sales force satisfaction with these factors?

6. During one of the sessions at an upper-management skunk camp, Al Jorgenson mentioned the rapid growth of CHEMCO's sales force, the reps' relative inexperience, and their alarming rate of turnover. One of the other participants mentioned that her company had solved a similar problem by developing a mentoring system. Later, she explained to Al the details of her company's program. How might mentoring be used as a motivational tool to improve the situation at CHEMCO? How would it help or hinder the female sales reps in Division 1?

PART FIVE

CONTROLLING
AND EVALUATING
THE SALES FORCE

15

ANALYSIS OF SALES, COSTS, AND PROFITABILITY

LEARNING OBJECTIVES

When you finish this chapter, you should understand:

▲ The sales manager's responsibility for profits
▲ The need for sales volume, costs, and profitability analyses
▲ Various sources of sales information
▲ How to conduct sales analysis by territory, sales representative, product line, and customer
▲ The concept of input-output efficiency
▲ The value of marketing and accounting cooperation
▲ The benefits of marketing cost (profitability) analysis
▲ The procedure for marketing cost (profitability) analysis
▲ The arguments for using contribution costs versus full costs
▲ The concept of return on assets measured and how to compute it
▲ Approaches to increasing sales force productivity

Phil Coty appears to be a supersalesperson. He is always among the top 10 percent in sales for the company. Phil, or "Big Time," as he is usually called, is extroverted and well-liked by his customers, partly because he entertains them lavishly. He takes his prospects and customers to the finest restaurants and frequently provides tickets to professional sports events or popular stage shows. Mary Steiner, on the other hand, is much more low-key and usually has a difficult time reaching her sales quota each month. Mary seldom entertains her prospects and customers and is known for being "strictly business." Some sales managers may jump to the conclusion that Phil is a much better salesperson than Mary. But a closer analysis of the revenues versus costs generated by these two salespeople may show that Phil contributes less to overall profits than does Mary. With today's high costs of personal selling, it is increasingly important that sales managers emphasize profitability of sales efforts. This chapter will help sales managers attain sharper focus on "the bottom line" through sales volume, costs, and profitability analyses by market segments.

However, the *Ethics* scenario on page 493 is presented to illustrate how expenses and, therefore, profitability can sometimes be beyond the control of the sales manager.

THE SALES MANAGER'S RESPONSIBILITY FOR PROFITS

Too many sales managers overstress selling activities and sales volume while neglecting cost controls and profitability analysis. Although sales volume analysis is helpful in evaluating and controlling sales efforts, it neglects the profitability of these efforts—and high volume does not ensure high profits. Even when sales managers focus on profits, they often look at total profits and do minimum analysis by major market segments (customers, products, territories, salespeople) if the aggregate figures are favorable. Thus, many sales force efforts continue to be assigned perfunctorily and equally among territories, product lines, or customer classes. To increase the efficiency of sales force efforts, sales managers need to pay more attention to cost and profitability analyses by important market segments and organizational units. From such analyses, sales managers can direct resource efforts and expenditures to those areas in which the return per dollar spent is highest.

In a survey of 273 manufacturers nearly all claimed that they performed profitability analyses for product lines. Two-thirds analyzed by sales territories, 57 percent by salespeople, and 54 percent by customers. But 19 percent of the large firms and 23 percent of the medium-sized ones conducted analyses on only one of these four bases.[2] Many companies do not have a good system for gathering, classifying, and analyzing sales and marketing cost and profit data. Yet it is the overriding responsibility of sales managers to utilize all their resources so as to accomplish that balance between sales volume and costs that will result in the highest long-run organizational profits. This chapter is concerned with providing an understanding of the purpose, approach, process, problems, and opportunities involved in analyzing sales volume and marketing costs for better sales management decisions and higher organizational productivity.

In analyzing the productivity of sales force efforts, sales managers need to understand the linkages among sales volume, selling costs, and profits by market segments. In determining the profitability of different market segments, the logical sequence is first to analyze the sources of sales volume and then to subtract the costs for producing those sales to arrive at individual segment profitability. Although the analytical task seems straightforward, it is fraught with difficulties, especially in assigning marketing costs (such as advertising, administration, or warehouse and office rent) that are indirect or common to more than one segment.

Since selling costs are really a subcategory of marketing costs, and because a combination of selling and marketing costs is required to produce sales, the more general term "marketing cost analysis" will be used. Furthermore, because sales managers are really more interested in profitability than costs, "marketing profitability analysis" will be referred to in describing this overall process of sales volume, cost, and profitability analysis.

Marketing profitability analysis can be described as an in-depth analysis of the elements making up an organization's profit-and-loss, or income, statements. Such an analysis reclassifies the traditional accounting statement expenses into cost centers according to the purposes, or functions, for which the expenses (costs) were incurred. For example, salaries for a sales organization may be paid to employees for performing such functions as direct selling, order processing, or sales administration. These salaries may be further allocated to territories, products, customers, or salespeople. Analyses of this type can be invaluable to sales managers in making decisions to eliminate or add new marketing activities or to change the allocation of current efforts.[3] Sales volume analysis will be discussed first.

SALES ANALYSIS

Sales analysis may be described as the collection, classification, comparison, and evaluation of an organization's sales figures. All organizations collect and classify sales data as the framework upon which their accounting records and statements are constructed. To sales managers, sales figures are the most immediately visible and available means for judging how well the organization is performing. Sales managers regularly use sales analyses to evaluate current performance compared with past sales, competitors' sales, or forecasted sales. From these evaluations, management decides the direction and scale of future sales efforts.

The Definition of a Sale

Before starting a sales analysis, management must decide when a sale takes place—whether at the time an order is received, shipped, or paid for. Most companies consider a sale to have taken place at the time of shipment, but some companies keep records for all three definitions of a sale to analyze what volume and type of orders make it through each of the three stages. Whatever the definition, it must be applied consistently if sales comparisons across time periods are to be meaningful.

Sources of Sales Information

Depending upon the depth of sales analyses and the breakdown desired, the sources of sales information will vary widely. In a simple sales analysis, only aggregate sales figures are needed by the desired market segment. But for comparisons with quotas, market potential, historical sales, or industry averages, considerably more information must be collected and classified. Even though

EXHIBIT 15-1

Sources and Types of Sales Information

- *Sales invoice.* Customer name and address; products or services bought, sales in units and dollars; name of salesperson; customer's industry and/or trade channel; terms of sales, including discounts and allowances; method of payment; mode of shipment; and freight costs

- *Salesperson's call reports.* Prospects and customers called upon; names of persons contacted; products presented or discussed; prospect's or customer's product needs and usage; orders obtained

- *Salesperson's expense accounts.* Itemized daily expenses for travel, lodging, food, and entertainment of prospects and customers

- *Individual prospect/customer records.* Prospect or customer name and address; customer's industry or trade channel; number of calls by company salesperson; sales in dollars and units; estimated annual usage of each product type sold by the company; annual purchases from the company

- *Internal financial records.* Sales by major market segments (territories, customers, products, or salespersons); direct selling expenses; administrative costs; costs and profits by market segments

- *Warranty cards.* Basic demographic data on customers; where purchased; price paid; reasons for purchase; service expected

- *Store audits.* Dollar or unit sales volume; market share in product category

- *Consumer diaries.* Dollar or unit purchases by package size, brands, prices, special deals, and type of outlets where purchased

- *Test markets.* Dollar or unit purchases; market share; effect of different marketing mixes on sales

the sales invoice is the most important single source of sales information, most companies select other sources as well, depending upon the types of analysis desired. Major sources and types of sales information are provided in Exhibit 15-1.

Collection of Sales Data

Sales figures are usually reported in both dollars and units, since inflation can distort dollar comparisons across different time periods. Sales data are frequently subcategorized by territories, product types, customer classes, order sizes, methods of sales, time periods, organizational units, or salespersons to provide more meaningful information to management. Each subcategory may be further subdivided for more in-depth analysis. For example, sales by territory can be subcategorized by product types, customer classes, and so on, as shown in Exhibit 15-2.

Total Sales Volume

In any sales analysis, total sales volume figures are the first ones studied. Sales managers want to know the trend of sales over the past several years in terms

EXHIBIT 15-2

Subcategories of a Sales Territory

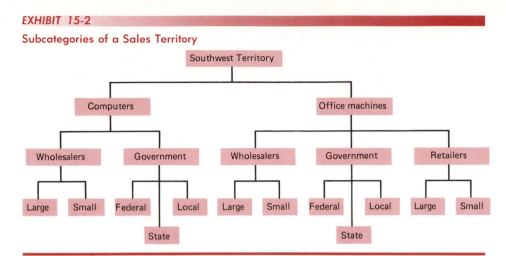

of units and constant (uninflated) dollars. By comparing relative changes in total industry sales with company sales, the sales manager has a benchmark for performance versus competition. Trends in company market share (company sales ÷ industry sales) are excellent indicators of relative competitive performance. As seen in Exhibit 15-3, AHB Manufacturing Company's sales volume has risen faster than industry sales from 1987 through 1993, and sales (in constant dollars) have continued to increase. Even though these aggregate sales figures indicate that all is going well, an aggressive sales manager would resist the temptation to be complacent and would go about the task of more in-depth sales analysis to see how sales force productivity might be improved. With the press of other duties, sales managers are often lulled into inattention to sales analyses when total sales figures appear favorable, because they forget the *iceberg principle*. Only about 10 percent of a floating iceberg is visible above the surface of the water; yet it is the underlying 90 percent that can sink a mighty ship (like the *Titanic*). The captain may superficially evaluate the iceberg on the basis of

EXHIBIT 15-3

AHB Manufacturing Company Sales versus Industry Sales (In Thousands of Dollars)*

Year	Industry Sales	Company Sales	Company Market Share
1987	$15,689	$2,359	15.04%
1988	16,912	2,782	16.45
1989	17,776	3,373	18.98
1990	18,234	3,519	19.30
1991	18,982	3,712	19.56
1992	19,871	3,916	19.71
1993	20,466	4,231	20.67

*In constant 1987 dollars.

EXHIBIT 15-4

AHB Manufacturing Company:
Hierarchical Analysis of Sales Volume by Market Segments

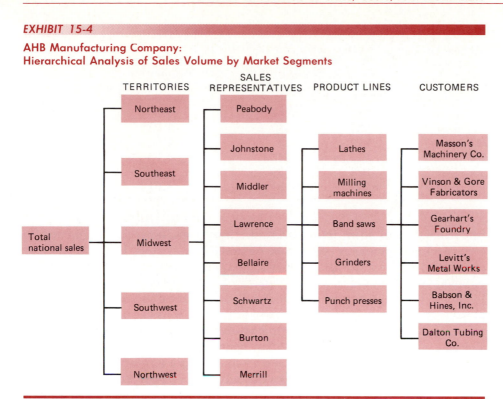

its visible part. In terms of business operations, favorable total figures can easily hide unprofitable market segments and unproductive sales activities. To uncover all the "iceberg," it is necessary to divide total sales figures into their successively smaller components. For example, we might start with an analysis of sales volume by territory and then subdivide territorial sales to the salesperson who generated those sales. Next, we might assign each salesperson's sales into product lines. Finally, we can subdivide product-line sales into customer classes. Each sales manager will need to decide what type and how many breakdowns are needed to get at the underlying explanations for sales volume figures. Through this sequential process, sales managers can unravel the outer covering at each top-to-bottom hierarchical level to see exactly where sales revenue is coming from, as illustrated in Exhibit 15-4. Thus, the 1993 sales data in Exhibit 15-3 can be initially broken down by geographic territory.

Sales Analysis by Territory

Scanning the territorial classification in Exhibit 15-5, we can quickly see that all the territories met or exceeded their quotas for the year, except for the midwest region, which achieved 98 percent of quota and had the highest total sales. Although everything looked good, AHB Manufacturing Company's new sales manager, Kathy Bennett, decided to investigate sales in each of the territories

EXHIBIT 15-5

AHB Manufacturing Company: 1993 Sales Analysis by Territory ($000's)

Territory	Quota	Actual	Index Performance (Actual Sales ÷ Quota)
Northeast	845	848	1.00
Southeast	820	840	1.02
Midwest	890	870	0.98
Northwest	815	843	1.03
Southwest	830	830	1.00
Totals	4,200	4,231	1.01

by breaking them down into subclassifications. First, however, the procedure for assigning sales quotas ought to be reviewed (see Chapter 11) to ensure that each quota was assigned fairly and based on one or more sound measurements of potential—for example, *Sales & Marketing Management*'s Buying Power Index. In addition, to guide further sales analysis, consideration should be given to any unusual conditions in the individual territories (such as more intense competition or a union strike that has an adverse impact on sales or, conversely, an anticipated shortage of the company's product that creates windfall sales to customers who are "stocking up"). If quota was barely achieved in a territory where industry demand was sharply up during the year, further investigation would be called for. After considering each territorial circumstance for the period, the sales manager can start with the territory that suggests the most promise for productivity improvement. Since the midwest territory fell a little short of quota, sales manager Bennett began with that region's sales, broken down by sales representative.

Sales Analysis by Sales Representative

From Exhibit 15-6, Bennett noted that five sales representatives made or exceeded their quotas and two others barely missed. Only Lawrence, with a per-

EXHIBIT 15-6

AHB Manufacturing Company, Midwest Territory: 1993 Sales by Sales Representative

Sales Representative	Quota	Actual	Performance Index (Actual Sales ÷ Quota)
Peabody	106	110	1.04
Johnstone	95	93	0.98
Middler	110	112	1.02
Schwartz	115	117	1.02
Bellaire	110	109	1.02
Lawrence	130	106	0.82
Burton	116	116	1.00
Merrill	108	107	0.99
Totals	890	870	0.98

EXHIBIT 15-7

EXHIBIT 15-7

AHB Manufacturing Company:
Sales Representative Lawrence's 1993 Sales by Product Line

Product Line	Quota	Actual	Performance Index (Actual Sales ÷ Quota)
Lathes	26	25	0.96
Milling machines	22	23	1.05
Band saws	30	6	0.20
Grinders	24	24	1.00
Punch presses	28	28	1.00
Totals	130	106	0.82

formance index of 0.82, fell significantly below his sales quota. Before calling Lawrence in for an explanation, Bennett wanted to get a more detailed breakdown of Lawrence's sales by product line.

Sales Analysis by Product Line

As revealed in Exhibit 15-7, Lawrence did an excellent job of reaching product quotas for all goods except band saws; he achieved only 20 percent of his band saw quota. Checking with the company's production manager, Bennett learned that there had been no unusual quality control problems, shortages, or delivery problems on band saws. Furthermore, the marketing vice president said that there had been no recent change in the marketing mix for band saws in any territory and that total sales for band saws were running slightly ahead of last year. To probe a little deeper, the sales manager decided to ask her sales administration assistant for a breakdown of Lawrence's sales of band saws by customer.

Sales Analysis by Customer

Exhibit 15-8, the analysis of band saw sales by customer, shows that one customer, Babson & Hines, Inc., accounted for Lawrence's poor performance on

EXHIBIT 15-8

AHB Manufacturing Company:
Sales Representative Lawrence's 1993 Sales of Band Saws by Customer

Customer	Quota	Actual	Performance Index (Actual ÷ Quota)
Masson's Machinery Co.	1	1	1.00
Vinson & Gore Fabricators	2	2	1.00
Gearhart's Foundry	1	1	1.00
Levitt's Metal Works	1	1	1.00
Babson & Hines, Inc.	24	0	0.00
Dalton Tubing Co.	1	1	1.00
Totals	30	6	0.20

that product line. Babson & Hines was Lawrence's biggest customer and had been targeted for 80 percent of his entire sales quota for band saws. However, there was a change of purchasing agent at Babson & Hines, and the company subsequently switched to another supplier, leaving Lawrence out in the cold. Embarrassed about losing such a large account, which he had begun to take for granted, Lawrence said nothing to the new sales manager, hoping that he might regain some of the business later in the year or make it up by increasing sales on other product lines. Lawrence did not expect his little deception to be picked up, because the previous sales manager seldom analyzed sales by market segments as long as overall sales were favorable. Sales manager Bennett had a private conference with Lawrence after the next monthly sales meeting. She explained to him that, in the future, she expected to be alerted immediately about sales problems so that she might provide assistance. Lawrence was relieved that he was not reprimanded for his mistake in judgment, and he left Bennett's office feeling sincere respect for the thoroughness of her analysis of sales force operations.

Analysis of Lawrence's sales by customer illustrated the validity of the *concentration principle* (sometimes called the "80-20 principle"), which asserts that the major portion of any organization's sales, costs, or profits often comes from a small proportion of business segments—for example, customers or products. If Lawrence had allocated his selling time with customers in proportion to sales, he might have retained the Babson & Hines, Inc., account. As an outstanding application of the concentration principle, USV Pharmaceutical increased sales 250 percent over a four-year span by directing its sales force to stop calling on 330,000 small accounts in order to focus on 70,000 major ones.[4]

Beyond revealing all kinds of valuable information about "who, what, where, when, and how" sales revenue is generated, sales volume analysis lays the foundation for the next stage in profitability analysis: the in-depth study of the costs of marketing in achieving sales.

MARKETING COST ANALYSIS

Sometimes called "distribution cost analysis," marketing cost analysis goes beyond sales volume analysis to investigate those costs incurred in generating sales volume.[5] By subtracting the marketing costs identified with the sales revenue from various market segments or organizational units, we can determine the profit contributions of the segments and units.

Sales managers try to allocate resources to obtain the most profitable balance between sales volume and marketing costs. But it is difficult to decide how to allocate these resources because the precise impact of expenditures on different elements of the marketing mix (e.g., advertising, sales promotional materials, sales calls, and postpurchase service) is not readily measurable. Any effective marketing cost analysis requires cooperation among the sales manager, the headquarters marketing team, and the accounting department. One way to understand this need for integrated efforts is to consider input-output efficiency.

Input-Output Efficiency

Different mixes and levels of selling and supporting marketing efforts are needed to achieve different sales objectives. The relationship between the inputs (marketing efforts) and the outputs (sales objectives) is a measure of a sales organization's efficiency.[6] To illustrate, if a regional sales organization has the objective of selling 2,000 new office machines during the year, the input would be the mix and level of direct selling and supporting marketing efforts required to achieve the output—that is, the sales target. Specifically, the expected inputs are that the sales force will have to make 3,000 additional sales calls during the year and that twenty advertisements will be needed in selected trade magazines to help introduce the new product to prospective customers. In addition, the sales manager estimates that the inside office sales force will accept about 600 collect telephone calls (many long-distance) inquiring about the new machines. A summary of these activities is presented below:

Sales Efforts (Inputs)		Sales Objectives (Outputs)	
3,000 sales calls @ $100	$300,000	Sell 2,000 new office machines	
600 telephone calls @ $1.50	900	($1,000 each) @ $500 gross margin	
Totals	$300,900		$1,000,000

By dividing the dollar outputs by the dollar inputs ($1,000,000 ÷ $320,900), one can derive an efficiency ratio of 3.116.

Many organizations do not function in the most efficient manner because they fail to operate near the optimum point on their average cost curves representing selling and supporting marketing costs. Instead of making 3,000 sales calls, it may be more efficient to mail out 6,000 sales promotion brochures about the new product and make only 1,500 sales calls on the best prospects as identified by marketing research. By reallocating the mixture of direct selling and marketing support activities, a company might achieve the same sales with greater efficiency ($1,000,000 ÷ $186,900 = 5.35), as shown in the following table:

Sales Efforts (Inputs)		Sales Objectives (Outputs)
1,500 sales calls @ $100	$150,000	Sell 2,000 new office
600 telephone calls @ $1.50	900	machines
1 market survey @ $10,000	10,000	($1,000 each) @
6,000 sales promotion brochures @ $1.00	6,000	$500 gross margin
20 trade magazine ads @ $1,000	20,000	
Totals	$186,900	$1,000,000

Sales organizations often incur high average costs for selling tasks because they overutilize direct selling activities and underutilize the marketing support team. By cooperating with the marketing specialists in advertising, marketing

EXHIBIT 15-9

Average per Unit Sales Cost Curve for Direct Selling

research, or sales promotion, the sales force can often function much more efficiently. It behooves the sales manager to attempt to operate at the optimal point on his or her average selling cost curve. As seen in Exhibit 15-9, there is usually an optimum number of sales calls required to operate at the lowest average selling cost per unit. At S_1 the number of sales calls being made is insufficient to produce desired sales, so per-unit costs are high at C_1. At S_3 the sales manager is relying too heavily on costly sales calls, so per-unit costs remain too high at C_3. Only at S_2 is the optimal number of sales calls being made, thereby achieving the lowest per-unit costs at C_2. Beyond this optimal point, the sales manager ought to shift from direct selling to other marketing and promotional activities.

Marketing and Accounting Cooperation

Historically, accounting systems have been mainly concerned with reporting aggregate financial data to stockholders and creditors in order to raise outside funds. Gradually, accounting statements were redesigned to provide analysis of production costs for internal management use. Only in recent years, with the widespread use of computers, have accountants seriously turned their attention to marketing cost analysis.

Because of their critical function as the revenue-producing arm of the company, marketing activities often constitute a company's largest total expenditures. To progressive accounting and marketing departments, marketing cost analysis offers rewarding opportunities for cooperation in seeking ways to improve overall company productivity. Three continuing problems underlie the tendency to neglect marketing cost analyses by accounting systems: inadequate communication, lack of marketing cost standards, and inability to collect and analyze the huge volume of marketing data.

Inadequate communication between marketing and accounting managers arises partially from their different perspectives on the use of cost data. Accountants tend to see costs as an end—that is, something to be reduced. Marketers, however, see costs largely as means to an end or benefit—usually sales. Sales managers are particularly sensitive to potentially adverse effects on sales if marketing expenditures are curtailed too much.

Accounting cost analysis is primarily designed to provide a historical financial record of overall company operations and to ensure that production costs stay within established standards. By contrast, marketing cost analysis is more concerned about future decisions in that it seeks to learn the specific cost and profit contributions of different marketing efforts. While recognizing their different perspectives on cost analysis, marketing and accounting managers should try to cooperate with one another for the overall benefit of company productivity.

Lack of marketing cost standards has slowed the development of marketing cost analysis. The labor, material, and machinery resources needed to produce a certain output are reasonably controllable and predictable or testable in pilot plant operations, so standard costs can be established. Standard costs serve as predetermined cost norms, or guidelines, based on past experience and research. Unfortunately, the marketing outlays needed to produce a given level of sales are much less predictable because results vary widely, depending upon the marketing mix selected for changing marketing scenarios. While production managers can control the costs of most of their inputs (labor, material, and hours of operation) to yield a certain output, marketing managers seldom can precisely determine the costs of inputs needed to achieve a desired sales level. Instead of operating within a self-contained, controlled manufacturing plant, marketers must operate in a relatively vast, uncontrollable marketing environment of intense competition, fluctuating economic conditions, and varying customer responses. Moreover, the results of many marketing expenditures, such as advertising and customer service, do not have an immediate, readily measurable impact on sales. Because they work over a period of time, it is difficult to identify sales results in one period with the marketing costs incurred to achieve those sales. In conventional accounting practice, most marketing expenses are charged off in the period incurred, while production costs are identified with per-unit output and held in inventory until sold. The differentiated use of the terms "costs" and "expenses" in referring to production and marketing inputs reflects the accountant's difficulties with marketing operations. Accountants tend to speak of "production costs" and "marketing expenses," suggestive of their different levels of specificity. Less precisely, marketers often use "costs" and "expenses" interchangeably. The challenge remains for accountants and marketers to find new approaches to managing marketing costs for improved profitability.

Inability to collect and analyze the huge volume of marketing data has long hindered the progress of marketing cost analysis. But with the coming of low-cost, high-speed computers, the mass of marketing data has become increasingly manageable. Today, even small firms have access to the latest computer technology, which can handle the countless calculations necessary to compile and analyze marketing information in a timely fashion for decisions on sales force efforts and other marketing activities. In addition, many of today's sales managers are receiving directly from computers full-color managerial charts and graphs that summarize the mountains of marketing sales volume, cost, and profit data in almost any form desired. Computer graphics enable sales managers to respond more quickly to opportunities and challenges in the marketplace instead of having to wait several weeks as an artist attempts to translate massive computer printouts into managerially comprehensible formats.

Benefits of Marketing Cost Analysis

Marketing cost analysis recognizes that sales are achieved through marketing expenditures and that each expenditure contributes uniquely to profits. By identifying the productivity of different marketing expenditures, sales managers are able to improve the precision and productivity of their decisions in allocating sales force efforts and sales department resources, preparing sales department budgets, and obtaining support for the sales force from other elements of the headquarters marketing mix.

Key Terms

Before proceeding, it will be beneficial to pause and define some terms that will be used in the discussion of the marketing cost (profitability) analysis procedure.

- *Natural expenses.* The traditional expense categories (salaries, rent, depreciation, and the like) used in accounting statements.
- *Functional costs.* Natural expenses reclassified into the activities or functions for which they were incurred (e.g., "salary expense" reclassified into direct selling, transportation, or advertising function salaries).
- *Costs* versus *expenses.* Two terms that are often used interchangeably in describing marketing cost analysis. Costs tend to be specific and directly related to volume output, while expenses are more general or indirect expenditures. The distinction will not be of serious concern here.
- *Direct costs.* Costs that can be entirely identified with or traced to a particular function or segment such as a territory, customer, or product. In a territorial analysis, for example, each territory would be assigned the cost of salaries for the salespeople working exclusively in that territory.
- *Indirect costs.* Costs that are incurred for more than one function or segment and thus must be allocated on some reasonable basis; sometimes called "common costs." For example, the sales manager's salary or office utilities would have to be spread among sales functions and segments.
- *Fixed costs.* Costs that do not change with sales volume (e.g., salaries of the sales administration staff, office rent, and fire insurance).
- *Variable costs.* Costs that vary with sales volume (e.g., travel outlays for salespeople calling on customers or commissions based on sales volume).
- *Standard costs.* Predetermined costs, based on experience and research studies, for achieving certain levels of volume. In production there are usually standard costs for direct labor, materials, and factory overhead. Marketing costs are much more difficult to standardize, since they tend to be generated from nonrepetitive activities.

Marketing Cost (Profitability) Analysis Procedure

In conducting a marketing profitability (or cost) analysis for a sales organization, sales managers ought to approach the analysis systematically by following these steps: (1) Specify the purpose of the analysis, (2) identify functional cost centers, (3) convert natural expenses into functional costs, (4) allocate functional costs to segments, and (5) determine profit contribution of segments.

Specifying the purpose. Before commencing the profitability analysis, sales managers must decide its precise purpose. That is, what do they want to determine the profitability of—sales territories, sales representatives, customers, product lines, or organizational units such as district or branch offices? Depending upon the answer to this question, the treatment of marketing costs will vary. Some costs may be direct for one segment but indirect for another. For instance, a salesperson's salary is a direct cost to an assigned territory but an indirect cost with regard to the different product lines or customer classes that he or she sells in that territory. Even the compensation of salespeople can usually be broken down into fixed costs (salary) and variable costs (commission based on sales). Only by specifying the precise purpose of the analysis is the sales manager able to classify costs as *direct* or *indirect* and as *fixed* or *variable*.

Identifying functional cost centers. As shown in Exhibit 15-10, functional cost centers for sales organizations can be broadly categorized into order-getting costs and order-filling costs. Order-getting costs pertain to activities that obtain sales orders, such as direct selling and advertising expenditures. Order-filling costs relate to activities that follow the sale (such as order processing, packing, shipping, and delivery) and are necessary to fill a customer's purchase order. Each functional cost center should contain a homogeneous group of directly related expenses instead of arbitrarily allocated ones.

Converting natural expenses into functional accounts. In marketing cost analysis, natural accounting expenses must be reassigned to categories based on the purpose of each expenditure. Because nearly all expense data are collected by the organization's accounting system, analysis ought to start with the traditional

---

EXHIBIT 15-10

Functional Accounts for Marketing Profitability (Cost) Analysis

Order-Getting Costs	Order-Filling Costs
Direct selling	Order processing
Sales promotion	Packing, shipping, and delivery
Advertising	Customer service
Sales discounts and allowances	Billing and controlling accounts receivable
Credit	Warehousing
Warranties	Inventory control
Marketing research	Material handling
Sales administration	

accounting statements. The most important of these is the profit-and-loss (or income) statement, which takes this basic form:

Sales − cost of goods sold = gross margin

Gross margin − expenses = net profit (loss)

Traditional income statements are of limited value to sales managers because they fail to reveal the specific purpose of expenditures—that is, the costs of performing different marketing activities. Working with the simplified income statement for the Baylor Company sales department in Exhibit 15-11, we have assigned the natural-expense accounts to functional accounts in Exhibit 15-12.

Salaries were spread to the functional areas where the recipients work. About $590,190 went to twelve salespeople and the sales manager, $21,400 to a sales promotion specialist employed in the sales office, $25,650 to an advertising specialist, $64,250 to three people in sales administration, $31,000 to two billing clerks, $27,340 to a marketing research staff specialist, and $71,280 to five people in the shipping department. Besides being paid their regular salaries, all salespeople received a commission of 2 percent on sales. Since these commissions were directly related to sales, the entire $169,334 was charged off to the direct selling function. Travel expenses included $150,488 for food, lodging, and entertainment expenses incurred in direct selling efforts, and $1,003 spent by the marketing research specialist while coordinating a market study. As both natural and functional accounts, advertising in selected trade magazines required $45,000 and sales promotion materials cost $20,115. Postage expenses were incurred to some degree by every functional cost center but primarily by the packing and shipping area. Expenditures for supplies amounted to $160,623 and were also spread over all the functional accounts—again, mainly for packing and shipping. Finally, the sales department had to pay $188,606 in rent, which

---

EXHIBIT 15-11

Baylor Company Sales Department Income Statement

Sales		$11,466,683
Cost of goods sold		6,923,491
Gross margin		$ 4,543,192
Sales expenses:		
Salaries	$831,110	
Commissions	169,334	
Travel	151,491	
Sales promotion	20,115	
Advertising	45,000	
Postage	62,078	
Supplies	160,623	
Rent	188,606	
		$ 1,628,357
Net profit (loss)		$ 2,914,835

EXHIBIT 15-12

Baylor Company: Natural Expenses Assigned to Functional Areas

					Functional Accounts			
Natural Expenses	Direct Selling	Sales Promotion	Adver- tising	Sales Adminis- tration	Order Processing and Billing	Marketing Research	Packing and Shipping
Salaries	$ 831,110	$590,190	$21,400	$25,650	$64,250	$31,000	$27,340	$ 71,280
Commissions	169,334	169,334						
Travel	151,491	150,488					1,003	
Sales promotion	20,115		20,115					
Advertising	45,000			45,000				
Postage	62,078	3,000	9,671	212	689	794	493	47,219
Supplies	160,623	7,716	21,247	2,023	183	928	2,101	126,425
Rent	188,606	79,186	8,200	5,300	15,100	23,400	12,150	45,270
	$1,628,357	$999,914	$80,633	$78,185	$80,222	$56,122	$43,087	$290,194

was allocated to the functional areas in proportion to the floor space used by each activity.

Allocating functional costs to segments.   To discover the profitability of separate organizational units or particular market segments, the sales manager must allocate the functional costs incurred by the unit or in the process of serving the segment. Each marketing function or activity needs to be examined to find the factor that most affects the volume of work. In making the cost allocations, sales managers can consider several bases, including selling time, number of sales calls, or actual space occupied. Another frequently used, but improper, basis for allocating functional costs is sales volume; this tends to penalize sales productivity and efficiency. For example, if one sales territory accounted for 20 percent of total regional sales, it would be charged 20 percent of the sales administration functional costs of $80,222 in Exhibit 15-12, regardless of the actual expenses and proportion of time spent by the sales manager and his or her staff in working with that territory. In contrast, a particularly worrisome territory that took up 40 percent of total sales administration expenses and personnel time may be allocated only 5 percent of those functional costs to match its low sales volume. Using sales volume to allocate functional costs contravenes the very purpose of marketing cost analysis, since it ignores the actual costs incurred in different business segments and relies only on a simple but irrelevant base factor. Therefore, functional costs should be allocated according to measurable variables that have a cause-and-effect relationship with the functional cost category. That is, the costs should change in proportion to the performance of the activity—for example, direct selling costs increase directly with the number of sales calls. Several alternative bases for allocating functional costs to different identifiable segments are provided in Exhibit 15-13.

EXHIBIT 15-13

Functional Cost Centers and Bases of Allocation

Functional Costs	Bases of Allocation		
	To Sales Territories	To Products	To Customers
Direct selling costs: Salaries, incentive pay, travel, and other expenses of salespeople	Direct	Selling time devoted to each product	Number of sales calls multiplied by average time per call
Indirect selling costs: Sales administration, sales training, marketing, research, field supervision	Equal charge to each salesperson	Selling time devoted to each product	Selling time devoted to each customer
Sales promotion costs: Consumer or trade promotions—e.g., trade discounts, coupons, contests, point-of-purchase displays	Direct	Direct	Direct
Advertising expenditures: Advertising department salaries and expenses, media costs	Direct or by circulation of media	Direct or by media space given each product	Charged equally to each account
Marketing research: Cost of gathering information	Time spent researching each territory	Time spent researching each product	Time spent researching customer
Transportation: Cost of delivering goods to customers	Classification rate × weights of products	Classification rate × weights of products	Bills of lading
Order processing and billing	Number of customer orders	Number of customer orders	Number of customer orders
Packing and shipping	Number of shipping units, weights, or size of units	Number of shipping units, weights, or size of units	Number of shipping units, weights, or size of units

Full costs or contribution margin?   Since marketing costs contain direct, indirect, fixed, and variable amounts, another major decision must be made: whether to allocate full costs or only marginal costs (direct and variable) to the segments. Costs that are fixed and indirect are usually impossible to assign to segments except arbitrarily. Advocates of the *full-cost* (or *net-profit*) *approach* argue that all costs can be allocated on some reasonable basis. Using the full-cost approach, total costs (whether variable, fixed, direct, or indirect) are allocated, and the profitability of each segment is determined by deducting cost of goods sold from net sales to arrive at gross margin. Then all other costs or operating expenses are deducted to derive net income for the segment.

On the other side of the controversy, proponents of the *contribution margin approach* claim that it is misleading to allocate costs that are not controllable and, therefore, not considered in marketing decisions. They believe that only costs that are controllable (direct and variable) and traceable to a particular segment should be subtracted from the revenue produced by that segment. The reasoning is that these variable and direct costs would disappear if the segment were eliminated, while all other costs (fixed and indirect) would continue and have to be absorbed by other segments. Moreover, any segment that produces revenues in excess of its direct and variable costs is making a contribution to profits by helping cover the organization's fixed expenses or common costs. In Exhibit 15-14, one can see the essential differences in the full-cost and the contribution margin approaches to marketing cost analysis. Under the contribution margin concept, costs are categorized as either variable or fixed regardless of whether they pertain to manufacturing, marketing, or administrative activities. Then all the variable costs are deducted from dollar sales to determine the segment's contribution analysis.

Advantages of contribution margin. The trend in marketing profitability analysis favors the contribution margin approach for two primary reasons. First, arbitrarily allocating fixed and indirect costs to segments merely confuses managerial profitability analysis, since these costs continue even if the apparently unprofitable segments are eliminated. Second, the contribution margin approach considers the interrelationships among marketing activities and the synergism of their efforts. One marketing activity, such as advertising, benefits from as well as aids other activities, such as personal selling or sales promotion. Similarly,

---

EXHIBIT 15-14

Marketing Cost (Profitability) Analysis:
Full-Cost versus the Contribution Margin Approach

Full-Cost Approach		Contribution Margin Approach	
Sales		Sales	
Less:	Cost of goods sold	Less:	Variable manufacturing costs
Equal:	Gross margin	Less:	Other variable costs directly traceable to the market segment
		Equal:	Contribution margin
Less:	Operating expenses (including the segment's allocated share of company administrative and general expenses)	Less:	Fixed costs directly traceable to products; fixed costs directly traceable to the market segment
Equal:	Segment net income	Equal:	Segment net income

EXHIBIT 15-15

Baylor Company Income Statement by Product Lines Using Full-Cost Approach

	Totals	Product A	Product B
Sales	$11,466,683	$5,287,141	$6,179,542
Cost of goods sold	6,923,491	3,562,734	3,360,757
Gross margin	$ 4,543,192	$1,724,407	$2,818,785
Expenses:			
Sales	$ 1,628,357	$ 698,177	$ 930,180
Administrative	2,234,169	1,027,718	1,206,451
Total expenses	$ 3,862,526	$1,725,895	$2,136,631
Net profit (loss)	$ 680,666	$ (1,488)	$ 682,154

one product in a multiproduct line helps promote the image and sell the entire line. The income statement for the Baylor Company, as given in Exhibit 15-11, will be used to compare the two approaches to allocating functional costs. As seen in Exhibit 15-15, the full-cost method shows product A suffering a net loss of $1,488 and product B earning a net profit of $682,154. From this analysis the decision might be made to deemphasize or even drop product A. However, the full-cost approach allocated $1,027,718 of administrative expenses on the basis of product A's percentage of total sales ($5,287,141 product A sales ÷ $11,466,683 total sales = 0.46 × $2,234,169 total administrative expenses = $1,027,718 product A administrative expenses). Thus, the arbitrary allocation of fixed costs was responsible for product A's net loss. Switching to the contribution margin approach (Exhibit 15-16) reveals that product A contributes

EXHIBIT 15-16

Baylor Company Income Statement by Product Lines Using the Contribution Margin Approach

	Totals	Product A	Product B
Sales	$11,466,683	$5,287,141	$6,179,542
Variable costs:			
Cost of goods sold	6,923,491	3,562,734	3,360,757
Sales expenses	1,628,357	698,177	930,180
Total variable costs	$ 8,551,848	$4,260,911	$4,290,937
Contribution margin	$ 2,914,835	$1,026,230	$1,888,605
Fixed costs:			
Administrative expenses	2,234,169		
Net profit	$ 680,666		

$1,026,230 to covering total fixed administrative expenses of $2,234,169. If product A were eliminated, current total net profit of $680,666 would turn into a net loss of $345,564 because product B's contribution margin would be insufficient to absorb the additional burden of administrative costs. Progressive companies like Pillsbury keep track of the profit contribution of sales regions and products on a monthly basis so timely marketing-mix adjustments can be made.

Determining profit contribution of segments.   Although some sales managers still avoid cutting costs because they fear sales will simultaneously decline, most professional sales managers want to identify unprofitable customer accounts, products, or territories that can be serviced less frequently or dropped for increased overall profitability. Unprofitable segments are endemic problems in virtually all sales organizations. In some companies, up to 50 percent of the business elements lose money. Illustrating the *concentration principle,* studies have found that often one-third of products, customers, orders, sales territories, and salespeople account for two-thirds of profits.[7] Studying profit contributions by segments invariably rewards the sales manager far beyond the time spent in the analysis.

Profit contributions of segments can be examined in two basic ways: by individual segments or by cross-classification of segments. When studied individually, segment categories are examined sequentially; thus, the analysis determines the profitability of one segment category, such as product class, then moves to territory or customer type, and so on, until all segments are investigated. In a cross-classification analysis one segment is defined more specifically by other segments. For instance, the sales manager may want to know the profitability of product X, sold to customer B, in territory 2.

In Exhibit 15-17, the profitability of segments is analyzed separately. All segments (products, territories, and customers) appear profitable when examined one at a time. But when we conduct cross-classification analysis of the three segments in Exhibit 15-18, we learn that product Y is losing money with customer A in territory 1 but is yielding a high profit contribution with customer C in territory 2. An alert sales manager would probably want to probe further by requesting a cross-classification that includes a breakdown by salesperson as

---

EXHIBIT 15-17

Profitability of Individual Market Segments (Figures in Thousands of Dollars)

Market Segments	Product X	Product Y	Territory 1	Territory 2	Customer A	Customer B	Customer C	Customer D
Sales	$805	$ 2,955	$ 1,610	$ 2,150	$ 710	$ 900	$ 800	$ 1,350
Variable costs	−520	−2,340	−1,210	−1,650	−540	−670	−550	−1,100
Direct fixed costs	−198	−460	−308	−350	−138	−170	−145	−205
Market segment Profit contribution	$ 87	$ 155	$ 92	$ 150	$ 32	$ 60	$ 105	$ 45

EXHIBIT 15-18

Profitability of Market Segments Analyzed Using Cross-Classification

	Territory 1		Territory 2	
	Customer A	Customer B	Customer C	Customer D
Product X				
Sales	$ 190	$ 120	$ 185	$ 310
Variable costs	−115	−73	−128	−204
Direct fixed costs	−41	−32	−39	−86
Market segment profit contribution	$ 34	$ 15	$ 18	$ 20
Product Y				
Sales	$ 520	$ 780	$ 615	$ 1,040
Variable costs	−425	−597	−422	−896
Direct fixed costs	−97	−138	−106	−119
Market segment profit contribution	$ (2)	$ 45	$ 87	$ 25

well. Without seeing the interrelationships of segment profitability as provided in a cross-classification analysis, a sales manager might erroneously assume that all the individual segments are profitable.

Underlying problems. Merely determining that certain cross-classified segments are unprofitable is not sufficient. The sales manager must next discover *why* the segments are unprofitable. Have the salespeople been adequately motivated? Are they making efficient and effective use of their time? Is the competitive situation in these segments unique? Are product quality, customer service, and warranties satisfactory? Are prices competitive? How compatible and effective is the marketing mix supporting the field sales representatives? These plus many other questions should be asked and answered.

As important as marketing profitability analysis is to professional sales managers, it merely uncovers symptoms of problems. It is up to the sales manager to discover the specific underlying problems before attempting to improve profitability by making various decisions, such as dropping segments, changing incentive plans, retraining or firing salespeople, or altering the marketing mix. Sales managers should not hesitate to obtain the help of marketing research specialists to identify problems and recommend solutions for improved segment profitability.

Return on assets managed (ROAM). Marketing profitability analysis is invaluable to sales managers insofar as it enables them to compare sales productivity by segment with the cost of activities performed to achieve those sales. Yet a critical financial management tool missing from profitability calculations is the total value of company assets (e.g., working capital in the form of accounts receivable and inventory) required to support the sales force functions. The *return* *on assets managed* (ROAM) by each segment of the business measures how productively the assets have been employed. We avoid using the term "return on investment" (ROI), since it usually refers more narrowly to capital investment (noncurrent assets) and owner's investment (net worth or equity capital). As shown below, ROAM is the product of the profit margin on sales (net profit ÷ sales) and inventory turnover (sales ÷ total assets):

$$\text{ROAM} = \frac{\text{net profit}}{\text{sales}} \times \frac{\text{sales}}{\text{total assets used}}$$

When applied to segment analysis on the basis of the contribution margin, the formula becomes

$$\text{ROAM} = \frac{\text{segment contribution margin}}{\text{segment sales}} \times \frac{\text{segment sales}}{\substack{\text{additional assets} \\ \text{used by the segment}}}$$

Using the data in Exhibit 15-16, ROAM can be computed for product A. Assume that product A required an investment in accounts receivable of $2,493,889 plus an inventory of $8,763,498 (for total current assets of $11,257,387) in order to achieve its sales of $5,287,141 and its contribution margin of $1,026,230. By substituting these figures in the formula below, we derive a ROAM of 9.12 percent:

$$\text{ROAM} = \frac{\$1,026,230}{\$5,287,141} \times \frac{\$5,287,141}{\$11,257,387} = 0.09116$$

To increase the return on assets managed for specific segments, the sales manager can implement any of three strategies: raise the profit margin on sales, increase total sales while maintaining profit margins, or decrease the relative dollar value of assets necessary to achieve sales. *Raising the profit margins on sales* requires that the sales manager conduct profitability analyses by segments to identify those segments that are yielding inadequate contribution margins. Then the sales manager must decide to deemphasize or eliminate efforts in these segments.

Increasing total sales while maintaining profit margins on sales requires that the sales manager continually seek more effective and efficient marketing mixes so that the sales organization operates near its minimum average costs per unit of sales (as discussed earlier in this chapter). Market testing, under reasonably controlled conditions, may be necessary to find this optimal mix of headquarters and field marketing efforts. Therefore, it is vital that sales managers include on their staffs a marketing research specialist who works closely with the headquarters marketing research department as well as with the field marketing representatives.

Decreasing the assets needed to obtain sales requires that sales managers work closely with inventory managers to find the optimum trade-off between inventory levels and "out-of-stocks." Both sales managers and accounting managers need to monitor the level of accounts receivable to ensure that they remain within predetermined standards

INCREASING SALES FORCE PRODUCTIVITY

Unable to pass on rapidly rising costs to customers, companies have focused on internal cost cutting—and few costs have been climbing faster than those of maintaining a sales force in the field. Several approaches are being pursued: (1) reducing the size of the sales force; (2) hiring independent sales agents who are paid only on a commission basis; (3) increasing participation in trade shows to make product presentations to large numbers of customers simultaneously; (4) relying more on the telephone, direct mail, and videoconferencing to reach customers; (5) employing the latest communications and computer technology (e.g., portable computers, electronic beepers, cellular car phones) to aid the selling process; and (6) improving the sales management information system (SMIS).

Cost-conscious managements of today view the sales force as a profit-and-loss center, and several companies have created a new position called "marketing controller" to monitor marketing costs. Computers are being widely used by large and small organizations to identify cost problems and to analyze them for solutions. Various district and regional sales offices have their own computers hooked directly to headquarters so that field salespeople have access to huge data banks in managing costs for profitable sales activities.

More and more small companies are beginning to realize that computers can help them keep up with the big companies. Affordable software can now process sales leads and track a salesperson's follow-up all the way to the signing of the order. Computerized data bases can also help small businesses deal with industry segmentation and pinpoint small but potentially high-growth niche markets. Experts are predicting that within a decade the laptop computer will become as indispensable as the sample case for most small businesses.[8] By investing in computers for the sales force, even small businesses are able to achieve increases in productivity and profitability.

Customers are also suffering from rising costs—especially their purchasing costs, which account for about 50 cents of every dollar spent by large companies. Even many smaller companies, such as Magruder Color Company, a New Jersey manufacturer of printing inks, have converted to centralized computer purchasing for high-volume items. As customers develop their own management information systems for determining reorder points, size of orders, and suppliers, it becomes even more important that sales organizations improve their intelligence systems, as we discussed in Chapter 3.

Sales Management Information Systems

A sales management information system (SMIS) can seldom be created all at once. Instead, it nearly always evolves one function at a time. Most SMISs fall into one of the following stages, differing largely in terms of flexibility, complexity, and question-answering power: (1) data storage and retrieval systems, (2) systems for monitoring results of business activities, and (3) analytical systems for exploring and evaluating business alternatives.

Data storage and retrieval systems.   At this basic SMIS level, data are collected and stored either in the computer's memory or on a tape disk that can be accessed at any time. For example, a data storage and retrieval system might contain a historical record of sales by different market segments. In this stage, the SMIS is serving largely as a storage house for raw and random data that provide the input for producing managerially desired information in subsequent stages.

Monitoring systems.   Most SMISs are in this stage, in which routine reports and exception reports on sales operations are created for sales management. For example, weekly or monthly reports of sales by various segment classifications and cross-classifications allow managers to monitor sales and obtain early warnings of any problems. Still, the sales managers are limited to reviewing historical results.

Analytical systems.   At this most powerful level, the SMIS enables sales managers to obtain answers to exploratory, diagnostic, evaluative, or predictive questions such as these: Why did that happen? What impact will it have on the future of the business? What would happen if . . . ? Often, complex mathematical models and sophisticated analytical tools are integral to this system. An analytical system is required if the SMIS is to be of significant help in strategic sales planning.

Reasons for failure of SMIS.   Sales managers ought to be aware of several possible problems with any SMIS. These include:

- Too much information for comprehension
- Delivery of information that is so current that managers may react to a simple random movement instead of a real trend in the marketplace
- Information value that is less than the cost of producing it
- Inadequately defined management information needs
- Individual responsibility for information gathering not clearly assigned
- Lack of managerial acceptance for the SMIS
- Inadequate evaluation procedures to measure the SMIS against its stated objectives
- Failure in the system itself—for example, processing, storing, analyzing, or disseminating information
- Assumption that decision making automatically improves if sales managers have the desired information
- Belief that a manager does not have to understand the SMIS generally in order to utilize it properly

Control over Field Marketing Activities

Despite the growing availability of sales management information systems, many companies have inadequate control over their field marketing efforts. A study of large and small companies across different industries found that:

- Less than half the companies knew the profitability of their individual product lines.

- Nearly one-third had no regular review process for spotting and dropping weak products.

- Nearly half the companies did not regularly compare their prices to those of the competition, analyze their warehousing and distribution costs, analyze the reasons for returned merchandise, conduct formal evaluations of advertising effectiveness, or review their sales force call reports.

- Many company managements complained about delays of four to eight weeks in getting many control reports, which included numerous inaccuracies.[9]

The results of the above study may be discouraging to some, but to energetic, creative sales managers they indicate that there are real opportunities to improve sales force performance. In Chapter 16 we will turn our discussion to measuring and evaluating sales force performance.

SUMMARY

To increase the productivity and efficiency of sales force efforts, one of the most important jobs of the sales manager is to conduct sales volume, cost, and profitability analyses by important market segments in order to direct resources for the highest return per dollar spent. Sales analysis is the collection, classification, comparison, and evaluation of sales figures by such subcategories as product types, customer classes, territories, and salespeople. Although the sales invoice is the most important source of sales information, there are a number of other sources, too. Marketing cost analysis goes beyond sales volume analysis to determine the costs involved in generating sales. To determine the profit contributions of various market segments, marketing costs involved in generating the sales revenue must be subtracted from the sales revenue generated.

Using the concept of input-output efficiency, sales managers should consider several mixes and levels of selling and supporting marketing efforts to achieve different sales objectives. Especially important in improving overall company productivity is increased cooperation and understanding between the marketing and the accounting departments.

The marketing profitability (cost) analysis procedure involves these major steps: (1) Specify the purpose of the analysis, (2) identify functional cost centers, (3) convert natural expenses into functional costs, (4) allocate functional costs to segments, and (5) determine the profit contribution of segments. Since marketing costs include direct, indirect, fixed, and variable amounts, another critical decision is whether to allocate full costs or only marginal costs (direct and variable) to the market segments being analyzed. Proponents of the contribution margin approach claim that it is misleading to allocate costs that are not controllable and, therefore, not considered in marketing decisions. They believe that only costs that are controllable (direct and variable) and traceable to a particular market segment should be subtracted from the revenue produced by that segment. The trend in marketing profitability analysis favors the contribution margin approach.

Return on assets managed (ROAM) by each market segment measures how productively sales organization assets are being employed—for example, working capital in the form of accounts receivable and inventory. Few costs have been climbing as fast as those of maintaining a field sales force, and—unable to pass on these rising costs to customers—companies are trying various approaches: (1) reducing the size of the sales force, (2) hiring independent sales agents in place of direct salespeople, (3) increasing participation in trade shows, (4) using telemarketing, direct mail, and videoconferencing to reach customers, (5) employing the latest communications and computer technology to aid the selling process, and (6) improving the sales management information system (SMIS).

Many, if not most, companies still do not have adequate control over their field marketing activities, and knowledgeable, energetic sales managers have real opportunities to improve sales force productivity.

STUDY QUESTIONS

1. Do you think that we will ever develop accurate standard costs for marketing activities? Explain your answer.

2. What impact do you think computers will have on our ability to control marketing costs?

3. Why has accounting generally focused on production costs instead of marketing cost analysis?

4. What responsibility, if any, do you think a sales manager has to learn more about accounting and financial marketing? Why?

5. In the controversy between the full-cost and contribution margin approaches to allocating marketing costs, which side do you support? Why?

6. Do you think most sales managers are concerned about their ROAM? Why?

7. Do you know of a company that has a good SMIS? How does it work? Does its management really use it? Why or why not?

8. How might the sales manager obtain greater cooperation with the accounting manager or marketing controller? Do you think sales managers have a communication problem in dealing with accounting managers? Explain.

9. What are the major components of an SMIS? How would you go about developing one in a small company that you may own someday?

10. Why do so few companies have adequate controls over their field selling activities? What can you suggest to improve the situation?

IN-BASKET EXERCISE

You are the national sales manager for a large and successful consumer products company. Today, your in-basket contains a memo from the company's newly hired vice president of accounting. In the memo he indicates that although sales have been increasing steadily, he would like you to cut your selling costs by approximately 25 percent to prepare for a projected downturn in the economy. In addition, he feels that it would be beneficial to the organization if you could be more "precise" in determining the costs of the inputs needed to achieve the desired level of sales for next year. He would like to meet with you on Friday to discuss these issues.

1. How are you going to respond to this memo?

2. Can you successfully argue against the vice president's demands? If so, how?

CASE 15-1

ANALYZING SALES, COSTS, AND PROFITS AT ASI

Auto Stereo, Inc. (ASI), is a wholesale distributor for a line of automobile stereos targeted at passenger vehicles. A meeting has been scheduled by the company's marketing planning committee for its annual review of marketing operations. It is necessary for the company to formulate a marketing plan for the coming year. The plan will be based on a sales analysis and a marketing cost analysis for each of ASI's four regions for the automobile stereo line, which consists of three products: an AM/FM stereo, an AM/FM stereo

EXHIBIT 1

Sales by Account Size and Number

Size of Account	Number of Accounts	Number of Orders	Total Sales
Under $1000	15	45	$ 33,750
$1001–$2000	149	447	670,500
$2001–$3000	220	660	1,650,000
Over $3000	880	2640	8,948,230
Total	1264	3792	$11,302,480

EXHIBIT 2

Sales by Product and Account Size

Size of Account	AM/FM	AM/FM Cassette	AM/FM CD	Total Sales
Under $1000	$ 22,500	$ 7,500	$ 3,750	$ 33,750
$1001–$2000	447,000	195,562	27,938	670,500
$2001–$3000	1,031,250	412,500	206,250	1,650,000
Over $3000	5,965,487	994,248	1,988,495	8,948,230
Total	$7,466,237	$1,609,810	$2,226,433	$11,302,480

EXHIBIT 3

Cost of Sales and Units Sold by Product

	AM/FM	AM/FM Cassette	AM/FM CD
Cost of sales	$1,319,150	$879,439	$774,319
Advertising/sales promotion	$ 234,000	$156,000	$ 78,000
Number of shipping units sold	1,793,400	765,800	434,100
Weight per shipping unit	37 lb	32 lb	41 lb

with cassette player, and an AM/FM stereo with compact disc (CD) player. ASI has two major segments of customers: retailers and producers.

The task of developing the sales and cost analyses has been delegated to the sales manager in each of the four regions. Kimberly Magin, the newest sales manager at ASI, has been with the firm for ten years. She began as a clerical assistant for the former sales manager while she worked on her college degree at night. Upon graduation three years ago, she applied

for a sales position and has since worked as a sales rep in the field for ASI. Two months ago she was appointed sales manager when the former sales manager left ASI for another position. Kimberly is now in charge of two sales territories and manages the five full-time salespeople in those territories. She feels that her first task as a sales manager—developing the sales and cost analyses—is a monumental one. Her initial reaction is to go over to her PC and see if the former sales manager left anything that could help her ac-

EXHIBIT 4

Cross-Classification Analysis by Product, Customers, and Territories

| Product | Territory A | | Territory B | | |
	Retailers	Producers	Retailers	Producers	Totals
AM/FM:					
Sales	$1,842,201	$2,286,133	$1,287,342	$2,050,561	$7,466,237
Variable costs	1,448,724	1,658,350	1,003,195	$1,613,845	5,724,114
Direct fixed costs	271,636	324,934	235,908	386,519	1,218,997
Segment profit contribution	121,841	302,849	48,239	50,197	523,126
AM/FM cassette:					
Sales	506,713	391,459	431,235	280,403	1,609,810
Variable costs	390,212	312,844	388,490	198,302	1,289,848
Direct fixed costs	100,173	78,163	90,120	52,834	321,290
Segment profit contribution	16,328	452	(47,375)	29,267	(1,328)
AM/FM CD:					
Sales	678,665	556,003	541,366	450,399	2,226,433
Variable costs	529,288	446,162	434,293	351,411	1,761,154
Direct fixed costs	111,767	111,784	108,123	89,538	421,212
Segment profit contribution	37,610	(1,943)	(1,050)	9,450	44,067

	Totals	Sales	$11,302,480
		Variable costs	8,775,116
		Direct fixed costs	1,961,449
		Profit contribution	565,865

complish this task. After going through several diskettes, she feels that she has found some helpful information. This information is presented in Exhibits 1 through 4.

Questions

1. Is there any information here that can help Kimberly with a sales analysis? If so, what?
2. What specific types of information does Kimberly need to conduct a thorough sales analysis? Where could she go to locate such information?
3. How can ASI benefit from its sales manager's sales and cost analyses?
4. Will a marketing cost analysis help Kimberly increase profits in her region. How?
5. What recommendations could Kimberly make from a marketing cost analysis performed on the data she has to work with?

CASE 15-2

WOLFSON WRITING INSTRUMENTS, INC.: ANALYZING FINANCIAL REPORTS

Stuart Reeves had been Wolfson Writing Instruments' top sales representative for four of the past five years, yet he was surprised when he was promoted to national sales manager. The first month on the new job went very smoothly as Stuart traveled around the company's three sales regions getting to know the individual members of the sales force. During the next two months, Stuart found the job a bit tedious, since it involved so much paperwork. Stuart didn't enjoy spending so much time in the office and he certainly didn't like paperwork, but he knew that sales management required one to grasp the "big picture" and that demanded an understanding of the numerous reports that he continuously received. Although he never had any training in management, Stuart did his best and gradually began to figure out several of the reports.

At the end of his first quarter, Stuart received several reports from the financial department summarizing quarterly sales and profits, as shown in Exhibit 1. Reviewing these financial reports, Stuart saw that two of the company's regions had earned healthy net profits for the quarter, but the midwestern region had suffered a net loss of $40,269. Sales in the midwestern region were $2.1 million less than in the eastern region and nearly $2.7 million less than in the western region. Yet the total selling expenses among the three regions varied by only about $200,000. It seemed clear that selling expenses were too high in the midwestern region. Ninety percent of sales force compensation was straight salary, and Stuart remembered that the midwestern region had a lot of senior salespeople who were highly paid. Unless the compensation system changed, there wasn't much Stuart could do about selling expenses in the region. One way to solve the problem might be simply to drop the midwestern sales

EXHIBIT 1

Income Statement by Regions

	Eastern Region	Midwestern Region	Western Region
Sales	$8,697,328	$6,543,121	$9,214,864
Variable costs			
Cost of goods sold	5,128,540	5,210,533	6,420,432
Selling expenses	1,233,457	1,025,732	1,072,117
Fixed costs			
Administrative expenses	433,163	347,125	416,274
Total costs	$6,795,160	$6,583,390	$7,908,823
Net profit	$1,902,168	$ (40,269)	$1,306,041

EXHIBIT 2

Income Statement by Product

	Ballpoint Pens	Mechanical Lead Pencils
Eastern Region		
Sales	$5,362,192	$3,335,136
Variable costs		
Cost of goods sold	3,347,134	1,781,406
Selling expenses	703,118	530,339
Fixed costs		
Administrative expenses	245,791	187,372
Total costs	$4,296,043	$2,499,117
Net profit	$1,066,149	$ 836,019
Midwestern Region		
Sales	$3,612,446	$2,930,675
Variable costs		
Cost of goods sold	3,060,050	2,150,483
Selling expenses	678,694	347,038
Fixed costs		
Administrative expenses	189,987	157,138
Total costs	$3,928,731	$2,654,659
Net profit	$ (316,285)	$ 276,016
Western Region		
Sales	$5,423,517	$3,791,347
Variable costs		
Cost of goods sold	4,003,862	2,416,570
Selling expenses	621,664	450,453
Fixed costs		
Administrative expenses	250,123	166,151
Total costs	$4,875,652	$3,033,174
Net profit	$ 547,865	$ 758,173

EXHIBIT 3

Investments by Product and Region

	Ballpoint Pens	Mechanical Lead Pencils
Eastern Region		
Accounts receivable	$3,120,449	$1,872,312
Inventory	8,881,479	5,122,376
Midwestern Region		
Accounts receivable	$2,120,287	$1,540,601
Inventory	7,297,128	6,482,120
Western Region		
Accounts receivable	$2,311,483	$2,481,040
Inventory	8,421,677	7,120,432

that the only unprofitable product was ballpoint pens sold in the midwestern region. Again, Stuart wondered what would happen to overall company profits if ballpoint pens were dropped in the midwestern region.

Looking at several other reports provided by the financial department, Stuart was drawn to one that showed each region's investment in inventory and accounts receivable, as shown in Exhibit 3. He wasn't sure what to do with this report, but he was extremely surprised to see that heavy investments were made in these two items.

Overall, Stuart felt a little frustrated by all the reports for they indicated some problems, but he did not feel confident about how to analyze the data.

Questions

1. What else besides high selling expenses might be contributing to the midwestern region's problems?

2. Compute the return on assets managed (ROAM) for each product for each region. How could this information help Stuart?

3. What corrective action might Stuart take given the results of the ROAM analysis?

4. Should Stuart drop the midwestern region? Or stop selling one of the products in the midwestern region? Why or why not?

5. What other financial reports would you advise Stuart to request from the financial department in order to conduct further analysis? Why?

region. It certainly did not make sense to keep losing money there. Stuart wondered what the impact on the company would be if the midwestern sales region were dropped.

Another financial report dealt with sales and profits by product in each region, as shown in Exhibit 2. The company sold only two basic products: ballpoint pens and mechanical lead pencils. This breakdown showed

REFERENCES

1. Bill Kelley, "How Much Help Does a Salesperson Need?" *Sales & Marketing Management*, May 1989, pp. 32–35.

2. Richard T. Hise, "Have Manufacturing Firms Adopted the Marketing Concept?" *Journal of Marketing*, July 1975, pp. 9–12.

3. For further understanding of marketing cost (profitability) analysis, see Frank H. Mossman, Paul M. Fisher, and W. J. E. Crissy, *Financial Dimensions of Marketing Management*, Wiley, New York, 1978; James M. Hulbert and Norman E. Toy, "A Strategic Framework for Marketing Control," *Journal of Marketing*, April 1977, pp. 12–19; Bruce M. Smackey, "A Profit Emphasis for Improving Sales Force Productivity," *Industrial Marketing Management*, vol. 6, 1977, pp. 135–140; Stephen L. Buzby and L. E. Heitger, "Profit-Oriented Reporting for Marketing Decision Makers," *MSU Business Topics*, Summer 1976, pp. 60–68; Charles Ames, "Build Marketing Strength into Industrial Selling," *Harvard Business Review*," January–February 1972, pp. 48–60; V. H. Kirpalani and Stanley S. Shapiro, "Financial Dimensions of Marketing Management," *Journal of Marketing*, July 1973, pp. 40–47; Dick Berry, "Sales Performance: Fact or Fiction?" *Journal of Personal Selling and Sales Management*, August 1986, pp. 71–79; Roger Calantone and René Darmone, "Salesforce Decisions: A Markovian Approach," *Journal of the Academy of Marketing Science*, Fall 1984, pp. 124–144.

4. Robert F. Vizza and T. E. Chambers, *Time and Territorial Management for the Salesman*, The Sales Executives Club of New York, New York, 1971, p. 97.

5. Dana Smith Morgan and Fred W. Morgan, "Marketing Cost Controls: A Survey of Industrial Practices," *Industrial Marketing Management*, vol. 9, 1980, pp. 217–221; Robert D. Buzzell and Paul W. Farris, *Industrial Marketing Costs: An Analysis of Variations in Manufacturers' Marketing Expenditures*, Marketing Science Institute, Cambridge, Mass., 1976.

6. This analysis is based on a concept of efficiency described in Bert Rosenbloom, *Marketing Channels: A Management View*, 3d ed., Dryden Press, Hinsdale, Ill., 1987, pp. 31–33. Also see Raymond W. LaForge and David W. Cravens, "Empirical and Judgment-Based Sales Force Decision Models: A Comparative Analysis," *Decision Sciences*, Spring 1985, pp. 177–195.

7. For better understanding of this concentration principle and its importance to profitability analysis, see Harry Deane Wolfe and Gerald Albaum, "Inequality in Products, Orders, Customers, Salesmen, and Sales Territories," in Robert Gwinner and Edward M. Smith (eds.), *Sales Strategy, Cases and Readings*, Appleton-Century-Crofts, New York, 1969, pp. 515–520; Leland L. Beik and Stephen L. Buzby, "Profitability Analysis by Market Segments," *Journal of Marketing*," July 1973, pp. 48–53; C. Davis Fogg and Josef W. Rokus, "A Quantitative Method for Structuring a Profitable Sales Force," *Journal of Marketing*, July 1977, pp. 83–94; Merrett J. Davoust, "Analyzing a Client's Customer Profitability Picture," *Management Advisor*, May–June 1974, pp. 15–19.

8. "What Would Willy Loman Have Done with This?" *Wall Street Journal*, Nov. 26, 1990, p. B1.

9. Philip Kotler, *Marketing Management: Analysis, Planning, and Control*, 4th ed., Prentice-Hall, Englewood Cliffs, N.J., 1980, p. 628.

16

MEASURING AND EVALUATING SALES FORCE PERFORMANCE

LEARNING OBJECTIVES

When you finish this chapter, you should understand:

▲ How well contemporary sales forces are performing
▲ Some key characteristics of top sales forces
▲ The major steps in the sales force performance measurement and evaluation process
▲ The numerous quantitative and qualitative performance standards for measuring sales force performance
▲ The three successive stages in an effective performance evaluation monitoring system
▲ The strengths and weaknesses of the most widely used performance appraisal techniques
▲ The types of performance reviews generally utilized
▲ The limitations of most traditional evaluation systems
▲ Behaviorally anchored rating scales
▲ How to use sales audits and when to conduct a horizontal, as opposed to a vertical, sales audit

A DAY ON THE JOB

Clay Garner, vice president of H. R. Chally Group, a company that specializes in assessing sales forces, believes there are many different types of high-performing salespeople. "Research that we've done shows that experience, education, and practice are the essentials to becoming a productive salesperson," says Garner. Furthermore, "We recognize different kinds [of salespeople]. A consultant-type, for example, who must come up with individually designed solutions, is different from a relationship salesperson, who provides products to companies where the customer is the expert." Garner firmly believes that high-performing salespeople are "made" and not "born" that way. With the proper training and enough practice, almost any individual can become a great salesperson. When asked to define greatness, Garner says, "Foremost, it's understanding the needs of each customer. And after recognizing each client's needs, matching them with the appropriate selling style." Given the vast individual differences among salespeople today, how does a sales manager develop the right criteria for effectively measuring and evaluating an entire sales force without alienating or demotivating any of the reps?[1]

Bill Davis, a sales representative for a large pharmaceutical company, starts work every morning at seven o'clock, makes sales calls all day long, and then usually does sales paperwork at home late into the evening. Bill is a very dedicated employee who is well liked by his customers, but he is a classic "plugger" who works a lot harder than most people to achieve just average results. As a sales manager, how would you evaluate Bill's performance?

Every member of an organization, either directly or indirectly, affects sales, but the ultimate success of the organization depends largely on the performance of individual salespeople. While top salespeople usually receive a lot of recognition and rewards, it is "the average performer" who characterizes most sales organizations. Not everyone can develop into a supersalesperson, but the primary job of the sales manager is to help every salesperson achieve his or her full potential. Thus, measurement and evaluation of the sales force must consider a wide range of salesperson performances across a great diversity of measures. Few sales organizations, however, have satisfactory performance measurement and evaluation systems in place. In fact, many are remiss in even collecting the basic data needed to measure and evaluate sales force performance. If a sales organization is to prosper in today's environment of tighter profit margins and intense foreign and domestic competition, a well-conceived and skillfully implemented computer-based sales management information system is increasingly important.

In order for sales managers to derive significant decision-making benefits from the sales management information system (SMIS), they must (1) identify key performance measures, (2) set specific standards of performance for salespeople, (3) continuously monitor actual performance compared with preset standards, and (4) periodically provide individual performance evaluation feedback to each sales representative. Unless these basics are well executed, it is difficult to promote the behaviors required for sales organization success.

HOW WELL ARE SALES FORCES PERFORMING?

Just because many companies are failing to measure sales force performance adequately, it should not be presumed that sales performance is satisfactory. A recent study looked at sales productivity in nineteen industries for the period 1977 to 1987 and revealed that nine industries had negative annual growth rates when the figures were adjusted for inflation. Moreover, the average sales volume per sales representative for all industries actually declined by 0.9 percent per year during that ten-year period.[2] Another study of 1,000 buyers at U.S. supermarkets also revealed some disenchanting results. While the buyers had some positive things to say about the salespeople who call on them, many of them rated salespeople low on knowing about promotional techniques, providing buyers with assistance, keeping them informed, following up on queries, and especially, motivating store personnel.[3] Yet another survey on salesperson effectiveness indicated that buyers are most upset regarding how often salespeople call on them. The majority of buyers reported being visited by a salesperson an average of 2.5 times a month, and the next major group of buyers reported being visited no more than 1.8 times a month. This finding was amplified by smaller customers who reported that certain salespeople did not call on them for two and even three years.[4] These glaring deficiencies in sales force performance vividly point to the need for systematic performance measurement and evaluation procedures.

IN SEARCH OF SALES FORCE EXCELLENCE

According to the Bureau of Labor Statistics' Economic Growth and Employment Projections program, the number of salespeople in manufacturing industries will increase 4, 9, or 14 percent by the year 1995, depending on whether the United States has a low-, moderate-, or high-growth economy. However, over the same period, manufacturing output will expand much faster: 19 percent in a low-growth economy, 24 percent in a moderate-growth economy, and 39 percent in a high-growth economy. This discrepancy in growth rates implies that the average salesperson will have to handle 15 percent more business by 1995 in a low-growth economy and as much as 25 percent more in a high-growth economy.[5] Obviously, sales force productivity will have to increase significantly, or alternative selling methods and channels will be utilized.

What factors are most important in developing a highly productive, top-notch sales force? *Sales & Marketing Management*'s 1986 Best Sales Force survey of 900 sales executives from eight industries identified ten major qualities of a well-run sales force, as shown in Exhibit 16-1. Nearly 77 percent of the responding sales executives said that *a company's reputation with its customers* is

EXHIBIT 16-1

Characteristics of Top-Performing Sales Forces

	Percentage of Sales Executives Saying		
	Extremely Important	Very Important	Totals
Reputation among customers	76.9%	19.2%	96.1%
Holding old accounts	61.5	36.1	97.6
Quality of management	51.5	40.7	92.2
Ability to keep top salespeople	44.6	43.1	87.7
Product/technical knowledge	37.7	46.1	83.8
Innovativeness	37.7	38.4	76.1
Quality of training	34.6	54.6	89.2
Opening new accounts	33.8	48.8	82.6
Meeting sales targets	26.9	46.9	63.8
Frequency of calls/territory coverage	14.6	41.5	56.1

Source: Sales & Marketing Management, June 1986, p. 55.

"extremely important" to the success of the sales effort, and another 19 percent rated it "very important." Ranking second and third were *holding old accounts* and the *quality of management.* However, if you combine the percentage of respondents who rated each characteristic either "extremely important" or "very important," *holding old accounts* narrowly wins. Ranking fourth was *ability to keep top salespeople.* The other six factors in the survey were: *product/technical knowledge, innovativeness, quality of training, opening new accounts, meeting sales targets,* and *frequency of calls/territory coverage.* One company, Cooper Tire & Rubber, placed first in eight out of ten categories in the rubber and plastic products industry.[6]

MEASURING SALES FORCE PERFORMANCE

The ultimate responsibility of sales managers is to make sure that sales organization goals and objectives are being accomplished effectively and efficiently, as planned. *Effectiveness* is results-oriented and deals with whether or not organization objectives are being achieved. *Efficiency* focuses on costs and the economical use of resources. A sales organization can be effective without being efficient, or, conversely, it can be efficient without being effective. The sales manager's job is to maximize both levels of performance. This necessitates continuous monitoring of the selected sales performance measures to compare *where one is* with *where one should be* in order to take timely actions to correct unacceptable deviations.

Effectiveness and efficiency should always be related to a time perspective—the short run (less than one year), the intermediate run (one to four years), and the long run (five or more years). In some industries, the time dimension for measuring effectiveness and efficiency may need to be extended. Volkswagen of America has a comprehensive sales and marketing program to acquaint sales managers, dealers, and salespeople with the planning and organizing process to meet objectives five years "down the road." While skillfully acquiring and employing resources to satisfy its goals and societal expectations in the near run, the sales organization must adapt to environmental opportunities and threats in the intermediate future. Foremost in the long run, the organization must survive in a world of uncertainties,[7] as depicted in Exhibit 16-2.

There can be no single criterion of effectiveness or efficiency, such as short-run profit, in today's marketing environment. Sales managers are compelled to satisfy a set of often-conflicting internal objectives and goals, such as increasing market share while improving net profits. Managers also deal with complex, conflicting requirements imposed by various external stakeholders—including governments, consumers, shareholders, the community, and various special interest groups. For example, consumers may demand lower-cost products while governments impose costly safety and environmental protection standards—a dilemma facing America's automobile manufacturers.

In a systematic approach to sales force measurement and evaluation, the first step is to determine goals and objectives for the sales organization. Next, the sales plan is developed with specific strategies and tactics for achieving the objectives and goals. Performance standards are set for all sales activities, and the sales manager decides how best to allocate resources and sales force efforts. Then the plan is put into action. Finally, performance is monitored continuously and compared with preestablished standards; if needed, corrective decisions are made by sales managers to minimize or eliminate deviations. Exhibit 16-3 presents major steps in the performance measurement and evaluation process.

EXHIBIT 16-2

Sales Organization Focus over Time

Short run (one year):
Achieve sales objectives.
Efficiently acquire and employ scarce human, material, and financial resources.
Satisfy various organizational stakeholders (customers, top management, employees, shareholders, government, etc.).

Intermediate run (two to four years):
Create and identify new opportunities while adapting to competitive and environmental threats.
Continuously strengthen resource base.

Long run (five or more years):
Survive in an uncertain and increasingly competitive world.

EXHIBIT 16-3

Sales Force Performance Measurement and Evaluation System

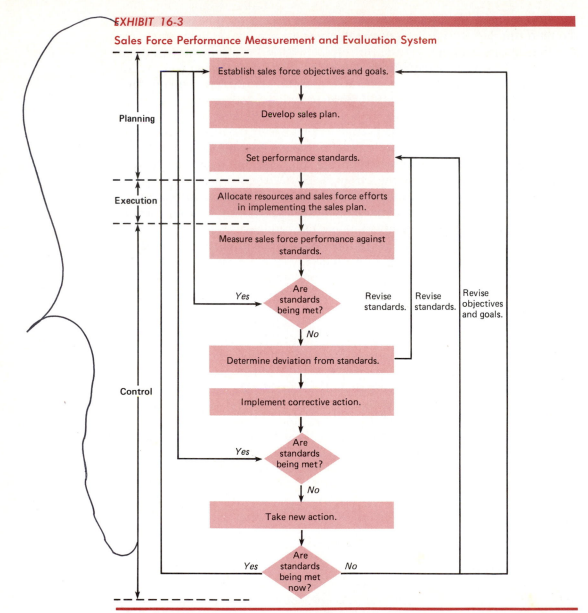

Source: Adapted from Douglas J. Dalrymple and Leonard J. Parsons, *Marketing Management*, 2d ed., Wiley, New York, 1980, p. 622.

Establishing Sales Goals and Objectives

Shortly after company goals and objectives are passed down from top management through the chain of command to the sales manager, the performance measurement and evaluation process for the sales organization begins. The initial step is to formulate the sales goals (long-run aspirations, which are usually not very quantifiable). For instance, the sales organization goal may be recognition by customers as the most service-oriented sales force in the industry. After establishing long-run sales goals, the sales manager can focus on the shorter-run, more quantifiable targets called sales objectives. Several objectives may be sought simultaneously. For example, annual objectives might include reaching 100 percent of sales quota, keeping sales expenses within assigned budgets, improving the ratio of selling to nonselling time by 20 percent, or increasing profitability on sales by 10 percent.

After sales goals and objectives have been agreed upon by sales management, it is important to secure the salespeople's comprehension, approval, and enthusiastic support through open, two-way communication that connects their personal goals with the larger organizational goals. Without this, sales goals and objectives may become little more than "wish lists" that do not receive sufficient organizational commitment to reach fulfillment.

Developing the Sales Plan

Goals and objectives indicate the "destination"; a sales plan provides the "road map" showing how to get there. A sales plan is one of several unit operational plans (e.g., distribution, promotion, new-product development) comprising and derived from the marketing plan. The sales plan is then coordinated with other departmental plans (production, finance, research) to complete the company plan.

A sales plan, as outlined in Exhibit 16-4, includes four major parts: *situation analysis*, which identifies where the sales organization is now; *opportunities and problems*, which indicate where it should go; *action programs*, which outline how to get there; and *performance evaluation systems*, which measure progress toward the destination.

Setting Performance Standards

Having established sales force objectives and goals and having developed the sales plan, the sales manager's next step is to set performance standards for the sales force. *Performance* standards are planned achievement levels that the sales organization expects to reach at progressive intervals throughout the year. An individual performance standard is an agreement between a subordinate and superior as to what level of performance is acceptable in some future period.[8] One of the best ways to formalize this general agreement is to draw up a detailed job description for the subordinate. An example of a job description for a re-sale marketing representative in a major oil corporation is provided in Exhibit 16-5.

In setting performance standards for the sales force, *efforts expended* as well as *results obtained* need to be considered. Not all relevant variables bearing on performance are under the control of sales representatives, so results alone may not be objective measures. With many types of selling, there is a time lapse between efforts expended by salespeople and the achievement of results. Thus, a method for appraising efforts qualitatively as well as quantitatively is necessary.

EXHIBIT 16-4

The Sales Plan

Situation analysis: "Where are we now?"
1. Market situation and competitive environment
   a. Size of the market (by major segments)
   b. Dynamics in the marketplace (e.g., shifts in customer purchasing behavior and competitive strategy changes)
   c. Market shares (by competitors, products, and customer classes)
   d. Strengths and weaknesses (of each competitor's products and sales organization relative to ours)
2. Product sales situation
   a. Product types (by line items, sizes, models, etc.)
   b. Sales and distribution data (by geographic regions, territories, customer categories, or sales representatives)
   c. Markets served (by types of customer segments or end users)
   d. Customer profiles (by purchasing patterns and servicing needs)

Opportunities and problems: "Where do we want to go?"
1. Internal (marketing and sales, R&D and technical, manufacturing/operations, financial, organization, personnel, etc.)
2. External (market segments, competition, economic, political, legal, social, or international)
3. Planning assumptions and constraints
   a. Internal company environment (estimate stability of objectives, goals, resources, management)
   b. External market environment (estimate short-run and long-run marketing environment conditions)
4. Sales forecasts
5. Contingency planning (based on different sets of assumptions from those in 3, above)

Action programs: "What is the best way to get there?"
Strategies and tactics (convert sales forecasts into resource, production, service, quotas, and budget needs)

Performance evaluation systems: "How much progress are we making toward our destination?"
1. Set standards of performance
2. Evaluate actual performance versus planned standards
3. Take necessary corrective action on variances from plan

This is especially true in industrial sales—that is, selling to other businesses rather than consumers. In introducing new products or selling costly capital goods, tangible results may require several months of intense sales efforts before the prospective buyer makes a final decision.

Management by objectives. Sales managers are responsible for setting many sales performance standards for salespeople, but the salespeople must understand and accept these standards before developing their own plans for achievement. *Management by objectives (MBO)* involves mutual goal setting between the sales

---

EXHIBIT 16-5

Job Description

Position: Resale Marketing Representative
Immediate Supervisor: Area Manager

Purpose of job: To manage a territory so that assigned objectives are achieved in the following categories: sales/profits, accounts receivable, rent income, and retail efficiency. These objectives can be accomplished by developing a strong network of dealers, salaried service station managers, consignees, agents, and distributors.

Regular assigned duties:
1. Plans and organizes work in accordance with the team system to achieve sales/profit plan in all categories.
   a. Analyzes the accounts in the territory, using the *Quarterly Review and Replanning Guide,* to determine the opportunities and problems that can affect sales/profits, accounts receivable, rent income, and retail efficiency; determines what action plans would realize the opportunities and solve the problems.
   b. Prioritizes opportunities and problems, determines which should be accomplished each quarter, and sets objectives accordingly.
   c. Schedules and plans calls and sets target dates to accomplish objectives.
2. Calls on accounts on a planned basis.
   a. Solicits orders.
   b. Counsels dealers/managers and wholesalers on money management, hours, planned merchandising, appearance, and driveway service; implements plans, programs, and methods that will contribute to the territory's objectives.
   c. Keeps accounts receivable within established credit limits and collects all monies as required.
   d. Maintains dealer business in line with company objectives. Renews existing dealers' leases with consideration given to the interests of both dealers and/or wholesalers as well as the company.
   e. Conducts dealer meetings on subjects that can best be handled by group counseling and selling.
3. Recruits and interviews lessee dealer/manager prospects following selection procedures; recommends acceptable candidates for management approval; arranges for training; negotiates and proposes loans where applicable; installs new dealers/managers under installation guide. As required, recruits consignees.
4. Investigates customer complaints; resolves or, where necessary, refers to others for their handling.
5. Recommends appropriate maintenance of corporation-owned buildings and equipment.
6. Keeps abreast of competitive activity in territory and, as required, advises dealers and the area manager.
7. Handles correspondence and reports pertinent to the territory and maintains adequate records.

---

manager and the sales representative. Specifically, both parties agree on the salesperson's particular goals or performance targets for the coming period. By helping to set their own performance targets, salespeople are more likely to be committed to those goals and to devise realistic plans for their accomplishment.[9]

In many companies, sales representatives must prepare an annual "territorial marketing plan" outlining their strategy for obtaining new customers and increasing sales to current customers. This ensures that salespeople and sales supervisors agree on how goals are to be achieved—particularly when salespeople participate in setting objectives and have give-and-take discussions with sales managers about how to improve performance. Information derived from these territorial plans helps sales managers evaluate more objectively the individual performance of sales representatives. Moreover, this process encourages sales representatives to do a better job of planning their work and reporting their activities. At Brown & Sharpe Machine Tool Division, each salesperson has a written plan that is reviewed quarterly with the sales manager.

Periodic performance monitoring ensures acceptable progress toward goals while providing guidance for altering the planned strategies and tactics to get back on target. The final step is an annual performance appraisal, which leads to the setting of new objectives for the coming year. The MBO cycle, including its planning and control phases, is illustrated in Exhibit 16-6. The process is essentially the same whether applied to the entire sales force or to an individual salesperson. With each successive MBO cycle, sales managers and salespeople will find the process proceeding more efficiently.[10]

Sales managers should stress four principles in using MBO:

- *Open communication.* There needs to be a free exchange of views between sales manager and salesperson in order to make realistic future commitments and decide on specific actions needed to achieve goals and objectives.

- *Mutual participation and agreement.* The salesperson must be an uninhibited, full participant in the MBO process with the sales manager so that there is mutual understanding and agreement on objectives, plans, and performance evaluation.

EXHIBIT 16-6

The MBO Cycle for the Sales Force

PLANNING PHASE

Step 1

Set sales objectives.

Step 2

Develop sales plans and implement them.

Recycle.

Step 4

Conduct annual performance appraisal of salespeople.

Step 3

Periodically monitor performance and alter sales tactics to stay on target.

CONTROL PHASE

- *Coinciding goals.* The individual's personal goals must be integrated with the organization's overall goals so that they are mutually reinforcing.

- *Rewards for performance.* Salespeople with superior performance records ought to be rewarded through public recognition as well as increased financial compensation. Public recognition for superior performance enhances the value of the reward for the high achievers and generally helps inspire other salespeople to do better.

Finally, sales managers who implement MBO need to be aware of some reasons why it may not be successful:

- *Inadequate top-management commitment.* If salespeople perceive that sales managers are only perfunctorily implementing MBO, their commitment to the program will atrophy. At all levels of the sales organization, management must go beyond mere lip service and show strong support for the MBO process.

- *Insufficient participation of salespeople.* Imposed objectives tend to be perceived as "theirs," while joint agreement on objectives by sales managers and salespeople tends to be perceived as "ours." Sales managers must evince sufficient trust to share the objective-setting, planning, and evaluation process with salespeople.

- *Unrealistic expectations.* MBO is not a panacea that will yield dramatic, early results. Often, five years or more may be required to implement a smoothly functioning MBO system. In the early trial-and-error phase, management needs to show patience, support, and encouragement for all participants.

- *Lack of a performance evaluation monitoring system (PEMS).* Sales managers should not presume that an MBO system negates the need to have a PEMS to measure individual performance. MBO focuses exclusively on the accomplishment of objectives; thus, it overlooks significant behavioral or personal characteristics measured by the PEMS.

Key performance factors.   Most companies use a balance of several variables to control sales operations because reliance on a single index or even just a few can be misleading and even dangerous. For instance, if a company overstresses keeping service expenses low, customer satisfaction and repeat sales might deteriorate. But it is not necessary that busy sales managers attempt to monitor a hundred different measures of performance—they need focus on only a few critical factors. Successful sales organizations usually employ a mixture of quantitative and qualitative performance standards, chosen from a list such as the one in Exhibit 16-7.

Quantitative standards, like the number of sales calls made, tend to affect sales or expenses directly and can be measured objectively. *Qualitative* performance criteria, such as the salesperson's product knowledge, have a more indirect and longer-run impact on sales and expenses and thus must be evaluated largely on a subjective basis. Both quantitative and qualitative measures are important to sales force success and should be part of the evaluation process.

EXHIBIT 16-7

Sales Force Performance Evaluation

Quantitative Measures

Sales Results	Sales Efforts
Orders:	**Sales calls:**
Number of orders obtained	Number made on current customers
Average order size (units or dollars)	Number made on potential new accounts
Batting average (orders ÷ sales calls)	Average time spent per call
Number of orders canceled by customers	Number of sales presentations
	Selling time versus nonselling time
Sales volume:	Call frequency ratio per customer type
Dollar sales volume	
Unit sales volume	**Selling expenses:**
By customer type	Average per sales call
By product category	As percent of sales volume
Translated into market share	As percent of sales quota
Percent of sales quota achieved	By customer type
	By product category
Margins:	Direct selling expense ratios
Gross margin	Indirect selling expense ratios
Net profit	
By customer type	**Customer service:**
By product category	Number of service calls
	Displays set up
Customer accounts:	Delivery cost per unit sold
Number of new accounts	Months of inventory held by customer type
Number of lost accounts	Number of customer complaints
Percent of accounts sold	Percent of goods returned
Number of overdue accounts	
Dollar amount of accounts receivable	
Collections made of accounts receivable	

Qualitative Measures

Sales-related activities:
Territory management: sales call preparation, scheduling, routing, and time utilization
Marketing intelligence: new-product ideas, competitive activities, new customer preferences
Follow-ups: use of promotional brochures and correspondence with current and potential
  accounts
Customer relations
Report preparation and timely submission

Selling skills:

Knowing the company and its policies	Product knowledge
Knowing competitors' products and sales strategies	Customer knowledge
Use of marketing and technical backup teams	Execution of selling techniques
Understanding of selling techniques	Quality of sales presentations
Customer feedback (positive and negative)	Communication skills

Personal characteristics:
Cooperation, human relations, enthusiasm, motivation, judgment, care of company property, appearance, self-improvement efforts, patience, punctuality, initiative, resourcefulness, health, sales management potential, ethical and moral behavior

Innumerable performance standards can be established, depending upon sales objectives and goals, the marketing situation, and the sales manager's control needs. But all standards should be (1) relevant to job performance, (2) stable and consistent irrespective of the evaluator, and (3) able to discriminate between outstanding, average, and poor performance. Because the sales force is a subsystem of the larger marketing system, sales force performance can be influenced by many factors beyond the direct control of the sales organization. Variables such as product quality, price differences, and the level of promotional support should not distort the performance standards selected for measurement of sales force achievement.

Quantitative performance standards.   The following factors are some of the quantitative performance standards considered by companies in the control of sales operations.

Sales quotas.   Derived from sales forecasts, sales quotas are usually perceived as motivational targets as well as performance standards for the entire sales organization, territorial sales teams, or individual salespeople. Expressed in either units of products or dollars, sales volume quotas are the most pervasive of all the quantitative standards. If sales quotas are to be effective control and evaluation devices, however, it is mandatory that they be realistically and equitably assigned according to valid differences in territorial potentials.

Gross-margin or net-profit ratios.   To gain control over the relative profitability of the sales mix (of products and customers), the sales manager may set a target *gross-margin ratio* for the sales force. This will encourage salespeople to sell certain products to selected customers to obtain the highest gross margins. But gross-margin targets neglect the other half of final profit calculations—that is, the expenses incurred in obtaining and filling orders.

Net-profit ratios will cause sales representatives to be concerned about selling expenses as well as gross margins. Both gross-margin and net-profit ratios have disadvantages as performance standards. First, each ratio tends to stress short-run, high-margin sales (and minimum expenses in the case of the net-profit ratio). Such an emphasis can lead to lower profits over the long run as development of new accounts, customer service, and account maintenance are neglected. Second, salespeople may feel that gross-margin or net-profit ratios are unfair if factors beyond their control (such as pricing policies, advertising efforts, or delivery costs) differ among territories. Finally, there is the *full-cost* versus *contribution margin* controversy (discussed in Chapter 15) in figuring net-profit ratios. The contribution-to-profit approach would seem the most equitable, since it considers only direct selling expenses traceable to a particular territory.

Sales expense ratio.   Sales expenses as a percent of dollar sales volume is a commonly used ratio. The salesperson can improve his or her performance on this criterion by either increasing sales or controlling expenses more effectively. But selling expenses vary by territory, depending upon the territory's geographic size, class of customer, or cost-of-living index. Sales expense ratios are employed more often as performance standards in industrial product sales; these sales tend to involve heavier selling expenses than do consumer product sales, which involve stronger advertising support in the selling effort. For fairness,

it tells very little about competencies. The difference between the two can be seen in the job of gas station attendant: to do the job, a person will need certain fundamental skills such as pumping gas, making change, checking automobile batteries and oil levels, and so on; however, to be effective in the job, he or she will need personal competencies such as friendliness, reliability, honesty, and resourcefulness. To satisfy customers and ensure profitable repeat business, the owner would want to employ attendants with these competencies.

Traditionally, salespeople have been evaluated according to quantitative, or "output-based," measures of performance. Perhaps sales managers have felt more comfortable basing their evaluations on such objective, bottom-line criteria. However, there appears to be a trend toward including more qualitative, or "behavior-based," measures in the sales evaluation process. As the sales environment is increasingly characterized by relationship selling, salespeople are required to be more customer-oriented, which involves placing greater emphasis on nonselling activities than on short-run sales volume. Additionally, researchers are beginning to investigate and develop more reliable behavior-based measures of salesperson performance.[11]

Allocating Resources and Sales Force Efforts

The real test of any sales manager is how well he or she allocates human, financial, and material resources while implementing the sales plan. If goals are not met, it is the sales manager who receives the blame, not the salespeople. According to a survey by *Productivity,* a monthly management newsletter, about 80 percent of 221 top managers cite poor management as the major reason for poor productivity.[12]

At Worthington Diagnostics, sales managers can sit down at desktop terminals to analyze a data base that has profiles of every customer and prospect who has come into contact with the company. From direct-mail responses, prospects who are interested in a new product can be researched and the salesperson provided with a comprehensive profile before making the sales call.

Loctite uses a computerized matrix of its 11,000 customers to classify them on the basis of potential, using an A-B-C scale. Customers that are classified "A" get the largest share of sales force time because their market potential is the highest. With computerized planning, Loctite can scientifically decide which accounts its salespeople should call on, which ones can be turned over to distributors, and which ones can be solicited by direct mail.

Orion Research, a Cambridge, Massachusetts, marketer of sophisticated analytical instrumentation equipment, uses a computerized inquiry-handling system called the *comprehensive computerized marketing system (CCMS)* to rank sales leads according to potential, generate precise prospect information for the salespeople in preparing for sales calls, and provide sales managers with up-to-the-minute data on salesperson and distributor performance. The CCMS selects, from over 150 pieces of company literature, the appropriate ones for each prospect; helps the salespeople manage their time and territories so that the focus is on leads that have the highest profit potential; monitors the selling efforts until the order is either won or lost; and builds a continuous data base for periodic analytical reports to sales management. In the first six months after the CCMS was implemented, Orion Research's sales jumped 31 percent with no increase in the sales force.[13]

Diverse sales objectives and goals must be separated into meaningful components for achievement by individual salespeople. The MBO process described earlier in this chapter is one sound approach for doing this. Assigning sales territories, routing salespeople, setting sales quotas, and determining sales budgets are the principal tools sales managers use in allocating sales force efforts. Since the *budgeting* process was described in Chapter 3, *territorial management and routing* were covered in Chapter 10, and *sales quotas* were discussed in Chapter 11, these topics will not be discussed further here.

Evaluating Sales Force Performance

Every organization has some sort of performance evaluation monitoring system (PEMS). In smaller companies, this system may be largely informal, relying on the firsthand observations of supervisors. As an organization grows, managers are less able to monitor closely each employee's daily activities—so they turn to a more formalized PEMS. Companies differ greatly in their approach to a PEMS. Martin Marietta requires that managers in its AeroSpace Division write broad essays describing the designated employee's strengths and weaknesses. Most companies, however, try to quantify managerial observations and judgments by performance results, behavior, or personal characteristics. In the obsessive drive to develop quantifiable scores, many organizations lose sight of what they want the PEMS to do. Performance appraisal systems should do three essential things for the sales manager and salespeople:

- Provide feedback to each salesperson on individual job performance.
- Help salespeople modify or change their behavior toward more effective work habits.
- Provide information to sales managers on which to base decisions on promotion, transfer, and compensation of salespeople.

These are the successive stages in the effective implementation of a PEMS:

1. *Performance planning.* Probably the most important phase of the PEMS because it allows the salesperson to obtain the counsel of the sales manager in deciding three key questions: "Where am I going?" "How will I get there?" "How will I be measured?"

2. *Performance appraisal.* A continuous interpersonal process whereby sales managers give individual salespeople immediate feedback on each specific task, project, or objective accomplished. In their supervisory role, sales managers should provide some form of recognition, praise, correction, or comment after any salesperson's performance.

3. *Performance review.* A periodic review of the preceding performance appraisals to summarize where the salesperson is in his or her personal development. It should answer the question "How am I doing?" and lead into the next performance planning stage.

Even though the three stages in the PEMS overlap, sales managers should not assume that all three can be dealt with simultaneously in once-a-year, overall performance appraisals. *Performance planning* lays out objectives and plans for achieving them and explains how the individual will be evaluated. A well-constructed MBO program can be invaluable in this stage. *Performance appraisals* are day-by-day, mini-evaluations on specific performances. The *performance review* is a periodic summing up of these daily appraisals so that the salesperson can see where he or she stands.

Performance appraisal techniques.   Today's appraisal techniques are about the same as those that have been used for years. About three-fourths of companies use both ratings and narratives as appraisal techniques. Organizations that rely primarily on one of the appraisal techniques usually require backup support by the other technique. Narrative statements are preferred for work planning and review as well as for the documenting of critical incidents of both positive and negative performances. But narratives can be so subjectively written and interpreted that many sales managers' and sales representatives' careers have been stagnated by superiors who engaged in the process of "damning by faint praise" in written evaluations or who could not effectively prepare written performance evaluations. Nevertheless, ratings are critical for administering compensation programs and for defending an organization against charges of discrimination in compensation or promotion.

For most organizations, a nagging problem is how to develop one overall individual performance rating, that is, determining whether a salesperson's performance is outstanding, above average, average, below average, or poor. A simple quantitative total score rating, such as 83 out of 100 possible points, implies an unrealistic degree of measurement precision, ignores the relative importance of different performance criteria, and neglects the important subjective input of managers concerning their subordinates. While most companies are still struggling with the imperfections of their performance appraisal systems, a survey of national and international corporations identified these trends:

- Use of both ratings and narrative descriptions of employee behavior in the same appraisal system. Higher-level positions tend to rely more on narrative evaluations.

- Tying compensation more closely to performance, as pay raises are based more on merit than on cost-of-living increases.

- Frequent changes in appraisal systems in response to new types of jobs, more complex composition of employees, and concern for equal opportunities for all employees in compensation and promotion processes.[14]

Types of performance reviews. Periodically, sales managers should be required to summarize the performance of each salesperson in a permanent record for the benefit of the salesperson in tracking his or her progress and for the review of other sales and marketing managers. Although various types of rating forms are used, three popular ones are descriptive statements, graphic rating scales, and behaviorally anchored rating scales.

Descriptive statements. Usually used in conjunction with some form of graphic rating scale, descriptive statements about a salesperson may be short responses to a series of specific criteria such as job knowledge, territorial management, customer relations, personal qualities, or sales results. Another approach, which various organizations (including the military) use, calls for an overall portrait of the individual's abilities, potential, and specific performance during the marking period. This essay-type evaluation backs up and should be consistent with quantitative ratings on different performance criteria. An over-riding problem with descriptive statements is their subjectivity, both in writing and interpreting them, and many sales managers fall into a predictable pattern of being too harsh, too lenient, or too neutral in their comments so that the appraisal is not well balanced. Moreover, many evaluators are simply not very capable writers, so their use of words may fail to provide an accurate portrayal of the salesperson. All sales managers need specific training in performance evaluation, particularly when descriptive statements are utilized.

Graphic rating scales. Numerous formats may be considered for this "report card" type of rating, but in all cases the sales manager must assign to an individual a scale value on various traits, skills, or sales-related results. Two commonly employed devices for doing this are the semantic differential and Likert-type scales. The *semantic differential* uses bipolar adjective extremes to anchor several scale segments, usually five or seven, as shown in Exhibit 16-8. The salesperson is rated on a quality such as product knowledge and given a scale value from a numerical low of 1 (poor) to a high of 7 (excellent).

Likert-type scales provide descriptive anchors for each segment of the scale, as shown in Exhibit 16-9, so that the sales manager can select which overall term best applies.

Sales managers ought to avoid these graphic report card–type ratings of generalized abilities, traits, or performances of individual sales representatives. The word anchors are not very meaningful because of their subjective interpretation by the rater, the wide variance in comparison groups of salespeople, and the anchors' vague connection with actual performance. Specifically, tra-

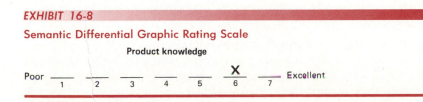

EXHIBIT 16-8

Semantic Differential Graphic Rating Scale

EXHIBIT 16-9

Likert-Type Graphic Rating Scale

Product knowledge

Unsatisfactory	Below average	Average	Above average	Outstanding
	X			

ditional evaluation systems usually suffer from one or more of the following limitations:[15]

- *Halo effect.* This occurs when sales managers tend to let one "key factor" influence their ratings of a salesperson on all other factors.

- *Central tendency.* Some sales managers may be reluctant to take a stand, so they rate salespeople near the middle of the scale on all rating factors. Thus, little distinction is made among salespeople, and minimal information is provided for compensation or promotion decisions.

- *Psychological resistance to negative evaluations.* A few sales managers suffer emotional distress when giving negative evaluations to salespeople, so they tend to avoid making negative evaluations.

- *Political concerns.* In order to "look good" themselves and prevent problems on their "watch," some sales managers will avoid giving any rating that is not acceptable to the individual salesperson.

- *Fear of reprisal.* Out of fear of reprisal for "discriminating" among employees, some sales managers are especially careful to avoid giving negative ratings to anyone who might take legal action (e.g., women, minorities, or older salespeople).

- *Varying evaluation standards.* Sales managers may have different evaluation standards. Some may have very high standards and rate very harshly, while others may be relatively lenient.

- *Interpersonal bias.* The personal likes and dislikes of the sales manager may influence his or her evaluations of salespeople. The "chemistry" between two people may not work, and resultant friction can lead to evaluation bias. Conversely, salespeople can use personal influence techniques with the sales manager to bias their evaluations upward.

- *Questionable personality traits.* Although many rating forms include personality traits (such as enthusiasm, resourcefulness, or intelligence) as indicators of selling performance, there is little evidence to support this trait approach.

- *Organization use.* Depending upon their internal purpose and use, performance ratings can be influenced. Sales managers often give higher ratings to salespeople when the evaluations are for compensation or promotion purposes because they want to keep their people happy and see them do well in comparison to those in other organizational units. When appraisals are mainly for personal development of subordinates, however, sales managers tend to be more objective and to point out areas needing improvement.

- *Recent performance bias.* Some sales managers are influenced too much by recent performance when evaluating individual performance; consequently, behavior earlier in the rating period is neglected.

- *No outcome focus.* Too many rating systems seem to have questionable validity and limited value for directing the growth and development of salespeople. They tend to rely on rating factors believed to be related to performance and fail to indicate how the salesperson might improve performance.

- *Inadequate sampling of job activities.* Some sales managers either may not know about or may not adequately observe all the activities in a given salesperson's assignment. Thus, the evaluation fails to include all important aspects of the job, or job tasks may be included that are not part of the current job.

The limitations associated with traditional evaluation systems can also bring about ethical issues, as illustrated in the *Ethics* scenario below.

Many rating systems attempt to overcome some of the above limitations by asking the sales manager to justify extremely high or low ratings. The explanations, however, are seldom insightful with regard to performance, and requiring such comments tends to cause managers to avoid the use of scale extremes and thus results in a "clustering" of ratings. One approach to coping with the problems of traditional rating systems is to use *behaviorally anchored rating scales (BARS),* as shown in Exhibit 16-10. BARS measure key performance behaviors that the individual salesperson can control. Consideration of specific

---

**ETHICS IN SALES MANAGEMENT:
PERSONALITIES AND THE EVALUATION PROCESS**

You have just discovered that a friend of yours—a fellow sales manager—may be putting too much subjectivity into his annual evaluations of his salespeople. You are very familiar with his sales district and the respective performance levels of his sales reps, so you were quite surprised when you saw the sales force evaluations he recently prepared. In particular, one of his sales reps, who is among the top-performing salespeople in the entire company, received a very marginal evaluation despite the fact that he had, in your opinion, a very successful sales year. Your company uses quantitative and qualitative criteria equally in assessing salesperson performance. You personally know this salesperson, and you also know that your friend (his sales manager) despises him because of his very aggressive, outgoing personality. He is very conceited and often obnoxious, yet he is a very successful salesperson. You feel that his personality is the cause of his less-than-fair evaluation.

1. Is it ethical for sales managers to place too much subjectivity into their yearly evaluations? Why or why not?

2. What would you do in this situation? Should one sales manager tell another how to run his or her district?

3. Should the company's method of performance evaluation be changed? Why or why not?

Behaviorally Anchored Rating Scale

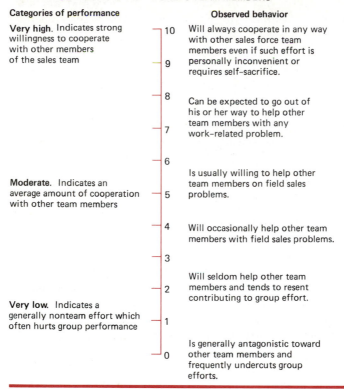

COOPERATION WITH SALES TEAM MEMBERS

Categories of performance		Observed behavior
Very high. Indicates strong willingness to cooperate with other members of the sales team	10 9	Will always cooperate in any way with other sales force team members even if such effort is personally inconvenient or requires self-sacrifice.
	8 7	Can be expected to go out of his or her way to help other team members with any work-related problem.
	6	
Moderate. Indicates an average amount of cooperation with other team members	5	Is usually willing to help other team members on field sales problems.
	4	Will occasionally help other team members with field sales problems.
	3 2	Will seldom help other team members and tends to resent contributing to group effort.
Very low. Indicates a generally nonteam effort which often hurts group performance	1 0	Is generally antagonistic toward other team members and frequently undercuts group efforts.

behaviors allows different sales managers to arrive at more consistent and objective evaluations, since the rating factors have similar interpretations.

Behaviorally anchored rating scales.   In constructing sales-oriented BARS, there are four basic steps:

1. *Identify critical incidents.* Some sales managers, salespeople, and customers are asked to describe specific critical incidents of effective and ineffective sales performance behavior. When an individual identifies a critical incident, he or she is asked to provide an actual example. These critical incidents are then condensed into a smaller number of performance categories. Kirchner and Dunnette obtained over a hundred critical incidents for a sales job, and these were reduced to thirteen sales performance dimensions.[16]

2. *Refine critical incidents into performance dimensions.* The sales managers and salespeople who are developing the performance appraisal analyze the reduced set of critical incidents and then refine them into a still smaller set of performance dimensions—usually five to twelve—that are defined in general terms. The critical incidents are then provided to another knowledgeable

group of salespeople, who are asked to assign the incidents to the appropriate performance dimensions. An incident is usually retained for the final BARS if 60 percent or more of the second sales group assign it to the same dimension as did the first group.

3. *Rate the effectiveness of the described behaviors.* The second sales group is asked to rate (usually on a scale of zero to ten) the behavior described in the critical incidents as to how accurately it represents a performance level on the dimension. Those incidents that have the lowest standard deviations (indicating greater agreement among raters) are kept for the final BARS.

4. *Select a set of incidents as behavioral anchors for the performance dimension.* Usually, six to eight critical incidents are selected for use as behavioral anchors for each performance dimension. The final BARS consist of vertical scales, one for each dimension to be evaluated, anchored by the retained incidents. Though a true behavior rating system takes time to develop, it allows for more precise ratings of salesperson performance behaviors.

Overall performance of the sales force. One danger in performance appraisal systems is that sales managers may become so preoccupied with the proper application of the techniques that they neglect a comprehensive evaluation of the composite sales force. The *sales audit,* as outlined earlier in Chapter 3, is a frequently used device to evaluate thoroughly and objectively an organization's marketing organization, environmental opportunities and challenges, goals, objectives, policies, strategies, and results. A sales audit seeks to answer two critical questions: *''Are we doing things correctly?''* and, more important, *''Are we doing the correct things?''*

In conducting sales audits, there are two basic approaches: horizontal and vertical. The *horizontal sales audit* is systems-oriented in that it is an examination of the entire sales effort. By contrast, a *vertical audit* is an in-depth study of one major component of selling efforts—such as the compensation plan or the effectiveness and efficiency of sales force territorial assignments. Although a sales audit suggests that selling efforts should be analyzed in isolation from other marketing efforts, such an approach is seldom feasible or desirable. This is because personal selling is a major component of the promotional mix, which, in turn, is a key element of the marketing mix. Since all elements of the marketing mix influence each other, the results from any vertical audit ought to be reexamined in relationship to results from other vertical audits. In the final analysis all marketing efforts must be compatibly integrated to achieve the desired synergistic impact in the marketplace.[17]

A sales audit consists of several relatively independent components that permit a comprehensive evaluation of the selling organization and efforts according to the priorities of the sales manager. Sales managers may choose to add other categories tailored specifically to their particular situations, but the following audits would seem applicable to most sales organizations.

Sales environment audit. This is an analysis of developing trends in the selling environment (customer preferences, competitors' strategies, government regulations, and so forth) that may create special opportunities or challenges for the sales organization. For instance, Xerox thinks that it has spotted an opportunity to capture a 20 percent share of the typewriter market (80 percent of which is dominated by IBM): its Memorywriter is sold by its copier and duplicator sales force; this puts 4,000 salespeople, making 5 million sales calls a year, behind the product.

Sales goals and objectives audit.　This audit appraises the sales organization's goals and objectives. Although salespeople usually have a general understanding of their organization's short-run objectives, they are typically vague about the longer-run, less measurable goals of the sales organization. It is up to the sales manager to specify goals and objectives for the salespeople. In addition, it is the manager's responsibility to ensure that these goals and objectives are consistent with those of the overall marketing organization and the company.

Sales policies audit.　Personal selling policies need to be reviewed periodically to see that they coincide with sales goals. For example, a policy of promoting top salespeople to sales management without giving them additional managerial training may not be compatible with the goal of dropping unprofitable products, customers, or territories. As another example, competitive insurance, brokerage, and real estate firms will have to review their policies of selling only through agents now that Sears is utilizing electronic marketing. Likewise, because of the accelerating costs of sales calls and the small sizes of average orders, Bliss and Laughlin Industries, Inc., suppliers of industrial products such as precision tools and construction materials, has changed from a strict policy of selling through personal contact only to one of using mail-order catalogs for several products.

Sales strategies and tactics audit.　This audit consists of a critical appraisal of how well selling strategies and tactics are exploiting market opportunities and dealing with challenges. Japanese companies have successfully executed the strategy of focusing on small-volume users of such products as photocopying machines and computers. Their selling tactics have included special customer services and prompt attention to customer complaints so that there are few dissatisfied customers.

Avon Products was the first company to try the unique strategy of selling cosmetics and toiletries door-to-door instead of through intermediaries. By positioning its salespeople as "beauty consultants" offering personal advice to homemakers, Avon captured about 20 percent of the total $5 billion market. But it has had to shift its strategy and tactics toward mail and telephone sales in order to adapt not only to the increasing number of women working outside the home but also to its own salesperson turnover ratio of over 100 percent a year.

Recognizing the increased availability of part-time experienced salespeople, Xerox made a strategy decision to hire 1,300 of them as independent representatives on a straight commission to develop small-town markets for low-end copiers.

Sales organization audit.　This is an appraisal of the sales organization's ability to implement the selling strategy and tactics. Does the sales organization optimally fit the current market situation? For example, with increasingly more complex or technical products, the sales manager may see the need to switch from a sales operation organized by geographic territory to one centered on the product being sold.

Sales productivity audit. This audit analyzes the profitability of different sales force units and the cost-effectiveness of various selling expenditures. In order to evaluate sales force productivity, the sales manager should be familiar with the concepts and techniques discussed in Chapter 15, on sales volume, cost, and profit analysis. In essence, a sales productivity audit requires that sales managers compare various breakdowns of sales data, such as by geographic region, product category, customer class, method of sale (mail, telephone, or personal sales call), size of order, or financial arrangement. The information needed for these market-segment breakdowns can be found in various sales department documents (call reports, expense accounts, sales invoices, prospect and customer records, credit memos, warranty cards, store audits, or consumer purchase diaries). The segment data should then be compared with the organization's historical sales data, industry averages, and organizational expectations or forecasts. With the aid of computers to analyze huge data banks of performance information, sales force evaluation should become increasingly more precise and objective. Selzer-Ivice (a manufacturers' agent firm and division of Control Data), which sells automotive and electronic parts to some 500 OEM and end-user accounts in the midwest, uses a system that presents its monthly sales data in four separate reports:

- *Manufacturer's customer analysis.* A listing of sales by product line to each customer

- *Sales report by customer and manufacturer.* A breakdown of each salesperson's sales by customer and by product line to that customer

- *Sales report by manufacturer.* A summary of each salesperson's total volume with each manufacturer to identify each salesperson's strengths and weaknesses by line handled

- *Manufacturer salesperson analysis.* A listing of each manufacturer's sales by each of Selzer-Ivice's salespeople

A special benefit of this system is the improved preparation of sales representatives for sales calls on customers. Representatives know what the customer has and hasn't bought recently and can tailor their sales presentations to overlooked products. A sales productivity analysis often reveals that profitable sales tend to come from particular categories of products, customers, or territories in a disproportionate ratio to effort expended. For example, a survey of over 500 companies, conducted by the New York Sales Executives Club, found that 27 percent of the sales force accounted for over 52 percent of sales.[18] Productivity increases may sometimes come easily, simply by focusing more effort on the more profitable customers or by ensuring that sales call objectives are clearly in mind. For instance, Bell Telephone Company salespeople are taught to plan all their sales calls keeping one or more of three objectives in mind:

- *Market development efforts.* Seeking to generate new business by educating customers and developing relationships with prospective buyers
- *Sales-generating activities.* Focusing on selling particular products to certain customers on specific sales calls
- *Market protection work.* Attempting to determine the strategies and tactics of competitors and to protect relations with current customers

More often, the increases in productivity do not come easily, and the sales manager will need to carry out some intensive computer-assisted data analysis for various market segments.

While trying to improve the productivity of the sales organization, sales managers will have to adjust to an even more rapidly changing marketing environment in the years ahead. Many of the changes will dramatically help sales managers in their efforts, while others may seriously hinder their efforts. Some of these changes will come in subtle sociological or political form rather than through technological innovations. In the next chapter, we turn to a discussion of ethics, social responsibility, and the legal environment of selling and sales management.

SUMMARY

The ultimate responsibility of the sales manager is to ensure that sales organization goals and objectives are achieved effectively and efficiently. Effectiveness is results-oriented; efficiency focuses on economical use of resources. A sales organization can be effective without being efficient, or vice versa. There must be multiple criteria to measure effectiveness and efficiency in today's intensely competitive marketing environment.

The major steps in the performance measurement and evaluation process include (1) establishing sales goals and objectives, (2) developing the sales plan, (3) setting performance standards, (4) allocating resources and sales force efforts in implementing the sales plan, and (5) evaluating sales force performance and implementing corrective actions, if needed.

Management by objectives (MBO) is a managerial approach that involves mutual goal setting between the sales manager and the salesperson. By helping set their own performance targets, salespeople are more likely to be committed to them and to devise realistic plans for their accomplishment. Successful sales organizations usually employ a mixture of quantitative and qualitative performance standards. Competence assessment, which tries to determine the characteristics needed to do a job rather than the specific tasks of the job, has been successfully used to select high achievers among sales applicants.

There are three successive stages in an effective performance evaluation monitoring system (PEMS): performance planning, performance appraisal, and performance review. Although several types of rating forms are used, three popular ones are descriptive statements, graphic rating scales, and behaviorally anchored rating scales (BARS). BARS measure key performance behaviors that the individual salesperson can control. Constructing BARS involves four basic steps: (1) identifying critical incidents, (2) refining critical incidents into performance dimensions, (3) rating the effectiveness of the described behaviors, and (4) selecting a set of incidents as behavioral anchors for the performance dimension.

To evaluate the overall performance of the sales force, the sales manager ought to consider a sales audit. The horizontal sales audit is an examination of the entire sales effort, while a vertical sales audit is an in-depth study of one major aspect of the selling effort, such as the compensation plan.

STUDY QUESTIONS

1. Assume the role of a buyer of office supplies for a medium-sized manufacturing firm. What qualities would you want in the salespeople who call upon you? What qualities would turn you off?

2. What are the four major components of a sales plan? Which component do you think would be most difficult to develop? Explain why.

3. Which, if either, do you think is more important for evaluating salespeople—quantitative or qualitative measures? Explain why you answered as you did.

4. What is meant by ''competence assessment''? Provide an example of how you might apply this technique in selecting new salespeople from many candidates.

5. Name the three stages in a performance evaluation monitoring system (PEMS), and describe the sales manager's role in each stage. In your work experience, how were you evaluated by your boss?

6. What type of performance appraisal techniques would you prefer your boss to use in evaluating you? What variables does your answer depend upon?

7. Name and describe some of the limitations of traditional evaluation systems. Have you ever had any personal experience with these limitations as either a rater or a ratee? Tell your story.

8. How might the objectivity of overall ratings of a salesperson be increased when several different sales supervisors or managers are providing evaluations?

9. Discuss the purpose and components of a sales audit, and describe the two different approaches to conducting one.

10. Do you think the increasing use of computers in sales management will change the sales force performance measurement and evaluation process? If so, how?

IN-BASKET EXERCISE

You were just hired as the new vice president of sales for a large retail organization, and your first task is to assess the company's sales force evaluation system. You asked several of the sales managers how they evaluate their salespeople, and they all basically indicated that their sales reps are ranked according to quarterly sales volume and that raises are given out on the basis of the rankings. The sales managers all feel that this is a fairly good, objective appraisal system.

1. How do you feel about this sales force evaluation system?
2. Could any other evaluation criteria be used here? Why or why not?

CASE 16-1

CENTRAL STATES RISK MANAGEMENT, INC.: DEVELOPING THE PERFORMANCE EVALUATION SYSTEM

Douglas Powell, the southern district sales manager for Central States Risk Management, has just returned from his company's annual sales and marketing meeting with a difficult problem. At the meeting, the vice president of marketing announced the company's intentions to expand into the professional liability insurance market. Doug was instructed to take five salespeople from his sales staff of twenty-five and have them start developing the professional liability markets in his area, concentrating on lawyers and CPAs. In addition, he was given a first-year operating objective of obtaining a 10 percent penetration for the professional liability market in the southern district.

The selling tasks required in developing the market for professional liability insurance products are quite different from those needed to sell the personal lines of insurance and risk management products. Doug was confident his district salespeople could do the job, but he was unsure about how to effectively assess their performance.

Background

The Central Insurance Agency was started in 1957 by Bill Henderson and William Fenway, each of whom had considerable experience working as life insurance agents for national companies. The firm started out as an independent agency selling personal lines of insurance, such as life, accident, and health coverage. After five years, the agency had almost $30 million of life, accident, and health coverage in force and em-

ployed ten agents who worked on commission and covered three states in the midwest.

In 1978, the name of the company was changed to Central States Risk Management, Inc., to reflect its geographic growth and plans for product diversification. By this time, the company had approximately seventy agents working in four regional offices, with customers in five midwestern states. The agency began to offer basic employee benefit plans, consisting of participative life, accident, and health insurance programs to small businesses with less than fifty employees. By 1988, Central States had over $150 million of life, accident, and health insurance coverage in effect, with a sales force of 105 agents in five states.

Doug Powell has been the sales manager for the southern district since 1985. Under his supervision, the district has been either first or second in premium income generated. In addition, the level of turnover among the southern district's sales force was traditionally the lowest of the four regional offices in the company.

Central States agents sold life, accident, and health insurance policies underwritten by various national insurance carriers. Central States collected the premiums from the individual customers and kept an agreed-upon percentage of each premium payment to cover its sales expenses, administrative overhead, and profits. Part of that premium percentage went to pay the commissions of the agent who sold the policy.

The agents were paid commissions based on a percentage of the premiums they generated. In addition,

Case prepared by Dan L. Sherrell, Louisiana State University. Used with permission.

they received a base salary and quarterly bonuses for attainment of quotas. The sales force's quotas were developed by evaluating the market potential for writing new policies or adding to existing coverage. This potential was compared with the current estimated level of market penetration. Then, quarterly quotas were derived on the basis of expected seasonal fluctuations in each market.

Doug attributed the productivity of the southern district to the talent of the sales force personnel and his ability to identify and reward the most effective salespeople. The current appraisal system consisted of Doug's comparison of each agent's premium income produced for the current year compared with the income generated from the previous year. Deviations were noted and discussed with the individual agent. Doug then prepared an evaluation of each individual on the district sales force along with recommendations for increases in commission rates or salary bases. This report was forwarded to the vice president of marketing and was approved or revisions were suggested. This system had been developed by Doug when he became district manager and he felt confident about it. The people on his sales force had told him they felt the process adequately rewarded the best performers.

Current Situation

Lawyers, CPAs, engineers, or any individual who provides advice or services based on acquired expertise needs protection from lawsuits by clients. Professional liability insurance is designed for such needs. Frequently, one of the benefits provided by professional organizations is the endorsement of various insurance products for organization members at group rates. The individual members are typically contacted by the endorsed company through direct mail, followed by a sales call from the representative.

Doug knows that the company's decision to enter the professional liability insurance market will require that his salespeople perform a set of sales tasks quite different from those they are accustomed to performing. If Central States could become the endorsed supplier of professional liability coverage for bar associations or CPA organizations in each market of the southern district, the sales force would have access to a customer group of high potential. Gaining the endorsement of local professional organizations would do much to ensure the successful market penetration for professional liability insurance.

The salespeople involved in the professional liability market will spend a large portion of their time contacting officers of the target professional organizations, making presentations, and performing other missionary selling tasks in an attempt to win the organizations' endorsements. Consequently, any evaluation of the performance of the professional liability salespeople should take into account the amount of effort devoted to "nonselling" tasks.

In an attempt to handle the problem, Doug wrote down the selling tasks required to sell life, accident, and health insurance (see the accompanying exhibit). Beside the list of activities, he noted the percent of total effort his district salespeople typically devoted to the job. Doug listed the selling tasks he envisioned as necessary in developing and servicing a market for

---

EXHIBIT

Description of Required Selling Tasks

Life, Accident, and Health Insurance	Percent of Effort	Professional Liability Insurance	Percent of Effort
1. Prospecting for new accounts	0.20	1. Prospecting for new accounts (identifying new professional groups)	?
2. Contacting prospects	0.10	2. Obtaining endorsements for client-affiliated professional groups	?
3. Qualifying prospects	0.05	3. Contacting prospects (group contacts through mass mailings)	?
4. Presenting the sales message	0.20	4. Qualifying prospects	?
5. Meeting customer objections	0.10	5. Presenting the sales message	?
6. Closing the sale	0.05	6. Meeting customer objections	?
7. Servicing the account	0.30	7. Closing the sale	?
		8. Servicing the account	?
		9. Maintaining client and professional group relationships	?

professional liability insurance. In the last column of the table he placed question marks alongside the entries, since he was uncertain about the percent of effort needed for each task.

Looking at the two lists of activities, Doug began to realize that the selling tasks themselves were not so different but that the amount of time devoted to each task by the two types of salespeople was what differed. Keeping that fact in mind, Doug began to try to think of ways in which he could develop an evaluation system that was flexible enough to encompass the activities of both types of sales jobs.

Questions

1. Could Central States' vice president of marketing be premature in expanding into the professional liability market? Develop a sales plan for Doug to follow as he enters this new market.

2. Evaluate Doug's current appraisal system for his agents. What are the current strengths and weaknesses of this system?

3. Given the operating objectives for the professional liability market, which selling activities should be emphasized for the professional liability sales force? How much effort should be devoted to each sales task?

4. How would you develop standards of performance or quotas for the professional liability sales force?

5. How would you compare the productivity of the professional liability sales force with the performance of the life, accident, and health insurance sales force?

CASE 16-2

REWARDING PERFORMANCE AT MARCO ELECTRONICS

MARCO Electronics is a large multinational electronics firm which manufactures and distributes a wide range of consumer and industrial electronic products throughout the world. The company takes pride in its ability to compete effectively in the highly competitive electronics industry. Senior executives want to foster an aggressive, risk-taking environment in an effort to keep the organization among the leaders of the industry in the United States and around the world.

Within the context of this aggressive, results-oriented environment district sales managers are asked to evaluate their salespeople using the Job Skills Guide for Salespeople (Exhibit 1), which is a primary element of the performance management system. This system is used to evaluate performance and set quotas, and it is a significant factor in determining bonuses at the end of the year. As part of the evaluation process the manager and sales representative have a "management appraisal interview." In this interview the salesperson presents an appraisal of his or her own performance (Exhibit 2, page 554) over the previous year. The sales manager discusses the Job Skills Guide, which has been completed prior to the meeting.

Neil Mennon was hired by MARCO Electronics three years ago, right after his college graduation. Neil was one of the top students at the company sales training sessions, and he has been labeled as a future top performer at MARCO. Sales bonuses for Neil were rather marginal during his first two years with the company, but he accepted the low bonuses as they were given during a period that was characterized for him by a great deal of learning and self-improvement.

Neil has just finished his third year with MARCO, and this time he is rather upset with his year-end bonus. He believes that the past year was his best year yet and that he deserves a bigger bonus. Neil's evaluation from his sales manager on his Job Skills Guide was outstanding. He received a rating of 1 ("exceeds expectations") on all items except 3f, 4a, and 4b. For these items, he received a rating of 2 ("meets expectations"); yielding a total score of 25. Neil feels that he did exceptionally well on his Self-Appraisal Form. All the objectives that Neil set for the year have been met and any weaknesses that were listed have been overcome. Everything seemed to go well during Neil's management appraisal interview, as the sales manager was impressed with Neil's progress and performance. However, after talking with several of his close friends on the sales force, Neil has found out that some of his peers with scores of 35 or higher on the Job Skills Guide received similar or even higher yearly bonuses.

Case prepared by Mark W. Johnston, Louisiana State University. Used with permission.

EXHIBIT 1

EXHIBIT 1

Job Skills Guide for Salespeople

Name of sales representative _____   Name of district sales manager _____   Date____

DIRECTIONS: Please use the rating scale provided to evaluate the demonstrated job skills of the sales representative whose name is listed above.

RATING SCALE
1 = Exceeds expectations   3 = Below expectations
2 = Meets expectations   N/A = Not applicable

1. **Assessing territory market potential, setting objectives, and developing territory marketing plans**
   a. Analyzing sales and market data   1 2 3 N/A
   b. Setting sales and product support objectives   1 2 3 N/A
   c. Developing territory marketing plans   1 2 3 N/A
   SCORE (this section) _____

2. **Managing the territory**
   a. Maintaining customer records   1 2 3 N/A
   b. Developing work plans   1 2 3 N/A
   c. Preparing call plans   1 2 3 N/A
   d. Budgeting and controlling expenses   1 2 3 N/A
   e. Handling administrative work   1 2 3 N/A
   SCORE (this section) _____

3. **Influencing and selling**
   a. Maintaining relationships with key influentials   1 2 3 N/A
   b. Establishing productive relationships with customers and their staffs   1 2 3 N/A
   c. Identifying and confirming customer needs   1 2 3 N/A
   d. Making effective sales presentations   1 2 3 N/A
   e. Handling objections and closing   1 2 3 N/A
   f. Implementing corporate policies   1 2 3 N/A
   g. Developing new business opportunities   1 2 3 N/A
   SCORE (this section) _____

4. **Communicating and maintaining effective working relationships**
   a. Maintaining productive relationships with sales managers   1 2 3 N/A
   b. Developing productive relationships with appropriate corporate officers   1 2 3 N/A
   c. Contributing to the development of a strong team effort in the organization   1 2 3 N/A
   SCORE (this section) _____

5. **Managing self-development/acquiring product knowledge**
   a. Gaining and maintaining product knowledge   1 2 3 N/A
   b. Participating in development programs   1 2 3 N/A
   c. Evaluating and improving job skills   1 2 3 N/A
   d. Managing his/her own career development   1 2 3 N/A
   SCORE (this section) _____

   TOTAL SCORE _____

quantitative characteristics
personal

Questions

1. What might be some of the reasons for Neil's unsatisfactory year-end bonus?

2. Do you see any weaknesses with MARCO's sales force evaluation procedures? What are they? Comment on both the Job Skills Guide and the Self-Appraisal Form.

3. Are there areas of evaluating sales performance that are not included in MARCO's Job Skills Guide? If so, what are they? Should weights be assigned to any of the factors listed in the Job Skills Guide? Why or why not?

4. What should Neil do?

5. Help Neil in developing an alternative evaluation procedure for MARCO Electronics. Thoroughly support your recommendation.

EXHIBIT 2

Your Self-Appraisal Form

DIRECTIONS

As part of a management review of performance being conducted throughout the division, you are asked to complete a self-appraisal of your performance. The subject matter should include an opinion of what you feel are your major strengths and weaknesses and your accomplishments in attaining goals and objectives—or if not met, the reasons you feel contributed to not attaining the goals. It would be well to define areas concerning the job in which you and your sales manager agree as well as areas where you feel you don't quite see eye to eye. Also, make a few notes as to what you think can be done to help you do a better job.

It is important to understand that the performance review session is a vehicle that enables you and your manager not only to discuss your performance, but also to agree mutually on goals and seek ways to meet your needs as well as those of the organization. The session is not to be considered an inquisition or fault-finding venture. When you sit with your manager, be sure to discuss freely all matters pertaining to your performance and your job.

After your appraisal session the manager will submit your self-appraisal form and Job Skills Guide plus a summary of your discussion to the personnel office, which will maintain a confidential file on the events that have transpired. Remember that this session is designed to help you progress in this organization. Its success depends upon the rapport that occurs between you and your sales manager.

STRENGTHS

1. _____
2. _____
3. _____
4. _____
5. _____

WEAKNESSES

1. _____
2. _____
3. _____
4. _____
5. _____

OBJECTIVES (Met and not met: If not met, explain.)

_____
_____
_____
_____

REFERENCES

1. Arthur Bragg, ''Are Good Salespeople Born or Made?'' *Sales & Marketing Management,* September 1988, pp. 74–78.
2. William A. O'Connell, ''A 10-Year Report on Sales Force Productivity,'' *Sales & Marketing Management,* December 1988, pp. 33–38.
3. Hugh Lendrum, ''What's Wrong with These Sales Forces?'' *Sales & Marketing Management,* March 1990, pp. 54–56.
4. ''Have You Seen a Salesperson Lately?'' *Sales & Marketing Management,* March 1990, p. 56.
5. *Sales & Marketing Management,* Feb. 3, 1986, p. 16.
6. ''1986 Best Sales Force Survey,'' *Sales & Marketing Management,* June 1986, p. 55.
7. For other time perspectives, see Noel B. Zabriskie and John Browning, ''Measuring Industrial Salespeople's Short-Term Productivity,'' *Industrial Marketing Management,* April 1979, pp. 167–171; Jon R. Katzenback and R. R. Champion, ''Linking Top-Level Planning to Salesmen Performance,'' *Business Horizons,* vol. 9, 1966, pp. 91–100; James C. Cotham III and David W. Cravens, ''Improving Measurement of Salesman Performance,'' *Business Horizons,* vol. 12, 1969, pp. 79–83; Michael J. Etzel and John M. Ivancevich, ''Management by Objectives in Marketing: Philosophy, Process, and Problems,'' *Journal of Marketing,* vol. 38, 1974, pp. 47–55; Eugene H. Fram and Andrew J. DuBrin, ''Our Use of Time Determines Both Leadership Style and Managerial Effectiveness,'' *Personnel Journal,* January 1980, pp. 47–48, 61 ff.

8. For different perspectives on performance standards, see F. R. Widdap, "Why Performance Standards Don't Work," *Personnel*, March–April 1970, p. 15; O. A. Davis and R. B. Woodruff, "An Approach for Determining Criteria of Sales Performance," *Journal of Applied Psychology*," June 1973, pp. 242–247; Ronald E. Turner, "Market Measures from Salesmen: A Multidimensional Scaling Approach," *Journal of Marketing Research*, May 1971, pp. 165–172; Roger A. Layton, "Controlling Risk and Return in the Management of a Sales Team," *Journal of Marketing Research*, August 1968, pp. 277–282; James M. Hulbert and Norman E. Toy, "A Strategic Framework for Marketing Control," *Journal of Marketing*, April 1977, pp. 12–20.

9. Additional insights on mutual goal setting can be found in Thomas R. Wotruba and Michael L. Thurlow, "Sales Force Participation in Quota Setting and Sales Forecasting," *Journal of Marketing*, April 1976, pp. 11–16; J. Taylor Sims, "Industrial Sales Management: A Case for MBO," *Industrial Marketing Management*, vol. 6, 1977, pp. 44–45; Robert A. Else, "Selling by Measurable Objectives," *Sales Management*, May 14, 1973, pp. 22–24; James O. Leathers, "Applying Management by Objectives to the Sales Force," *Personnel*, August 1973, pp. 45–50.

10. For further reading about MBO, see Joseph W. Leonard, "Why MBO Fails So Often," *Training and Development Journal*, June 1986, pp. 38–39; "The Pros and Cons of an MBO Program," *Best's Review*, January 1981, pp. 72–73; Donald W. Jackson, Jr., and Ramon J. Aldag, "Managing the Sales Force by Objectives," *MSU Business Topics*, Spring 1974, pp. 53–59; Richard T. Hise and Peter L. Gillett, "Making MBO Work in the Sales Force," *Atlanta Economic Review*, July–August 1977, pp. 32–37; Donald W. Jackson, Jr., and John L. Schlacter, "Do Sales Managers Really Manage by Objectives?" in Richard P. Bagozzi et al. (eds.), *Marketing in the 80's, Changes and Challenges, 1980 Educators' Conference Proceedings*, American Marketing Association, Chicago, 1980, pp. 248–251; J. Singular, "Has MBO Failed?" *MBA*, October 1975, pp. 47–50; Dale D. McConkey, "20 Ways to Kill Management by Objectives," *Management Review*, October 1972, pp. 4–13.

11. For more on behavior-based measures, see Erin Anderson and R. L. Oliver, "Perspectives on Behavior-Based versus Outcome-Based Salesforce Control Systems," *Journal of Marketing*, October 1988, pp. 76–88; Robert P. Bush, Alan J. Bush, David J. Ortinau, and Joseph F. Hair, Jr., "Developing a Behavior-Based Scale to Assess Retail Salesperson Performance," *Journal of Retailing*, Spring 1990, pp. 119–136.

12. *Wall Street Journal*, Jan. 6, 1981, p. 1.

13. Thayer C. Taylor, "Giving Sales Leads a Leading Edge," *Sales & Marketing Management*, Sept. 14, 1981, pp. 35–37.

14. Hermine Zagat Levine, "Performance Appraisals at Work," *Personnel*, June 1986, pp. 63–66; Kenneth S. Tell, "Performance Appraisal: Current Trends, Persistent Progress," *Personnel Journal*, April 1980, pp. 296–316. Other perspectives on performance appraisal techniques can be found in Craig Eric Schneier, Richard W. Beatty, and Lloyd S. Baird, "Creating a Performance Management System," *Training and Development Journal*, May 1986, pp. 74–79; Charles J. Fombrun and Robert L. Laud, "Strategic Issues in Performance Appraisal: Theory and Practice," *Personnel*, November–December 1983, pp. 23–30; Roger J. Plachy, "Appraisal Scales That Measure Performance Outcomes and Job Results," *Personnel*, May–June 1983, pp. 57–65; Ed Yager, "A Critique of Performance Appraisal Systems," *Personnel Journal*, February 1981, pp. 129–132; Bill R. Darden and Warren French, "An Investigation into the Salesman Evaluation Practices of Sales Managers," *Southern Journal of Business*, July 1970, pp. 47–56; Richard S. Sloma, *How to Measure Managerial Performance*, Macmillan, New York, 1980; Thomas R. Wotruba and Richard Mangone, "More Effective Sales Force Rating," *Industrial Marketing Management*, June 1979, pp. 236–245; R. Kenneth Teas and James Horrell, "Salespeople Satisfaction and Performance Feedback," *Industrial Marketing Management*, February 1981, pp. 49–57; Charles M. Futrell, John E. Swan, and John T. Todd, "Job Performance Related to Management Control Systems for Pharmaceutical Salesmen," *Journal of Marketing Research*, February 1976, pp. 25–33.

15. Benton Cocanougher and John M. Ivancevich, "BARS' Performance Rating for Sales Force Personnel," *Journal of Marketing Research*," July 1978, pp. 87–95. To better understand the linkage between BARS and MBO, see William J. Kearney, "Behaviorally Anchored Rating Scales—MBO's Missing Ingredient," *Personnel Journal*, January 1979, pp. 20–25.

16. Wayne K. Kirchner and Marvin D. Dunnette, "Identifying the Critical Factors in Successful Salesmanship," *Personnel*, vol. 34, 1957, pp. 54–59.

17. For more understanding of marketing and sales audits, see Louis M. Capella and William S. Sekely, "The Marketing Audit: Methods, Problems, and Perspectives," *Akron Business & Economic Review*, Fall 1978, pp. 37–41; J. Bardley-Simpson, "Sales Analysis: A Visual Approach," *European Journal of Marketing*, Spring 1974, pp. 57–74; Ed Roseman, "An Audit Can Make the 'Accurate Difference,'" *Product Marketing*, August 1979, pp. 24–25; Philip Kotler, "From Sales Obsession to Marketing Effectiveness," *Harvard Business Review*, November–December 1977, pp. 67–75; Louis M. Capella and William S. Sekely, "The Marketing Audit: Usage and Application," in Robert S. Franz, Robert M. Hawkins, and Al Toma (eds.), *Proceedings 1978 Southern Marketing Association Annual Conference*, University of Southwestern Louisiana, Lafayette, pp. 411–414; Fred W. Morgan, Jr., "Marketing Control Systems: Their Relationship to Company Size," in Henry Nash and Donald Robin (eds.), *Proceedings 1977 Southern Marketing Association Annual Conference*, Southern Mississippi University, Hattiesburg, pp. 90–91.

18. *Business Week*, Feb. 1, 1964, p. 52.

CONTROLLING AND EVALUATING THE SALES FORCE AT CHEMCO

Unable to relax because of the stress he was experiencing over having to evaluate his sales force, John Benson, a newly appointed regional manager for CHEMCO, was sitting at his desk reviewing what information he had concerning the performance of his sales force. In less than one week John would have to report on this evaluation to his division manager.

John's primary objective was to ultimately determine profitability per sales representative. His secondary objective was to measure his sales force's performance on nonselling tasks. In addition, he wanted to be able to provide appropriate feedback to all his employees in order to give them an indication of how they were doing. However, as he reviewed the information that he had available, John was uncertain about whether or not he would be able to accomplish all these objectives.

In an effort to get some advice on where to begin, John called Doris Armstrong, his predecessor, to ask how she had handled evaluating the sales force. (John had replaced Doris only three weeks earlier, but the two were unable to find the time necessary to discuss all the transitional details.) Doris's response was that she simply had a one-on-one discussion with each salesperson on a monthly basis. The discussion would take place over coffee if the salesperson was located nearby; otherwise, it would be conducted over the telephone. Doris

Case prepared by E. Stephen Grant, Memphis State University.

Divisional Sales and Profitability Summary

Division	December Market Profitability			Year-to-Date Market Profitability		
	Sales	Amount	Percentage	Sales	Amount	Percentage
1	3,500	840	24.0	39,200	10,555	26.9
2	1,500	467	31.1	18,999	5,999	31.6

Source: Company records.

explained that she believed this was the only way to do it: "It is surprising what you can learn over coffee, especially if the atmosphere is an informal one." John was alarmed by Doris's response. While hanging up the telephone, John thought to himself that he had inherited an unorganized and very poorly controlled group of salespeople. The call did nothing to improve his level of stress, for he now believed he would have to design an evaluation process from scratch because he had no intention of "fluffing off" evaluations as Doris had done.

THE INFORMATION

At his disposal, John had only three sources of information. One was a profitability report that highlighted the current-month and year-to-date sales and profitability levels of CHEMCO's two divisions (see Exhibit 1). Another information source was a computer-generated summary of monthly sales and profit contributions per salesperson (see Exhibit 2).

In addition, John had a floppy diskette that contained the results of a sales personnel survey that had recently been administered to company salespeople

Monthly Sales Contribution Summary (Partial)

Employee Number and Name	Gross Sales	Gross Profit	PR/Travel Expense	Direct Profit	Marketing Overhead	Market Profitability	
						Amount	Percentage
3 Jones	52,520	26,049	4,032	22,017	6,040	15,977	30.4
4 Grant	10,520	6,599	3,339	3,261	1,185	2,075	20.1
5 Remsie	9,870	7,118	8,035	(917)	1,135	(2,052)	0.0
9 Lalla	76,764	40,580	12,509	28,071	8,828	19,243	25.1
10 Wren	83,348	45,636	7,439	38,197	9,585	28,612	34.3
11 Kerr	7,436	4,505	17,403	(12,898)	855	(13,753)	185.0
12 Baret	51,341	29,395	2,681	26,714	5,904	20,809	40.5

Source: Company records.

by an independent consultant. Reviewing the items listed on the diskette's label, he noted that there were three sections of the questionnaire that possibly could be of relevance for his evaluation task, so he booted up the disk. As he investigated the contents of the questionnaire, John discovered that the sections pertaining to perceived areas of personal improvement, perceived working environment, and perceived degrees of personal competence were indeed relevant to his task.

After reviewing the information on the diskette, he decided that it would be useful to evaluate individuals' responses to questions in the relevant sections of the survey. Also, he thought it would be useful to compare the questionnaire results with individuals' monthly sales and profit contributions (see Exhibit 2) in order to determine if there was a relationship between employees' reported perceptions and their sales performance.

THE FUTURE

Realizing that an adequate evaluation process was not in place, John began brainstorming in order to develop a process that would standardize the evaluation of his sales force. In doing so, John realized he had more questions than answers. However, he was able to determine the fundamentals that he believed would have to underlie the new evaluation process. John grabbed a sheet of paper and listed the following:

1. Salespeople should be involved in the process so that they understand and accept my expectations of them.

2. Performance should be monitored on a periodic basis so that there are no surprises for me or them.

3. Both qualitative and quantitative measures of performance should be incorporated in order to adequately measure all the factors that are important for our success.

4. The performance review should result in an essay-type evaluation of each individual's performance relative to the performance expectations that were established for that salesperson.

5. There should be no secret evaluation forms, processes, steps, and the like. Each individual has to possess complete faith in the process and be able to participate in it without fear of reprisal.

Although John was new to his position of regional manager, he had a total of ten years' experience with CHEMCO and knew that a standardized evaluation process was needed companywide. Given that need, John decided to schedule the time necessary to develop such a process; he planned to present his ideas to his division manager at the meeting in which he was to report the results of the evaluation that had been the source of his concerns. That meeting was scheduled for the following week; therefore, John had less than one week to develop his evaluation process.

QUESTIONS

1. With the information John has, complete John's evaluation task by providing a brief analysis of the performance of the following salespeople: Jones, Grant, Remsie, and Lalla. Review the survey results, and use all relevant question responses that aid in your evaluation. (*Note:* Your CHEMCO diskette contains the survey results that John has been reviewing. The employee numbers referred to in Exhibit 2 correspond with the employee numbers on your CHEMCO diskette.)

2. Assuming that the five fundamentals John has listed are valid, develop a flowchart of an evaluation process that possesses all five. Briefly explain your reasoning for each step of the process.

3. How could John improve his evaluation procedures? Provide a detailed response; for example, if you believe he needs more information, identify exactly what he needs and why he needs it.

4. Given your knowledge of the CHEMCO organization (review the Integrated Cases in Parts One, Two, and Four), do you agree with John concerning the evaluation fundamentals he has listed? If so, explain why you agree; if not, explain why not and list the fundamentals you believe would be appropriate.

PART SIX

THE ENVIRONMENT FOR PERSONAL SELLING AND SALES MANAGEMENT

17

ETHICS, SOCIAL RESPONSIBILITY, AND THE LEGAL ENVIRONMENT

LEARNING OBJECTIVES

When you finish this chapter, you should understand:

- ▲ The different concepts of business ethics and the conflicts among them
- ▲ The ethical concerns of salespeople in dealing with the company, coworkers, customers, and other salespeople
- ▲ The major ethical concerns of sales managers
- ▲ An approach to making ethical decisions in selling and sales management
- ▲ The evolution of corporate social responsibility concepts
- ▲ The different levels of social responsibility at which a company can operate
- ▲ A decision-making process for social responsibility issues
- ▲ The use and value of social audits and how to report results
- ▲ The legislation affecting selling and sales management in local, state, federal, and international sales situations

563

A DAY ON THE JOB

Rick Huddleston, a client-services consultant for a financial-services firm, deals with ethical issues on a day-to-day basis. "Men and women, from warehouse workers to CEOs, are under increasing pressure to set aside their values for financial gain," says Huddleston. "Budget cuts, compensation compression, the soaring cost of living, and increased competition are some of the factors that pressure individuals into doing things that may conflict with their personal values." Huddleston believes sales managers and the organization can do a great deal to foster and promote ethical standards among the sales force. "While individuals bring their own values into a sales position, there are many other factors, such as industry standards, competitor's standards, and guidance from management, that can help an individual deal with ethical issues on the job," says Huddleston. When asked how he deals with the temptations of unethical behavior in the workplace, Huddleston states: "It's important to realize that while unethical activities may result in temporary gains for the individual in the short run, they can ultimately lead to financial ruin and personal humiliation in the long run. Most successful people find that an honest, ethical approach to all business transactions will eventually lead to successful and profitable lifetime careers."[1]

One of your most promising new salespeople is stopped for running a red light . . . and is arrested when nearly a pound of cocaine is found in his car trunk. Your top salesperson has been accused of offering bribes to win some major accounts. A young woman who applied for a job as a salesperson came in for an interview today and turns out to have a severe handicap. Your company has just been slapped with a lawsuit because one of your sales representatives has slandered a competitor. Handling such issues as these is becoming increasingly commonplace for today's professional sales manager. In this chapter, we will study the numerous ethical, social, and legal influences on decision making in today's rapidly changing sales environment.

BUSINESS ETHICS

Business ethics are among the most important, yet perhaps most misunderstood, concerns in the business world today.[2] The study of business ethics deals with questions about whether specific practices are acceptable or not. Throughout the text various *Ethics* scenarios were presented in an attempt to place the reader in a position to judge whether the behavior in each situation was ethical or not. As you have probably discovered by now, there is no one right answer when it comes to judging the behavior presented in these situations. Therefore, by its very nature, the field of business ethics is controversial, and there is no universally accepted approach for resolving its questions. However, since ethical considerations are such an integral part of the sales manager's job, this chapter will help you to recognize and resolve ethical issues in the selling environment.

Webster's Third New International Dictionary defines "ethics" as: "the discipline dealing with what is good and bad or right and wrong or with moral duty and obligation; a set of moral principles or values; the principles of conduct governing an individual or a profession."

Frequent use of the term "morals" to define "ethics" implies that there is a close relationship between the two. In general, morals refer to the *practice* of right conduct, whereas ethics pertain to the *theory* of right conduct. Ethics deal not with things as they are but with the way they ought to be. This suggests the need for analysis, evaluation, and development of normative criteria for deciding ethical issues.

Business ethics deal largely with the relationship between business practices and the moral concept of right and wrong. In business, judgment of what is right or wrong has been traditionally based mainly upon economic considerations. But when discussing business ethics, we must be careful to specify whether we are talking about *individual, organizational,* or *professional* ethical standards. Ethical issues in business often involve conflicts between these three standards, as depicted in Exhibit 17-1.

All individuals develop their own standards of ethical behavior for their personal lives. But as soon as a person becomes a salesperson or sales manager, he or she must think about what is good for the company, too. Because companies compete with each other, the organizational goals of profit, growth, and survival may override the goals of individual ethics. It is managerial power that enforces the organizational value system or concept of acceptable and unacceptable business practice. An individual who opposes the organizational value system jeopardizes his or her career advancement.

Professional ethics differ from individual ethics by emphasizing the collective viewpoint and acceptable practices of the members of the profession. They differ from organizational ethics by stressing the norms or values of the profession, rather than those of the organization, as a basis of authority. Too often, one's allegiance to a profession (e.g., advertising, marketing research, accounting, law, or sales) and its own ethical codes of self-interest can lead to a very narrow perspective and the inability to consider outside criticism or opposing viewpoints objectively. "Ethical" bans on advertising professional medical, dental, or legal

EXHIBIT 17-1

Ethics: Balance between Individual, Professional, and Organizational Values

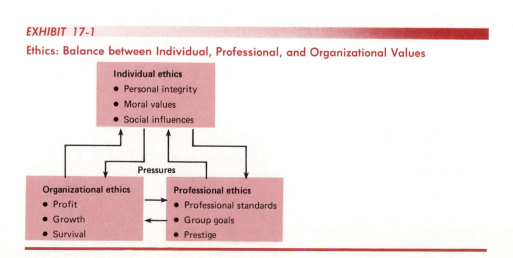

services, for instance, might be criticized by outsiders as an indirect means of preventing price competition for these services.

These three types of ethics—individual, organizational, and professional—provide valuable checks and balances on each other. *Professional ethics* can enforce standards of business practice (e.g., in market research, selling, or advertising) when the organization attempts to justify some proposed unethical action as "just doing what other companies are doing" or "fighting fire with fire." *Organizational ethics*, stressing profits and growth, serve to check overzealous self-serving professional ethics such as those of a lawyer who applies "unreasonable" standards before approving new product labels for a company. A person's *individual ethics* may oppose any excessive organizational or professional control that might violate personal standards—for example, the coercion of a sales manager who tries to persuade salespeople to offer bribes to important customers in order to win their business.

Sales managers will be in a better position to prevent any questionable behaviors if they have a good understanding of what salespeople go through when confronted with a potentially unethical situation. The framework presented in Exhibit 17-2 attempts to identify the factors that influence ethical decision making by focusing on three variables that affect a salesperson's behavior: individual salesperson factors, significant others, and opportunity. *In-*

EXHIBIT 17-2

A Contingency Framework for Ethical Decision Making in the Selling Environment

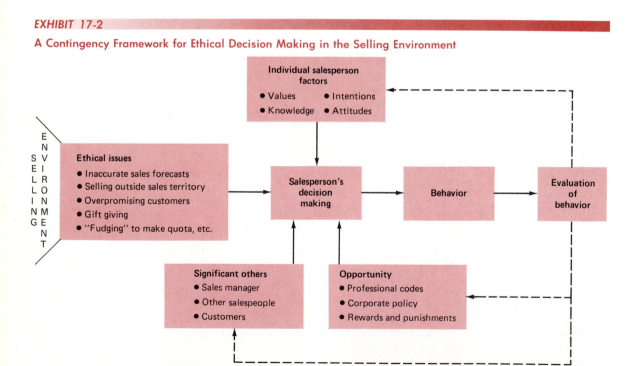

Source: Adapted from O. C. Ferrell and Larry Gresham, "A Contingency Framework for Understanding Ethical Decision Making In Marketing," *Journal of Marketing,* Summer 1985, pp. 87–96.

dividual salesperson factors include the moral philosophies or principles that sales-people use to decide what is right or wrong. Hopefully, this textbook has illustrated through the *Ethics* scenarios that people are guided by different moral philoso-phies when making decisions in an ethical situation. *Significant others* incorpo-rates the influence of people such as sales managers, other salespeople, and customers. For example, if a sales manager continually makes promises to cus-tomers that he or she cannot keep, a salesperson may come to believe that he or she can also make such promises. Therefore, a sales manager's behavior can do a great deal to influence, if not change, an individual salesperson's behavior. Finally, *opportunity* results from conditions that either limit barriers or provide rewards for the salesperson. Rewards can be either internal or external to the salesperson. Internal rewards include the personal self-worth or job satisfaction that salespeople experience because of their behavior. External rewards are the things salespeople expect to receive because of their behavior; examples include anything from monetary compensation to recognition and status. Thus, indi-vidual factors, significant others, and opportunity interact to influence a sales-person's perception of and response to an ethical issue. Sales managers can be an important part of this decision-making framework by developing a good understanding of the individual, being an influential significant other, and em-phasizing the most relevant opportunities to the sales force.

Ethical Concerns of Salespeople

Two very important and influential components of an individual salesperson's ethical decision-making framework are significant others and opportunity. Sales-people must constantly be aware of their dealings with their own company, coworkers, customers, and competitors.

Dealing with the company.   Most salespeople would probably admit that they occasionally "harmlessly" bend the rules when dealing with their own employer. But when small, seemingly insignificant abuses are condoned by many em-ployees, they can significantly increase the employer's cost of doing business, and this, in the long run, can boomerang to hurt all employees as well as customers.

Misusing company assets.   Padding expense accounts, taking company sup-plies or equipment for personal use, making personal telephone calls on company phones, using company time to conduct personal business, keeping company premiums or promotional items meant for customers, and driving a company car on unauthorized personal business trips are a few of the many ways that salespeople can abuse their relationship with their employer.

Cheating in sales contests.   Some salespeople are so driven to win a sales contest that they will try to persuade customers to load up on products, with the promise that the goods will be taken back after the contest is over. This practice not only hurts fellow salespeople but also increases the company's expenses without benefit.

Falsifying sales records.   When their performance is at least partially based on sales activities as well as sales results, some salespeople are tempted to "fudge a little'' on their reported number of sales calls, service calls, or promotional mailings.

Moonlighting. A few audacious salespeople, who are not closely supervised, may be tempted to accept part-time jobs during the hours in which they are supposed to be working for their main employer.

Going around company policy. Although few salespeople always operate strictly ''by the book,'' most recognize that there are usually important reasons for following company policies. Salespeople who are always ''wheeling and dealing,'' trying to get around company policy (e.g., attempting to get special delivery, service, or billing treatment for their favored customers), can create dissension among coworkers, upset customers, and embarrass their company.

Dealing with coworkers. A few excessively competitive salespeople may resort to various unethical behaviors in an effort to outdo their coworkers.

Taking customers from other salespeople. Intruding on another salesperson's territory to obtain sales and persuading a customer with offices in two different territories to make all purchases from one's own territory are examples of customer poaching that will inevitably lead to retaliation and counterproductive disputes among the salespeople.

Undercutting coworkers. Occasionally, salespeople have gotten so caught up with internal competition that they deliberately undercut their coworkers. For example, covering up one's own mistake by claiming that a secretary failed to relay a telephone message and telling a customer that another salesperson doesn't provide good postpurchase service to customers are self-serving deceptions that are clearly unethical.

Dealing with conflicts of interest. Some salespeople, such as real estate agents and stockbrokers, must deal daily with potential conflicts of interest in working with both buyers and sellers. For example, should a real estate agent try to persuade the potential buyer to pay the highest price for a seller's house and thereby earn a higher commission, or should the agent try to secure a fair price on the house, that is, approximately what the agent knows the seller will accept? Most real estate agents must walk a fine ethical line in working closely with both buyers and sellers.

Dealing with customers. Over the long run, it is seldom ''smart'' to engage in unethical practices with customers even if the customer is the instigator.

Overpromising. In order to win a sale, some salespeople promise much more than they can reasonably expect to deliver, believing that the customer will accept a plausible excuse later. For example, promising an unrealistic delivery date in order to make a sale is an ethical violation that will likely boomerang on the salesperson and harm future relations with the customer.

Distorting the truth. Whether covering up their own company's product and service problems or lying about the problems of competitors' products, a few salespeople distort the truth or lie outright in order to make a sale. These kinds of salespeople seldom last long because they quickly lose their credibility with customers.

Overselling.   Customers may not always be aware of how much inventory they need, so the unethical salesperson may try to persuade them to overbuy.

Revealing confidential information.   In an attempt to ingratiate themselves with a favored customer, some salespeople reveal confidential and potentially harmful information about their customer's competitors.

Giving gifts.   Bribes, kickbacks, and payoffs are strictly illegal and can create serious problems for the salesperson and his or her company. Nevertheless, some salespeople try to ''show their appreciation'' by secretly providing their customers with expensive gifts. Unfortunately, customers sometimes drop not-too-subtle hints that they expect a nice gift, especially around the holiday season. Legally, only $25 per year per individual can be given to customers, and many companies refuse to allow their employees to accept any gifts from suppliers.

Misusing entertainment.   Although playing golf with a customer or prospect or taking him or her to dinner or a ball game is an acceptable and often expected part of doing business, entertainment cannot be a disguised bribe to influence a buyer to purchase.

Playing favorites.   There are always some customers that a salesperson will like better than others, but the ethical salesperson cannot afford to show favoritism (e.g., by manipulating orders when products are in short supply). Other customers will deeply resent such unequal treatment and may refuse to deal with salespersons even suspected of such behavior.

Dealing with competitors.   Perhaps it can be argued that all is fair in love and war, but this is certainly not the case for ethical salespeople in relation to competition.

Disparaging the competition.   Making exaggerated, negative comments about competitors' products not only is unethical but also usually backfires because the customer will wonder what is being said behind his or her back.

Disturbing competitors' product displays.   Whether in stores, at trade shows, or elsewhere, it is not only unethical but also illegal for salespeople to tamper with competitors' products—for example, reducing the number of product facings in a store or damaging competitors' displays or products in any way.

Spying on competitors.   Salespeople may use many guises to obtain competitively useful information. For example, they may pump competitors' salespeople at social gatherings, encourage customers to put out phony bid requests to get information on competitors' price offerings, or pretend to be customers at professional conferences, at trade shows, or on plant tours. Although not illegal (and some would argue that ''nearly everybody does it''), such practices are ethically questionable.

Employer dealings with salespeople.   Not only do salespeople need ethical standards in dealing with their companies, but top executives must deal ethically with their salespeople. In some companies, salespeople must function in impossible situations in which they have to compromise their personal ethics, refuse to do what is asked, or leave the company. Salespeople have a right to expect the following basics from the company.

Compensating employees. Timely payment of salary, commissions, and bonuses plus prompt reimbursement of expenses are basic requirements for a company in dealing ethically with its salespeople.

Assigning sales territories. Initially, management must carefully assign sales territories to ensure that the basis of allocation is as fair as possible. Then, whenever territories must be reassigned, split up, or moved to national accounts, the salesperson should have early warning of the impending change and be given an opportunity to negotiate a new territorial assignment.

Pressuring salespeople. Setting unrealistically high goals for salespeople, along with maintaining constant pressure on them to produce sales, is viewed as unfair or unethical behavior unless the salespeople are involved in setting the quotas and fully understand the reasons for intense pressure to produce.

Employing, promoting, and firing. Although the Equal Employment Opportunity Act prohibits discrimination except on the basis of clearly performance-related criteria, there is continuing evidence that sexism, racism, and ageism still influence managerial decisions in hiring, promoting, and firing salespeople.

Ethical Concerns of Sales Managers

As the company's personal contact with customers, the sales force must contend with a variety of ethical problems in product quality and service, pricing, distribution, and promotion. Even though many of these problems are largely the responsibility of headquarters marketing, salespeople and sales managers must bear "the heat" from angry customers who complain to them.

According to a nationwide sample of 2,500 households studied by the U.S. Office of Consumer Affairs (OCA), 75 percent of all consumer complaints are about the poor quality of products and services and 70 percent of these complaints are never remedied. OCA researchers concluded that most private industries and government agencies are inept in handling consumer complaints and do an inadequate job of informing the public about how to file and follow through on complaints. Other major findings of the OCA study were:

- A third of households had one or more consumer problems in the last year.

- The largest number of consumer complaints was directed at the automobile industry, followed by appliances, mail service, clothing, telephones, food, and household items.

- Twelve percent of the consumers said that the problems they had with shoddy products were so severe that personal injury could have resulted.

- One-sixth of the consumers said they lost time from school or work trying to remedy problems with products or services, resulting in an average loss to consumers of about $142.

- Seventy-five percent of consumers will complain if they have problems with a product costing $6 to $10, while 95 percent will complain if the product costs between $500 and $1,000.

- Ten percent of consumers have complaints regarding products or services but do not follow up on them because they feel it is not worth the time and effort, they do not know how or where to complain, or they believe no one will care or bother to solve the problem.[3]

Product quality and service.   Intense domestic and world competition has led some companies to lower their ethical standards to maintain short-run sales and profit levels. Sales managers need to accept the role of spokesperson for customers—if only to protect the company's reputation and long-run profits—whenever they spot any questionable activities. Such activities might include potentially deceptive product advertising, misleading product warranties, odd-sized packages that make price comparisons difficult, concave-bottom bottles that appear to contain more liquid than they do, oversized packages for small products (to gain shelf visibility), or "surrogate indicators" that imply the product has a quality it does not actually possess. Furthermore, sales managers should instruct salespeople to conscientiously avoid any misleading statements to customers about delivery dates, prices, product life, and so forth. It is also a good idea to refrain from making unfairly disparaging remarks about competitive products or services, as Minnesota Mining and Manufacturing (3M) learned when its Static Control Systems Department was accused of using sales demonstrations that "unfairly" denigrated competition by purposely misusing materials and static-measuring devices.[4] Consultative salespeople who are trying to build long-run relationships of mutual trust and confidence with customers should avoid any statements or actions that may result in a loss of personal integrity in the eyes of customers.

Price.   Because some customers buy strictly on price, a few companies will give them a low price but ship them inferior-quality goods, short-weight them, or remain indifferent to their postpurchase service needs. Other companies may routinely inflate price quotes to customers so that they can appear to give a discount later. Although professional sales organizations do legitimately offer price and quantity discounts, trial-use periods, and free samples, it would be clearly unethical to offer prospects or customers cash, free gifts, free goods, or kickbacks to win their business. Even when prospects or customers ask for such gratuities, the ethically sensitive professional salesperson will politely state company policy. Otherwise, the salesperson's and the company's reputations may be compromised. Both parties degrade themselves in such transactions, and even the unethical buyer will usually come to respect and buy from ethical sellers. Moreover, such unethical practices can lead to a serious disruption of normal or profitable sales, as competitors may offer even higher bribes.

There are many vague areas in pricing ethics. For instance, do salespeople have the responsibility to warn customers about upcoming price changes, discounts, or special allowances? In the final analysis, it is up to sales managers to set the professional ethical tone for their salespeople through their words and, more importantly, their actions.

Distribution.   The major ethical concerns in distribution revolve around the proper degree of control over the channel and whether channel policies are applied fairly and consistently. For example, should a subsidiary or franchisee be compelled to purchase all parts, supplies, materials, or services from the parent organization? Should reciprocity be required from suppliers; that is, should you insist that suppliers buy from you if you are going to buy from them? Should customers involved in ethically questionable business activities be permitted to buy? Should marginal customers who buy only small quantities of a product be served?

Products and services distributed to low-income minority neighborhoods have often been inferior to those delivered to other market segments. Shoddy products, stale food, poor housing, inferior educational systems, inadequate public services (e.g., garbage collection and transportation), price discrimination, and unethical sales practices have from time to time been inflicted on minority markets. Poor people, whether members of a minority or not, are vulnerable to exploitation by greedy sellers because they are generally unaware of their legal rights, dependent on credit, uneducated, and even nonconversant in English. In all fairness to the seller's position, theft, vandalism, bad debts, and robbery are more common in the inner city, where most of the poor live, so business insurance costs are exorbitant. Thus the poor pay more, but ghetto sellers earn less.[5]

Promotion.   Advertising, which is largely under the control of headquarters marketing, is often a source of customer complaints since it is the most visible and maligned of all promotional activities. Salespeople will need to acquaint themselves with perceived ethical problems in advertising and other forms of promotion and report these attitudes to sales management for forwarding to headquarters. Ethical questions in recent years have focused on misleading or deceptive advertising; advertising to children; sexually oriented appeals; and stereotyped portrayals of women, minority groups, and senior citizens in advertisements. Promotion to children, even in subtle forms (such as brand names of cigarettes and beers on beach blankets, hats, or food hampers) has come under frequent attack, especially since children spend or influence their parents to spend more than $30 billion annually.

Antidiscrimination laws and government enforcement agencies have helped erode sex, race, age, and other forms of discrimination. Today, differences in lifestyles, family positions, and occupations of women, blacks, Hispanics, gays, the disabled, senior citizens, and various other minority groups are acknowledged in the promotional efforts of all but the least sensitive sellers.

MANAGING UNETHICAL SALES FORCE BEHAVIOR

Ethical conflicts arise in many selling situations. Since ethics deal to a great extent with individuals' personal moral philosophies and values as well as organizational or even customer values, conflicts are sure to arise. Ethical issues

EXHIBIT 17-3

Business Practices Causing Conflict between Company Interests and Personal Ethics

Percentage of Respondents Reporting:	Sometimes
Giving of gifts and kickbacks	29.3
Fairness and discrimination	22.4
Price collusion and pricing practices	18.4
Firings and layoffs	18.1
Honesty in internal communications (e.g., reports, memos)	16.5
Honesty in executing contracts and agreements	15.5
Honesty in external communications	7.8

Source: Scott J. Vitell and Troy A. Festervand, "Business Ethics: Conflicts, Practices and Beliefs of Industrial Executives," *Journal of Business Ethics*, February 1987, p. 114.

are bound to surface from conflicts between a business's attempts to achieve its organizational objectives and its salespeople's efforts to achieve their own goals. Exhibit 17-3 lists the business practices that most often cause conflict between company interests and personal interests. As the percentages show, ethical conflict arises most frequently from the giving of gifts and kickbacks. Salespeople often encounter this situation when they are attempting to win over customers or when customers pressure them into giving gifts, as illustrated in the *Ethics* scenario below.

Whenever individuals offer or accept gifts they place their own self-interest ahead of those of the organization. Other areas of conflict between company interests and personal ethics include fairness and discrimination, price collusion and pricing practices, firings and layoffs, honesty in internal communications, honesty in executing contracts and agreements, and honesty in external communications. Clearly, these issues and the conflicts they produce do exist in the business environment. Business executives and educators alike recognize this fact and are continually increasing their efforts to resolve such conflicts.

ETHICS IN SALES MANAGEMENT: ON PAR WITH COMPANY POLICY?

You are a sales manager for a large sporting goods manufacturer. Over the years you have become very good friends with the president of your largest account. Recently, while you were playing golf with this person, she mentioned that her game would be improved with a new set of golf clubs. She repeatedly makes such hints, and on one occasion she even said that it "shouldn't be any problem for you to go into the warehouse and pick up a new set of clubs for your best customer. No one would really know!" The fact is that your friend is probably right, as you've heard of this kind of thing going on with other sales executives.

1. What would you do in this situation? Remember, you don't want to upset your best customer.

2. You check into your company's policy regarding gift giving and entertainment and find that no formal written policy exists. Will this change your behavior? Why or why not?

How does a firm manage or even upgrade its ethical standards? A recent survey of senior executives indicated that a firm's ethical standards can be improved through (1) the adoption of a business code of ethics, (2) a more humanistic curriculum in business education, and (3) legislation.[6] Others believe that questionable behavior must be curbed through proper managerial feedback.[7] However, sales managers have a very difficult time monitoring the ethical behavior of their salespeople since the reps often work alone and the managers may therefore not be aware of ethical violations. Sales managers may have difficulty not only in supervising behavior that is not observed or reported but also in supervising behavior that is reported if there is no benchmark or code of ethics to compare the reported behavior with. Clearly, curbing unethical selling practices poses very unique problems for sales managers.

Regardless of their own views on ethical codes, professional sales managers and salespeople ought to be aware of the increasing trend toward personal accountability. Managers are finding it increasingly difficult to hide in the bureaucratic shadows of their organizations. Greater personal accountability will probably influence managers to make more conservative decisions. Some sales executives will always feel that ethics are so complex that a company is better off without a policy. But the mere preparation and distribution of even a general policy can have a positive impact by letting salespeople know that top management is concerned about the company's reputation and the personal ethics of its employees.

Business Codes: Guides to Ethical Behavior

Three types of ethical codes exist in the American commercial environment:

- *Professional codes* for occupational groups such as doctors, lawyers, accountants, marketing researchers, advertisers, or sales representatives
- *Business association codes* for companies engaged in the same line of activity—for example, the American Association of Advertising Agencies
- *Advisory group codes* suggested by government agencies or other special interest groups

The move toward sales and marketing professionalism is being led by various groups such as the Sales and Marketing Executives International, the American Marketing Association, and the American Association of Advertising Agencies—each of which has adopted a code of ethics. Formal codes of ethics for organizations must satisfy two requirements if they are to encourage ethical conduct. First, the codes must refer to specific practices such as kickbacks, payoffs, record falsification, and misleading sales claims. General platitudes about good business practice or professional conduct are not very effective. Second, organizational codes of ethics must be supported by top management and equitably enforced through a system of rewards and punishments. No code of ethical business practices is likely to be observed by the sales force unless violators are promptly disciplined commensurate with the degree of transgression.

Since the passage of the Foreign Corrupt Practices Act (FCPA) in 1977, most large companies have devised or revised written codes of conduct concentrating on overseas payments to increase sales. These codes range from Gulf Oil's one-page "Statement of Business Principles" to codes of worldwide business conduct running ten pages or longer. Unfortunately, some codes seem to be little more than public relations efforts. For example, Grumman Aerospace Corporation adopted a written policy prohibiting overseas payoffs. But when the board of directors asked an outside committee to conduct an audit, it was discovered that not only Grumman salespersons but also high-ranking managers had established a pattern of hiding questionable overseas payments and withholding information from the board.[8]

A Process for Ethical Decision Making

No one can successfully impose his or her ethical value system on others because everyone's background, experiences, beliefs, and perceptions differ so widely. But we should all be consciously aware of the impact of our decisions. Every decision we make reveals our existing selves and serves to mold (for better or worse) our future selves. Quaker Oats tells its employees, "Ethical behavior wouldn't embarrass you, your family or your company if it were revealed publicly." Koppers Company feels that the best test is to think about whether you'd be willing to explain your contemplated action on TV.[9]

John Dewey, a great American educator and philosopher, was impressed by the thorough analysis scientists make of each step in an experiment, and he felt that this approach could be applied to ethical problems. He believed that many decisions are made and actions taken not only without consideration of their moral quality but with little thought at all, almost impulsively. People often excuse themselves from the consequences of some action that turned out badly by declaring that they meant well. In all probability, however, they took no pains to think through the possible consequences of what they proposed to do. To avoid plunging into decisions with merely good intentions, Dewey developed an approach to ethics that he called "reflective morality." It is a method for ethical decision making that leaves the selection of values to the individual. According to Dewey, reflective thought or deliberation is an imaginative rehearsal and evaluation of various courses of action prior to reaching a final decision. Borrowing from Dewey's framework, sales managers and salespeople can follow five steps toward more ethical decision making:

1. List all possible decision-making choices and the possible consequences of each.

2. List people or groups who will be affected by each decision. Remember that "no one is an island." Your decisions touch many other lives and may have far-reaching impact.

3. Try to put yourself in the place of those people most affected by each decision. By putting yourself in the place of others and seeing things from the standpoint of their interests, values, and needs, you help minimize your own needs until they reach the level they would be at from the perspective of an impartial observer.

4. Compare values of the various alternatives, and rank them from the viewpoint of each affected group. Values are things of worth, and each individual assigns worth or lack of it according to the values important to him or her.

5. Make a decision and implement it.[10]

Even though salespeople and sales managers may find this process less than perfect for every situation, what is most important is that they consider the impact of their decisions on all parties and recognize the forces that lead to the final decision.

SOCIAL RESPONSIBILITY

Any discussion of ethical practices in commerce will soon lead to the closely related topic of social responsibility. Kenneth Boulding, in *The Organizational Revolution*, reveals the close relationship between ethics and social responsibility when he defines ethical conduct as "that which is motivated by the larger and more objective interest as against the smaller and more personal interest."[11] Ethics and social responsibility are closely aligned in the minds of most business managers, although sales managers have widely varying views as to the exact meaning of the terms. Most, however, would probably agree that social responsibility implies that business decision makers have some obligation, beyond their individual self-interest, to protect and improve the welfare of society as a whole.

Evolution of Corporate Social Responsibility

Social responsibility in commercial organizations has evolved through three historic phases: profit-maximizing management, trusteeship management, and "quality-of-life" management.

Phase 1: Profit-maximizing management. Throughout most of the nineteenth century and the early part of the twentieth century, management's openly professed objective was to maximize profits. It was widely believed that by operating in its own selfish interest within a competitive marketplace, each business would be guided by an "invisible hand" to create the greatest wealth for the public good. Adam Smith's "laissez-faire" doctrine,[12] Spenser's social Darwinism,[13] and the Protestant work ethic combined to help justify the "rightness" of competitive business activity. Powerful business leaders such as John D. Rockefeller (oil), J. P. Morgan (finance), Cornelius Vanderbilt (railroads), and Andrew Carnegie (steel) were prominent in this profit-maximization era of U.S. business. Derisively referred to as "robber barons," these businessmen competed fiercely. For example, Rockefeller forced the railroads, to whom he gave so much transporting business, to give him a kickback on every barrel of oil that he or his competitors shipped. Enabled thereby to sell his oil at a lower price, Rockefeller eventually bought out his faltering competitors. If his oil company could not economically drive out a competitor, a price-fixing agreement was arranged, benefiting both companies at the consumer's expense.[14] Whole industries operated unscrupulously. Railroads set low freight rates on routes that had competing sources of transportation, but on routes that had little or no competition, rates were much higher. Sometimes, the total cost of transporting goods 300 miles was cheaper than the cost of shipping the same goods only 100 miles. Perhaps Rockefeller himself expressed the collective view of the barons best: "I believe the power to make money is a gift of God . . . to be developed and used to the best of our ability for the good of mankind. Having been endowed with the gift I possess, I believe it my duty to make money . . . and still more money, according to the dictates of my conscience."[15]

Contrary to the view of the barons, the concept of laissez-faire was not working for the benefit of society. If commerce and industry had consisted of only small entrepreneurs, the invisible-hand doctrine might have been valid. But with huge concentrations of economic power, market entry for new competitors was extremely difficult. The "Let the public be damned" attitude held by industrial leaders led to fluctuating economic conditions, monopolistic pricing structures, and finally the Great Depression of the 1930s, which ended wide support for the laissez-faire and invisible-hand doctrines in U.S. business.

Phase 2: Trusteeship management.   In the 1920s the concept of trusteeship management began developing in response to two structural changes: the diffusion of ownership of U.S. businesses and the emergence of a pluralistic society. By the 1930s the largest stockholders in most corporations owned less than 1 percent of the outstanding shares. Although they were legally the owners, individual stockholders were largely powerless to influence corporate operations. Under trusteeship management, corporate executives are responsible for balancing the interests of various groups of company stakeholders—stockholders, employees, customers, suppliers, creditors, and the community. An increasingly pluralistic society brought additional pressures from numerous exogenous groups, including labor unions, government, and consumers.

Phase 3: "Quality-of-life" management.   In the United States, until about 1960, society's major demand on business was that it should raise the standard of living of the people by producing increasing quantities of want-satisfying goods and services. In 1958 John Kenneth Galbraith called the United States "an affluent society." Yet amid all this prosperity the nation suffered pockets of poverty, polluted air and water, a deteriorating landscape, dissatisfied consumers, and social injustice. Faced with a declining social and physical environment, society began to reorder its priorities in favor of the "quality" rather than the "quantity" of life.

Contemporary Views on Management's Social Responsibility

As U.S. managerial philosophy evolved, each subsequent phase tended to connect and integrate with the earlier phase rather than replace it. Thus managerial views on social responsibility today reflect aspects of all previous eras, with prominent scholars and business executives serving as spokespersons for each perspective. Nobel prize–winning economist Milton Friedman advocates the managerial philosophy of phase 1 to maximize return on investment.[16] He contends that a corporate manager is an agent of the stockholders and that any diversion of resources from the task of maximizing profit amounts to spending the stockholders' money without their consent. In his view, governments, not business, are best equipped to handle social problems. Opponents of this view argue that spending stockholders' money to help solve social problems maximizes profits in the long run by avoiding costly interference from government and various special interest groups. One of the more elegant criticisms of the profit-maximizing orientation comes from Kenneth Mason, former president of the Quaker Oats Company:

> I know of no greater disservice to American business in my lifetime than Milton Friedman's widely publicized assertion that business' only reason for being is to generate profits for stockholders. What a dreary and demeaning view of the role of business and business leaders in our society! Making a profit is no more the purpose of a corporation than getting enough to eat is the purpose of life. Getting enough to eat is a requirement of life; life's purpose, one would hope, is somewhat broader and more challenging. Likewise with business and profit.[17]

Understanding the pluralistic nature of our society and the necessity of dealing equitably with the concerns of various contributors and external interest groups, most contemporary managers tend to apply the phase 2 concept of social responsibility in their decision making. However, an increasing number of companies—IBM, Xerox, Coca-Cola, Eli Lilly, Chase Manhattan Bank, Levi Strauss, and Quaker Oats—are especially active in social action programs.

Levels of Social Responsibility

An organization's specific socially responsible actions will depend on the moral and ethical value systems upon which executive decisions are based, beyond legal requirements and market competition. The U.S. Chamber of Commerce states that an organization can be at one of four basic attitude levels with regard to social responsibility, as shown in Exhibit 17-4.

Obeying the law.   At the first level of social responsibility, the organization merely adheres to legal requirements. Refusing to give or accept kickbacks, insisting on truthfulness in personal sales presentations and other promotional efforts, and providing equal opportunity for all employees, regardless of age, sex, or race, are examples of obeying the law as well as applying sound managerial practices.

Meeting recognized public expectations.   Moving to the second level, corporate executives try to satisfy public expectations beyond what is required by law. For example, Polaroid Corporation maintains a 300-person consumer service de-

EXHIBIT 17-4

Levels of Corporate Social Responsibility

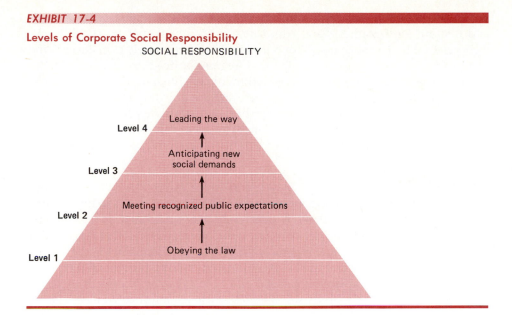

SOCIAL RESPONSIBILITY

Level 4 — Leading the way

Level 3 — Anticipating new social demands

Level 2 — Meeting recognized public expectations

Level 1 — Obeying the law

partment to perform such chores as rewriting advertisements that might mislead buyers and dropping in on Polaroid camera repair centers to check on quality. And because small stores sometimes fail to redress customer complaints, the department makes sure that Polaroid's free service phone number is printed in big type on every product.

Anticipating new social demands.   At the third level, the corporation addresses consumer concerns before problems arise. For example, Oscar Mayer & Company was one of the first meat-packers to date its packages, list the meat's nutrients on the package, and use clear packaging so that consumers can see what they are buying. Stressing product quality while responding in advance to consumer concerns before they become generally recognized has enabled Oscar Mayer to earn consistently higher profits than the industry median.

Leading the way.   At the fourth level of social responsibility, the corporation takes on a leadership role in setting new standards of business social perform-ance. Levi Strauss, IBM, Xerox, and other companies encourage employees to take leaves to participate in social projects. Xerox Corporation has a social service leave program that gives employees a six-month to one-year leave of absence to work on community development programs of their choice. Participants have contributed to a wide variety of programs for the inner city, prisons, and the handicapped. Xerox employees have built wheelchair ramps, cleared land and built picnic tables in a public park, and served as juvenile probation officers. Top management fully supports the program and guarantees that the same or at least an equivalent job will be waiting when the employee returns.

Several banks, particularly those in urban areas, have designated target neighborhoods for community economic development and special housing fi-nancing projects. The Chase Manhattan Bank focused such community redevelopment efforts in the predominantly minority areas of Jamaica, Woodside, and Bedford Stuyvesant in New York City. As Chase chairperson David Rockefeller has said: "The business sector is undertaking increasingly to make genuine headway against major urban problems. More must be done . . . more to promote cooperative efforts among business, government, and the minority communities. But the heartening signs of progress to date suggest a willingness on the part of this vital triad to cooperate, fully recognizing that in striving for solutions they are living up not only to the best of American ideas but also to the widest of American self-interest."[18]

Social Audits

To appraise how they are performing in achieving social goals, many organizations are utilizing social audits. A *social audit* may be defined as a systematic evaluation of and report on some of the company's activities that have social impact. A survey of the annual reports of the 500 largest companies in the United States revealed social responsibility disclosures in over 91 percent of them.[19]

To develop and implement a social audit, an organization needs to assess its selling environment, identify social issues, set social improvement objectives, allocate resources to achieve those objectives, and then regularly measure and evaluate progress in terms of both organizational and societal costs versus benefits. Some form of social accounting is required to let various constituencies or stakeholders know what and how the company is doing. To date, most social accounting has reported on product safety, environmental cleanup or protection, recycling of waste material, and opportunities for women and minorities. Monsanto Company used an audit team, headed by an outside director and drawn from the firm's standing social audit committee, to determine whether it had been involved in bribery or illegal political contributions overseas.

Increasingly, organizations are integrating social responsibility into the mainstream of practice. Instead of being merely an add-on program, social responsibility is becoming an important managerial function for many companies. Gillette has a vice president for corporate integrity who has the authority to take products off the market, stop new-product introductions, halt promotional campaigns and selling tactics, or cancel any proposed actions that might reflect negatively on the integrity of the company.

Some approaches used to collect and report social audit information are:

- *Inventory.* Enumeration of all socially responsible organizational activities, such as minority hiring, training, and promotion programs
- *Cost.* Dollar expenditures on social programs
- *Program management.* MBO approach to establish goals for each socially oriented activity and to monitor progress toward achievement
- *Benefits versus costs.* Various programs' real contribution to society compared with the expenditure of resources in carrying out the program[20]

Many companies are conducting cost-benefit analyses to project the long-run return from various social investments. A managerial flowchart for social de-

EXHIBIT 17-5

The Decision-Making Process for Social Responsibility Issues

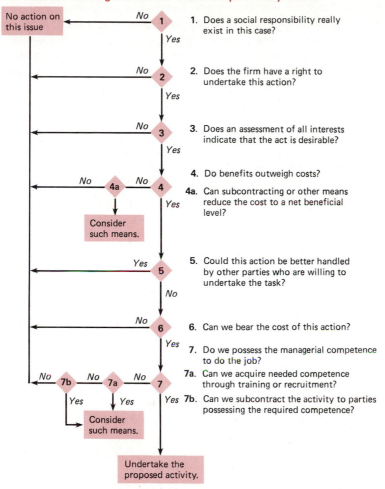

1. Does a social responsibility really exist in this case?

2. Does the firm have a right to undertake this action?

3. Does an assessment of all interests indicate that the act is desirable?

4. Do benefits outweigh costs?

4a. Can subcontracting or other means reduce the cost to a net beneficial level?

5. Could this action be better handled by other parties who are willing to undertake the task?

6. Can we bear the cost of this action?

7. Do we possess the managerial competence to do the job?

7a. Can we acquire needed competence through training or recruitment?

7b. Can we subcontract the activity to parties possessing the required competence?

Source: Adapted from Ramon J. Aldag and Donald W. Jackson, Jr., "A Managerial Framework for Social Decision-Making," *MSU Business Topics*, Spring 1975, p. 34. Reprinted by permission of the publisher, Division of Research, Graduate School of Business Administration, Michigan State University.

cision making (such as the one presented in Exhibit 17-5) can help avoid ill-conceived and poorly executed social actions.

LEGISLATION AFFECTING SELLING AND SALES MANAGEMENT

State and Local Regulation

Among the most important state and local laws and ordinances designed to regulate selling activities are the Uniform Commercial Code, the Green River ordinances, and the "cooling-off rule." The *Uniform Commercial Code* is a basic set of guidelines adopted by most states that sets forth the rules of contracts and the law pertaining to sales. The code includes specific provisions regarding the performance of goods, sellers' warranties, and the maximum allowable rates of interest and carrying charges. Court actions under this code usually concern buyers' claims that salespeople misrepresented the goods or made promises that were not kept. It is critical that the selling organization, in defending itself, be able to provide the court with substantiating sales documentation, including contracts, letters of agreement, and the like.

The *Green River ordinances,* originally passed in Green River, Wyoming, in 1933, are local ordinances requiring nonresidents to obtain a license from city authorities to sell goods or services direct to consumers in that vicinity. Adopted by most metropolitan areas, the laws tend to discourage many companies from trying to distribute their products and services door-to-door on a national basis.

Closely connected to the Green River ordinances is the "cooling-off rule" imposed by the Federal Trade Commission. The rule requires that door-to-door salespeople give written notice to customers who place orders of $25 or more that they can cancel their purchases within three days. This FTC ruling came after years of complaints about high-pressure tactics in selling magazines, jewelry, encyclopedias, cosmetics, and other merchandise house-to-house. Consumers complained about salespeople who gained entrance to their homes by claiming to be pollsters or government inspectors and then gave a sales pitch misrepresenting the product's price or quality.

Federal Regulation

United States legislation regulating business can be divided, according to intent, into two major categories: *protection of companies* from each other and *protection of consumers and society* from unfair business practices. Exhibit 17-6 shows the major federal legislation that has a direct or an indirect impact on selling and sales management activities.

Among the many federal laws regulating business competition, the most important are the Robinson-Patman Act, the Sherman Act, and the Clayton Act. These acts cover a number of issues, including the following: price discrimination, collusion, price fixing, exclusive dealing, restraint of trade, reciprocity, tie-in sales, unordered goods, orders and terms of sale, business descriptions, product descriptions, secret rebates, customer coercion, and business defamation.

Price discrimination.   Section II of the Clayton Act states that it is unlawful for a seller to discriminate in price among different customers when the discrimination has a harmful effect on competition. It is also unlawful for a buyer knowingly to induce or receive a discriminatory price. In order to ensure equality of opportunity for all, sellers are required to treat similar buyers equally with respect to price and terms of sale.

Section III of the Robinson-Patman Act goes so far as to make it a criminal offense to be a party to or to assist in discrimination between competing purchasers. Under the Robinson-Patman Act, a seller cannot sell at different prices in different markets or charge different prices to different purchasers of the same quality and quantity of goods. A price differential or different terms of sale can be defended only on the following grounds: (1) The price differential was given in good faith to meet (not beat) a price offered by a competitor, or (2) the price differential was based upon a *cost saving* that reflects a difference in the cost of manufacture, sale, or delivery resulting from the differing methods or quantities in which products are sold or delivered. For example, price reductions are allowed when based on volume ordered, closeout sales, lower shipping and selling costs, good-faith meeting of competition, and lower commissions paid by the seller to its employee salespeople. All these "cost defenses" will justify a difference in price or terms of sale. For legal protection, sellers should be sure that their accounting procedures reflect cost differences that permit the firm to reduce prices or terms of sale to certain customers.

It is unlawful for competitors to agree to fix prices or stabilize prices, agree to any formula to determine prices, or enter into any agreement that may have even an indirect effect on prices. None of the following arrangements (regardless of whether they are written, oral, formal or informal, or merely mutual expectations) between competitors are legal: dividing or allocating markets, territories, or customers; rigging bids or submitting bids knowing that they will be unacceptable; charging a maximum price; limiting production, setting quotas, or discontinuing a product; boycotting third parties; depressing the prices of raw materials with other raw materials purchasers; establishing uniform discounts or credit terms or eliminating discounts; establishing a system for determining delivered prices or a specific method of quoting prices.

Any discussion of prices, warranties, uniform practices, or industry conditions between competitors is prohibited; in order to avoid any suggestion of cooperation, salespeople and sales managers should refrain from contact with competitors at trade shows and social gatherings.

Collusion. Competitors who conspire to set prices, agree to divide territories on a noncompetitive basis, or join together to act to the detriment of another competitor are involved in illegal collusion.

Price fixing. Competitors who conspire to set or maintain uniform prices and profit margins are involved in price fixing. Even the informal exchange of price information with competitors or discussion of pricing policies at trade association meetings has been found illegal by the courts.

Exclusive dealing. Agreements in which a manufacturer or wholesaler grants one dealer exclusive rights to sell a product in a certain trading area or insists that the dealer not carry competing lines are illegal under the Clayton Act.

Restraint of trade. Under the Sherman Act and the Clayton Act, agreements made with competitors to divide a market into noncompetitive territories or to restrict competition in a market are restraints of trade. Also, dealers cannot be required to refrain from selling competitors' products as a condition of receiving the right to sell the manufacturer's product. However, a unilateral refusal to deal with a price-cutter is not illegal so long as there is no effort on the manufacturers' part to raise or maintain prices in doing so.

EXHIBIT 17-6

Key Legislation Affecting Selling and Sales Management

Intended to Regulate Business Competition

- *Sherman Antitrust Act (1890).* Prohibits "monopolies or attempts to monopolize" and "contracts, combinations, or conspiracies in restraint of trade" in interstate and foreign commerce.

- *Federal Trade Commission Act (1914).* Established the FTC as a body of specialists with broad powers to investigate and to issue cease-and-desist orders to enforce Section V, which declares that "unfair methods of competition in commerce are unlawful."

- *Clayton Act (1914).* Supplements the Sherman Act by prohibiting certain specific practices (certain types of price discrimination, tying clauses, exclusive dealing, intercorporate stockholdings, and interlocking directorates) "where the effect . . . may be to substantially lessen competition or tend to create a monopoly in any line of commerce." Provides that violating corporate officials can be held individually responsible.

- *State Unfair Trade Practices Acts (1930s).* Prohibit "loss-leader" pricing (selling below cost). Laws are still in effect in about half the states.

- *Robinson-Patman Act (1936).* Amends the Clayton Act by strengthening the prohibition of price discrimination (subject to certain defenses). Provides the FTC with the right to establish limits on quantity discounts; to forbid brokerage allowances except to independent brokers; and to prohibit promotional allowances, services, or facilities except where made available to all "on proportionately equal terms."

- *Wheeler-Lea Act (1938).* Amends the FTC Act; prohibits unfair and deceptive acts and practices whether competition is injured or not.

- *Lanham Trademark Act (1946).* Regulates brands and trademarks.

- *Consumer Goods Pricing Act (1975).* Repeals federal "fair-trade laws" and state laws allowing manufacturers to set retail prices.

- Deregulation laws for specific industries:
  Natural Gas Policy Act (1978)   Staggers Rail Act (1980)
  Airline Deregulation Act (1978)   Depository Institutions Act (1981)
  Motor Carrier Act (1980)

Intended Primarily to Protect Consumers

- *Pure Food and Drug Act (1906).* Regulates labeling of food and drugs and prohibits manufacture or marketing of adulterated food or drugs. Amended in 1938 by Food, Drug, and Cosmetics Act.

- *Meat Inspection Act (1906).* Regulates meat packing houses and provides for federal inspection of meats.

- *Textile labeling laws.* Require manufacturers to indicate what their product is made of:
  Wood Products Labeling Act (1939)   Flammable Fabrics Act (1953)
  Fur Products Labeling Act (1951)   Textile Fiber Products Identification Act (1960)

- *Automobile Information Disclosure Act (1958).* Prohibits car dealers from inflating the factory price of new cars.

- *Kefauver-Harris Drug Amendments (1962).* Requires that drugs be labeled with their generic names, that new drugs be pretested, and that new drugs are approved by the Food and Drug Administration before being marketed.

- *Fair Packaging and Labeling Act (1966).* Provides for the regulation of the packaging and labeling of consumer goods. Requires manufacturers to state what the package contains, who made it, and how much it contains. Permits industries' voluntary adoption of uniform packaging standards.

- *National Traffic and Motor Vehicle Safety Act (1966).* Provides for safety standards for tires and automobiles.

- *Child Protection Act (1966).* Bans sales of hazardous toys and other unsafe articles. Amended in 1969 to include articles that pose electrical, mechanical, or thermal hazards.

- *Cigarette Labeling and Advertising Acts (1966, 1969).* Requires manufacturers to label cigarettes as being hazardous to health and prohibits TV advertising of cigarettes.

- *Consumer Credit Protection Act (1968).* Truth-in-lending law that requires lenders to state the true costs of a credit transaction, outlaws the use of actual or threatened violence in collecting loans, and restricts the amount of garnishments.

- *Fair Credit Reporting Act (1970).* Ensures that a consumer's credit report will contain only accurate, relevant, and recent information and will be confidential unless requested for an appropriate reason by a proper party.

- *Consumer Product Safety Act (1972).* Established the Consumer Product Safety Commission and authorized it to set safety standards for consumer products as well as exact penalties for failure to uphold the standards.

- *Consumer Goods Pricing Act (1975).* Prohibits the use of price maintenance agreements among manufacturers and resellers in interstate commerce.

- *Magnuson-Moss Warranty/FTC Improvement Act (1975).* Authorizes the FTC to determine rules concerning consumer warranties and provides for consumer access to means of redress, such as the class action suit. Also expands FTC regulatory powers over unfair or deceptive acts or practices.

- *Equal Credit Opportunity Act (1975).* Prohibits discrimination in a credit transaction because of sex, marital status, race, national origin, religion, age, or receipt of public assistance.

- *Fair Debt Collection Practice Act (1978).* Makes it illegal to harass or abuse any person and make false statements or use unfair methods when collecting a debt.

- *FTC Improvement Act (1980).* Provides the House of Representatives and Senate jointly with veto power over FTC trade regulation rules. Enacted to limit the FTC's powers to regulate "unfairness" issues. In effect, it reverses the trend toward more FTC protection of consumers.

Reciprocity. Selecting only suppliers who will also purchase from the buyer ("You buy from me and I'll buy from you") is illegal, but not so illegal as to prevent companies from doing it. Some companies even have a "trade relations" department to keep track (by computer) of reciprocal buying arrangements with various suppliers.[21] The Federal Trade Commission took nearly a year to investigate the competitive practices of American Standard Company, a manufacturer of plumbing, heating, and air-conditioning products. American had a director of sales coordination whose job was to coordinate the firm's reciprocal trade agreements. With the cooperation of American's purchasing, sales, finance, and traffic departments, detailed information was maintained on purchases from

American by its suppliers. Beyond this, American kept its funds in banks whose borrowers were involved in building projects utilizing American Standard products. Since these practices are prohibited by Section V of the Federal Trade Commission Act, American Standard agreed to stop such activities and even eliminated the position of sales coordinator.

Surveys indicate that the majority of purchasing agents and sales managers dislike reciprocity, and many sales managers feel it should be an illegal practice.[22] Unless the buyer is getting competitive prices, quality, and service from the reciprocating seller, the practice is seldom economically justifiable. A study of company practices indicates that reciprocity has been declining as a result of more aggressive enforcement of antitrust laws.[23]

Tie-in sales. Purchasers cannot be forced to buy an unwanted item or items in return for being allowed to purchase a product in heavy demand.

Unordered goods. Section V of the FTC Act prohibits companies from shipping unordered goods or shipping larger amounts than ordered, hoping the buyer will pay for them.

Orders and terms of sale. Under the FTC Act, it is illegal for sellers to substitute goods different from those ordered, misrepresent delivery dates, fail to fill an order, or not fill an order within a reasonable time. Terms or conditions of sale cannot be misrepresented. Key terms of sale include warranties or guarantees, the ability of the buyer to cancel a contract or obtain a refund, and the important facts in a credit or financing transaction.

Business descriptions. Often during a sales presentation, a salesperson will provide information about his or her company. Salespeople must never misrepresent their company's financial strength; length of time in business; reputation; or facts concerning its plant, equipment, or facilities.

Product descriptions. Salespeople must not misrepresent the method by which a product is produced. For example, it is illegal to state that a product is "custom-made" or "tailor-made" when it is ready-made. Furthermore, no statements can be legally made about "proven" claims unless scientific or empirical evidence has been obtained to establish the truth of such claims.

Secret rebates. It is illegal to reward a dealer's sales team for sales of your company's products without the consent of the salespeople's employer. Also, even if the dealer management approves such an incentive, this practice may still be a violation of the Sherman Act if it results in unfair discrimination among competing dealers.

Customer coercion. It is unlawful to make fictitious inquiries which irritate a competitor or which pressure anyone into buying a product through coercion, intimidation, or scare tactics.

Business defamation. Hundreds of companies and manufacturers' agents have been sued by competitors for making slanderous statements about the competitors that resulted in financial damage, lost customers, unemployment, or lost sales. Not only can private lawsuits be brought against offenders, but also the Federal Trade Commission is empowered to impose a cease-and-desist order or injunction on companies that engage in unfair or deceptive practices through their salespeople. Business defamation can include the following offenses:

- *Business slander.* If an unfair and untrue oral statement is made about a competitor, the statement becomes actionable when it is communicated to a third party and can be interpreted as damaging the reputation of the competitor or the personal reputation of an individual in that business.

- *Business libel.* If an unfair and untrue statement is made about a competitor in writing (usually a letter, sales literature, advertisement, or company brochure), the statement becomes actionable when it is communicated to a third party and can be interpreted as damaging the competitor's reputation or the personal reputation of an individual in that business.

- *Product disparagement.* If false or deceptive comparisons or distorted claims are made concerning a competitor's product, services, or property, the defamation is actionable when made during or after the sales presentation.

- *Unfair competition.* Injury to a competitor may also result from falsely advertising one's own product, misrepresenting the qualities or characteristics of the product, or engaging in a related unfair or deceptive trade practice.

Negative statements made by a salesperson during or after the sales presentation can be especially troublesome. The law treats these statements as defamatory per se; that is, a company or defamed individual does not have to prove actual damages to successfully win a verdict—proof that the statement is untrue is sufficient. Below are the kinds of statements that are personally defamatory:

- Untrue comments depicting a competitor as engaging in illegal or unfair business practices

- Untrue remarks claiming that a competitor fails to live up to contractual obligations and responsibilities

- Untrue statements regarding a competitor's financial condition

- Untrue statements implying that a principal in the competitor's business is incompetent, of poor moral character, unreliable, or dishonest

In order to avoid this kind of trouble, it is recommended that the sales manager do the following:

1. *Review all promotional material and sales correspondence before distribution* to minimize the possibility that defamatory material is inadvertently distributed by the sales force. In one recent case, a company offered a free roll of film with each roll developed. The company being sued had distributed sales literature claiming that such practices were inflationary and made possible

only by the use of inferior developing practices. The court found that the assertions were personally defamatory because they implied that the competitor's president was deceptive and dishonest in his business. It further found that the statements disparaged the quality of the competitor's product. As a result, the court awarded damages of $394,400.

2. *Tell the salespeople not to repeat unconfirmed trade gossip,* particularly about the financial condition of a competitor.

3. *Tell salespeople to avoid statements that may be interpreted as damaging to the reputation of a business or individual.* One company was ordered to pay $105,000 because it had circulated an unfairly critical letter about a competitive product to potential customers.[24]

4. *Ensure that salespeople avoid making unfair or inaccurate comparisons about a competitor's product.* Mere "puffing," or claiming superiority over a competitor's product, is not disparagement as long as the comparison attempts to enhance the quality of your product without being unfairly critical of the competitor's product. But it is unlawful to make a statement or pass along untrue or misleading information that tends to influence a person not to buy.

5. *Avoid sending customers written comparisons of competing products.* In one court case, a company was sued for $1 million after it bought a competitor's product, analyzed it, and distributed a printed pamphlet through its sales force that was unfairly critical of the competing product.[25] One way to make comparisons is to support factual claims with scientific facts or statistical evidence documented or prepared by an independent research firm.

International Regulation of Sales

International sellers must cope with three different sets of laws restricting their operations. First, a multinational company must comply with U.S. laws, which, for instance, forbid U.S. companies to trade with some foreign countries such as North Korea, Cambodia, and Vietnam. Second, the multinational firm must also obey the laws of any country in which it operates even though they may differ sharply from U.S. laws. Many times, foreign laws are less stringent, perhaps allowing the sale of banned U.S. products such as cyclamates as food sweeteners; thus moral and ethical issues are raised for the company. In other cases, foreign laws are more restrictive; for example, France prohibits door-to-door selling. At times, foreign regulations may be applied somewhat capriciously, as Colgate discovered in Greece. Although free samples, coupons, and contests have been widely used to promote products abroad, Greece sued Colgate for giving away razor blades with its shaving cream.[26] Finally, the multinational firm is subject to international laws that are enforced across national boundaries. Both the United Nations and the European Economic Community are standardizing commercial codes, such as environmental and product safety standards, that are binding on all companies whose nations consent.[27]

In some countries, personal selling must be done inconspicuously. For example, in Europe, door-to-door salespeople are considered an intrusion on personal privacy, and European industrial buyers do not like to be seen with sales representatives in public. Therefore, private areas are set aside at trade shows where negotiations between buyers and sellers can be conducted out of sight of potential competitors.[28] Sometimes, the salesperson-customer relationship is even ritualistic, as buyers and sellers prefer to know and trust one another on a personal basis before conducting business. A Rockwell International vice president and salesperson made seven trips to Venezuela trying to close a sale for three jet transports. Prospect contact was always long, with several four-hour lunches, yet the product and terms of sale were barely mentioned on several visits. Instead, conversation ranged from foreign policy to women, as the prospects wanted to size up the U.S. sales representative before getting down to business. Such negotiations are common even in dealing with suppliers. An Associated Dry Goods manager seldom could persuade his Italian suppliers to discuss business until dinnertime—around 10 P.M.—each day.[29] As irritating as such idiosyncracies may seem to U.S. salespeople, it is wise to adapt if one expects to sell successfully outside the United States.

When first planning to sell products or services to a foreign country, sellers should check with the U.S. Department of Commerce for information about each country's legal restrictions on imports and U.S. restrictions on exports. For example, sales of some categories of technological equipment and processes are restricted by U.S. law or by edict of the State Department or Defense Department, and such items will not be allowed to leave the country. Then, before beginning any transactions within the foreign country, the sales manager should contact the commercial attaché at the U.S. embassy for information on the legal requirements for conducting business there.

Because the United States has been experiencing adverse trade balances, the U.S. Commerce Department is providing special incentives and substantial assistance to sellers who seek international markets. Already, the Department of Commerce has developed a computerized international trade information system to provide data on foreign business contacts, market conditions, and international trade shows. Tie-ins with private vendors allow sales organizations to obtain worldwide market data through telephone, telex, or computer terminals. Countries such as Japan, the United Kingdom, and The Netherlands have more experience than the United States in selling internationally, since they sell well over half their output abroad. However, several U.S. companies already derive more than 50 percent of their revenue from abroad; they include Pan Am World Airways, Exxon, Citicorp, Texaco, Mobil, Colgate-Palmolive, Caterpillar, Coca-Cola, Dow Chemical, Ford, Gillette, Gulf Oil, IBM, ITT, Kodak, Pfizer, and Xerox.[30]

People in the United States have already seen how successful "export strategies" have been in increasing the economic power and standard of living in Japan and other Asiatic countries. As one British manager put it: "Our home market has become someone else's international market. Either we must build products for international markets or not build products at all."[31] The United States is in this very situation today. Unless U.S. businesses can develop and market products that equal or exceed those of any world competitor, the domestic market will be lost to foreign imports. The nation's sales executives can ill afford to be complacent about foreign competition when it is so strong in their own country, and among the most respected and best-rewarded executives of the decade ahead will be those who strengthen their companies' competitiveness in world markets.

SUMMARY

Ethics, social responsibility, and the legal environment all affect selling and sales management activities. Business ethics deal with the relationship between business practices and the moral concept of right and wrong. Salespeople and sales managers are subject to three different perspectives on ethical standards, which may not coincide. In fact, organizational, professional, and personal ethical standards may frequently come into conflict. It is the job of the sales manager to guide salespeople in balancing such pressures and to try to bring the three ethical perspectives into healthy harmony. Salespeople must be sensitive to their ethical behavior in dealing with the company (their employer), their coworkers, and customers. John Dewey suggested reflective thought, or evaluation of various courses of action and their impact on others, in a five-step guide to ethical decision making.

Closely related to ethics is the concept of social responsibility, which implies that business decision makers have some obligation, beyond their self-interest, to protect and improve the welfare of society as a whole. Social responsibility in commercial organizations has evolved through three phases: profit-maximizing management, trusteeship management, and quality-of-life management. The U.S. Chamber of Commerce states that corporations can be functioning at one of four distinct levels of social responsibility: obeying the law, meeting recognized public expectations, anticipating new social demands, or leading the way. Social audits can help companies appraise how they are performing in achieving social goals.

Domestic and international selling and sales management activities are regulated by state and local laws and ordinances, federal regulation, international laws, and legislation within a particular foreign country. Some laws are designed to protect companies from vicious competition among themselves, while other laws are designed to protect consumers and society from harmful business practices. Interpretation of laws covering such offenses as business slander, business libel, product disparagement, and unfair competition can be subtly applied, and sales managers must accept full responsibility for ensuring that salespeople avoid violations in the heat of battle with competitors. Every member of a sales organization must remain up to date on all the regulations and laws that affect selling activities.

STUDY QUESTIONS

1. Why should business ethics be a topic of concern for sales managers? Isn't it enough for the sales force to operate within the law? Why or why not?

2. As a sales manager, would you try to develop a code of ethics for the sales force? If so, what role would individual salespeople have in developing the code? What penalties would you exact for violations?

3. When selling in a foreign country, should you apply your company's ethical standards or the standards of the country you are in? What problems might your choice of standards create for you?

4. Which of the levels of social responsibility discussed in the chapter most closely fits your own philosophy? Explain why.

5. Do you think corporate social audits are a good idea? Why or why not?

6. What personal guidelines do you utilize in deciding what is ethical behavior for you?

7. Project yourself ahead to the year 2010. Do you think sales managers will be less or more concerned about the issues of ethics and social responsibility? Why?

IN-BASKET EXERCISE

You are a district sales manager for an electronics firm that markets to industrial users, and you have recently been receiving complaints from customers about late deliveries. It appears that, on occasion, several of your salespeople promised customers certain delivery dates without checking with the product and shipping departments. As a result, the products reached the customers a day or two after the promised delivery date. When you confronted your salespeople with this issue, they claimed, "Everyone in the industry does it," and said, "The competition is getting so intense that we have to do it to compete." Moreover, your salespeople told you that an "on-time delivery is more of an exception than the rule for the industry."

1. Should anything be done in this situation? Why or why not?

2. Would establishing a code of ethics on the issue of "overpromising" help in this situation? Why or why not?

3. How would you develop a code of ethics for your company in this situation, and how would you enforce it?

CASE 17-1

ALTOR, INC.: DEVELOPING A COMPREHENSIVE CODE OF ETHICS FOR ITS SALES FORCE

ALTOR, Inc., is a manufacturer of a wide range of parts and equipment for the music industry. The company, established in 1965, is located in Nashville, Tennessee. ALTOR started as a supplier of parts and equipment to the recording studios in the Nashville area. As the popularity of country and western music grew during the 1970s and 1980s, so did sales at ALTOR. Originally, the company operated with three central partners: Johny Carter, who was in charge of production; Vickee Dee, who managed the finances; and Conrad Cash, who represented the sales force for ALTOR.

By 1992, ALTOR, Inc., was a major supplier of a variety of musical parts and equipment throughout the United States. During the 1980s, it moved its sales operations into the Memphis, New Orleans, and Detroit markets. ALTOR's goal was to be a viable competitor in the Los Angeles and New York City markets by the mid-1990s. The company's sales force grew to twenty salespeople in 1992, and there are plans to hire an additional six more in the next several years. Since ALTOR is a relatively small company, its strategy has been to hire reps who have selling experience in a music-related industry. Hiring experienced salespeople has worked well for ALTOR, as sales training has been limited to product knowledge. Compensation is a combination of salary plus commission, and sales force turnover for the company has been very low.

As a result of the increasing awareness of business ethics in the 1980s and 1990s, management at ALTOR is beginning to get concerned about whether or not the salespeople can handle ethical dilemmas. The music industry is a very competitive, cutthroat business. All three managing partners of ALTOR have been in the music business all their lives and are well aware of the ethical dilemmas that can arise on a day-to-day basis. While there have not been any major complaints or problems with their salespeople, the partners believe that it is time to investigate the possibility of developing a usable code of ethics for the sales force. They feel that such a code will do a great deal to preserve the first-class company image they have built over the last twenty-five years.

Questions

1. What influences a salesperson's behavior concerning ethical decision making? Why is this important for management to consider?

2. Are there any unique problems sales managers may have in dealing with ethics that other types of managers may not have? What are they?

3. How might the contingency framework for ethical decision making that was presented in the chapter help ALTOR in dealing with ethical dilemmas?

4. Develop a code of ethics for the sales force at ALTOR. What specific points are needed in this code? Why?

CASE 17-2

ETHICS AND LEGISLATION IN THE INTERNATIONAL SELLING ENVIRONMENT

The personal jet taking Joe Carter to his sale's presentation in Africa was just cleared for arrival in Wonderbloom, Senegal. Joe always wanted to work in the field of international marketing, and now his first job after college, a sale's position with Quazelle Aviation, is affording him the opportunity to do just that. While his permanent residence is in Memphis, Joe has made a number of sales visits to Europe over the last two years. This trip, his first sales visit to Africa, will give him his first exposure to how business is conducted in developing nations. To take his mind off his nervousness, Joe returned to reviewing the presentation he would soon make to several government procurement ministers.

Quazelle Aviation has been selling aircraft parts and supplies for many years. Recently, the company has expanded its product line to include equipment that reduces noise levels in older jet aircraft. This product-line expansion is in response to regulations several nations have passed that prohibit loud aircraft from landing at their airport terminals. The market for noise-reduction equipment is a new one for Quazelle, and it is largely found in developing nations. This is because the noise prohibitions have not been a problem for major airlines with modern fleets, as the newer airplanes have technological advances already built in that reduce the noise. In the developing world, airlines cannot afford to buy new airplanes, so they are forced to purchase older, used planes from the world's major airlines. For the most part, the planes are years behind the latest technology and suffer tremendously in regard to high noise levels. This has created a promising opportunity for Quazelle Aviation.

Managers at Quazelle have specifically targeted African nations as needing the noise-reducing equipment. The aviation industry in Africa has been growing rapidly over the last decade, despite the fact that the number of passengers flying in Africa has actually decreased. The low demand for air travel, coupled with the growth of government-owned airlines, has created an overcapacity in the airline industry. There are now over thirty national airlines serving the continent of Africa. Most of these airlines regularly lose vast sums of money, and their operations must be subsidized by the governments. Besides low demand for their services, there are numerous other problems facing the airlines in Africa, including the need for large capital investments, inadequate airport facilities, lack of trained personnel, and obsolete and dangerous fleets.

With these severe problems plaguing the airlines, it is clear that financial considerations play a small role in the growth of national airlines. In fact, the development of the aviation industry has largely come about because many African governments perceive national airlines to be a showpiece of their nations. Furthermore, national pride has led these African countries to require aircraft that can land at major noise-restricted cities such as London and Paris. Without equipment like that made by Quazelle, it would be difficult to comply with the imposed noise restrictions, as the cost of purchasing new fleets of modern aircraft would be prohibitive.

Joe was the leader of the marketing team that was arriving in Africa to attempt to sell Quazelle's equipment. Wonderbloom, Senegal, was the team's first stop. A short layover was required to refuel and service the plane after the ten-hour flight from the United States.

The Senegalese were very hospitable to the American sales team, offering the group a ride into town to eat and take a brief tour of the city while the plane was being serviced. After accepting the offer, Joe had a good dinner at the Hilton Hotel and took a short drive around town. Then he headed back to the airport with the sales team to continue their journey. At the airport, Joe was somewhat bewildered by the situation he encountered. The airplane had been moved to a far corner of the airfield and was surrounded by armed soldiers. The crew had been removed from the plane and was observing the situation from the tarmac. Upon discussing the situation with the pilot, Joe discovered that the authorities had decided to inspect the airplane while the sales team was away. Besides providing transportation, the private jet served as a demonstration model for a number of Quazelle's advanced products. When the authorities discovered the plane had several expensive modifications, they decided to raise the predetermined landing fee of $500 to $20,000. The inspectors had concluded that since Joe and his team were flying an expensive aircraft, they could also afford to pay an expensive landing fee.

Joe was furious and could not figure out how to get his plane returned. He had certainly never encountered such a situation on his trips to Europe. When negotiations with the inspectors did not produce results, Joe decided to call a business associate, Buddy Thompson, in the United States. Buddy handled the international operations of a major airline and was familiar with business conditions in Africa. Buddy laughed when he heard Joe describing the incident in a panicked voice. "Don't worry, Joe," he said, "just take the $500 you carry with you, go see the airport manager, and tell him that the people of Memphis hope he will accept this $500 donation on their behalf for airport improvements." Joe did what Buddy instructed. After accepting the gift, the airport manager said, "As a matter of fact, we are planning on paving the taxiway where your plane is now sitting, and it is therefore most important that the plane be moved immediately and without delay." Joe was more than happy to comply. The landing fee was waived, and the inspectors wished the team a safe trip and a quick return. Joe later learned from Buddy that the delay he experienced was a common occurrence. Not surprisingly, the taxiway that needed repair had not been paved in twenty years of operation and probably never would be.

The next stop for Joe was the country of Lughawe. His plane landed smoothly, and Joe gathered his luggage and the materials that the team would need for the presentation the next day. He also brought with him samples of some of the equipment that he would be attempting to sell. Joe proceeded to customs and declared the items he was bringing into the country. The customs agent appeared to be stalling; he reinspected the samples several times and questioned Joe in depth about their origin and content. Confused at the delay and interrogation, Joe assumed that he had encountered another situation in which a little cash would be needed to get things moving. "Well, how much money do you want so that I can pass?" Joe asked the customs agent in a rather smug voice. The agent suddenly became visibly irritated and marched off. Just then, a man standing behind Joe pulled him aside and whispered, "It is not a good idea to bribe these officials openly with cash. You can get the agent into a lot of trouble and find yourself spending a while in jail. Here, when the agent returns, thank him for his help and give him these few packs of cigarettes for his kindness." Joe followed the man's instructions and the agent let Joe pass. Outside the airport Joe again thanked the man who had given him the advice. John Turner introduced himself and explained to Joe that he was a salesman with a British farm implement company and had been doing business in Africa for over twenty years. "It is not easy to do business in this area of the world," Turner confessed. "One of the difficulties in Africa is knowing which officials to bribe and how to do it. In some cases it's necessary; in other cases, it can land you in jail." Joe could see that foreign business practices, especially in Africa, were much more complex than he had first anticipated.

Joe awoke the next morning in his hotel in Lughawe. The first meeting of the day was with Lughawe's minister of transportation. As in many African countries, Lughawe's airline was owned and operated by the government. Management of the airline was handled by the Transportation Ministry, and major purchases were decided personally by the minister. Joe had been briefed about the minister before arriving in Lughawe. The current socialist government had come into power shortly after the country's independence from a colonial power, and the minister of transportation had obtained his post because he was a friend and supporter of the general who led the revolt. His primary qualification for the position was that he had been a bus driver before the revolution. Joe knew that if any equipment was to be sold to the national airline, approval would need to come from the minister.

The meeting with the Transportation Ministry was pleasant. Because the minister was unable to read, a secretary was brought in to read aloud all written documents and brochures that Joe and his team had brought with them. After listening to Joe's presentation and hearing the cost of the equipment, the minister agreed that he would like to purchase the equipment for the country's aircraft. The secretary was asked to prepare a letter of introduction to the finance minister so that financial arrangements for the purchase could be worked out.

Unlike the transportation minister, the finance minister was well trained for his post, having received his graduate degree in economics from a university in the United States. Minister Tendahi explained to Joe that while some officials had obtained their positions because they had been active participants in the revolution, others, like himself, had recently returned to Lughawe to help the country prosper and develop.

After reading the letter the transportation minister had provided, Minister Tendahi agreed that the country would indeed like to purchase the equipment Joe was selling, but he added that regrettably it did not have the cash to do so and, because of the country's poor credit rating, probably could not obtain financ-

ing. Joe became discouraged upon hearing this. "But we might be able to work something out," Minister Tendahi said in an eager voice and with a smile. "Oh no," thought Joe, "is this another situation where someone wants a bribe? What am I supposed to do this time? If bribing the customs agent can land you in jail, I wonder what the penalty for bribing a minister might be. On the other hand, what if that is the only way to get things done, as was the case in Senegal." But to Joe's relief, the minister went on to suggest that Joe consider a trade arrangement in which copper from Lughawe could be exchanged for the equipment. Joe's company could then find a buyer for the copper in the United States and eventually receive payment.

Questions

1. What should Joe have done before taking his international sales trip to help him cope with the cultural changes?

2. With so many problems facing African nations, do you feel that national pride is sufficient justification for maintaining airlines? Why or why not?

3. Should Joe have paid the airport manager to get his plane back and leave the country? Should he have given the customs agent the packs of cigarettes? Is there a difference between the $500 paid to the airport manager and the cigarettes given to the customs agent? Should Joe have paid off the Minister of Finance if he had been asked to do so. Why or why not?

4. Could there be an international business code of ethics? Why or why not? Would it be practical?

REFERENCES

1. Personal interview with Rick Huddleston, November 1990.
2. O. C. Ferrell and John Fraedrich, *Business Ethics: Ethical Decision Making and Cases*, Houghton Mifflin, Boston, 1991.
3. *Marketing News*, Feb. 22, 1980, p. 8.
4. *Sales & Marketing Management*, May 18, 1981, p. 32.
5. See Walter B. Wentz, *Marketing*, West, St. Paul, Minn., 1979, p. 550; David Caplovitz, *The Poor Pay More*, Free Press, Glencoe, Ill., 1963; Bureau of Labor Statistics, *Retail Food Prices in Low and Higher Income Areas*, U.S. Government Printing Office, Washington, D.C., 1974; Donald F. Dixon and Daniel J. McLaughlin, "Do the Inner City Poor Pay More for Food?" *Economic and Business Bulletin*, Spring 1968, pp. 6–12; Robert G. Mogull, "Where Do We Stand on Inner City Prices?" *Southern Journal of Business*, July 1971, pp. 32–40; Charles Goodman, "Do the Poor Pay More?" *Journal of Marketing*, January 1968, pp. 18–24; Donald E. Sexton, Jr., "Comparing the Cost

of Food to Blacks and to Whites—A Survey," *Journal of Marketing,* July 1971, pp. 40–46; Donald E. Sexton, Jr., "Do Blacks Pay More?" *Journal of Marketing Research,"* November 1971, pp. 420–426; Robert B. Settle, John H. Faricy, and Richard W. Mizerski, "Racial Differences in Consumer Locus of Control," in Fred C. Allvine (ed.), *1971 Combined Proceedings,* American Marketing Association, Chicago, 1971, pp. 629–633; Alan R. Andreasen, *The Disadvantaged Consumer,* Free Press, New York, 1975; Howard Kunreuther, "Why the Poor Pay More for Food: Theoretical and Empirical Evidence," *Journal of Business,* July 1973, pp. 368–383.

6. "Ethical Behavior," *Wall Street Journal,* Jan. 18, 1988, p. 13.

7. Patrick E. Murphy and Mark G. Dunn, "Marketing Ethics: Empirical Views," paper presented at American Marketing Association Winter Educators Conference, 1988; Joseph A. Bellizzi and Robert E. Hite, "Supervising Unethical Salesforce Behavior," *Journal of Marketing,* April 1989, pp. 36–47.

8. Jack G. Kaikati and Wayne A. Label, "American Bribery Legislation: An Obstacle to International Marketing," *Journal of Marketing,* Fall 1980, pp. 38–42. Also see Barbara J. Coe, "The Questionable Foreign Payments Controversy: Dimensions of the Problem," in Barnett A. Greenberg and Danny N. Bellenger (eds.), *Contemporary Marketing Thought, 1977 Educators Proceedings,* American Marketing Association, Chicago, 1977, pp. 473–476.

9. William J. Maus, "Business Ethics: An Inside View," *Pennsylvania CPA Spokesman,* September 1981, p. 29.

10. John Dewey, *Ethics,* Holt, New York, 1908; John Dewey, *Logic: The Theory of Inquiry,* Holt, New York, 1938; John Dewey, *The Theory of Moral Life,* Holt, 1960.

11. Kenneth Boulding, *The Organizational Revolution: A Study in Ethics of Economic Organization,* Quadrangle Books, Chicago, 1968.

12. Adam Smith, *The Wealth of Nations,* Random House, New York, 1937. Original printing 1776.

13. Richard Hofstadter, *Social Darwinism in American Thought,* rev. ed., Beacon-Press, Boston, 1955.

14. Matthew Josephson, *The Robber Barons,* Harcourt Brace, New York, 1934, p. 196.

15. Ibid., p. 10.

16. Milton Friedman, *Capitalism and Freedom,* University of Chicago Press, Chicago, 1962.

17. *Business Week,* Aug. 13, 1979, p. 14.

18. David Rockefeller, "Corporate Responsibility: A Call for Joint Business Investments in Society," *Black Enterprise,* March 1972, p. 85.

19. *Social Responsibility Disclosures: 1977 Survey of Fortune 500 Annual Reports,* Ernst & Ernst, Cleveland, Ohio.

20. A. H. Kizilbash, William O. Hancock, Carlton A. Maile, and Peter Gillett, "Social Auditing for Marketing Managers," *Industrial Marketing Management,* January 1979, pp. 1–6. Other insights on social audits are found in Raymond A. Bauer, "Corporate Social Audit: Getting on the Learning Curve," *California Management Review,* Fall 1973, pp. 5–10; Donald R. Hudson, "Measuring the Quality of Life," *Atlantic Economic Review,* May–June 1977, pp. 15–21; Robert W. Nason, "Internalization of Corporate Social Costs," in Howard S. Gitlow and Edward W. Wheatley (eds.), *Developments in Marketing Science, Volume II, Proceedings of the Third Annual Conference of the Academy of Marketing Science,* 1979, pp. 354–358.

21. Velma A. Adams, "The Rise of the Trade Relations Directors," *Dun's Review,* December 1964, p. 35; Edward McCleary, Jr., and Walter Guzzardi, Jr., "A Customer Is a Company's Best Freind," *Fortune,* June 1965, p. 180; "Trade Relations Men Walk Shaky Tightrope," *Business Week,* Oct. 5, 1968, p. 96; Reed Moyer, "Reciprocity: Retrospect and Prospect," *Journal of Marketing,* October 1970, pp. 47–54; Reed Moyer, "Reciprocity Is Dead," *Sales Management,* Oct. 15, 1970, p. 27.

22. F. Robert Finney, "Reciprocity: Gone but Not Forgotten," *Journal of Marketing,* January 1978, pp. 54–59.

APPENDIXES

THE PERSONAL SELLING PROCESS

Professional selling requires sales representatives to develop an effective, systematic approach adaptable to the particular customer type and selling situation. Although several different steps may be identified in the selling process, depending upon the degree of specificity desired, there are seven major stages: (1) prospecting, (2) planning the sales call (often called the "preapproach"), (3) approaching the prospect, (4) making the sales presentation, (5) dealing with prospect objections, (6) closing the sale, and (7) following up on the sale.

PROSPECTING

If sales representatives hope to increase or even maintain sales volume, they must continually seek out or prospect for new customers. In fact, more salesperson time is required for prospecting than any other selling activity.[1] In prospecting, salespeople must obtain *leads* on people who may have a need for the company's product or service. To turn a lead into a *prospect*, the lead must be qualified in terms of need or want, ability to buy, authority to buy, and eligibility to buy.

Qualifications

Need or want. Trying to sell your product or service to people who don't need or want it is simply a waste of time and effort. Industrial salespeople often find that initial contact with their leads usually enables them to determine whether there is a genuine need or want. Sometimes, however, people's needs or wants can be unrecognized or latent until the salesperson points them out. For example, an office manager may not feel the need for a word processor until the salesperson points out the advantages. Experienced salespeople do not try to sell products to people who do not want them. Not only would this probably be futile, but it would also be unethical even if successful over the short run. Salespeople want to sell products to customers in such a way that the products don't come back but the customers do.

The SIC codes (discussed in Chapter 4) can often be valuable in generating leads for industrial products and services. But for many consumer products, telephone solicitations or direct mail inviting people to ask for additional information may be preferred means for generating leads.

Ability to buy. The individual or organization must have the ability to buy. Local credit services, banks, Better Business Bureaus, other customers, or even competitors can provide information about the lead's ability to buy. For organizations, credit rating services such as Dun & Bradstreet can indicate financial condition. Usually, those without ready cash can buy on credit or can rent the item. If the lead just doesn't have the wherewithal to buy or make payments, there is little use in pursuing the negotiations, for the item may have to be repossessed later.

Authority to buy. Most sales representatives have wasted many hours talking to some person with an official-sounding title who did not have the authority to make the purchase decision. Although a purchasing agent may have the formal authority to buy a piece of machinery, sometimes the final decision may have to come from the operations manager or the machine operator. In organizations, the purchasing decisions are usually made by buying committees instead of any one individual.

Even at the consumer level, salespeople may find that a decision to buy a household appliance is shared. Perhaps one spouse decides what brand to buy, while the other chooses the model or features.

Eligibility to buy. Life insurance salespeople know that many unhealthy people who would like to buy life insurance at regular rates cannot pass the medical examination and thus are ineligible. Similarly, many people would like to purchase products at wholesale, but manufacturers and wholesalers would alienate and lose their retail customers if they sold to the general public.

When the lead qualifies on all four criteria—need, ability, authority, and eligibility to buy—the individual or firm can be declared a *prospect*. There are several approaches to locating and qualifying prospects, as outlined in Exhibit A-1. Six major ones will be discussed here.

Prospecting Methods and Strategies

- *Centers of influence*. Join various organizations or participate in activities where you can meet and interact with influential people who may become customers or refer prospects to you.

- *Spotters*. Persuade ordinary working people (such as retail clerks and secretaries) to provide leads and information to you about prospects, usually for a fee.

- *Endless chain*. Ask everyone you call on for the names of potential buyers.

- *Observation*. Be alert to changes or events in your territory that might affect your sales, for example, births, graduations, marriages, and job promotions. Reading daily newspapers is one basic way to find such leads.

- *Advertising*. Effective advertising should stimulate interest in your offerings and encourage potential customers to initiate the contact.

- *Cold canvassing*. Simply knocking on doors in a promising neighborhood or calling people listed in the telephone book to uncover prospects is inefficient but oftentimes effective in generating sales.

- *Internal records*. Obtaining information from company records (for example, customer lists for other products) may reveal many potential prospects.

- *Service personnel*. Ask repair people and other personnel who visit customers to tell you when customers need to buy again. For example, garage mechanics can tell you who is in need of a new car.

- *Directories or mailing list*. In this computer age, a directory or mailing list has been or can be compiled for just about any group of people you might be interested in—for example, people who subscribe to a type of media (sports, financial, homemaking), different professional groups (doctors, lawyers, college professors, architects), or people who have recently achieved something (those who have just graduated from high school or who have just been listed in *Who's Who in America*).

- *Contests*. Contests to obtain inquiries from people who may be interested in your product are frequently conducted through the mail by organizations selling real estate, vacations, or magazines.

- *Group or party plans*. Tupperware, Aloe Charm, and other party plan approaches are used to show many people the products at once, saving time and stimulating word-of-mouth interaction.

- *Trade shows and exhibits*. Displaying and demonstrating products at trade shows or exhibits where interested people tend to gather is a way to acquire many names and addresses for later follow-up sales calls or mailings. For example, computer software exhibits are good ways to introduce new software to innovators who will influence others.

- *Sales representatives*. Exchange information on prospects with other sales representatives (either colleagues or competitors). For instance, a salesperson may sell a new heating plant system to a customer and notice that the customer also can use a new fire alarm and protection system.

Major Prospecting Methods

Centers of influence. By joining country clubs, civic organizations, professional associations, fraternal orders, and other groups, salespeople have the opportunity to meet influential people who may become customers or who can assist the sales reps in meeting potential customers. While interacting in these centers of influence, salespeople need to operate in a low-key and gracious manner that makes their occupation seem only incidental to, and not the reason for, meeting people.

Spotters. Sales associates, or "spotters," are people who seek out leads for salespeople and are sometimes paid a fee. Probably the best spotters are current customers who provide referrals to potential prospects. But nearly anyone who deals with the public can be a spotter, including secretaries, retail clerks, taxi drivers, route drivers, mail carriers, police officers, and even competitive salespeople.

Endless chain. Current customers and especially new buyers have a vested interest in praising your product because they want to alleviate their own anxiety by justifying their purchase.[2] Frequently, they are even willing to provide testimonial letters as satisfied customers. By using referrals and recommendations from satisfied customers, the sales representative can develop an endless chain of leads. But the salesperson must ensure that all customers receive satisfaction; otherwise, the referral chain can be broken. Paying a fee for referrals is not uncommon, as shown in the following example about the self-professed "best salesperson" in the world.

THE WORLD'S BEST SALESPERSON?

According to the *Guinness Book of World Records*, Joe Girard is the world's greatest salesperson. Girard, who was the top car salesperson in America for over a decade, sold nearly a thousand cars yearly out of a Detroit Chevrolet dealership. Today, he makes even more money by writing books (e.g., *How to Sell Anything to Anybody*), making videotapes, and conducting eight-week training courses for salespeople.

Girard has great confidence in himself and works at keeping it. Every morning when he gets out of bed, he looks in the mirror and says: "You are the most terrific, most beautiful guy in the whole world." He even wears a gold pin on his lapel proclaiming himself as No. 1, and as he puts it: "I am the best. Numero uno. And you know why I'm the best? I believe in myself. . . . If you want to sell anything, you have to sell yourself, you must have self-respect, that is, you must believe you're number one."

When he sold cars, he used two full-time assistants. The assistants greeted prospective customers and took them on demonstration rides. Once the customers were prepped, Joe Girard took over. He took each customer into a tiny office where they sat 2½ feet from each other—never more because "you've got to keep the electricity going, maintain close eye contact, shut everything out but me and what I've got to say. People always look at salesmen like they're liars, cheats, out to rob them of their money. But I'm their friend. I give everyone this button which says: 'I like you.'"

Girard believes in paying close attention to prospects' body language. If their eyes narrow or they perspire or cross and uncross their legs, he changes the subject and talks about the football game or politics—anything to make them relax. And then he moves back in. Girard insists that he's not a phony. People sniff out phoniness, he claims, and he elaborates: "No one who's insincere will ever be a successful salesman. Sixty-five percent of my customers are repeats. That's because I treat them the way they want to be treated. I take care of them because if I treat them right, they'll bring in more customers." (To help ensure that they do, he pays a $25 commission for any referral of a potential car buyer.) "I never stop working," says Girard, "I'm the best—but I can be better."

Joe Girard's Sales Tips

1. Let the prospective customer know that you want to be a friend—and don't give the customer a chance to decline your offer of friendship. Never ask questions that can be answered yes or no.

2. Let the customer try the product to his or her heart's content. Girard tells the prospective buyer to take any car, and he suggests, "Maybe you should drive it by your house and show it to your wife." According to Girard, "Once the wife sees her husband in a brand new car, she's going to feel excited. And he's bound to feel important." Thus, it's going to be really tough to bring it back to the dealership.

3. Use flattery, but be certain the flattery is sincere. "How can anyone walk away from someone who's interested in him?"

4. Never interrupt or attempt to upstage a prospective buyer.

5. Make your customers work for you. The most important selling begins after the sale when you make sure that the customer is satisfied.

6. Follow through after your sale. "I'll go all the way to the top people at General Motors to help someone who got stuck with a lemon," says Girard.

7. Quote a reasonable price, regardless of the customer's knowledge on this point. Sooner or later, the customer is going to find out whether or not the price was fair, so if you want repeat business and a good reputation, treat all customers fairly.

8. Never pressure a customer—and not just because it isn't nice to do. "I don't use hard-sell techniques," Girard claims, "because they don't work."[3]

Observation. Organized observation, especially reading local newspapers, can provide salespeople with many leads. Local newspapers contain information on marriages, births, deaths, automobile accidents, fires, new construction, job offerings, and promotions; such items are all sources of leads, since they indicate a change in people's needs for various products or services. Also, by merely driving around or talking to various people doing everyday activities, salespeople can gather information about possible prospects. For example, if a salesperson hears that certain companies are seeking new employees, he or she can conclude that they are probably expanding and will need to purchase new production and office equipment.

Advertising. Many sales organizations do not adequately follow up on direct telephone or letter inquiries from people who come across the company's advertisements in newspapers, the Yellow Pages, direct-mail pieces, and trade or popular magazines or on bulletin boards, television, and radio. A survey by the Center for Marketing Communications found:

- Eighteen percent of all people requesting information never got any material.

- Forty-three percent of the people got it too late to be of value.

- Seventy-two percent of the inquirers were never contacted by a sales representative.[4]

Not responding quickly to inquiries is rather like ignoring customers who walk into your retail store. All companies need a systematic response procedure for following up *all* inquiries because these are usually "hot prospects."

Cold canvassing. With tangible products that nearly everyone can use, such as cosmetics or vacuum cleaners, cold canvassing can be productive, especially if other lead-generating methods aren't working.

Securing appointments with people by telephone can be an effective way simultaneously to secure and to qualify leads, because people who agree to sales interviews are likely prospects. Preplanning steps for telephone prospecting are listed in Exhibit A-2.

PLANNING THE SALES CALL (THE PREAPPROACH)

After qualifying a prospect as a potential customer, the sales representative must plan how best to approach the prospect. In this preapproach stage, the salesperson needs to obtain strategic information about the prospective buyer, and ensure a favorable reception. A call-sheet format needs to be developed to record valuable prospect information. One example of a call sheet for an industrial customer is provided in Exhibit A-3.

EXHIBIT A-2

Precall Planning for Telephone Prospecting

1. Establish criteria for qualifying prospects, for example, type and size of the prospect's business, financial condition, and probably applications of the product or service.

2. Develop a list of prospects (using the criteria above) from sources such as (a) the Yellow Pages, (b) trade journals, (c) membership lists of trade associations, (d) the local chamber of commerce.

3. Determine each prospect's ability to pay (credit rating) through (a) Dun & Bradstreet, (b) local credit rating bureaus, (c) your own credit department.

4. Set specific objectives for your call.
   a. Try to sell at least a small order over the telephone, so you can get the prospect on your account books.
   b. Gather valuable information by preparing fact-finding questions.
      (1) Use basic questions to help you determine if the potential customer is a valid prospect: "Do you currently use the product?" "Do you have a need for a product like this?"
      (2) Use searching questions that require a detailed response: "What questions do you normally ask in considering a product like this?"
      (3) Use questions that begin with *who, what, where, why,* and *how:* "About how much time does it take you to complete the task using your current product?" "What do you think is the best benefit you'll derive from the product?" "How would you change the product if you could?"

5. Prepare an opening statement.
   a. *Identify yourself and your company:* "Good morning, Mr. Banning. How are you today? I'm Paul Rafferty of Cosmos Computers."
   b. *Make an interest-creating comment* that will focus the prospect's attention on your product or service: "I just heard that Dream Kitchens has added another branch in Center City. Congratulations on your continuing growth. I'm calling because I know you'll want to see a demonstration of our fantastic new computer software program that will allow your customers (while in your showroom) to design graphically what they want in a new kitchen by keying in answers to just a few questions. It's unbelievable how much communication with customers is enhanced when you both can see what you're talking about directly on the computer screen."
   c. *Establish rapport* to reduce negative reaction to the call.
      (1) Make a friendly remark about something of general interest such as the weather or holiday season coming up: "As cold as it's been lately, I'll bet you're getting new customers from people just intending to duck into your beautiful showrooms to get that free cup of coffee and to keep warm while looking at the latest kitchen styles."
      (2) Mention something that you and the prospect have in common: "Do you sometimes find it difficult to understand what customers really want from their verbal descriptions?"
      (3) Say something to stimulate pride: "Since your company won the 'Most Progressive Business' award last year, I know that you are in the forefront of innovation."
      (4) Tactfully acknowledge that he or she is a busy person: "I know that you are a very busy person, especially during this time of the year, so just let me briefly describe how the program works."

6. Prepare the sales message.
   a. Stress benefits over features of products and services.
   b. Use a positive, upbeat, and vivid sales vocabulary: (1) expressive, emotion-creating adjectives; (2) dynamic, powerful words with unique impact; (3) personal words, such as "you, me, we, I"; (4) phrases that paint positive mental pictures.

7. Anticipate and prepare responses to potential prospect objections. Usually, the prospect simply wants a major reason to buy or more explanation to support the purchase decision.

8. Prepare potential closes of the sale. Practice different closes until you become familiar with a close for any given situation.

9. Prepare the wrap-up when a sale is made over the telephone: (a) confirming the order and its details, (b) arranging for the next call, (c) expressing your thanks.

10. Prepare your request for an appointment with the prospect, especially if no sale is made:
    a. Include a lead-in such as the following: "I would like to meet with you to show you how our system works and how it can significantly increase your sales while reducing costs."
    b. In requesting the appointment, give your prospect a choice: "Would eleven o'clock Thursday morning or two o'clock Friday afternoon be better for you?"

Call-Sheet Example

Firm   Barring Manufacturing Company

Address: Street   48th and Downing Streets

City and State   Canyon View, Wyoming

Telephone   (278) 984-2761

CUSTOMER CHARACTERISTICS

Type of Business: [X] Manufacturer   [ ] Utility   [ ] Retailer   [ ] Process

[ ] Wholesaler   [ ] Foundry   [ ] Mine/Quarry   [ ] Service

[ ] Service   [ ] Not-for-profit   [ ] Petroleum

[ ] Other _____

Buying Pattern: [ ] Weekly   [ ] Monthly   [ ] Semiannually   [ ] Yearly

[X] As needed   [ ] Seasonal   [ ] Other _____

Products Bought	Annual Purchases	Our Share	Brand Preferred	Other Suppliers
1. Power tools	$ 2,800	$ 500	Baxton	Baxton Industries Acme Electronics
2. Ball bearings	$ 1,400	$ 250	Wilson	Wilson Company Peabody Corp
3. Electrical parts	$ 3,600	$ 850	Barring	Baxton Industries North Electronics Cannon Corp
4. Valves	$ 2,200	$ 400	Superior	Superior Supply Peabody Corp Sand Valves Co.
5. Gaskets	$ 1,800	$ 600	Barring	Superior Supply Wilson Company
6. Pipe	$ 1,300	$ 200	Superior	Peabody Corp Wilson Company
7. Chain drives	$ 2,800	$ 800	Peabody	Superior Supply Derk & Jon, Inc
8.				
9.				
Totals	$15,900	$3,600		

KEY CUSTOMER CONTACTS

Calling Hours	Department	Names/Responsibilities
8 - 11 a.m. M,W,F	Purchasing	1. Mac Burns - Electrical Parts 2. P. D. Jones - Ball Bearings 3. L. J. Bergman - Purchasing Dir. 4.
9 a.m. - 2:30 p.m. M,T,W,Th	Engineering	1. Sam Katz - Gaskets 2. Bill Midgley - Valves 3. "Ace" Thompson - Chain Drives 4.
8 a.m. - 4 p.m. M,W,Th	Production	1. J. K. Brodbeck - General Manager 2. Pete Rocowski - Head Foreman 3.

Obtaining Strategic Information

Nearly everything you can learn about prospects can be strategically useful. At a minimum you should learn the potential buyer's full name, position, title, educational background, level of technical knowledge, authority in the company with respect to buying your product, normal buying behavior, and personality traits. Moreover, the salesperson ought to take time to learn as much as possible about the prospect's family, hobbies, interests, political views, and lifestyle.

When approaching organizations, the salesperson needs to understand the total buying situation. This includes the relative competitive position of the firm in the industry, its formal and informal organizational structure (especially with regard to purchase influences), basic objectives and goals of the company, and its major customers, current problems, and opportunities. Some of this information can be obtained from general sources such as trade associations, chambers of commerce, government and public libraries, and investment houses. Some valuable sources for specific information on potential customers are listed in Exhibit A-4. In addition to gathering secondary data, salespeople may make a preliminary call on the prospect to obtain firsthand preapproach information. Industrial buyers know that a sales representative should fully understand and analyze their purchasing needs before he or she can prescribe solutions, so they tend to cooperate in providing necessary information in fact-finding preliminary call interviews.

Ensuring a Positive Reception

One way to help ensure a favorable initial reception is to ask one of your company's top executives to set up an appointment with a top executive in the prospect company so that key members of the seller team can meet the buyer team. Another way the salesperson can improve his or her reception is to send the prospect a useful sales promotion gift (such as a nice ballpoint pen or calculator), along with a personal letter and brochure providing basic product information, in advance of the actual sales call. Where possible, the letter and information should be tailored specifically to meet each prospect's needs and to meet sales call objectives. Many sales managers utilize the management-by-objectives (MBO) system to make sure that salespeople understand and agree on what accomplishments are expected. If the sales organization does not use MBO, sales representatives should set up their own personal planning objectives in writing, using convenient, workable formats, such as those shown in Exhibits A-5 and A-6.

Prior to outlining their travel routes, sales representatives must call for appointments in order to avoid noncontact and excessive waiting time in the prospect's office. After appointments have been confirmed, the sales call route should be planned to minimize traveling time and expense. It is a good idea to reconfirm each appointment ahead of time on the scheduled day to make sure your prospect is not absent from work and has not been called into an unexpected meeting.

Sources of Information on Potential Customers

Trade Association Directories

Encyclopedia of Associations (Gale Research Company, Detroit):
Vol. 1, *National Organizations of the U.S.*, lists organizations alphabetically (by name, address, convention schedules).
Vol. II, *Geographic and Executive Index*, contains an alphabetical list of the association executives with a cross-reference to Vol. I by city and state.
Vol. III, *New Associations and Projects*, continuously updates information between editions of Vols. I and II.

National Trade and Professional Associations of the United States and Labor Unions (Columbia Books, Washington, D.C.) contains data on over 4,700 organizations, trade and professional associations, and national labor unions.

Directory of Corporate Affiliations (National Register Publishing Company, Skokie, Ill.) cross-references 3,000 parent companies with their 16,000 divisions, subsidiaries, and affiliates.

Business Guides

Moody's Industrial Manual (Moody's Investor Service, New York) provides seven years of statistical records and financial statements on each company, principal officers and directors, major plants, products, and merger and acquisition records.

Reference Book of Corporate Managements (Dun & Bradstreet, New York) identifies over 30,000 executives who are officers and directors of 2,400 large corporations.

Standard & Poor's Corporation Services (Standard & Poor's Corporation, New York) provides various services, including: *Industry Surveys* (trends and projections); *Outlook* (weekly stock market letter); *Stock Guide* (monthly summary of data on 5,000 common and preferred stocks); *Trade and Securities* (monthly listing of statistics on business, finance, stocks and bonds, foreign trade, productivity, and employment).

Standard & Poor's Register of Corporations, Directors and Executives (Standard & Poor's Corporation, New York):
Vol. I includes an alphabetical listing of 36,000 national corporations, with names and titles of top executives, and annual sales.
Vol. II contains an alphabetical list of 75,000 directors and executives in the United States and Canada.
Vol. III indexes corporations by SIC and geographical area.

Standard Directory of Advertisers (National Register Publishing Company, Skokie, Ill.) lists over 17,000 companies and their agencies doing national and regional advertising, grouped by type of business and by state and city. Entries include names of top executives in finance, marketing, advertising, and purchasing, along with annual sales and product distribution methods.

Indexes

Business Periodicals Index (H. W. Wilson, New York) is a cumulative subject index listing business articles from over 160 periodicals.

The Wall Street Journal Index (Dow Jones, Princeton, N.J.) is an index of all *Wall Street Journal* articles arranged into corporate news and general news.

F&S Index of Corporations and Industries (Predicasts, Cleveland, Ohio) covers company, industry, and product information on American companies from 750 business-oriented newspapers, financial publications, and trade magazines.

F&S Index of International Industries, Countries, Companies (Predicasts, Cleveland, Ohio) provides information on foreign companies classified by SIC code and alphabetically by company name.

Applied Science & Technology Index (H. W. Wilson, New York) is a cumulative subject index to periodicals in the fields of science (for example, aeronautics, chemistry, construction, engineering, telecommunications, and transportation).

Government Publications

Survey of Current Business (U.S. Department of Commerce, Bureau of Economic Analysis, Washington, D.C.) updates 2,600 different statistical series in each monthly issue. Includes data on gross national product, national income, international balance of payments, general business indicators, employment, construction, real estate, domestic and foreign trade.

Monthly Catalog of United States Government Publications (Superintendent of Documents, U.S. Government Printing Office, Washington, D.C.) is a comprehensive list, by agency, of federal publications issued each month.

Monthly Checklist of State Publications (Superintendent of Documents, U.S. Government Printing Office, Washington, D.C.) lists state publications received by Library of Congress.

Census data. Extensive source of information on the United States. Includes:

- *Bureau of the Census Catalog of Publications.* An index of all Census Bureau data, publications, and unpublished materials.
- *Census of Retail Trade.* Provides data on the number of retail operations, sales, payroll, and personnel by primary metropolitan statistical areas (PMSAs), counties, and cities with populations of 2,500 or more by kind of business.
- *Census of Wholesale Trade.* Same as above but for wholesalers.
- *Census of Selected Services.* Data on hotels, motels, beauty parlors, and other retail service organizations.
- *Census of Housing.* Detailed data on various housing characteristics, including occupancy, financing, equipment, and facilities by state, metropolitan areas, and city block.
- *Census of Manufacturers.* Various data on manufacturers, including value added, employment, payrolls, new capital expenditures, cost of materials, and value of shipments for 450 manufacturing industries classified by geographic region and state, employment size, and type of establishment.
- *Census of Population.* Number, social and economic description, and cross-classification of inhabitants for metropolitan statistical areas, urban areas, and all locales of 1,000 people or more.
- *Census of Agriculture.* Data for all farms and for farms with sales of $2,500 or more by county and state.

EXHIBIT A-5

Major Account Sales Plan

Date 1/6

Sales Engineer Ed Yardley   Region/District Office Miami

Customer/Prospect Colfax Co.   Address 219 W. River St.

Objective	Achievement Date	Primary Contact	Specific Actions	Achievement Date
Win contract for heating plant system	9/15	Max Coates, Purchasing Agent	1. Take Max to see Superior Co's system—set up with Bob Star.	8/15
			2. Get computer analysis of cost savings with new system.	8/20
			3. Develop financial plan for Colfax Co.	8/30
Increase annual order for APX lubricant by 25%	10/10	Jim Box, Plant Mgr. Sam Yorski, Plant Supr.	1. Make appointment with Jim and Sam to demonstrate new, improved APX.	10/1
			2. Use computer analysis to show APX's cost advantages over "Big Man" brand lubricant.	10/5
			3. Offer 10% discount to increase order size by 25%.	10/7

EXHIBIT A-6

Territory Sales Plan

Fiscal Year 1987/88

Sales Engineer Ed Yardley   Region/District Miami

Customer	Sales History*			Sales Forecast, 1988	Sales by Product*		
	1985	1986	1987		X	Y	Z
Clemons	287	293	295	300	200	75	25
Giant	189	191	188	195	105	60	30
Bullman	175	182	194	210	120	80	10
Sampson	110	114	119	125	70	42	13
Actipro	105	101	97	100	68	22	10
UDB	93	94	94	95	57	20	18
Billips	74	81	82	84	61	15	8
CanDoCo	66	68	71	73	55	7	11
Penticap	45	48	51	53	44	3	6
Balltop	36	29	33	35	27	5	3
Sacko	22	26	27	28	19	8	1
Brothers	8	9	9	10	6	2	2
Peter & Sons	0	0	4	5	2	2	1

*Sales reported in $000.

APPROACHING THE PROSPECT

Depending upon the selling situation, several methods can be effectively used to approach the prospect, including the introductory approach; mutual acquaintance, or reference, approach; customer benefit approach; compliment, or praise, approach; free gift, or sample, approach; question approach; product, or ingredient, approach; and dramatic approach.

Introductory Approach

Too many salespeople use a perfunctory introductory approach followed by a second approach. Salespeople never get a second chance to make a first impression, so they should make sure their introduction is well thought out and smoothly executed. Initial greeting of the prospect should not be trite or too glib. A friendly, smiling greeting and a sincere, firm handshake are the key both at the beginning and end of the sales call. In their introduction, sales representatives should identify themselves by name and by company (for instance, ''Good morning, Mr. Webster, I'm Charlie Bivens from General Mills, here for our 9 A.M. appointment''). Many sales representatives present a business card at this point so that the prospect can refer to it, if needed, to call them by name. Some salespeople prefer to wait until the close of the interview, for emphasis.

Mutual Acquaintance, or Reference, Approach

Mentioning the names of several satisfied customers who are respected by the prospect (even if they are competitors) can be a very compelling approach (e.g., ''Your colleague Bob Franklin, at Magna Chemical Products, has just switched to our process, and so have four of the top five chemical companies in the area''). One top salesperson always asks new customers to give him the names of their five most influential friends who might be interested in the product or service. Testimonial letters from satisfied customers can be especially valuable in selling products or services that involve high investment or social risk—for example, home computers, consulting services, or jewelry. Salespeople must avoid mere name dropping because prospects will often contact the referenced person before buying. Therefore, be sure that the individual will verify your testimonial.

Customer Benefit Approach

Prospects, whether individuals or organizations, seek to solve problems or obtain benefits through their purchases. Moreover, they generally have one predominant or determinant buying motive, which the salesperson should identify and appeal to. Examples of the customer benefit approach include the following:

- ''Do you know that you can save 20 percent or more on your fleet automobile expenses by using our leasing plan?''
- ''Did you know that our Model 600 microcomputer is faster, more powerful, and easier to carry than any other microcomputer available?''

- "Independent research companies have judged our electronic typewriter to be the best value in the market for companies like yours."
- "By converting your insurance policy to our new family plan, you can get $50,000 more coverage at the same price you're paying now."

Compliment, or Praise, Approach

If conveyed subtly, a sincerely delivered compliment can be a positive approach to a prospect and can set a pleasant atmosphere for the interview. Many prospects (or, for that matter, people in general) are anxious for positive feedback or praise. An indirect compliment is often more effective than a direct one, which may be dismissed as mere flattery. Some examples of complimentary approaches are:

- "Congratulations on your recent promotion to assistant purchasing director."
- "Your secretary is really efficient and thoughtful. She called me Thursday morning to let me know that you would be out of town last Friday and couldn't keep our appointment. I wish that all my customers had such considerate secretaries."
- "Your office is so attractively designed, and your staff so congenial, that one of the highlights of my week is calling on you."

Free Gift, or Sample, Approach

Door-to-door salespeople long ago discovered that a cosmetic sample or free brush can help establish goodwill and gain entry to a prospect's home. Similarly, professional salespeople can offer a luncheon invitation, a free seminar, trial use of a product, or a small sample of services (e.g., an estate planning suggestion, a home estimate, or investment advice) as a means of approaching prospects. Salespeople must keep in mind, however, that legal and ethical guidelines must not be violated in using this approach.

Question Approach

Asking questions involves prospects in two-way communication early, since responses are required. Moreover, other information (such as the level of prospect interest) is inadvertently provided when prospects respond to questions. One type of question helps qualify prospects—for example, "If I could show you how your organization can increase profits by 15 percent or more by using our Salesperson Routing Program, would you be willing to give me a half hour of your time?" Such a question necessitates thoughtful consideration by the prospect, quickly separates the "lookers" from the "buyers," and moves the salesperson along the path to an early sales close if the subsequent sales presentation meets prospect expectations. Most salespeople avoid asking questions that prospects are likely to answer negatively. The classic "May I help you?" which many retail salesclerks use mechanically makes it all too easy for the prospect to brush the salesclerk aside with an equally mechanical response, "No thanks, I'm just looking." A customer benefit approach might call for a question format to involve the prospect in a conversation (e.g., "What features or benefits do you want most in a new television?") leading to a potential sale.

Product, or Ingredient, Approach

Some salespeople like to carry a sample of the product or at least a graphic mock-up when first approaching prospects. This allows prospects to see exactly what the salesperson is selling and permits smooth transition into the sales presentation or demonstration. A cutaway cross section of a new type of heavy-duty truck battery or hydraulic pump or a customized computer printout for a prospect can significantly enhance the impact of the first contact with potential customers.

Dramatic Approach

Should other approaches fail, the salesperson can turn to a dramatic or attention-getting gimmick. Vacuum cleaner salespeople have been known to scatter sawdust or dirt around a room prior to demonstrating their product. Some salespeople have placed $5 on the prospect's desk and announced, "If I can't show you in the next twenty minutes how our product will do all that I said it would, keep the five dollars." Often, they let the prospect keep the $5 anyway, since it is a relatively inexpensive way of ensuring attention. More dramatic approaches are sometimes employed, such as setting fire to a bogus dollar bill while declaring, "Let me show you how you can stop burning up your hard-earned dollars."

The danger in using the dramatic approach is that the prospect may resent such blatant showmanship and become defensive. Salespeople should use this approach only when they are confident that the prospect will be receptive to it. Although the approach should spark prospect interest and create a positive atmosphere for the sales interview, the main persuasive effort should be focused on the presentation.

MAKING THE SALES PRESENTATION

Each prospect will project a different personality, but salespeople can usually classify prospects into one of several basic categories, which aids in developing an appropriate selling strategy. Exhibit A-7 outlines some common prospect categories and suggests a general selling strategy for each.

Various communication tools can aid the sales representative in the sales presentation by bringing into play more dramatically all the prospect's senses: sight, hearing, touch, smell, and taste. Where possible, it is particularly effective to allow the prospect to participate in a demonstration of the product or service. Videotape players, video cameras, videodisc players, overhead projectors, tape recorders, filmstrip projectors, movie projectors, slide projectors, and portable

EXHIBIT A-7

Prospect Categories and Strategy

- Skeptical *Sid and Sally*. Be very conservative in the sales presentation. Avoid puffery, stay with the facts. Understate a little, especially in areas where the prospect is very knowledgeable.

- Silent *Sam and Sue*. To get Silent Sam or Sue to talk, ask questions and be more personal than usual. Get them to tell you about some of their interests, problems, successes.

- *Paula and Pete* Procrastinator. Summarize benefits that will be lost if they don't act quickly. Reassure them that they have the authority and the ability to make decisions. Use a little showmanship to overcome their indecision.

- *Gussy and Garfield* Grouch. Ask questions to get at any underlying problems. Try to get them to tell their story.

- *Edith* Ego *and Ollie* Opinionated. Listen attentively to whatever they say, agree with their views, cater to their wishes, and flatter their egos.

- *Irma and Irwin* Impulsive. Speed up the sales presentation, omit unneeded details, and hit the highpoints. Try to close early if the situation seems right.

- *Mary and Melvin* Methodical. Slow down the sales presentation to adjust your tempo to theirs. Provide additional explanations for each key point and include many details.

- *Teresa and Tim* Timid or *Carol and Corey* Cautious. Talk at a gentle, comfortable, deliberate pace. Use a simple, straightforward, logical presentation. Reassure them on each key point.

- *Tom and Thelma* Talkative. Don't allow their continuous "small talk" to take your sales presentation off on a tangent. Listen politely, but try to get back on track as quickly as possible. To get back on track, say something like, "By the way, that reminds me that our product has. . . ." Then, try to wrap up the sales presentation as quickly as you can.

- *Cathy and Charlie* Chip-on-the-Shoulder. Don't argue or become defensive with them. Remain calm, sincere, and friendly. Agree with them as much as you can. Try to show respect for them.

compact computer terminals are some of the many tools available to salespeople. Over 77 percent of companies use audiovisual (AV) support in sales activities.[5] Salespeople should not overlook some of the more traditional but effective visual aids such as product samples or models, flip charts, sales manuals, presentation boards, posters and tables, charts, graphs, and maps. One example of a unique sales aid—a traveling showroom—is described in the next example.

COFFEE ANYONE?

Who said ingenuity has lost its place in selling? One who recently proved otherwise is Melitta, Inc., which strategically and comfortably outfitted a van as a traveling salesroom, then drove around from headquarters to headquarters inviting everyone from buyers to top management of chains and wholesalers to get out of the office and enjoy a cup of fresh coffee and pastry.

The occasion was the introduction of the Melitta coffee maker system into New York and Philadelphia area supermarkets. The problem was showing not only a product but also a different way of brewing coffee—a bit more complex and time-consuming than talking about canned vegetables. The solution was the van. So squarely were the tables turned, in fact, that salespeople—not buyers—were in shirtsleeves on their own turf. Buying committees, usually beyond a salesperson's reach, were cheerfully available.

"We were able to talk to the buyers in a relaxed atmosphere, free from telephone interruptions, with all the facilities we needed for demonstration," says Melitta's national sales manager. "Frequently six or seven top chain executives would visit the van, rather than the one or two we would have been able to see during ordinary office calls. They stayed longer too—and they bought."[6]

In order to prepare an effective sales presentation to achieve precise objectives, sales representatives must understand alternative strategies, summarized in Exhibit A-8: stimulus response, formula, problem solution, need satisfaction, team selling, and depth selling.

EXHIBIT A-8

Basic Sales Presentation Strategies

Strategy	Method	Success Key
Stimulus response	Walks the prospect through a series of leading questions (such as, "Wouldn't you like to earn more on your investments?").	Conditions the prospect to say "yes" all the way through the steps of the selling process until the purchase decision.
Formula	Leads the prospect through the mental states of the buying process (attention, interest, desire, and action).	Leads the prospect to buy, one positive step at a time.
Problem solution	Consults with the prospect to identify problems and alternative solutions.	Helps develop mutual trust while focusing on the prospect's reason for buying.
Need satisfaction	Tries to find the prospect's dominant buying needs; this helps the prospect to clarify his or her real needs.	Focuses on buyer needs and helps salesperson to learn buyer motivations. Generally ensures buyer satisfaction.
Team selling	Uses the talents of several people to deal with the multiple concerns and influences of the buying team.	Increases salesperson's effectiveness and saves time by putting key experts from the buying and selling teams together at the same time. Promotes teamwork and morale.
Depth selling	Utilizes a tailored mix of the above strategies.	Maximizes the impact of the sales presentation and increases the probability of sales success.

Stimulus Response

Stimulus-response strategies call for stimuli (selling points) to be presented in such a way as to obtain favorable responses from prospects while leading them down a desired path to the sales close. While demonstrating the product, the sales representative may ask leading questions (e.g., "Aren't you surprised to see how quietly and smoothly this new electronic typewriter works compared with your current one?") in order to obtain a series of "yes" responses from the prospect. Although this technique is widely used for training new salespeople, it can come across as being artificial and mechanical if too rigidly adhered to. Professional salespeople who deal with sophisticated buyers should use the stimulus-response approach only briefly in conjunction with the product demonstration.

Formula

While permitting more prospect focus and participation, formula strategies still tend to emphasize product features rather than customer needs. AIDA, one commonly employed formula, tries to move prospects toward a purchase decision by sequential development through four mental states: *attention, interest, desire,* and *action.*

Problem Solution

In applying problem-solution strategies, the sales representative makes full use of his or her professional consultative selling abilities. This approach is typically used with more technical selling, in which several solutions or alternatives are explored while a long-run relationship of trust, confidence, and respect is developed. It may require considerable research and the aid of a team of backup technical specialists to prepare a written proposal analyzing the problem, including the advantages and disadvantages of each alternative solution. An electronics company deciding between purchasing robots for an assembly line and upgrading its current equipment would benefit from a problem-solving sales presentation strategy that would analyze the pros and cons of each possible solution.

Need Satisfaction

Need-satisfaction strategies call for no talk about the product or service until the sales representative has discovered exactly what the dominant needs or wants of the prospects are. Prospects are encouraged to reveal their psychographic makeup (attitudes, interests, opinions, personality, and lifestyle) through skillful questioning by the salesperson. Want-satisfaction strategy requires that the salesperson be a patient, perceptive listener and observer of body language in order to really understand "where the prospect is coming from" and what is really wanted. Usually utilized in more economically and psychologically significant selling-purchasing situations, it demands considerable selling practice and experience to be effective. Misunderstanding or misreading of the prospect's dominant buying motives will cause the sale to be lost.

Team Selling

As organizations grow larger, buying becomes more centralized and buying committees or centers become more expert. The salesperson acts as the coordinator and contact person for the sales team, which may consist of various technical specialists in marketing, finance, engineering, production, or research and development. When the sales representative is dealing with various members of a purchasing committee or group of people influential in the buying decision, team selling strategies are necessary. Each member of the buying team may be interested in a different product characteristic (e.g., engineering specialists may focus on structural strength, production specialists may emphasize quality and timely delivery, and purchasing specialists may be mainly concerned about price). Therefore, the sales team must be prepared to adapt to the dominant buying motives of each member of the group in one-on-one sales negotiations. In addition, while making a presentation to a buying committee, the sales team must appeal to the collective dominant buying motive of the assembled group as well as the criteria of each member.

Depth Selling

All the above strategies in the sales presentation are applied in depth selling strategies, with two or more often employed simultaneously. For example, a sales representative might use an overall formula strategy (AIDA) while starting with probing want-satisfaction questions to discover buying motives, then turn to stimulus-response questions to get the prospect thinking positively about the product, and finally move to the problem-solving strategy to suggest alternative solutions and win the prospect's confidence. Depth selling is a strategic mix of sales presentation strategies. Therefore, the effective use of this approach requires a very bright and perceptive salesperson.

DEALING WITH PROSPECT OBJECTIONS

Prospect objections should be seen as a positive sign of interest and involvement. Often, objections are indirect ways of asking for more information. In other words, the prospect may be saying, "Convince me, give me more assurance." To avoid the risk of making a buying mistake, prospects will often make negative statements such as, "This typewriter doesn't seem very sturdy. I'll bet it has a lot of plastic parts." What they are really doing is asking the salesperson to assure them that the parts will not break or wear out quickly.

Hopefully, the salesperson can respond honestly along this line: "On the contrary, this is one of the strongest machines on the market. It is made of a new lightweight metal that is one and a half times as strong as the standard metal in typewriters. Its repair record is one of the best on the market." Each time salespeople can overcome such apparent objections, they remove barriers to the sale.

Sometimes an objection serves as a stalling device or a way for the prospect to get out of the selling situation. When prospects say they want to think it over,

---

EXHIBIT A-9

Methods and Strategies for Dealing with Objections

- *Indirect denial.* Initially agree with the prospect, then gently take issue with the statement.
- *Boomerang.* Turn the objection into a reason for buying, but avoid making the prospect look ignorant for raising the objection.
- *Counterbalance.* Counter an objection that cannot be denied by citing an even more important buying benefit.
- *Denial.* When the objection is invalid, tactfully but forthrightly deny the objection.
- *Question.* Use questions to clarify objections and to "answer" objections indirectly.
- *Failure to hear.* Seemingly unimportant comments made under the prospect's breath should not be ignored by salespeople unless no response is the best alternative.

---

would like to talk to their spouse first, or cannot afford to buy now, they may be giving a valid reason for delay. But more often such statements indicate purchase anxiety, which must be offset with risk-reducing benefits or the sale will be lost.

Various methods have been developed and tested to handle prospect objections successfully, as outlined in Exhibit A-9.

Indirect Denial Method

This method is sometimes called the "Yes, but" approach because salespeople respond to objections by agreeing with the prospect's comment and then gently following up with a disclaimer. For instance, a prospect may say, "Your company's forklift trucks have a reputation for transmission problems." With the indirect denial method, the sales rep may respond, "Yes, we did have that problem with our earlier models, but in the last two years our engineers solved it by changing the design of the transmission so that it undergoes less wear and tear. Now our transmission is as good as any make available."

Boomerang Method

Using the boomerang method, salespeople turn the objection into a reason for buying. If the prospect asserts, "This word processing equipment is too expensive for an office of this size," the salesperson might state in response, "Mr. Vinson, you said you were planning to hire a new secretary for $16,000 a year. Well, this equipment costs only $7,000, and your present secretary can more than double her productivity with it, thereby making it unnecessary to hire another secretary." In exercising this method salespeople must take care that prospects do not feel they are being condescended to or made to look stupid for raising objections; otherwise, the boomerang will knock down the sale.

Counterbalance Method

When the prospect's objection is valid and undeniable, the salesperson should try to counterbalance the disadvantage with an offsetting advantage of the same feature. A prospect might complain, "This photocopying machine door is heavy and hard to open," and the salesperson might counter with, "Yes, we purposely designed it that way to keep unauthorized and untrained personnel from tampering with the intricate machinery inside. It has cut down on repair problems significantly by making it a little more difficult to gain access to the internal workings of the machine."

Denial Method

Sometimes the prospect makes a sincere but erroneous statement, such as: "I don't want to take a chance and buy from you because I hear that your company is near bankruptcy." To overcome this objection, the salesperson has no choice but to deny it politely and firmly with a comment such as, "I've heard that rumor, too, but it just isn't true. We are in strong financial shape, and I'll be glad to show you our latest annual report." A less forthright answer may cause the prospect to think the salesperson is hedging.

Question Method

By responding to a prospect's objections with a specific question, the sales representative can often deflate the objection. If a prospect says, "I don't like the design of this photocopying machine," the salesperson can ask, "What specifically don't you like about the design, Mr. Capuci?" Such questions may lead the prospect to see that the objection is not well thought out or may cause the prospect to talk himself or herself into minimizing its significance. Moreover, responding with a question throws the ball into the prospect's court and allows the salesperson to deal with a specific objection and to have more time to think of a reply.

Failure-to-Hear Method

Salespeople should seldom deliberately ignore a prospect's objection even if muttered under the breath. Seemingly minor objections that receive no answer can block a sale. Sensitive salespeople are careful to stay "tuned in" to the prospect in every way possible, including paying attention to tone and inflection of voice and body language.

Farmland Industries gives its salespeople six basic rules to follow in dealing with prospect objections; these rules are explained in the next example.

RULES FOR OVERCOMING OBJECTIONS

1. *Don't argue.* Never begin talking by saying "no." Begin by appearing to agree. Never use the word "but." The old "Yes, but . . ." opening is just another way of saying no. Don't use the word "objection" in your answer. Refer to it as a "question" or an "interesting point."

2. *Don't answer too quickly.* Pause for a moment and reflect on what the customer has said. If you jump right in, the customer feels you're pressuring him or her.

3. *Don't overanswer.* Some salespeople attach too much meaning to an objection. Just answer it; don't bury it. People don't buy because of your skill in answering objections. They buy because they want the benefits of your product. After answering the objection, go back to your positive sales story.

4. *Don't be drawn into pointless wrangles.* Some objections may be unanswerable. No product can have all the advantages. Some customers won't accept even the most skillful answer. There comes a time to simply move on to another point: "I perfectly understand the point you are making, Mr. Jones, and I've given you the best answer I can at the moment. There's another thing I want to mention to you about the. . . ."

5. *Don't guess at an answer.* If you don't know how to answer an objection, don't try. Promise to get the information and come back later.

6. *Don't doubt your own answer.* Never appear to doubt that you have answered the objection completely. Don't say, "Have I answered your objection completely?" You are asking the customers to admit they are wrong for objecting. They'll probably pile on another objection just to save face.[7]

CLOSING THE SALE

Unless the close is effective, the sale seldom happens. Salespeople must learn not only *how* to close but *when* to close, as the "closing cues" in Exhibit A-10 show. *Trial closes* may be used at various times in the selling interview, depending upon the complexity and cost of the product or service. A trial close is simply

EXHIBIT A-10

Closing Cues

Lights, Camera, Action . . . Begin a Trial Close

- When the prospect makes a positive statement about the product . . .
- When the prospect begins handling the product . . .
- When the prospect plays with the pen or order form . . .
- When the prospect asks about product price, installation, use, or delivery . . .
- When the prospect asks who else is using the product . . .
- When the prospect's tone of voice turns more positive . . .
- When the prospect unconsciously reaches for his order pad or wallet . . .
- When the prospect is testing or trying out the product . . .
- When the prospect asks if there are any special incentives to buy . . .
- When the prospect's worried or defensive expression is replaced by a more relaxed or happy expression . . .
- When you complete your full sales presentation . . .
- When you successfully answer a prospect's objection to buying the product . . .
- When you answer all the prospect's questions . . .

a means of seeing whether the prospect is ready to buy and thus might be ready to close the sale. Trial closes might take these verbal and nonverbal forms:

- "Do you like Model I or Model II best?"
- "Do you think you would like the maintenance contract that can be obtained at a discount with the purchase?"
- "Would you be interested in comparing the lease versus buy options?"
- Run your hand over the product (e.g., a wool-lined topcoat) and comment, "I'll bet you'll keep warm as toast in this coat this winter."
- Give the product (say, a calculator or package of cosmetics) to the prospect to touch, hear, or smell. Let all the prospect's senses come into play.

Salespeople should continue to sell when their trial close is met by such caution signs as these:

- The prospect seems to want more information about a technical product or service.
- The prospect makes an objection or asks for more information.
- An interruption upsets the prospect's buying frame of mind.
- A trial close fails to get any positive prospect interest.
- The sales presentation is too hurried or sketchy for the prospect to follow adequately.
- The prospect is defensive or hostile and essentially refuses to meaningfully communicate with the salesperson.

As presented in Exhibit A-11, there are many sales closing techniques. Any one or a combination of these closes can be effectively applied when the selling situation is appropriate.

Choice Close

Instead of asking prospects whether or not they want to buy, the choice, or alternative, close gently leads them to choose between two items the seller has— for example, "Which do you want, the compact model or the regular model?" This close avoids giving the prospect the option of saying "no" by setting up a choice decision. Even restaurant employees routinely use this close when they ask, "What would you like to drink—coffee, milk, or a soft drink?"

Minor Points Close

This approach leads prospects toward progressively larger decisions by starting out with minor points. The salesperson may successively ask, "If you buy, which color would you like?" "Would you prefer the deluxe or regular model?" "Are you interested in the installment plan?" "How soon would you need it

---

EXHIBIT A-11

Closing Techniques and Explanations

- *Choice close.* Offer alternative products to choose from.
- *Minor points close.* Obtain decisions on minor points leading to gradual acceptance of the total product package.
- *Assumptive close.* Assume the purchase decision is already made in order to compel the prospect to buy.
- *Stimulus-response close.* Ask a sequence of leading questions to make it easier for the prospect to say "yes" when asked for the order.
- *Summary close.* Summarize advantages and disadvantages before asking for the order.
- *Standing-room-only (SRO) close.* Imply that the opportunity to buy is fleeting because demand is great and few are left.
- *Special deal close.* Make a "special" offer to get prospect to buy now.
- *Success story close.* Tell about a customer who had a similar problem but solved it by buying the product.
- *Closing on resistance.* Answer the objection by turning the problem into a benefit, and then ask for the order.
- *Contingent close.* Get the prospect to agree to buy if the salesperson can demonstrate the benefits promised.
- *Turnover close.* Turn the closing over to another salesperson with a fresh approach or better chance to make the sale.
- *Trial close.* Use a question or a nonverbal action to elicit some commitment.
- *Ask-for-the-order close.* Simply ask for the order directly or indirectly.
- *Pretend-to-leave close.* Pretend to leave but "just happen to remember" another benefit or special offer after the prospect has relaxed sales resistance.
- *Puppy dog close.* Let the prospect take the product home to use and like a puppy dog, he or she will probably become emotionally attached to it.
- *No-risk close.* Agree to take the product back and refund the customer's money if the product does not prove satisfactory.
- *Lost sale close.* When nothing seems to have worked to close the sale, apologize for not being able to satisfy the customer and ask what it would have taken to get him or her to buy; then offer that.

---

delivered?" Through this line of questioning the prospect usually develops an increasingly favorable disposition toward purchasing the product.

Assumptive Close

Here the salesperson assumes that the prospect will purchase and conveys this assumption through his or her comments and nonverbal actions. Salespeople may say something like, "Do you want to take it with you or have it delivered?" "Will that be cash or charge?" "We accept either Visa or MasterCard—which card do you have?"

Nonverbal actions might include handing the prospect an order blank and a ballpoint pen, handing the product to the prospective customer, starting to wrap the package, or getting out the credit card charge-plate machine.

Stimulus-Response Close

Leading the prospect through a series of selling points or stimuli by eliciting consistently favorable responses is a closing strategy often used by inexperienced salespeople, since it can be readily learned. By asking leading questions (e.g., "You would prefer a product that uses less energy, wouldn't you?"), the salesperson conditions the prospect to respond "yes" right up to the sale. Applying the stimulus-response close risks irritating some prospects, since the presentation is often memorized and requires little participation by the prospect except to provide positive responses.

Summary Close

Listing all the advantages and disadvantages of buying the product is a good means of letting the prospect see how benefits outweigh costs or disadvantages. With more business-oriented prospects, the summary can be presented in a *T-account* or *balance sheet* format.

Standing-Room-Only (SRO) Close

To encourage prospects to make the decision to buy now, some salespeople may apply psychological pressure by stressing that a lot of people are anxious to buy the product and it may not be available later. Although the SRO close can be very honest, it is sometimes associated with questionable ethics. Some real estate people, for instance, deliberately schedule overlapping appointments with potential buyers so that it appears that a lot of people are interested in the property, thereby pressuring prospects to make a quick decision to buy. In retail stores salesclerks sometimes tell a shopper, "These coats have been selling like hot cakes, so I can't guarantee any will be available later unless you want to put a down payment on one, which will allow me to hold it for you until three o'clock."

Special Deal Close

When a salesperson has done his or her best to close but the prospect remains resistant, the special deal, or one-time offer, close may be the clincher. The salesperson might state, "If you buy today, I can give you a 15 percent discount on the maintenance contract," or, "If you order today or tomorrow so that I can reach my monthly quota, I'll throw in this $30 adapter free."

Success Story Close

Citing the successful solution to a similar prospect's problem can help close on a reluctant buyer. The salesperson might explain, "Fred Murphy, who, as you may know, is the purchasing director for your competitor, Kentland Poultry Company, switched to our feed grains for Kentland's chickens, and he says their average weight has increased nearly half a pound. I'm confident our feed formula 943 can do the same for your company's chickens."

Closing on Resistance

If the prospect puts up a final objection when the close seems near, the salesperson may be able to turn that resistance into a reason for purchasing. A prospect may object, "I need a photocopier with wheels so that it can be moved around our office. The stationary models you've shown me would be too inconvenient." The salesperson might respond, "If you'll sign this purchase order, I'll have one of our machinists install some rollers on the bottom of the model you prefer, which will make it easily movable by your secretaries."

Contingent Close

By setting up a presales presentation contingency, the sales representative can obtain a commitment to buy if the product does what the representative claims it will do. A salesperson might ask, "If I can show you how this heat pump will cut your fuel bills by 20 percent or more yearly, will you buy it?" This places a burden on the salesperson to prove his or her contention, but it simultaneously puts the onus on the prospect to buy if the point is demonstrated.

Turnover Close

If the prospect is not yielding to the sales closing techniques of a particular salesperson, it may be effective to turn the prospect over to another salesperson. This needs to be smoothly handled so that the prospect will not think that the first salesperson has simply lost patience. An appropriate transitional phrase might be, "I'd like to ask Mark Cohen to talk to you about the special benefits of using the navigational system, since he is a boat enthusiast like yourself. He can answer your more technical questions and give you a personal feel for how it handles in the water."

Trial Close

Subtle attempts to find out how close the prospect is to making the purchase decision enable the salesperson to adjust selling tactics. In a trial close, the salesperson might ask the prospect, "Which do you prefer—the Apple IIGS or the Macintosh Plus?" If the prospect indicates even a partial commitment at this point, the salesperson should continue presenting benefits or reasons to buy before trying another trial close. Even nonverbal trial closes can be effective. Depending upon the product, the salesperson might start using the product (a word processor), give it to the prospect to try on (jewelry) or hold (a camera), or simply caress the product (a cashmere sweater). By participating in or observing such nonverbal actions, prospects tend to become more committed toward purchase.

Ask-for-the-Order Close

Probably the most obvious but often overlooked close is to simply ask for the order. Naturally, this must be done in a graciously assertive manner, such as, "Won't you let me order one for you now so that you can start enjoying these benefits as soon as possible?"

Pretend-to-Leave Close

After completing the basic sales presentation and trying various closes, the salesperson may pretend to leave the prospect to attend to other customers or do some other tasks. This causes the prospect to relax his or her guard and become more receptive when the salesperson returns to mention one final benefit or extra inducement to buy that he or she "forgot" to mention earlier.

Puppy Dog Close

Few people can resist a friendly puppy, and if they take one home with them, they'll probably keep it. Analogously, if a salesperson lets prospects take products (e.g., an automobile, videocassette player, television, or computer) home with them, they'll probably find it difficult to return the products. An experienced salesperson will probably say something like this: "Ms. Piermont, I know you're undecided about buying the Honda Accord, so why don't you just take it home for the weekend to try it out? Then, when you come in Monday, we'll see what you've decided." After the neighbors have seen Ms. Piermont driving the new car and her husband and children have enjoyed riding around in it, she will find it very difficult to lose neighborhood prestige and disappoint her family by taking the car back to the dealer.

No-Risk Close

To reduce the customer's fear that he or she may make a buying mistake, the salesperson can offer a money-back guarantee if the customer is not fully satisfied. This technique works much like the "puppy dog close" because once customers take the product home, they will find it difficult to return the product and ask for their money back. Even if not fully satisfied with the product's performance, they'll probably accept a substitute product or some adjustment arrangement from the salesperson.

Lost Sale Close

When the salesperson appears to have failed to close the sale, a final closing technique is to apologize to the customer for not being able to satisfy him or her and then to ask what it would have taken to make the sale. Prospects are often unprepared for this approach and may blurt out their real objection or explain what it would have taken to make the sale. When this happens, the salesperson can offer whatever the customer wanted or deal with the specific objection.

THE FOLLOW-UP

After making any sale, salespeople should make special efforts to follow up with customers to ensure that they are satisfied and to express thanks for the business. Experienced salespeople know full well that their best future customers are present customers. Many buyers suffer postpurchase anxiety about the wisdom of their purchase decision, and the salesperson's follow-up call may help alleviate this dissonance by reassuring customers. Furthermore, additional sales of complementary products can often be easily made through postpurchase follow-ups. Also, salespeople should follow up to handle any potential complaints about a product or service. At British Vita, salespeople are encouraged to look for complaints in order to make sure that customers are satisfied and thus more likely to remain brand-loyal. Vita requires that its salespeople keep in frequent contact with customers after they have purchased the product to spot problems and solve them before they become too large. No matter what the complaint, the salesperson on the account is responsible for solving it. If the salesperson cannot settle it to the customer's satisfaction, a company product manager is called in, too.

Every sales representative needs an occasional inspirational boost in order to keep going when things are not going well. So, in closing, we would like to recite these words:

> If you want a thing bad enough to go and fight for it,
> Work day and night for it,
> Give up your time and peace and sleep for it,
> If only desire of it
> Makes you quite mad enough
> Never to tire of it,
> If you'll gladly sweat for it,
> Fret for it, plan for it,
> If you'll simply go after the thing you want,
> With all your capacity,
> Strength and sagacity,
> Faith, hope and confidence, stern pertinacity,
> If neither cold nor poverty, famished and gaunt,
> Nor sickness nor pain
> Of body or brain
> Can turn you away from the thing you want
> If dogged and grim, you besiege and beset it,
> YOU'LL GET IT![8]

REFERENCES

1. Gerald I. Manning and Barry I. Reece, *Selling Today: A Personal Approach*, Brown, Dubuque, Iowa, 1980, p. 223.
2. See Rolph E. Anderson, "Consumer Dissatisfaction: The Effect of Disconfirmed Expectations on Perceived Product Performance," *Journal of Marketing Research*, February

1973, pp. 36–42; John J. Withey, "Reducing Post-Purchase Dissonance: The Role of Industrial Salespeople," in E. James Randall (ed.), *Pi Sigma Epsilon's National Conference in Sales Management Proceedings,* 1986, Georgia Southern College, Statesboro, Ga., pp. 29–33.

3. *US,* Jan. 10, 1978, p. 49; *Philadelphia Inquirer,* July 3, 4, 1978, p. 12-A.

4. "How Well Do They Handle Inquiries? Don't Ask," *Sales & Marketing Management,* Special Report 117, Nov. 23, 1976, p. 4.

5. *Sales & Marketing Management,* Jan. 18, 1982, p. 63.

6. *Progressive Grocer,* October 1973, p. 13.

7. Farmland Cooperative Training Division brochure, Farmland Industries.

8. Robert S. Tralins, *How to Be a Power Closer in Selling,* Prentice-Hall, Englewood Cliffs, N.J., 1971, p. 188.

B

STARTING YOUR CAREER IN SALES

CHOOSING A CAREER

One of the most important decisions in your life is deciding upon your career. Not only will a career choice affect your income and lifestyle, but also it will have a major impact on your happiness and self-fulfillment.

Many people find their career opportunity in marketing. Nearly a third of all civilian jobs are in marketing-related fields. Sales offers more jobs by far than any other area of marketing. In fact, if you are a marketing major, the chances are high that your first job will be in sales. Personal selling and sales management opportunities are available in a wide range of product and service organizations, both profit and not-for-profit. Every consumer is familiar with door-to-door salespersons, life insurance agents, real estate agents, and salespeople in retailing and wholesaling. But many people do not readily think of stockbrokers, industrial sales representatives, or manufacturers' agents as salespeople. Every product or service you can think of has to be sold by a salesperson, either to a consumer, retailer, wholesaler, manufacturer, government agency, or not-for-profit organization such as a university or hospital.

Women and minorities are finding that sales careers offer exceptional opportunities for rapid advancement because job performance tends to be measured more objectively than in most other career fields. To put it directly, you either make the sales or you don't. Women may even have special advantages over men in personal selling because of their highly developed social skills, cultural conditioning, and interpersonal abilities.[1]

The *College Placement Annual* describes sales as an often overlooked area of employment for college graduates.[2] According to the *Annual*, sales is a very promising career field as it is common to all industries and always has job openings. Moreover, a good salesperson is always in demand, whether it be good economic times or bad.[3]

The American Almanac of Jobs and Salaries lists sales as one of the most financially rewarding occupations.[4] Beyond being *one of the highest-paying fields*, sales offers considerable freedom and independence compared with most jobs and is seldom boring because it deals directly with people and their ever-changing needs. Another appealing aspect of a sales career for many new salespeople (especially in international sales) is the *lifestyle*, that is, the opportunities it offers such as traveling and entertaining customers on an expense account. Some salespeople also enjoy *tax deductions* for a home office or automobile expenses.

Starting in personal selling and sales management jobs is also one of the *fastest routes to the top* of any organization; more CEOs come from sales and marketing backgrounds than from any other field. As examples, Lee Iacocca (Chrysler), Phil Lippincott (Scott Paper), John Akers (IBM), John Sparks (Whirlpool), and Bruno Bich (Bic Pen) came up through sales and marketing. Typically, a college graduate enters selling as a sales trainee and advances to a sales position, senior salesperson, sales supervisor, then sales manager at the district, regional, and national levels. If you prefer to advance through the ranks of marketing management, you can usually make a career move into product or brand management or another marketing headquarters job after serving for a couple of years in the initial sales position.

Salaries for salespeople, sales managers, and top sales executives vary widely across industries and company size, so it is more realistic to present ranges of earnings for general categories, as shown in Exhibit B-1.

Skills, Aptitudes, and Abilities of Salespeople

The sales field is so large and diverse that there is a sales job that will fit virtually everyone's personality, skills, aptitude, and abilities. Some sales jobs require outgoing people to call on prospects who are nearly always strangers, while others need low-key, soft-sell people who can develop and maintain close consultative relationships with customers who are called on frequently. Some sales jobs demand considerable travel, which entails being on the road for days or even weeks at a time; other sales jobs require very little travel and allow the salesperson to be home virtually every night; still other sales jobs allow the salesperson to stay in one place, making telephone calls to potential customers. Some selling jobs (e.g., a stockbroker) require a strong educational and training background before the salesperson can function successfully, whereas other sales jobs (e.g., a door-to-door encyclopedia salesperson) may require relatively little

EXHIBIT B-1

Salary Ranges for Different Sales Jobs

Senior sales manager	
National sales manager	$50,000–$200,000+
Vice president of sales	
Sales manager	$40,000–$100,000+
Salespersons:	
Sales trainee	$20,000–$30,000+
Senior salesperson	$40,000–$65,000+
Sales supervisor	$50,000–$80,000+
Salespersons in different fields:	
Real estate agent (broker)	$20,000–$100,000+
Insurance agent (broker)	$22,000–$150,000+
Manufacturers' agent (representative)	$25,000–$150,000+
Securities salesperson (stockbroker)	$30,000–$200,000+

Source: Adapted from "1990 Survey of Selling Costs," Sales & Marketing Management, Feb. 26, 1990, p. 77; Business Week's Guide to Careers, Spring–Summer 1985, p. 23; 1984 American Marketing Association Marketing Compensation Report, American Marketing Association, Chicago, 1984, p. 18; and authors' estimates.

education or training for the salesperson to be successful. Probably the most difficult part of job hunting is deciding exactly what type of work you would like. Many students have had no working experience other than summer jobs, so they are not sure what career to pursue. Too often, college students and their parents rush toward occupational fields that seem to offer the highest monetary payoff or are currently "hot," instead of looking at the long run over a forty- to fifty-year working life. One straightforward approach to deciding what type of job to undertake is to do a "self-analysis." This involves honestly asking yourself what your skills, abilities, and interests really are and then identifying occupational fields that match up well with your personality profile. Some students prefer to take various vocational aptitude tests to help identify their interests and abilities. Your college's placement office or psychology department can inform you about the availability of these tests.

Contributions of Salespeople

Salespeople with all kinds of talents selling millions of products and services are essential to a healthy, growing economy. Salespeople who really care about solving people's problems can perform a great service to society while earning a good living for themselves. Professional salespeople learn to think of their customers' problems as more important than their own, at least during the working day. They remain alert to the changing needs of consumers and organizational buyers, thereby helping stimulate industrial innovation to better satisfy people's needs and wants. In addition, by anticipating and forecasting annual sales, they enable producers to improve overall operational planning, production, marketing, and distribution efficiency. Dedicated salespeople provide a great service by efficiently and effectively bringing buyers and sellers together for mutual satisfaction.

YOUR FIRST SALE

Selling yourself to a prospective employer is usually the first big sale of a successful salesperson. With your services (as represented by your qualifications, education, training, and personal characteristics) as the product, you must convince prospective employers that they should buy your services over those of many other candidates for the job. All the steps of the personal selling process apply: prospecting for potential employers, planning your approach to them, approaching with a résumé and cover letter, making your sales presentation and demonstrating your qualifications in a personal interview, dealing with objections or giving reasons why the employer should hire you over other candidates, attempting to close the sale by enthusiastically asking for the job and employing appropriate closing techniques, and following up by thanking the prospective employer for the interview and reinforcing a positive impression.

Prospecting for a Potential Employer

After you have determined what you're selling (your skills, abilities, interests, and so forth) and identified the type of job you think you would like, you might begin your personal selling process by looking at the *College Placement Annual* at your college placement office. The *College Placement Annual* provides a variety of information about prospective employers and lists the organizations according to the types of jobs they have available—for example, advertising, banking, marketing research, and sales. Other sources of information about prospective employers include directories such as those published by Dun and Bradstreet, Standard & Poor's, and trade associations; the annual American Marketing Association membership directory (company listings); the Yellow Pages of telephone books in cities where you would like to live and work; and classified sections of *The Wall Street Journal* or city newspapers. Before contacting a particular company, look up its annual report and stock evaluation (from *Value Line* or various other sources) in your college library to learn as much as possible about the company and its prospects for the future. You might also obtain a list of articles on the company from the *Business Periodicals Index* (BPI).

College placement office.   Use your college placement office to find out which companies are going to be interviewing on campus on what dates; then sign up for interviews with those companies that seem to best match your job skills and requirements. Usually, the college placement office has books, pamphlets, or files that will give you leads on other prospective employers that may not be interviewing on campus that term.

Job-hunting expenses.   Although campus interviews are convenient, students seldom get a job without follow-up interviews with more senior managers—

usually at company headquarters. These additional interviews generally take a full day and may involve long-distance trips. You should be forewarned that job hunting can be expensive. Printing your résumé, typing cover letters, buying envelopes and stamps, making long-distance telephone calls, incurring travel expenses, and buying new clothing will require a sizable outlay of money. Even though most companies eventually reimburse you for all expenses incurred on a company visit, they seldom pay in advance. Reimbursement can take several weeks, so you may encounter some cash-flow problems over the short run.

Employment agencies. Although many employment agencies receive fees from employers for providing good job candidates, others charge job seekers huge fees (sometimes thousands of dollars) for helping them find jobs. Therefore, make sure you fully understand the fee arrangement before signing up with an employment agency. Some employment agencies may not be worth your time and/or money because they use a programmed approach in helping you write your résumé and cover letter and in prospecting for potential employers. Potential employers have seen these "canned" formats and approaches so many times that your personal advertisement (your résumé and cover letter) will appear almost indistinguishable from others.

The hidden job market. It has been estimated that nearly 90 percent of available jobs are never advertised and never reach employment agency files,[5] so creative resourcefulness often pays off in finding the best jobs. Consider every reasonable source for leads. Sometimes, your professors, deans, or college administrators can give you names and contact persons at companies that have hired recent graduates.

Do not be bashful about letting other people know that you are looking for work. Classmates, friends, and business associates of your family may be of help not only directly but also indirectly, acting as extra pairs of eyes and ears alert to job opportunities for you.

Planning Your Approach (the Preapproach)

After conducting your self-analysis and identifying potential employers looking for people with your abilities and interests, you need to prepare a *résumé* (or personal advertisement) for yourself. Your résumé should focus on your achievements to date, your educational background, your work experience, and your special abilities and interests. Some students make the mistake of merely listing their assigned responsibilities on different jobs without indicating what they accomplished on the job. If you achieved something on the job, say it—for example, "Helped computerize office files," "Increased sales in my territory by 10 percent," "Received a 15 percent raise after three months on the job," or "Promoted to assistant store manager after four months." When looking for a job, remember that employers are looking for a *track record of achievement;* and you must distinguish yourself from those who may have had the same assigned job responsibilities as you did but performed poorly. If your work experience is minimal, consider a "skills" résumé, in which you emphasize your particular abilities, such as organizing, programming, or leadership skills, and give supporting evidence whenever you can. Examples of various types of résumés can be found in the *College Placement Annual* and in various other job-hunting publications that your college business reference librarian can direct you to.

Remember that there is no one correct format for your résumé. A little tasteful creativity can help differentiate your résumé from countless look-alike résumés. If you are a young college graduate, your résumé will usually be only one page long, but do not worry about going to a second page if you have something important to present. One student so blindly followed the one-page-résumé rule that he left out having served in the military—a fact that is usually viewed very positively by prospective employers, especially if it involved significant leadership responsibilities or work experience.

If you know what job you want, you may want to put your *job objective* near the top of your résumé. If you are not sure what job you want or want to send out the same résumé for several different jobs, then you can describe your job objective in your *cover letter*. In the cover letter, a key element is convincing the prospective employer to grant you an interview. Thus, you must talk in terms of the employer's interests, not just your own. You are answering the question: "Why should we hire you?" You may need to send a letter with your résumé enclosed to a hundred or more companies to obtain five to ten interviews, so do not be discouraged if you do not get replies from all companies or are told by many companies that there are no present job opportunities. You will probably need only a few interviews and just one job offer to get your career started.

Review some of the publications and sources mentioned in the previous section on prospecting (e.g., *College Placement Annual,* Dun and Bradstreet directories, and annual reports) to learn as much as you can about your prospective employer so that you can tailor your cover letter. Remember, the employer is thinking in terms of the company's needs, not yours. For one example of a résumé, see Exhibit B-2. A cover letter is illustrated in Exhibit B-3.

Making Your Approach

Prospective employers can be approached by mail, telephone, or personal contact. Personal contact is best, but this usually requires that you know someone with influence who can arrange an interview for you. Of course, a few enterprising students have devised elaborate and sometimes successful schemes to get job interviews. For example, we know of one young man who simply went to the headquarters of the company he wanted to work for and asked to see the president. Told that the president of the company could not see him, the student said that he was willing to wait until the president had time. This audacious individual went back three different days until the president finally agreed to see him, perhaps mainly out of curiosity about what sort of young man would be so outrageous in his job search.

Fortunately for this young man, he had a lot to offer and was able to communicate this to the president, so he was hired. We certainly don't recommend such an unorthodox approach, but it shows how far people have gone

RACHEL E. SANFORD
2935 Mountain View Road
Ellington, PA 19401
(216) 567-0000

JOB OBJECTIVE	Sales representative for a consumer products company
EDUCATION	Graduated "cum laude" with B.S. in Marketing Management (June 1993), University of Southern Pennsylvania. Career-related courses included Selling and Sales Management, Public Speaking, Business Writing, Public Relations, Marketing Research, Computer Programming, and Multivariate Data Analysis.
ACTIVITIES AND HONORS	*President*, Student Marketing Association; *Vice president*, Chi Omega Sorority; *Captain*, women's varsity tennis team; sportswriter for the *Campus View* student newspaper. Named to Who's Who among American College Students, 1992–1993. On Dean's List all four years. Overall grade point average = 3.65.

WORK EXPERIENCE

Summer 1992	*Sales representative*, Peabody Manufacturing Company. Sold women's blouses to boutiques and small department stores in southeast Pennsylvania. Exceeded assigned sales quota by 20%; named "outstanding" summer employee for 1992.
Summer 1991	*Buyer,* Hamm's Department Stores, Inc., Midway, Pa. Developed purchase plan, initiated purchase orders, monitored and controlled expenditures for nearly $1 million worth of women's clothing. Made monthly progress reports (written and oral) to Hamm's Executive Committee. Received 15% bonus as #2 buyer in the six stores of the Hamm's chain in special "Back to School" purchasing competition.
Summer 1990	*Retail clerk,* Hamm's Department Stores, Inc., Midway, Pa. After 3 months, received 10% pay raise and promotion to evening salesclerk supervisor over seven part-time salesclerks. Devised new inventory control system for handbags and accessories that cut costs over $30,000 annually.
Summer 1989	*Cosmetics salesperson*, Heavenly Charm, Inc., Midway, Pa. Sold $43,000 worth of Heavenly Charm cosmetics door to door. Named #1 salesperson in the sales region. Offered full-time job as sales supervisor.
INTERESTS	Tennis, golf, public speaking, short story writing, and reading biographies.

EXHIBIT B-3

Sample Cover Letter

Rachel E. Sanford
2935 Mountain View Road
Ellington, PA 19401

Mr. Samuel Abramson
District Sales Manager
Hixson Appliance Company
Philadelphia, PA 19103

Dear Mr. Abramson:

Hixson has been a familiar name to me ever since I was barely able to see over my mother's kitchen counter. Virtually every appliance we had was a Hixson, so I know firsthand what fine quality products you sell. My career interest is in sales, and there is no company that I would rather work with than Hixson Appliance.

I will be graduating this June from Southern Pennsylvania University with a B.S. in marketing management and I would like you to consider me for a job as a sales representative with your company. As you can see in my enclosed resume, I have successfully worked in sales jobs during three of the last four summers. My college course electives (e.g., public speaking, business writing, and public relations) have been carefully selected with my career objective in mind. Even my extracurricular activities in sports and campus organizations have helped prepare me for working with a variety of people and competitive challenges.

Will you please grant me an interview so that I can convince you that I'm someone you should hire for your sales team? I'll call you next Thursday afternoon to arrange an appointment at your convenience.

Look forward to meeting you soon.

Sincerely,

Rachel E. Sanford

Enclosure

to impress potential employers. A personal contact within the company can win you some special attention and enable you to avoid competing head-on with the large number of other candidates looking for a job. However, most students start their approach in the traditional way by mailing their résumé and cover letter to the recruiting department of the company. Unless your résumé matches a particular need at that time, it will probably be filed away for possible future reference or merely discarded. To try to get around the system, some students send their letter by express mail or mailgram or address it to a key executive, with "Personal" written on the envelope. These students believe that bypassing the company's personnel office will increase the likelihood that their cover letter and résumé will be read by someone with authority to hire. You can be sure that using gimmicks, no matter how creative, to get a job interview will offend some executives and thus cause you to be rejected from consideration for a job. But you can probably also be sure that a few executives will admire your efforts and grant you an interview.

Only you know how comfortable you feel with different approaches to obtaining a job interview. We advise you not to use an approach that is out of character for you and thus will make you feel awkward and embarrassed.

Making Your Sales Presentation

Your personal sales presentation will come during the interview with the prospective employer's recruiters or interviewers. Review Chapter 7, "Selecting the Sales Force," to prepare yourself for the personal interview. Take particular note of Exhibit 7-5, which identifies negative factors about interviewees that frequently lead to rejection. Some typical questions asked in an interview include those listed in Exhibit B-4.

Try to make a positive impression on everyone you encounter in the company, even while waiting in the lobby for your next interview. Sometimes managers will ask their receptionists and secretaries for an opinion of you, and your friendliness, courtesy, professional demeanor, personal habits, and the like, will all be used to judge you. Even the magazines you choose to read while waiting can be a positive or negative factor. For instance, it will probably be less impressive for you to read a popular magazine like *People* or *Sports Illustrated* than to read something more professional such as *Business Week* or *The Wall Street Journal.*

During the interviews, do not become merely a passive respondent to the interviewer's questions. Being graciously assertive by asking reasonable questions of your own will indicate to the interviewer that you are alert, energetic, and sincerely interested in the job. The personal interview is your opportunity to persuade the prospective employer that you should be hired. To use a show business analogy, you will be onstage for only a short time (during the personal interview), so try to present an honest but positive image of yourself. Perhaps it will help you to be alert and enthusiastic if you imagine that you are being interviewed on television.

Sometimes, prospective employers will even ask you to *demonstrate* certain abilities by having you write a timed essay about some part of your life, sell something (such as a desk calculator) to the interviewer, or respond to hostile questions. Be calm and confident during any such unorthodox interviewing approaches and you will make a good impression. Remember, most employers want you to perform well because they are looking for the best people they can find in a given time frame for the money they have to offer. If you are given intelligence, aptitude, or psychological tests, you should try to be honest so that you do not create unrealistic expectations that you will not be able to fulfill. It is just as important that you do not create a false impression and begin with a

EXHIBIT B-4

Some Questions Frequently Asked in a Job Interview

- Of the jobs you've had to date, which one did you like best? Why?

- Why do you want to work for our company?

- Tell me what you know about our company.

- Do any of your relatives or friends work for our company? If so, in what jobs?

- Tell me about yourself, your strengths, weaknesses, career goals, and so forth.

- Is any member of your family a professional salesperson? If so, what do they sell?

- Why do you want to start your career in sales?

- Persuade me that we should hire you.

- What extracurricular activities did you participate in at college? What leadership positions did you have in any of these activities?

- What benefits have you derived from participation in extracurricular activities that will help you in your career?

- Where do you see yourself within our company in five years? In ten years? Twenty years?

- What is your ultimate career goal?

- What do you consider your greatest achievement to date?

- What is your biggest failure to date?

- What is (was) your favorite subject in school? Why?

- Are you willing to travel and possibly relocate?

- How would the people who know you describe you?

- How would you describe yourself?

- What do you like most about selling?

- What do you like least about selling?

- If we hire you, how soon could you start work?

- What is the minimum we would have to offer you to come with us?

company that is not right for you as it is to secure employment in the first place. Many experts say that it is not very difficult to "cheat" on aptitude or psychological tests if you are able to "play the role" and provide the answers that you know the company wants to read. Usually, the so-called safe approach in most personality and preference (interest) tests is to not take extreme positions on anything that is not clearly associated with the job you are applying for. For sales jobs, it is probably safe to come across as highly extroverted and interested in group activities, but it may not be safe to appear to be overly interested in literature, music, art, or any solitary activity. In addition, the "right" answers tend to indicate a conservative, goal-oriented, money-motivated, and gregarious personality.

Dealing with Objections

Sometimes interviewers will bluntly ask, "Why should we hire you?" This requires that you think in terms of the employer's needs and present in cryptic form all your major "selling points." Also, sometimes the interviewer may bring up reasons why you are not the ideal candidate. For example, he or she may mention such things as the following: (1) "We're really looking for someone with a little more experience"; (2) "We'd like to get someone with a more technical educational background"; or (3) "We need someone to start work within two weeks." These kinds of statements are similar to *objections* or requests for additional information. In other words, the interviewer is saying, "Convince me that I shouldn't rule you out for this reason." To overcome such objections, you might respond to each along the following lines: (1) "I've had over a year's experience working with two different companies during my summer vacations, and I've worked part-time with a third company all during college. I'm a fast learner and I've adapted well to each of the three companies, so I feel that my working experience is equivalent to that of someone who has three or four years' experience with the same company"; (2) "Although I didn't choose to earn a technical undergraduate degree, I've taken several technical courses in college, including basic engineering courses, chemistry, physics, and two years of math. I'm very confident that I can quickly learn whatever is necessary technically to do the job, and my real strength is that my education has been a blend of technical and managerial courses"; (3) "Well, I do have one more term of school, so I couldn't start full-time work in two weeks, but perhaps we could work out an arrangement in which I could work part-time . . . maybe Friday, Saturday, and Sunday or on weekends until I graduate."

Good "salespeople" do not allow an objection to block a sale. Providing reasonable solutions or alternative perspectives can often overcome objections or, at least, allow room for further negotiation toward a compromise solution.

Closing the Sale

Although it is not likely that a prospective employer will offer you a job promptly after the job interview, you should nevertheless let the interviewer know that you definitely want the job and are confident that you will do an excellent job for the employer. You will need to use your best judgment as to whether or not to use other closing techniques such as the *summary* close or the *standing-room-only* close. For example, with the summary close, you can summarize your strong points that match up with the company's needs to reinforce in the interviewer's mind that you are right for the job. With the standing-room-only close, you let the prospective employer know that you have other job offers and will need to make a decision within a limited time; this may be appropriate when you sense that the employer is very impressed with you but needs a little push to offer you the job now rather than interview more candidates. This puts the onus on the prospective employer to make a good offer quickly or risk losing you to another company.

In each of the stages of the personal selling process, you should be looking for feedback from the interviewer's body language and voice inflections or tone.

Following Up the Interview

Within a few days after any job interview, whether you want the job or not, it is business courtesy to write thank-you letters to interviewers. In these letters you can reinforce the positive impression you made in the interview and again express your keen interest in working for the company. If you do not hear from the company within a few weeks, it may be appropriate to write another letter expressing your continuing interest in the job and asking for a decision so that you can consider other options if necessary. As a possible reason for this follow-up letter, you might mention an additional personal achievement since the interview, more fully answer one of the interviewer's questions, or perhaps send a newspaper or magazine article of interest. A neat, well-written, courteous follow-up letter gives you a chance not only 'o make a stronger impression on the interviewer but also to exhibit positive qualities such as initiative, energy, sensitivity to others' feelings, and awareness of business protocol.

YOUR EARLY WORKING CAREER

Even though you want to choose a company that you will stay with throughout your working life, it is realistic to recognize that you will probably work for three, four, or more companies during your career. If you are not fully satisfied with your job or company during the first few years of your full-time working life, remember that you are building experience and knowledge that will increase your marketability for future job opportunities. Keep a positive outlook and do the best you can in all job assignments, and your chance for new opportunities will come. Do not be too discouraged by mistakes that you may make in your career; nearly every successful person has made and continues to make many mistakes. View these mistakes largely as *learning experiences*, and they will not be too traumatic or damaging to your confidence.

Good luck in your sales career!

REFERENCES

1. David King, ''The Best Salesman Is a Woman,'' *Business Week's Guide to Careers*, Fall–Winter, 1983, p. 95.
2. John D. Shingleton, ''The Economics of the Job Market, *College Placement Council Annual*, 34th ed., CPC Inc., Bethlehem, Pa., 1990, pp. 14–19.
3. Ibid., p. 15.
4. John W. Wright and Edward J. Dwyer, *The American Almanac of Jobs and Salaries*, Hearst Corporation, New York, 1990, pp. 373–384.
5. Tom Jackson and Davidyne Mayless, *The Hidden Job Market*, Quadrangle Books, New York Times Book Company, New York, 1976, pp. 95–122.

INDEXES

NAME INDEX

SUBJECT INDEX